Child Care and Education

SECOND EDITION

Carolyn Meggitt
Tina Bruce
Julian Grenier

HODDER
EDUCATION
AN HACHETTE UK COMPANY

Orders: please contact Bookpoint Ltd, 130 Milton Park, Abingdon, Oxon OX14 4SB. Telephone: (44) 01235 827720. Fax: (44) 01235 400454. Lines are open from 9.00 - 5.00, Monday to Saturday, with a 24 hour message answering service. You can also order through our website www.hoddereducation.co.uk

If you have any comments to make about this, or any of our other titles, please send them to educationenquiries@hodder.co.uk

British Library Cataloguing in Publication Data
A catalogue record for this title is available from the British Library

ISBN: 978 1 4441 7099 3

This Edition Published 2012
Impression number   10 9 8 7 6 5 4 3 2 1
Year   2015, 2014, 2013, 2012

Hachette UK's policy is to use papers that are natural, renewable and recyclable products and made from wood grown in sustainable forests. The logging and manufacturing processes are expected to conform to the environmental regulations of the country of origin.

Cover photo © BRAD–Fotolia
Typeset by Datapage (India) Pvt. Ltd.
Printed in Italy for Hodder Education, An Hachette UK Company, 338 Euston Road, London NW1 3BH.

Contents

Acknowledgements

We would like to thank the following people for their contributions: Chris Rice for her help with the section on operant conditioning; Ruth Forbes and the parents for the case studies of babies; Michelle Samson and Judith Stevens for their help on special needs and inclusion; Cathal Ryan for invaluable insights into safeguarding; Anne-Louise de Buriane and the staff and families of Langford Extended Primary School; Laura Meggitt, Community Play Specialist, for her valuable insights and for providing many of the early years case studies; everyone on the staff team at Kate Greenaway Nursery School and Children's Centre.

Thank you also to: the editorial team at Hodder Education, particularly Colin Goodlad, Publisher, and Chloé Harmsworth, Desk Editor, for all their hard work and support; Llinos Edwards, Freelance Copy-editor, who always manages to make everything clearer at each stage of writing.

The publishers would like to thank Teena Kamen for her help in preparing the manuscript.

Please note that all legislation, policies and so on were correct at time of publication.

Photo credits

All photos © Justin O'Hanlon, except:

Figures: 1.1 © Gideon Mendel/Corbis; 1.2 © tungphoto – Fotolia; 2.4 © philipus – Fotolia; 2.5 © Tamas Vargyasi – Fotolia; 3.5 © Louth Eastfield Infants' & Nursery School; 4.11 © Courtesy of Community Hygiene Concern; 4.12 © DR P. MARAZZI/SCIENCE PHOTO LIBRARY; 6.1 photography © Save the Children; 6.5 © FASawareUK; 8.1 © Sergej Khackimullin – Fotolia; 8.4 © Elly Godfroy/Alamy; 8.5 © Dalia Drulia – Fotolia; 8.7 © Vally – Fotolia; 9.1 © Foundation for the Study of Infant Deaths; 9.3 © ASTIER/ SCIENCE PHOTO LIBRARY; 9.4 © Gusto Images/Science Photo Library; 9.5a © PHOTOTAKE Inc./Alamy; 9.5b © Medical-on-Line/Alamy; 9.6 © Arvind Balaraman – Fotolia; 9.7 © HATTIE YOUNG/SCIENCE PHOTO LIBRARY; 9.8 © Aleksandar Kosev – Fotolia; 9.9 © Wong-Baker FACES Foundation 1983; 9.10a © Ian Hooton/Science Photo Library; 9.10b © Carolyn A Mckeone/Science Photo Library; 10.2 © Vadim Ponomarenko – Fotolia.com; 10.4 © micromonkey – Fotolia; 10.5 © Monkey Business – Fotolia; 11.5 © Brian Mitchell/Corbis; 11.6 © Jaren Wicklund – Fotolia; 11.7 © Fotosearch/Getty Images; 12.2 © Monkey Business – Fotolia.com; 13.1a © outlook/Alamy; 13.1b © TEMISTOCLE LUCARELLI – Fotolia; 13.1c © BSIP, Bajande/Science Photo Library; 13.1d © Reagan Pannell/Alamy; 13.1e © Stephanie Rausser/Iconica/Getty Images; 13.2a © Vivid Pixels – Fotolia; 13.2b © Lev Olkha – Fotolia; 13.2c © 2009 Benjamin Loo – Fotolia; 13.2d © ImageState Media; 13.2e © Creatas/Photolibrary.com; 13.2f © lisalucia – Fotolia; 13.4 © David Taylor/Alamy; 13.6 © Stephen Coburn/Fotolia.com; 13.7 © Julian Rovagni/Fotolia.com.

Figures 1.3, 6.6, 8.3, 8.6, 10.3 © Andrew Callaghan.

Figures 6.7, 8.2, 12.1 © David Meggitt.

Figure 4.10 © Tom Bruce.

Figures 6.3 (Just Eat More Portion Poster) and 10.1 (The Eatwell Plate) © Crown copyright material as reproduced with permission of the Controller of HMSO and the Queen's Printer for Scotland.

Illustrations by Barking Dog Art, Oxford Designers and Illustrators and Kate Nardoni/Cactus Design and Illustration.

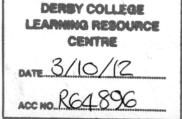

1 An introduction to working with children: Unit 1

Learning outcomes

In this chapter, you will learn:

1. The range of provision for children.
2. An initial understanding of the roles and responsibilities in promoting the rights of children.
3. What is meant by professional practice.
4. The principles and values that underpin working with children.
5. How to develop relevant study and time management skills.

Section 1: The range of provision for children

The main types of provision for children

Provision for children means the whole range of services that are specifically provided for children. Provision includes education and care services, health services, social services, and leisure and recreation services.

Services for children may be divided into four categories:

1 **Statutory services**: these are provided by the government (or state). The services that are provided are set by laws passed in Parliament.
2 **Voluntary services**: these are provided by organisations such as charities. Volunteers and paid staff provide services in the same way as in the statutory sector. Some or all of their funding comes from donations, and some are subsidised by the state.
3 **Private services**: these are profit-making services offered by private providers, and include private nurseries and private preparatory schools. They are inspected to ensure that the health and safety of the children are maintained.
4 **Independent services**: these are provided independently of the state and do not receive government funding; they include independent schools, which do not have to comply with the national curriculum of their home country because they are independent of the state.

Chapter 8 describes all these services and their roles in providing for children in detail.

Health services for children and their families

Most health services for children are statutory and free. The government's Department of Health is responsible for providing health care through the National Health Service (NHS), which was set up in 1948 to provide free health care to the entire population. Children are entitled to receive free health services provided by:

- GPs – or family doctors
- health visitors
- clinics
- hospitals.

Social services for children

Most social care services for children are statutory and free. Statutory social services were brought together under a director of children's services in each local authority following the Children Act 2004.

Social services provide a range of care and support for children and families, including:

- social workers
- residential child care

1

- foster care
- outreach service through Children's Centres.

Education services for children: integrated care and education

Statutory services

Most education services are statutory and free. Statutory education services include the following:

- The **Sure Start programme** (introduced in 1999) which brought together services for pre-school children and their families including early education, child care, health and family support.
- The **Early Years Foundation Stage** (EYFS): a comprehensive statutory framework (introduced in England in 2008 and in force until 31 August 2012, when a revised, simpler EYFS is being introduced 1st September 2012) that set the standards for the care, learning, and development of young children from birth to five.

- **Children's Centres**: the majority of these were developed from Sure Start local programmes, Neighbourhood Nurseries and Early Excellence Centres. Sure Start Children's Centres are places where children under five years old and their families can receive seamless holistic integrated services and information, and where they can access help from multidisciplinary teams of professionals.

- **Maintained nursery schools**: these offer either full-time or part-time places for children of three years to the equivalent of the end of the Reception Year. Some children may start at two years, but only if there is a recommendation and joint decision by the education, health and social services departments.

- **Nursery classes and nursery units**: nursery classes are attached to primary schools. The headteacher of the primary school may or may not be an expert in early years education. Nursery units are usually in a separate building with a separate coordinator.

Figure 1.1 Children's Centres provide a wide range of services for children and their families

- **Infant schools**: children start at infant school between the ages of four and five in a Reception class. Reception is the final part of the Foundation Stage. Pupils then transfer to Year One in the September following their fifth birthday, and to Year Two the following year. At the end of this time, pupils will move to a linked junior school.

Voluntary services

These services include:

- **Community nurseries**: these are often funded by voluntary organisations, such as Barnardo's, the Royal National Institute for the Blind (RNIB), Sense and Scope.
- **Pre-schools and playgroups**: many (but not all) are affiliated to the Pre-school Learning Alliance, which was set up in 1961 at a time when there was concern from parents at the lack of nursery education available. They usually offer part-time services, and offer perhaps two or three half-day sessions a week, often in a church hall. This type of provision is often the only one available in rural areas.
- **Day schools**, residential special schools, or specialist voluntary groups which support children in mainstream education.

Private services

These services include:

- **Private nurseries**, **nursery schools** and **day nurseries**: these are legally required to be registered and inspected, and to follow the current Early Years Foundation Stage (EYFS) statutory framework.
- **Private infant schools**: these are usually called preparatory schools. These schools are also required to follow the EYFS in Reception year.
- **Childminders, nannies and grandparents**: children are looked after in the childminder's home (HLE = Home Learning Environment), or in their own homes by grandparents or nannies. Childminders are offered training through the National Childminding Association, CACHE and childminding networks in local authorities. Nannies sometimes live with a family, but not always. Sometimes, they look after children from several different families.

Key terms

Sense – Sense is a national charity that supports and campaigns for children and adults who are deafblind. SENSE provides tailored support, advice and information as well as specialist services to all deafblind people, their families, carers and the professionals who work with them. It also supports people who have a single sensory impairment with additional needs.

Scope – Scope is a charity that works with disabled people of all ages and their families, across England and Wales.

Leisure and recreation services

Some of these services are statutory and are provided by the local authority, while others are privately owned and managed:

- sports centres, children's gyms
- music groups
- parks
- adventure playgrounds and soft play areas
- holiday schemes and activities
- lessons, such as dance and drama
- clubs, for example, Beavers, Cubs and Scouts; Rainbows, Brownies and Guides; Woodcraft Folk
- libraries.

The implications of funding for the statutory and independent sectors

Statutory services

These services are provided free of charge. Some statutory services are provided by central government and are funded from central taxation – for example, the National Health Service (NHS). Others are provided by local government and funded by a combination of local and central taxation – for example, education and social service departments.

Voluntary services

These organisations (mostly charities) rely on most or all of their funding from donations. They may also provide some of the statutory services, and will be paid by the local authority or government for these services. They are often staffed by volunteers and do not make any profit; any spare income is used to improve the quality of their service.

Private and independent services

These services include private day nurseries, private nursery schools, preparatory schools and kindergartens. They are available for those parents who can afford them, although some financial support is available through government schemes.

Government financial schemes

Childcare Tax Credit

Those parents who are eligible for Tax Credits may be eligible for Childcare Tax Credit which can help with up to 70 per cent of their childcare costs. This help is based on the parents' income.

Nursery Education Grant (NEG)

The government has recently introduced a scheme under which all three- and four-year-olds will get a free place at a nursery for at least 15 hours per week: over three days per week for five hours per day, or over five days per week for three hours per day. This money is available for public and private nurseries, registered playgroups and childminders who are accredited members of a childminding network. Because early years education places run on the school schedule, they are only available in term time and do not cover holiday provision. They are available for at least 38 weeks per year. The local authority pays the grant directly to the early education provider up to a certain maximum for three terms. If parents use a nursery for full daycare, the grant will pay for part of the day and parents will continue to pay for the rest.

Figure 1.2 Many local authorities provide play facilities for children

Section 2: Promoting the rights of children

What are children's rights?

Children are entitled to basic human rights such as food, health care, a safe home and protection from abuse. However, children are a special case because they cannot always stand up for themselves. They need a **special** set of rights which take account of their vulnerability and which ensure that adults take responsibility for their protection and development.

The UN Convention on the Rights of the Child (1989)

This is an international treaty that applies to all children and young people under the age of 18 years. It spells out the basic human rights of children everywhere. All children – without discrimination – have the right to:

- survive
- develop to their fullest potential
- be protected from harmful influences, abuse and exploitation

- participate fully in family, cultural and social life
- express and have their views taken into account on all matters that affect them
- play, rest and enjoy leisure.

This important treaty has been signed by almost every country in the world.

Children and young people have **responsibilities** as well as rights. Many have jobs, some care for relatives, a large proportion are school or college students; they all must respect other people's rights and act within the law. However, these responsibilities do not detract from their human rights, which everybody has from the moment of their birth.

A parent is responsible for the care and upbringing of their child. The Children and Young Persons Act 1933 imposes criminal liability for abandonment, neglect or ill treatment upon any person over the age of 16 years who is responsible for a child under 16 years. Because parental responsibility cannot be surrendered or transferred, parents are liable for neglecting their child if they choose an inadequate babysitter.

The rights embodied by the UN Convention which particularly relate to child care and education are these:

- Children have the right to be with their family or with those who will care best for them.
- Children have the right to enough food and clean water for their needs.
- Children have the right to an adequate standard of living.
- Children have the right to health care.
- Children have the right to play.
- Children have the right to be kept safe and not hurt or neglected.
- Disabled children have the right to special care and training.
- Children must not be used as cheap workers or as soldiers.
- Children have the right to free education.

Activity

Exploring children's rights

'In the UK it is still both legal and socially acceptable for parents to smack their children'

After considering the case of a boy who had been beaten regularly by his stepfather with a three-foot garden cane between the ages of five and eight, the European Court of Human Rights ruled in 1998 that the British law on corporal punishment in the home failed to protect children's rights. The stepfather had been acquitted (found innocent) by a British court of causing actual bodily harm. The stepfather had argued that the beating was 'reasonable chastisement'; this means that parents could use a degree of force in order to discipline their children. Recent changes to the law have removed this defence, which dates back to 1860. Current legislation, enforced under the Children Act 2004, still allows parents in England and Wales to administer moderate punishment as long as there is no reddening of the skin or if it causes harm such as bruising or mental harm.

Task 1

Individually, find out all you can about:

- the arguments **against** smacking children – in particular, investigate the work of the Children are Unbeatable! Alliance whose aims are

(a) to seek legal reform to give children the same protection under the law on assault as adults, and

(b) to promote positive, non-violent discipline (www.childrenareunbeatable.org.uk).

- the arguments **for** parents' right to smack their own children. For example, look into the Parents Have Rights campaign which is against any legislation that interferes with a parent's right to punish their children as they see fit (www.families-first.org.uk).

Task 2

In two groups, organise a debate on the issue of smacking children.

Group A will argue that 'The law should be changed so that physical punishment of children is never permitted'.

Group B will argue that 'Parents have the right to use whatever method of discipline works best for their children'.

Task 3

Prepare a fact file on the debate on smacking for the use of future students. Include a list of useful addresses and websites. Ensure that you find out about any recent changes to these laws in Scotland and elsewhere in the UK.

Value diversity, promote inclusiveness and differentiate activities

Planning the general learning environment

Planning begins with the observation of the child as a unique, valued and respected individual, with their own interests and needs. We could say this is all about getting to know the child. But further general planning is also necessary, because there is only so much that children can learn on their own. They need an environment that has been carefully thought through, along with the right help in using that environment. This aspect of planning ensures that the learning environment indoors and outdoors is balanced in what it offers, so that it helps all children in general but also caters for individual children.

All children deserve the best possible start in life and support that enables them to fulfil their potential. Children develop quickly in the early years and a child's experiences between birth and age five years have a major impact on their future life chances. A secure, safe and happy childhood is important in its own right. Together with good parenting, high quality early learning provides the foundation which children need to make the most of their abilities and talents as they grow up.

EYFS 2012

The EYFS:

- **ensures quality and consistency** across early years settings, so that every child makes good progress and no child gets left behind

- **provides a secure foundation** through learning and development opportunities which are planned around the needs and interests of each individual child, assessed and reviewed regularly

- **supports partnership working** between professionals and parents, and between different early years settings

- **provides equality of opportunity** and **anti-discriminatory practice**, ensuring that every child is included and supported.

The four overarching principles of the EYFS are:

1 A unique child

2 Positive relationships

3 A positive environment

4 Children develop and learn in different ways and at different rates.

Each principle is supported by four commitments which emphasise inclusive practice (children's entitlements, early support, equality and diversity). (See Section 4 of this chapter, page 17, for more details about these principles.)

A curriculum which includes all children

Most children learn in a rather uneven way. They have bursts of learning and then they have plateaux when their learning does not seem to move forward (but really they are consolidating their learning during this time). This is why careful observation and assessment for learning of individual children plus a general knowledge of child development are all very important. In the EYFS, observation, inclusion, assessment and record-keeping will be supported by DfES guidance (Enabling Environments, EYFS). Catching the right point for a particular bit of learning during development is a skill. So is recognising the child's pace of learning. Children have their own personalities and

moods. They are affected by the weather, the time of day, whether they need food, sleep or the lavatory, the experiences they have, their sense of wellbeing and their social relationships with children and adults.

Gifted and talented children

People who are talented in music, dance and mathematics tend to show promise early in their lives. The most important thing is that adults provide a rich and stimulating learning environment, indoors and outdoors, which encourages children to develop and extend their thinking, understand and talk about their feelings, and understand themselves and others. It is frustrating for gifted children when they are constrained and held back in their learning.

It is also important to remember that however gifted or talented a child may be in a particular respect, he or she is still a child. They need all the things that any child needs, and should not be put under pressure to behave and learn in advance of their general development.

Children with special educational needs (SEN) and disabilities

Some children will be challenged in their learning, and those working with children with SEN and disabilities will need to be particularly resourceful, imaginative and determined in helping them to learn.

Many children with SEN and disabilities are underestimated by the adults working with them. For example, most six-year-old children can run confidently across a field. However, in general, visually impaired children in mainstream settings are not expected to try to do this, and so they do not attempt it. No one suggests it to them or offers them help to do it. With the right help, the child might manage it, becoming physically more confident and mobile as a result. The experience of running across a field depends on the child's development, personality and mood. Walking hand-in-hand first might be important. Talking as you go helps. The child may need tips about picking up their feet, and eventually perhaps running towards your voice. If the child tumbles he will need reassurance, and not an anxious adult. Saying 'Can I help you up?' is more helpful than rushing over and asking 'Are you hurt?'.

Valuing and respecting the child's culture and family background

Every child needs to be included and to have full access to the curriculum, regardless of their ethnic background, culture, language, gender or economic background. No child should be held back in their learning due to restricted access to learning opportunities.

In order to plan, it is important to work closely in partnership with the child's parents or carers. Practitioners sometimes talk about 'my children', but children are unique individuals. When parents and practitioners work well together, respecting what they each bring to the partnership in a spirit of respect and trust, with a genuine exchange of information and knowledge, the child gains and so do the parents and staff (EYFS Positive Relationships; Parents as Partners).

Section 3: Professional practice

All those working with children and young people are bound by the law to respect the rights of children, young people and their families. In addition to the legal aspects, being a professional means that you must ensure that all children feel included, secure and valued; this is the cornerstone of a positive, integrated environment. As a professional, your practice should adhere to the CACHE values (see page 10) and also to any policies and codes of practice in your work setting. Professional practice should include:

- developing **positive relationships with parents** in order to work effectively with them and their children
- understanding the extent of your **responsibilities** and being answerable to others for your work
- working effectively as part of **a team**
- knowing **the lines of reporting** and how to get clarification about your role and duties
- understanding what is meant by **confidentiality** and your role in the preserving of secret or privileged information that parents or others share with you about their children or themselves.

What qualities make a good early childhood practitioner?

Above all else, an early childhood practitioner needs to like children and enjoy being with them. Caring as a quality is largely invisible, difficult to quantify and more noticeable when absent than when present. The main individual characteristics required are shown in the box below.

Guidelines for important personal qualities in an early childhood practitioner

1   **Listening**: attentive listening is a vital part of the caring relationship. Sometimes a child's real needs are communicated more by what is left unsaid than by what is actually said. Facial expressions, posture and other forms of body language all give clues to a child's feelings. A good carer will be aware of these forms of non-verbal communication (EYFS Positive Relationships – Listening to Children).

2   **Comforting**: this has a physical side and an emotional side. Physical comfort may be provided in the form of a cuddle at a time of anxiety, or by providing a reassuring safe environment to a distressed child. Touching, listening and talking can all provide emotional comfort as well (EYFS Positive Relationships – Key Person).

3   **Empathy**: this should not be confused with sympathy. Some people find it easy to appreciate how someone else is feeling by imagining themselves in that person's position. A good way of imagining how

Guidelines for important personal qualities in an early childhood practitioner (cont.)

a strange environment appears to a young child is to kneel on the floor and try to view it from the child's perspective.

4 **Sensitivity**: this is the ability to be aware of and responsive to the feelings and needs of another person. Being sensitive to other people's needs requires the carer to anticipate their feelings; for example those of a child whose mother has been admitted to hospital, or whose pet dog has just died.

5 **Patience**: this involves being patient and tolerant of other people's methods of dealing with problems, even when you feel that your own way is better.

6 **Respect**: a carer should have an awareness of a child's personal rights, dignity and privacy, and must show this at all times. Every child is unique, and so your approach will need to be tailored to each individual's needs.

7 **Interpersonal skills**: a caring relationship is a two-way process. You do not have to like the child you are caring for, but warmth and friendliness help to create a positive atmosphere and to break down barriers. Acceptance is important: you should always look beyond the disability or disruptive behaviour to recognise and accept the person.

8 **Self-awareness**: a carer is more effective if they are able to perceive what effect their behaviour has on other people. Being part of a team enables us to discover how others perceive us and to modify our behaviour in the caring relationship accordingly.

9 **Coping with stress**: caring for others effectively in a full-time capacity requires energy, and it is important to be aware of the possibility of professional burn-out. In order to help others, we must first help ourselves: the carer who never relaxes or develops any outside interests is more likely to suffer 'burn-out' than the carer who finds his or her own time and space.

Key term

Empathy – The ability to understand and share the feelings of another.

Your role – boundaries and limits

The skills required by the professional early childhood practitioner need to be practised with regard to certain responsibilities. (These aspects are covered more fully in Chapter 5.)

Guidelines for your responsibilities as a professional early childhood practitioner

1 **Respect the principles of confidentiality**: confidentiality is the preservation of secret (or privileged) information concerning children and their families which is disclosed in the professional relationship. It is a complex issue which has at its core the principle of trust. The giving or receiving of sensitive information should be subject to a careful consideration of the needs of the children and their families; for example, a child who is in need of protection has overriding needs which require that all relevant information be given to all the appropriate agencies, such as social workers, doctors, etc. Within the child care and education setting, it might be appropriate to discuss sensitive issues, but such information must never be disclosed to anyone outside the setting.

Guidelines for your responsibilities as a professional early childhood practitioner (cont.)

2 **Commitment to meeting the needs of the children**: the needs and rights of all children should be paramount, and the early childhood practitioner must seek to meet these needs within the boundaries of the work role. Any personal preferences and prejudices must be put aside; all children should be treated with respect and dignity, irrespective of their ethnic origin, socio-economic group, religion or disability. The equal opportunities code of practice involved will give detailed guidelines, together with EYFS.

3 **Responsibility and accountability in the workplace**: the supervisor, line manager, teacher or parent will have certain expectations about your role, and your responsibilities should be detailed in the job contract. As a professional, you need to carry out all your duties willingly and to be answerable to others for your work. It is vital that all workers know the lines of reporting and how to obtain clarification of their own role and responsibility. If you do not feel confident in carrying out a particular task, either because you do not fully understand it or because you have not been adequately trained, then you have a responsibility to state your concerns and ask for guidance.

4 **Respect for parents and other adults**: the training you have received will have emphasised the richness and variety of child-rearing practices in the UK. It is an important part of your professional role that you respect the wishes and views of parents and other carers, even when you may disagree with them. You should also recognise that parents are usually the people who know their children best; and in all your dealings with parents and other adults, you must show that you respect their cultural values and religious beliefs (EYFS Positive Relationships – Parents as Partners).

5 **Communicate effectively with team members and other professionals**: the training you have received will have emphasised the importance of effective communication in the workplace. You will also be aware of the need to plan in advance for your work with young children: knowledge of children's needs in all developmental areas will enable you to fulfil these within your own structured role.

Developing appropriate relationships with children

See also Chapter 3, page 143 for developing relationships with adults and children.

The CACHE values

In line with the CACHE values, you need to ensure that the child or young person is at the centre of your practice – that their needs are paramount.

Treat children and young people with respect

This means you:

- give only essential directions and allow children to make choices
- set appropriate directions which are realistic and consistent
- ask open-ended questions to encourage language development
- avoid labelling children
- are warm and positive in a way which affirms children.

Keep children and young people safe

This means you:

- ensure they are supervised at all times
- ensure children are safe at all times: make sure that all potentially dangerous materials and objects are kept out of their reach and that consideration is made of a child's stage and individual ability in the use of scissors, knives, etc.

Value and respect children and young people

This means you:

- listen to them
- do not impose your own agendas on them
- do not single out any one child for special attention
- ensure that children maintain control over their own play
- are friendly, courteous and sensitive to their needs
- praise and motivate them; display their work
- speak *to* the child not *at* the child; with young children, this means getting down to their level; with young people you should ensure that you maintain eye contact
- respect their individuality
- develop a sense of trust and caring with each child and young person.

Emotional attachment to children

Child care practitioners are often concerned, or feel that parents are anxious, about young children becoming too attached to staff. However, babies and young children need to form close attachments with significant adults in their lives, and they cannot become too closely attached. Some young children spend many hours in group settings outside the home – they need and ought to develop attachments to their key person. Parents who work long hours may experience a conflict of emotions. They want their child to be happy and secure in nursery care, but they do not want to feel forgotten or pushed out; parents often feel a real anxiety when their child shows affection for their key person.

Figure 1.3 Babies and children need to form emotional attachments

Physical contact with babies, children and young people

Babies and very young children need physical contact – they need to be held and cuddled in order to develop emotionally. Hugging a baby, comforting a child when they are upset, putting a plaster on them, changing their wet pants – all these are everyday ways in which adults care for young children. However, there is a growing concern among child care professionals about touching children in their care. Researchers say that there is anxiety and uncertainty about what is acceptable and what is not when it comes to innocent physical contact with children. If teachers and other child care professionals are no longer allowed to offer comforting hugs – or sometimes even to put on a plaster or sun cream – their relationship with the children they look after will certainly suffer.

Your setting should have a code of conduct which will give clear guidelines on appropriate physical contact with the children or young people in your care. What is appropriate physical contact with a baby or toddler – such as hugging them when upset or sitting them on your lap to explain something – will not be seen as appropriate with an older child (the EYFS also gives guidance on this).

Maintaining a professional attitude

It is important to remember that your relationship with the children in your care is a professional one. You should always be friendly and approachable but not try to take the place of the child's parents. Similarly, you should communicate with each child at a level which is appropriate to their stage of development and their holistic needs – you should not yourself behave as a child when interacting with them.

Developing appropriate relationships with colleagues and other adults

Most early years practitioners work with colleagues within a team. There are certain benefits for each individual from working in a team. These include:

- the sharing of responsibility – as well as knowledge
- a sense of belonging and a sharing of problems, difficulties and successes
- staff weaknesses being balanced by other people's strengths
- children and young people benefit from seeing people working well together.

There will always be areas in your work where you experience conflict or stress – these are discussed in Chapter 4.

Communication skills

Although your main job is to care for and educate young children, you will also need to develop positive relationships with adults. These adults will (for the most part) be your colleagues and parents of the children. However, you may also need to interact or communicate with other family members and other professionals involved with the children.

Communication has many different forms: verbal, non-verbal (including signing), written and pictorial.

Verbal communication

For verbal communication to be effective, consideration needs to be given to:

- tone of voice: this can be as important as the words actually spoken
- pace of speech: some parts of the message may be missed if you talk too quickly
- clear pronunciation: words that are mumbled may not be heard easily
- volume of speech: speaking too softly or too loudly
- language used
- accent or dialect.

When talking on the telephone, even though the other person cannot see you, he or she will usually be able to sense when you are not giving your full attention to the conversation.

Figure 1.4 (a) An open posture encourages communication (b) A closed posture inhibits communication

Non-verbal aspects of communication

Non-verbal communication is widely used by everyone, often without any words being spoken. Waving hello or goodbye, beckoning someone, a smile or 'thumbs up' sign convey messages. Used in conjunction with speech they aid understanding.

- **Eye contact**: perhaps the most important aspect of non-verbal communication is eye contact. It is extremely difficult to hold a conversation or communicate in any way without it. A practitioner who is listening to a child, young person, parent or carer will therefore use eye contact to express sincerity and empathy – and to show that he or she is attending carefully. However, it is important to be aware that, in certain cultures, mutual eye contact is considered disrespectful. Practitioners should adapt their use of eye contact accordingly.
- **Body language**: refers to the way we stand or sit (upright, slouched, tense, relaxed), the way we hold ourselves, or our posture.

- **Gestures**: most of us use gestures when we speak: shrugging, shaking the head or perhaps to point to something. Indeed, some people cannot communicate without using their hands and arms!
- **Touch**: sometimes it may be appropriate to use touch as a gesture of sympathy, reassurance or guidance, or particularly when communicating with a person who is visually impaired.
- **Facial expressions**: our facial expressions are important in conveying what we mean and how we feel. We judge whether another person has understood what we are saying and how they feel about it by watching facial expressions.

Failure to make eye contact and a 'closed' body stance (arms folded or held across body, hunched body) can make effective communication very difficult. Similarly, an adult with a tense, possibly aggressive, body stance also poses difficulties in communicating effectively. When faced with either of these examples, it is important to interact and respond in a way that reassures him/her.

Barriers to communication

There can be many barriers to communication:

- a visual or hearing impairment
- a different first or 'preferred' language
- strong accent or dialect
- technical or specialist language not being understood
- too much background noise or poor acoustics
- poor lighting so that facial expressions cannot be seen clearly.

Activity

Active listening

Working in threes, with one observer, one sender (parent, in this case) and one receiver (practitioner), carry out a conversation in which the parent talks about his/her difficulty sleeping and his/her tiredness.

- In the first instance, the receiver should not give any eye contact or indication that he or she is listening – no nodding, grunting or murmuring.
- How long can the sender try to make conversation? Discuss how the sender feels.
- Then change to active listening: the receiver should try to adopt an 'open' posture, maintain eye contact (without staring), indicate that he or she is listening and, at an appropriate point in the conversation, reflect back what he or she has been told.
- Change roles so that everyone tries each one.

Active listening

Developing good listening skills is very important. Most importantly, active listening involves eye contact (or, for visually impaired people, a light touch on the hand or arm to show your presence), an open body position, an interested facial expression and some murmurs of encouragement or nodding to reassure the speaker or sender that attention is being paid. To be an effective listener, you need to concentrate on the sender and understand the message that is being sent. This is different from an ordinary conversation in which you may exchange information about similar experiences and compare them. To ensure that you have understood the message, you should 'reflect back' the main points or concerns using some of the same words and checking before the sender continues. However, it is important to be aware that, in certain cultures, mutual eye contact is considered disrespectful. Practitioners should adapt their use of eye contact accordingly.

In the following example, the early years practitioner immediately recalls her own experiences rather than focusing on and responding to the parent.

Parent: I slept very badly last night, I just couldn't get comfortable.

Practitioner: I'm really tired too. My little boy kept crying and I couldn't get him off to sleep till 3 o'clock this morning.

See Chapter 5 for more on communication skills.

Section 4: The principles and values underpinning work with children

All people working with children and young people must work within a framework that embodies sound principles and values (see also Chapter 5).

The welfare of the child and young person is paramount

There are a number of basic principles that you should bear in mind when working with children and young people:

- Put children and young people first by treating their opinions and concerns seriously.
- Show compassion and sensitivity.
- Be aware that your body language can give away what you are really feeling.
- On no account must you slap, smack, shake or humiliate a child or young person. Besides going against the principles of child care, this is also abuse.

- As the responsible adult, it is your job to remain in control of every situation while respecting the child.

Every Child Matters (ECM)

The Children Act 2004, Every Child Matters, Change for Children and the EYFS set out an expectation for services to improve the way they work together to give all children and young people the best possible opportunity to grow up by experiencing the following outcomes:

- being healthy
- staying safe
- enjoying and achieving
- making a positive contribution
- achieving economic wellbeing.

Being healthy

This involves promoting a healthy lifestyle so that children and young people are able to enjoy good health. The Plan aims to:

- provide parents and carers with access to advice, information and support to promote healthy choices
- provide a range of services to promote children and young people's physical health – for example, sports sessions, healthy eating classes
- develop integrated services to promote the mental health of children and young people
- reduce alcohol consumption and smoking among young people, for example, by running peer support programmes on drug misuse
- identify and respond to additional health needs of children and young people experiencing health inequalities because of long-term parental health difficulties or because they are looked after in public care
- develop services to ensure that children and young people with disabilities or long-term health needs receive integrated assessment and responses to their health and development needs.

Staying safe

This involves ensuring that children and young people are being protected from harm and neglect and are growing up able to look after themselves. The Plan aims to:

- support parents and carers to provide safe homes and stability as their children grow
- help children and young people make choices, build their confidence and avoid harm; for example, by running anti-bullying projects, safe cycling groups, after-school clubs and self-defence groups
- identify people and circumstances that represent a serious risk to children and young people, and respond to such threats quickly and effectively
- assist children and families experiencing violence or discrimination (in the home, at school or in the community) to bring about change
- identify and safeguard children and young people who are looked after in public or private care settings
- encourage communities to create a supportive and stimulating environment in which children and young people can play safely while developing protective skills.

Enjoying and achieving

This involves helping children and young people to maximise their potential and develop skills for adulthood. The Plan aims to:

- support children and young people, their families and communities to have high aspirations and expectations
- raise achievement for all
- raise the achievement of vulnerable and underachieving groups, including the lowest-attaining 20 per cent of children and young people
- improve outcomes for looked-after children
- increase attendance in schools and enjoyment in learning
- improve access to enjoyable, challenging and enriching opportunities for children and young people, with particular focus on those with special and additional needs and those in disadvantaged and isolated communities; for example, with theatre arts groups, self-advocacy skills programmes, and cultural dance and music projects.

Labour terminology (Pre-11 May 2010)	Coalition terminology (Post-11 May 2010)
England will be the best place in the world for children to grow up	Make Britain the most family-friendly place in Europe
Targeted services	Fairer services
Targets and outcomes	Results and impact
Children's trusts	Local areas, better, fairer services
One children's workforce framework/tool	Local areas self-assessment tool
Five outcomes/ECM	Help children achieve more
Narrow the gap	Close the gap, vulnerable and disadvantaged
Integrated working	People working better to provide better services
Safeguarding children	Child protection
Family Intervention Projects (FIPs)	Key workers providing intensive support to families

Table 1.1 Changes in terminology were revealed in an internal DfE memo, split into two columns for words used before 11 May 2010 (when the Coalition Government took office) and those with which they should be replaced (CYP, 2010)

Making a positive contribution

This involves enabling children and young people to use their skills and abilities in ways that enhance their own lives and the lives of their community. The Plan aims to:

- support parents, carers, families, schools and communities to promote positive behaviour
- encourage children and young people to participate in a wide range of service planning and development activities; for example, conservation schemes, recycling programmes and mentoring projects
- provide young people with access to a range of safe spaces and facilities in which they can meet and engage in positive activities
- provide young people with increased opportunities to take up volunteering and community involvement
- provide children and young people who are at risk of school or social exclusion with access to preventative services that will help them stay out of trouble.

Achieving economic wellbeing

This involves helping children and young people to overcome income barriers and achieve their full potential in life. The Plan aims to:

- support families who are dependent on benefits or low incomes to improve their wellbeing and be economically active

- ensure that children are offered the best start in life through children's centres and high-quality early years and play provision
- improve transport accessibility and promote sustainable transport solutions for young people in rural areas
- work with local schools, colleges and employers to create opportunities for all 14- to 19-year-olds to pursue a course of study where they will learn in a style that suits them and in subject areas which motivate them
- ensure that impartial, comprehensive and high-quality information, advice, guidance and support are available to all young people, in proportion to need, to assist them in making successful transitions to further learning and work; for example, by preparation for work and training, and financial literacy classes for young people
- support homeless and vulnerable young people or families with dependent children to sustain safe, secure and stable accommodation and engage in employment, education or training.

Since the Coalition Government took office in May 2010 there has been some confusion as to the relevance and future of the Every Child Matters agenda. The Children's Workforce Development Project understands that while there has been a shift away from using the *terminology* of ECM (see Table 1.1 above), the ethos of the five outcomes is being retained on a local level in many areas by those working to support children and young people. The phrase ECM is not officially banned but since the Coalition Government came to power, the agenda in name is gone. In March 2011, Education Secretary Michael Gove argued that he had no problem with ECM as a list, but suggested it should be 'policed in a hands-off way' (Children and Young People's Workforce, 2011).

Four guiding themes shape the requirements of the EYFS, and should shape practice in early years settings. The themes are:

1 Every child is a **unique child**, who begins learning at birth and can become resilient, capable, confident and self-assured.
2 Children learn to be strong and independent through **positive relationships** with their parents and carers and with others, including their key person at their early years setting.
3 A positive **environment** – in which children's experiences are planned to reflect their needs and help build their confidence, and in which there is a strong partnership between early years practitioners, parents and other professionals – is crucial if children are to fulfil their potential and learn and develop well.
4 **Children develop and learn in different ways and at different rates**. All areas of learning and development are important and are inter-connected.

Section 5: Study skills

Organising and planning your time

Any activity can seem preferable to working on an assignment or settling down to revision: tidying your room, staring at the wall, fetching just one more small snack or even doing the washing up! However, when work is postponed regularly, deadlines and examination dates can increase

feelings of disorganisation and panic and can trigger a 'flight' response. It can become tempting to produce the minimum work possible or even to abandon assignments completely. Excuses have to be invented, deadlines renegotiated, further assignments become due before the last ones are completed and before long the course begins to feel overwhelming and unmanageable. Of course, people can have very good reasons for finding their workload difficult to manage: child care or other family responsibilities, the need to earn money through part-time work, and unexpected traumas or illnesses can all increase the pressure on students. However, if you are generally enjoying your course and finding the work stimulating and interesting, you are likely to want to find a way of organising your time so that you can keep a balance between your work, your social life and your other interests and commitments.

Planning time

There are only so many hours in a week. Although keeping rigidly to a 'weekly planner' or timetable will not always be easy or desirable, it should help you to focus on what free time you have in a week and which 'chunks' of it can be used for coursework and revision.

Activity

Planning your time

Draw up a table or print one out from a calendar program on a computer, showing the seven days of the week as headings and hourly blocks of time down the left-hand side. (For example 8–9 am, 9–10 am through to 9–10 pm.)

Now mark on:

- your college or school timetabled commitments (your lectures and lessons)
- any paid work, housework or child care/family commitments
- travel times

- times you normally spend with friends/sports activities/other leisure pursuits

- any 'unmissable' television programmes (not too many!).

What 'chunks' of time have you left for studying:

- in the day?

- in the evening?

- at weekends?

Do not forget that the half-term or end-of-term holidays can be a good time to catch up on assignments and revision. Remember to include these in your long-term calculations. However, having completed your planner, will you need to re-adjust any commitments to give you enough time to complete coursework. How important will it be for you to spend some time studying in the day as well as in the evening?

Motivation during study periods

It is important to find a place where you can work without interruptions and distractions. Even if you have the luxury of a room and a desk of your own at home, you will probably need to consider using your school, college or public library for some study periods. Settling down to a period of study is easier if you follow these suggestions:

- Remove all distractions of hunger, noise, cold and sociable friends!

- Try not to study if you are feeling angry or upset.

- Keep a pad of paper or digital equivalent next to you as you work. When ideas or other things occur to you, you can note them down before you forget them.

- Give yourself realistic targets and decide for how long you will study before you start. Try not to work for more than an hour without a short break. Reward yourself for completing what you planned to do.

- Try to give yourself a variety of activities to work on.

- Have the phone number of someone else from your class or group handy in case you need to check what you need to do or want to discuss the best way to go about a task.

Compiling a portfolio

A portfolio is a collection of the different types of evidence which can be used to show successful completion of the course. Examples of evidence include:

- Completed assignments, projects or case studies, including action plans and evaluations. These can be in written form or word-processed, although work in the form of video recordings, audio-tape recordings, photographs, logbooks or diaries may also be acceptable where they contain evidence of the practical demonstration of skills. Check with your teacher or tutor.

- Past records of achievement, qualifications, work experience or other evidence of 'prior learning'.

- Samples of relevant class or lecture notes, lists, personal reading records or copies of letters written (perhaps regarding work experience, to request information or advice, or related to job or higher education applications).

Equipment and materials

As soon as you know how many mandatory and optional units you will be taking for the course, it will be worthwhile taking advantage of any cheap stationery offers at high street stores and equipping yourself with:

- at least four large A4 lever arch files and sets of extra wide file dividers (or large A4 box files). One of these files will become your portfolio; the others can be used for organising and storing notes for each mandatory or optional unit and for a 'college and course administration' file

- a hole punch

- file paper, plain and lined

- plastic pockets or report files. These are not essential but you may feel better if finished assignments are presented neatly in a binder or pocket of some sort. However, do not enclose each individual sheet of an assignment within a plastic pocket. This is expensive, ecologically unsound and drives your teachers and assessors crazy when they have to remove sheets to make comments on your work!

- post-it index stickers can be useful to help 'flag up' important pieces of work in your completed portfolio
- small exercise books or notebooks, to act as logbooks or diaries.

If you are dyslexic or have another disability which prevents or makes it difficult for you to take notes in lectures, you might consider using a recording device to enable you to record lectures and play them back at another time.

Reading, note-taking and using a library

Textbooks such as this can offer you a basic framework for the ideas and information you need for the different subject areas covered in the course, CACHE Level 3 Child Care and Education. Your lectures and classes will supply you with additional material. However, you will need to carry out your own reading and research, making your own notes and updating information in areas where there is constant change (such as child care legislation). It will be useful for you to find out how the national organisation of care and education services works in the area and in the community in which you live.

You cannot do this successfully without making full use of libraries (including their computers), newspapers and journals, television and film, and information produced by a range of national, local and voluntary organisations. If you have personal access to the internet, you may find such research decidedly easier, and this book contains many references to websites worth exploring. Make sure that you are shown how to use all the relevant facilities of your library, whether school, college or public.

Using the internet

Think before reaching for the mouse. Using the internet can be highly productive but it can also take up a lot of your time. Before you start, work out:

- what you need to know
- how much you need to know
- when you need the information by
- whether you have a sensible search strategy. Do you have a list of recommended sites, or know the best way to use a search engine such as Google or Yahoo!?
- whether you could find the information you need more easily in books or a journal.

Strategies for reading and note-taking

We have all had the experience of reading a sentence, paragraph, or even a whole page, without being able to remember what we have just read. To be of most use to you, reading will often need to be combined with note-taking.

Taking notes is time-consuming and requires active concentration. Students often:

- worry if they are spending too much time taking endless, detailed notes without really understanding what they will be used for
- give up note-taking because they cannot seem to work out what to write down and what not to. This can be a particular problem when taking notes in lessons and lectures.

Essentially, note-taking is a strategy for helping you to think, understand and remember. There are many situations in life when it is important to focus on the key issues or points being communicated. For example, you may have to know exactly what to do if a child in your care has an asthma attack or needs adrenaline for a peanut allergy. You may have to explain these things quickly to another person, summarising essential information.

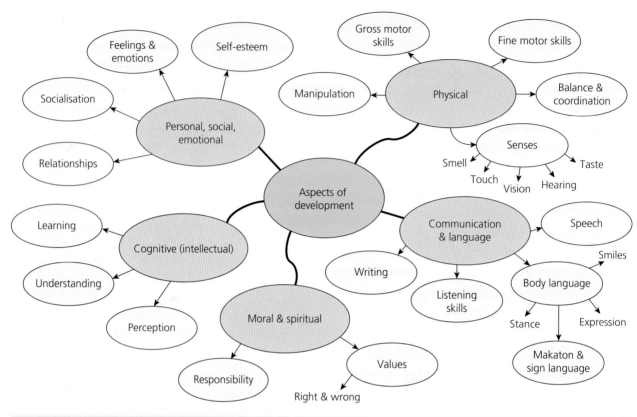

Figure 1.5 An example of a mind map

Deciding what to write down when you take notes is easier if you think about why you are taking notes. You may need to take different types of notes for different reasons. You will get better at working out methods of note-taking which suit you, the more you try out different approaches. It also helps to think about ways to store your notes so that they are easily accessible to you when you need them. If they are written or designed in such a way that you can make use of them again, you will be more likely to come back to them.

Everyone develops a personal style of note-taking which is best suited to their personality.

Mind-mapping

If you work better visually or spatially rather than in writing, you can make graphic 'notes': flow charts, block designs, family trees, spider plans or other forms of mind map. This method can be used for generating ideas and planning your work as well as, later on, note-taking and revising.

- In the centre of your page, draw a picture of, or name in words, your main topic or theme.
- Draw branches from this main topic in thick lines (use different colours or patterns). Label your branches with key words and/or images.
- Draw sub-branches from the main branches to represent sub-topics or to elaborate and extend your ideas. Again, use key words, phrases, images, pictures and colour. Use italics, underlining and capitals to highlight your work.
- Let your ideas flow and develop. Add more detail to your mind map as ideas occur to you. However, the mind map is not meant to be an art form, more a way to focus your attention on the essential components of a piece of work, topic or report.

Activity

Which method of note-taking suits me best?

Three different methods for taking notes are summarised below. Working individually or as a small group, experiment with each of these methods for:

1 taking notes from this textbook

2 taking notes from a lecture

3 taking notes from a relevant television documentary.

Discuss and compare the results of your experiments with each method. Which method did you feel most comfortable with? Did you find yourself writing too little or too much? How much time did the exercises take? Would you find the notes useful to read again? What would you use the notes for?

Underlining and highlighting

If you own the book or article you are taking notes from, highlighting, underlining and marking the margin with asterisks or other symbols can be a quick and effective method of skim-reading a text, focusing your attention on it and getting to grips with the material as a whole. Again, the most important part of this activity is that you are concentrating on what you are doing.

Writing assignments, observations and reports

Approximately two-thirds of the CACHE Level 3 Child Care and Education course is assessed through coursework and the completion of practical evidence records (PERs). Most of this written coursework is set in the form of assignments and projects – although some is assessed through multiple choice question papers (MCQs). There are five main reasons for this emphasis on coursework:

1 to allow you to make your own contribution to (or put your own stamp on) each subject or topic-related assignment

2 to support and encourage you to use your own initiative in solving problems, answering questions and completing tasks

3 to enable you to use each assignment to acquire a deeper knowledge and understanding of the area you are studying and to reflect critically on the ways in which you learn

4 to provide opportunities to work with others and gain confidence in approaching your teachers, tutors, lecturers, friends and others working in child care and education for help, extra information, the exchange of views, work experience and the acquisition of practical skills

5 ultimately, to put you in charge of your own learning:

- to enable you to work out, after you have finished a piece of work, what you have learnt and what you still need to know, what was easy and what was more difficult, and how you would improve it given another chance
- to give you the ability to know when your work is good or good enough without over-relying on the approval and assessments of others
- to allow you to transfer the appropriate skills and knowledge to any future study or work.

When you can do this you will have well-developed meta-cognitive skills: you can 'think about thinking' and reflect upon your own learning style and strategies, choosing those most appropriate to a task.

Planning and prioritising tasks

If you use a planner regularly it is easier to break up assignments, plans and observations into a series of smaller tasks, each of which you could aim to complete within a manageable time such as an hour or two. Sub-dividing your coursework in this way also allows you to prioritise the tasks. In what order are they best done? Which really needs to be done straight away?

- Make a list of small tasks in order of priority with the time you estimate they will take and target dates for completion.
- Leave room on your action plan to amend these dates when and if your plan is modified.

Monitoring and revising your work

There are likely to be many points during the completion of a piece of coursework when you will change direction or modify your original plan in some way. On your action plan, keep a note of:

- the reasons for changing your plans
- what new plans you have for the work.

Writing a bibliography

You will be expected to write a bibliography (a list of books, articles, and other resources used) for each assignment or observation you submit. To do this properly, you need to make a note of your materials and references as you study. There is nothing worse than finishing an assignment and then spending valuable time hunting down the name of a book you read in the library but did not note the details properly. As a general rule, you need to note:

- the title of the book or article (or website address)
- the author(s)
- the publisher
- the date of publication
- the place of publication.

Examples:

- Book: Bruce, T. (2005) *Early Childhood Education*. 3rd edn. London: Hodder and Stoughton.
- Article: Bruner, J., Wood, D. and Ross, G. (1976) 'The role of tutoring in problem-solving', *Journal of Child Psychology and Psychiatry* 17, 89–100.

The **Harvard system of referencing** is most often used. The references within your text use the author's name and the date of publication. Then the full details of the book or article are listed – alphabetically – in the bibliography and/or reference list at the end of the assignment.

Other sources of information or references in your work may come from the internet (give the website address), workplace (acknowledge the source), television programmes, video or film (give the title and date), or friends, family and teachers (attribute information as accurately as you can).

Memorising key ideas

There are many situations in working life where, under pressure, it will have been important or even crucial (for example, where first-aid knowledge has had to be applied) to have memorised key information or ideas. In more routine working situations, it will of course be possible to check your understanding or memory by consulting reference manuals, books or colleagues. The ability to use this skill will also become more automatic with practice. In any case, being required to memorise something is good rehearsal for real-life pressures and crises.

Case Study · Using your knowledge

Parminda is an early years worker at a day nursery for children aged five years and under. Parents usually pick up the children by 6 pm. On Friday, Lorna's father Richard turns up 15 minutes early, clearly drunk, and demanding to take his daughter home immediately. Richard does not live with Lorna's mother Pat, and there is an agreement that he picks up Lorna on Mondays and Tuesdays, and Pat picks her up on the other three weekdays.

Parminda has answered the door to Richard, who is now shouting at her in the reception area of the nursery building. He is swearing and threatening to push Parminda out of the way if she does not let him into the room where the children are playing.

Case Study | Using your knowledge (cont.)

Though feeling nervous, Parminda has fortunately remembered three key pieces of advice given her at a training course on facing aggression in the workplace:

1 Stay calm and use positive, not negative, words and phrases to help change the emotion of the aggressor.
2 Show that you value and appreciate good behaviour.
3 Firmly and gently explain how the aggressor's behaviour is affecting you.

Parminda suggests to Richard that she can help him if he stops shouting. She says that she will talk to her supervisor to see what she can do to help, adding that his shouting is making her feel nervous, although she is sure that a solution to the problem could be found. Although still tense and red-faced, Richard calms down enough to listen to the nursery manager, who has now arrived at the scene. He agrees to wait to talk to Pat and, in the intervening ten minutes, reveals that there have been problems between Pat and himself over access to Lorna.

Taking a test

When the day of a test arrives, have breakfast, give yourself plenty of time to check equipment, and arrive on time but not too early. Try not to talk about the test with friends before you start. Have a last look at any brief notes or summaries you have made. As soon as you are allowed to:

- read the questions
- make sure you understand the test instructions
- ask for help if necessary
- take your time
- highlight key words and note down any key facts you will have to use at some point but may forget as the test proceeds.

Assessment practice

Unit 1

Check that you know:

- the different types of settings from the statutory, voluntary and private sectors for children in your local area
- the main legislation in your country that supports the rights of children
- the principles and values that underpin working with children
- the professional skills you need when working with children
- the characteristics of working in a multi-agency team
- the importance of a child-centred approach.

 Useful resources

Foundation Years website (developed by 4Children) is the 'one stop shop' for resources, information and the latest news on the foundation years. The website provides advice and guidance for practitioners on working effectively with parents as partners in their children's learning: http://www.foundationyears.org.uk/

2 Development from conception to age 16 years: Unit 2

Section 1: How to apply the general principles and theoretical perspectives to all areas of development

Child development is an essential subject of study for everyone who works with young children. Looking after other people's children gives you different responsibilities compared to having your own children. So people who work with other people's children need to be trained properly and carefully. They need to be informed about how children develop and learn.

The key to understanding child development is 'wholeness'. Studying **holistic** child development is a way of seeing children in the round, as whole people.

Aspects of development

The various aspects of development are intricately linked: each affects and is affected by the others.

For example, once children have reached the stage of emotional development when they feel secure being apart from their main carer, they will have access to a much wider range of relationships, experiences and opportunities for learning. Similarly, when children can use language effectively, they will have more opportunities for social interaction. If one aspect or area of development is hampered or neglected in some way, children will be challenged in reaching their full potential.

The whole child may be looked at under the following headings or aspects of development:

- Physical
- Communication and language
- Intellectual and learning
- Social, emotional and behavioural.

The contextualised child

Researchers in the field of child development now realise that when, for example, children quarrel, it is almost impossible to say which aspect of their behaviour is:

- emotional (anger)
- physical (stamping with rage)
- intellectual or language (what they say or do).

Researchers now know that, in order to understand what is going on, it is also very important to identify who or what made a particular child angry, starting the quarrel. This is the **context** of the behaviour. So, it is important to contextualise the child when studying child development. By looking at child development in context we recognise that the biological part of development (physical development and genetic factors) is integrated with the cultural part of development (social, cultural, intellectual and linguistic factors).

Key terms

Holistic – Seeing a child in the round as a whole person, emotionally, intellectually, socially, physically, morally, culturally and spiritually.

Development – The general sequence in the way that the child functions in terms of movement, language, thinking, feelings, etc. Development continues from birth to death and can be likened to a web or network.

Context – This is made up of people and provision. It creates both the access to learning and the ethos in which the child learns.

Ethos – The characteristic spirit of a group of people or community, for example, a happy ethos or a caring ethos.

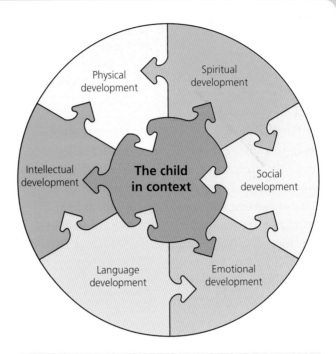

Figure 2.1 We can think of studying integrated development as being like looking at the pieces of a jigsaw

The difference between sequence of development and rate of development

Sequence of development

Children across the world seem to pass through similar sequences of development, but in different ways and different rates according to their culture. The work of Mary Sheridan on developmental sequences has been invaluable, but she suggests that children move through rigidly prescribed stages that are linked to the child's age: the child sits, then crawls, then stands, then walks. In fact, this is not the case. Not all children crawl: blind children often do not. Some children 'bottom-shuffle', moving along in a sitting position. For example, Mark moved around by bottom-shuffling and did not walk until he was two years old. He went on to run, hop and skip at the normal times. Walking late was not a cause for concern, and he did not suffer from any developmental delay.

A traditional approach to child development study has been to emphasise **normative measurement**. This is concerned with 'milestones' or stages in a child's development. These show what *most* children can do at a particular age. In reality, there is a wide range of normal development, and this will be influenced by genetic, social and cultural factors. Children have been labelled as 'backward' or 'forward' in relation to the so-called 'normal' child, which is not always helpful.

Rate of development

It is important to be aware that normative measurements can only indicate general *trends* in development in children across the world. They may vary according to the culture in which a child lives. It is important to understand that while the sequence of development is fairly general to all children, the *rate* – or speed – of development can vary a great deal. When children do things earlier than the milestones suggest is normal, it does not necessarily mean that they will be outstanding or gifted in any way. Parents sometimes think that because their child speaks early, is potty-trained early or walks early, he or she is gifted in some way. You should handle these situations carefully, as the child may not be gifted at all.

African children living in rural villages estimate volume and capacity earlier than European children who live in towns. This is because they practise measuring out cups of rice into baskets from an early age as part of their daily lives.

Learning about volume and capacity early does not mean that children will necessarily go on to become talented mathematicians. Children who learn these concepts later might also become good mathematicians.

Children with special educational needs often seem to 'dance the development ladder': they move through sequences in unusual and very uneven ways. For example, they might walk at the normal age, but they may not talk at the usual age. As researchers learn more about child development, it is becoming more useful to think of a child's development as a network that becomes increasingly complex as the child matures and becomes more experienced in their culture. So, instead of thinking of child development and learning as a ladder, it is probably more useful to think of it as a web.

Key term

Norm – The usual or standard thing.

The difference between growth and physical development

Growth

Growth refers to an increase in physical size, and can be measured by **height** (length), **weight** and **head circumference**. Growth is determined by:

- heredity
- hormones
- nutrition
- emotional influences.

Physical development

Physical development involves the increasing skill and functioning of the body, including the development of:

- motor skills (or skills of movement)
- skills of coordination (for example, hand–eye coordination)
- balance.

Common patterns in physical growth and development

Height

The most important factors controlling a child's growth in height are the genes and chromosomes inherited from the parents. From birth to adolescence there are two distinct phases of growth:

- **From birth to two years**: this is a period of very rapid growth. The baby gains 25 to 30 cm in length and triples his or her body weight in the first year.
- **From two years to adolescence**: this is a slower but steady period of growth. The child gains five to eight cm in height and about three kg in body weight per year until adolescence.

Body proportions

As a child grows, the various parts of his or her body change in shape and proportion, as well as increasing in size. The different body parts also grow at different rates – for example, the feet and hands of a teenager reach their final adult size before the body does. At birth, a baby's head accounts for about one-quarter of the total length of his or her body, whereas at seven years old, the head will be about one-eighth of the total length. This difference in body proportions explains why newborn babies appear to have such large eyes, and also why adolescents often appear to be clumsy or awkward in their physical movements.

Measuring growth

Centile charts are used to compare the growth pattern of an individual child with the normal range of growth patterns that are typical of a large number of children of the same sex. The charts are used to plot height (or, in young babies, length), weight and head circumference.

Physical development is the most visible of all the abilities shown in childhood and includes the less observable development of all the **senses**: hearing, vision, touch, taste and smell. Development follows a sequence:

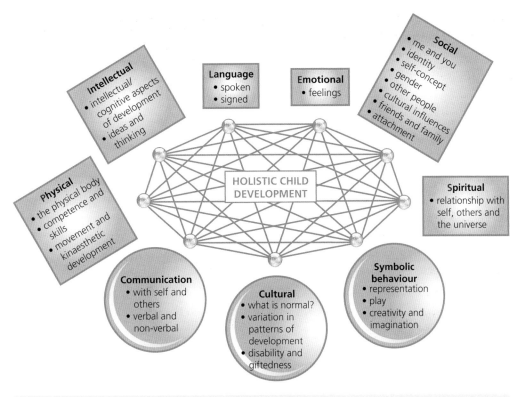

Figure 2.2 Thinking of child development as a web

- **From simple to complex** – for example, a child will walk before he or she can skip or hop.
- **From head to toe** – for example, head control is acquired before coordination of the spinal muscles. Head control is important from birth in order for the baby to feed.
- **From inner to outer** – for example, a child can coordinate his or her arms to reach for an object before he or she has learned the fine manipulative skills necessary to pick it up.
- **From general to specific** – for example, a young baby shows pleasure by a massive general response (eyes widen, legs and arms move vigorously). An older child shows pleasure by smiling or using appropriate words and gestures.

The development of motor skills

The sequence of physical development involves gross motor skills first – these involve control of large muscles in the body. This is followed by development of fine manipulative skills, which depend on small muscle coordination – these are sometimes called skills of **movement**.

- **Gross motor skills** use the large muscles in the body – the arms and legs – and include walking, running and climbing.
- **Fine motor skills** use the smaller muscles and include:
  - **gross manipulative skills**, which involve single-limb movements, usually the arm – for example, throwing, catching and sweeping arm movements
  - **fine manipulative skills**, which involve precise use of the hands and fingers for drawing, using a knife and fork, writing, and doing up shoelaces and buttons.

The skills of locomotion and balance

- **Locomotion** is the ability to move around on one's own. It is central to the pattern of development changes that occur at the end of the baby's first year, and it begins with crawling or bottom-shuffling.
- **Balance** is the first of all the senses to develop. It is crucial to posture, movement and **proprioception** (see page 30).

The eight-month-old child who rolls backwards and forwards across the floor, with no particular goal in sight, is preparing her balance for sitting, standing and walking.

Hand–eye coordination

The ability to reach and grasp objects in a coordinated way requires months of practice and close attention:

- In the first months after birth, hand–eye coordination takes effort.
- By around nine months of age, a baby can usually manage to guide his or her movements with a single glance to check for accuracy – for example, when feeding themselves with a spoon.

There are several aspects of physical development, which are outlined in Table 2.1 below.

Sensory development

Sensation is the process by which we receive information through the senses. These include:

- vision
- hearing
- smell
- touch
- taste
- proprioception (see page 30).

Perception is making sense of what we see, hear, touch, smell and taste. Our perception is affected by previous experience and knowledge, and by our emotional state at the time. There are therefore wide variations in the way different individuals perceive the same object, situation or experience.

Visual development

A newborn baby's eyes are barely half the size of an adult's, and although they are structurally similar they differ in two ways:

1 A baby's focus is fixed at about 20 cm, which is the distance from the baby to his or her mother's face when breastfeeding. Anything nearer or further away appears blurred. The baby will remain short-sighted for about four months.
2 The response to visual stimuli is slower in babies because the information received by the eye takes longer to reach the brain via the nervous pathway. A newborn baby is able to fix his or her eyes on objects and follow their movement only poorly. Head and eye movement is also poorly coordinated; in the first week or two, the eyes lag behind when the baby's head is turned to one side – a feature known by paediatricians as the 'doll's eye phenomenon'.

Research has shown that babies prefer looking at:

- patterned areas rather than plain ones, especially stripes
- edges of objects in 3D
- anything that resembles a human face – babies will actually search out and stare at human faces during their first two months of life
- brightly coloured objects.

Gross motor skills (locomotion or movement)	Fine motor skills (manipulation)	Balance and stabilisation
walking	throwing	bending
running	catching	stretching
skipping	picking up	twisting
jumping	kicking	turning
hopping	rolling	balancing
chasing	volleying	squatting
dodging	striking	transferring
climbing	squeezing	landing
crawling	kneading	hanging

Table 2.1 A summary of activities related to physical skills development

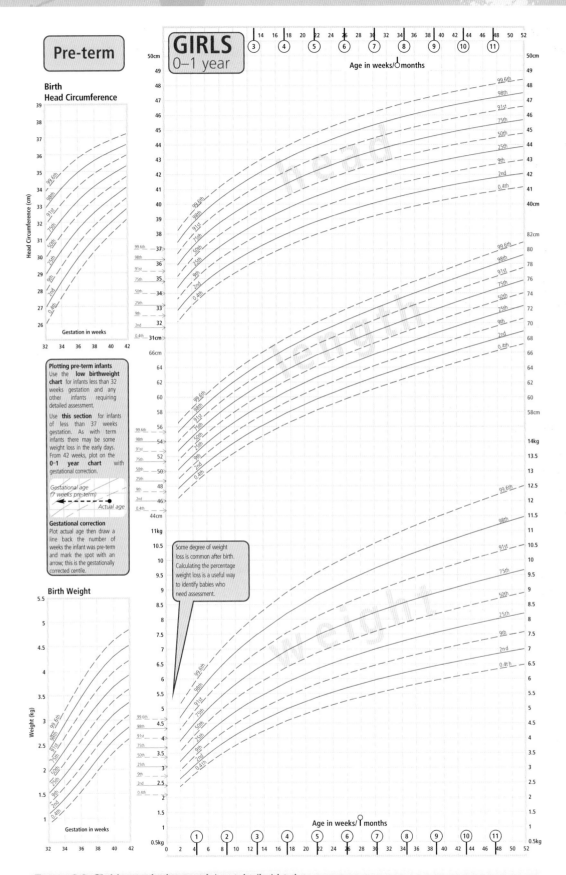

Figure 2.3 Child growth chart: girls' weight (kg) birth to one year

By around four months a baby can focus on both near and distant objects, and his or her ability to recognise different objects is improving steadily. By six months the baby will respond visually to movements across the room and will move his or her head to see what is happening. By one year the baby's eye movements are smoother and he or she can follow rapidly moving objects with his or her eyes – a skill known as **tracking**. A squint is fairly common and normal at this point.

The development of hearing

Newborn babies are able to hear almost as well as adults do.

- Certain rhythmic sounds – often called 'white noise' – seem to have a special soothing effect on babies. The drone of a vacuum cleaner or hairdryer is calming!
- The sound of a human voice evokes the greatest response, and the rhythms of lullabies have been used for centuries in all cultures to help babies to sleep or to comfort them.
- A baby can recognise his or her own mother's voice from the first week and can distinguish its tone and pitch from those of other people.
- Sudden changes in noise levels tend to disturb very young babies and make them jump.
- From about six months, a baby learns to recognise and distinguish between different sounds – for example, the sound of a spoon in a dish means that food is on its way.
- Babies can also discriminate between cheerful and angry voices, and will respond in kind.

The development of smell, taste and touch

The senses of smell and taste are closely linked. If our sense of smell is defective – for example, because of a cold – then our sense of taste is also reduced. A baby as young as one week old who is breastfed is able to tell the difference between his or her own mother's smell and other women's smells. From birth, babies are also able to distinguish the four basic tastes – sweet, sour, bitter and salty.

The sense of touch is also well developed in infancy, as can be demonstrated by the primitive reflexes (see Chapter 13, page 497). Babies seem to be particularly sensitive to touch on the mouth, the face, the hands, the soles of the feet and the abdomen. Research has shown that babies would rather be stroked than fed.

Sensory deprivation

A congenitally blind baby (a baby who is born blind) will develop a more sophisticated sense of touch than a sighted baby, although they both start life with the same touch potential. As the sense of touch develops, so the area of the brain normally assigned to touch increases in size for the blind baby, and the area of the brain normally assigned to sight decreases.

Similarly, in a congenitally deaf baby, the part of the brain that normally receives auditory stimuli is taken over by the visual and movement input from sign language.

Key terms

Proprioception – The sense that tells the baby the location of the mobile parts of his or her body (such as the legs) in relation to the rest of him or her – in other words, where his or her own body begins and ends.

Tracking – The smooth movements made by the eyes in following the track of a moving object (sometimes called 'smooth pursuit').

Physical development in relation to other areas of development

Physical development is linked to other areas of development, such as emotional and social development, and cognitive and language development. Each affects and is affected by the other areas. For example:

- Once babies have mastered crawling, they are free to explore the world on their own – they become more independent and confident when away from their familiar adults.
- The ability to reach and grasp objects (usually achieved at around six months) develops their

understanding of the nature of objects. This often results in a surprise – for example, when they try to pick up a soap bubble or a shaft of sunlight. Babies are interested in edges (of a book or a floor, for example). Where does one object end and the next object begin?

Physical activity and exercise

Exercise is essential for children's growth and development, because it:

- reduces their risk of developing heart disease in later life
- strengthens muscles
- helps strengthen joints and promotes good posture
- improves balance, coordination and flexibility
- increases bone density, so bones are less likely to fracture.

Apart from these obvious physical benefits, regular exercise develops a child's **self-esteem** by creating a strong sense of purpose and self-fulfilment; children learn how to interact and cooperate with other children by taking part in team sports and other activities.

Figure 2.4 The majority of babies start walking around the age of one year to 15 months, but this varies greatly

Figure 2.5 Threading large beads promotes hand–eye coordination, spatial awareness and the development of fine motor skills

Activity

A learning experience

Chloe walks towards a ball. She wants to pick it up. She leans over to touch the ball, but instead her foot hits it and the ball slides across the floor. She walks towards it again, and this time she tries to kick the ball on purpose. She misses the ball; her foot goes past the left side of the ball. Chloe tries again and again. She kicks it and begins to run after the ball, tries to stop in front of it and falls forward. She stands up and kicks it to a new location and she laughs.

1 How old do you think Chloe is?

2 What has Chloe learnt during this activity? Try to list at least six things and then compare them with the list at the end of this chapter (page 114).

Communication and language development

Communication is the exchange of messages or meanings. It uses all the senses, although we often focus on language and speech because they convey the most complex meanings. **Language** is a structured system that conveys meaning. We usually use spoken language, but can also communicate using writing or sign language. Language is more formal than communication, following a set of rules that allows the user to express new ideas and to convey complex meanings. Different languages use different sounds and follow different rules from one another. **Speech** is made up of the sounds that are used to communicate words and sentences in spoken language. Children acquire the ability to use speech as they gain control over the muscles of the mouth and face.

An overview of the stages of physical development

The first month

Gross motor skills	Fine motor skills
• The baby lies **supine** (on his or her back).	• The baby turns his or her head towards the light and stares at bright or shiny objects.
• When placed on his or her front (the **prone** position), the baby lies with head turned to one side, and by one month can lift the head.	• The baby is fascinated by human faces and gazes attentively at carer's face when fed or held.
• If pulled to sitting position, the head will lag, the back curves over and the head falls forward.	• The baby's hands are usually tightly closed.
	• The baby reacts to loud sounds but by one month may be soothed by particular music.

From one to four months

Gross motor skills	Fine motor skills
From four to eight weeks:	
• The baby can now turn from side to back.	• The baby turns her head towards the light and stares at bright or shiny objects.
• The baby can lift the head briefly from the prone position.	• The baby will show interest and excitement by facial expression and will gaze attentively at carer's face while being fed.
• Arm and leg movements are jerky and uncontrolled.	• The baby will use his or her hand to grasp the carer's finger.

An overview of the stages of physical development (cont.)

From one to four months

- There is head lag if the baby is pulled to sitting position.

From eight to twelve weeks:

- When lying supine, the baby's head is in a central position.
- The baby can now lift head and chest off bed in prone position, supported on forearms.
- There is almost no head lag in sitting position.
- The legs can kick vigorously, both separately and together.
- The baby can wave his or her arms and bring his or her hands together over the body.

- The baby moves his or her head to follow adult movements.
- The baby watches his or her hands and plays with his or her fingers.
- The baby holds a rattle for a brief time before dropping it.

From four to six months

Gross motor skills

- The baby is beginning to use a **palmar grasp** and can transfer objects from hand to hand.
- The baby is very interested in all activity.
- Everything is taken to the mouth.
- The baby moves his or her head around to follow people and objects.

Fine motor skills

- The baby now has good head control and is beginning to sit with support.
- The baby rolls over from back to side and is beginning to reach for objects.
- When supine, the baby plays with his or her own feet.
- The baby holds his or her head up when pulled to sitting position.

From six to nine months

Gross motor skills

- The baby can roll from front to back.
- The baby may attempt to crawl but will often end up sliding backwards.
- The baby may grasp feet and place them in his or her mouth.
- The baby can sit without support for longer periods of time.
- The baby may 'cruise' around furniture and may even stand or walk alone.

Fine motor skills

- The baby is very alert to people and objects.
- The baby is beginning to use a **pincer grasp** with thumb and index finger.
- The baby transfers toys from one hand to the other and looks for fallen objects.
- Everything is explored by putting it in his or her mouth.

From nine to twelve months

Gross motor skills

- The baby will now be mobile – may be crawling, bear-walking, bottom-shuffling or even walking.
- The baby can sit up on his or her own and lean forward to pick up things.

Fine motor skills

- The baby's pincer grasp is now well developed and he or she can pick things up and pull them towards him or her.
- The baby can poke with one finger and will point to desired objects.

An overview of the stages of physical development (cont.)

From nine to twelve months

- The baby may crawl upstairs and onto low items of furniture.
- The baby may bounce in rhythm to music.

- The baby can clasp hands and imitate adults' actions.
- The baby can throw toys deliberately.
- The baby can manage spoons and finger foods well.

From one year to two years

Gross motor skills	Fine motor skills

At 15 months:

- The baby probably walks alone, with feet wide apart and arms raised to maintain balance. He or she is likely to fall over and often sit down suddenly.
- The baby can probably manage stairs and steps, but will need supervision.
- The baby can get to standing without help from furniture or people, and kneels without support.

- The baby can build with a few bricks and arrange toys on the floor.
- The baby holds a crayon in palmar grasp and turns several pages of a book at once.
- The baby can point to desired objects.
- The baby shows a preference for one hand, but uses either.

At 18 months:

- The child walks confidently and is able to stop without falling.
- The child can kneel, squat, climb and carry things around with him or her.
- The child can climb onto an adult chair forwards and then turn round to sit.
- The child can come downstairs, usually by creeping backwards on his or her tummy.

- The child can thread large beads.
- The child uses pincer grasp to pick up small objects.
- The child can build a tower of several cubes.
- The child can scribble to and fro on paper.

From two years

Gross motor skills	Fine motor skills

- The child is very mobile and can run safely.
- The child can climb up onto furniture.
- The child can walk up and down stairs, usually two feet to a step.
- The child tries to kick a ball with some success but cannot catch yet.

- The child can draw circles, lines and dots, using preferred hand.
- The child can pick up tiny objects using a **fine pincer grasp**.
- The child can build a tower of six or more blocks (bricks) with longer concentration span.
- The child enjoys picture books and turns pages singly.

From three years

Gross motor skills	Fine motor skills

- The child can jump from a low step.
- The child can walk backwards and sideways.

- The child can build tall towers of bricks or blocks.
- The child can control a pencil using thumb and first two fingers – a **dynamic tripod grasp**.

An overview of the stages of physical development (cont.)

From three years

- The child can stand and walk on tiptoe and stand on one foot.
- The child has good spatial awareness.
- The child rides a tricycle, using pedals.
- The child can climb stairs with one foot on each step – and downwards with two feet per step.

- The child enjoys painting with a large brush.
- The child can use scissors to cut paper.
- The child can copy shapes, such as a circle.

From four years

Gross motor skills	Fine motor skills
- A sense of balance is developing – the child may be able to walk along a line. - The child can catch, kick, throw and bounce a ball. - The child can bend at the waist to pick up objects from the floor. - The child enjoys climbing trees and frames. - The child can run up and down stairs, one foot per step.	- The child can build a tower of bricks and other constructions too. - The child can draw a recognisable person on request, showing head, legs and trunk. - The child can thread small beads on a lace.

From five to eight years

Gross motor skills	Fine motor skills
From five years: - The child can use a variety of play equipment – slides, swings, climbing frames. - The child can play ball games. - The child can hop and run lightly on toes and can move rhythmically to music. - The sense of balance is well developed. - The child can skip.	 - The child may be able to thread a large-eyed needle and sew large stitches. - The child can draw a person with head, trunk, legs, nose, mouth and eyes. - The child has good control over pencils and paintbrushes. He or she copies shapes, such as a square.
From six to seven years: - The child has increased agility, muscle coordination and balance. - The child develops competence in riding a two-wheeled bicycle. - The child hops easily, with good balance. - The child can jump off apparatus.	 - The child can build a tall, straight tower with blocks and other constructions too. - The child can draw a person with detail, e.g. clothes and eyebrows. - The child can write letters of alphabet at school, with similar writing grip to an adult. - The child can catch a ball thrown from one metre with one hand.

An overview of the stages of physical development (cont.)

From eight to eleven years

Gross motor skills	Fine motor skills
From eight to nine years: • The child can ride a bicycle easily. • The child has increased strength and coordination. • The child plays energetic games and sports.	• The child can control his or her small muscles well and has improved writing and drawing skills. • The child can draw people with details of clothing and facial features. • The child is starting to join letters together in handwriting.
From ten to eleven years: • Children differ in physical maturity. Girls experience puberty earlier than boys do and are often as much as two years ahead of them. • The child's body proportions are becoming more similar to adults.	• The child tackles more detailed tasks such as woodwork or needlework. • The child is usually writing with an established style – using joined-up letters.

From 12 to 19 years

Physical development during adolescence is known as **puberty**. The age at which puberty starts varies from person to person but on average it begins between 9 and 13 in girls and 10 and 15 in boys. Many physical changes occur during puberty:

- **Growth** accelerates rapidly – often called a **growth spurt**. This usually happens in a particular order from outer to inner:

  1. the head, feet and hands grow to adult size
  2. the arms and legs grow in length and strength
  3. the trunk (the main part of the body from shoulder to hip) grows to full adult size and shape.

This sequence of growth means that, for a brief period, adolescents may feel gawky and clumsy, as they appear to be 'out of proportion'. The average boy grows fastest between 14 and 15. Girls start earlier, growing fastest when 12 and 13. Girls also finish their growth spurt earlier, at 18, while boys need another two years before they finish growing aged 20.

- **Secondary sex characteristics** develop; these are external traits that distinguish the two sexes, but are not directly part of the **reproductive system**; for example, the growth of pubic hair in both sexes, facial hair and deepened voice for males, and breasts and widened hips for females.

- Primary sex characteristics develop; these are the penis and sperm in males and the vagina and ovaries in females. During puberty, hormonal changes cause a boy's penis and testicles to grow and the body to produce sperm. Girls start to menstruate – to have their monthly period. Both these events signal **sexual maturity** – the ability to reproduce.

The first *external* sign of puberty in girls is usually breast development, often accompanied by a growth spurt. The main features of physical development in puberty in girls are as follows.	The first *external* sign of puberty in most boys is an increase in the size of the testicles and then the penis. This is followed by the growth of pubic and underarm hair. At the same time, the voice deepens and muscles develop. Lastly, boys grow facial hair.

An overview of the stages of physical development (cont.)

From 12 to 19 years

- **Breasts develop:** at first, the nipples start to stick out from the chest (often called 'budding'). Behind the nipple, milk ducts begin to grow. Next, the flat, circular part of the nipple, the areola, rises and starts to expand. Glands that make sweat and scent develop beneath it. The breast begins to fill out as fat is deposited around the nipple. Some girls feel a tingling sensation or have tender breasts. Initially, the breasts stick out or have a conical shape. As growth continues, they gradually round off into an adult shape.

- **Body size and shape** grows taller. Hips widen as the pelvic bones grow. Fat develops on the hips, thighs and buttocks, and the ratio of fat to muscle increases. The waist gets smaller and the body develops a more curved shape.

- **Menstruation** – having periods – is part of the female reproductive cycle that starts when girls become sexually mature during puberty. During a menstrual period, a woman bleeds from her uterus (womb) via the vagina. This lasts anything from three to seven days. Each period begins approximately every 28 days if the woman does not become pregnant during a given cycle. The onset of menstruation is called the menarche; it can occur any time between the ages of 9 and 16, most commonly around the age of 12–13. It means that the body is capable of **reproduction**.

The main features of physical development in puberty in boys are as follows.

- **Voice breaking:** testosterone causes the voice box or larynx to enlarge and the vocal cords to become longer. Sometimes, as the voice changes to become deeper, it may change pitch abruptly or 'break' at times. The voice box tilts and often protrudes at the neck – an 'Adam's apple'. (Many boys start to develop breasts in their teenage years, but this disappears as testosterone levels increase.)

- **Body size and shape** grows taller. The body takes on a new, more muscular shape as the shoulders and chest become broader and the neck becomes more muscular.

- **Chest hair** may appear during puberty, or some years later.

- **Penile erections** – these occur spontaneously, even from infancy, but during puberty they become more frequent. Erections can occur with or without any physical or sexual stimulation and can cause acute embarrassment.

- **Sperm:** once the testicles begin to grow, they also develop their adult function – to produce sperm. Mature sperm is present in the male body towards the end of puberty (most commonly between ages 13–15) and means that the body is capable of **reproduction**.

Some physical developments occur during puberty in both girls and boys:

- **Pubic hair** starts to grow around the genitals, and becomes coarse, dark and curly. In girls, pubic hair forms an upside-down triangle shape; in boys, the hair grows between the legs and extends up from the penis to the abdomen.

- Hair grows in the armpits and on the legs.

- A different kind of **sweat** is now produced in response to stress, emotion and sexual excitement. It is produced by the apocrine glands and occurs only in the armpits, belly button, groin area, ears and nipples. As bacteria break down the sweat it starts to smell strongly – this is known as body odour (BO).

- **Oil-secreting glands** in the skin can become over-active. This can cause skin to become greasier and may cause acne.

Table 2.2 An overview of the stages of physical development

Communication and language development (cont.)

Language development is very closely linked with **cognitive development** and a delay in one area usually affects progress in the other.

Language development is the development of communication skills. These include skills in:

- **receptive speech** – what a person understands
- **expressive speech** – the words the person produces
- **articulation** – the person's actual pronunciation of words.

Normative language developmental milestones

From birth to one year

Babies are born with a need and a desire to communicate with others before they can express themselves through speaking. Learning how to communicate – to listen and to speak – begins with **non-verbal communication**. This includes:

- **body language**: for example, facial expression, eye contact, pointing, touching and reaching for objects
- **listening** to others talking to them
- **making sounds** to attract attention
- **copying** the sounds made by others.

These skills develop as babies and young children express their needs and feelings, interact with others and establish their own identities and personalities.

The first year of a baby's life is sometimes called 'prelinguistic'. This is a rather misleading term. It is more positive and helpful to think of a baby as someone who communicates without words, and who is developing everything needed for conversations in spoken/signed language. This is sometimes called the period of emerging language.

From one to four years

From the second year of the baby's life until about the age of four years, there is a period of language explosion. Every aspect of language seems to move forward rapidly at this time. It is the best time to learn other languages, or to become bilingual or multilingual.

From four to eight years

From four to eight years of age, children are consolidating their communication and language learning. They build on what they know about communication with themselves, with other people, developing better articulation, and using more conventional grammar patterns. They think about who they are talking to, with greater sensitivity and awareness. They are also more attentive to the context in which they are talking, and the situation. They can put their ideas and feelings into words more easily than when they were toddlers.

To learn more about the detail of the sequence of communication and development, look at the charts of normative development on pages 42–44.

Activity

Observe one of the following either in the home setting or the early childhood setting:

- baby aged six to twelve months
- child aged one to three years
- child aged three to five years
- child aged five to seven years.

Note sounds: vowels (ah, eh, ee, aye, oh, yu) and consonants such as p, g, b. Then look at the charts of normative development on language development on pages 42–44 and analyse your observations.

Does the baby/child use single words or holophrases (single-word utterances that express several thoughts, ideas or feelings)? Does the child speak in sentences? Evaluate the language development of the child.

How does spoken/signed language help us to develop and learn?

Language helps children (and adults) to:

- talk to ourselves – children and adults often talk out loud to themselves; as we develop our language skills, what we say out loud becomes 'internal speech', so that we are increasingly able to think of the words rather than saying them out loud

- move from the here and now into thoughts about the past or the future, and back again
- use and make different symbols, from spoken/signed language to the languages of dance, music, mathematical symbols, drawings, sculptures and models
- develop ideas, some of which become concepts, and put them into words
- express creative and imaginative thoughts and ideas
- express and communicate personal ideas
- think in abstract ways
- plan
- express feelings, think about their emotional responses and manage them, becoming increasingly self-disciplined.

Communicating feelings

Children experience difficulties when they are not able to put their feelings into words or to express them in any way. This has a damaging impact on their sense of self and identity, and on their self-confidence. If children are full of anger, anxiety, frustration or fear, they need to express this. Talking about feelings is just as important as talking about ideas. Children who cannot explain or put into words/signs how they feel often have temper tantrums or show other kinds of challenging behaviour.

Communicating ideas and thoughts

As they begin to develop spoken or signed language, children are able to think about their own thinking. Thinking about your own thinking is called **metacognition**. Children begin to say things like, 'I've got a good idea' or 'That was a bad idea', as they reflect on their own thought processes. Typically, by about four years of age they are beginning to think about what they say. This is called **metalinguistics**. Children make jokes and 'play' with words, devising nonsense words for fun.

Children often talk out loud to themselves when they:

- feel frustrated and they are trying to understand something

Figure 2.6 Although there is a conversation going on here, there are quite long pauses while the practitioner does the next bit of face-painting. She holds the little girl's chin gently and the child trusts her. The child chose to have her face painted with a butterfly, and they have talked about the colour and the antennae on her forehead. Both are taking this seriously, so there are no jerky movements or loud talking. This needs to be a quiet time, with words said calmly

- need to talk to themselves about how they feel
- are trying to organise an idea they are developing
- are trying out an idea and want to talk it through with themselves
- want to tell themselves what to do (give themselves an instruction).

Talking out loud to themselves is often described by researchers as 'egocentric speech'. It is helpful for children, as the bullet points above show. Gradually children begin to be able to put themselves in someone else's shoes, providing that person's experience links with their own. They move from being self-centred to being self-relating to being other-people-centred. This does not mean the child is selfish, it just means they are becoming increasingly able to see something from someone else's point of view as well as their own.

Key terms

Metacognition – Being aware of your own thinking and being able to analyse this.

Metalinguistics – Being aware of the structure of the language you use, such as something rhyming; for example, four-year-olds love to make nonsense words and to play with language rhymes of their own making.

In Practice

Observe a small group of three or four children with an adult. Note examples of turn-taking and any of the things you would expect to find in a conversation that have been identified in this chapter. Was there a difference in the number of times individual children spoke in the group? In what way? Evaluate the pros and cons of small groups and large groups.

Language and feelings

Unless children develop the language of emotion, they will not be able to express their feelings in ways that others find acceptable. This will cause difficulties with relationships and will have a damaging influence on their social development.

Figure 2.7 In this photo the adult is talking to the child, getting down to her level and showing that she finds it interesting through her body language (putting her head on one side and looking directly at the child to establish contact). The child shows that she welcomes this by her relaxed facial expression and her arms. Note that her arms are bending onto her shoulders, which is what we do when we feel relaxed, and her hands are opened out too (clenched hands would indicate that the child felt tense). All of this is non-verbal communication, but it tells us a great deal about the warmth, sensitivity and respect in the social interaction and relationship of the child and adult

Language and movement

The parts of the brain dealing with movement are near to each other, with interconnected networks developing, so that hands move as the baby makes sounds, for example. We use our hands as we speak as part of the way we communicate throughout our lives. We point a finger to show someone something. We wag a finger to show anger or when we are being insistent. We open out our hands when we welcome what others say.

Figure 2.8 Children learn the language of 'Please be gentle', 'That hurts', 'Please could you stop doing that because I don't like it', 'I'm a bit worried that if you squeeze my ears it might hurt me', and so on. These two have a trusting relationship, knowing that they have a boundary around hurting each other

Research shows that the way we move our head and hands is very important in communicating and speaking and listening (expressive and receptive language).

Language – vision and sound

Babies love to look at faces. They stare at them and find them fascinating, and we love to look at the baby in response. If you talk to a baby, you will be helping him or her to learn that you make different shapes with your mouth, and they will gradually imitate these. Even at three months, if you say 'coo' and then pause, the baby will very likely say 'oo' back to you. Babies begin to work out that sounds come out of mouths.

Case Study   Analysing language

Look at the photographs in this chapter. Each one represents a case study. What do the photographs tell you about language and movement, and about language – vision and sound? Use the two previous sections of this chapter to help you analyse and evaluate the photographs.

Language and representing experiences

Language development is closely linked with the processes of representation. This means being able to keep hold of an experience. But it is more than just keeping an experience in our memory. Representation is about quite literally being able to 're-present' that experience in some way.

The 'hundred languages of children'

There are many ways of communicating, using different kinds of symbols other than spoken/signed language – for example, through dance, music, the visual arts, mathematical symbols and stories. The Italian educator Loris Malaguzzi called these the 'hundred languages of children'. They are all important ways in which children begin to communicate their feelings, ideas and relationships.

A symbol is something that stands for something else. In order to 're-present' an experience, humans have developed the ability to use and make symbols. From the time children begin to walk, talk and pretend, they become symbol-users and makers. This means that children are increasingly able to represent and communicate their experiences in a variety of forms.

Spoken/signed language makes it easier for us to keep hold of (represent) experiences, and to share (communicate) them. Language is one kind of symbol system that helps us to develop abstract concepts, ideas and thoughts. Words stand for things. The word 'table' is not the real table; it is a symbol that stands for the table.

For more information on the development of language and communication in children, see Chapter 13.

The stages of communication and language development

The first month

- Babies need to share language experiences and cooperate with others from birth onwards. From the start babies need other people.
- The baby responds to sounds, especially familiar voices.
- The baby quietens when picked up.
- The baby makes eye contact.
- The baby cries to indicate need, e.g. hunger, dirty nappy, etc.
- The baby may move his or her eyes towards the direction of sound.

From one to four months

From four to eight weeks:

- The baby recognises the carer and familiar objects.
- The baby makes non-crying noises such as cooing and gurgling.
- The baby's cries become more expressive.

From eight to twelve weeks:

- The baby is still distressed by sudden loud noises.
- The baby often sucks or licks lips when he or she hears sound of food preparation.
- The baby shows excitement at sound of approaching footsteps or voices.

During the first three months:

- The baby listens to people's voices. When adults close to the baby talk in motherese or fatherese (a high-pitched tone referring to what is around and going on) the baby dances, listens, replies in babble and coo.
- The baby cries with anger to show they are tired, hungry, and to say they need to be changed.
- The baby is comforted by the voices of those who are close to them and will turn especially to the voices of close family members.

From four to six months

- The baby becomes more aware of others so he or she communicates more and more.
- As the baby listens, he or she imitates sounds he or she can hear, and reacts to the tone of someone's voice. For example, the baby might become upset by an angry tone, or cheered by a happy tone.
- The baby begins to use vowels, consonants and syllable sounds, e.g. 'ah', 'ee aw'.
- The baby begins to laugh and squeal with pleasure.

From six to nine months

- Babble becomes tuneful, like the lilt of the language the baby can hear (except in hearing-impaired babies).
- Babies begin to understand words like 'up' and 'down', raising their arms to be lifted up, using appropriate gestures.
- The baby repeats sounds.

The stages of communication and language development (cont.)

From nine to twelve months

- The baby can follow simple instructions, e.g. kiss teddy.
- Word approximations appear, e.g. 'hee haw' to indicate a donkey, or more typically 'mumma', 'dadda' and 'bye-bye' in English-speaking contexts.
- The tuneful babble develops into 'jargon' and the baby makes his or her voice go up and down just as people do when they talk to each other. 'Really? Do you? No!' The babble is very expressive.
- The baby knows that words stand for people, objects, what they do and what happens.

From one year to two years

- The child begins to talk with words or sign language.
- **By 18 months:** The child enjoys trying to sing as well as to listen to songs and rhymes. Action songs (e.g. 'Pat-a-cake') are much loved.
- Books with pictures are of great interest. The child points at and often names parts of their body, objects, people and pictures in books.
- The child echoes the last part of what others say (echolalia).
- The child begins waving his or her arms up and down which might mean 'start again', or 'I like it', or 'more'.
- Gestures develop alongside words. Gesture is used in some cultures more than in others.

From two years

- Children are rapidly becoming competent speakers of the languages they experience.
- The child over-extends the use of a word, e.g. all animals are called 'doggie'.
- The child talks about an absent object when reminded of it; e.g. seeing an empty plate, they say 'biscuit'.
- The child uses phrases (telegraphese), 'doggie-gone' and the child calls him- or herself by name.
- The child spends a great deal of energy naming things and what they do – e.g. 'chair', and as they go up a step they might say 'up'.
- The child can follow a simple instruction or request, e.g. 'Could you bring me the spoon?'
- The child increasingly wants to share songs, dance, conversations, finger rhymes.

From three years

- The child begins to use plurals, pronouns, adjectives, possessives, time words, tenses and sentences.
- The child might say 'two times' instead of 'twice'. The child might say 'I goed there' instead of 'I went there'. The child loves to chat and ask questions (what, where and who).
- The child enjoys much more complicated stories and asks for his or her favourite ones over and over again.
- It is not unusual for the child to stutter because he or she is trying so hard to tell adults things. The child's thinking goes faster than the pace at which the child can say what he or she wants to. The child can quickly become frustrated.

From four years

- During this time the child asks why, when and how questions as he or she becomes more and more fascinated with the reasons for things and how things work (cause and effect).
- Past, present and future tenses are used more often.
- The child can be taught to say his or her name, address and age.
- As the child becomes more accurate in the way he or she pronounces words, and begins to use grammar, the child delights in nonsense words that he or she makes up, and jokes using words.

The stages of communication and language development (cont.)

From five to eight years

- The child tries to understand the meaning of words and uses adverbs and prepositions. The child talks confidently, and with more and more fluency.
- The child begins to be able to define objects by their function, e.g. 'What is a ball?', 'You bounce it.'
- The child begins to understand book language, and that stories have characters and a plot (the narrative).
- The child begins to realise that different situations require different ways of talking.

From eight to eleven years

From eight to nine years:

- The child uses and understands complex sentences.
- The child is increasingly verbal and enjoys making up stories and telling jokes.
- The child uses reference books with increasing skill.

From ten to eleven years:

- The child can write fairly lengthy essays.
- The child writes stories that show imagination, and are increasingly legible and grammatically correct.

From 12 to 19 years

During this period, young people become increasingly independent and spend much of their day outside the home – at school or after-school activities, and with peers.

- The young person has a fast, legible style of handwriting.
- The young person communicates in an adult manner, with increasing maturity.
- The young person understands abstract language, such as idioms, figurative language and metaphors.
- The young person is able to process texts and abstract meaning, relate word meanings and contexts, understand punctuation, and form complex syntactic structures.

Table 2.3 An overview of the stages of communication and language development

Intellectual development

Intellectual development – or cognitive development – is the process of knowing and becoming aware through reasoning, using the senses to perceive how things are, and out of this forming concepts (ideas that can be shared) and judgements. **Cognition** involves thoughts (the thinking we do), which helps us to develop and form ideas and **concepts** and to know things. The cognitive/intellectual life of a child cannot be separated from other areas of development.

Key terms

Concepts – Ideas that can be shared, such as fairness, weight and time.

Cognition – The thinking that helps us to develop ideas.

Concentrating and attending, being engaged and involved

Children concentrate best when they:

- find something interesting and enjoyable
- have a choice of experiences
- are with an adult who is interested in what they are doing
- are with an adult who will help them, but without doing things for them.

Activity

Look at the photographs in this chapter and link each of them with the bullet points about when children concentrate best.

Figure 2.9 Children sit, then crawl, before walking, running, jumping, hopping and skipping, but they do all of these things with increasing range as they develop more and more control of their bodies and thoughts. It really is true that minds and bodies work together

Figure 2.10 Thinking about kicking a ball is hard to do and it takes several years to manage the coordination of thinking and physical development

In Practice

Make a den in the garden or under a table indoors, using drapes, with string to fasten them together. It is best to do this with the children. Provide several drapes, so that children can join in the den-making if they wish to do so.

1. Do the children have ideas about a den they want to make for themselves?

2. What differences do you note in the way children are interested in the den when they are two to three years old, four to five years old and six to seven years old?

3. Try this with babies who crawl. Do they go into the den or look into it? What happens if you put objects inside the den? Do they like the den to be dark inside or fairly light?

Figure 2.11 The adult lends a helping hand when needed to the child who is learning to use a spoon

Figure 2.12 The boy is fascinated by the egg. This is not the moment for a conversation; it is the time to fully experience what is happening

In Practice

Children's ideas about the past

With the children, look for some worms, ants, spiders and other mini beasts in the garden. Talk about the experiences as you do so, explaining what each creature is, how many legs it has and what it does – for example, worms turn the soil and aerate (introduce air into) it; ants live in colonies, with worker ants finding food and taking it back to the others; spiders eat flies.

Later in the day, show the children a book about mini beasts, with photos of them in it. Chat about this together. Let the children talk about what interests them in the photos. What do the children remember and enjoy talking about with you?

Imagining and planning the future

As children begin to walk, talk and pretend, they are able to think about the future. A child might decide that when he or she gets to nursery he or she will do some cooking. The child might bake a cake and take it to eat with Grandma because he or she knows Grandma will like this.

In Practice

Children's ideas about the future

Make a book with simple cookery instructions and use it with a small group of children (two to four children aged three to seven years). About a week later, have a chat with the children in a group and ask them how to make the recipe. What will they need? How will they do it? Note what they say. What does this tell you about their thinking?

Figure 2.13 Cooking for someone's pleasure involves advance planning

Figure 2.14 Boys cooking

Theory of mind – me and you

Being able to appreciate another person's way of thinking from their point of view is an incredible thing to be able to do. The neuroscientist Sarah-Jayne Blakemore outlines the sequence of development:

- Until they walk, talk and pretend, babies concentrate on what they see, want and feel.
- Once they pretend, they begin to have some understanding of what is real and unreal.
- Gradually, they begin to talk about their beliefs (that the biscuits are in the kitchen cupboard).
- By the end of the first five years, typically they are beginning to know that people can have different beliefs to theirs, and that theirs can be changed too.

There are two approaches to studying theory of mind: one is to set up laboratory experiments to test it and the other is to observe children within their own families.

The Sally-Anne false belief task – the laboratory test approach, often used as an early detection test for autism

The Sally-Anne experiment involves placing a doll on a table and telling the child that this is Sally. Sally has a basket. Then a doll called Anne is introduced and she is placed next to Sally. Anne has a box.

Sally has a marble, which she places in her basket. She goes for a walk. Anne takes the marble out of the basket while Sally has gone. Anne puts the marble in her box. Sally comes back. She wants to play with the marble. The child is asked, 'Where will Sally look for the marble?'

The child may or may not realise that Sally will not know that Anne has moved the marble to her box while she is away. The answer the child gives will show whether the child understands what it is like to see things from either Sally's or Anne's point of view in terms of their 'knowledge' of the situation. If the child says that Sally will look in Anne's box for the marble, it shows they do not understand that Anne has moved it there, but that Sally would not know this as she had left the room when this was done. They are not yet looking at this from Sally's point of view.

In Practice

Carry out the Sally-Anne false belief task with a child aged three years and a child aged four years. What does this tell you about each child's thinking? Make sure the children do not observe each other doing the task.

Observing children in natural situations

Judy Dunn, observing children in their homes, found that even toddlers showed a practical grasp of how to annoy or comfort other children. From the time they walk, talk and pretend, they begin to understand other people's feelings, but only within the circle of people who love them and whom they love.

This confirms the pioneering work of Jean Piaget in the 1930s, that children are – and Piaget admitted this was an unfortunate description – intellectually egocentric (selfish) until the age of about four or five years. Margaret Donaldson, using laboratory techniques in the late 1970s, and Judy Dunn, observing in natural situations in the 1980s, have demonstrated that children perform at a more advanced level:

- in surroundings that they know and in which they feel comfortable
- when they are with people who love them and whom they love
- when a situation makes what Donaldson called 'human sense' to them.

Case Study   Theory of mind

Mandie, who is three years old, gives her mother the celery stick because she know she likes this. She gives Granny a cucumber stick for the same reason. She takes a carrot stick from the plate because she likes those the best. If she was with people she did not know, she would not have the knowledge to demonstrate her understanding of others.

Instead of talking as Piaget did, about children gradually shedding intellectual egocentricity, we now talk about developing theory of mind (ToM), which is more positive.

In Practice

Observe a child over the course of a day to see where he or she is in his or her journey towards understanding how other children and adults feel and think. Observe the child in the familiar setting, and when he or she is with adults who know and care for the child. Link your observations to what you have read in this chapter.

Problem-solving and making hypotheses and theories

Children are natural problem-solvers from the moment they are born. It used to be thought that, at first, children tried to solve problems through trial and error, and that only later could they develop a theory or hypothesis. More recently, however, researchers have found that even newborn babies can make a hypothesis. Making a hypothesis means having a theory that can be tested to see if it is right. It is amazing to think that babies can do this, rather than the cruder trial-and-error approach to solving problems.

Case Study   Baby makes a hypothesis

This experiment, conducted in the 1970s, would be considered unethical today because honey is now known to be dangerous to some babies under one year of age, but it does show how a baby makes a hypothesis. A newborn baby turned towards the sound of a buzzer and was given a honeyed dummy to suck on. The baby also turned to the sound of a bell, but was not given a honeyed dummy. Soon the baby turned only for the buzzer. Once the baby had tested the hypothesis – that the buzzer signified honey and the bell did not – the hypothesis was confirmed. Soon the baby was bored with confirming the hypothesis again and again, so the baby did not turn to either buzzer or bell.

Figure 2.15 How do you fill a bottle with water? A funnel solves the problem

into a maximum of three numbers per chunk, some chunks with two numbers.

Imitation and memory are linked: if you poke out your tongue at a newborn baby, they will imitate you.

Short-term memory relies hugely on hearing (acoustic) and also on seeing (visual). This is why it is difficult to remember words that sound similar (bog, dog, log, fog). The difference between 'dog' and 'cat' is easier for the brain to hear.

Short-term memories do not last long in the brain; they are limited. Neuroscientists now know that our feelings, sensory perceptions and memories are all bound together in a seamless whole. This means that the feelings children have are of central importance in the way memory develops.

Key term

Hypothesis – A hypothesis makes a prediction that something will happen and tests it out in a scientific way to see if it is true or not.

Making a false hypothesis is an important part of childhood

Children can be very obstinate about a theory they have! Experts think that finding out that a hypothesis is wrong is a very important part of learning to solve problems. In order to learn about problem-solving, children need to test out their incorrect hypotheses as well as correct ones. The reasoning they employ is invaluable for intellectual development.

Memory

Memory is about the way in which experiences are stored, retained and recalled in the brain. There are different kinds of memory: short-term memory and long-term memory.

Short-term memory

When you make a phone call, you need to remember the number for long enough to dial. Remembering ten or so digits is quite hard to do. It becomes easier for the brain if the numbers are 'chunked', ideally

Long-term memory

We remember things that engage our interest and hold meaning for us. One famous example comes from Jean Piaget's daughter Jacqueline when she was a toddler. She saw a friend (aged 18 months) have a temper tantrum. She was very impressed by this dramatic event, and the following day she tried it out on herself, imitating the tantrum.

Whereas short-term memory relies on sound and sight, long-term memory depends on meaning

Case Study — Learning by hypothesis

Segun (four years) saw some paint that glowed in the dark. His mother told him (wrongly) that it was called fluorescent paint. He asked his mother for some. Having painted the stone owl from the garden, Segun put it in his bed, so that it would glow in the dark. It did not glow in the dark! He then painted all sorts of stones from the garden. He put them in his bed each night. They did not glow in the dark either! Next he painted sticks from the garden and put them on his bed each night. They did not glow in the dark!

Segun's uncle visited him and told him that what he needed was iridescent paint. Segun, however, carried on with his idea of making objects glow

in the dark using fluorescent paint. Then he saw a pot that glowed in the dark. He asked the owner what sort of paint they had used. The answer was, 'Iridescent.' He decided to try the new paint, and his own glowed in the dark; so did his sticks and stones.

Segun had worked out, thorough exploration, that the hypothesis that fluorescent paint glows in the dark was incorrect. He will now know this for the rest of his life. He also knows from experience that iridescent paint does make things glow in the dark. This is real learning that no one can take away from him. It shows he is making predictions through his hypothesis, reasoning and problem-solving.

(semantics). Unless something makes sense, it cannot find its way into the long-term memory.

Between the ages of two and three years, children are able to remember more. The advantage of developing a longer-term memory is that they can organise their thinking a bit more. They remember what they have done before in similar situations with people, and they can use this memory to think about what to do in a new situation. This is called 'inhibition to the unfamiliar'. It means children begin to 'think before they do'.

Early concepts

Concepts take time to form because they rely on being able to organise information. Children develop concepts of time, space, love, beauty and number (to name just a few), which continue to develop over the years. Some aspects of concept formation are biological and some are social and cultural. Our brains quite literally change according to whom we meet and the experiences we have. This can be summed up by the phrase 'nurture shapes nature'.

Case Study — An emerging concept of faces

Hannah cried when her Uncle Dan, who was bald, came to the house. This happened every time she saw her Uncle Dan for a month or so. She had to adjust to her new knowledge that some people do not have hair on the top of their heads.

Babies get to know the faces of people in their family and of their carers. They begin to develop an early concept of what faces look like. By the age of about six to nine months, typically, they find faces that seem different rather frightening because they do not fit with what they know. At first, Uncle Dan was very upset, but he was reassured when this was explained.

Schemas – part of concept formation

A schema is a pattern of behaviour that is repeatable. It helps children to take in experiences. Schemas become generalised and tried out in a variety of situations. They become coordinated with each other and grow increasingly complex as children develop and learn. Knowing about schemas helps parents and practitioners to relate to children more easily and to enjoy their company more. It helps adults to understand some of the annoying things children do too, and to work positively with children. Schemas, which are part of brain development, help children to learn.

There is a developmental sequence in schemas:

- At first, babies develop action schemas, using their actions, senses and movement. These develop out of the reflexes that they are born with, and include, for example, sucking and gazing. These remain throughout life.
- Then the sensory motor action schemas begin to develop into two deeper levels:
  - symbolic (making one thing stand for another)
  - cause and effect (understanding that if I do this, then that will happen).

Figure 2.16 Trajectory schema – at a cause-and-effect level

Name of schema	Description
Transporting	A child may move objects or collections of objects from one place to another, perhaps using a bag, pram or truck.
Positioning	A child may be interested in placing objects in particular positions, for example on top of, around the edge of, or behind something. Paintings and drawings also often show evidence of this.
Orientation	This schema is shown by interest in a different viewpoint, as when a child hangs upside down or turns objects upside down.
Dab	A graphic schema used in paintings, randomly or systematically, to form patterns or to represent, for example, eyes, flowers or buttons.
Dynamic vertical (and horizontal)	A child may show evidence of particular interest by actions such as climbing, stepping-up and down, or lying flat. These schemas may also be seen in constructions, collages or graphically. After schemas of horizontality and verticality have been explored separately, the two are often used in conjunction to form crosses or grids. These are very often systematically explored on paper and interest is shown in everyday objects such as a cake-cooling tray, grills or nets.
The family of trajectories	(a) VERTICAL (up) and HORIZONTAL (down) A fascination with things moving or flying through the air – balls, aeroplanes, rockets, catapults, frisbees – and indeed, anything that can be thrown. When expressed through the child's own body movements, this often becomes large arm and leg movements, kicking, or punching, for example. (b) DIAGONALITY Usually explored later than the previous schemas, this one emerges via the construction of ramps, slides and sloping walls. Drawings begin to contain diagonal lines forming roofs, hands, triangles, zig-zags.
Containment	Putting things inside and outside containers, baskets, buckets, bags, carts, boxes, etc.
Enclosure	A child may build enclosures with blocks, Lego or large crates, perhaps naming them as boats, ponds, beds. The enclosure is sometimes left empty, sometimes carefully filled in. An enclosing line often surrounds paintings and drawings while a child is exploring this schema. The child might draw circles, squares and triangles, heads, bodies, eyes, wheels, flowers, etc.
Enveloping	This is often an extension of enclosure. Objects, space or the child him- or herself are completely covered. The child may wrap things in paper, enclose them in pots or boxes with covers or lids, wrap him- or herself in a blanket or creep under a rug. Paintings are sometimes covered over with a wash of colour or scrap collages glued over with layers of paper or fabric.
Circles and lines radiating from the circle	(a) SEMI-CIRCULARITY Semi-circles are used graphically as features, parts of bodies and other objects. Smiles, eyebrows, ears, rainbows and umbrellas are a few of the representational uses for this schema, as well as parts of letters of the alphabet. (b) CORE and RADIALS Again common in paintings, drawings and models. Spiders, suns, fingers, eyelashes, hair and hedgehogs often appear as a series of radials.
Rotation	A child may become absorbed by things which turn – taps, wheels, cogs and keys. The child may roll cylinders along, or roll themselves. The child may rotate their arms, or construct objects with rotating parts in wood or scrap materials.

Name of schema	Description
Connection	Scrap materials may be glued, sewn and fastened into lines; pieces of wood are nailed into long connecting constructions. Strings, rope or wool are used to tie objects together, often in complex ways. Drawings and paintings sometimes show a series of linked parts. The opposite of this schema may be seen in separation, where interest is shown in disconnecting assembled or attached parts.
Ordering	A child may produce paintings and drawings with ordered lines or dabs; collages or constructions with items of scrap carefully glued in sequence. They may place blocks, vehicles or animals in lines and begin to show interest in 'largest' and 'smallest'.

It is important to remember that the sensory-motor stage of the schema is at an earlier level, and that the cause and effect, together with the symbolic levels, both emerge out of this.

Table 2.4 Schema focus sheet

 In Practice

Schemas

Observe a child throughout one day – either a baby, a toddler or a child up to five years old – using narrative observations and, if possible, photography. Then analyse your observations to see if you have any examples of consistent use of a schema or schema cluster (rotation is often strong when enclosure is present; the two schemas form a cluster). Use Table 2.4 to help you identify schemas.

1. Note the child's favourite experiences in the setting. Can you see if there are links with the child's schemas?

2. Ask the parent(s) what the child is interested in at home and share your observations with them. Are there any connections between what the child enjoys and finds interesting in the setting and at home?

3. What can you do to support and extend the child's schemas? For example, if the child is particularly interested in rotation, you might add whisks and spinners to the water tray.

The stages of intellectual development

The first month

Babies explore through their senses and through their own activity and movement.

Touch

- From the beginning babies feel pain.
- The baby's face, abdomen, hands and the soles of his or her feet are also very sensitive to touch.
- The baby perceives the movements that he or she makes, and the way that other people move them about through his or her senses.
- For example, the baby gives a 'startle' response if they are moved suddenly. This is called the 'moro' or startle reflex.

Sound

- Even a newborn baby will turn to a sound. The baby might become still and listen to a low sound, or quicken his or her movements when he or she hears a high sound.
- The baby often stops crying and listens to a human voice by two weeks of age.

The stages of intellectual development (cont.)

Taste

- The baby likes sweet tastes, e.g. breast milk.

Smell

- The baby turns to the smell of the breast.

Sight

- The baby can focus on objects 20 cm (about eight inches) away.
- The baby is sensitive to light.
- The baby likes to look at human faces – eye contact.
- The baby can track the movements of people and objects.
- The baby will scan the edges of objects.
- The baby will imitate facial expressions (e.g. he or she will put out their tongue if you do). If you know any newborn or very young babies, try it and see!

From one to four months

- The baby recognises differing speech sounds.
- By three months the baby can even imitate low- or high-pitched sounds.
- By four months the baby links objects they know with the sound, e.g. mother's voice and her face.
- The baby knows the smell of his or her mother from that of other mothers.

From four to six months

- By four months the baby reaches for objects, which suggests they recognise and judge the distance in relation to the size of the object.
- The baby prefers complicated things to look at from five to six months and enjoys bright colours.
- The baby knows that he or she has one mother. The baby is disturbed if he or she is shown several images of his or her mother at the same time. The baby realises that people are permanent before they realise that objects are.
- The baby can coordinate more, e.g. see a rattle, grasp the rattle, put the rattle in his or her mouth (they coordinate tracking, reaching, grasping and sucking).
- The baby can develop favourite tastes in food and recognise differences by five months.

From six to nine months

- The baby understands signs, e.g. the bib means that food is coming.
- From eight to nine months the baby shows that he or she knows objects exist when they have gone out of sight, even under test conditions. This is called the concept of object constancy, or the object permanence test (Piaget). The baby is also fascinated by the way objects move.

From nine to twelve months

- The baby is beginning to develop images. Memory develops and the baby can remember the past.
- The baby can anticipate the future. This gives the baby some understanding of routine daily sequences, e.g. after a feed, changing, and a sleep with teddy.
- The baby imitates actions, sounds, gestures and moods after an event is finished, e.g. imitate a temper tantrum he or she saw a friend have the previous day, wave bye-bye remembering Grandma has gone to the shops.

From one year to two years

- The child understands the names of objects and can follow simple instructions.
- The child learns about things through trial and error.

The stages of intellectual development (cont.)

- The child uses toys or objects to represent things in real life (e.g. using a doll as a baby, or a large cardboard box as a car or a garage).
- The child begins to scribble on paper.
- The child often 'talks' to him- or herself while playing.

From two years

- The child has improved memory skills, which helps his or her understanding of concepts (e.g. the child can often name and match two or three colours – usually including yellow and red).
- The child can hold a crayon and move it up and down.
- The child understands cause and effect (e.g. if something is dropped, he or she understands it might break).
- The child talks about an absent object when reminded of it (e.g. he or she may say 'biscuit' when seeing an empty plate or bowl).

From three years

The child develops symbolic behaviour. This means that:

- The child talks.
- The child pretend plays – often talking to him- or herself while playing.
- The child takes part in simple non-competitive games.
- The child represents events in drawings, models, etc.
- Personal images dominate, rather than conventions used in the culture, e.g. writing is 'pretend' writing.
- The child becomes fascinated by cause and effect; the child is continually trying to explain what goes on in the world.
- The child can identify common colours, such as red, yellow, blue and green – although may sometimes confuse blue with green.

From four years

- At about age four, the child usually knows how to count – up to 20.
- The child also understands ideas such as 'more' and 'fewer', and 'big' and 'small'.
- The child will recognise his or her own name when it is written down and can usually write it.
- The child can think back and can think forward much more easily than before.
- The child can also think about things from somebody else's point of view, but only fleetingly.
- The child often enjoys music and playing sturdy instruments, and joins in groups singing and dancing.

From five to eight years

Communication through body language, facial gestures and language is well established, and opens the way into literacy (talking, listening, writing and reading).

- The child includes more detail in their drawings – e.g. a house may have not only windows and a roof, but also curtains and a chimney.
- Thinking becomes increasingly coordinated as the child is able to hold in mind more than one point of view at a time. Concepts – of matter, length, measurement, distance, area, time, volume, capacity and weight – develop steadily.
- The child enjoys chanting and counting (beginning to understand numbers). The child can use his or her voice in different ways to play different characters in pretend play. The child develops play narratives (stories), which he or she returns to over time. The child helps younger children into the play.

The stages of intellectual development (cont.)

- The child is beginning to establish differences between what is real and unreal/fantasy. This is not yet always stable, so the child can easily be frightened by supernatural characters.

From eight to eleven years

From eight to nine years:

- The child has an increased ability to remember and pay attention, and to speak and express their ideas.
- The child is learning to plan ahead and evaluate what they do.
- The child has an increased ability to think and to reason.
- The child can deal with abstract ideas.
- The child enjoys different types of activities – such as joining clubs, playing games with rules, and collecting things.
- The child enjoys projects that are task-orientated, such as sewing and woodwork.

From ten to eleven years:

- The child begins to understand the motives behind the actions of another.
- The child can concentrate on tasks for increasing periods.
- The child begins to devise memory strategies.
- The child may be curious about drugs, alcohol and tobacco.
- The child may develop special talents, showing particular skills in writing, maths, art, music or woodwork.

From 12 to 19 years

Around this time, young people experience a major shift in thinking from concrete to abstract – an adult way of thinking. Piaget described this as the formal operational stage of intellectual development. This involves:

- thinking about possibilities – younger children rely heavily on their senses to apply reasoning, whereas adolescents think about possibilities that are not directly observable
- thinking ahead – young people start to plan ahead, often in a systematic way; e.g. younger children may look forward to a holiday, but they are unlikely to focus on the preparation involved
- thinking through hypotheses – this gives them the ability to make and test hypotheses, and to think about situations that are contrary to fact
- thinking about their own thought processes – this is known as metacognition; a subcategory of metacognition is metamemory, which is having knowledge about your memory processes – being able to explain what strategies you use when trying to remember things (e.g. for an exam)
- thinking beyond conventional limits – thinking about issues that generally preoccupy human beings in adulthood, such as morality, religion and politics.

They approach a problem in a systematic fashion and also use their imagination when solving problems.

Table 2.5 An overview of the stages of intellectual development

Social, emotional and behavioural development

Social, emotional and behavioural development is made up of the following aspects:

- **Dispositions and attitudes**: how children develop interest in – and become excited and motivated about – their learning.
- **Self-confidence and self-esteem**: how children have a sense of their own value and develop an understanding of the need for sensitivity to significant events in their own and other people's lives.

- **Forming relationships**: this refers to the importance of children forming good relationships with others and working alongside others sociably.
- **Behaviour and self-control**: how children develop a growing understanding of what is right and wrong and why, along with understanding the impact of their words and actions on themselves and others.
- **Self-care and independence**: how children gain a sense of self-respect and concern for their own personal hygiene and care and how they develop independence.
- **Sense of community**: how children understand and respect their own needs, views, cultures and beliefs and those of other people.

Emotional development involves the:

- growth of feelings about, and awareness of, **oneself**
- development of feelings towards **other people**
- development of **self-esteem** and a **self-concept**.

Key terms

Self-esteem – The way you feel about yourself (good or bad) leads to high or low self-esteem.

Self-concept – How you see yourself, and how you think others see you; sometimes called **self-image**.

Personality and temperament

Everyone has a different **personality**. Research is increasingly suggesting that a child's temperament in early childhood is the foundation of his or her adult personality. It used to be thought that personality was fixed at birth (just as it used to be thought that intelligence was fixed at birth and unchangeable thereafter). As in other areas of development, it seems that a child's temperament is partly biological, but is also influenced by other factors:

- life experience and culture
- physical challenges, including special needs and disabilities
- the people children meet.

Temperament is the style of behaviour that is natural to the child. So the child's temperament influences the personality that emerges later on, during late childhood and early adolescence.

Figure 2.17 The thoughtful and sensitive presence of a familiar adult gives these three children a feeling of security

Laura E. Berk (2006: p. 412) summarises Mary Rothbart's important theory that babies and young children have differing levels of **reactivity**. Reactivity describes their:

- levels of activity
- capacity to pay attention for a time
- fearful distress, especially when faced by new situations
- irritable distress, especially finding it difficult to get comfortable, 'fussing'
- positive emotional response and state: how often they appear to be happy and experiencing pleasure.

It is very important that adults working with young children do not favour smiling children at the expense of those children who seem more 'difficult' or seem inactive and 'slow to warm up'. It is also critical that they do not form negative opinions of children with more difficult temperaments. Working professionally with children means being determined to uphold principles of equality of opportunity and inclusivity (see Chapter 5).

Babies and young children can also take some control themselves and be resilient. This is called **effortful control** – for example, managing their frustration by turning their attention to something else, rather than becoming increasingly angry or just giving up on difficult things.

As children grow, their temperament can change with their development. The 'easy' baby who is content to lay back may be very fearful about exploring and crawling, while the 'fussy', wriggly baby who never seems to settled may love the physical sensations of movement and enjoy getting around.

Key terms

Effortful control – Children's capacity to override their immediate wants, desires and responses with a more socially acceptable and effective response. Children who can see that there are cakes on the table, but wait for the adult to say it is okay to have one, are showing high levels of effortful control.

Reactivity – This refers to the intensity and speed of the child's emotional responses, the child's ability to focus attention and the child's movement.

The interdependency between physical, emotional, intellectual and social development

It is important to remember that it is not possible to isolate emotional and social development from any other areas of development. The process of **social referencing** is an example of how areas of development overlap: the child who feels prevented from playing with a new toy or approaching another child in the park by his carer's look of anxiety and fear is not only affected emotionally (perhaps becoming anxious and shy), but also cognitively by missing out on new play experiences.

Similarly, if carers do not try to think about what a child means when he or she cries or gets angry, the child in turn might be unable to think about how

other people feel. Peter Fonagy, a psychoanalyst and clinical psychologist, uses the term **mentalisation** to describe the ability, through imagination, to interpret what other people do and say. Mentalisation is needed to develop friendships, which depend on being able to imagine how another person is feeling; and it is also needed in order to take part in role play, enjoy books and a whole host of other experiences. For example, Julia Donaldson's book, *The Gruffalo*, depends on the reader or listener being able to imagine that the animals are afraid of a mysterious big monster in the forest.

In Practice

Observe a two-year-old child for an hour.

1. How many examples of social referencing do you see?

2. How do adult responses (facial expressions, tone of voice, words spoken) help the child to feel confident exploring?

3. How do they help the child to take care and be aware of danger?

Progress check

Putting theories into practice

- Know how children's temperaments might affect their wellbeing in nursery.
- Work as a team to use words like 'thinking', 'imagining' or 'wondering' to match children's developing theory of mind.
- Spend blocks of time with a child who seems fearful to explore and play, showing your interest in what the child is doing.

Key terms

Mentalisation – The ability to understand another person's mental state through observing their behaviour – for example, a child saying, 'I think Sophie wants to be my friend; she is trying to hold my hand'.

Social referencing – This is when a baby or young child checks an adult's emotional response before deciding on their own. If the adult looks pleased as a child moves to pick up a toy, the child is likely to smile too. If the adult looks fearful, the child is likely to shy away.

Research Activity

1. Are children being damaged by a culture in Britain that is too focused on individualism, competition and having expensive electronic toys and branded clothes?

2. Are children becoming more fearful because they are kept at home in front of televisions and computers instead of being allowed to play outside?

Read more about these questions in *A Good Childhood* by Richard Layard and Judy Dunn (2009) and *No Fear: Growing Up in a Risk-averse Society* by Tim Gill (2007).

Relating to others

From the start, it seems as if babies are born to relate to other people: they are interested in others and want to gain people's attention and respond to them. It is important to encourage sociability by providing opportunities for babies and young children to meet other children and adults. As early as six months of age, babies can enjoy each other's company. When they sit together, they touch each other's faces. They look at each other and smile at each other. They enjoy peek-a-boo games with adults and older children. This is an early example of **cooperative social behaviour**. It involves turn-taking and is the foundation of having a conversation with someone else. Babies delight in having a shared idea, and they really laugh with pleasure.

- Toddlers' behaviour also shows how very young children cooperate socially. One child might pick up a toy and another will copy. They laugh together. There is plenty of eye contact. One drops the toy intentionally, and the other copies. They laugh with glee. They have a shared idea that they can enjoy together.
- By the age of two or three years, the widening social circle becomes important. Children need varying amounts of help and support as they have new social experiences. This might include joining an early childhood group of some kind.

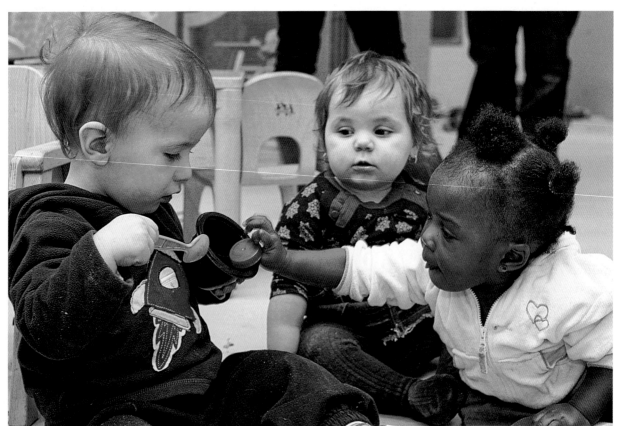

Figure 2.18 Young children in nursery showing cooperative social behaviour

Getting on with other children

A young child, seeing a friend distressed, may make a gesture spontaneously – such as giving them a treasured teddy bear – to ease the pain and provide comfort. This means that young children can be, in their own way, very *giving*. They are also very *forgiving*. Being able to give means that a young child has managed to think of someone else's needs and control his or her own behaviour accordingly. It takes enormous effort for young children to do this. It is an ability that will come and go depending on the situation, the people involved and how tired the child is. Children who become skilled in this way are often popular leaders, and other children want to be with them.

Children tend to behave according to the way they experience life. If they are ridiculed or smacked, they are likely to laugh at and hit others, especially children younger or smaller than themselves. This is because children use social referencing to guide their behaviour and responses to others. Some children need a great deal of support to play well and get on with other children. Children who know how to join in get on better with other children. They have good **access strategies**:

1 First, a child will tend to circle around the edge of an activity, perhaps on a tricycle, trying to work out what is happening, or will watch what is happening from the safe viewpoint of being at the sand tray or water tray.
2 Then they will imitate what the other children are doing – for example, pouring sand in and out of pots and laughing as each pot is upturned. We call this using a **side-by-side** strategy. Doing the same helps the child to join in with other children.

How you can support a child to join in

You might say to the child, 'Do you want to join in? Let's look at what they are doing, shall we? Don't ask if you can do the same as them, just do the same as them.' This advice is given because if children ask if they can join in, they are usually rejected. If, on the other hand, children simply do what the other children are doing, they are very likely to be accepted into the group. This is an important access strategy that adults can help children to develop. It is also a useful strategy

for adults to use if they are joining a group of children. Adults can also support young children by modelling phrases such as, 'Can I have a go next?' or 'Can I have that when you're finished?', which can help children to find a way between being left out and never getting a turn, or being impulsive and grabbing things to force their way in.

In Practice

Spend some time observing a child who is finding it difficult to play with others. Set up an activity based on what you have observed the child is interested in, and see if you can help the child to play with another child with similar interests.

Progress check

Supporting play

- Know about some of the ways that play helps children's emotional and social development.
- Work within your team to help children find appropriate ways to join in with play when they feel left out.
- Spend time with a child who is finding it difficult to share and play alongside others, acting as a positive model by suggesting phrases like, 'I would like a turn when you have finished.'

Helping children to manage their feelings in their social relationships

Learning to be assertive

Children might bully others because they feel bad about themselves, or because others have bullied them. They can pick on weaker children or children who are different – for example, they tease or make racial, gender or disability insults. Teaching all children to value the way others are different, rather than to mock or be nervous, and to be assertive in their response to name-calling or hitting, can help to prevent bullying.

Supporting children to develop assertiveness

- Try not to use labelling words like 'bully' or 'disruptive'. These can give a child a bad name that the child will then live up to – and often children do not really understand what these words mean anyway. Instead, talk to children in ways they understand, about what they can see or feel; for example, 'When you shout like that, it makes Adam sad. Can you see he is crying now? What would be a better way to get your turn on the bike?'; 'When someone tries to grab things off you, you can shout "No!" Let's practise saying "no" in a loud voice.'

- Swearing can create similar problems to name-calling. Often it is simply the case that swearing is an everyday part of the child's language experience. However, it is quite a different thing when children swear in order to shock. Any child who swears needs help in:
  - learning which words they cannot use in the early years setting
  - finding new words to replace the swear words (they still have to be able to express their thoughts and feelings)
  - building up their vocabulary so that they have wider choice of words.

Discussion point

It has been a difficult week in the nursery. There seems to be a lot of conflict between the children, and a small group of older children seem to be going round snatching toys from the younger ones. One of your colleagues says, 'As soon as we see *anything* we should get straight in there and clamp down on them. We need to stop this bullying.'

Do you think this approach will help the children to learn more sociable behaviour? Discuss your thoughts with another learner or in a group.

Supporting children to manage strong feelings

Children live life to the full. This means that they have powerful feelings. They need adult help to learn to deal with the strength of their feelings. Feelings are hard to manage – even adults do not always succeed in dealing with how they feel. These strong feelings can quickly overwhelm children. This can lead to:

- sobbing and sadness
- temper tantrums that are full of anger and rage

- jealousy that makes a child want to hit out
- joy that makes a child literally jump and leap with a wildness that is unnerving to many adults.

Children's body language

Children need to express their feelings, and not just through words. They do so through:

- **physical actions** – like stamping with rage, screaming with terror, hitting out, jumping with joy or seeking a cuddle
- **facial expressions** – a pout tells the adult the child is not happy, compared with eyes that are shining with joy
- **the position of the body** – playing alone with the dolls' house or hovering on the edge of a cooking session might indicate that the child wants to join in but does not know how; playing boats right in the centre of a group of children tells an adult something quite different
- **body movements** – children who keep twisting their fingers together are not at ease, compared with children who sit in a relaxed way.

Figure 2.19 Facial expressions can say a lot about how you are feeling; children enjoy being with adults who reflect their body language and emotions

Putting feelings into words

It helps children to manage their feelings if they can put them into words. The child who can say, 'Stop hitting me! That hurts! I don't like it!' has found an appropriate way to deal with an unpleasant situation.

- The cries that a baby makes are early attempts to 'tell' others how he or she feels. By trying to 'tune in' to the baby and understand the cause of his or her distress, you help the baby's developing confidence by showing that he or she is understood by other people.

- It takes time, experience and adult support for young children to learn how to express their feelings in words and to negotiate in dialogue with others. It can help to give them examples of sharp-sounding words, such as 'Stop it!' so that they can take control of situations. Children learn the language of feelings through real situations that hold great meaning and that engage their whole attention.

- Stories that relate to an area of difficulty for the child can help them to develop more understanding. Some children find it hard to say goodbye to their parents at the start of nursery. Hearing a story such as *Owl Babies* by Martin Waddell might be a way to start talking about those feelings of loss, and the relief the babies feel when their mother returns.

Helping children under emotional stress

When children do not experience warm, loving relationships, they react differently according to their personality. They may:

- become aggressive
- be very quiet, watchful and tense
- begin bedwetting or soiling themselves
- find it difficult to eat
- return to babyish ways – they may want a bottle again or a comforter; they might want to be held

and cuddled or carried about; they might want help with eating and dressing.

When children are under emotional stress, their behaviour can change quite quickly. It is important, therefore, that early years workers are alert to the changes listed above and that they respond sensitively and with understanding. If you suspect a problem of this kind, it is important to talk with your line manager about your observations and consider how best to discuss it with the child's family. The discussion will probably open up to the staff team. You will all look at the child's progress and agree what steps should be taken, depending on whether the situation is a temporary one for the child or one that is more likely to be long-term. Where children continue to experience difficulties of these kinds for more than a few weeks, and where there is no obvious cause – for example, a new baby or a sick parent – it may be important to involve another professional, such as a clinical child psychologist.

 Progress check

Helping children to be assertive

- Know about some strategies to use when children show angry feelings and act these out by being aggressive.
- Work within your team to help children to become appropriately assertive.
- Acknowledge children's emotions of all kinds – happy, sad and angry.

Guidelines for helping children to understand their feelings and manage their emotions positively

1 Children need to begin to understand, express and manage their feelings.

2 Children need to develop positive relationships with people.

3 Children feel things deeply and need a great deal of help in coming to terms with their emotions. Feelings are hard to deal with. Anyone – child or adult – can be overwhelmed by their emotions for a time, and need someone sympathetic to stay with them and look after them.

4 Children need help to learn how to make up when they have hurt someone else. Insisting children say 'sorry' can lead to a half-hearted apology, while putting the problem back to the child and saying, 'How can we make Iqbal feel a bit better now?' can be more productive.

Children who express themselves or relate to others in particular or challenging ways

The shy or withdrawn child

Although it is important for every child to have his or her own personal space and be allowed opportunities to do things alone, some children have difficulty socialising with other children or with adults. These children have too much personal space. There are a number of things that you can do to support a child to overcome his or her shyness.

- **Making introductions**: when an adult is new to the child, you can introduce them. 'Michael, this is Jane. Jane wants to do a painting. Can you help her to get started? Can you tell her how to find the colours she wants?'
- **Being welcoming**: if a child is shy with adults it can be helpful to join the child with a warm smile, but to say nothing. You might find that a welcoming gesture, such as handing the child a lump of clay if they join the clay table, reassures them.
- **Observing children**: keeping good observations of children's social relationships is important. If a child who is normally outgoing and has the full range of social behaviour suddenly becomes quiet, withdrawn and solitary, this should be discussed with the team and parents should be included in the discussion. Multi-professional help from outside may be required if the problem cannot be solved within the team.

The over-demanding child

Having too much individual adult attention can lead to children being labelled as 'spoilt' or 'over-demanding'. This negative image of the child is not helpful. Some children – for example, children with no brothers or sisters – are the main focus of their family and are given one-to-one attention by adults most of the time. They have not experienced waiting for things or taking turns. Is it the child's fault if he or she seems demanding of adult attention, insecure or ill at ease with other children? This child needs sensitive help to become involved in parallel, associative and cooperative social behaviour with other children.

Some children gain attention by being dominant and demanding. These are the so-called 'bossy' children. But this is another negative and unhelpful image. Such children need help in turn-taking and learning to give and take. They are usually afraid of losing control of situations – for example, in the play and home areas, they may control the other children by saying what the storyline is going to be and by making the other children do as they say. These children need an adult to help them to see that the 'story' will be better if other children's ideas are allowed in. It takes a bit of courage for the child to dare to let the play 'free-flow', because no one knows quite how the story will turn out.

Sibling jealousy

When a new baby is born, it can be hard for a child who is used to having a lot of attention. Sibling jealousy often results in very demanding behaviour, which may last for some time, until the family adjusts to its new social relationships. Recent research shows that the older child needs to feel that he or she is being treated in exactly the same way as the new baby – for example, getting some special attention at times.

Key term

Behavioural, emotional and social difficulties (BESD) – Signs that a child may have BESD include withdrawn or isolated behaviour, highly disruptive or disturbing behaviour, hyperactivity and significant difficulties with social interactions. It is difficult to assess whether a young child has BESD, and an educational psychologist or clinical child psychologist should always be involved.

Children and 'status possessions'

Children in Britain today are growing up in a very materialist society, where they may see adults putting great emphasis on having the latest car, smart phone or television. From two years of age they may become eager to own objects. Owning possessions helps them to gain attention and enables them to control things. Children who have not experienced secure social relationships are often especially anxious to possess fashionable objects that carry high status – for example, a special toy or particular clothes and shoes. Advertisers pressurise children into wanting goods branded with their favourite characters: there are now hundreds of Thomas the Tank Engine products for example, including clothes, bedding, games and rucksacks.

Adults can help children in a number of ways. It is probably best to avoid any kind of branded goods in a nursery setting: it is inevitable that a Bob the Builder hammer will create a huge amount of conflict. Branded goods are also restrictive: you can only be Batman in a Batman suit, while with a length of dark fabric you can be Batman, or a monster, or a baby wrapped up for sleep. Playing with equipment and materials like this can help children to see that branded objects are not vital for having friends and being part of the group. Children need to learn that friends like you because of who you are, not because you have a certain type of trainers.

Angry children

Hitting, kicking, spitting, biting, swearing and disrupting other children's activities are behaviours that children use to demand attention. When children behave like this, they can soon become labelled as naughty or impossible to manage, and it is only a short step to these children starting to live up to their label, and staff starting to speak and act towards them in an anxious or hostile way. So it is important to break this cycle, to try to hold on to the positive aspects of the child's behaviour and appeal to these. The following strategies may help:

- Try to imagine what it might be like to be a child in the setting. Does it sometimes feel like there is a great mass of children, all demanding attention and seeking the same equipment? You can help by taking time with individual children, listening to them and observing them, encountering them as special individuals and not just one many in the group.
- Try to become aware of your own feelings. Angry children provoke angry responses from adults. Can you work on your responses and become calmer and clearer, and reduce confrontations? Saying, 'I can wait a minute, but then I really do need you to come and sit down,' will often work much better than demanding 'Sit down now!'
- Look for patterns in children's behaviour. If a child is often angry at a particular time of the day, during a particular activity or in response to particular children, try to plan the day to minimise these times.

Dealing with temper tantrums

Temper tantrums can be:

- **noisy** – the child might hurl themselves about, perhaps hurting themselves, usually in rather a public way
- **quiet** – the child holds their breath and might even turn blue.

It is almost always best to deal with temper tantrums in a quiet and matter-of-fact way, however much you sense your own feelings boiling up. Try to give as little attention as possible to the tantrum and encourage other children away. It can be helpful to stay near the child, offering quiet reassurance, but it is usually best not to talk: the child is in no state for discussion. At the end, you might say something like, 'Now you are calmer, we can talk about this and see what we can do about it,' and help the child return to playing with others.

Stages of emotional, social and behavioural development

The first month

- A baby's first smile in definite response to carer is usually around five to six weeks.
- The baby often imitates certain facial expressions.
- The baby uses total body movements to express pleasure at bathtime or when being fed.
- The baby enjoys feeding and cuddling.
- In the first month babies are learning where they begin and end, e.g. his or her hand is part of them but mother's hand is not.

From one to four months

Four to eight weeks:

- The baby will smile in response to an adult.
- The baby enjoys sucking.
- The baby turns to regard nearby speaker's face.
- The baby turns to preferred person's voice.
- The baby recognises face and hands of preferred adult.
- The baby may stop crying when he or she hears, sees or feels her carer.

Eight to twelve weeks:

- The baby shows enjoyment at caring routines such as bath time.
- The baby responds with obvious pleasure to loving attention and cuddles.
- The baby fixes his or her eyes unblinkingly on carer's face when feeding.
- The baby stays awake for longer periods of time.

From four to six months

- The baby shows trust and security.
- The baby has recognisable sleep patterns.

From six to nine months

- The baby can manage to feed herself using his or her fingers.
- The baby is now more wary of strangers, sometimes showing stranger fear.
- The baby might offer toys to others.
- The baby might show distress when his or her mother leaves.
- The baby typically begins to crawl and this means he or she can do more for him- or herself, reach for objects and get to places and people.
- The baby is now more aware of other people's feelings. For example, he or she may cry if their brother cries.

From nine to twelve months

- The baby enjoys songs and action rhymes.
- The baby still likes to be near to a familiar adult.
- The baby can drink from a cup with help.
- The baby will play alone for long periods.
- The baby has and shows definite likes and dislikes at mealtimes and bedtimes.
- The baby thoroughly enjoys peek-a-boo games.
- The baby likes to look at him- or herself in a mirror (plastic safety mirror).

Stages of emotional, social and behavioural development (cont.)

- The baby imitates other people – e.g. clapping hands, waving bye-bye – but there is often a time lapse, so that he or she waves after the person has gone.
- The baby cooperates when being dressed.

From one year to two years

- The child begins to have a longer memory.
- The child develops a sense of identity (I am me).
- The child expresses his or her needs in words and gestures.
- The child enjoys being able to walk, and is eager to try to get dressed – 'Me do it!'
- The child is aware when others are fearful or anxious for him or her as he or she climbs on and off chairs, and so on.

From two years

- The child is impulsive and curious about their environment.
- Pretend play develops rapidly when adults encourage it.
- The child begins to be able to say how he or she is feeling, but often feels frustrated when unable to express him- or herself.
- The child can dress him- or herself and go to the lavatory independently, but needs sensitive support in order to feel success rather than frustration.
- By two and half years the child plays more with other children, but may not share his or her toys with them.

From three years

Pretend play helps the child to decentre and develop theory of mind (the child begins to be able to understand how someone else might feel and/or think).

- The child is beginning to develop a gender role as they become aware of being male or female.
- The child makes friends and is interested in having friends.
- The child learns to negotiate, give and take through experimenting with feeling powerful, having a sense of control, and through quarrels with other children.
- The child is easily afraid, e.g. of the dark, as he or she becomes capable of pretending. The child imagines all sorts of things.

From four years

- The child likes to be independent and is strongly self-willed.
- The child shows a sense of humour.
- The child can undress and dress him- or herself – except for laces and back buttons.
- The child can wash and dry his or her hands and brush their teeth.

From five to eight years

- The child has developed a stable self-concept.
- The child can hide their feelings once they can begin to control them.
- The child can think of the feelings of others.
- The child can take responsibility, e.g. in helping younger children.

From eight to eleven years

At eight or nine years old:

- The child may become discouraged easily.
- The child takes pride in their competence.

Stages of emotional, social and behavioural development (cont.)

- The child can be argumentative and bossy, but can equally be generous and responsive.
- The child is beginning to see things from another child's point of view, but still has trouble understanding the feelings and needs of other people.

At eleven or twelve years old:

- The child may be experiencing sudden, dramatic, emotional changes associated with puberty (especially girls, who experience puberty earlier than boys).
- The child tends to be particularly sensitive to criticism.
- The child prefers to spend leisure time with friends and continues to participate in small groups of the same sex, but is acutely aware of the opposite sex.
- The child succumbs to peer pressure more readily and wants to talk, dress, and act just like friends.

From 12 to 19 years

- The young person may become self-conscious or worried about physical changes (e.g. too short, too tall, too fat, too thin).
- The young person develops a sexual identity; self-labelling as gay or lesbian tends to occur around the age of 15 for boys and 15 and a half for girls, although first disclosure does not normally take place until after the age of 16 and a half years for both sexes.
- The young person often feels misunderstood.
- The young person can experience wide emotional swings (e.g. fluctuate between emotional peaks of excitement and depths of moodiness).
- The young person wants to become accepted and liked.
- The young person tends to identify more with friends and begin to separate from parents; they are less dependent on family for affection and emotional support.

Table 2.6 An overview of the stages of emotional, social and behavioural development

Theories of child development

A theory of child development is someone's idea about how a child might develop. Theories help people to predict, for example, that before children talk, they usually babble. Theories about how children develop are products of research, so are influenced by the culture in which they are thought out. Research by human beings provides all the evidence for and against various theories of child development. It is very important to remember this, because humans are not objective – they agree and disagree. You must realise that there is no such thing as 'the truth' about child development. We always need to stop and ask: Who is doing the research? Who is formulating the theory?

Two examples illustrate this point.

- The child psychologist **Vygotsky** grew up in the Soviet Union, where Marxist and Communist ideas dominated. He came from a large family. Is it coincidence that his theory emphasises social relationships and the community?
- The psychologist **Piaget** grew up in Europe. He was an only child. Is it coincidence that his theory emphasises the child as an individual and as an active learner, trying to experiment and solve problems?

Using theories in your work

You need to have an open mind and to look at various different theories, bringing together those ideas that are useful from each one, so that you can use them in your work. Some theories will help you

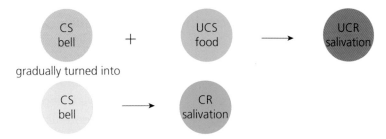

Figure 2.20 A summary of Pavlov's experiment

to make predictions about a child's learning. You need to see how theories like those of Vygotsky and Piaget are the same and how they are different. Both these theories help us to look at how children learn.

Historically, theories of child development have tended to fall into one of two groups. Some theories take the view that learning is closely linked with development. Examples of this type of theory are '**leave it to nature**' theories and **social constructivist** theories. The other group of theories dismisses the importance of a child's development as the basis of learning. These theories follow the **transmission** model, which says that children learn what they are shown by adults. When describing how children learn, therefore, it is important to say which theory is being used.

Transmission models of learning

In the seventeenth century, the British philosopher John Locke thought that children were like lumps of clay, which adults could mould into the shape they wanted. At the beginning of the twentieth century, an American psychologist, Watson, and the Russian psychologist Pavlov were developing similar theories about how people learn. In the past, these theories have had a strong influence on thinking about development.

Classical conditioning

Ivan Petrovich Pavlov (1849–1936) experimented with conditioned responses in dogs. He liked to be described as a physiologist, rather than as a psychologist, because he believed that psychological states (such as conditioning) are identical to physiological states and processes in the brain. He thought this approach was useful and scientific. In his experiments, there was a neutral conditioned stimulus (CS), which was a church bell ringing. This

was paired with food, which was an unconditioned stimulus (UCS). The dogs were fed when the church bells rang. This produced an unconditioned response (UCR), which was saliva flowing in the dog's mouth when the food appeared. Gradually, the sound of any bell would produce a conditioned response (CR) in the dogs, which would produce saliva, ready for the food that usually accompanied the ringing of the bell.

Classical conditioning is the way in which responses come under the control of a new stimulus. In this case, food normally produces salivation. Classical conditioning changes the stimulus, so that the sound of a bell produces salivation. Pavlov would have fed the dogs whether or not they salivated at the sound of the bell.

Figure 2.21 Pavlov's dog: an illustrated summary of the experiment

Case Study   An example of learning through classical conditioning

Year 2 children (aged six and seven years) in a primary school were working in groups. One group was painting, one was writing, one was involved in a maths game and one was cooking. The school bell rang. Immediately, the children stopped what they were doing and started to tidy up quickly and go out to play. The children were conditioned to expect playtime when the bell sounded, so they tidied up in readiness. They would have tidied up even if they had not subsequently been allowed to go out to play.

Bell (CS) + Playtime (UCS) = Tidy up (UCR)

Bell (CS) = Tidy up (CR)

Operant conditioning

Burrhus Frederic Skinner (1904–90) was a behavioural psychologist who worked in the USA. He did not believe it was useful to theorise about mental states that could not be observed. He thought this was unscientific.

Whereas Pavlov fed his dogs when the bell rang whether they salivated or not, Skinner only fed his rats or pigeons if they behaved as he required. For example, Skinner gave rats a reward of food if they pressed a lever. This was **positive reinforcement**: the desired behaviour was rewarded.

Conversely, undesired behaviour could be **negatively reinforced**. For example, the rats might receive an electric shock each time they went near one area of a maze. They would then begin to avoid that area. The undesired behaviour was extinguished and the desired behaviour was encouraged.

Chris Rice is a lecturer in early childhood courses at Clydebank College in Scotland, and explains how positive and negative reinforcement can work for children:

Positive and negative reinforcement

Positive reinforcement is concerned with a child behaving in a certain way, leading to a pleasing outcome; then the behaviour will be repeated. For example, a baby points to a toy monkey and looks at the adult. The adult hands the baby the toy, making appropriate monkey noises, which they both find funny. The baby then repeats the behaviour with other objects, in order to be similarly amused (positive reinforcement).

Negative reinforcement is concerned with a child behaving in a particular way in order to avoid something unpleasant, to stop pain or to prevent discomfort. For example, the baby cries because he or she has a wet nappy and feels uncomfortable. The adult responds by changing the nappy and the baby feels better. The next time the baby feels discomfort he or she will repeat the behaviour – that is, repeat the crying – in order to stop the unpleasant feeling.

A **reinforcer** causes the behaviour to be repeated; it may be some form of reward for showing a desired behaviour or something that is linked to the avoidance of unpleasantness or pain.

In the positive reinforcement example, the monkey noises are the reinforcer – the entertaining reward for asking for the toy.

In the negative reinforcement example, getting a nappy change is the reinforcer – the reward for crying. In both these situations, the baby is learning that a certain behaviour will elicit a certain response from other people.

As long as these responses occur, the baby will repeat the behaviour. If the adult ignores the behaviour instead of rewarding it, it will stop eventually (this is called **extinction**).

Links to practice

Another example of negative reinforcement would be that while playing at the water tray, a toddler might try to take a jug from another child. Neither child will let go and both will look to the nearest adult, with cries of distress to get attention. If in the past this has led to a satisfactory conclusion – the adult finding a bottle that one child accepts as a substitute – the children will repeat the behaviour in the future.

Bribery and behaviour shaping

Bribery is quite different to **behaviour shaping** or **behaviour modification**. We might want a child to put away the floor puzzle that he or she has been working on that is spread all over the floor. If we tell the child that he or she can have a sweet if he or she tidies it up, this is bribery. The child, understandably, feels that he or she is being given a choice, and weighs the behaviour against the reward. Is it worth it? The child may decide it is not – and he or she will be baffled if the adult is displeased with his or her choice. (Older children may see this as an opportunity to negotiate, asking for two sweets!) With bribery, the child learns that the point of the behaviour is to please the adult and gain the reward – in this case, a sweet – not to ensure that all the pieces of the puzzle are stored safely for another time.

Link to practice

In behaviour shaping or modification, there is no 'if' and no mention of reward. The reinforcer comes only *after* the behaviour has appeared, usually in a way that is linked to the behaviour. 'Well done,' the adult might say, 'you have tidied that up quickly.' When using behaviour shaping, the only time that there is any mention of future outcome is in terms of what will be happening next – for example, 'When everyone is sitting quietly, then we can start the story.'

Just as positive reinforcement must not be confused with bribery, negative reinforcement must not be confused with **punishment**. Ignoring undesirable behaviour (leading to extinction), together with clear and consistent reinforcement of desired behaviour, is more effective than punishment.

Problems with behaviourist techniques

It is important that adults are very clear about their purpose if they use these techniques.

- What behaviour is to be extinguished?
- What behaviour does the adult want to increase?

The adult must make sure that what they intend is what actually happens, and that the child does not pick up an entirely different message. For example, a child may learn that if he says sorry within an adult's hearing and quickly enough after hitting another child, he may avoid punishment, irrespective of whether or not he has any feelings of remorse.

Subject	Behaviour	Reinforcer	Outcome
child	has tantrum in supermarket	GETS sweets	POSITIVE REINFORCEMENT –
salesperson	meets sales target	GETS bonus	
teenager	pushes over old woman in street	GETS money from handbag	
dog	sits up and begs	GETS food	BEHAVIOUR WILL BE REPEATED
baby	points to toy	GETS toy handed to them	
holidaymaker	puts on suntan oil	AVOIDS sunburn	NEGATIVE REINFORCEMENT –
tutor with headache	takes aspirin	STOPS headache	
driver	slows down before speed camera	AVOIDS speeding ticket	
student	hands medical certificate in	AVOIDS losing bursary	BEHAVIOUR WILL BE REPEATED
baby with wet nappy	cries	STOPS discomfort (adult changes nappy)	
neighbour	complains about loud music next door	STOPS noise	
(With permission from Chris Rice, Clydebank College)			

Table 2.7 Operant conditioning

Often, adults ignore children when they are behaving appropriately, only giving them attention when they are disruptive. However, children need to realise the advantages (enjoyment and satisfaction) of cooperating with others in different situations, so that enjoyment and satisfaction become the reinforcers. Other kinds of reward are then not necessary.

Key term

Transmission – Shaping the child's behaviour so that the child has the knowledge the adults wants to transmit (or send) to him or her.

Leave it to nature: a laissez-faire model

In the eighteenth century, the French philosopher Jean-Jacques Rousseau thought that children learned naturally, and that they were biologically programmed to learn particular things at a particular time. He thought that just as a flower unfolds through the bud, so a child's learning unfolds – for example, babbling leads into language, and then on into reading and writing; and kicking the arms and legs leads to crawling and walking.

In this approach, adults help children to learn by making sure that the environment supports the child's learning as it unfolds. For example, children learn the language that they hear spoken as they grow up. If children hear Chinese, they learn to speak Chinese. If they hear English, they learn to speak English. If children hear more than one language, they are able to learn more than one language and become bilingual or multilingual. This model of learning suggests that children are naturally programmed to learn languages.

This view of learning suggests that children naturally do what they need to in order to develop and learn. It sees children as active in their own learning. Children may be helped by other people or may learn on their own. Because adults do not need to act, according to this theory, it is sometimes referred to as a *laissez-faire* (letting things take their own course) view of how children learn.

Arnold Gesell

In the 1930s, Arnold Gesell mapped out some norms of development (normative measurement was discussed earlier in this chapter – see page 25). These were used to chart milestones in the child's development as it unfolded. Gesell believed that normal development progressed according to a set sequence. His milestones could be used to check that the pattern of development was 'normal'. Gesell's developmental scales looked at motor, adaptive, language and personal–social areas. If children reached particular milestones, such as walking, within the 'normal' age range, then their development was said to be making 'normal' progress. This approach is depressing if used with children with special educational needs, as they are constantly labelled 'abnormal'.

Case Study — An example of learning through a 'leave it to nature' approach

Because most children of around three to four years of age begin to enjoy drawing and painting, the rooms in a nursery school were set up to support this. Great care was taken in the way that a variety of colours were put out in pots, with a choice of thick and thin paintbrushes. Children could choose paper of different sizes. A drying rack was close to the area and children could choose to paint at a table or on an easel.

Adults would be on hand to help if needed, but would be careful not to talk to children while they were painting, in case they cut across the children's thinking. Adults would not 'make' children paint, because not all children would be ready to do so. Readiness is important in this approach to learning.

Advantages	Disadvantages
• Adults can learn about how to offer the right physical resources, activities and equipment for each stage of development.	• Adults may hold back too much because they are nervous of damaging the child's natural development: for example, by not talking to a child while she is drawing or by holding back from playing with children.
• Children can actively make choices, select, be responsible, explore, try things out and make errors without incurring reproach or a feeling of failure.	• Adults only support children in their learning, rather than extending the learning children do.
• Adults value observing children and act in the light of their observations. This might mean adding more materials, and having conversations with children to help them learn more.	• Children might be understimulated because adults are waiting for signs of readiness in the child. The signs might never come! Adults wait too long before intervening.
• Adults are able to follow the child's lead and be sensitive to the child.	• Children might not be shown how to do things in case it is not the right moment developmentally to teach them, which leaves them without skills.
	• Children with special educational needs or from different cultures might be labelled 'abnormal' or 'unready'. In fact, they might reach a milestone earlier or later, but still within the normal sequence. They might develop unevenly but in ways which make 'normal' life possible. Milestones in one culture might be different in another culture.

Table 2.8 Advantages and disadvantages of the 'leave it to nature' view of development and learning

The social constructivist/interactionist approach

In the eighteenth century, the German philosopher Kant believed that a child's learning was an interaction between the developing child and the environment. He said that children constructed their own understanding and knowledge about things. The approach is called a **social constructivist** view of how children learn. This model:

- is the approach currently most favoured by early years workers
- has the best support from research into child development in the western world
- draws on both the transmission model and the *laissez-faire* model of a child's learning, rearranging elements of both into something that is helpful to those working with children.

Piaget, Vygotsky and Bruner all used a social constructivist/interactionist approach; their work is discussed below.

Jean Piaget (1896–1980)

The important elements of Piaget's theory of how children learn are that:

- children go through **stages** and **sequences** in their learning
- children are active learners
- children use **first-hand experiences** and prior experiences in order to learn
- children **imitate** and transform what they learn into **symbolic behaviour**.

Piaget did not explicitly emphasise the importance of the social and emotional aspects of learning, and he did not dwell on social relationships as much as the other social constructivists. This means that he took social and emotional development for granted and did not write about it in detail. Instead, his writing emphasises intellectual or cognitive development and learning. Piaget's theory is called **constructivist** (rather than social constructivist) for this reason.

Lev Vygotsky (1896–1934)

Vygotsky stressed the importance for development of someone who knows more than the child and who can help the child to learn something that would be too difficult for the child to do on his or her own. He described:

- the **zone of proximal development (ZPD)**, sometimes called the zone of potential development – this means that the child can do with help *now* what it will be possible for him or her to do alone with no help *later in life*
- the **importance of play** for children under seven years, allowing them to do things beyond what they can manage in actual life (such as pretend to drive a car) – it is another way through which children reach their zone of potential development
- the **zone of actual development** – this is what the child can manage without help from anyone.

Vygotsky believed that **social relationships** are at the heart of a child's learning, so his theory is called a social constructivist theory.

Jerome Bruner (b.1915)

The essence of Bruner's theory is that children learn through:

- **doing** (the **enactive** mode of learning)
- **imaging** things that they have done (the **iconic** mode of learning)
- making what they know into **symbolic codes** – for example, talking, writing or drawing (the **symbolic** mode of learning).

Scaffolding

Adults can tutor children and help them to learn. They do this by 'scaffolding' what the child is learning in order to make it manageable for the child. This means that children can learn any subject at any age. They simply need to be given the right kind of help. For example, when a baby drops a biscuit over the side of the high chair, the baby can learn about gravity if the adult 'scaffolds' the experience by saying something like: 'It dropped straight down to the floor, didn't it? Let's both drop a biscuit and see if they get to the floor together.' Bruner's theory is also called a social constructivist theory, as social relationships are central to 'scaffolding'.

Key terms

Enactive learning – This is about learning by doing, through first-hand experiences.

Iconic thinking – When an image stands for a person, experience or object, perhaps through a photograph.

Case Study

An example of a social constructivist/interactionist view of development and learning

Using a team approach to record-keeping in an early years setting, staff had built up observations of children. They noted that Damian (five years old) kept punching; he punched other children, furniture and other objects. It seemed to be his main way of exploring.

The staff decided to introduce activities that allowed punching.

- They put huge lumps of clay on the table.
- They made bread and encouraged energetic kneading.

- They sang songs like 'Clap your hands and stamp your feet' and 'Hands, knees and bumps-a-daisy'.
- They encouraged vigorous hand-printing and finger-painting.
- They helped children to choreograph dance fights when acting out a story.
- Damian told the group about 'baddies' from another planet.
- He helped to beat the carpet with a beater as part of spring cleaning.

Case Study   **An example of a social constructivist/interactionist view of development and learning (cont.)**

- He spent a long time at the woodwork bench, hammering nails into his model. He soon stopped hitting other children, and began to talk about what he was doing in the activities with adults and other children.

Observation enabled adults to support Damian's learning in educationally worthwhile ways. Adults were also able to extend his learning, so that hitting people stopped and became learning to hit in a rich variety of ways that did not hurt anyone.

The nature–nurture debate

The nature–nurture debate is concerned with the extent to which development and learning are primarily to do with the child's natural maturing processes, and the extent to which development and learning progress as a result of experience.

The debate has been very fierce, and it is not over yet. Modern psychologists such as Sir Michael Rutter believe that the child's learning is probably about 60 per cent nature and 40 per cent nurture. Neuroscientists such as Colin Blakemore stress the importance of relationships (nurture), and how these actually cause the brain to change and be altered physically.

We can think about the developmental theories in terms of nature and nurture:

- The transmission approach stresses experience and nurture.
- The 'leave it to nature' approach stresses maturation and nature.
- The social constructivist approach to learning stresses both nature and nurture. A modern way of describing this is to say that both the biological and sociocultural paths of development are important for learning.

Intelligence – fixed or elastic?

The idea that children are born with a fixed amount of intelligence, which is measured and does not change throughout their lives, was not seriously challenged until the 1960s.

Before the 1960s, children were frequently tested to find their IQ (intelligence quotient), using scales such as the Stanford-Binet or Merrill-Palmer tests.

Because these tests were developed by white, male psychologists with middle-class ways of looking at life, they favoured white, middle-class, male children, who therefore scored higher than other groups of children. This began to worry some researchers, who found that IQ tests:

- favour children from the culture from which the tests emerged, which means the tests are not as objective as they were first thought to be
- measure particular types of intelligence, such as memory span and ability with numbers and language, so that intelligence is only looked at in a narrow way, which does not help us to consider outstanding ability in dancing, music or sensitivity to others, for example
- lead to children being labelled 'bright', 'average' or 'low ability'
- cause practitioners to have predetermined expectations of children (for example, 'Well, she's only got an IQ of 80')
- are sometimes useful if used as part of a range of tests (especially for children with special educational needs), but they are not useful used in isolation from other forms of assessment
- do not show the motivation (will) a child has to learn; two children might have the same IQ, but the one with the greater will to learn is likely to do better.

During the 1960s, Jean Piaget's work made researchers think again about what intelligence/cognition is. His theory (which has been confirmed by later work in neuroscience) suggested that intelligence is not fixed and unchangeable, but elastic. This means it can stretch, grow and increase. We now know that intellectual/cognitive development is helped if children:

- engage with adults and other children who are interesting to be with and who are interested in them
- experience a stimulating environment that encourages thinking and ideas, emotional intelligence and social interaction.

Case Study — The Brooklands experiment

A group of children with severe learning difficulties were taken from the wards of the Fountain Hospital in London in 1960. They were placed in a stimulating environment of people and first-hand interesting experiences. Their intelligence was found to develop rapidly. This research project, led by Jack Tizard of the University of London, was called the Brooklands experiment. Research like this led, in 1971, to children with special needs living in hospitals or attending day care centres, receiving education as well as care, by law. Until then, it was considered impossible to educate children with IQs below 50.

Educating children: compensating for deficits or building on nature?

Following either of these two approaches leads to entirely different ways of working with babies and young children.

An approach based on the idea of compensating for deficiencies prevailed in the late 1960s in the USA (Headstart programmes) and in the early 1970s in the UK (Halsey studies). This was because researchers were beginning to realise that intelligence is elastic. Children who were growing up in non-stimulating environments were placed in education programmes that compensated for the poverty and social disadvantage of their lives. However, this approach did not place enough emphasis on:

- the language and cultural background of the children
- the importance of the child's parents and family life.

By contrast, the Froebel Nursery Research Project, directed by Chris Athey from 1972 to 1977, worked in close partnership with parents. The home language of

the children was respected and valued, and they were offered interesting, real experiences through a quality curriculum. This included gardening, cooking, indoor and outdoor play, a home area, woodwork, clay, painting and drawing, and modelling with found materials.

The IQs of the children rose, especially the younger children who joined the Froebel project as babies. This approach builds on what children do naturally and biologically, as well as placing great emphasis on the social and cultural aspects of learning in a caring educational community. Children learn to talk and communicate, and develop their thoughts and ideas more easily, when they spend their time with adults who care about what they think and are interested in them.

Activity

Remembering our learning

Think back to your own schooldays. Were any of the lessons based on a transmission model of learning? Evaluate your learning experience.

Guidelines for using the different approaches to development and learning

1. Figure 2.22 shows that in a 'leave it to nature' approach to learning, children make a very high contribution to the learning they do, but adults hold back and take a very small part.

2. This is very different from the transmission model. In this approach, the adult has a very high input into the child's learning, taking control over the child's learning. The child's contribution is quite low.

3. The 'by the book' approach to learning is not valuable and has not been covered in this unit. Here, both the adults and the children have a very low level of participation. It is not really an approach to learning; it is just a way of keeping children occupied. Worksheets, colouring in, tracing, templates, filling in gaps and joining the dots all fall under this heading.

4. In the social constructivist (sometimes called interactionist) approach to learning, both the adult and the children put an enormous amount of energy into active learning.

Advantages	Disadvantages
• This approach is very rewarding and satisfying because adults and children can enjoy working together, struggling at times, concentrating hard, stretching their thinking and ideas, celebrating their learning, and sharing the learning together.	• It is very hard work compared with the other two approaches to learning that we have looked at in this chapter. This is because there is much more for adults to know about, more to think about, more to organise and do.
• Trusting each other to help when necessary creates a positive relationship between children, parents and staff. It means taking pride in the way that indoor and outdoor areas of the room are set up, organised, maintained and cared for.	• It is much more difficult for those who are not trained to understand how to work in this way.
• It means teamwork by the adults, which is the way to bring out everyone's strengths in a multiprofessional group of teachers and early years workers.	
• It means sharing with parents and children all the learning that is going on.	
• It means adults need to go on learning about children's development. When adults continue to develop as people professionals, learning alongside children, they have more to offer the children.	
• In Sweden there are now local plazzas where early years workers explain the way they work to parents, those working with older children, governing bodies and politicians.	
• Adults and children respect and value each other's needs and rights, and help each other to learn.	
• Although it takes time, training and experience for adults to build up skills for working in this way, it is very effective in helping children to learn during their early years.	

Table 2.9 Advantages and disadvantages of the social constructivist/interactionist view of learning

Activity

Models of learning

Make a chart with these three headings:

- Transmission model of learning

- *Laissez-faire* or 'leave it to nature' model of learning

- Social constructivist or interactionist model of learning.

Which of the following sentences go under which heading?

1 Adults should mould children's learning. After all, adults know more than children.

2 Children know what they need in order to learn.

Activity

Models of learning (cont.)

3 Do you want to have a story first, or tidy up first?

4 We need to tidy up; we'll have the story after.

5 Children are full of ideas if they are encouraged to have them.

6 Do it because I say so.

7 That child has been off-task all morning.

8 Children are born with everything they need in order to learn.

9 Children enjoy conversations with adults.

10 Children must be free to try things out.

11 Children will learn when they are ready and not before.

12 That child performed the task successfully today.

13 Nature knows best.

14 Adults know best.

15 Children must be free to try things out and to learn from the mistakes they make.

Compare your answers with a working partner. Discuss your answers together.

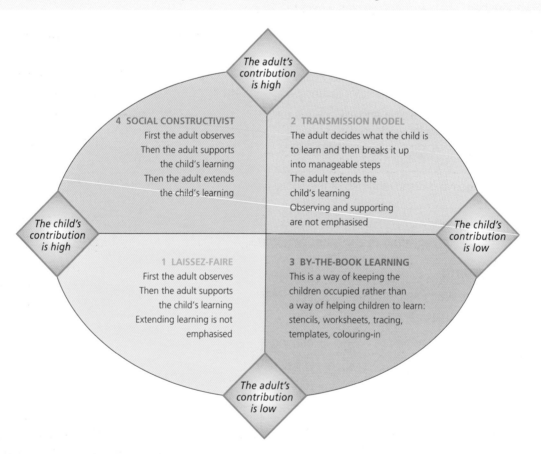

Figure 2.22 The four approaches to development and learning

The theories described above have been arranged (loosely) in the same sequence as the normative charts: (1) theories about communication and language development; (2) theories about intellectual development, and (3) theories which focus mainly on emotional, social and behavioural development.

Theories about communication and language development

There are different approaches to the study of language. Useful ones to consider are the normative, behaviourist, nativist and social constructivist approaches.

The normative approach: vocabulary building

In the 1930s and 1940s, experts like Arnold Gesell studied the development of language in young children mainly by using vocabulary counts. They counted the number and types of words that children used. They looked at whether children used single words, phrases and different types of sentences. This approach tended to stress what children could do at particular ages, and it could be very misleading.

For example, recent research suggests that babies say words like 'up' and 'gone', but this is not recognised by adults. Instead, adults seize on babble like 'ma-ma-ma', as they are longing for babies to say, 'Mama'.

Research shows that in fact the first word children in different parts of the world say is usually a comment on how either objects or people have 'gone'. In Korea, when adults give babies a drink in a cup, they say, 'It's moving in'. In Western cultures, adults are more likely to say something like, 'Here's your cup'. As a result, Korean babies say 'moving in' before they say 'cup', and Western babies say 'cup' before they say 'moving in'. This shows that there is more to language development than vocabulary building.

The behaviourist approach

In 1913 James Watson, an American psychologist, established behaviourism. The idea was that human behaviour is a response to environmental stimuli.

The behaviourists thought that language had to be 'put into' children, because they are rather like empty vessels. Children were thought to learn language by imitating the people around them, such as their parents and the practitioners working with them. This meant that they thought children would only learn the language they heard or were taught directly.

The nativist approach

Noam Chomsky

An exciting revolution occurred when the behaviourist view was challenged in 1968 by Noam Chomsky. He showed that young children invent sentences that they definitely have not heard before. He suggested that we are not like empty vessels, born with nothing inside us mentally. Instead, human babies are born with what he called a **language acquisition device** (LAD) inside their brain.

Chomsky said that:

- babies are born with the predisposition to learn, talk and listen
- children learn to talk because they are genetically equipped to do so; they learn partly through the people they meet, communicate and socialise with.

Researchers studied the mistakes or errors that children make when they talk. They found that these gave important clues about innate language rules that children all over the world seem to be born with (including children who use sign language).

Chomsky has been criticised because he ignores the context in which children learn to talk. He is not interested in what the words mean (the semantics). His focus is on the structure of the language (the grammar).

The social constructivist approach

Jerome Bruner

Although Bruner agrees with Chomsky that there is a language acquisition device (LAD), he does not think this is enough. He argues that there also needs to be a **language acquisition support system** (LASS). By this he means that the child's family and the whole context in which the child learns language is important. Mealtimes, bedtimes, and going shopping are all an important part of the way children learn to speak and socialise using language.

Bruner stresses the importance of relationships and a warm affectionate atmosphere in supporting language development. In games like peek-a-boo, for example, the child learns about 'here', 'gone', 'bye-bye' and the words to go with these situations, in a relaxed way, with people they love and who love him or her.

Jean Piaget and language development

Piaget thought it was thanks to language development that children were able to think beyond the immediate situation. In his view, language also helps them to see that things are not always as they appear. But although he suggested that language is very important in developing thinking, it is not entirely responsible for this. He sees language as a social part of development, something that needs other people, so that ideas can be shared and developed. But he also stressed the importance of the very individual and personal symbols that appear at the same time as language emerges.

Lev Vygotsky and language development

Vygotsky thought that language emerged from social interactions and relationships. In that sense, language begins outside the child. But as the child takes part in the cultural life of the family, it becomes the way in which children begin to reflect on and elaborate their experiences. Language development takes children on a personal journey in their individual thoughts, but it also gives them social experiences that are important in their culture and society.

Vygotsky believed that language and thought were interrelated in profound ways. He thought that the talking aloud and to themselves that we see young children do gradually becomes internalised. It becomes inner speech, which is silent. In this way, children

begin to gain control over their thoughts, so that they can plan, organise, remember and solve problems.

He suggested that this silent inner speech and spoken social speech are connected to the way concepts and the understanding of shared ideas develop together. In other words, there are two strands of development in learning to talk which have a deep influence on the way a child develops their ability to think:

- inner speech (silent and inside yourself)
- social communication using speech.

Activity

Theories of language development

Note three key messages from each theory that you find helpful in your work. How will you use this in your practice?

Theories about intellectual development

Piaget's theory of concepts

Although Piaget pioneered work on schemas and concepts, a great deal more is now known, allowing our knowledge of these to develop.

Young children become increasingly able to think forwards and backwards in time in quick succession, because every event is a bit like a separate photograph. They need to focus (or centre) on one thing at a time. Piaget calls this **centration**.

As children begin to link their previous experiences more easily, the experiences they have become more like a moving film than a sequence of still photographs. Piaget calls this period of development 'pre-operational'. However, most early years workers do not like the idea that children are 'pre' anything, because it concentrates too much on what children cannot do, giving a negative image of the young child. It is much more useful to think in terms of developing operations, which provides a more positive emphasis.

As a child's early concepts emerge and develop they begin to:

- link past, present and future around a particular idea
- develop memory, which helps them to know more
- organise their thinking
- understand sequences, with a beginning, middle and end
- understand transformations
- seriate, so that they understand the differences between things (different shapes, sizes, colours, objects and animals)
- classify, so that they see the similarities between things (cats and dogs are animals)

- organise previous experience – Piaget calls this **assimilation**
- predict things about the future
- take in new knowledge and understand it – Piaget calls this **accommodation**
- bring together their ideas, thoughts, feelings and relationships.

As children's concepts begin to develop they begin to understand that things are not always as they appear. This typically occurs in middle childhood (between seven and twelve years) according to Piaget. Children begin to be able to hold in mind several things at once, and they can run back and forth in their minds as they think. Their thinking is becoming more mobile at this point.

Guidelines on promoting cognitive development

1 Observe children's thinking and the ideas they develop; carefully note your observations and share them with parents and colleagues.

2 Remember the sequences of development in thinking, so that you can help the child in ways that tap into this.

3 Use your observations to make sure that you do not underestimate or overestimate a child's thinking.

4 Offer a wide range of experiences (not narrow activities and tasks that allow little choice on the part of the child).

5 Ensure a wide range of experiences but make sure that you think of what would be of particular interest to individual children.

6 Help the child while respecting and showing sensitivity to their ideas, helping only when needed.

7 Adapt experiences to suit children with special educational needs, complex needs and disabilities.

Key term

Centration – The child cannot hold in mind several ideas at once, so focuses (centrates) on one aspect. This is centration. The child might focus on the height of a mug, for example.

Assimilation – This is the process by which new information and experience is taken into (assimilated) the existing structures (schemas or concepts) in the brain.

Accommodation – Sometimes it is not possible to simply take in experiences, and then alterations can be made which adapt/alter (accommodate) the brain.

- **biological sequences** of development (the way children grow, develop and mature) .
- **social** knowledge (other people and the way children relate to them)
- the **equilibrium** of learning (accommodating to new ideas and assimilating experiences into what is already known); because we are always learning, we are always balancing (as we do on a two-wheel bicycle)
- the importance of **experience** in development and learning – Piaget pioneered the idea that experience is important in the development of intelligence and cognition (thinking).

There are several ways of exploring Piaget's theory. One is to look at the way he explores:

Usually, Piaget's work is looked at through the biological sequences of development rather than through the other aspects of his theory.

The following section outlines the stages of development that occur in a child according to Piaget. The exact ages vary, and are different in different cultures and for children with complex needs and disabilities, but the sequences are still thought to be useful.

Piaget's stages of cognitive development

Sensory-motor stage (birth to about 18 months)

There are six stages:

1 Ready-made behaviours (reflexes) that the baby is born with are adapted and used – for example, the baby actively tries to reach for the nipple (teat) with his or her hands as soon as it touches the baby's lips.
2 Hands become coordinated with sucking; sounds are looked for; objects are seen and reached for; hand-watching is important.
3 Babies begin to show intention. They try to prolong or repeat something that interests them.
4 Babies begin to experiment with making things happen. They begin to work out that although they do the same thing (for example, throw) each time, the object they throw might behave in a different way – a ball will bounce, a biscuit will crumble, milk will spill.
5 Around the end of the first year, babies deliberately modify their actions in order to produce the result they want. They like trying out new things, and they follow through and search for a ball if it rolls under the sofa, expecting to find that it has rolled out the other side.
6 They can think about the past and the future. They might imitate the action of eating a lollipop the day after they had one as a treat.

Developing operations (about 18 months to seven years)

Children are involved in:

- imitation (and increasingly imitating things after the event)
- pretending (imagining things from the past or in the future)
- forming images inside their heads.

The first part of this phase is often called the period of symbolic behaviour. This is linked to play, imagination and creativity. We see the child becoming more and more able to think about and reflect on things he or she actively experiences. The second part of this phase is known as intuitive. The child develops a sense of right and wrong.

In Practice

Conservation of number

Show a child two rows of identical buttons. Check that the child agrees that the rows have the same number of buttons. Spread out one row to make it longer. Ask the child which row has the most buttons. Children under seven years usually do not conserve number in a formal task situation like this. This means they are likely to think that the spread-out row has more buttons. Children cannot yet hold in mind more than one thing at a time.

Concrete operations (about seven to 12 years)

Although children are beginning to be able to think in more abstract ways, they still need plenty of real and first-hand experiences in order to understand things. There is a Chinese proverb that says, 'I do and I understand'. During these years of middle childhood, children become increasingly able to:

- hold in mind several things at once
- deepen the way they use symbols as they draw, make models, dance, make music, write, read, make stories and use mathematical numbers and mark-making
- conserve ideas (be able to see beyond the superficial appearance of how things look) about shape, number, quantity, volume, and so on – for example, to work out that although five sweets look like more when they are spread out than when they are bunched up, there are still five sweets
- understand the rules of games, such as football or snakes and ladders.

Formal operations (about 12 years to adulthood)

In the stage of concrete thinking, children need real and present situations so that they can have their deepest thoughts – for example, they can understand a great deal about what is fair and unfair if one child is given a present and the other is not. But formal operations allow older children and adults to think in abstract ways.

- Supposing only your class survived a global disaster. How would you create rules and laws to live fairly together?
- What do we mean by peace and justice? These are abstract ideas.

Some adults never reach this stage, and for most of the time adults continue to rely on concrete, real situations when they think. It is hard to think in the abstract, without a real situation to help the thinking along, so we do not manage it all the time.

Figure 2.23 Through their play children begin to sort out their thinking. They need experience in order to do this

In Practice

Permanence of the object

Piaget used a test called 'the permanence of the object'. He would cover an object, and the baby had to sit and watch this. By nine months of age, the baby would reach for the object by uncovering it and picking it up; younger babies did not do this. It is now thought that babies have to realise that two objects (the object and the cover) can be in one place in order to complete the test.

Later researchers gave babies of five months of age an object which might be put in either their right hand or their left hand. When the light went out they found that the babies reached for the object as soon as it was dark. The object could not be seen, but the babies still reached out and almost always they reached out in the right direction. The babies seemed to know that the object was still there, even though they could not see it in the dark. They also know that they only have one mother and so become disturbed if they are shown multiple images of her as early as five months old.

Using the information provided, carry out Piaget's permanence of the object test. You will need to find the equipment needed, and a sitting/crawling baby who is relaxed and wanting to play with you.

1. What are your findings?
2. What does this tell you about the baby's thinking and ideas?

Social and cultural relationships

These are now thought to be just as central to a child's development as the other kinds of experience that Piaget emphasised more, such as the way that children build up an understanding of objects. Recent research is helping us to remember that it is important to have a balanced approach which emphasises:

- the importance of people and positive relationships for thinking and learning
- first-hand experiences that are physical, cultural and social
- learning and thinking in indoor and outdoor situations

the importance of children having experiences that are of interest and that hold meaning for them

- that children are active learners, but they are not isolated learners – they need other children and adults to help them learn and think.

Children perform less well in test situations

When children are put into laboratory test situations, they find it harder to do their best thinking. They find it difficult to understand exactly what the experimenter is asking them. When they are in a situation that makes 'human sense' to them – at home or in their early years setting with their mother or key person – they are in a familiar situation and they can think better.

Cultural sensitivities

Recent researchers are beginning to look more at the importance of context. One of Piaget's conservation tests, to see if a child has a concept of looking at a view from different visual perspectives, involves asking a child to look at model mountains. The child is asked to say what a doll will see when placed at different points around the model. A child growing up in the Norfolk Broads where the land is flat will not experience the mountains of Switzerland in the way that the children whom Piaget studied did. The Swiss children saw views from different angles as they moved round the mountains, in a way that children living in Norfolk would not, so children living in flat countryside might appear to be less able according to the conservation test. In this example, the conservation test is culturally biased in favour of the Swiss children. Biases like this are called cultural sensitivities.

Transforming – you are never the same again

Piaget's stages of development are now seen as too linear. Instead, researchers look at the way networks of behaviour develop in sequences. Piaget's basic idea is that one stage transforms as it changes into the next persists, but we now know that it is a very complex series of biological transformations, and we are trying to understand and learn about the detail.

Gaps in Piaget's theory

Although Piaget's is still the most overarching theory of cognition (thinking), it left a lot of gaps that recent researchers have been trying to fill. It is a bit like putting more pieces into a jigsaw puzzle so that we can have a fuller picture than the one Piaget gave us.

Helping children to remember experiences

Children need books with pictures, displays on walls and interest tables with objects that remind them of prior experiences. After a visit to the park, there might be photographs on the wall of children splashing in puddles in their wellington boots, and on the table next to the wall, daffodil bulbs growing in a pot and a pair of wellies to help children remember what they saw and did. Bruner calls this **iconic thinking**.

Symbolic codes

In Bruner's theory, a code is something that can be shared with other people. Languages are symbolic codes. The word 'dog' is not actually a dog; the word stands symbolically for a dog – it is a code meaning a dog.

The way that children are helped by adults to participate in their culture is of great importance in Bruner's theory. He made a very important statement: any subject can be taught at any age in an intellectually honest fashion. The baby who drops custard and then a spoon over the edge of the high chair, he would argue, is learning about gravity (physics) at a very basic level. Physics is another kind of code that the child is learning as he or she begins to participate in his or her culture.

Learning to read and write are symbolic codes too, but at first children participate by learning to talk and use language, and by making marks on paper and being read to.

Progress check

What can you do to help children think and have ideas?

Children enjoy thinking about all sorts of things, and they appreciate your help in developing their ideas and thoughts. It is important that you:

- see children as active learners
- offer a wide range of experiences through which they are able to develop and learn
- develop your observation skills so that you tune in to children as unique individuals
- use what you have found in gathering observations of a child to plan experiences based on what interests them and helps their thinking and ideas to develop
- try not to expect children to do things that are boring for them
- do not expect children to perform tasks that are too difficult for them and therefore put them off
- encourage children to have ideas and to be creative and imaginative
- encourage children to try new things
- give children sensitive help in carrying out their ideas
- adapt experiences to suit children with special educational needs and disabilities.

Chris Athey: learning through schemas

Chris Athey developed Piaget's idea of schemas when working on The Froebel Nursery Research Project, which she directed in 1972–7, working in close partnership with parents. Schema theory derived from Athey's work has a strong place in early years practice in England, and indeed some other countries too, most notably New Zealand. It is used successfully in many nursery schools and other settings. Features of Athey's pioneering work include the following:

- the home language of the children was respected and valued
- children were offered interesting, real experiences through a quality curriculum. This curriculum included:
  - gardening

- cooking
- play indoors and outdoors
- a home area
- woodwork
- clay
- painting and drawing
- modelling with found materials.

The objective of the Project was to support children from less socially advantaged homes, and was very successful. The IQs of the children rose, especially the younger children who joined the Froebel project as babies. This approach builds on what children naturally and biologically do, as well as placing great emphasis on the social and cultural aspects of learning in a caring educational community. Children learn to talk and communicate, and to develop their thoughts and ideas more easily when they spend their time with adults who care about what they think and are interested in.

Theories about emotional and social development

Psychodynamic theories: Freud and Erikson

Sigmund Freud is the founder of psychoanalytic theory. Freud linked thinking, feeling, and sexual and social relationships with early physical behaviour, such as breastfeeding, toilet-training and separation from parents. He believed that:

- our unconscious feelings direct the way we behave; we are not aware of these feelings, and this means that we often do not know why we behave as we do in a particular situation
- our earliest childhood experiences deeply influence what we believe and how we feel as adults
- people go through psychosexual stages of development which he called oral, anal, phallic, latency and genital stages
- he could help the people he psychoanalysed to understand their behaviour and feelings, and even to change.

Freud thought that people have:

- an **id**, which makes 'want' demands
- an **ego,** which tries to resolve conflicts between the id and the superego
- a **superego,** which conveys the demands made by parents or society about how to behave.

Erik H. Erikson (1902–94)

Erikson took Sigmund Freud's work as the rock on which he based his own personality theory. He was also a pupil of Anna Freud, Sigmund's daughter. Erikson concentrated on the superego and on the influence of society on a child's development. He showed how, when we meet a personal crisis or have to deal with a crisis in the world (for example, living through a war), we are naturally equipped to face the difficulties and to deal with them. Erikson thought that there were eight developmental phases during a person's life (five during childhood and three during adulthood). He said that during each phase we have to face and sort out the particular kinds of problem that occur during that phase.

In the days before equal opportunities, Erikson called his developmental stages the eight phases of Man. It is important to bear in mind that theories evolving from Freud's ideas are based on white, middle-class patients in Western Europe. The theories need to be used carefully for that reason. However, they still seem to be useful in many of Erikson's eight developmental phases.

1 **Babyhood**: we have to sort out whether we feel a basic sense of trust or mistrust in life. This phase is about being a hopeful person or not.
2 **The toddler and nursery years**: we develop either a basic sense of being able to do things ourselves (autonomy), or a basic sense of doubt in ourselves, leading to shame. This phase is about our self-identity.
3 **The infant school years**: we either take the initiative and go for it or we feel guilty and hold back in case we upset people. This phase is about leading an active life with a sense of purpose, or not.
4 **The junior years**: we either begin to be determined to master things or we do not try hard

in case we cannot manage something. This phase is about becoming skilled.
5 **Adolescence**: we either begin to be at one with ourselves or we feel uncertain and unsure. We learn to have faith in ourselves, or not.
6 **Young adults**: we begin to have a sense of taking part in our society and of taking responsibility in it as a shared venture, or we think only of ourselves and become isolated.
7 **Middle age**: we begin to be caring of the next generation and the future of our society, or we reject the challenge.
8 **Old age**: we return to our roots and overcome feelings of despair, disgust about new lifestyles or fear of death, or not. This is Erikson's phase of wisdom.

Attachment theory: John Bowlby

John Bowlby (1907–90) drew on ideas from animal studies, psychology and psychoanalysis to develop a body of work known as **attachment** theory (1969). Babies and the people who care for them usually form close bonds. As the baby is fed, held and enjoyed, these emotional, loving relationships develop and deepen. Babies who find that adults respond quickly to their cries become trusting of life and are securely attached in stable, warm relationships. They know that they will be fed, changed when soiled, comforted when teething, and so on. Babies and parents who, for one reason or another, do not make close emotional bonds experience general difficulty in forming stable, warm and loving relationships.

John Bowlby looked at:

- how babies become attached to the mother figure (**attachment**)
- what happens when babies are separated from the mother figure (**separation**)
- what happens when babies experience **loss and grief** after being separated from the people to whom they feel close.

Mary Ainsworth, who worked with Bowlby, found that if adults responded quickly to a baby's cries, the child was less demanding by three years of age than those babies who had generally been left to cry. The individual temperament of a baby becomes obvious very early on and has an effect on the carers. For instance, some babies become hysterical very quickly when hungry, while others have a calmer nature. **Bonding** is partly about adults and babies adjusting to and understanding each other, learning how to read each other's signals.

Bowlby thought that early attachment was very important – that the relationship between the mother figure and the baby was the most important. This was because in the 1950s mothers tended to be at home with their babies. He did not believe that the most important attachment figure *must* be the natural mother, but he did say that babies need one central person, or a mother figure. It is now understood that babies can have deep relationships with several people – mother, father, brothers, sisters, carers and grandparents. Indeed, babies develop in an emotionally and socially healthy way only if they bond with several different people. In many parts of the world and in many cultures, this is usual. Babies might enjoy playing with one person and having meals with another. It is the quality of the time which the child spends with people that determines whether or not the child becomes attached to them.

Attachment can be difficult at first, especially in cases where it is hard for the adult and child to communicate; for example:

- the birth has caused mother and baby to be separated, and the mother is depressed
- the child is visually impaired and eye contact is absent
- the child is hearing-impaired and does not turn to the parent's voice; eye contact is also harder to establish here because the child does not turn to the parent's face when he or she speaks
- the child has severe learning difficulties and needs many experiences of a person before bonding can become stable.

Links to practice

Bowlby's work on attachment was important because it led to the following changes in practice:

- the introduction of the **key person** system in early years settings. (For more information on the key person system, see Chapter 13, page 524.
- parents can often stay in hospital with their children; there may be a bed for a parent next to the child's bed
- social workers are more careful about separating children and parents when families experience difficulties
- most early years settings have policies on how to settle children so as to make it a positive experience
- children are fostered in family homes rather than placed in large institutions.

Separation anxiety

By five or six months, many babies are so closely attached to the people they know and love that they show separation anxiety when they are taken away from these attachment figures. Researchers have found that toddlers will happily explore toys and play with them if an attachment figure (usually their parent) is present. If the parent goes out of the room however, young children quickly become anxious, and stop exploring and playing. They need the reassurance of someone they know to be able to explore, play and learn. Children who have had many separations from those with whom they have tried to bond find it very difficult to understand social situations and relationships.

Key term

Attachment – An enduring emotional bond that an infant forms with a specific person. Usually the first attachment is to the mother, formed between the ages of six and nine months.

Transitional objects: D.W. Winnicott

Donald Winnicott (1896–1971) emphasised the importance of play for the emotional and social development of the child, but stated that all developmental stages in a child's play are related to the child's capacity to learn.

His work has helped early years practitioners in nurseries and crèches to be sensitive to how children feel when they separate from those they live with and love. Winnicott taught us to see the importance of the teddy bears and other comforters that children seem to need to carry about with them. He called these **transitional objects**. Parents often describe them as 'comfort objects'.

- He believed that children need such objects to help them through the times when they begin to realise that they are a separate person. The teddy might stand for the mother, when she leaves the baby in the cot; it is a symbol of the mother who will return. It helps children through being alone or feeling sad.
- Naturally, the child might enjoy the teddy's company more when the mother is there. This reinforces the value of the teddy as a transitional object when the mother is absent.

Many adults still use transitional objects when they first leave home, or when their partner goes away. It is not only children who have to deal with feelings of being separated from someone they love.

Until recently, children were not allowed to take teddy bears into hospital in case they carried germs. In some early years settings, transitional toys are still taken away from children when they arrive, in case they get lost. Some children have imaginary friends. These are another kind of transitional object, but they are imaginary rather than real. Children may use other early comfort behaviour such as sucking, stroking or smelling. These do not have an imaginative dimension as in the case of a transitional object or imaginary friend.

Social learning theory: Albert Bandura

Social learning theory emphasises that young children learn about social behaviour by:

- watching other people
- imitating other people.

Albert Bandura (1925–) found that children tend to imitate people in their lives who they believe hold status, especially if those people are warm or powerful personalities. This research study did not replicate a natural situation for the children, but it does suggest that adults can be very influential on a child's behaviour. This should lead us to think about our own behaviour and the effect we have on children:

- If children are smacked by adults, they are likely to hit other children.
- If children are shouted at by adults, they are likely to shout at others.
- If children are given explanations, they will try to explain things too.
- If children are comforted when they fall, they will learn to do the same to others.

People who work with young children are very important status figures in the child's social learning.

The Bobo doll study

The Bobo doll is an inflatable doll, five feet tall with a weighted base. No matter how hard the doll is hit, it always springs back. Bandura showed three groups of children a film in which an adult was hitting a Bobo doll and shouting at it. The film had a different ending for each of the three groups:

- **First ending**: the adult was given a reward for hitting the doll.
- **Second ending**: the adult was punished for hitting the doll.
- **Third ending**: nothing was done to the adult for hitting the doll.

Then the children were given a Bobo doll like the one in the film. The children who saw the adult rewarded for hitting the doll tended to do the same.

Link to practice: Role play as social learning

Children copy directly what adults do, but they also *pretend* to be adults (that is, they role-play being adults) when they begin to play imaginatively. The child's home – or the home area in a nursery setting – is an important area for this, and so is the outdoor area, which can become all sorts of places (shops, markets, streets and building sites, for example). The problem with this approach is that it does not see role play as children experimenting with different ways of doing things: it suggests that children merely copy what they see. We now know that role play is a more complex activity than the social learning theory would suggest.

Factors that influence development

Many factors affect the healthy growth and development of children and young people. These include personal factors such as genetic influences and health status, and external factors such as poverty and deprivation.

Personal factors influencing development

Genetic influences

Scientists believe that both our environment and our genes influence the person we become. Genes are found in our chromosomes, and parents pass these on to their offspring in their sex cells (the egg and the sperm). Different versions of the same gene are called alleles, and these can determine features such as eye colour, and the inheritance of disorders such as cystic fibrosis. A baby's development can also be affected during pregnancy, at the time of birth and after the birth. In the very early weeks of pregnancy, a woman may not even know she is pregnant; however, the first twelve weeks of life in the womb (or uterus) are the most crucial as this is when all the essential organs are being formed.

- **Antenatal** – the time from conception to birth. Aspects of the mother's lifestyle affect the development of the child, such as her diet, whether she smokes and consumes alcohol, and whether she is fit and healthy.
- **Perinatal** – the actual time of the birth. A baby who is born prematurely (before 37 weeks' gestation) may need intensive care and may have problems which affect development. Difficulties around the birth itself (such as the baby lacking adequate oxygen) can also affect future development.

Health status

Children and young people's health status is determined by their genetic inheritance as well as other factors, such as diet, environment and the health care that they receive. Some children and young people are born with a condition that could adversely affect their holistic development; for example, cystic fibrosis, Down's syndrome or a heart defect. Children and young people who develop a chronic illness (such as diabetes or asthma) may find that their activities are restricted by their condition, or that their schooling is interrupted by frequent hospital visits.

External factors influencing development

External factors that influence development include the following:

- poverty and deprivation
- family environment and background
- personal choices
- being a looked-after child
- education.

Poverty and deprivation

Many of the factors that adversely affect child health and development are closely interrelated, and make up a **cycle of deprivation**. For example, poorer families tend to live in poorer housing conditions and may also have an inadequate diet; this may not include sufficient minerals and vitamins, leading to an increased susceptibility to infectious diseases, and so on. Poverty is the single greatest threat to the healthy development of children and young people in the UK. Growing up in poverty can affect every area of a child's development: physical, intellectual, emotional, social and spiritual.

- **Accident and illness**: children and young people living in poverty are four times more likely to die in an accident and have nearly twice the rate of long-standing illness than those children living in households with high incomes.
- **Quality of life**: a third of children and young people in poverty are deprived of the meals, toys or the clothes that they need.
- **Poor or unbalanced diet**: living on a low income means that children and young people's diet and health can suffer. Eating habits developed in early

life are likely to be continued in adulthood. This means that children and young people who eat mainly processed, convenience foods will tend to rely on these when they leave home. Conditions that occur in early life are directly related to a poor or unbalanced diet, such as anaemia and an increased susceptibility to infections such as colds and bronchitis.

- **Space to live and play**: poorer children and young people are more likely to live in sub-standard housing and in areas with few shops or amenities, where children have little or no space to play safely.
- **Growth**: they are also more likely to be smaller at birth and shorter in height.
- **Education:** children who grow up in poverty are less likely to do well at school and have poorer school attendance records.
- **Long-term effects**: as adults they are more likely to suffer ill health; be unemployed or homeless; become involved in offending, drug and alcohol abuse; become involved in abusive relationships.

Family environment and background

A child who is miserable and unhappy is not developing in a healthy way, although he or she may *appear* physically healthy. All children need:

- **love and affection**: to receive unconditional love from their parents or primary carers
- to feel **safe** and secure
- **stimulation**: healthy growth and development can be affected when a child receives too little (or too much) stimulation
- **opportunities to play**: all children need to play and young people need to have leisure opportunities, such as playing a sport or a musical instrument, or joining a club.

Children's social and emotional development is strongly influenced by family and culture. The majority of parents provide a nurturing environment for their children. However there are some parents who for a variety of reasons do not manage to provide the secure base that every child needs. Common problems within the home occur when one or both parents neglect their children because of:

- mental health problems, such as depression
- drug misuse, particularly alcoholism
- marital conflict and domestic violence.

Personal choices

The lifestyle choices that young people make can also affect their development. Young people may choose to smoke, drink alcohol or take drugs – all of which can impact on the healthy development of their brain. These lifestyle choices are often difficult to give up, so setting an unhealthy pattern for the future.

Looked-after children

Children and young people who are in the care of local authorities are described as 'looked-after children'. They are one of the most vulnerable groups in society. The main reason for children being under the care of their local authority is that they lack a stable, warm and consistent environment, and many of them will not have formed secure attachments. This impacts on their emotional and social development – particularly developing trust in others – and also affects their ability to do well at school. The majority of children who *remain* in care are there because they have suffered some sort of abuse or neglect. Some children are in residential care or living with foster families. Others who also have *care status* may live with their parents, but are the responsibility of the local authority.

Key term

Care status – When a child is the subject of a care order that places him or her under the care of a local authority. The local authority then *shares* parental responsibility for the child with the parents, and will make most of the important decisions about the child's upbringing, such as where they live and how they are educated.

Education

The quality of education received in childhood is very important. This is not just the formal education received in schools, but the quality of the learning environment children experience, both within their families and in wider social and cultural networks, such as sports clubs and places of worship. Some children do not benefit from quality education. They may fail to attend school regularly, and this will affect their future cognitive development as well as their employment opportunities.

Section 2: How to use a range of observation techniques appropriate to different stages of development and circumstances

Becoming skilled in observation and assessment is one of the most important parts of your training and developing practice.

- By **observation**, we mean closely watching, listening to and generally attending to what a child is doing, and recording your findings as accurately as you can. While you are observing, you should try to avoid drawing any conclusions, and to stay as focused on the child as possible.
- By **assessment**, we mean making judgements about what your observation says about the child's development, learning, health and wellbeing.

Through careful observation, you can start to:

- get to know each child as an individual
- evaluate each child's health and wellbeing
- think about each child's interests, strengths and needs
- reflect on each child's development and think about how to support and extend their learning
- gather information to share with parents, and show how you value parents' observations of their own children
- gain an impression of how children experience life in nursery, how they interact with others and how they behave
- think about the quality of care routines and interactions

- evaluate the quality of the learning environment and the curriculum.

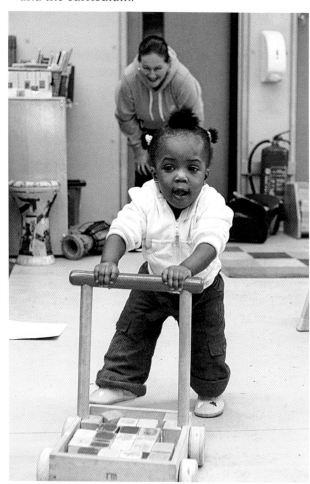

Figure 2.24 Noticing and celebrating what children can do is an important part of working in the early years

There is a long tradition of using written observations (sometimes called **narrative observations**) to gather and record information about children. The biologist Charles Darwin kept a notebook about his first son William, and wrote it up in his book *A Biographical Sketch of an Infant*. The psychologist Jean Piaget filled his early books with beautiful observations of his children Laurent, Jacqueline and Lucienne.

In British nursery schools, traditional practice has always emphasised carefully observing young children (Bartholomew and Bruce, 1993). There are many different methods for observing children, and these are discussed later in this section.

EYFS 2012

Observation in the **2012 EYFS** ensures that learning and development opportunities are planned around the needs and interests of each individual child, assessed and reviewed regularly. Observation and assessment in the early years must reflect the overarching principles of the EYFS, listed in Chapter 1, page 7.

The range of techniques used in observation and recording

It is generally accepted good practice to observe children in a familiar environment, playing and interacting with family and friends. In educational and care settings, the EYFS promotes observation-based assessment. Observations are assessed using the 'Development matters' scales or the EYFS Profile (at the end of the Reception year); see Section 3.

There are other scales to help assess particular areas of development – for example, in the Every Child a Talker (ECAT) programme. Observations can be:

- **narrative** – an account of what you saw when you observed a child for a period of time
- **anecdotal** – a brief note of the key point you observed (for example, Charlie did a painting for the first time today).

Practitioners are increasingly using video, photography and audio recording of children. There are many advantages that have come with new technology, especially as digital cameras and MP3 recorders are cheap and easy to use. If you want to study a child's language development and discuss it with parents, then an audio or video recording might be a very good way of doing this. Likewise, nothing records a child's construction or model as well as a carefully taken photograph.

As you become more skilled at making observations of children, there are many further approaches that will complement your work and give you a broader picture. Some of these are explored below.

 In Practice

Using cameras, camcorders and MP3 recorders

❏ Before you make an audio or video recording of a child, or take photographs, check the policy of the setting.

❏ Think about how you will store data safely and with parental consent. It is not advisable to download photos or video onto your personal computer, for example. Best practice would be to keep everything on a computer in the setting, with password protection or encryption.

❏ Think about how you will position yourself. You will need to be quite close to the children to pick up their voices clearly, for example.

❏ Analysing video and audio recordings is extremely time-consuming. You may get the best results if you record for just a minute or two at the right moment – when a child is really engaged in his play or in full conversational flow. Accurately transcribing even a few minutes of children's conversation can take half an hour or more.

❏ Think about how you will display and share information:

   ❏ Digital slideshows of well-taken photos can be a powerful and accessible way of showing a child's learning story, for example, or how a range of children play and learn in a particular area.

   ❏ Many settings put together profile books of individual children. These usually consist of photos with written observations and assessments. You will need to take care that a profile book is not merely a scrapbook of photos, without any commentary on the child's learning and development.

Leuven Involvement Scale

The Leuven Involvement Scale (developed by a team at the Research Centre for Experimental Education at Leuven University, Belgium, under the supervision of Dr. Ferre Laevers in 1994) is a method for assessing the quality of children's learning. There are associated scales in children's wellbeing and practitioner sensitivity. Taken all together, these can give you valuable information about how effective your setting is. But because children are only observed for very short lengths of time (two minutes), the scales will tell you more about the overall quality of the setting than about the learning and development of particular children. The scale is used by settings involved in the popular Effective Early Learning programme (Bertram and Pascal, 1997).

Target Child Observation

The Target Child Observation (Painter, Roy and Sylva, 1980) is a technique based on narrative observation, which also includes a coding system to help you interpret your findings. The Target Child Observation involves observing individual children for 10 or 20 minutes, allowing you to gain in-depth information

Figure 2.25 The look of concentration on this girl's face as she waters her plants, and the careful way she is holding and tipping the watering can, show that she is deeply involved

RP = role play, SOL = solitary, SG = small group, LG = large group, TC = target child, C = child, A = adult, BC = book corner, SW = small world, W = waiting
Child initials: JG   Gender: M   Age: 3 yrs 10mths   Date/Time: 1/10/05 2.15p.m.

ACTIVITY RECORD	LANGUAGE RECORD	TASK	SOCIAL
1. min TC on carpeted area, playing with farm animals and buildings.	TC→C My cow wants to come in your field. C→TC No. You'll have to wait till my tractor has finished.	SW	SG
2. min TC sitting at edge of carpet, looking at wall display.		W	SOL
3. min Now in dressing-up area, putting on a floppy hat and laughing.	C→TC You look funny in that. TC→C Let me see. Where's the mirror?	RP	SG
4. min Sitting in a small chair at a table, holding a knife and fork in his hands.	TC→C Where's my tea? I want my tea. Not fish fingers again!	RP	SG
5. min Standing at 'cooker' and stirring something in a pan.	A→TC What are you cooking? TC→A I'm a good cooker. It's basgetti.	RP	SG
6. min Taking off hat and tidying equipment.		RP	SOL
7. min Sitting in story corner, looking at book.		BC	LG

Figure 2.26 Example of a target child observation

about each child. You will need time for the observation and then allow at least the same amount of time again for the coding and analysis of your results. The Target Child Observation approach was used in the Oxford Pre school Research project in the 1970s and the EPPE (Effective Provision of Pre school Education) project, which has been in progress since 1997.

Time-sampling

Time-sampling involves making a series of short observations (usually up to two minutes each) at regular intervals over a fairly long period. The interval between observations and the overall duration is your decision, depending on exactly what you are observing and why. For example, you may choose to record at 20-minute intervals over the course of a whole day, or every 15 minutes during a half-day session.

It can be a useful way of finding out how children use particular toys or resources, to monitor how a new child has settled in or to observe the behaviour of an individual child. When observing an individual child's behaviour, time sampling can raise awareness of positive aspects which may be overlooked in the normal run of a busy day. Staff can then make a point of noticing and appreciating the incidents of positive behaviour and encourage these as part of a strategy to reduce unwanted aspects.

Child observed = HR Teacher = T Other children = A, B, C, D, E.
LG = large group, SG = small group, P = pair of children
Aim: To find out how well a child, newly arrived from another school, has settled in, looking particularly at interaction with other children.

Time	Setting	Language	Social group	Other
9.00	Registration – sitting on carpeted area.	None	LG	At back of class group, fiddling with shoelaces and looking around the room.
9.20	At a table, playing a language game.	HR: 'It's *not* my turn.'	SG	One parent helper and 3 other children.
9.40	On floor of cloakroom.	HR: 'You splashed me first and my jumper's all wet, look.'	P	Had been to toilet and is washing hands.
10.00	In maths area, carrying out a sorting activity using coloured cubes.	T: 'Can you find some more cubes the same colour, HR?' HR: 'There's only 2 more red ones.'	SG	Concentrating and smiling as he completes the task.
10.20	Playground – HR is standing by a wall, crying.	Sobbing sounds – won't make eye contact with or speak to T on duty.	SOL	Small group of children look on.
10.40	Music activity – playing a tambour to beat the rhythm of his name.	Says his name in 2-syllable beats.	LG	Showing enjoyment by smiling – T praises him.
11.00	Tidying away instruments with another child.	A→HR: 'We have instruments every week. It's good, isn't it?' HR→A: 'Yeh. I liked it.'	P	
11.20	Playing with construction equipment with A and B.	B→HR + A: 'I've got loads of Lego at home.' HR→B + A: 'So have I. I like the technical stuff best.' B→HR: 'What's that like?'	SG	Children working together to build a garage for toy cars.
11.40	HR fetching reading book to read to T.	Humming to himself.	SOL	
12.00	Lining up with other children to go for lunch.		LG	Nudging A, who is standing in front of him. A turns round and grins.

Figure 2.27 Example of a time sample in a Year 1 class

It is difficult to keep stepping away at regular intervals from whatever else you are doing, in order to make the record. Negotiation with colleagues is essential so that children's safety is not put at risk. You can choose your own headings for the chart format to match the detail you need to include. Usual headings are 'Time', 'Setting or location', 'Language' and 'Social group', but you may want to include 'Actions' and 'Other'.

Diary description

This is usually kept to monitor the learning and development of an individual child (but can also be used for a group) and provides a day-to-day account of significant events. It may include anecdotal records (see below) and other forms of observation. A diary is time-consuming to keep and you need to be sure that the information gathered is helpful and remains objective, rather than being mundane, repetitive and subjective. This type of observation can help to record the progress of every child in a group over time.

Anecdotal record

This is a brief description of an incident written soon after it has occurred. This is a widely used method of observation and is useful because it is recorded only a short time after the incident. The adult records a

significant piece of learning, perhaps the first steps a baby takes unaided, or an important development in relationships with other children. Anecdotal observations can be made in a different coloured pen, to show that they are not 'on-the-spot' but recalled events.

Flow diagram (or movement chart)

This method allows you to present information about an individual child or a group of children, activities, safety in a work setting or use of equipment. It can be very simple, with very basic information (see Figure 2.28), or more detailed to highlight more than one aspect (see Figure 2.29). If you want to track one child from one area or activity to another during the course of a morning session, it might help to have a prepared plan of the room on which to map her or his movement.

From this type of observation you can see:

- which activities the child visited
- the order in which he or she visited them
- how long he or she spent at each one
- which activities he or she visited on more than one occasion
- which activities he or she did not visit at all.

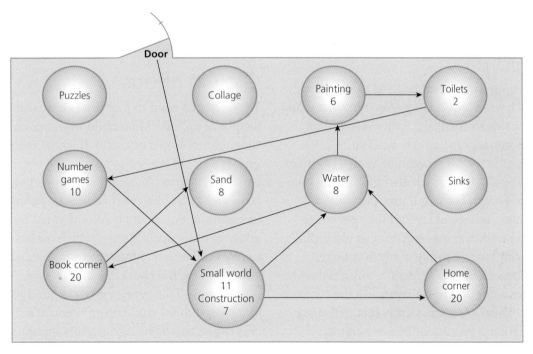

Figure 2.28 Example of a flow chart

The more detailed version provides the following additional information:

- which activities had adult-led tasks
- which ones had an adult permanently supervising or helping

- which other children were at an activity when the observed child arrived.

From this level of detail you may gain further insight into the child's movements. Repeated observations may enable you to find out if the child never visits

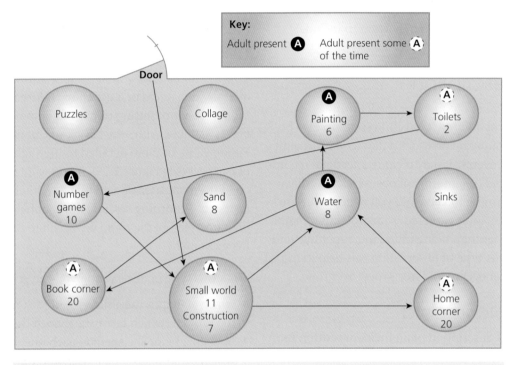

Figure 2.29 Flow chart – with extra detail

the sand, always heads for an activity with an adult present or always follows another child.

Sociogram

This is a diagrammatic method used to show an individual child's social relationships within a group, or to find out about friendship patterns between several children within a group (see Figure 2.30). Identifying girls and boys separately can sometimes make it immediately clear whether girls play with girls, and boys with boys, or if they play in mixed gender groups. You should record the ages of the children involved. You may find that an older child habitually plays with a group of much younger children. You will be able to identify any child who always plays alone or who always seeks the company of an adult. There are many factors that will affect the play relationships – friendship of parents,

proximity of homes, presence of siblings and, not least, pattern of attendance. These factors need to be taken into account when drawing your conclusions.

Growth charts

These can be used to plot the height and/or weight of an individual child over a period of time. (An example of a growth chart is shown on page 29.) Make sure you use one for the correct gender as there are variations between boys and girls. The chart cannot be submitted in isolation, but must be accompanied by your analysis of the information which makes reference to percentiles and shows your understanding. You must use the chart to interpret 'your' child's information. This type of chart is good to include in a longitudinal study. Even if you are studying a child aged two years or over, it is quite likely that

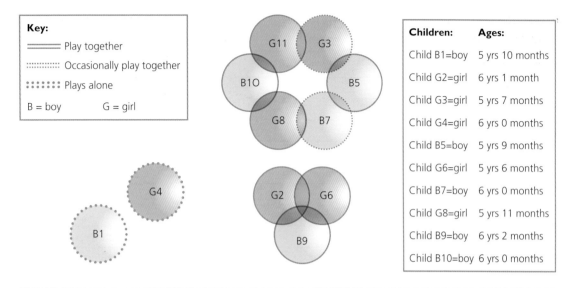

Figure 2.30 Sociogram

the parents will have a record of length/height and weight at birth and at some intervening intervals that you can plot.

Checklists

This form of recording has its limitations, including the following:

- giving no detail or supporting evidence
- being narrow in focus
- making practitioners feel that they have more information than they really do
- being time-consuming to create.

However, if these limitations are appreciated and the checklist is well thought out, it can be a very straightforward method of recording your observation. It should only be used in addition to other methods. It can be used to help:

- monitor developmental progress of an individual child or several children
- assess children on a regular basis over a period of time
- staff to plan for children's changing needs
- consideration of one area of development
- assess a child's behaviour.

Longitudinal study

A longitudinal study consists of a series of observations of different aspects of development, recorded using a variety of techniques over a period of time – a few weeks, months, a year or more. It provides opportunities to look at the 'whole' child by observing and assessing progress in all areas of development. As a student you are most likely to carry out such a study on a child whom you know well or whose family you know well. In this case, you may be given permission to include photographs and/or video footage. The initial part of the study will involve gathering background and factual information, followed by observations carried out at agreed intervals (not necessarily regular). You may get the chance to observe special events, such as outings, birthdays, clinic visits, as well as the child's time spent in a setting.

When you have recorded all your observations you can collate the information. You might choose to present them in strict chronological order or in groups of observations of different developmental areas. This will depend on the focus of your study and the individual observations.

	CHILD 1 yrs m	CHILD 2 yrs m	CHILD 3 yrs m
1. WALKING			
Looks ahead			
Walks upright			
Avoids objects			
Small steps			
Strides			
Walks heel to toe			
Arms by side			
Arms swinging			
Other observation			
2. BALANCE			
Stands on one foot			
Balances for 3–4 seconds			
Balances for longer			
Leans to one side			
Arms stretched out			
Arms by side			
Arms folded			
Can walk on narrow line			
Other observation			
3. RUNNING			
Runs on tiptoe			
Runs flat-footed			
Swings arms			
Arms by side			
Arms folded			
Able to change speed			
Changes direction			
Runs round corners			
Other observation			

You can add to this chart for other gross motor skills, such as skipping, hopping, climbing, swinging etc., by identifying the important components of the action.

Figure 2.31 Example of a gross motor skills checklist

Possible use: for monitoring reading skills
Title of book used: *The Birthday Cake* Date:

Skill	Child 1	Comment	Child 2	Comment
1. Holds book right way up	✔	Held book correctly in both hands	✔	Took book from me and turned it right way
2. Knows which is the front of a book	✔	Looked at front cover before opening book	✔	Pointed to character on cover picture
3. Follows text/pictures left to right	✔	Followed pictures as story was read	✔	Head movements showed was doing this
4. Knows text 'works' top to bottom	✔	As above	✔	As above
5. Can point to known characters in illustrations	✔	Pointed to Chip and Floppy	✔	Named characters as they appeared in illustrations
6. Can talk about illustrations	✔	Did so when prompted	✔	Pointed to things in pictures which he found funny
7. Can recap the story partway through	✗	Needed prompting and had to turn back through pages	✔	Good recall of what had happened
8. Can suggest what might happen next	✗	Could offer no ideas	✔	Good suggestions with reasons
9. Identifies some individual letters	✔	Named and pointed to 'c', 'd' and 'a'	✔	Named and pointed to 'c', 'd', 'a', 'g', 'h', 'l', 'b', 'n', 'w', 't', 's', 'r', 'y', 'p'
10. Can identify a capital (upper-case) letter	✔	Named and pointed to 'C' – own initial letter	✔	Named and pointed to 'C', 'F', 'B', 'H', 'T', 'R'
11. Can identify a full stop	✗		✗	

Figure 2.32 Example of an expanded checklist showing reading development

In work settings, a longitudinal study can be useful in planning long-term strategies for a child with special needs.

 Progress check

Using a range of tools for observation and assessment

- Experiment with different ways to observe a child's development.
- Talk as a team about any checklists that you use, and consider whether these are useful.
- Share different types of observations and assessments with parents in order to develop a dialogue about children's progress and areas of difficulty.

Research Activity

You can learn more about observation techniques in detail, with sections of film to develop your skills, with the Observation Technique DVDs produced by Siren Films (www.sirenfilms.co.uk/products/observation-techniques).

Observation in practical contexts

Assessment should occur as part of early years practitioners' ongoing interaction with young children. Ongoing assessment should also be informed by feedback from the child's parents and other adults who interact with the child. Assessment must not entail prolonged breaks from interaction with children and should not require excessive paperwork. Key achievements and any concerns should be recorded periodically. Practitioners must give parents and carers regular updates on their children's progress and achievements as part of their ongoing partnerships with families (DfE, 2011).

 In Practice

It is important to become skilled in observing and assessing children so that you can:

- ❏ get to know the children
- ❏ have purposeful discussions with parents, carers and colleagues
- ❏ think about what to plan next
- ❏ identify children's strengths and also their areas of difficulty
- ❏ monitor children's progress and offer help if a child does not seem to be accessing a particular area of the curriculum or does not seem to be making good progress
- ❏ reflect on the quality of your work as a practitioner and the overall quality of your setting.

You might notice that a child is making lots of progress in their communication, but you have no observations of their exploratory play and early scientific learning. You will need to plan to look out for the child's play and learning in that area. You might need to think of ways of encouraging the child to participate in those sorts of experiences. Sometimes settings might identify that there are patterns in their observations and assessments.

- If there are many observations of boys in the block play area, but none of girls, you will need to think of how you will encourage girls to take part in construction play.
- If boys spend little time in the book area, you might need to change the types of books on display, or try adding homemade books about children's play and interests.
- If the bilingual children in the setting make less progress than those who speak English as a first language, you will need to focus on whether your setting is providing enough appropriate support.

However, all this depends on the quality of your observations and assessment. If your observations are poor, you will not get any useful information from them.

In Practice

Develop your skills in observation and assessment

The following points will help you to develop your skills, both as you start out on your work with children and as you develop into an experienced practitioner.

❏ **Plan ahead**: think about when the majority of the children are likely to be settled enough in what they are doing so that you can start your observation.

❏ **Think about exactly what you need information about**: if you are observing a baby's feeding routine and the baby's responses, you will need to know exactly how much milk the baby has, how the baby likes to be held, what interaction soothes the baby and makes the experience enjoyable, and what happens at the end of the feed. Equally, if you have pages of observations of a child's early writing and lots of examples, you will need to plan to gather information about an area you know less about.

❏ **Choose your approach with care**: if you are building up a profile of a child, you might plan to observe him or her systematically over a number of days, choosing different times and places. You can gather information about the start of the day, different types of play inside and out, mealtimes, settling to sleep or resting, and so on. If your focus is assessment for learning, you need to find times when the child is involved in something worthwhile, so you will have plenty of material to think about. An observation of a child drifting from one table to the next and looking bored will tell you little about the child's development and learning – it might be better to help the child there and then.

❏ **Respond quickly, on the spur of the moment**: life with young children is unpredictable, which is what makes it so interesting. You may be busy with a hundred different things, but notice out of the corner of your eye that William has gone to the easel and is doing a painting for the first time. You might be cooking with three children and need to concentrate totally on helping them with the recipe, but be noticing lots of things about what they can do. These are times to write a quick note on a post-it when you get a moment, or at the end of the session, to add to children's records. Just state very briefly what you saw that was important and always include the date.

❏ **Try to observe as accurately as possible**: focus on what you see and hear, and try to get everything down with as much detail as possible.

❏ **Take photos or collect examples where possible**: subject to the policies of your setting, a series of photos of a child painting will really bring an observation to life. Photocopy a child's early attempts at writing his or her name, as well as observing how he or she went about this.

❏ **Share your thoughts with others**: ask the child to talk to you about what you observed, share the observation with a colleague and talk to the child's parents. You will find that you will deepen your understanding this way.

The Welsh Government has produced a brief and helpful guide to observation in the Foundation Phase that will give you more ideas. You can find the guide by searching online for 'Foundation Phase Observing Children'.

The importance of appropriate sharing of confidential information

Many difficult issues arise when professionals record and share information about children. These include the following.

Consent

Information on a child should only be collected and stored with the consent of the child's parents, who should have free access to this information on request. Information should only be shared between professionals with the express consent of parents, which should be gained formally with a signature. The only exceptions are the very small number of cases where the child might otherwise be at risk of immediate and significant harm if you shared a piece of information with the parent. (See Chapter 3 for specific guidance on safeguarding.)

Confidentiality

It is important that information is securely stored so that it cannot be freely accessed by anyone. Practitioners, including students, should not discuss

Figure 2.33 This boy is concentrating very intently as he sits on his teacher's lap, shaving a piece of wood; observing this carefully can tell you about his confidence and concentration, his physical development and his understanding of the properties of materials

or otherwise share this information – for example, when chatting in the staffroom or with friends at the weekend. If information is kept on computers or sent by email, steps must be taken to ensure that it could not fall into the hands of other people (for example, the use of encryption software).

However, where good, cooperative working is achieved between professionals, with clear consent, there are numerous benefits for parents:

- **Openness**: a Common Assessment Framework (CAF) is shared, so parents can see what the different views of the professionals are, and can put across their own viewpoint too.
- **Not having to repeat the same information over and over again**: if information is shared, a parent will not have to tell each professional in turn about something distressing, like their baby's difficult birth. They need only tell their story once.

- **Not being bombarded with different advice**: if there is a CAF in place for a child, there will be a single agreed set of advice and action plan. Otherwise, a parent might find that everyone has a different opinion about how to help their child, and might feel overwhelmed or confused.

When professionals and parents cooperate well and share information in this way, children benefit.

- **They do not have to be constantly assessed by different people**: if a paediatrician has information about a child's development and learning in nursery, she or he will not need to undertake a long assessment at the clinic, but can focus instead on areas of particular importance.
- **Consistent programmes can be put together to help the child**: if a child has received speech and language therapy in a clinic, with the target of putting two words together, then consistent help with this at home and in nursery will provide significantly more benefit.

It is important to focus on children holistically, and think about their all-round development. The child who has a speech and language delay might be a strong and graceful mover. If we fail to think of the whole child, we can end up seeing children with problems that need fixing, rather than as individuals with strengths and special qualities as well as needs.

Figure 2.34 A photo can tell you a great deal about a child's development and learning, like the concentration and high level of physical skill shown by this four-year-old child

 Progress check

Assessment that helps children's development and learning

- Work within the team on assessment for learning, so that all the observations you gather are used to help with planning.
- Use observations and assessment to pick up on children who are not making progress, so they can be given additional help.
- Contribute to a CAF to help the different professionals and the family to work together in a more coordinated way.

In Practice

If you are on placement in a setting and you are going to observe a particular child over a period of time, you should take into account the following.

❏ First, speak to your supervisor or mentor: make clear the requirements of your course, and think together about which child or children might be suitable. For example, if a child is subject to a safeguarding plan, then he or she will already be being observed and assessed by many different people. Also, some children are very self-conscious: being observed might stop them from playing. Ask for advice and help.

❏ Ask the parent or primary carer for consent: it is helpful if the child's key person or the nursery manager/head meets the parent with you. This provides reassurance. Explain the requirements of your course, and how having opportunities to observe children will help you to become a better practitioner. Answer any questions openly and honestly, and if you are not sure of something,

say so, and assure the parent that you will find out and answer the question in due course. Offer parents regular opportunities to look at your observations.

❏ Ask for a signature to show formal consent.

❏ Maintain anonymity (for example, refer to children only by their initials, not their full names) and **confidentiality** – do not discuss what you find out about children with friends or family.

❏ Plan when, where and how often you will observe the child: make sure that everyone on the staff team is aware of this. You do not want to create a situation where staff are expecting you to supervise an area and play with children, but you are expecting to be able to hold back and spend time observing.

❏ Share your observations with staff in the setting: this will be a way in which you can help them with their record-keeping, assessment and planning.

Here is an example of a letter to a parent, asking for consent.

Dear parent of [*child's name*]

My name is [*your name*] and I am on placement in [*name of setting*] for [*dates of your placement*].

One of the things I will be learning about is how children play, develop, learn and socialise with each other. To help me do this, I will be observing some individual children over time and I would like to ask for your consent to observe your child.

I would like to make it clear that:

• you are free to give or withhold your consent
• you can withdraw your consent at any time, without having to give a reason – just let me know
• you can ask to see my observations and notes at any time.

I will keep my observations and notes in a safe place where they cannot be read by other people. I will only share them with my tutors and with staff here at the nursery.

I will offer times to meet with you to share what I have observed. It will be very helpful if you are able to tell me about your child too, as you will know so much more than me.

Please sign below if you agree to allow me to observe your child.

Name:

Signature:

Date:

The rights of children

It is very important to remember that everything that happens in the nursery must, as far as possible, be in the children's interests. Children cannot give informed consent in the way that adults can. But you can follow the same principles with the children:

- If you think your observation might be causing distress or discomfort, you should stop. Look out for times where the child:
  - keeps looking at you and seems inhibited from playing
  - seems uncomfortable
  - shrinks or looks away when you get close enough to observe
  - indicates through body language or words that she does not want you to observe her.
- If a child asks you what you are doing or shows interest:
  - explain that you are watching his or her play and that you are very interested in what he or she is doing
  - show the child your notebook or paper and explain that you are writing things down
  - wait patiently for the child to go back to his or her play or activity, without trying to shoo the child away; you will usually find that children get used to observations and stop noticing you.
- If a child might be about to have an accident, or if you think a child is about to be hurt or bullied, you will need to stop your observation and intervene (or ask a member of staff to help).

It is also good practice to share your observations with children, taking account of their age and development. With very young children, you may want to look at photos together and consider the child's responses (such as smiles, frowns, lack of interest). Many children from the age of three years upwards will be able to talk to you for a time.

In Practice

Share your observations with children

- ❑ Show a child some photos you have taken and talk about them together. Try to find out the child's point of view. What does the child think he or she was playing or learning to do?

- ❑ Tell a child about what you have observed and what you think, and ask for his or her comments. For example, 'I've noticed you spending lots of time with the blocks. What do you like about playing with them?'

- ❑ Ask a child what they would like to do next or make suggestions. For example, 'I know you like playing with the trains a lot. Shall we go to the station one day and see some real trains?'

Article 12 of the United Nations Convention on the Rights of the Child says that children have a right to express an opinion. Their opinion should be taken into account if any matter or procedure affects them.

Progress check

Consent

- Know the policies of the setting on consent, and the legal requirements.
- Make sure you ask parents and carers for informed consent.
- Explore ways of seeking consent from children of different ages.

Key term

Informed consent – Informed consent means that you check carefully that someone has understood your request. If you said to a parent in passing, 'Do you mind if I do an observation of your child today?', you have not obtained informed consent. You need to arrange a time to meet, explain what you are planning to do, make time to answer any questions and obtain the parent's signature.

The importance of antibias practice

When you are observing and assessing children, you will need to be able to work towards putting into practice the anti-discriminatory, antibias approaches outlined in Chapter 5, ensuring that diversity and inclusive practice is promoted.

Child development charts, including the 'Development matters' section in the EYFS, can be criticised for trying to 'normalise' each child. In other words, instead of seeing development as varied and influenced by different cultures and backgrounds, charts can present an 'ideal child'. This is a problem if any child who develops differently is seen as abnormal and problematic.

For example, Laura E. Berk (2006: p. 333) summarises a large number of American research studies which suggest that the communication styles of some ethnic minority families are very different to the styles that are expected and valued in schools. Observations indicated that wealthier, white families were likely to ask questions such as: 'How many beads have you got' and 'What colour is that car?' Children who are used to answering questions like this do well in schools where such exchanges are common.

On the other hand, in many of the ethnic minority families observed, only 'real' questions were asked – where the parent genuinely does not know the answer. Often, questions asked by parents called for individual responses, not 'right' answers – for example, 'So, what do you think of that car then?'

Any observation and assessment system that focuses on children giving correct answers to questions would be likely to favour those from wealthier, white backgrounds. Children who could not answer lots of direct questions about the colour and numbers of things might be seen as deficient. But a more flexible observation and assessment system would be able to recognise the particular strengths of children with a range of conversational styles.

Observations that try to record accurately what children do and say will be less biased. One child's discussion of his views about a car can be valued just as much as another's correct description of the car's colour and features.

It is not possible to avoid cultural bias, or any other kind of bias, when observing children. You can minimise bias however by:

- focusing on what children actually do and say
- raising your awareness of cultural diversity
- learning from parents about how they play and talk with their children at home, and what they value
- involving children – ask them to tell you what their thoughts are about what you have noticed and heard.

It is important not to confuse unbiased practice with holding back from making judgements. If you never make judgements about children's development, you will never notice which children are experiencing difficulties and therefore who needs to be offered extra help. Although you will be trying to uphold equal opportunities, the result will be that children with special needs and other difficulties will miss out on the extra help they need.

When you are observing and assessing children, you need to make robust judgements about:

- the child's approach to play and learning – for example, involvement, enjoyment and toleration of frustration
- the child's rate of progress – can you see development over time?
- whether the child is making sound progress or needs extra help.

The important thing is that you try to base your judgements on the information you have recorded, not merely on your opinions and impressions. You should also be open to the views of others – parents, carers and your colleagues, for example. Be prepared to explain why you have formed your opinion, but be open to changing your mind.

Key term

Antibias practice – Antibias practice means going beyond equal opportunities and actively opposing forms of discrimination and prejudices in your work – for example, letting all children take part in woodwork upholds equal opportunities. Inviting a woman joiner into the nursery and displaying pictures and books about women doing woodwork, and talking these issues through with children, is an antibias approach.

Limits of professional role and competence

Even the most experienced early childhood practitioners may find that, although they have observed a child and made efforts to adapt their provision, they need help from outside the setting. This is particularly true if there is a specific medical condition or developmental delay. In these cases the people who best know the child – almost always the parents or main carer – will provide the most valuable suggestions, alongside the advice and guidance of other expert or specialist professionals.

The development of an individual 'care plan' or special educational programme will take account of evidence gathered from different sources – for example, from parents, early childhood practitioners, health visitors, doctors, social services, speech and language therapists, and so on. These provisions can only meet the child's needs when there is cooperation between all the services involved, and those who are competent to do so make accurate assessments. This is called integrated multi-agency working. For some children with additional needs, the CAF is used to give a fuller picture of the child. It gives information from the child, parents and all aspects of development, including health, education and social.

Interpreting and evaluating observations

Your observations of children need to be interpreted and evaluated to assess development and meet individual needs.

Using developmental theory to interpret observations

Theories about the way in which children learn, think and behave can help when making observations of children. Applying your knowledge of a particular theory can help in a number of ways. For example, using theories can help you to:

- understand the reasons behind children's thinking and behaviour
- plan activities which are developmentally appropriate
- decide which aspects of development to observe
- assess a child's strengths or identify any gaps in learning
- adapt your practice to take account of different theoretical approaches.

Example: Linking Vygotsky's theory to practice

As we saw earlier in this chapter, Vygotsky stressed children's active role in human development and (unlike Piaget) believed that a child's development occurs as a result of the child's attempts to deal with everyday problems. He also thought that in dealing with these problems, the child always develops strategies collaboratively, that is, in interaction with others. A significant proportion of children's everyday activities take place in Vygotsky's zone of proximal development (ZPD). He said:

'In play a child always behaves beyond his average age, above his daily behaviour; in play it is as though he were a head taller than himself.'

The following case study shows the ZPD 'in action' as the practitioner provides the 'scaffolding' of the activity.

Case Study — Vygotsky's zone of proximal development

A group of children aged four loved to run down a steep grassy slope in the outdoor play area. Margo, an early years practitioner, noticed that they were always keenly watched by the younger children, who could also climb to the top confidently, but then hesitated when they looked down. When the younger children asked for help, she would hold their hands and take them slowly down the slope, gradually increasing the pace each time as they increased in confidence. Once the children were ready to 'go it alone', Margo stood at the bottom to catch them as they came down. Then they did it all by themselves.

The evaluation of individual needs through observation

Effective planning for children's early learning is based on every child's individual needs, abilities and interests; this is why accurate observations and assessments are so important. These needs have to be integrated into the curriculum requirements for your particular setting and the age groups of the children you work with, for example the learning and development requirements of the EYFS.

All early years practitioners must consider children's individual needs, interests, and levels of development, and must use this information to plan a challenging and enjoyable experience for each child in all seven areas of learning and development.

There are three **prime areas** which are particularly important for igniting young children's curiosity and enthusiasm for learning. The three prime areas are:

- personal, social and emotional development
- physical development
- communication and language.

Early years providers must also support children in four **specific areas** of learning and development, through which the three prime areas are strengthened and applied. The specific areas are:

- literacy
- mathematics
- understanding the world
- expressive arts and design.

Throughout the early years, if a child's progress in any prime area gives cause for concern, practitioners must discuss this with the child's parents and continue to provide focused support in that area, reducing the risk that the child will struggle when starting Key Stage 1. Practitioners should consider whether a child may have a disability or special educational need, which requires specialist support, and should link with and/or help the family access relevant services as appropriate.

For children whose home language is not English, practitioners should provide opportunities to develop and use the child's home language in play and learning, supporting their language development at home. Children should also have sufficient opportunities to learn and reach a good standard in English language during the EYFS so that they can benefit from the opportunities available to them when they begin Key Stage 1. When assessing communication, language and literacy skills, practitioners must assess children's skills in English. If a child is not reaching the expected level in English, practitioners should explore with parents the child's skills in the home language to establish whether there is a language delay (DfE, 2011).

Section 3: How to assess the development of children and reflect upon the implications for practice

Careful observations enable you and your colleagues to make objective assessments concerning children and their individual care needs, behaviour patterns, levels of development, skills/abilities, and their learning needs and achievements. Assessment of this information can help highlight and celebrate a child's strengths as well as identifying any gaps in their learning. This can then form the basis for the ongoing planning of appropriate care routines, play opportunities and learning activities and they may also be a useful starting point for future learning goals.

Assessing and recording

You should draw on everyday observations and your knowledge of individual children to inform your assessments. After you have provided play and learning activities, you will need to assess and record the child's progress. Some assessment and recording may occur during the activities, providing continuous assessment of each child's performance

ASPECT	PRIME AREA OF LEARNING
	Personal, social and emotional development
Self-confidence and self-awareness	Children separate from their main carer with support and encouragement from a familiar adult. They begin to recognise danger and know who to turn to for help. They seek to do things for themselves, knowing that an adult is close by, ready to support if needed.
Managing feelings and behaviour	Children are aware that some actions can hurt or harm others. They seek comfort from familiar adults in the setting, when needed. They respond to the feelings and wishes of others, and their own needs and feelings.
Making relationships	Children seek out others to share experiences. They play alongside others and can be caring towards each other.
	Physical development
Moving and handling	Children gain increasing control of their whole bodies and are becoming aware of how to negotiate the space and objects around them.
Health and self-care	Children can communicate their physical needs for things such as food and drink and can let adults know when they are uncomfortable. They are beginning to be independent in self-care, e.g. pulling off their socks or shoes or getting a tissue when necessary, but still often need adult support for putting socks and shoes back on or blowing their nose.
	Communication and language
Listening and attention	Children listen with interest when adults read stories to them. They recognise and respond to many familiar sounds, e.g. turning to a knock on the door, looking at or going to the door. They can shift attention to a different task if their attention is fully obtained.
Understanding	Children can identify action words by pointing to the right picture, e.g. 'Who's jumping?' They understand 'who', 'what', 'where' in simple questions and are developing understanding of basic concepts (e.g. big/little).
Speaking	Children learn new words very rapidly and are able to use them in communicating. They use action, sometimes with limited talk, that is largely concerned with the 'here and now'. They talk in basic sentences and use a variety of questions, e.g. what, where, who?

Table 2.10 Development at age 24 to 36 months (DfE, 2011; adapted from Appendix 3)

(for example child observations and checklists). Some assessment and recording may occur shortly afterwards (for example record sheets and formal assessments). It is important to assess and record children's progress so that you can:

- Discover if the activity has been successful (have the aims and learning outcomes have been met?).
- Consider how the activity might be modified/ adapted to meet the needs of the child or children.
- Inform a senior practitioner, teacher, SENCO or other professionals whether or not a particular activity has been successful.

Assessment in the 2012 EYFS

Assessment in the 2012 EYFS plays an important part in helping parents and practitioners to understand children's needs and plan activities to meet them, supporting children's progress. It is particularly important that parents are left in no doubt about their child's progress and development, and that learning and development needs are identified early and addressed in partnership with parents and other relevant practitioners (DfE, 2011). Early years providers must assess young children's progress on an ongoing basis, and also complete assessments at two specific points which are described below.

Summary of development at 24 to 36 months

Early years practitioners must supply parents or carers with a short written summary of their child's development at age 24 to 36 months. The content of this summary of development must be based on the three prime areas of learning: personal, social and emotional development, physical development, communication and language (see Table 2.10 above). Beyond these areas, it is for practitioners to decide what the summary should include, reflecting the development level and needs of each individual child.

The written summary must highlight observations about a child's development, noting areas where a child is progressing well, but particularly focusing on any areas where practitioners are concerned that a child

may have a developmental delay, special educational need, or disability. It must describe the activities and strategies the provider intends to adopt to address any issues or concerns. Practitioners should discuss with parents how the summary of development can be used to support learning at home. Practitioners should encourage parents to share the summary of progress with other relevant professionals (DfE, 2011).

The concept driving this is the idea that the earlier children receive tailored support to catch up, the stronger their later chances of healthy development. A targeted plan to support a child's future learning and development in the setting will help to ensure a good level of achievement by age five so that the child is well prepared for school.

The EYFS Profile

The second point at which a report on progress is required is the final term of the year in which the child reaches age five, and no later than 30 June in that term. At this point, the EYFS Profile must be completed for each child. This provides parents, practitioners and teachers with a well-rounded picture of a child's knowledge, understanding and abilities, their progress against expected levels, and their readiness for school. The Profile should help teachers to plan activities for children starting Key Stage 1. Providers must make arrangements for each child to be assessed throughout the final year. The Profile report must reflect ongoing observation and should also take account of all relevant records held by the setting, and of any discussions with parents and other relevant adults.

Each child's level of development must be assessed (and recorded) against the 17 early learning goals. Practitioners must indicate whether children are meeting expected levels of development, if they are exceeding expected levels, or not yet reaching expected levels ('expected', 'exceeding' or 'emerging'). The 'expected' levels are the Early Learning Goals (ELGs) – see Table 2.11 below.

The Profile must be completed for all children, including those with special educational needs and disabilities. Children will have differing levels of skills and abilities across the Profile and it is

ASPECT	EXPECTED LEVEL OF DEVELOPMENT
Personal, social and emotional development	
Self-confidence and self-awareness	Children are confident to try out new activities and can say why ... than others. They are confident to speak in a familiar group and w... ideas, and choose the resources they need for activities they have ... can say when they do or do not need help.
Managing feelings and behaviour	Children can talk about how they and others show feelings and know ... behaviours are acceptable. They can talk about their own and others' b... and its consequences. They can work as part of a group or class and u...rstand and follow the rules. They can adjust their behaviour to different situations and take changes in routine in their stride.
Making relationships	Children can play cooperatively, taking turns when playing. They can take account of one another's ideas about how to organise their activity. They can show sensitivity to the needs and feelings of others and form positive relationships with adults and other children.
Physical development	
Moving and handling	Children show good control and coordination in large and small movements. They move confidently in a range of ways, safely negotiating space. They handle equipment and tools effectively, including pencils for writing.
Health and self-care	Children know the importance for good health of physical exercise and a healthy diet and can talk about ways to keep healthy and safe. They can manage their own basic hygiene and personal needs successfully, including dressing and going to the toilet independently.
Communication and language	
Listening and attention	Children listen attentively in a range of situations. They listen to stories, accurately anticipating key events and respond to what they hear with relevant comments, questions or actions. They can give their attention to what is being said to them and respond appropriately, while remaining involved in an activity.
Understanding	Children can follow instructions involving several ideas or actions. They answer 'how' and 'why' questions about their experiences and in response to stories or events.
Speaking	Children express themselves effectively, showing awareness of listeners' needs. They use past, present and future forms accurately when talking about events that have happened or are to happen in the future. They develop their own narratives and explanations by connecting ideas or events.
Literacy	
Reading	Children read and understand simple sentences in stories and information books, using phonic knowledge to decode regular words and read them aloud accurately. They demonstrate understanding when talking with others about what they have read, or what has been read to them.
Writing	Children write their own labels, captions, messages and simple stories which can be read by themselves and others. They use their phonic knowledge to spell words in ways which match their spoken sounds, and make use of high frequency spellings.
Mathematics	
Numbers	Children use numbers up to ten in order to do simple addition and subtraction to solve practical problems. They can find a total by counting on, and can calculate how many are left from a larger number by counting back.

	EXPECTED LEVEL OF DEVELOPMENT (Cont.)
Personal, social and emotional development	
Shape, space, and measures	Children use everyday language to describe and compare size, weight, capacity, time, position and distance. They know and talk about patterns and the properties of flat and solid shapes.
Understanding the world	
People and communities	Children talk about past and present events in their own lives and the lives of family members. They know that other children do not always enjoy the same things and are sensitive to this. They know about similarities and differences between themselves and others, and among families, communities and traditions.
The world	Children know about similarities and differences in relation to places, objects, materials and living things. They can talk about the features of their own immediate environment and how environments might vary from one another. They can make observations of animals and plants and explain why some things occur, and talk about changes, including in simple experiments.
Technology	Children recognise that a range of technology is used in places such as homes and schools. They select and use technology for particular purposes.
Expressive arts and design	
Exploring and using media and materials	Children sing songs, make music and dance and experiment with ways of changing them. They use and explore a variety of materials, experimenting with colour, design, texture, shape and form.
Being imaginative	Children use what they have learned about media and materials in purposeful and original ways. They represent their own ideas, thoughts and feelings through art and design, music, dance, role play and stories.

Table 2.11 Early Learning Goals (ELGs) (DfE, 2011; adapted from Appendix 4)

important that there is a full assessment of all areas of their development to inform plans for future activities. Parents, carers and practitioners working with the child need to have a clear, rounded picture of all of a child's needs.

The planning cycle

Figure 2.35 shows how observation and assessment inform the planning process. The cycle is a continuous one and settings adapt their provision to suit the needs of the children and families they are working with at any one time. It is through close observation, monitoring and assessment that staff can ensure that they introduce appropriate changes in their practice to meet the specific needs of individual children, as well as the whole group. This is particularly relevant to identifying children's schemas (see earlier in this chapter, page 52) which can be taken into account when planning. It ensures

that practitioners plan next steps that take account of a child's development, interests and needs. It marks significant points in a child's learning journey and helps assessment for learning as a continual process.

Use information from other professionals and colleagues

For a long time it has been the role of health and medical professionals to carry out regular checks, measurements and assessments on children, initially as foetuses in the womb during pregnancy, through birth and into the early years.

● **Health visitors** oversee infant health, including immunisations, referring to paediatricians when necessary. They monitor weight, diet, general growth and development, usually until the child begins school.

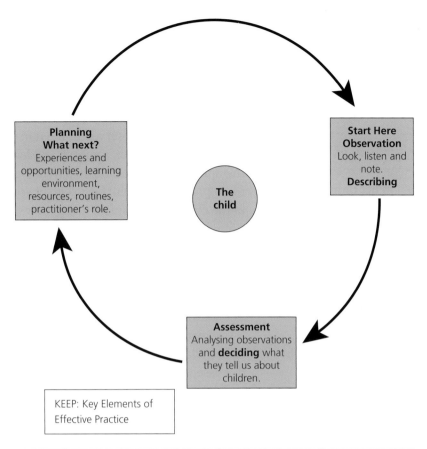

Figure 2.35 Observation, assessment and planning are a continuous cycle of activity in the early years

- **School health services** continue sight and hearing tests, and may administer immunisations or vaccinations (for example, in cases of hepatitis or meningitis outbreaks).
- **Child clinics, family health centres and paediatric wards** in hospitals also monitor children's health, relying on observation and assessment of children.

It has been common for the professionals in different agencies – health, social services, child care and education – to keep their observations and records to themselves. The English Government's Every Child Matters programme is prompting professionals to work together more, and in closer collaboration with parents. The same theme is emphasised in the Scottish Government's commitment to Early Intervention, Cymorth in Wales, and the Sure Start programme in Northern Ireland.

In the past, a child's development at the age of two years would have been assessed in a clinic by a health visitor using a tick-list. Clinics are unfamiliar places for children, and they are places we go to when we are sick – not the best places for children to play, talk and move around. In a more integrated approach, the health visitor might meet the child's parent and key person from nursery, and base the development assessment on the conversation they have.

Sometimes, a child is being helped by more than one agency. For example, an overweight child might be in nursery, and also under the care of a paediatric dietician. In these cases, the professionals will work together to assess the child's development, in partnership with parents, using the CAF. The CAF will help everyone to assess the child in a holistic, or all-round, way. For example, it will be just as important to find out how physically active the child is at home and in nursery, as it will be to find out what the child is eating. The CAF will then be used to agree a plan of action, involving the parents, to meet the child's needs.

Find out more about the CAF by visiting www.cwdcouncil.org.uk/caf or by searching online for 'Common Assessment Framework'.

Multi-professional working is important, but remember that it involves a team approach. No single person is a multi-professional in her or his own right. As an early years practitioner, you will be able to observe how children:

- play and learn in nursery
- interact with other children
- move, inside and outdoors
- manage disputes and conflicts
- eat, drink, rest and sleep
- respond when they part from their parents and are reunited.

Assessment practice

Unit 2

Choose an area of development from the list below:

- physical development
- communication and language development
- intellectual development and learning
- social and emotional development
- behavioural development.

Carry out three observations on the same child – using different methods, and describe how observations may be used to support planning to meet the child's needs.

These observations will make an important contribution to a CAF. However, some children – especially those with medical conditions, disabilities and special educational needs – will also need to be observed and assessed by other specialist professionals. For example, a child with Down's syndrome may be observed in the nursery by an occupational therapist, a speech and language therapist, and an educational psychologist. Each of these professionals will be able to observe aspects of the child's development using their specific training and professional knowledge. It is also most important to remember that the child's parents will almost certainly be the people with the most knowledge and expertise.

The information from these observations and assessments will inform the child's Individual Action Plan (IAP). Early intervention and IAPs are discussed more fully in Chapter 11 (Unit 14).

Activity

A learning experience: answers to activity on page 32

1 Chloe has just had her second birthday.

2 These are some of the things you may have listed – you may have found more. Chloe has learned:
- that you need to watch your feet as well as your hands
- if you hit something with your foot it moves
- you have to aim at the ball, not just swing your leg
- not to give up even when it's difficult
- not to run too fast when you go after a ball
- to slow down before trying to stop
- to start stopping at a certain distance ahead, depending on the speed you are moving at
- how to assess speed, distance, force
- the connections between 'cause and effect'
- to keep trying because you can succeed
- that learning is fun.

Useful resources

Websites and organisations

Anna Freud Centre – The centre was established in 1947 by Anna Freud to support the emotional wellbeing of children through direct work with children and their families, research and the development of practice, and training mental health practitioners:
www.annafreud.org

JABADAO – A national charity that works in partnership with the education, health, arts and social care sectors to bring about a change in the way people work with the body and movement:
www.jabadao.org

Talk to Your Baby – This organisation is part of the National Literacy Trust, and has campaigned for front-facing pushchairs which encourage adults to talk to children and show them exciting experiences. There is a huge problem in that many adults use the mobile phone and ignore children as they push them along, so that babies and toddlers do not have the opportunity for interesting and shared conversations with their parents/carers:
www.talktoyourbaby.org.uk

Siren Films – Siren Films produces high-quality DVDs covering a wide range of topics, such as the first year of life, two-year-olds, play, attachment and key person, three- and four-year-olds, early literacy and schemas in toddlers:
www.sirenfilms.co.uk

High/Scope – Information and resources about the High/Scope approach to early years education and care, which emphasises children's autonomy and a carefully structured environment:
www.high-scope.org.uk

Ofsted – Inspection reports and guidance on best practice from England's Office for Standards in Education:
www.ofsted.gov.uk

Robertson Films – Website about the classic and harrowing films made in the 1950s by James and Joyce Robertson, about children going into hospital and to nursery:
www.robertsonfilms.info

Kidscape – This charity was established specifically to prevent bullying and child sexual abuse. The website includes resources for parents, children and professionals, and details of campaigns and training events:
www.kidscape.org.uk

The National Strategies (Early Years) – The government's programme for developing practice in the early years, including statutory requirements, advice on best practice, and research findings:
http://www.education.gov.uk/schools/toolsandinitiatives/nationalstrategies

Books and articles

Axline, V. (1971) *Dibs, In Search of Self: Personality Development in Play Therapy*. London: Penguin.
Bain, A. and Barnett, L. (1980) *The Design of a Day Care System in a Nursery Setting for Children under Five*. London: Tavistock Institute for Human Relations.
Berk, Laura E. (2006) *Child Development* (seventh edn). Boston, MA: Pearson International Edition.

Useful resources (cont.)

Bowlby, J. (1969) *Attachment and Loss. Vol. I: Attachment*. London: Hogarth Press.

Browne, A. (2009) *Developing Language and Literacy 3–8* (3rd edn). London: Sage.

Bruce, T. (2011) *Early Childhood Education* (4th edn). London: Hodder Education.

Clark, A. and Moss, P. (2001) *Listening to Young Children: The Mosaic Approach*. London: National Children's Bureau.

Cole, M. and Cole, S.R. (1993) *The Development of Children*. New York: Scientific American.

Dahlberg, G., Moss, P. and Pence, A. (2007) *Beyond Quality in Early Childhood Education and Care: Languages of Evaluation*. London: Routledge.

Dowling, M. (2010) Young children's personal, social and emotional development (3rd edn). London: Sage Publications.

Ecclestone, K. and Hayes, D. (2009) *The Dangerous Rise of Therapeutic Education*. London: Routledge.

Elfer, P. and Dearnley, K. (2007) 'Nurseries and emotional well-being: Evaluating an emotionally containing model of continuing professional development', *Early Years: An International Journal of Research and Development*, 27(3): 267–79.

Elfer, P., Grenier, J., Manning-Morton, J., Dearnley, K. and Wilson, D. (2008) 'Appendix 1: The key person in reception classes and small nursery settings', *Social and Emotional Aspects of Development: Guidance for Practitioners Working in the Early Years Foundation Stage*. Nottingham: DCSF Publications, available at http://nationalstrategies.standards.dcsf.gov.uk/node/132720.

Freud, A., in collaboration with Dorothy Burlingham (1973) *The Writings of Anna Freud. Vol. III: Infants Without Families [and] Reports on the Hampstead Nurseries*, 1939–1945. New York: International Universities Press.

Gill, T. (2007) No Fear: *Growing Up in a Risk-averse Society*. London: Calouste Gulbenkian Foundation.

Isaacs, S. (1945) *Childhood and After: Some Essays and Clinical Studies*. London: Agathon Press.

Layard, R., Dunn, J. and the panel of The Good Childhood Inquiry (2009) *A Good Childhood: Searching for Values in a Competitive Age*. London: Penguin.

Manning-Morton, J. and Thorp, M. (2006) *Key Times: A Framework for Developing High-quality Provision for Children from Birth to Three*. Maidenhead: Open University Press.

Meggitt, C. (2012) *An Illustrated Guide to Child Development* (3rd edn). Oxford: Heinemann.

Nyland, B., Ferris, J. and Dunn, L. (2008) 'Mindful hands, gestures as language: Listening to children', *Early Years*, 28(1): 73–80.

Paley, V.G. (1981) *Wally's Stories*. Cambridge, Mass.: Harvard University Press.

Sylva, K. and Lunt, I. (1982) *Child Development: A First Course*. Oxford: Blackwell.

Trevarthen, C. (2004) *Learning about ourselves from children: Why a growing human brain needs interesting companions*. Edinburgh: Perception-in-Action Laboratories, University of Edinburgh.

Waddell, M. (1995) *Owl Babies*. London: Walker Books.

Whitehead, M. (1999) *Supporting Language and Literacy Development in the Early Years*. Buckingham and Philadelphia, PA: Open University Press.

Whitehead, M. (2010) *Language and Literacy in the Early Years 0–7* (4th edn). London: Sage.

Winnicott, D.W. (1964) *The Child, the Family and the Outside World*. London: Penguin Books.

Section 1: The implications of relevant legislation on working practices with children

Children's needs and rights

As well as their basic rights to life, health and education, children are viewed as having a much wider range of rights including the right to engage in play activities, to express their views and to participate in making decisions that affect them directly. Children's rights, as stated in the UN Convention on the Rights of the Child, are clear and universal: they apply to *all* children. See Chapter 1, page 5 for more information on children's rights, including the UN Convention on the Rights of the Child.

Also, while children's individual needs may differ, they all have the same rights. Children's rights are based on their needs, but emphasising rights rather than needs demonstrates a commitment to viewing and respecting children as valued citizens (see also The Children's Rights Alliance for England: www. crae.org.uk/).

Human Rights Act 2000

The Human Rights Act 1998 incorporated the European Convention on Human Rights (ECHR) into domestic law. It came into force in England and Wales in October 2000. It enables citizens of the UK (including children and young people) to seek to protect their ECHR rights through domestic courts. In addition, they can still seek protection through the European Court of Human Rights in Strasbourg, France.

National legislation relating to children's rights

As an early years practitioner you must know and understand the basic requirements of national legislation relating to children's rights. You also need to know and understand how to carry out research on children's rights and identify the implications for your setting.

The Children Act 1989

This Act provided a step in the right direction towards implementing the articles of the UN Convention on the Rights of the Child within the UK (see Chapter 1, page 5 for the articles). The Act came into force in 1991 and is concerned with families and the care of children, local authority support for children and their families, fostering, childminding and day care provision.

The Children Act 1989 is particularly important because it emphasises the importance of putting the child first. In summary, the Act makes the following statements:

- What is best for the child must always be the first consideration.
- Whenever possible, children should be brought up in their own family.
- Unless the child is at risk of harm, a child should not be taken away from their family without the family's agreement.
- Local authorities must help families with children in need.
- Local authorities must work with parents and children.
- Courts must put children first when making decisions.
- Children being looked after by local authorities have rights, as do their parents.

The Children Act 2004

This Act was introduced following high profile enquiries into child protection (for example, Victoria Climbié) and the introduction of the government's Green Paper 'Every Child Matters'. As this Act affects the way you should work with other professionals to benefit children and their families, it is important that you have a sound knowledge of its contents. Briefly, it states that there are four key themes and five outcomes that must be considered when working with children.

Four key themes of the Children Act 2004

- Supporting parents and carers.
- Early intervention and effective protection.
- Accountability and integration – locally, regionally and nationally.
- Workforce reforms.

Five outcomes for children

- **Stay safe** from: maltreatment, neglect, violence and sexual exploitation; accidental injury and death; bullying and discrimination; crime and anti-social behaviour in and out of school; insecurity and instability.
- **Be healthy**: physically healthy; mentally and emotionally healthy; sexually healthy; healthy lifestyles; choose not to take illegal drugs.
- **Enjoy and achieve**: ready for school; attend and enjoy school; achieve stretching national educational standards at primary school; achieve personal and social development and enjoy recreation; achieve stretching national educational standards at secondary school.
- **Achieve economic wellbeing**: engage in decision-making and support the community and environment; engage in law-abiding and positive behaviour in and out of school; develop positive relationships and choose not to bully or discriminate; develop self-confidence and successfully deal with significant life changes and challenges; develop enterprising behaviour.
- **Make a positive contribution**: engage in further education, employment or training on leaving school; ready for employment; live in decent homes and sustainable communities; access to transport and material goods; live in households free from low incomes.

See also page 121 below: Legislation for safeguarding children in the UK.

Research Activity

1. Investigate children's rights in your local community.
2. Find out what local provision is being made to meet these rights, such as statutory services and voluntary organisations.

Key terms

Children's needs – These include basic welfare needs such as food, shelter and physical care, as well as communication and interaction with others. In addition, educational needs are also important, such as opportunities for play and learning which are appropriate for each child's age/level of development.

Children's rights – The universal entitlements to life, health, education, play and consultation which applies to all children from birth to age 18 years.

The Childcare Act 2006

The needs of children and their parents are at the heart of this Act, with local authorities as the champions of parents and children, ensuring that their views are heard in the planning and delivery of services which reflect the real needs of families. The Act:

- requires local authorities to improve the outcomes of all children under the age of five and close the gaps between those with the poorest outcomes and the rest, by ensuring that early childhood services are integrated, proactive and accessible
- places a duty on local authorities to take the lead role in facilitating the child care market, to ensure that it meets the needs of working parents, in particular those on low incomes and with disabled children
- ensures that people have access to the full range of information they may need as a parent
- introduced the Early Years Foundation Stage – to support the delivery of quality integrated education and care for children from birth to age five.

The Equality Act 2010

The Act replaced previous anti-discrimination laws (such as the Disability Discrimination Act 1995) with a single Act to make the law simpler and to remove inconsistencies. The Act also strengthened protection in some situations.

The Act covers nine protected characteristics, which cannot be used as a reason to treat people unfairly. Every person has one or more of the protected characteristics, so the Act protects everyone against unfair treatment. The protected characteristics are:

- age
- disability
- gender reassignment
- marriage and civil partnership
- pregnancy and maternity
- race
- religion or belief
- sex
- sexual orientation.

The Equality Act sets out the different ways in which it is unlawful to treat someone, such as direct and indirect discrimination, harassment, victimisation and failing to make a reasonable adjustment for a person with disabilities.

The fundamental difference between this Act and previous equality legislation is that new groups are now provided the same levels of protection from discrimination across all the protected characteristics and all sectors.

Guidelines of the key changes introduced by this Act

1 Protecting people from discrimination in the recruitment process: it is now unlawful for employers to ask job applicants questions about disability or health before making a job offer, except in specified circumstances.

2 Protecting people discriminated against because they are perceived to have, or are associated with someone who has, a protected characteristic (such as protecting carers from discrimination).

3 Protecting pregnant women and mothers from discrimination: mothers can breastfeed their children in public places such as cafes and shops and not be asked to leave. The new law makes it clear that it is

Guidelines of the key changes introduced by this Act (cont.)

against the law for a mother to receive less favourable treatment because she is breastfeeding when receiving services. However, there is no right to breastfeed at work. The Act also prohibits schools from discriminating against pupils who are pregnant or new mothers.

4 Changing the definition of gender reassignment, by removing the requirement for medical supervision.

5 Harmonising the thresholds for the duty to make reasonable adjustments for disabled people.

6 Extending protection in private clubs to sex, religion or belief, pregnancy and maternity, and gender reassignment. (Source: EHRC 2010)

Special Educational Needs and Disability Act 2001

The Special Educational Needs and Disability Act 2001 amends Part 4 of the Education Act 1996 to make further provision against discrimination on the grounds of disability in schools and other educational establishments. This Act strengthens the right of children with special education needs (SEN) to be educated in mainstream schools where parents want this and the interests of other children can be protected. The Act also requires local education authorities (LEAs) to make arrangements for services to provide parents of children with SEN with advice and information. It also requires schools to inform parents where they are making special educational provision for their child and allows schools to request a statutory assessment of a pupil's SEN.

The **Special Educational Needs Code of Practice 2001** gives practical advice to LEAs, maintained schools and others concerning their statutory duties to identify, assess and provide for children's SEN. This code came into effect in 2002 and reinforces the right for children with SEN to receive education within a mainstream setting, advocating that schools and LEAs implement a graduated method for the organisation of SEN.

Special Educational Needs and Disability Green Paper

The Coalition Government has published its proposals for changing the system through which families of children and young people with SEN and disabilities receive their support. The Green Paper entitled **Support and Aspiration: A New Approach to Special Educational Needs and Disability** provides details of how the government intends to reduce bureaucracy and improve transparency in how resources are allocated. It would also do the following:

- Abolish the categories of early years/school action and early years/school action plus and replace them with one SEN category that will cover both early years settings and schools.
- Simplify the assessment process by replacing statements of SEN with one assessment that will cover support from education, health and social care. The government intends to introduce these education, health and care plans by 2014.
- Make assessments more independent by exploring whether voluntary and community organisations could coordinate them.
- Give parents and families a greater degree of control of their services by introducing more personal budgets.
- Improve the support for young people as they move into adulthood.
- Improve the way in which agencies work together to support children and families, with consideration being given to what role the voluntary and community sector can play. (Source: DfE 2011.)

Key term

Special educational needs – All children have individual needs, but some children may have additional needs due to physical disability, sensory impairment, learning difficulty or emotional/behavioural difficulty.

Research Activity

Find out about the legislation covering equality and inclusion and how it relates to your setting; for example, the setting's equal opportunities policy and/or inclusion policy.

Legislation for safeguarding children in the UK

Safeguarding children in England

Working Together to Safeguard Children (2010)

This document applies to those working in education, health and social services as well as the police and the probation service. It is relevant to those working with children and their families in the statutory, independent and voluntary sectors. The document covers the following areas:

1 A summary of the nature and impact of child abuse and neglect.
2 How to operate best practice in child protection procedures.
3 The roles and responsibilities of different agencies and practitioners.
4 The role of Local Safeguarding Children Boards (LSCBs).
5 The processes to be followed when there are concerns about a child.
6 The action to be taken to safeguard and promote the welfare of children experiencing, or at risk of, significant harm.
7 The important principles to be followed when working with children and families.
8 Training requirements for effective child protection.

It is not necessary for all practitioners to read every part of *Working Together to Safeguard Children* in order to understand the principles and to perform their roles effectively. However, those who work regularly with children and young people and who may be asked to contribute to assessments of children and young people in need should read the relevant sections.

Framework for the Assessment of Children in Need and their Families (2000)

This provides a systemic framework to help professionals identify children and young people in need and assess the best approach to help them and their families (see also Chapter 6, Promoting a healthy environment for children).

What to do if you're worried a child is being abused (2003) is a guide for professionals working with children which explains the processes and systems contained in *Working Together to Safeguard Children* and *Framework for Assessment of Children in Need and their Families*.

Protection of Children Act 1999

As a further safeguard to children's welfare, this Act requires child care organisations (including any organisation concerned with the supervision of children) not to offer employment involving regular contact with children, either paid or unpaid, to any person listed as unsuitable to work with children on the Department of Health list and the Department for Education and Employment's List 99. The Criminal Records Bureau (CRB) acts as a central access point for criminal records checks for all those applying to work with children and young people.

The Children Act 2004

- Sections 1–9 of this Act created a Children's Commissioner for England. However, the English Commissioner does not have the remit to promote children's rights, unlike the commissioners for the rest of the UK.
- This Act also placed a duty on local authorities to appoint a Director of Children's Services and an elected lead member for Children's Services, who is accountable for the delivery of services.

- It placed a duty on local authorities and their partners (including the police, health service providers and the youth justice system) to cooperate in promoting the wellbeing of children and young people and to make arrangements to safeguard and promote the welfare of children.
- The Act put the new *Local Safeguarding Children Boards* on a statutory footing (replacing the non-statutory Area Child Protection Committees), and gave them powers of investigation and review procedures which they use to review all child deaths in their area, as required by the Working Together to Safeguard Children statutory guidance.
- The Act also revised the legislation on physical punishment by making it an offence to hit a child if it causes mental harm or leaves a lasting mark on the skin. This repealed the section of the Children and Young Persons Act 1933 which provided parents with the defence of 'reasonable chastisement'.

Safeguarding children in Wales

The Children Act 1989 legislates for England and Wales. The current guidance for Wales is *Safeguarding children: Working together under the Children Act* 2004 (Welsh Assembly Government, 2006).

The Children's Commissioner for Wales Act 2001 created the first Children's Commissioner post in the UK. The principal aim of this position is to safeguard and promote the rights and welfare of children. In January 2011 the Welsh Assembly passed the Rights of Children and Young Persons (Wales) which embedded the principles of the UN Convention on the Rights of the Child into Welsh law.

Safeguarding children in Scotland

The Children (Scotland) Act 1995 has similar principles to the law in England and Wales, but has its own guidance: *Protecting children: a shared responsibility: guidance on inter-agency cooperation* (Scottish Office, 1998). Subsequent legislation created a Children's Commissioner for Scotland (Commissioner for Children and Young People

(Scotland) Act 2003) to safeguard and promote the rights and welfare of children.

Safeguarding children in Northern Ireland

The Children (Northern Ireland) Order 1995 has similar principles and has its own guidance: *Cooperating to safeguard children* (DHSSPS, 2003). In addition, in Northern Ireland it is an offence not to report an arrestable crime to the police, which by definition, includes most crimes against children. Subsequent legislation created a Children's Commissioner for Northern Ireland (Commissioner for Children and Young People (NI) Order 2003) to safeguard and promote the rights and welfare of children.

The impact of legislation on working practices

There is one aspect of work with babies, toddlers and young children that must always come first: the requirement to keep them safe, and to protect them from significant harm. Schools and early years settings are places where children and young people spend a considerable amount of their lives. Early years practitioners are some of the most important adults that young children will come into contact with. As a staff team, they can create an atmosphere and ethos which profoundly affects the child's experience of being cared for, listened to, valued, guided and stimulated. Early years settings and schools therefore play a considerable part in promoting children's best interests. All early years settings are bound by the laws described above – and by the many laws relating to health and safety (see Chapter 4: Keeping children safe).

The responsibility of the setting to have policies and procedures in place

All early years settings in the UK must be registered by the appropriate organisation and are also regularly inspected. Each of the home countries of the UK has its own system for registering and inspecting settings. All settings must demonstrate (through policies and codes of practice) how they intend to ensure that they meet the legal, regulatory requirements. All workplace policies and codes of practice must be drawn up within the framework of current legislation. A code of practice is not a legal document, but it does give direction and cohesion to the organisation for which it has been designed. Policy documents cover areas of ethical concern and good practice, such as those shown in Figure 3.1.

Equal opportunities policy

An equal opportunities policy represents a commitment by an organisation to ensure that its activities do not lead to any individual receiving less favourable treatment on the grounds of:

- gender
- race
- ethnic or national origin
- age
- disability
- marital status
- religious belief
- skin colour.

Having such a policy does not mean reverse discrimination, but *equality for all*. An effective policy will establish a fair system in relation to recruitment, training and promotion opportunities, as well as to the staff's treatment of children, parents and one another.

The policy statement

Every employing organisation should set out a clear policy statement that can be made available to employees and service-users. The statement should include:

- a recognition of past discrimination
- a commitment to redressing inequalities
- a commitment to positive action.

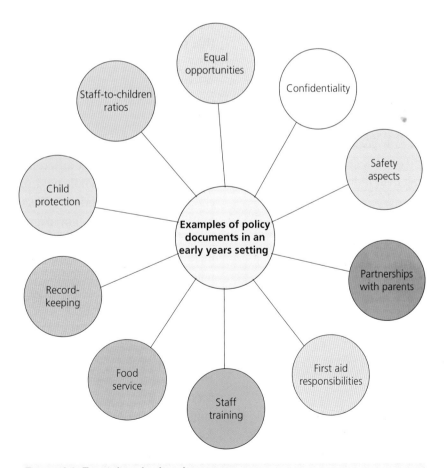

Figure 3.1 Examples of policy documents

Training should be provided to explain to all staff the implications and practical consequences of the policy. The organisation must also provide information about the law on direct and indirect discrimination.

Any policy which attempts to promote equality is only effective if the individuals working in the organisation incorporate its principles into their individual practice.

Section 2: How to recognise and promote strategies which are fair, just and inclusive

Practitioners should work in a fair, just and inclusive way, taking into account both the statutory legal framework in the UK and the policies and procedures in your setting. You need to value, and show respect to, all those you encounter in your setting as individuals. Examples of ways of working inclusively are given below.

Definitions of inclusion have developed from being primarily focused on integrating children with special educational needs into a much broader concept concerning social justice and equality for all. Inclusion is the process by which early years settings develop their ethos, policies and practices to include all learners with the aim of meeting their individual needs.

Key term

Inclusion – Ensuring that every child, young person, adult or learner is given equality of opportunity to access education and care, by meeting their specific needs.

How to promote diversity, equality and inclusive strategies

As early years practitioners, we are responsible for ensuring inclusive practice and equal opportunities within our settings. There are many ways in which we can promote such practice. We can do this using the following guidelines.

Promote a sense of belonging

As children grow up, they need to feel that they belong to the group, whether that group is their family, their culture, the community they live in and experience, or their early years setting. Belonging to a group is the result of either:

- being allocated to a group defined by someone else – for example, being British-born
- deciding to join a group – for example, choosing to be a vegetarian or joining a football club.

Until recently, people tended to be seen as belonging to a particular ethnic group if they shared a culture, language, physical features (such as skin colour) or religion. This way of grouping people is no longer thought to be useful. Increasingly, people *choose* the groups they want to be identified with. The early childhood setting is often the first group outside the family and its friendship network that the child joins. It is important when welcoming families to a setting that they feel a sense of belonging.

Value cultural diversity and respecting difference

In the UK we live in a diverse and multicultural society. This means that it is important to appreciate, understand and respect different cultural and religious ideas. The whole environment of the early childhood setting needs to reflect a multicultural and multilingual approach. For example, the home area, like every other area of the environment, should include objects that are familiar to children and link with their homes and culture. These are often called **cultural artefacts**.

Give individual children individual help

There may be children with special educational needs using the home area for example, and they might need special arrangements to allow them access: a child in a wheelchair will need a lower table so that a mixing bowl can be stirred; it might be necessary to make a toy cooker of an appropriate

Figure 3.2 Reading a picture book in Portuguese

height. Children love to construct their own play props; allowing them to do so makes for a much more culturally diverse selection, because they can create what they need in order to make a play setting like their own homes.

Understand religions

In order that every child feels accepted beyond their home, those working with children and young people and their families need to learn about belief structures other than their own. It is also important to remember not to judge people or make assumptions about their values or behaviour based on whether or not they believe in a god or gods. Some children are brought up in families that follow more than one religion. For example, there might be a Roman Catholic Christian father and a Muslim mother, or a Hindu father and a Quaker Christian mother.

Include children with disabilities

Inclusion is about being able to support, encourage and provide for all with individual needs, whether they are temporary or permanent. Excluding children with disabilities from everyday experiences can lead to a lifetime of segregation. In addition, lack of contact with disabled people can lead to fear and ignorance of those who seem 'different'.

 Progress check

Understanding and promoting equality of opportunity

Practitioners should:

1. Know their Equalities Lead Officer or Equalities Coordinator
2. Receive support and ongoing training in this area
3. Work to improve his or her own practice
4. Report all incidents of discrimination (an incident is discriminatory if it is felt to be so by anyone involved, even an onlooker)
5. Take active steps to make sure that everyone knows about the available services and is able to access them.

Have an awareness of gender roles

Creating an environment where girls and boys are respected and cared for equally in early childhood is the first step towards breaking cycles of discrimination and disadvantage, and promoting a child's sense of self-worth as it relates to their gender. It is important to remember that some children will have learned narrow gender roles. In the traditional home situation, mothers usually do housework and fathers mend cars. Children need to see adults taking on broader gender roles, and to learn about alternative ways for men and women to behave as themselves.

Avoid stereotypes

When adults fill in forms, they decide whether to be described as Mr, Ms, Mrs or Miss, and whether or not they wish to describe themselves according to different ethnic categories. An adult with a hearing loss can also choose whether to be described as deaf, hearing impaired or aurally challenged. Children need to be given as much choice as possible about these aspects of their lives. If adults describe a child as 'the one with glasses', or comment 'What a pretty dress,' or talk about 'the Afro-Caribbean child', they are stereotyping these children and seeing them narrowly rather than as whole people. Children and young people need to hear and see positive images of themselves and of other people.

Reflective practice: Promoting equality of opportunity

Think about different ways in which you have encouraged equality of opportunity in your work with children and young people. How can you ensure that your practice is not discriminatory? How can you promote equality of opportunity? Write a short account of ways in which you can ensure that no child, young person or adult is treated unfavourably compared with others.

Key terms

Diversity – The differences in values, attitudes, cultures, beliefs, skills, knowledge and life experience of each individual in any group of people.

Equality – Ensuring that everyone has a chance to take part in society on an equal basis and to be treated appropriately, regardless of their gender, race, disability, age, sexual orientation, language, social origin, religious beliefs, marital status and other personal attributes.

Section 3: Where to access the policies of the setting and how to follow the procedures for safeguarding children

Access to policy documents

Policies and codes of practice are usually kept in the staff room or manager's office. It is the employer's duty to ensure that each member of staff knows about the policies and procedures within the setting. However, it is your responsibility to ensure that you have read and understood the documents. If you come across any policy matter that you are unsure about, you should know where to find the relevant document in order to find out what is expected of you in practice.

Following the procedures for safeguarding children

All the legislation and guidance in recent decades, including the Children Act 2004, make it clear that the child's interests must come first. All professionals must work together to promote the child's welfare before all else. For example, imagine that you found out that a father has slapped his child on the face, leaving a mark. You may have developed a very close relationship with this parent and you may be very sympathetic to the difficulties he is experiencing. You may feel that this incident is a 'one-off', that he genuinely loves and cares for the child, and that he would be devastated if you did not keep this to yourself. All the same, you are required to put the child's interests before your feelings about the family. The actions you might take are discussed later in this chapter (page 131).

Legal requirements for all settings

All early years settings and schools must nominate a member of staff to oversee safeguarding and child protection. This person must be specifically trained to undertake this role. The whole team (including volunteers and students) must work together to promote children's welfare and keep them safe. The whole team will need regular training and updating, and it is best practice that such training provides staff with time to explore different experiences, attitudes and opinions as steps towards agreeing policy and practice. Every adult working in the setting must be a *suitable person* to work with young children, and must have been checked by the Independent Safeguarding Authority. This includes students on placements and regular volunteers. The legislation, policies and procedures for safeguarding children are described on pages 121–2.

What is safeguarding?

For some children, universal services such as early years education and health visiting are not enough to ensure their healthy, safe and happy development. These children might, for periods of time, be vulnerable. They may experience emotional difficulties, fall behind in their development or learning, or suffer the adverse effects of poverty, poor housing or ill health. The Common Assessment Framework (CAF) in England exists to support children and families with appropriate help and advice for a brief period.

There are also children in need, who are judged to be unlikely to reach or maintain a satisfactory level of health or development unless they are offered additional services. This group includes children

with disabilities. Finally, there are children who are subject to an inter-agency child protection plan. These children are judged to be at risk of significant harm without the provision of additional services, as well as close and careful monitoring by specialist children's social workers. All this work with children and families falls under the umbrella term of **safeguarding**.

The government has defined safeguarding as:

'the process of protecting children from abuse or neglect, preventing impairment of their health and development, and ensuring they are growing up in circumstances consistent with the provision of safe and effective care that enables children to have optimum life chances and enter adulthood successfully.'

Key term

Safeguarding – This term includes: all the steps you would take in an early years setting or school to help children to feel safe and secure; protecting children from neglect or abuse; ensuring that children stay safe, healthy and continue to develop well.

This chapter offers concise, useful and accurate information about safeguarding. If you have any doubts or concerns about a child, however trivial you might think they are, we strongly advise you to speak to the manager or headteacher of the early years setting or school where you are working. Always ask for information and guidance.

Factors which make child abuse more likely to occur

Child abuse is more likely to occur when people (often parents or carers):

- have little knowledge about children's needs or how children develop
- find it hard to use the knowledge that they have about the way children develop
- experience a great deal of stress in their lives
- are poor decision-makers

- find it hard to take responsibility for things that they do
- find it difficult to relate to or communicate with other people
- are inconsistent
- find it hard to change their ideas, to change what they have always done, or to change what was done to them when they were children.

All sections of society produce adults who abuse or neglect children. It is very dangerous to form stereotypes about the kind of people who might violate a child's rights or about the situations which could lead to child abuse or neglect.

As evidence gathers on the subject of safeguarding children, it is becoming apparent that:

- the abusive or neglectful person is almost always known to the child; for example, a parent, a family member, a friend of the family, a carer or cohabitee
- premature babies and children from birth to age four are most likely to be abused or neglected
- separation of the mother and the baby for a period of time after birth can be associated with child abuse or neglect
- children who cry a great deal are much more likely to be abused or neglected
- children who do not enjoy eating are more likely to be abused or neglected
- step-children are vulnerable
- children with disabilities are more likely to be abused or neglected
- children who are boys when parents wanted girls, or vice versa, are more likely to be neglected.

Children at risk

Certain factors within the family home can mean that children are at a higher risk of being abused:

- Drug or alcohol abuse by parents can lead to children being put at risk, even if the parents are not actually mistreating them; such abuse is a familiar trigger for violence in the home and it can also lead to parents having a disordered lifestyle which can leave children in danger.
- Mental illness: although this does not prevent individuals from being good parents, it can

sometimes move a child up the scale from being one in need to one at significant risk of harm.

Definitions of abuse and neglect

'Abuse and neglect are forms of maltreatment of a child. Somebody may abuse or neglect a child by inflicting harm, or by failing to act to prevent harm. Children may be abused in a family or in an institutional or community setting, by those known to them or, more rarely, by a stranger, for example, via the internet. They may be abused by an adult or adults, or another child or children.' (*Working Together to Safeguard Children: A Guide to Inter-agency Working to Safeguard and Promote the Welfare of Children,* DCSF, 2010)

There are four categories of abuse: physical, emotional and sexual abuse, and neglect. These are outlined below.

Physical abuse

Physical abuse is the most apparent form of child abuse. It includes any kind of physical harm to a child, which can include hitting, shaking, throwing, poisoning, burning or scalding, drowning and suffocating.

Physical harm may also be caused when a parent or carer fabricates the symptoms of illness in a child, or deliberately induces illness – for example, giving a child so much salt that he or she becomes very ill, so that medical staff think the child has a gastric illness or a brain condition.

Emotional abuse

Emotional abuse is difficult to define and can be difficult to detect. It involves continual emotional mistreatment which results in significant damage to the child's emotional development. The child may come to feel worthless, unloved, inadequate or valued only if they meet the expectations or needs of another person. Emotional abuse includes the following:

- The parent having expectations that are well outside what is suitable for the child's age and development. This includes unreasonable expectations, like continuously trying to force a child to achieve more, and then constantly criticising the child for his or her failures. At the other end of the spectrum, some parents may fail to stimulate their child adequately – for example, keeping a two-year-old in a playpen with only a couple of baby toys.

- Preventing a child from participating in normal social interaction with other children, either by keeping the child at home, or by taking the child out but being so overprotective, fearful or controlling that the child cannot join in.
- Failing to protect the child from witnessing the mistreatment of others – for example, cases of domestic violence.

All children will experience some emotional difficulties as part of the ordinary processes of growing up. It becomes abusive if the result is significant damage to the child's emotional development. All cases of child abuse will include some degree of emotional abuse.

Sexual abuse

Sexual abuse involves forcing or encouraging a child to take part in sexual activities. The child may or may not be aware of what is happening. Activities may involve physical contact – for example, rape, including forced anal sex or oral sex – or non-penetrative acts like touching or masturbation.

The abuse may include non-contact activities, such as involving children in looking at or in the production of sexual images online or on mobile phones, watching sexual activities or encouraging children to behave in sexually inappropriate ways.

Neglect

Neglect means that the parent persistently fails to meet the child's basic physical needs, psychological needs or both. The result is that the child's health or development is significantly impaired.

Neglect can occur during pregnancy if the mother abuses drugs or alcohol, which can have serious effects. Neglect of babies and young children includes the failure to:

- provide adequate food, clothing and shelter
- keep the child safe from physical and emotional harm or danger
- supervise the child adequately, including leaving the child with inadequate carers
- make sure the child is seen promptly by medical staff when ill
- respond to the child's basic emotional needs.

Research Activity

This section on Definitions of abuse and neglect draws on guidance from *Every Child Matters*. Find out more by reading the guidance in full – search online for 'Working Together to Safeguard Children'.

Recognising child abuse

Early years practitioners are good at recognising when all is not well with a child. Historically, the biggest difficulty has not been in recognising problems, but in communicating concerns to others (including the child's parents) and acting on them. Often practitioners worry about the consequences of passing on information, and worry that it might lead to the family being split up. It is important to remember that in the vast majority of cases the different services will work *with* the family to ensure the child's safety. But the decision about what is best for the child should be made by a trained social worker, acting on the best possible information. When practitioners feel worried but do not communicate their concerns to others, a child can be put in danger.

The National Society for the Prevention of Cruelty to Children (NSPCC) states:

> 'Children and young people often find it very difficult to talk about the abuse they are experiencing. So adults have a vital role to play in looking out for the possible signs.'

The following section draws on the NSPCC's guide, *Learn how to recognise the signs of child abuse*. It is not always possible to be completely certain that a child is being abused, but there are signs and indicators that all early years practitioners should look out for:

- A baby or toddler who is always crying.
- A child who often has injuries or bruises.
- A child who is often very withdrawn. Withdrawn children are not simply quiet or shy – they shrink from adult attention, lack interest in their surroundings and try to occupy themselves without being noticed.
- A child who is often in very dirty clothes, looks unwashed for a period of time or is very smelly.
- A child who is frequently very hungry.
- A child who is often not appropriately dressed for the weather or time of year. This would include children who often come to the setting in thin T-shirts, shorts or dresses through the winter. It would also include children who come into the setting on a hot day in very warm clothes.
- Any indication that a child is being left home alone, or left unsupervised in risky circumstances at home.
- A child who does not receive the medical treatment he or she needs.
- A child who is mocked, sworn at, constantly joked about and made to feel foolish or useless.
- A child who expresses fear about particular adults, or seems reluctant to be picked up by a particular adult or afraid to be left alone with that person.
- A child with very strong mood swings – anxiety, depression, uncontained anger or severe aggression.
- A child whose sexual knowledge, use of sexual words or sexual behaviour is not appropriate for their age or development.
- A child who is witnessing domestic violence.
- A child who is witnessing significant drug or alcohol abuse.

There may be valid explanations for some of these signs. Equally, there are many other indications of possible abuse, and other circumstances that could be unsafe for a child. The NSPCC advises:

'The most important thing to remember is that if you have a gut feeling that something is not right, **trust your judgement** and take action.'

Research Activity

You can read the full NSPCC guide 'Learn how to recognise the signs of child abuse' at www.nspcc.org.uk

Allegations

Sometimes a child may allege information that leads you to think that he or she is being abused. With young children, this may happen in a number of ways. A child might tell you something directly: 'Mummy and daddy went out yesterday, and me and Scarlet were scared because we were all alone.' Or a child might use play to communicate – for example, you might observe a child in the home corner shouting at and slapping one of the dolls.

In all cases, your role when a child alleges is to listen very carefully and show concern. Reaffirm that it is good for the child to tell you things that are worrying or upsetting him or her. Say that you believe the child. If you are not sure about something the child has said, then ask for clarification: 'I'm not sure I quite understood – did you say it was your arm that hurts?'

However, there are also some things that you must *not* do. You must not question or cross-examine a child or seem to put words into a child's mouth. So you would not ask a question like, 'Does this happen every day?' because the child might just agree with you, or repeat your words. You are there to listen and observe – you are not an investigator.

A child may make an allegation to anyone – their key person, the caretaker, the dinner supervisor, a student on placement. For that reason, it is very important that everyone who comes into contact with children has training on safeguarding and knows what to do if they have any reason to be worried about a particular child.

• Discuss your concerns as a matter of urgency with the named member of staff for safeguarding, however busy that person seems to be.

In most cases, the named member of staff will discuss the concerns with the parent and then make a judgement about what to do next. You should be told what action (if any) is being taken, and why. Responses might include:

- **No action** – for example, in a case where a parent gives a reasonable explanation for their child's injury or behaviour.
- **Advice given** – for example, a parent is advised on what sort of clothes will keep their child warm enough in winter. Staff can then check that the child is appropriately dressed on subsequent days.
- **Support offered** – for example, a parent might agree that she is finding it difficult to manage the child's behaviour, and might welcome the offer of support from a parenting group or an appointment with a clinical psychologist.
- **Referral to family support at the local Children's Centre** – this will provide structured support and help for the family on a voluntary basis. A similar type of referral might be made to a specialist social work team (Disabled Children's Team, Domestic Violence Project).
- **Referral to Children's Social Care (social services)** – if the named person judges that the child is at risk of significant harm, a written referral will be made to Children's Social Care.

If you have raised a concern and you think that the action being taken is inadequate, meet the named person again. Explain your opinion, referring to what you have observed or heard. Although such conversations are very difficult, they are essential if we are to uphold to the principle that the child's welfare and safety comes first.

If you are a student, discuss your concerns in confidence with your tutor. Any worried adult is also entitled to contact Children's Social Care or the NSPCC directly. If you have reason to believe your concern is not being acted on, you should do this.

Key term

Allegation – This is when a child alleges information that causes an adult to be concerned about the child's safety and wellbeing. This can happen through children talking, acting things out in their play, or drawing and painting. It is essential that early years practitioners listen and watch very carefully, but do not question the child or put words into the child's mouth.

Procedure for when abuse is suspected

Early intervention is recommended to help the child and family when there are difficulties, with different professionals and agencies working together: they should not wait until something serious happens before taking action. For example, a health visitor might notice that a mother is getting very stressed by the behaviour of her toddler and is struggling to cope. Early intervention might involve talking to the mother, showing sympathy, and perhaps finding some support for her at the local Children's Centre or setting up a programme of home visits. This would be much better than waiting to see if the situation gets any worse before doing anything.

Key term

Early intervention – This approach seeks to offer extra help and support to a family before the child starts to lag behind in development or experience neglect or abuse. Early intervention is about working cooperatively with parents and carers, giving them a chance to make choices about which services they need.

If a child alleges (makes an allegation) to you, or if you are worried for one or more of the reasons listed by the NSPCC (see page 130):

- Make a note that is as exact as you can make it, recording exactly what the child said, and anything you noticed (signs of an injury, child seeming upset, stressed, angry or ashamed while talking to you). If you have had ongoing concerns, summarise what these are; again, be as accurate as you can.

Research Activity

Revise the main points of the last pages by answering the following questions:

1. What are the four categories of child abuse?

2. What should you remember to do, if a child alleges to you? What should you avoid doing?

3. Why would early years staff share concerns about a child's welfare or wellbeing with the child's parents, rather than just keeping a record or making a referral?

Confidentiality and 'need to know'

In general, you must keep sensitive information confidential. If information circulates too freely, parents can feel very exposed and vulnerable. They may stop sharing information with staff.

Allegations made against staff

Schools and early years settings are usually some of the safest places for children to be. However, sadly there have been incidents when children have been harmed or abused by the adults who work with them and care for them. Cases include the murders of Holly Wells and Jessica Chapman by their school caretaker Ian Huntley in 2003, and the discovery in 2009 that a nursery nurse, Vanessa George, had sexually assaulted and made and distributed indecent pictures of some of the children in her care.

Generally, an early years setting or school keeps children safe by having good procedures around safer recruitment, management and its general operating policy; for example, if children are encouraged to speak out when they feel unhappy or uncomfortable, they will be much less vulnerable to abuse. Children's intimate care – nappy-changing, toileting, dressing and undressing – should be coordinated by a key person. This means that children do not have the experience that anyone can take them aside and undress them, and their right to privacy is upheld. It is good practice, where developmentally appropriate, to ask children to consent to offers of intimate care and to give them as much control as possible. So you might say to a toddler in the toilet, 'Would you like me to help pull your pants down?' rather than just going ahead and doing it.

Guidelines for confidentiality

- **Where appropriate, seek consent before you share information** – you might find out on a home visit that a child's mother has a serious mental health difficulty, which is well managed by medication and therapy. However, the medication can make her feel rather tired first thing in the morning, and she tells you that she can struggle to take on information or hold a conversation then. So you might say, 'I'll need to tell my manager this, but shall we also let the staff team know, so they can talk with you at the end of the day and not in the morning?' The parent can then give or withhold consent freely.

- **Never disclose any information about a child's welfare in an inappropriate way** to people outside the setting or school – for example, you would not tell friends or family about a child protection conference you had attended.

- **Put the child's interests first** – if sharing information will help to ensure a child's safety, you must do this. In nearly all cases, you would start by explaining to the parent why you wish to share the information and how this would help the child. If a parent refuses, ask for advice and guidance from the named person for safeguarding or the manager/head of the setting. If a parent says something like, 'I did smack her round the head, but you won't tell anyone will you? They'll take her into care,' you will need to explain clearly that you are legally required to pass on information like this.

However, no system alone can protect children. What matters, beyond good policies and procedures, is that adults are confident to raise concerns, and that children are encouraged to say if they are unhappy or uncomfortable with anything that happens to them.

All early years settings and schools are required to have a policy to deal with allegations made against staff. This will cover cases where a child makes a disclosure, or an adult is seen or overheard behaving in an inappropriate way. But there are other examples that might give rise to a concern, without a specific allegation being made:

- a child who seems fearful of a particular member of staff
- a member of staff seeming to try to develop a very close relationship with a child – for example, offering small presents and special treats, or arranging to meet the child outside of the setting or school
- a parent expressing a general concern about how a member of staff relates to their child, without being able exactly to say what is wrong.

In cases like these, you will need to discuss your concerns with the named person for safeguarding. Discussions like these are awkward, but it is important to share any concerns you have – the child's welfare is paramount.

Whistleblowing

Sometimes a person inside an organisation knows that something is going wrong and is being covered up. This could affect the safety and wellbeing of children. Examples of this in early years settings and schools include the following:

- A member of staff has reported a number of concerns about a child's welfare. The child's parents are on the management committee of the nursery, and the manager says, 'They are not the sort of people who would harm their child.'
- There are consistently too few staff on duty in the nursery. When the local authority come to visit, supply staff are hired, and during an Ofsted inspection, management and office staff are brought into the room so that legal ratios are met.

In cases like these, it is very important that action is taken before there is a serious incident. If a member of staff has spoken to the manager, headteacher or other appropriate person and made clear that a situation is dangerous and illegal, and no action is taken, it is necessary to 'blow the whistle' and report the concerns directly to an outside body, such as the local Children's Services, Ofsted or the NSPCC.

Figure 3.3 Children need to be cared for by suitably qualified staff who enjoy their company

If you act to protect children or to keep them safe, you are clearly protected by the law. In general, employees who blow the whistle are legally protected against being bullied, sacked or disciplined, if they have acted in good faith.

Research Activity

Search online for 'Protection of whistleblowers' or find out more at ww.direct.gov.uk/en/Employment/ResolvingWorkplaceDisputes/Whistleblowingintheworkplace

Progress check

- Working in a team, you should discuss your concerns about children in meetings or with senior staff, as appropriate.
- Understand why you would ask a parent for consent before sharing confidential information with another professional.
- Understand that there are times when you would share information without consent.

Helping children and families to deal with the effects of child abuse or neglect

Children are best helped when early years practitioners are not judgmental about the child's family and, in particular, about the person who has abused the child.

Building self-esteem

It is important to build the self-esteem of both the child and the family. Low self-esteem is associated with children who have been abused or neglected, and also with adults who abuse or neglect children. Improving self-esteem can be difficult when parents who are required to bring their children under a child protection order to a family centre, day nursery or children's centre, do not appear responsive or positive to staff or to the child.

It takes time to build self-esteem. Staff who give messages of warmth, who respect other people's dignity and who value people, although they may reject what they have done, are more likely to help

Guidelines for helping children deal with abuse and neglect

- Encourage children to play.
- Some children will need to be supported by trained play therapists or psychologists. Where there has been sexual abuse, anatomically correct dolls are sometimes used with the child. With help from these professionals, you might also be able to use the dolls with the child. These can help children to play, acting out their experiences and expressing how they feel about what has happened to them.
- Be warm – just be there for the child. Do not ask questions.
- Encourage the child to try to enjoy activities with you.
- Remember that children who have been abused or neglected are often challenging. Remind yourself about ways of helping children who push boundaries and challenge (see Chapter 2).
- Help parents to feel confident in their parenting.
- Do not undermine parents with remarks such as 'He doesn't do that here!' Instead, tackle problems together. Try saying to parents, 'Let's both try the same approach. When she does it next time, either at home or in the nursery, shall we both make sure we have the same reaction?'
- The aim is to get parents and children relating well to each other.
- Remember that many people who work with young children were themselves abused as children. It is important to manage feelings about this subject in a professional way.

parents in this way. Feeling valued as an individual, whatever you have done, builds self-esteem.

Safeguarding systems

Common Assessment Framework (CAF)

It has been argued that approaches to child protection in the past put too much emphasis on monitoring and assessing children's wellbeing and safety, rather than providing families with extra help and services in a timely manner. There was, perhaps, a tendency to wait until a family met the 'threshold' for Children's Social Care involvement, rather than working with the family on identified needs and problems.

The CAF is an attempt to address these concerns, as part of the government's Every Child Matters programme. The Children Act 2004 requires different agencies – for example, across education, health, children's social care and housing – to cooperate in the best interests of children and young people. The CAF provides a structure to facilitate this cooperation. (Although the CAF is specific to England, the same approach of working together is recommended in all the countries of the United Kingdom.)

The CAF is informed by research which suggests that children and families can move in and out of difficult phases in their lives, and that early intervention can prevent longer-term or more serious difficulties arising.

Shared assessment

One of the many difficult issues when working with vulnerable children and families is making an assessment of what the needs of the child and the family are. In the example we will consider here, a health visitor may notice that a three-year-old girl presents as slightly more prone to infections than is usual, and appears a little low in energy. Her development may seem satisfactory in terms of number of words spoken and understood, walking and running, and building with blocks in the clinic.

However, the early years practitioners working with the child may have noticed that she appears sociable at first, but is not able to play with or alongside other children. It may have been observed that while the child remains playing in areas of the nursery for some time, this involvement is only superficial and she is merely repeating the same actions over and over again.

As a result of these concerns, the child's key person could arrange to meet with the parents and the health visitor to discuss the extent to which the child is:

- healthy
- safe from harm
- learning and developing well
- socialising and making positive relationships with others
- not significantly impaired by the effects of poverty.

Team Around the Child (TAC)

This type of meeting is called **Team Around the Child.** There is a pre-assessment checklist for the CAF which practitioners can consult before calling such a meeting. It is important to remember that meetings like this, and the process of drawing up a CAF, are voluntary. Practitioners should only proceed with the informed consent of parents.

Using our example of the three-year-old girl, in such a meeting the mother might explain that her child sometimes gets very little sleep at night because her older brother, with whom the girl shares a room, has disabilities and needs care through the night. The mother might explain that the family is feeling overwhelmed and very stressed, and that there is little time for positive attention for her daughter.

By bringing together the information from the health visitor, the early years practitioner and the parent, an assessment of needs can be made in the following areas:

- development of the child
- parents and carers
- family environment.

This assessment, and the action plan based on the assessment, will be recorded on a standard CAF form, or electronically (the eCAF). In this case, the possible benefits of the CAF could be:

- a referral to the children's centre family support service, in order to investigate whether the family could be entitled to disability carers' allowance with respect to the older sibling
- a local voluntary group might be contacted, to provide respite care for several hours a week so that the older brother can be cared for while the rest of the family have some time together
- an application for more suitable housing could be made, supported by the different agencies.

The parent will be asked to nominate a lead professional to coordinate this plan. With the CAF, the parents will not constantly need to fill out different forms and repeat the same information to different agencies.

It is possible that without this support, the child's development and play could have fallen further behind that of her peers in nursery, leading to her becoming more isolated and unhappy. The stress of the family's situation could have led to the child's needs being neglected at home. In a small number of cases, stress of this kind can lead to mistreatment of one or both children.

Research Activity

To read the guidance on the CAF, including the pre-assessment checklist, go to http://www.education.gov.uk or search online for 'CAF'.

Inter-agency child protection

You may have heard about children being 'on the child protection register', but technically they should be described as having an **inter-agency child protection plan**. To give an idea of the scale of child protection work in England (comparable statistics are not easy to come by for the other countries in the UK):

- there were 547,000 referrals to children's social care departments in the year ending 31 March 2009

- these referrals led to social workers completing 349,000 **initial assessments**
- 37,900 children became the subject of an **inter-agency child protection plan** – this is fewer than 0.5 per cent of all children, or fewer than one child in 200.

Initial assessments

Initial assessments are undertaken by specialist children's social workers in response to referrals made by schools, doctors, nurses and early years settings, for example. The initial assessment informs the decision of what to do next. Possible decisions include:

- **Offering services to support the child and family**, if it is judged that the child is not at immediate risk of harm but is at risk of poor developmental outcomes.
- **Urgent action to protect the child from harm** – for example, applying for a court order to take the child into care. Social workers cannot take children away from their parents – only the courts can direct this. However, a police officer can take a child into police protection in an emergency.
- **Holding a strategy discussion**. This would happen where the assessment indicates that the child may be suffering significant harm. Other professionals who know the child and family, such as GPs, health visitors, teachers and early years practitioners, may be invited to this discussion. Specialist police officers must always be represented in strategy discussions. Where appropriate, a child protection conference will be arranged.

It is important to remember that staff in early years settings and schools should *not* investigate possible abuse or neglect. The role of the early years practitioner is to refer concerns to children's social care, to contribute to the initial assessment and to attend meetings as requested.

The initial assessment can lead to:

- further work and assessment being undertaken by specialist children's social workers – this is called the Core Assessment

- help being offered to the child and family on a voluntary basis, usually coordinated under the CAF
- a Child Protection Conference being convened – key staff working with the family, along with the child's parents, will be invited to this conference; the meeting will be organised by an independent chairperson who has not previously been involved in the case in any way, and who reports to the Director of Children's Services.

Child Protection Conference

The Child Protection Conference seeks to establish, on the basis of evidence from the referral and the initial assessment, whether the child has suffered ill-treatment, or whether his or her health or development has been significantly impaired as a result of physical, emotional or sexual abuse, or neglect. A professional judgement must be made about whether further ill-treatment or impairment is likely to occur. It is possible to hold a Child Protection Conference pre-birth if there are significant concerns that the newborn baby will be at risk of immediate harm – for example, in a family where there has been significant previous child abuse, or where a mother has abused drugs or alcohol during pregnancy.

If this is established, the child will be made the subject of an inter-agency child protection plan. The child's early years setting or school should be involved in the preparation of the plan. The role of the school or early years setting to safeguard the child, and promote his or her welfare, should be clearly identified. Examples of this role might include:

- carefully monitoring the child's heath or wellbeing in the setting on a daily basis
- making referrals to specialist agencies – for example, educational psychology
- offering support and services to the parents – for example, a parenting class run at the setting
- monitoring the child's progress against the planned outcomes in the agreed plan.

Discussion point

One of your key children is subject to an inter-agency child protection plan, under the category of neglect. During the day, you notice that the child looks rather grubby. Other children are avoiding him because he smells.

Discuss how you would talk to the parent at the end of the day and what information you would pass on to the child's social worker.

Core Group

The Core Group of professionals and the child's parents must meet within ten working days of a child being made subject to a child protection plan. The group will be called together by the child's social worker in the role of the lead professional (sometimes called the key worker), and will then meet regularly as required. This group should include a member of staff from the child's early years setting or school. The Core Group develops the child protection plan into a more detailed working tool, outlining who will do what and by when. Both this working plan and the overall child protection plan should be based on the assessments undertaken by the specialist social worker and others, and should address the issues arising in relation to:

- the child's developmental needs
- parenting capacity
- family and environmental factors.

There should be a child protection conference review within three months of the initial conference. Further reviews should be held at least every six months while the child remains subject to a child protection plan.

The plan may be ended if it is judged that there have been significant improvements to the wellbeing and safety of the child. These improvements might have taken place as a result of:

- a change in circumstances – for example, the abusing parent has moved out of the family home and no longer has unsupervised contact with the child

- the family is responding positively to the requirements set out in the plan, and following advice given
- the child is being given the medical or other treatment that he or she needs.

At this stage, there might be no further involvement from Children's Services, or the family may continue to be offered further help and support by the different agencies, usually coordinated under the CAF. This only happens once Children's Services are satisfied that their involvement is not required because the child is no longer considered to be 'in need'.

Key term

Inter-agency protection plan – If a child's health or development has been significantly impaired as a result of physical, emotional or sexual abuse or neglect, an inter-agency protection plan may be drawn up. The plan will identify the steps that the family needs to take to safeguard the child, with the support of children's services and other agencies. The child's safety, health, development and wellbeing will be regularly monitored throughout the plan.

Progress check

- Working in a team, you should help work towards the plan in a CAF, or offer additional help to a child who has been identified as being vulnerable.
- Know about the definition of a child in need.
- Know who can take children into protective care if they are in immediate danger.
- Understand why a child might be made subject to an inter-agency child protection plan.

Safe working practices

Children learn some realities of safety the hard way, for example by banging their heads or grazing their knees. You cannot prevent them from hurting themselves altogether, but you can alert them and keep reminding them. You have an important role, not only in keeping children safe and secure but also in teaching them to be aware of safety issues.

Safe supervision of children while allowing risk and challenge

Safe supervision of children is vital to ensure their safety. Supervising children means far more than just preventing them from doing certain things in case they have an accident. It also involves knowing when to supervise 'at arm's length', to allow children opportunities to tackle more challenging activities. There are certain circumstances when close supervision is essential (for example, when children are playing near or with water) but there should also be times when adults can supervise unobtrusively to give children the chance to try something new. This subject is dealt with in more depth in Chapter 4, Keeping children safe.

Supporting children's safety when they move in and out of the setting

Every setting should have clear systems in place to ensure the safety of children:

- when being received into the setting
- when departing from the setting, and
- during off-site visits.

During these times, there is often a lot of movement and activity. When children are received into the setting, several children may arrive at once, parents may be in a rush to get to work, and children are keen to rejoin their friends. When leaving the setting, again many children will be leaving at the same time, parents chatting with others and children eager to say goodbye to their friends. During off-site visits, there is usually a great deal of excitement about being in a new place with lots to see and do. Every practitioner should be aware of the policy and procedures that relate to these times in their setting, and should be clear about his or her own role and responsibility.

Receiving children into the setting

All settings must register children on arrival. A daily register of the names of all the children in the setting at any given time is essential not only in case of an emergency evacuation of the setting, but also so that adequate staff supervision (or staffing ratios) is provided. Many early years settings have door entry phones and a password system for parents and staff to enter the premises. The entrance should be secure so that the door cannot be left open for people to wander in and out. In some settings, one member of staff is stationed at the door, greeting and sharing information with each family as they arrive. Some settings have a designated dropping-off area where a calm atmosphere can be created as parents and carers 'hand over' their child to their key person.

Ensuring safety on departure

Every setting will have a policy about correct procedure for when parents and carers come to collect their child. Again, the register must be kept so that it is clear which children are in the setting in case of an emergency. At home time, a member of staff must ensure that every child is collected by the appropriate person: the person registered as the child's own parent or carer, or a person who has written authorisation from the parent or carer. If parents know that they will not be able to collect their child on a particular occasion, they should notify the setting, giving permission for another named person to collect their child. The child's key person should, where possible, be responsible for handover at home times. Within the setting's safeguarding children policy, there should be a written statement of the procedures in place for an uncollected child.

Reflective practice: Safety at arrival and departure

1 Do you know the procedures for arrival and departure in your setting?
2 How do you ensure that the person who arrives is authorised to collect the child?
3 Do you know what to do if an unknown adult arrives to collect a child?
4 Think about the most welcoming and safe way to greet families when they arrive.

Case Study   Problems at home time

Anna is a three-year-old child who attends a private nursery group four days a week. Her key person, Leanne, has developed a good professional relationship with Anna's mother and suspects that she and her partner are having problems balancing their home life with their work commitments. Anna's mother, Kirsty, often arrives late to collect Anna; she is always very flustered and apologetic about it. Anna's father, David, works long hours as a sales rep and is often away from home for weeks at a time. He has only collected Anna on a couple of occasions before, and only when Kirsty had given prior permission. One Friday afternoon, David arrives at the nursery and explains to Leanne that Kirsty had rung him to say she was running very late and asked if he could collect Anna on this occasion. When Leanne replies that she must check with the nursery manager before allowing him to take Anna, David becomes very angry and starts to shout about his rights as a father. As Leanne is trying to reason with him, he suddenly pushes his way past her into the nursery room and scoops Anna up, grabbing her coat from her peg as he rushes out. Five minutes later, Kirsty arrives and becomes very distressed when she hears what has happened. She tells Leanne that she and David had had an argument that morning and that he had threatened to leave her.

Discuss this case study in class and answer the following questions:

1 If you were Leanne (Anna's key person), what should you do?

2 What are the main issues involved in this case study?

3 How can the nursery ensure every child's safety at home time?

Safety during off-site visits

Any outing away from the children's usual setting (such as trips to farms, parks and theatres) must be planned with safety and security issues as a top priority. When participating in off-site visits, all practitioners (including volunteers) have a duty to take reasonable care to avoid injury to themselves and others, and to cooperate to ensure that statutory duties and obligations are fulfilled. Adults in charge of children during an off-site visit have a duty of care to make sure that the children are safe and healthy. Practitioners have a common law duty to act as would a reasonably prudent parent, and should not hesitate to act in an emergency and to take life-saving action in an extreme situation. As a safeguard to children, volunteer helpers on off-site visits must:

- be appropriate people to supervise children
- be trained in their duties, and
- have had a CRB (Criminal Records Bureau) check.

Unqualified staff or volunteers must not be left in sole charge of children except where it has been previously agreed as part of the risk assessment. Practitioners and volunteers should not be in a situation where they are alone with one child away from the rest of the group.

Every setting must consider the following points:

Planning and risk assessment

Visit or find out about the place beforehand and discuss any particular requirements, such as what to do if it rains, or specific lunch arrangements. A risk assessment should be carried out to include consideration of potential risks in the environment, such as traffic, dogs, ponds or rivers, etc. (You can find out more about risk assessment in Chapter 4, Keeping children safe.)

Contact numbers

A copy of the children's contact information should be taken on the outing, and the person in charge should regularly check the names of the children against the day's attendance list.

Parental permission

Parents should be informed of what is involved on the outing, such as what the child needs to bring (such as packed meal, waterproof coat), spending money if necessary (state the advised maximum amount). Parents must sign a consent form that gives the setting permission to take their child off the premises.

Supervision and staff ratios

There should always be trained staff on any outing, however local and low-key. Usually help is requested from parents so that adequate supervision is ensured. The minimum staff:child ratios are set out in the welfare requirements for every home nation, and must be complied with:

- The adult to child ratio should never exceed one to four.
- If the children are under two years old or have special needs, then you would expect to have fewer children per adult.
- Swimming trips should be attempted only if the ratio is one adult to one child for children under five years old.
- The younger the children, the more adults are required, particularly if the trip involves crossing roads, when an adult must be available to hold the children's hands.

Head counts

Make sure that you all count the children regularly. Always accompany children to public toilets, telling a colleague how many children you are taking with you.

Transport

If a coach is being hired, check whether it has seat belts for children. By law, all new minibuses and coaches must have seat belts fitted, and minibus drivers must pass a special driving test.

Activity

Receiving children into the setting

Find out about the system for receiving children in your setting:

1 Who is responsible for registering the children?

2 How does the setting ensure that the entrance door is kept shut between arrivals?

3 How smooth is the transition from reception into the setting to each child being with his or her key person?

Section 4: How to empower children to develop self-confidence, self-esteem and self-reliance

Children develop a sense of self (self-conceptual sense of identity) during the first year of life, and this becomes more stable as they develop socially. The way we feel about ourselves is called our self-image, and this is deeply influenced by how we think that others see us. If we feel loved, valued, appreciated and that we matter to people who matter to us, then our sense of wellbeing is high. Developing a positive self-image is about:

- realising you exist
- developing self-esteem and good sense of wellbeing
- learning to like and respect yourself
- knowing who you are
- knowing and understanding yourself
- developing skills of caring for and looking after yourself
- feeling that you are making a caring contribution to others.

From an early age children are aware of differences between themselves and others. This can be a positive or negative aspect of their lives. Many things influence our **self-image**, including:

- ethnicity
- gender
- language
- particular and special needs
- abuse
- economic circumstances.

Strategies to develop self-confidence and self-reliance

In order for self-confidence and self-reliance to grow, children need to develop positive relationships with people. Children feel things deeply and they need a great deal of support to understand, express and deal with their emotions. Feelings are hard to deal with; it is important to remember that even adults do not succeed all the time in coping with how they feel. Helping children to express and deal with their feelings constructively and positively is probably one of the most important things an adult can do if children are to feel they matter, and are valued and respected.

Remember to work as a team to decide together on what is unacceptable behaviour and how to deal with it. Many early years settings now have behaviour policies. These should always use positive images of the child as the starting point. Negative images, for example that of a bully, can be made positive through visualisation techniques: the bully becomes a child who needs help to become assertive without being aggressive. Practitioners need to emphasise the development of self-discipline by the child, rather than adults managing the behaviour for the child.

It is important that adults working with young children be guided by each child's personality. What helps one child might not help another. Every child is different, but also remember that all children need:

- personal space
- one-to-one attention
- friends
- to feel part of the group
- to feel secure.

Supporting self-confidence and self-esteem in young children through the key person approach

The self-confidence and self-esteem of young children can be greatly boosted by a strong key person approach in the setting. Many aspects of this approach support the safeguarding of children.

- **Listening and tuning in to a child** – this will include noticing changes in a child's behaviour and emotional wellbeing, and developing a trusting relationship so that the child can tell you if things are upsetting him or her. Taking a child's concerns seriously is important. Often, when a child has been bullied or abused in some way, he or she will try to communicate what has happened. The child needs to know that you are there to listen and, most importantly, that you will believe what he or she tells you.

- **Allowing a child to express his or her feelings** – if a child is allowed to express sadness and anger, as well as happiness and enjoyment, he or she may feel more confident that it is all right to have a range of emotions. The child will be more likely to tell other people how he or she is feeling.

- **Increasing a child's confidence** – this involves making a child feel a sense of belonging, and that he or she is special for his or her unique qualities. It is important to show a genuine interest in what a child has to say, and to praise him or her for any achievements. A quick 'That's lovely, Suhail,' is really not enough to show a child that you value him.

- **Observing a child** and keeping **regular records** of his or her behaviour – the key person is in a strong position to note any changes of behaviour or signs of insecurity that could result from child abuse.

Emotional intelligence

Children's emotions have a huge impact on nursery and school life. Anger, in particular, has a damaging effect on the atmosphere in a setting. Emotional intelligence refers to the ability to recognise, understand, handle and appropriately express our emotions. It involves how we feel, think and behave.

The concept is associated particularly with the name of Daniel Goleman, an American psychologist. His work has been influential in the field of education (as well as in business circles) where it is seen as offering ways of improving pupils' achievement and of providing them with skills for their personal and working lives. Emotional Intelligence is often referred to as 'EQ – Emotional Quotient', contrasting with 'IQ – Intelligence Quotient'.

Goleman focused on five main areas of emotional intelligence:

1 **Self-awareness:** understanding our emotional responses or feelings is the most important factor in EI, as it gives us the potential to control our emotional state.

Figure 3.4 This toddler is able to explore the environment confidently because of the security he gains from the presence of his key person

2 Emotional control: we can use strategies to control our emotional state. This can be helpful when reacting appropriately to stressful situations.

3 Self-motivation: when we have a goal, the control of emotions will assist greatly in achieving it (for example, in focusing our feelings productively and controlling our impulses).

4 Empathy: the ability to recognise signs in others of how they are feeling is important if we are to establish good relationships with them. It involves 'tuning in' to how others feel, and can also help us to deal with conflict situations.

5 Handling relationships: good understanding of emotions can help us to manage other people's emotional states.

Children are now encouraged to explore their emotions in school and to learn about manners, respect and good behaviour in an attempt to raise school attendance and to improve learning. Schools which seek specifically to promote **emotional literacy** amongst pupils have provided evidence that it helps to raise achievement. Teachers use various different approaches. For example, they might:

- adopt key emotions such as anger and happiness or fear and excitement each half-term. This encourages awareness of the impact that emotions can have on our lives
- ask children to think about contrasting emotions: *when* they might experience them and *how* they might express them differently
- use fiction, themed displays or music to help children of any age feel more connected to their emotions.

Emotional literacy is the term mostly used in the UK to refer to emotional intelligence skills or competencies.

How to develop relationships with children and adults

This area is fully examined in Unit 1. See Chapter 1, pages 10–13 for advice on developing relationships with children and adults.

How to value children and give them attention

As you build and develop trusting relationships with the children in your care, they will learn to trust you. A good early years setting is one where adults support children to have high expectations of themselves, encourage self-esteem and are positive and warm – in other words, setting where children are valued. It is essential to create a learning context in which children feel appreciated and valued, and where those close to them, usually their families, are also valued. It is through other people that children learn to feel valued, or not. When children feel their efforts are appreciated and see them celebrated, they develop a positive self-image. This helps learning almost more than anything else, as every child is free from the pressure of having to produce perfect results. A child is therefore free to learn, from things going badly as well as from things going well. This helps children to be highly motivated and interested in their learning. On the other hand, if a child spends time with adults who only praise and recognise *results*, most children are bound to fail.

The importance of children's communication skills

Children need to be able to communicate, and the development of communication skills is one of the most important aspects of development. Being able to communicate helps children to:

- express their needs and preferences
- express their emotions and manage strong feelings, such as anger
- understand the feelings of others
- have increased self-esteem and social confidence
- develop friendships with other children
- prepare for reading and writing – pre-literacy skills
- share and take turns.

See Chapters 2 and 12 (Unit 16) for more information on communication.

In Practice

How to show a child that you are actively listening

1 **STOP**: pay attention. When a child or young person approaches you with something to share, stop what you are doing and pay attention. This lets her know that you are listening and that you value what she is saying.

2 **LOOK**: make eye contact. Get down to her level, face her directly and make eye contact. Also show that you are listening through body language, such as by smiling and nodding.

3 **LISTEN**: listen attentively. Focus your attention on what she is saying by listening to her words and tone of voice. Listen carefully to what she actually says as well as what she might be trying to say.

4 **RESPOND**: respond appropriately. Having listened carefully to what has been said, you could paraphrase what she has just said, ask open-ended questions, or prompt her to say more, by saying 'That's interesting' or 'Oh, I see'.

The importance of listening to children

Listening should be an active process, involving not just hearing, but interpreting, understanding and responding. Being able to attend to and 'actively' listen to what children and young people are saying is important in the development of self-esteem. When practitioners listen actively, they communicate to children and young people the message that they are important enough to have the adult's undivided attention. Active listening also supports children to solve problems and to take responsibility for their own learning.

Key term

Active listening – The process of actively seeking to understand the meaning of another person's communication, whether the communication is spoken or conveyed in a different way. Active listening includes the use of verbal and non-verbal skills.

How to show children you respect their individuality

In line with the CACHE values, you need to ensure that the child or young person is at the *centre* of your practice; their needs are paramount. This means that every child or young person is valued for his or her individuality. As a practitioner, your role is:

- to listen to children
- not to impose your own agenda on them

- not to single out any one child for special attention
- to ensure that children maintain control over their own play
- to be friendly, courteous and sensitive to their needs
- to praise and motivate them; display their work
- to speak to the child – not at the child; with young children, this means getting down to their level and maintaining eye contact
- to respect their individuality
- to develop a sense of trust and caring with each child.

How to be fair and consistent in supporting children

Children and young people need to feel safe and secure, and they need practitioners to react predictably to situations, showing fairness and consistency. If parents, carers and staff are not consistent in their approaches, children and young people become unsettled and confused, and they do not know what is expected of them. Behaviour then becomes increasingly inappropriate, as they have no real understanding of the acceptable boundaries. All children and young people need care and attention, support and practical help, but as each child or young person is unique, each will have different needs. It is important that practitioners do the following:

- **Provide a safe predictable environment**: it is very important for all staff to work as a team so that different messages are not given by different people. For example, if one adult allows children to sit on tables and another does not, it leads to boundary testing by children. Children will need to sort out their confusion about what is and is not allowed.

- **Address each child's needs**: for example, a confident, talkative child or a child with behavioural difficulties may take up a lot of your time, but it is important to watch out for the quiet child who seems not to need you when playing quietly alone.
- **Spend time with all the children** in your care: a team approach to planning activities will help to make sure that a balance is achieved for all, and that every child receives individual attention whenever possible.

The role of adults in promoting a positive self-image and sense of wellbeing in children

- Value children for who they are, not what they do or how they look.
- A child needs love, security and a feeling of trust. There is no single way to give these feelings to children: it will depend on where children live, their family and culture. There is no standard family or institution, or a single best way to love children and give them self-esteem.
- People who give children positive images about themselves (in terms of skin colour, language, gender, disability, features, culture and economic background) help children to develop good self-esteem. Look at the book area and the displays on the walls in your setting. Are you giving positive messages?
- Visitors to the nursery can provide positive images. The people children meet occasionally or on a daily basis will all have a strong influence on them. If children almost never see men working in early years settings or women mending pieces of equipment, they form very narrow ideas about who they might become. Books, pictures, outings and visitors can all offer positive images which extend children's ideas of who they might be.

- Adults who are positive role models help a child's self-esteem.
- Children need to feel some success in what they set out to do. This means that adults must avoid having unrealistic expectations of what children can manage, such as dressing, eating or going to the toilet. It is important to appreciate the efforts that children make.
- They do not have to produce perfect results: the effort is more important than the result.
- Adults help children's self-esteem if they are encouraging. When children make mistakes, do not tell them they are silly or stupid. Instead say something like, 'Never mind, let's pick up the pieces and sweep them into the bin. Next time, if you hold it with two hands it will be easier to work with.'
- Children need to feel they have some choices in their lives. Obviously, safety and consideration for others are important, but it is usually possible to allow children to make some decisions.
- Children need clear, consistent boundaries or they become confused. When they are confused they begin to test out the boundaries to see what is consistent about them.
- Children need consistent care from people they know. Many early years settings have now introduced a key worker or family worker system, which provides continuity.
- Children need to have a feeling of trust that their basic needs for food, rest and shelter will be met. Rigid rituals are not helpful, but days do need a shape or routine. This will give children a predictable environment. They will have the know-how to help in setting the table, for example, or washing their hands after going to the toilet.
- Children and their families need to be given respect so that they can then develop self-respect. Children, parents and staff need to speak politely and respectfully to each other.
- Children have strong and deep feelings. They need help, support and care from adults.

Section 5: How to support children to prepare for transfer or transition

What are transitions?

A transition is a change of passage from one stage or state to another. Children and young people naturally pass through a number of stages as they grow and develop. Often, they will also be expected to cope with changes such as movement from nursery education to primary school, and from primary to secondary school.

You may have just made the transition from secondary school to a tertiary college or sixth form. Along with the excitement of a new course and possibly making new friends, you are likely to have felt some apprehension about the change to your life. This is likely to affect you more if you have experienced many changes in your life. These changes are commonly referred to as transitions.

Types of transitions

Transitions can affect all areas of the development of children and young people:

- **Emotional**: personal experiences, such as parents separating, bereavement, entering or leaving care
- **Physical**: moving to a new educational setting, a new home or care setting
- **Intellectual**: moving from nursery to primary school, or primary to secondary school
- **Physiological**: puberty or a long-term medical condition.

Expected transitions

Many transitions are universal; they are experienced by almost everyone, and can usually be anticipated, or expected. **Babies** experience transitions when they:

- are weaned onto solid food
- are able to be cared for by others, such as at nursery or a childminder's home

- progress from crawling to walking
- move from needing nappies to being toilet-trained.

Children experience transitions when they:

- start nursery and then primary school
- move up to secondary school.

Young people experience transitions when they:

- go through the physical and emotional changes caused by puberty
- attend college or university
- leave home
- start work.

Adults experience transitions when they:

- get married
- become separated or divorce
- have children
- change jobs
- experience a death in the family, which changes the family structure.

Unexpected transitions

Not every transition is experienced by every child, and not all transitions can be anticipated. These unexpected transitions include:

- the birth of a new baby in the family (although this is a very common transition, it is not always expected)
- an unexpected change of school or childcare provider
- moving house
- violence or abuse within the family
- parents divorcing; having a new step-parent and perhaps new step-family
- serious illness, accident or death in the family.

Understanding the potential effects of transitions

You need to be able to identify transitions and understand what you can do to support children through them. Before we can fully understand the importance of transitions in children's lives, we need to learn about the concepts of attachment and separation, and the effects of multiple transitions in a child's life.

Attachment

Attachment means a warm, affectionate and supportive bond between a child and his or her carer that enables the child to develop secure relationships. When children receive warm, responsive care, they feel safe and secure.

- Secure attachments are the basis of all the child's future relationships. Because babies experience relationships through their senses, it is the expression of love that affects how they develop, and that helps to shape later learning and behaviour.
- Children who are securely attached will grow to be more curious, get along better with other children and perform better in school than children who are less securely attached.
- With children who have a strong attachment to their parent or primary carer, the process of becoming attached to the **key person** is easier, not harder, than it is for children with a weaker attachment (see below for the importance of the key person approach). Remember, though, that all parents find separation difficult, whether or not they have formed a strong attachment with their child.

Separation

Many of the times that prove to be difficult for children are connected with separation. Going to bed is separation from the main carer and is often a source of anxiety in children. Some young children can be terrified as a parent walks out of the room. How children react to separation is as varied as children's characteristics. For some children every new situation will bring questions and new feelings of anxiety; other children love the challenge of meeting new friends and seeing new things.

The effects of multiple transitions

Children who have had to make many moves or changes may feel a sense of loss and grief. These changes may have a profound effect on their emotional and social development. Reasons for transitions include:

- **Divorce or separation**: children whose parents have separated or divorced may have to live and get along with several 'new' people, such as stepfathers, stepmothers, half-brothers and sisters, etc.
- **Changes in childcare arrangements**: children who experience many different childcare arrangements; for example, frequent changes from one nanny or childminder to another.
- **Children who are in local authority care** – either in residential children's homes or in foster care.
- **Children whose families have moved house several times,** perhaps for employment reasons, or as Travellers.

How children feel when they transfer to a new setting

You need to be able to identify transitions and understand what you can do to support children through them. Many of the problems associated with transitions in childhood are associated with separation. As children become older, they start to cope better with being separated from their parents or main carers, but the way in which they cope will still depend on their early experiences of separation and how earlier transitions were managed. Children who have had multiple transitions (perhaps changing schools or homes many times, possibly caused by changes to a parent's job) often find it harder to settle in and make new friends and relationships.

Transitions can affect the development of children and young people in different ways. There can be positive as well as negative effects; they can also be short-term or long-term, depending on the individual child or young person and on how effectively they are supported. Possible effects of transitions are given in Table 3.1.

Experience of the child	Effect of this experience
Withdrawal	Children may withdraw from new relationships with other children and with carers, because they do not trust the separation not to happen again.
Disorientation	No sooner have children settled in one place and got to know a carer, they may be uprooted and have to face the same process again.
A sense of loss	Every time children and young people make a move, they lose the friends they have made and also the attachments they have formed with their carers.
Regression	Reverting to behaviour usually shown by younger children; for example, a child who was previously dry at night may start to wet the bed, or an older child might start to talk in a more 'babyish' way.
Depression	This may show in a number of ways: sadness, problems in sleeping, crying and lack of appetite.
Separation anxiety	Children become clingy and need to be near their parent or primary carer to feel reassured.
Changes in behaviour	Young children may have frequent tantrums; older children may show challenging behaviour.
Lack of motivation	Children and young people may have difficulty in concentrating on schoolwork and become easily distracted.

Table 3.1 Effect of transitions on children

One expected transition that all young people experience is puberty. Puberty is the physical process where a child's body develops into an adult body and becomes capable of reproduction. We all have to make the transition from childhood into adulthood and almost without exception, everyone experiences some self-doubt. Because there is a very wide variation in the ages at which young people experience puberty, the person who is the first or last one in their peer group to go through the physical and hormonal changes may feel awkward and embarrassed; they may also be teased by others in their group and this increases their feelings of insecurity.

Supporting the child and family through transitions

Children and young people need practitioners who are able to recognise the importance of attachment and emotional wellbeing during periods of transition, and who are able to identify the needs of an individual child and his or her family. The key person approach is vital to supporting young children through transitions, and is also frequently used in health care and social care settings when transitions are necessary.

Reflective practice: Transitions

Does your setting have a policy for transition and continuity which is shared with everyone involved, both in and beyond the setting?

How do you help children and families who are new to the area or your setting to settle in and get to know people? What is the role of the key person in supporting transitions?

Think about a child or young person you know who has experienced a transition. How was he or she supported, and could the experience have been improved?

 Progress check

Transitions

Choose three expected transitions and three unexpected transitions that may occur in children's lives. (For example: one expected transition for all children is starting school; one unexpected transition might be their parents separating or divorcing.)

For each transition, describe:

- the possible effects on the child when experiencing the transition
- how the child could be supported through the transition.

Case Study — A new baby in the family

Sean is two and a half years old. He has been attending nursery for three days a week since he was a baby and is a happy, sociable little boy who interacts well with the other children. Sean's mother is expecting her second child.

In the run-up to her due date, Sean is booked in occasionally for extra days and often dropped off by his father or grandparents. He seems to adjust very well to this and talks proudly about becoming an older brother. One Tuesday, after a few days away, Sean attends nursery with the news that he has a new little sister. He brings in photos and seems happy, if a little more tired than usual.

A week later, Sean is brought in by his mother (with his baby sister) for the first time in a few weeks. He becomes clingy and cries inconsolably for 20 minutes after she leaves. Over the next couple of weeks, Sean is brought in and picked up by his father, mother or grandparents. Sometimes he does not know who will be picking him up, or at what time. He is often late to arrive, missing the register time and morning song.

Sean becomes clingy to his key person and sullen when he has to share toys. He sometimes disrupts storytimes by wandering away and has started to have sudden tantrums. One day, Sean is playing with one of his friends, Jemima. They both want the same toy and Sean bites Jemima in frustration when she reaches for it first.

1 Identify all the changes in Sean's behaviour.

2 Why might having a new baby in the family affect Sean's behaviour and development?

In Practice

Helping children to settle in

This activity will help a child who is new to the setting to realise that he or she is not alone, and that other children also feel shy and alone at times.

- **Introduction**: choose a teddy and introduce him to the group, saying something like:

  'Teddy is rather shy and a little bit lonely. How can we help him to feel better?'

- **Discussion and display**: take photos of Teddy – using a digital camera if possible – with different groups of children, and in different places in the nursery (for example, playing in the sand, reading a book, doing a puzzle) and use later for discussion and display.

- **Circle time**: in circle time, pass Teddy round, and encourage each child to say something to him:

'Hello Teddy, my name is Lara' or 'Hello Teddy, I like chocolate . . .', etc.

- **Taking Teddy home**: every child takes it in turns to take Teddy home. Include a notebook and encourage parents to write a few sentences about what Teddy did at their house that evening. The children can draw a picture.

- **Storytime**: read and act out the story of Goldilocks and the Three Bears, with the different sized bowls, beds, and chairs.

- **Cooking**: use a shaped cutter to make teddy-shaped biscuits or dough teddies.

- **Teddy bears' picnic**: Arrange a teddy bears' picnic where each child brings in a favourite bear. What does your teddy like to eat? Are there enough plates, biscuits and cups for all the bears?

Progress check

Observing social needs

In your work placement, plan to observe an individual child's social needs during a whole session. Make a checklist that includes the following needs:

- **Interaction with other children**: observe how the child plays; for example, does he play alone (solitary play), alongside others but not with them (parallel play), or actively with other children?

- **Attention from adults**: does the child seek attention from one particular adult, or from any adult? Note the number of occasions on which a child seeks adult attention and describe the interaction.

- **Self-help skills and independence**: observe the child using self-help skills, such as putting on coat to go outside, washing hands and going to the toilet.

Identify the stage of social development the child is passing through and list the ways in which you can ensure that their social needs are met within the setting.

Strategies to support and prepare children for transfers and transitions

Being separated from our loved ones is difficult at any age, and a feeling of bereavement can be experienced. In situations where children are repeatedly separated from their families, through home circumstances or war and conflict, it helps when the adults with whom the child is left understand the elements discussed in this chapter, so that vulnerable children feel a sense of belonging and wellbeing, and feelings of being valued, loved and respected.

Supporting times of transition

- Remember that if the parent is anxious about leaving their child, the child will be anxious about being separated from the parent. Make sure that every adult and child is welcomed. Put notices in the languages of the community as well as in English.
- A notice board with photographs of staff and their role helps people to feel familiar with the environment.
- An attractive display of some of the recent experiences gained by the children helps people to tune in to the setting's way of working.
- A notice with the menu for the week gives valuable information to parents and carers.

- Something for children to do is vital; watching fish in a fish tank or having a turn on a rocking-horse are popular examples.

It is also important to remember that Anna Freud, working with children who had experienced the Holocaust, found that their friendships with each other were very important, and so was having a normal childhood with opportunities for sensitively supported play. Play seemed to have a self-healing power.

The importance of the key person

In many settings there is a system of a key person for the child. The important thing is that there are opportunities for warm, intimate relationships between practitioners and babies and young children. For this to be possible, children need constant and stable people, and to be in very small groups. Then there are opportunities to listen to children and tune in to them. Whether or not there is an allocated key person, it is this approach of respecting the child as unique, with emotional need for warm, affectionate relationships and feeling valued, which will truly support their transition.

Some families will have a lead professional working with them to ensure that there is more joined-up thinking and that different professionals link with each other. This has developed through the Children

Act 2004 and the embedding of the Every Child Matters agenda. It will also be an important way of reducing inequality, which became a local authority duty under the Childcare Act 2006.

How to promote communication between settings

It is important that times of transition are as positive as possible, both for the individual child and the family as a whole. Transitions can be painful, and some of the separations in the list of examples could never be happy experiences for children or those who love them and whom they love. However, it is always possible to ease the impact of difficult separations through thoughtful, organised and sensitive support.

From the home environment to the early childhood setting

This might be when the family visits the early childhood setting or it might be through a home visit. It is important that parents do not feel forced into accepting a home visit from staff. Often families welcome home visits as an opportunity to get to know the early years practitioner. A home visit, or a visit to the setting before the child starts there, gives staff the chance to find out what the parents are expecting from the setting. All this helps parents and children to make the transition from being at home to starting in a group setting. Childminders and nannies often make photograph albums with short captions in the same spirit.

Parents and children often appreciate having a booklet of their own to keep, and this can build into a record of the child's time with the setting, childminder or nanny. This often helps a child to make future transitions.

When settling a child and family, transitions are made easier if there is sensitivity about the way you use gesture and body language, such as eye contact. The photographs in the brochure can be invaluable when staff and family do not share the same language.

Settling children into the setting

Probably the most important thing an early years practitioner does is to settle a child into an early years group, in partnership with the parents or carers. Many settings have a very clear policy on admissions and settling in.

The importance of providing continuity of experiences for children

Whenever there is a transitional point for a child and family, it is important to look at *what went before*. This is so that we can learn about and tune in to the child, and support them and make as seamless a transition as possible. There should be **continuity**, not discontinuity of experience for the child and family.

This means that every practitioner working with children in the birth-to-16 years range should know what comes before and what comes after the time the child will spend with them. For example, a practitioner working in England will need to know about:

- Early Years Foundation Stage
- Curriculum Guidance for the Foundation Stage
- Key Stage 1
- Secondary school admission.

The DfES has developed a mainstream training package for the transition between the Foundation Stage and Key Stage 1, called *Continuing the Learning Journey*.

Research Activity

Transition from nursery to reception

Access the Birth to Five website (www.birthtofive. org.uk) and find out how one school in Lincolnshire helps to ease children's transition from nursery to reception class.

Find out how your setting prepares for transitions and supports the children and their families.

Welcome to our school

Louis is going to show you around

Figure 3.5 Managing transition to primary school

Supporting vulnerable parents

Parents who have experienced war and conflict are often anxious about leaving their children with those outside the family. They may appreciate:

- having their youngest children in the next room while they learn English and learn about life in Britain
- their older children being near them in school in the same building
- all their children joining them at the end of the session, to try out a story they have learnt, using props (such as Goldilocks and the Three Bears)
- meeting other parents who have experienced war, conflict and trauma
- meeting practitioners who help them and their children to develop and learn, and who care for their emotional wellbeing.

Accessing further support

Families need information about a wide range of topics. Much information can be gained from the media – radio, television and newspapers. The internet is also a valuable source of information, but not every family has easy access to computing and internet connections. Table 3.2 shows the sources of information generally available.

Section 6: The causes and effects of discrimination in society

What is discrimination?

Discrimination is the denial of equality based on personal characteristics, such as race and colour. Discrimination is usually based on **prejudice** and **stereotypes**.

- **Prejudice** means to prejudge people based on assumptions. For example, racial prejudice is the belief that physical or cultural differences (such as

Place of information	Resources and services
Public library	Usually with internet services; local information about a wide range of services for children and families; also a reference section with books giving information on benefits and other government services.
Citizen's Advice Bureau (CAB)	Most towns have a CAB; rural areas may have to access one by telephone. They offer independent legal and financial support.
Childcare Information Service	This service was set up by the government to provide information for parents about the range and costs of childcare in their area. Their website (www.childcarelinks.gov.uk) has links to all local authorities. Parents without internet access could write directly to their local authority for printed information.
Benefit agency	Most large towns have a Benefits agency office with a wide range of leaflets – often printed in different languages – and experienced staff to explain what is available.
Local authority (LA) or Council	Many local authorities have a separate department to provide support children and families who are vulnerable or need help with everyday living. They can be accessed directly or via the internet.
Voluntary organisations	Local charities often hold meetings and host events to publicise their work and to raise money; examples include: Gingerbread (a charity for the support of lone parents), The National Council for One Parent Families, The Daycare Trust (a national childcare charity) and Families Need Fathers.

Table 3.2 Accessing information and support

skin colour, religious beliefs or dress) are directly linked to differences in the development of intelligence, ability, personality or goodness.

- The word **stereotype** comes from the process of making metal plates for printing. When applied to people, stereotyping refers to forming an instant or fixed picture of a group of people, usually based on false or incomplete information. Stereotypes are often negative.

The causes of discrimination in child care and education

Discrimination occurs when someone is treated less favourably, usually because of a negative view of some of their characteristics. This negative (pejorative) view is based on stereotypes that do not have a factual basis.

Children may discriminate against other children on account of their differences. This often takes the form of name-calling and teasing, and may be directed at children who are either fatter or thinner than others in the group, or who wear different clothes.

Stereotypes and labels

Stereotypes and labels can lead to discrimination. It is important to avoid labelling or stereotyping people. Stereotyped thinking can prevent you from seeing someone as an individual with particular life experiences and interests, and lead to negative attitudes, prejudice and discrimination. Examples are:

- **Racism or racial discrimination**: the belief that some 'races' are superior to others – based on the false idea that different physical characteristics (like skin colour) or ethnic background make some people better than others. For example: refusing a child a nursery place because they are black; failing to address the needs of children from a minority religious or cultural group, such as children from Traveller families; only acknowledging festivals from the mainstream Christian culture, such as Christmas and Easter.

- **Sexism and sex discrimination**: this occurs when people of one gender reinforce the stereotype that they are superior to the other. For example: boys are routinely offered more opportunities for 'rough-and-tumble' play than girls; some early years practitioners may encourage girls to perform traditional 'female' tasks such as cooking and washing.
- **Ageism and age discrimination**: negative feelings are expressed towards a person or group because of their age. In Western society it is usually directed towards older people; however, young people are often excluded because they are thought to be too young to participate. For example, in the UK young people are not permitted to vote until they are 18.
- **Disablism and disability discrimination**: disabled people are seen in terms of their disability, rather than as unique individuals who happen to have special needs. Children and young people with disabilities or impairments may be denied equality of opportunity with their non-disabled peers. For example: failing to provide children with special needs with appropriate facilities and services; organising activities in a nursery setting in a way that ignores the special physical, intellectual and emotional needs of certain children.

There are many other stereotypes that can lead to discrimination – such as those concerning gay and lesbian groups, people from low socio-economic groups and those who practise a minority religion.

Scenarios: making assumptions

1 Sam, Jason, Laura and Fatima are playing in the role play area. The nursery teacher asks Sam and Jason to tidy away the train set and trucks, and asks Laura and Fatima to put the dolls and cooking pots away, as it is nearly storytime.

The assumption here is that dolls and cooking utensils are 'girl' playthings, whereas trains and

trucks are 'boy' playthings. The teacher is reinforcing this stereotype by separating the tasks by gender.

2 Paul's mother arrives at the school open day. She is in a wheelchair, being pushed by Paul's father. The teacher welcomes the parents and then asks Paul's father if his wife would like a drink and a biscuit.

This is a common feature of daily life for people who use wheelchairs. They are often ignored and questions are addressed to their companion, often because the other person is embarrassed by the unusual situation and afraid of making a mistake. The assumption here is that the person in the wheelchair would not be able to understand and reply to what is said to them.

3 Members of staff are having a tea break and discussing a new child who has just started at their school. Julie says, 'I can't stand the way these Travellers think they can just turn up at school whenever they feel like it – they don't pay taxes you know, and they live practically on top of rubbish dumps … poor little mite, he doesn't know any different.'

An assumption has been made which is based on prejudice and stereotyped thinking. In this case, Travellers are assumed to be 'scroungers' and to live in unhygienic conditions. Such attitudes will be noticed by all the children in the class and may result in the individual child being treated differently, damaging their self-esteem and leading to feelings of rejection.

4 Harry's mother is a registered heroin addict who has been attending a drug rehabilitation programme for the last few months. Whenever Harry behaves in an aggressive way to other children or to staff, one staff member always makes a jibe about his home life: 'Harry, you may get away with that sort of thing where you come from, but it won't work here. We know all about you.'

This is an extreme and very unkind form of stereotyping. It is assuming that, because his mother is a drug user, Harry is somehow less worthy of consideration and respect. By drawing attention to his home life, the member of staff is guilty of prejudice and discriminatory behaviour. There is also a breach of the policy of confidentiality.

The effects of discrimination

Children can experience discrimination in a number of ways. Discrimination can be direct or indirect:

- **Direct discrimination** occurs when a child is treated less favourably than another child in the same or similar circumstances. For example, when a child is bullied, by being ignored, verbally or physically abused, or teased (see also pages 61–2 on bullying).
- **Indirect discrimination** occurs when a condition is applied that will unfairly affect a particular group of children when compared to others; this may be either deliberate or unintended. For example, when children from a minority ethnic or religious group (such as Sikh, Muslim or Plymouth Brethren) are required to wear a specific school uniform which causes difficulties within their cultural code.

Discrimination of any kind prevents children and young people from developing a feeling of self-worth or self-esteem. The effects of being discriminated against can last the whole of a child's life. In particular, they may:

- be unable to fulfil their potential, because they are made to feel that their efforts are not valued or recognised by others
- find it hard to form relationships with others because of low self-worth or self-esteem
- be so affected by the stereotypes or labels applied to them that they start to believe in them and so behave in accordance with others' expectations. This then becomes a **self-fulfilling prophecy**: for example, if a child is repeatedly told that he is clumsy, he may act in a clumsy way even when quite capable of acting otherwise
- feel shame about their own cultural background
- feel that they are in some way to blame for their unfair treatment, and so withdraw into themselves
- lack confidence in trying new activities if their attempts are always ridiculed or put down
- be aggressive towards others: distress or anger can prevent children and young people from interacting cooperatively with other children and young people.

Key terms

Anti-discrimination – An approach which challenges unfair or unlawful treatment of individuals or groups based on a specific characteristic of that group (such as colour, age, disability, sexual orientation).

Discrimination – Treating a person less favourably than others in the same or similar circumstances.

Assessment practice

Unit 3

- How do policies and procedures help to safeguard children and promote fair, just and inclusive strategies?
- Give examples of how settings may prepare children for transfer or transitions
- Explain the causes and effects of discrimination on children.

Useful resources

Organisations and websites

National Society for the Prevention of Cruelty to Children (NSPCC) campaigns against cruelty to children, and runs Childline, the free, confidential helpline for children and young people. The NSPCC also offers services to support children and families, and can investigate cases where child abuse is suspected:
www.nspcc.org.uk

Working Together to Safeguard Children is the government's guide to inter-agency working to safeguard and promote the welfare of children:
www.everychildmatters.gov.uk

The Anna Freud Centre was established in 1947 by Anna Freud to support the emotional wellbeing of children through direct work with children and their families, research and the development of practice, and training mental health practitioners:
www.annafreud.org

Kidscape is a charity established specifically to prevent bullying and child sexual abuse. The website includes resources for parents, children and professionals, and details of campaigns and training events:
www.kidscape.org.uk

National Strategies (Early Years) is the government's programme for developing practice in the early years in England, including statutory requirements, advice on best practice, and research findings:
http://www.education.gov.uk/schools/toolsandinitiatives/nationalstrategies

Childnet – their Know IT All website contains resources designed to help educate parents, carers, teachers and young people about safe and positive use of the internet. Available free at:
www.childnet.com/kia/

Books

Axline, V. (1971) *Dibs, In Search of Self: Personality Development in Play Therapy*. London: Penguin.
Department of Health (2003) *What To Do If You're Worried A Child Is Being Abused*. London: Department of Health. Free copies of this booklet are available via the DH website: www.dh.gov.uk
Lindon, J. (2003) *Child Protection* (second edn). London: Hodder & Stoughton.
Lindon, J. (2012) *Safeguarding and Child Protection 0–8 Years* (fourth edn). London: Hodder Education.

Section 1: How to identify and develop strategies to establish and maintain healthy, safe and secure environments

Safety is a basic human need. When working with children and young people you need to know how to provide a safe, healthy environment. This involves knowing how to assess risks to children's safety and to ensure that any such risks are minimised. A fine balance must be achieved which allows children to explore their environment and to learn for themselves, but also ensures that the environment in which children are playing and learning is as safe and healthy as possible.

Health and safety legislation

There are many regulations, laws and guidelines dealing with health and safety. You do not need to know the detail, but you do need to know where your responsibilities begin and end. The most relevant laws relating to health and safety in the child care setting are listed in Table 4.1.

Relevant laws relating to health and safety	
Health and Safety at Work Act 1974	**Health and Safety (First Aid) Regulations 1981**
Personal Protective Equipment at Work Regulations 1992	Control of Substances Hazardous to Health Regulations 2002 (COSHH)
Reporting of Injuries, Diseases and Dangerous Occurrences Regulations 1995 (RIDDOR)	The Food Hygiene Regulations 2006
Fire Precautions (Workplace) Regulations 1997 (amended 1999)	Care Standards Act 2000
Data Protection Act 1998	Children Act 1989
Children Act 2004	Childcare Act 2006
Management of Health and Safety at Work Regulations 1999	Manual Handling Operations Regulations 1992

Table 4.1 Relevant laws relating to health and safety in the child care setting

Health and Safety at Work Act 1974

Employers have a duty to:

● make your workplace as safe as they are able display a Health and Safety Law poster or supply employees with a leaflet with the same information (available from the Health and Safety Executive)

- decide how to manage health and safety: if the business has five or more employees, this must appear on a written Health and Safety Policy.

As an employee, you have a duty to:

- work safely. If you are given guidance about how to use equipment, you should follow that guidance. You should not work in a way that puts other people in danger.

Fire Precautions (Workplace) Regulations 1997 (amended 1999)

Fire Safety Officers must check all child care premises while they are in the first registration process. They will advise on what is needed to make the workplace as safe as possible.

- Evacuation procedures should be in place, known to all the adults, and practised regularly using all available exits at different times, so that everyone can leave the building quickly and safely if an emergency occurs.
- Some exits may be locked to prevent children wandering away or intruders entering, but adults must be able to quickly open them in case of an emergency.
- Designated fire exits must always be unlocked and kept unobstructed. Fire extinguishers should be in place and checked regularly. A fire blanket is needed in the kitchen.
- In accordance with the Regulatory Reform (Fire Safety) Order 2005, the responsible person in the setting is required to carry out a fire risk assessment for all those who are on or around the premises.

Control of Substances Hazardous to Health Regulations 2002 (COSHH)

Solutions such as bleach or dishwasher powders, some solvent glues and other materials in your setting can be hazardous. You should have a Risk Assessment that tells you what these things are, and what to do to minimise the risks involved. Any new person coming to the team must be made aware of what to do.

Reporting of Injuries, Diseases and Dangerous Occurrences Regulations 1995 (RIDDOR)

An accident book must be kept in which incidents that happen to staff are recorded. If an incident occurs at work that is serious enough to keep an employee off work for three or more days, employers will need to fill in the relevant paperwork and send the report to the Health and Safety Executive. They may investigate serious incidents and give advice on how to improve practice if needed.

Health and Safety (First Aid) Regulations 1981

Employers should make sure that at least one person at each session has an up-to-date first aid qualification and is the 'Appointed' first aider. In child care settings regulated by OfSTED, there is also a requirement for a staff member to be trained in 'Paediatric First Aid'. Methods of dealing with incidents to adults and children are not the same, particularly where resuscitation is involved. Recommendations change, and for this reason, first aid qualifications must be renewed every three years.

The Food Hygiene Regulations 2006

If you prepare or handle food, even something as basic as opening biscuits or preparing food for a snack, you need to comply with Food Handling regulations. These cover what might be seen as common sense things:

- washing your hands before preparing food
- making sure that the surfaces and utensils you use are clean and hygienic
- making sure that food is stored safely at the correct temperature
- disposing of waste hygienically.

These regulations also include knowledge of safe practices in the use of chopping boards, having separate sinks for hand washing and preparing foods, how to lay out a kitchen and so on. There should always be people who have completed a Basic

Food Hygiene certificate available to ensure that guidance is properly carried out.

Personal Protective Equipment at Work Regulations 1992

Under these regulations, employers must make sure that suitable protective equipment is provided for employees who are exposed to a risk to their health and safety while at work. This is considered a last resort, for the risk should be prevented wherever possible. In child care the most important piece of personal protective equipment that is provided will be gloves, to be used when dealing with body fluids.

Employees and students should be made aware of the need to use these when changing nappies or dealing with blood spillage or vomit. Good hygiene protects both adults and children.

Data Protection Act 1998

Anyone who keeps records, whether on computers or on paper, should comply with this Act. It should be clear to service-users for what purpose the data is being kept. Information about a child should also be accessible to its parent/carer and shared with them. It is not necessary to do this 'on demand'. A convenient time to be able to discuss the information can be arranged.

Information should not be kept for longer than necessary, though accident and incident records will need to be kept in case they are needed for reference at some time in the future. Records must also be stored securely.

Children Act 1989

The Children Act 1989 brought together several sets of guidance and provided the basis for many of the standards we maintain with children. It first outlined the amount of space that should be available as well as the adult:child ratio for work with children aged under eight. This is based on the age of the children being cared for. The minimum ratio is set out in Table 4.2.

Age of children	Number of adults: children (ratio)
0–1	1:3
2–3	1:4
3–8	1:8

Table 4.2 The adult: child ratio in childcare settings

Some places have slightly different ratios depending on local conditions, such as the number of rooms used, or the location of the toilets if not directly off the main room. Local authority nursery classes and schools may also work on a ratio of one adult to ten children where a trained teacher is in charge. Children in Reception classes or older do not have specified ratios, though 1:6 is recommended for outings.

The Children Act also outlined some of the principles that we now take for granted:

- The welfare of the child is most important.
- Practitioners should work in partnership with parents.
- Parents should care for their children whenever possible.
- Children's opinions should be taken into account when matters concern them.

Childcare Act 2006

As we saw in Chapter 3, the needs of children and their parents are at the heart of this Act.

Working practices that contribute to healthy, safe and secure environments

Policies and procedures

Each early years setting will have **policy documents** covering such areas as:

- safety
- health and hygiene
- safety at arrival and departure times and on outings

- prevention of illness and first aid
- fire prevention
- staffing ratios and supervision.

In group care and education settings, a member of staff is usually nominated as being responsible for health and safety; in a childminder's home or if you are working as a nanny, you can contact the local Childminding Association or nanny agency for information on health and safety.

Lines of responsibility and reporting

Your setting's health and safety policy will contain the names of staff members responsible for health and safety. All practitioners are responsible for health and safety in any setting.

Your responsibilities include:

- taking reasonable care for **your own safety** and that of others
- working with your employer in respect of **health and safety** matters
- knowing about the **policies and procedures** in your particular place of work – these can all be found in the setting's **health and safety** policy documents
- not intentionally damaging any health and safety equipment or materials provided by the employer
- **reporting all accidents**, incidents and even 'near misses' to your manager. As you may be handling food, you should also report any **incidences of sickness** or diarrhoea. If you are unable to contact the sick child's parents or carer (or other emergency contact person), then you will need to seek medical advice. Always ask your supervisor or manager if in doubt.
- **reporting any hazards** immediately you come across them.

Apart from your legal responsibilities, knowing how to act and being alert and vigilant at all times can prevent accidents, injury, infections and even death – this could be in relation to you, your fellow workers or the children in your care.

Risk assessment

Risk assessment is a method of preventing accidents and ill health by helping people to think about what could go wrong and devising ways to prevent problems.

1 Look for the hazards.
2 Decide who might be harmed and how.
3 Weigh up the risk – a risk is the likelihood that a hazard will cause harm.
4 Decide whether existing precautions are sufficient.
5 If they are not, decide what further precautions are needed to reduce risk.
6 Record your findings.

Identifying hazards in childcare settings

General safety – slips, trips and falls

You will need to check before, during and after play sessions and remove any items that prevent children – and yourself – from getting from A to B safely. Always be aware of children with special needs – for example, those with mobility problems or a visual impairment. Whenever children are playing with or near water – even indoors at the water play area – they must be constantly supervised. Babies need to be protected from falls – again, close supervision is needed. Everyone who works with children should take a recognised 'baby and child' first-aid course and should periodically take refresher courses.

Moving and handling

Lifting and carrying children and moving the equipment used in childcare settings could lead to manual handling injuries such as sprains and strains.

If you do have to lift something or somebody from the ground, you should follow these rules:

- Keep your feet apart.
- Bend your knees and keep your back upright.
- Use both hands to get a secure hold.
- Keep your shoulders level, your back upright and slowly straighten your legs.
- To put the load down, take the weight on the legs by bending your knees.

COSHH – Control of Substances Hazardous to Health Regulations

Safe workplaces depend on the careful use and storage of cleaning materials and other potentially hazardous substances. Every workplace must have a COSHH file which lists all the hazardous substances used in the setting. The file should detail:

- where they are kept
- how they are labelled
- their effects
- the maximum amount of time it is safe to be exposed to them
- how to deal with an emergency involving one of them
- never mix products together: they could produce toxic fumes. Some bleaches and cleaning products, for instance, have this effect.

Being a good role model

You need to set a good example by always taking care with your appearance and your own personal hygiene. Often your early years setting will provide you with a uniform – usually sweatshirt and trousers – but if not, choose your clothing carefully, bearing in mind the sort of activity you are likely to be involved in.

Guidelines: being a good role model for personal hygiene

- Personal hygiene involves regular and thorough cleaning of your skin, hair, teeth and clothes.

  The most important defence against the spread of infection is hand-washing. Wash your hands frequently – especially before eating, and before and after touching your mouth or nose. You should not use the kitchen sink to wash your hands.

- Parents and carers must wash their hands after they blow the nose or wipe the mouth of a sick child.
- Use paper towels to dry your hands if possible; if cloth towels are used, make sure that they are washed daily in hot water.
- Keep your nails clean and short as long finger nails harbour dirt. Do not wear nail varnish because flakes of varnish could chip off into the snack you are preparing.
- Avoid jewellery other than a simple wedding ring and a watch.
- Avoid contact with the secretions (especially on stray facial tissues) of somebody with a runny nose, sore throat or cough.
- Cover any cuts or sores on the hands with a clean, waterproof plaster. Use a new plaster each day.
- Do not share utensils or cups with somebody who has a cold, sore throat or upper respiratory tract infection.
- Wear disposable gloves when changing nappies or when dealing with blood, urine, faeces or vomit.
- Hair should be kept clean, be brushed regularly and be tied back, if long.

Providing a safe, hygienic indoor environment

Children need a clean, warm and hygienic environment in order to stay healthy. Although most large early years settings employ a cleaner, there will be many occasions when you have to take responsibility for ensuring that the environment is kept clean and safe; for example if a child has been sick or has had a toileting accident.

All early years settings should have set routines for tidying up and for cleaning the floors, walls, furniture and play equipment; details may be found in the setting's written policy for health and hygiene issues.

Guidelines for providing a safe and hygienic indoor environment

1 Adequate ventilation is important to disperse bacteria or viruses transmitted through sneezing or coughing. Make sure that windows are opened to let in fresh air to the nursery – but also make sure there are no draughts.

2 Cleaning routines:

- All surfaces should be damp-dusted daily. Floors, surfaces and the toilet area must be checked on a regular basis for cleanliness.

- All toys and play equipment should be cleaned regularly – at least once a week. This includes dressing-up clothes and soft toys. Use antiseptic solutions such as Savlon to disinfect toys and play equipment regularly; toys used by babies under one year should be disinfected daily.

- Check that sandpits or trays are clean and that toys are removed and cleaned at the end of a play session; if the sandpit is kept outside, make sure it is kept covered when not in use. Keep sand trays clean by sieving and washing the sand regularly.

- Water trays should be emptied daily, as germs can multiply quickly in pools of water.

- The home area often contains dolls, saucepans and plastic food; these need to be included in the checking and in the regular wash.

- As well as routine cleaning, you should always clean up any spills straight away; both young children and adults often slip on wet surfaces.

3 Use paper towels and tissues, and dispose of them in covered bins.

4 Remove from the nursery any toy that has been in contact with a child who has an infectious illness.

5 Throw out any plastic toys that have cracks or splits in them, as these cracks can harbour germs.

6 Particular care should be taken to keep hats, head coverings and hairbrushes clean, in order to help prevent the spread of head lice.

7 Animals visiting the nursery or nursery pets must be free from disease, safe to be with children and must not pose a health risk. Children should always be supervised when handling animals, and make sure that they always wash their hands after touching any pet.

8 A 'no smoking' policy must be observed by staff and visitors.

Providing a safe and hygienic outdoor environment

Children benefit from playing in the fresh air, as long as they are dressed for the weather. All early years settings should be checked regularly to make sure that a safe and hygienic environment is being provided.

Guidelines for ensuring a hygienic outdoor environment

1 Check the outdoor play area daily for litter, dog excrement and hazards such as broken glass, syringes or rusty cans.

2 Follow the sun safety code: provide floppy hats and use sun cream (SPF 15) to prevent sunburn (if parents give their permission).

3 Check all play equipment for splinters, jagged edges, protruding nails and other hazards.

4 Supervise children at all times.

5 Keep sand covered and check regularly for insects, litter and other contamination.

6 Keep gates locked and check that hinges are secure.

Safety and security

One of the cornerstones of early childhood care and education is to offer an exciting range of experiences to children, which will stimulate them and extend their skills in all areas of development. As they grow, you need to be responsive to their changing safety needs at each stage of development. Close supervision is the most effective way of ensuring children's safety.

Supervising children's safety

The most important thing to remember when caring for children is to treat each child as an individual – with individual needs. Babies' and young children's abilities will differ over time; it may be surprising when they do things for the first time but you should be able to anticipate, adapt and avoid dangerous situations in order to maintain their safety and security. In particular, babies have no awareness of danger and are therefore totally dependent on their carers for protection and survival. Appropriate levels of supervision, provided by you, are therefore essential.

For example, babies under one year old are able to wriggle, grasp, suck and roll over and are naturally curious. Toddlers, too, can move very quickly, so accidents often happen in seconds. As children grow and their physical skills increase, they are better able to explore their environment, which means they are more likely to have knocks and bruises and you need to ensure that they can play in safety.

A safe environment

- Not only broken or damaged equipment and toys can be a risk to children's safety: you need to make sure that the activity or plaything a child uses is suitable for them. This means checking that the child is at the right stage of development to be able to play safely with the toy.

Special needs: children with special needs may need specialised equipment and playthings in order to participate safely in the daily activities in any childcare setting; more often, they just need to have very slight changes made to the environment. For example, a child with physical difficulties might benefit from having velcro straps attached to the pedals of a bike.

- **Doors, gates and windows** should be appropriately fastened to ensure the safety of the children. Any nursery or playgroup must be secure so that children cannot just wander off without anyone realising; there should also be a policy which guards against strangers being able to wander in without reason.
- Many early years settings now have **door entry phones**, and staff wear name badges or identifiable uniform. Be sure to challenge, politely, anyone who is unfamiliar to you in the setting or gives you cause for suspicion as to why they are there, and keep a record of any visitors.
- **Access points and fire exits** must be unobstructed at all times.
- **Play equipment**: all equipment used for children's play should be checked routinely and

any damaged items should be removed from the scene and reported to your supervisor. You will be expected to check for objects which stick out on equipment and could cut a child or cause clothing to become entangled, such as screws or bolts on trucks or playground equipment. Plastic toys and equipment can be checked for splits and cracks when you clean them. Check wooden equipment, such as wooden blocks or wheeled carts for splinters and rough edges.

- **Sandpits**: check that sandpits are covered overnight or brought indoors to prevent contamination from animals, such as cats. You should also check that no hazardous litter is in the sand – such as sharp sticks, broken glass or insects.
- **Safe storage**: sharp objects, such as scissors and knives, must be stored out of children's reach – scissors used for craft work should be children's safety scissors – and remember to remove knives from tables where children might grab them.
- **Water**: check that buckets or bowls of water are never left where children could trip into them, as children can drown in water that is only a few inches deep. If there is open water, such as a pond, drains or a pool, at or near to the setting, make sure that they are made safe and inaccessible to children, and that children are closely supervised at all times when playing with or near water.
- **Electrical equipment**: most early years settings have a variety of electrical equipment – including TV, DVD player, CD player and a computer. You need to check that the electric sockets are covered with socket covers when not in use and that there are no trailing wires on the floor or where children could grab them.
- **Outdoor safety**: before outdoor play sessions, you must check that surfaces are safe to play on – for example, not icy or slippery – and that objects which could cause children harm have been removed. Also ensure that children are properly equipped for outdoor play. They should always be dressed according to the weather, with waterproof coats and wellington boots in wet weather and warm hats and gloves on in cold weather. You also need to ensure that children are protected against strong sun – by following the Sun Safety Code. Children playing outside should be supervised at all times.

Risks and hazards

On a day-to-day basis, you need to be alert to the changing abilities and safety needs of children and also to identify and address hazards in the childcare setting. Your employer will do this on a formal basis, carrying out a health and safety risk assessment. To ensure children's safety, you need to be able to:

- **identify a hazard**: at every stage of a child's life, you must think again about the hazards that are present and what you can do to eliminate them. This could be play equipment left on the floor, obstructing an exit – or small items which have been left within reach of a baby.
- **be aware of the child's interaction with the environment**: this means understanding the different stages of child development – for example, babies explore objects with their mouths and run the risk of choking – and young children tend to run everywhere and could trip over toys on the floor.
- **provide adequate supervision**, according to each child's age, needs and abilities.
- **be a good role model**: ensuring that the child's environment is kept safe and that you follow the setting's health and safety guidelines.
- **know how to use the safety equipment provided**, e.g. safety gates, window locks, baby harnesses and security intercom systems.
- **teach children about safety**: encourage children to be aware of their own personal safety and the safety of others.

Key terms

Hazard – A source of potential harm or damage, or a situation with potential for harm or damage.

Risk – The possibility of suffering harm or loss; danger.

Risk assessment – The assessments that must be carried out in order to identify hazards and find out the safest way to carry out certain tasks and procedures.

The prevention of accidents

Accidents are the most common cause of death in children aged between one and 14 years, accounting for half of all child deaths. The pattern of accidents tends to vary with age, depending on the child's developmental progress and exposure to new hazards.

Why do accidents happen?

Babies are vulnerable to accidents because they have no awareness of danger and cannot control their environment; they are totally dependent on their parents or carers to make their world safe.

Children are naturally curious and need to investigate their surroundings. As children get older and their memory develops, they start to realise that certain actions have certain consequences – for example, touching a hot oven door hurts – so they begin to learn a measure of self-protection.

Carers of young children need to have a sound knowledge of child development in order to anticipate when an accident is likely to happen. Carers also have a duty to make the home, car and early years setting safer places, and should know where to go for advice and equipment.

Children need a safe environment so that they can explore and learn and grow. As they develop, older children need to learn how to tackle everyday dangers so that they can become safe adults. Children learn some realities of safety the hard way – for example, by banging their heads or grazing their knees. You cannot prevent them from hurting themselves altogether, but you can alert them and keep reminding them. You have an important role, not only in keeping children safe and secure, but also in teaching them to be aware of safety issues.

Teaching children about safety issues

Children under five years of age tend to be absorbed in their play and focus on the 'here and now'. However, young children *do* tend to avoid any hazard that has been identified for them. It is important that safety issues are talked about at the setting and that learning opportunities are structured into the *everyday* play curriculum. A variety of materials are available to support safety work with children, including books, pictures, posters, plays and puppets. These can support the development of awareness about road safety, water safety and fire safety in children. However, not all teaching needs to be *planned*. You can use any opportunities that arise naturally, such as an accident or a near miss that has happened to someone the children know. If children – even very young children – understand *why* the rules have been made, they will be more likely to abide by them.

When teaching young children about safety, you will need to find ways to communicate with each child according to their needs – for example, children with hearing difficulties will need both children and adults to face them so that they can see any signs and can lip-read, if the hearing loss is severe.

You should teach children:

- to carry things carefully
- never to run with anything in their mouths – this includes sweets and other food
- never to run while carrying a glass, scissors or other pointed objects; if a child falls, he or she can stab him or herself with something as simple as a pencil. Something in the child's mouth can choke him or her.

You also need to explain the reasons behind the rules you give them – for example, by saying:

- 'You must not throw sand because you will hurt your friend.'
- 'Never run into the road, because you could be hit by a car.'
- 'Do not run with a stick in your hand, as it would hurt you if you fall.'

For most children, you need to repeat these fundamental safety rules over and over again, so that they remember them.

Guidelines for preventing accidents

1 Be a good role model – set a safe example.

2 Make the home, garden and childcare setting as accident-proof as possible.

3 Teach children about safety – make them aware of dangers in their environment.

4 Never leave children alone in the house.

5 Always try to buy goods displaying the appropriate safety symbol:

- **The Kite Mark** (BSI) (see Figure 4.1(a)). This mark on any product means that the British Standards Institution (BSI) has checked the manufacturer's claim that its product meets specific standards.

- **The Lion Mark** (see Figure 4.1(b)). This symbol is only found on British-made toys and means that they have met the safety standards required.

- **The age advice safety symbol** (see Figure 4.1(c)). This symbol means 'Warning: do not give the toy to children of less than three years, or allow them to play with it'.

Note that toys and games bought from market stalls, and cheap foreign imports may be copies of well-known brand-name toys but may not meet the safety standards. Also, second-hand toys and games may not have original packaging/symbols, so checks will need to be made.

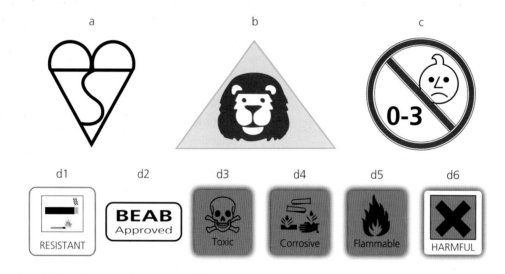

Figure 4.1 (a) the Kite Mark (b) the Lion Mark (c) the age advice safety symbol (d) other safety symbols

Guidelines for ensuring safety in the childcare setting

- Children should be supervised at all times.

- Premises must be large enough, and – in early years settings – should provide a separate area for the care of babies and toddlers.

- The nursery environment and all materials and equipment should be maintained in a safe condition.

- Low-level glass (such as in doors and cupboards) should be safety glass or must be covered with boarding or guards; sharp corners on low-level furniture should be padded.

- There must be adequate first aid facilities and staff should be trained in basic first aid.

- Routine safety checks should be made daily on the premises, both indoors and outdoors.

Guidelines for ensuring safety in the childcare setting (cont.)

- Fire drills should be held twice a term in schools and nurseries and every six weeks in day nurseries. Fire exits must be left accessible and unlocked at all times.
- Electric sockets should be covered.
- Floor surfaces should be clean and free of splinters.
- Access should be easy for prams, pushchairs and wheelchairs.
- Kitchen facilities must be adequate in terms of hygiene, storage and safety.
- Children should only be allowed home with a parent or authorised adult.

The importance of road safety

Some facts about children and road safety

- Every week, on average, nine children under the age of six years are killed or seriously injured on Great Britain's roads.
- Children under five years cannot judge how fast vehicles are going or how far away they are.
- If hit by a car travelling at 40 mph, four out of five child pedestrians will die. If hit by a car travelling at 30 mph, four out of five will survive. Children's survival rates increase even more, the lower the speed of the car.
- The peak time for child casualties is weekdays, 3 pm to 5 pm, coinciding with the end of the school day. Friday is the peak day for child casualties.

Educating children about road safety

Educating children about safety on the roads should begin at a very early age, the best method being by example. Children need to learn about road safety in the same way as they learn any new skill: the message needs to be repeated over and over again until the child really has learned it. Every local authority employs a Road Safety Officer, and the Royal Society for the Prevention of Accidents (RoSPA) runs campaigns for children of all ages.

When walking on the pavement, parents and carers should:

- set a good example, as young children will copy adults
- hold the child's hand and put reins on a younger child if he or she is not strapped in a pushchair
- not allow the child to run ahead
- look out for and encourage the child to be aware of hidden entrances or driveways crossing the pavement
- make sure the child walks on the side of the pavement away from the traffic
- not let the child out alone or even with an older child
- always use a zebra or light-controlled crossing, or a school crossing patrol, if there is one.

'Walking bus' schemes, which allow children to walk to and from school safely in supervised groups, can also help children learn how to negotiate roads safely.

Children should wear fluorescent jackets which fit over their normal clothing when out at dusk or when walking on country roads without pavements.

The Green Cross Code

The Green Cross Code is a very good method of teaching road safety to young children.

The Green Cross Code

1. Think first. Find the safest place to cross then stop.

2. Stop. Stand on the pavement near the kerb.

3. Use your eyes and ears. Look all around for traffic and listen.

4. Wait till it is safe to cross. If traffic is coming let it pass.

5. Look and listen. When it is safe, walk straight across the road.

6. Arrive alive. Keep looking and listening for traffic while you cross.

Figure 4.2 The Green Cross Code

Food hygiene and basic hygiene practices

What is food poisoning?

Any infectious disease that results from consuming food or drink is known as **food poisoning**. The term is most often used to describe the illness (usually diarrhoea and/or vomiting) caused by bacteria, viruses or parasites.

Most cases of food poisoning result from eating large numbers of pathogenic (or harmful) bacteria that are living on the food. Most food poisoning is preventable, although it is not possible to eliminate the risk completely.

At risk – babies and young children

Babies and very young children are at particular risk from food poisoning, partly because they have immature immune systems. Also, infection can spread very quickly in young children, if there is a lack of supervised thorough hand-washing after using the toilet and before eating, and from touching contaminated toilet seats and tap handles. Many young children also put their hands, fingers and thumbs in their mouths frequently, so hands should be kept clean.

How bacteria from food sources make you ill

Bacteria – or germs – found in food can lead to food poisoning, which can be dangerous and can kill (though this is rare). They are very hard to detect since they do not usually affect the taste, appearance or smell of food.

Bacteria can either be present in food, or can come from other people, surfaces or equipment, or from other food through cross-contamination.

The main causes of bacterial food poisoning are:

*   **Undercooking** – for example, when the oven is not hot enough (or used for long enough) to ensure that the inside of, for example, a chicken is completely cooked. It is essential that frozen raw meat and poultry is adequately thawed, followed by thorough cooking to ensure that any pathogenic bacteria are destroyed.
*   **Food prepared too far in advance and then not refrigerated** – for example, when a ham sandwich is left out of the fridge – uncovered or covered –

for several hours. Food poisoning bacteria can multiply rapidly at room temperature. All food prepared in advance must be refrigerated to ensure minimal bacterial growth. For this reason, fridges should operate between 0 °C and 5 °C.

- **Poor personal hygiene** – for example, when a person prepares food without washing their hands properly. Poor personal hygiene can result in food becoming contaminated with bacteria. Hands must be washed as frequently as necessary but definitely:
  - before handling food or equipment
  - after visiting the toilet
  - in between handling raw and cooked food, and
  - after handling waste food or refuse.

Cross-contamination – for example, when a knife that has been used to cut raw meat is not washed and is then used to cut cooked or ready-to-eat food. Food poisoning bacteria may be present in raw food such as meat and poultry. If these bacteria are allowed to contaminate food that is to be eaten without further cooking, food poisoning can result. Cross-contamination from raw food may happen as a result of poor storage, when the juices from raw meat are allowed to drip on to cooked food, or via a chopping board or utensils used for both raw and cooked food.

Infected food handlers – for example, a person who returns to work after a brief episode of vomiting and diarrhoea may still be a carrier of food-poisoning bacteria. Any person suffering from vomiting and/ or diarrhoea should not prepare or serve food until totally clear of symptoms for at least 48 hours. Even then, extra attention to hand-washing is essential. Septic boils and cuts are another potential source of pathogens. Uninfected wounds should be completely covered and protected by a waterproof dressing.

Failure to keep cooked food hot – for example, serving food that has been allowed to stand and become cool – under 63 °C – after cooking. As thorough cooking does not destroy spores, hot food kept below 63 °C can allow the spores to germinate and produce food-poisoning bacteria. For this reason, it is important to keep hot food above 63 °C.

Eating food from unsafe sources – for example, buying food from a shop that does not refrigerate its products properly.

Key terms

Gastroenteritis – Inflammation of the stomach and intestines, often causing sudden and violent upsets. Diarrhoea, cramps, nausea and vomiting are common symptoms.

Pathogen – A micro-organism, such as a bacterium or virus, which causes disease. The lay term is 'germ'.

Preventing food poisoning: why washing your hands is vital

Even healthy people carry food-poisoning bacteria on their bodies. These can be spread to the hands through touching parts of the body that contain them, such as the nose, mouth or bottom, and then from the hands to the food.

Hands are the most obvious way in which a person can contaminate food, because they touch utensils, work surfaces and the food itself when it is being prepared, served or eaten. Nails can also harbour dirt and bacteria and should be kept short and clean at all times.

If hands are not clean, they can spread food-poisoning bacteria around the kitchen. Washing your hands thoroughly is a good way to reduce the chance of passing on bacteria. This should include washing the backs of hands, wrists, between the fingers and under fingernails with soap and warm water, and then drying them thoroughly.

Guidelines on how to wash our hands effectively

We all think we know how to wash our hands but many of us do not do it properly. Figure 4.3 shows how we often miss certain parts of our hands – particularly our thumbs and between our fingers - when washing them. Follow this step-by-step guide to effective hand washing:

- Wet your hands thoroughly under *warm* running water and squirt liquid soap onto the palm of one hand.
- Rub your hands together to make a lather.
- Rub the palm of one hand along the back of the other and along the fingers. Then do the same with the other hand.
- Rub in between each of your fingers on both hands and around your thumbs.
- Rinse off the soap with clean running water.
- Dry hands thoroughly on a clean dry towel, paper towel or air dryer.

This should take about 15–20 seconds.

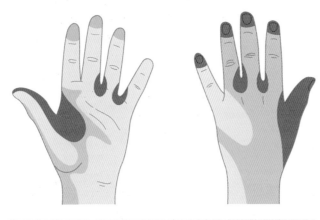

Figure 4.3 Parts commonly missed when washing hands. Red = parts commonly missed; orange = parts sometimes missed; cream = parts rarely missed

Preventing food poisoning: storing food safely

- Keep food cold. The fridge should be kept as cold as it will go without actually freezing the food (1–5 °C or 34–41 °F).
- Cover or wrap food with food wrap or microwave cling film.
- Never refreeze food that has begun to thaw.
- Do not use perishable foods that are past their use-by dates.
- Always read instructions on the label when storing food.

- Once a tin is opened, store the contents in a covered dish in the fridge.
- Store raw foods at the bottom of the fridge so that juices cannot drip onto cooked food.
- Thaw frozen meat completely before cooking.

Preparing and cooking food safely

- Always wash hands in warm water and soap, and dry on a clean towel, before handling food and after handling raw foods, especially meat.
- Wear clean, protective clothing that is solely for use in the kitchen.
- Keep food covered at all times.
- Wash all fruits and vegetables before eating. Peel and top carrots and peel fruits such as apples.
- Never cough or sneeze over food.
- Always cover any septic cuts or boils with a waterproof dressing.
- Never smoke in any room that is used for food.
- Keep work surfaces and chopping boards clean and disinfected; use separate boards for raw meat, fish, vegetables and so on, to avoid cross-contamination.
- Make sure that meat dishes are thoroughly cooked.
- Avoid raw eggs. They sometimes contain salmonella bacteria, which may cause food poisoning. (Also avoid giving children uncooked

cake mixture, homemade ice creams, mayonnaise or desserts that contain uncooked raw egg.) When cooking eggs, the egg yolk and white should be firm.

- When reheating food, make sure that it is piping hot all the way through, and allow it to cool slightly before giving it to children. When using a microwave, always stir and check the temperature of the food before feeding children, to avoid burning from 'hot spots'.
- Avoid leftovers – they are a common cause of food poisoning.

Keeping the kitchen safe

- Teach children to wash their hands after touching pets and going to the toilet, and before eating.
- Clean tin-openers, graters and mixers thoroughly after use.
- Cover cups/beakers with a clean cloth and air-dry where possible.
- Keep flies and other insects away – use a fine mesh over open windows.
- Stay away from the kitchen if you are suffering from diarrhoea or sickness.
- Keep the kitchen clean – the floor, work surfaces, sink, utensils, cloths and waste bins should be cleaned regularly.
- Ensure any washing-up by hand is done thoroughly in hot water, with detergent; you should use rubber gloves.
- Tea towels should be boiled every day and dishcloths boiled or disinfected.
- Keep pets away from the kitchen.
- Keep all waste bins covered and empty them regularly.
- Keep sharp knives stored safely where children cannot reach them.

Did you know?

- The number of bacteria on fingertips doubles after using the toilet.
- Bacteria can stay alive on our hands for up to three hours.
- 1,000 times as many bacteria spread from damp hands than from dry hands.

- Even after thorough washing, bugs (such as E. coli) can remain under long fingernails.
- Millions of bacteria can hide under rings, watches and bracelets.
- A 1 mm hair follicle can harbour 50,000 bacteria.

Section 2: The procedures for dealing with accidents, illnesses and other emergencies

Everyone who works with children should attend a first aid course. There are now specialist courses, such as the St John's **Early Years First Aid** (paediatric) and the British Red Cross's **First Aid for Child Carers**. Childminders must have attended a training course within six months of registration and must hold a current paediatric first aid certificate at the point of registration. Once you have learnt how to respond to an emergency you never lose that knowledge, and knowing how means that you could save a life one day.

Dealing with accidents and emergencies

How to get emergency help

- Assess the situation – stay calm and do not panic.
- Minimise any danger to yourself and to others – for example, make sure that someone takes charge of other children at the scene.
- Send for help – notify a doctor, hospital, parents, and so on, as appropriate. If in any doubt, call an ambulance: **dial 999 or 112**.

Calling an ambulance

Be ready to assist the emergency services by providing the following information:

- Give your name and the telephone number you are calling from.
- Tell the operator the location of the accident. Try to give as much information as possible – for example, are there any familiar landmarks, such as churches or pubs, nearby?
- Explain briefly what has happened – this helps the paramedics to act speedily when they arrive.
- Tell the operator what you have done so far to treat the casualty.

First aid box

All first aid boxes should have a white cross on a green background. There is no mandatory list of items to put in a first aid box, but guidelines published by the National Association of Child Minders NCMA, as well as Ofsted and experienced paediatric first aid trainers, recommend that the first aid box in a childcare setting should contain:

- one First Aid Guidance Leaflet
- one large sterile wound dressing
- one pair disposable gloves
- ten individually wrapped wipes
- two sterile eye pads
- one pair of scissors
- one packet hypoallergenic plasters – in assorted sizes
- three medium sterile wound dressings
- two triangular bandages
- five finger bob bandages (no applicator needed)
- four safety pins.

Large nurseries and schools may have more than one first aid box and the contents will vary according to individual needs; for example, a nursery setting will have a larger number of small adhesive dressings or plasters.

- The first aid box must be a strong container that keeps out both dirt and damp.
- It should be kept in an accessible place, but one that is out of reach of children.

- All employees should be informed where the first aid box is kept and it should only be moved from this safe place when in use.
- Supplies must be replaced as soon as possible after use.

It is recommended that you do not keep tablets and medicines in the first aid box.

Research Activity

Accident and incident reporting

Find out about policies and procedures relating to first aid in your work setting. In particular, find out the following:

- Where is the first aid kit kept, and is it easy to reach quickly?
- Who is responsible for replenishing the first aid box?
- Where is the accident report book kept?
- In what circumstances do you have to report an incident or accident at your work setting to the Health and Safety Executive?

Dealing with illness

Recognising signs of illness

The responsibility of caring for a child who becomes ill is enormous; it is vital that carers should know the signs and symptoms of illness and when to seek medical aid. When a child is taken ill or is injured, it is vital that the parents or carers are notified as soon as possible.

Provide comfort and reassurance

If a child becomes ill while at nursery, he or she may have to wait a while to be taken home. In the meantime you should:

- offer support and reassurance to the child, who may feel frightened or anxious
- always notify a senior member of staff if you notice that a child is unwell; that person will then decide if and when to contact the child's parents

or carers. A member of staff (preferably the child's key person) should remain with the child all the time and keep them as comfortable as possible.

You must deal with any incident of vomiting or diarrhoea swiftly and sympathetically to minimise the child's distress and to preserve their dignity. All settings have an exclusion policy that lets parents know when it is safe for their sick child to return to the group.

Serious conditions

A child who has sustained a serious injury or illness will need to be seen urgently by a doctor. For example:

- a head injury or any loss of consciousness
- a wound that continues to bleed after first aid treatment is given
- suspected meningitis (see Chapter 9)
- an asthma attack not relieved by child's inhaler
- fracture or suspected fracture, burns and scalds, foreign bodies
- life-threatening incidents such as seizures, poisoning, choking, anaphylaxis, loss of consciousness, respiratory and cardiac arrest.

Key terms

Anaphylaxis – A severe allergic reaction that affects the whole body. It can lead to anaphylactic shock.

Anaphylactic shock – A potentially fatal immune response when the body system literally shuts down. The most common causes are a severe allergic reaction to insect stings and certain drugs.

What to do in case of sudden serious illness or injury

If you think the child's life is in danger, dial 999 if you are in the UK, ask for an ambulance urgently and explain the situation. Contact the family doctor (GP) if the child has any of the symptoms listed above. If the doctor cannot reach you quickly, take the child to the accident and emergency department of the nearest hospital.

1 **Call for help**: stay calm and do not panic! Your line manager (or designated first aider) will make an assessment and decide whether the injury or illness requires **medical help**, either a GP or an ambulance. He or she will also **contact the parents or carers** to let them know about the nature of the illness or injury.
2 **Stay with the child**; comfort and reassure him or her.
3 **Treat the injury** or **assess the severity of the illness** and treat appropriately. You are not expected to be able to diagnose a sudden illness, but should know what signs and symptoms require medical treatment.
4 **Record exactly what happens** and what treatment is carried out.

Remember! It is essential that you do not make the situation worse, and it is better to do the minimum to ensure the child's safety such as putting them into the recovery position. The only exception to this is if the child is not breathing or there is no heartbeat.

Emergency help for children with existing medical conditions

The following chronic medical conditions – and their management in early years settings - are described fully in Chapter 10. You need to know how to respond and care for a child who has a sudden attack or flare-up while in the group setting.

Asthma

Not all asthma attacks can be prevented. When the child is having an acute attack of wheezing – the difficulty is in breathing out rather than in catching one's breath – he needs a reliever drug (a bronchodilator, usually in a blue inhaler case). Most children will have been shown how to deliver the drug by an aerosol inhaler, a spinhaler or a nebuliser.

Guidelines for helping a child who is having an acute asthma attack

- If the attack is the child's first, call a doctor and the parents.
- Stay calm and reassure the child, who may be very frightened.
- Encourage the child to sit up to increase lung capacity.
- If the child has a reliever inhaler or nebuliser, then supervise him while using it.
- Never leave the child alone during an attack.
- Try not to let other children crowd around.

If these measures do not stop the wheezing and the child is exhausted by the attack, call a doctor. He or she will either give an injection of a bronchodilator drug or arrange admission to hospital.

Epilepsy

A seizure is caused by a sudden burst of excess electrical activity in the brain, causing a temporary disruption in the normal message-passing between brain cells. This results in the brain's messages becoming temporarily halted or mixed up. Seizures can happen at any time and generally last a matter of seconds or minutes, after which the brain usually returns to normal. Seizures are also called **convulsions** or **fits**.

The most common causes of seizures in young children are high fever (known as a **febrile convulsion** or seizure), epilepsy, head injury and poisoning.

Guidelines for helping a child who is experiencing a seizure

Do:

- protect the child from injury by moving any furniture or other solid objects out of the way during a seizure
- make space around the child and keep other children away
- loosen the clothing around the child's neck and chest and cushion their head
- stay with the child until recovery is complete
- be calmly reassuring.

Do not:

- restrain the child in any way
- try to put anything in their mouth
- try to move them unless they are in danger
- give the child anything to eat or drink until they are fully recovered
- attempt to bring them round.

Call an ambulance if:

- it is the child's first seizure and you do not know why it happened
- it follows a blow to the head
- the child is injured during the seizure
- the seizure is continuous and shows no sign of stopping – a very rare condition called status epilepticus.

Diabetes

Hypoglycaemia is the most common complication in diabetes where there is not enough sugar in the blood – usually because of too much insulin. It must be treated promptly to avoid possible brain damage from prolonged low blood sugar levels. **Hypoglycaemic attacks** – or **hypos** – are especially likely to happen **before meals**. They can also happen as a result of:

- too much **insulin**
- **too little food** at any stage of the day
- cold weather
- not enough food to fuel an **activity**
- a **missed meal** or delayed meal or snack
- the child vomiting.

How to recognise a hypo

Hypos happen quickly, but most children will have **warning signs** that will alert them, or people around them, to a hypo. Signs include:

- weakness or hunger
- confused or aggressive behaviour
- loss of concentration or coordination
- rapid, shallow breathing
- sweating
- dizziness
- glazed eyes and pallor
- headache
- trembling or shakiness.

Guidelines for first aid: how to manage a hypo

- Stay with the child – never leave them alone or expect them to go and get their own food or drink.
- Sit the child down and reassure him or her.
- Give the child a sugary drink (such as a fizzy non-diet drink) or sweet food.
- If the child recovers quickly after a sweet drink or food, give some more and allow the child to rest.
- If the child does not recover quickly or becomes unconscious, **call an ambulance immediately** and place the child in the recovery position. Always inform the parents of any hypoglycaemic attack, so that adjustments can be made to the treatment.

Sickle cell anaemia

Sickle cell anaemia is an inherited blood condition caused by abnormal **haemoglobin**. Under certain conditions the red blood cells that contain the haemoglobin and are normally round become sickle- or crescent-shaped. They clump together and lodge in the smaller blood vessels, preventing normal blood flow and resulting in **anaemia** (a lack of haemoglobin).

You should contact the parents without delay if the child with sickle cell anaemia shows the following symptoms, because he or she needs urgent hospital treatment:

- suddenly becomes unwell or appears drowsy
- complains of severe abdominal or chest pain
- complains of headache or neck stiffness.

Emergency procedures: what to do in the event of a non-medical incident or emergency

There are many different types of emergency (apart from a medical emergency when a person is seriously injured or ill) and it is important to know what procedures to follow, for example:

- if a child goes missing
- in case of fire
- if there is a security incident.

Missing children

Strict procedures must be followed to prevent a child from going missing from the setting. However, if a child does go missing, an established procedure must be followed, for example:

- The person in charge will carry out a thorough search of the building and garden.
- The register is checked to make sure that no other child has also gone astray.
- Doors and gates are checked to see if there has been a breach of security whereby a child could wander out.
- The person in charge talks to staff to establish what happened.
- If the child is not found, the parent or carer is contacted and the missing child is reported to the police.

Case Study | Missing from a nursery

A two-year-old girl walked out of her pre-school nursery one winter morning, leaving her coat behind, and crossed a busy road as she wandered half a mile to her home. The first that the nursery knew of her disappearance was when her furious father turned up demanding to know why he had found his tearful daughter struggling to open their garden gate.

Fortunately, potentially dangerous events like this are very rare, but they should be preventable.

1 How do you think that this could have happened?
2 Consider your own setting and assess whether it could happen there.
3 How could such incidents be prevented?

In case of fire

In the case of fire or other emergency, you need to know what to do to safely evacuate the children and yourselves. Follow the following rules for fire safety:

- No smoking is allowed in any childcare setting.
- Handbags containing matches or lighters must be locked securely away out of children's reach.
- The nursery cooker should not be left unattended when turned on.
- Fire exits must be clearly signed.
- Fire procedures should be tested regularly; registers must be kept up to date throughout the day.
- Fire exits and other doors should be free of obstructions on both sides.
- Instructions about what to do in the event of a fire must be clearly displayed.
- You should know where the fire extinguishers are kept and how to use them.
- Electrical equipment should be regularly checked for any faults.

Evacuation procedures

A plan for an escape route and the attendance register must be up to date so that everyone – children and staff – can safely be accounted for at the meeting point of safety. The attendance record must be taken by the person in charge when the building is evacuated. Clearly written instructions for fire drills and how to summon the fire brigade must be posted in a conspicuous place in the setting.

Security issues and violence

Early years settings and schools should be secure environments where children cannot wander off without anyone realising. But they also need to be secure so that strangers cannot enter without a proper reason for being there. Occasionally you might encounter a problem with violence – or threats of violence – from a child's parents or carers. Your setting will have a policy that deals with this issue.

Recording and reporting emergencies

Reporting to parents

All accidents, injuries or illnesses that occur to children and young people in a group setting must be reported to the child's parents or primary carers. If the injury is minor (such as a bruise or a small graze to the knee), the staff will inform parents or carers when the child/young person is collected at the end of the session; or they may send a notification slip home if someone else collects the child. The parents/carers are notified about:

- the nature of the injury or illness
- any treatment or action taken
- the name of the person who carried out the treatment.

In the case of a major accident, illness or injury, the child's parents or primary carers must be notified as soon as possible. Parents/carers need to know that staff members are dealing with the incident in a caring and professional manner, and they will need to be involved in any decisions regarding treatment.

The Accident Report Book

Every workplace is, by law, required to have an Accident Report Book and to maintain a record of accidents. Information recorded includes:

- name of person injured
- date and time of injury
- where the accident happened (for example, in the garden)
- what exactly happened (Kara fell on the path and grazed her left knee)
- what injuries occurred (a graze)
- what treatment was given (graze was bathed and an adhesive dressing applied)
- name and signature of person dealing with the accident
- signature of witness to the report
- signature of parent or carer.

One copy of the duplicated report form is given to the child's parent or carer; the other copy is kept in the Accident Report Book at the early years setting. If you are working in the family home as a nanny, you should follow the same reporting procedure, even though you do not have an official Accident Report Book.

Reporting and recording illness

If a child becomes ill while in a group setting, you should first report it to your manager or supervisor and then record the following details in the child's Daily Record:

- when the child first showed signs of illness
- the signs and symptoms: for example, behaviour changes, a high temperature or a rash
- any action taken: for example, taking the temperature or giving paracetamol (with parental permission agreed beforehand)
- progress of the illness since first noticing it: for example, are there any further symptoms?

Activity

Policies and procedures

Find out what policies and procedures apply to your setting. Make sure you know what your role is in keeping children safe and healthy.

Establishing healthy and safe routines

Routines in daily care are beneficial for all children, and contribute greatly to the provision of a positive, safe and secure environment. Daily routines include:

- safety at home times
- safety at meal and snack times
- preventing cross-infection
- safety at sleep and rest times
- hygiene routines.

Safety at home times

Your setting will have a policy stating what to do when parents or carers come to collect their child. Many children's settings have door entry phones and a password system for parents and staff to enter the premises. At home time, staff must ensure that the child is collected by the appropriate person. If parents know that they will not be able to collect their child on a particular occasion, they should notify the setting, giving permission for another named person to collect their child. The child's key person should, where possible, be responsible for handover at home times.

Safety at meal and snack times

Meal and snack times should be enjoyable occasions for both staff and children. The following safety guidelines should be followed to ensure health and safety at these times:

- **Hygiene**: wipe all surfaces where food will be served, before and after meals and snacks. Make sure that children have washed and dried their hands before eating.
- **Serving food**: check that the food you are giving children is appropriate for them; check they have no allergies, for example to milk or wheat. Never give peanuts to children under four years old as they can easily choke or inhale them into their lungs, causing infection and lung damage. Food should be cut up into manageable pieces and should be served at the correct temperature – not too hot or too cold.
- **Seating**: babies should be securely strapped into high chairs, using a five-point harness.
- **Supervision**: supervise children carefully: never leave children unattended with drinks or food in case they choke. Never leave a baby alone, eating finger foods. Babies can choke silently when eating soft foods such as pieces of banana, so you should make sure that you know what to do if

choking occurs. Never leave babies propped up with a bottle or feeding beaker.

Preventing cross-infection

Children who play closely together for long periods of time are more likely than others to develop an infection – and any infection can spread very quickly from one child to another and to adults who care for them. Your setting's health and safety policy will establish procedures to reduce the risk of transferring infectious diseases. These include:

- providing staff members and parents with information on infection control policies and procedures
- stating the exclusion criteria that will apply when a child or a staff member is sick
- providing training for staff members so that they understand and can use the infection control procedures
- providing adequate supervision to make sure everyone follows the policies and procedures
- providing adequate supplies of protective equipment
- providing adequate facilities for hand-washing, cleaning and disposing of waste
- providing safe work practices for high-risk activities, such as dealing with blood and body fluids, nappy changing and toileting, handling dirty linen and contaminated clothing and preparing and handling food
- policies relating to health and safety issues.

Safety at sleep and rest times

Every setting will have its own routine, providing for the needs of both babies and young children for periods of sleep and rest. You should follow these guidelines:

- Treat each child uniquely – every child has his or her own needs for sleep and rest.
- Be guided by the wishes of the child's parent or carer.

- Keep noise to a minimum and darken the room; make sure that children have been to the toilet.
- Always put babies on their backs to sleep.
- Make sure that the cot or bed is safe and hygienic: no pillows, no small objects within reach and no ribbon fastenings on garments.
- Find out all you can about the individual child's preferences; some children like to be patted to sleep; others may need to cuddle their favourite comfort object.

- Make sure that someone is always with the child until they fall asleep; reassure them that someone will be there when they wake up.
- Provide quiet, relaxing activities for those children who are unable – or do not want – to sleep, such as reading a book to them, doing jigsaw puzzles and so on.
- Handbags containing matches or lighters must be locked securely away out of children's reach.

Case Study — A breach of health and safety regulations

A nursery owner was fined £35,000 in 2008 for breaking health and safety regulations, after a toddler died at the nursery as a result of trapping her neck in the drawstring of a bag. The 16-month-old toddler was described as lively, inquisitive and able to walk. She had been placed in a cot to sleep with a looped drawstring of a bag placed over the side, and became entangled in the loops. She was left unattended for 20 minutes, and when found, she was apparently lifeless. An inquest jury returned a verdict of unlawful killing after hearing that the toddler was in the care of a 17-year-old student and an unqualified member of staff while senior managers met upstairs.

This led to the case against the owner being reopened. The Crown Court judge said staff showed 'gross incompetence' by not acting on warnings from the toddler's parents that she did often wrap things around her neck. The judge said: 'This [*leaving a bag on the cot*] was

such an obvious risk that virtually no parent in their own home would have considered this, let alone professionals who should have been responsible.' The prosecuting counsel claimed that although toddlers at the nursery should have been checked every ten minutes, there was a 'conflicting understanding' among staff. He said that a proper risk assessment was not carried out, which meant that bags continued to be left on cots. The nursery owner said: 'There are no words I can say to excuse or lessen the terrible tragedy of [the toddler's] death. As a mother myself, I feel deep sadness and remorse. I accept fully that the ultimate responsibility for her safety lay with me, as the owner.' The judge noted that it was not a case of manslaughter but a breach of health and safety regulations: 'The death of this child is a tragic and heart-breaking incident. It was, however, an accident … which should have been foreseen.'

(Adapted from a report in The Guardian, 30 October 2008)

Section 3: How to plan and provide an enabling physical environment for children

Current initiatives and philosophies which influence the provision of environments for children

Throughout history, there have always been people who have been prepared to stand up and fight for what young children need. They are the pioneers who help everyone working with young children, past and present, to move forward. Not all of us have the kind of personality that makes us a pioneer, but we can all do our bit for the children in our care. The people featured in this chapter are often called educational pioneers, but each one of them cared for children as much as they educated them. They all believed in integrated early years provision. This has a long and respected heritage, and the greatest influence in the UK in the nineteenth century has been that of Friedrich Froebel. Other pioneers include Maria Montessori, Rudolf Steiner and Margaret McMillan.

Friedrich Froebel (1782–1852)

Friedrich Froebel was a forester and mathematician, and was the first person to write about the importance of the play in development and learning. He started a community school, where parents were welcome at any time. His staff were trained to observe and value children's play. Below is a summary of his beliefs and findings:

- It is important to talk with parents and learn with them how to help children learn through their play.
- He designed a set of wooden blocks (gifts), which are still used in early childhood settings today. He also designed many other kinds of play equipment

(occupations) and movement games (action songs and finger play rhymes and dancing) through which children learn by doing.

- Relationships with other children are as important as relationships with adults, and he had a strong belief in the value of imaginative and symbolic play.
- Froebel encouraged pretend play and play with other children.
- Both indoor and outdoor play are important.
- He helped children to make dens in the garden and to play with natural materials such as sand, water and wood.
- Teachers should be sensitive and approachable, and have qualities that the children can respect and imitate.
- He called his schools 'kindergartens' (for children aged two to eight). This word means 'children's garden' in German. Even today there are kindergartens all over the world. Froebel has had a profound influence on early childhood education and care.

Research Activity

Investigating Froebel's work

1 Research a set of wooden hollow blocks and wooden unit blocks (examples of these are made by Community Playthings). Can you find any mathematical relationships between the different blocks? Plan how you could help children to learn about shape, using wooden blocks. Implement your plan, and evaluate your observations with children of three to seven years of age.

2 Try to find 12 examples of finger rhymes. These are songs or rhymes using the fingers for actions. Make a book of them for children to enjoy. Make sure you include a multicultural range of action songs and also think about children with disabilities. Share the book with a child of between two and seven years of age. Evaluate your observations.

3 Research what children did in kindergartens in the twentieth century – for example, each child had his or her own little garden.

4 Imagine that you are Friedrich Froebel today. What do you think he might like or dislike about your early years setting?

In Practice

❑ Plan how you will organise a garden activity. What equipment will you need? Where will you do this? How will you clear up?

❑ Plant some flowers or vegetables with children, and watch them grow.

❑ Observe a child of between two and seven years of age, and evaluate your garden activity in relation to that particular child's cognitive and language development.

Maria Montessori (1880–1952)

Maria Montessori was an Italian doctor who worked in the poorest areas of Rome in the 1900s. She did not believe that pretend play was important. She thought children wanted to do real things, for example, not *play* at being cooks but to actually do some cooking. However, she did like Froebel's play equipment, and she designed more (didactic materials) to help them learn, for example, about shapes, weight, colour, size and numbers. A summary of her beliefs:

● All children have absorbent minds, and the way in which children learn is different from the way in which an adult learns. Children absorb information from the environment. Initially this learning is unconscious, but after the age of three the child absorbs information consciously. The ability to absorb language and to learn motor skills is initially without formal instruction but later children use language to question.

● Children pass through sensitive periods during which they are particularly receptive to developing specific skills. A child will develop a particular interest in one specific skill or action, which they will repeat time and time again.

● Children should be guided by a trained adult to use her equipment until they can use it confidently on their own and independently.

A Montessori teacher plays a very different role from that of a teacher in mainstream school provision. The teacher, who is known as the directress, is seen to guide or direct the children, putting them in touch with their environment so that they can learn for themselves.

Montessori called her schools Children's Houses and these are still to be found all over the world.

Margaret McMillan (1860–1931)

Margaret McMillan (and her sister, Rachel) fought for the education of young children to emphasise physical care and development. They campaigned and were successful in introducing free school meals under the Provision of School Meals Act 1906, and they introduced regular medical inspections for school children by opening the first clinic especially devoted to school children in 1908. A summary of her beliefs:

● Children cannot learn if they are undernourished, poorly clothed, sick or ill with poor teeth, poor eyesight, ear infections, rickets, etc. (Recent reports emphasise that poor health and poverty are challenges still facing those who work with families in the UK today.)

● Children learn by exploring and achieve their whole potential through play; she placed an emphasis on craft and water activities, singing and model-making.

● Outdoor play and being taught in the fresh air is important; gardening was a regular activity.

● The importance of hygiene and cleanliness: parents should be educated about keeping their children clean and hygienic.

● The role of the 'home' in supporting a child's learning capability is very important.

● She stressed the importance of having trained teachers, and opened a special training school for the teachers in her schools. Children were taught in small groups, and McMillan expected teachers to be imaginative and inventive.

● A very close partnership with parents is essential: she encouraged parents to develop alongside their children, with adult classes in hobbies and languages made available to them.

The British nursery school, as envisaged by McMillan, has been admired and emulated across the world. McMillan Nursery Schools have gardens, and are communities that welcome both parents and children.

In Practice

Investigating Margaret McMillan's work

Plan an outdoor area for an early years setting. Emphasise the child's need for movement and curiosity about nature, and provide an area for digging and playing in mud. Evaluate your plan.

Rudolf Steiner (1861–1925)

Rudolf Steiner encouraged play through natural materials, such as clay, beeswax, silk scarves for dressing up and irregularly shaped wooden blocks. A summary of his beliefs:

- Singing and dancing are important, and stories give children ideas for their play.
- Education is an *artistic* process. There must be a balance between artistic, creative and practical experiences on the one hand, and academic activities on the other.

He believed that children pass through three specific phases:

1 The **Period of Will** (birth to seven years) in which the *active* aspect predominates. Within this period there are three stages:
    - birth to three years – the main features are walking, speech and the ability to think in words
    - three to five years – the development of the imagination and memory are important
    - five years onwards – the stimulation for play tends to come less from external objects but more from ideas generated within the children.
2 The **Period of the Heart** (seven to fourteen years): the *feeling* phase. The child is now ready for formal learning, although the role of the imagination is still very important.
3 The **Period of the Head** (14 years onwards): the *cognitive* phase. The adolescent stage is considered to be the period of thinking. At this stage children develop a healthy idealism, and may be very sensitive about their feelings.

Steiner's schools are called Waldorf Schools and are now the largest independent school system in the world, with many of the schools situated in North America and Australia.

The Reggio Emilia approach

The Reggio Emilia approach to pre-school education was started by the schools of the city of Reggio Emilia in Italy after World War II. There is much about Reggio Emilia's approach to child care and education that distinguishes it from other efforts both inside and outside of Italy, and attracts worldwide attention. Of special interest is the emphasis on children's symbolic languages in the context of a project-oriented curriculum.

The key features of the Reggio Emilia approach are:

- **Community support and parental involvement**: the parents' role mirrors that of the community's, at both the school and classroom level. Parents are expected to take part in discussions about school policy, child development concerns, and curriculum planning and evaluation.
- **Administrative policies and organisational features**: every centre is staffed with two teachers per classroom (12 children in infant classes, 18 in toddler classes, and 24 in pre-primary classes), one teacher trained in the arts who works with classroom teachers in curriculum development and documentation, and several auxiliary staff. There is no principal, nor is there a hierarchical relationship among the teachers.
- **The role of the environment**: the pre-schools are generally filled with indoor plants and vines, and awash with natural light. Classrooms open to a central piazza, kitchens are open to view, and access to the surrounding community is assured through wall-size windows, courtyards and doors to the outside in each classroom. Entrances capture the attention of both children and adults through the use of mirrors (on the walls, floors, and ceilings), photographs, and children's work accompanied by transcriptions of their discussions. These same features characterise classroom

interiors, where displays of project work are interspersed with arrays of found objects and classroom materials, with clearly designated spaces for large- and small-group activities.

- **Long-term projects as vehicles for learning**: teachers often work on projects with small groups of children, while the rest of the class engages in a wide variety of self-selected activities typical of pre-school classrooms. The topic of investigation may derive directly from teacher observations of children's spontaneous play and exploration. Projects begin with teachers observing and questioning children about the topic of interest. Based on children's responses, teachers introduce materials, questions and opportunities that provoke children to further explore the topic.

- **The hundred languages of children**: as children proceed in an investigation, generating and testing their hypotheses, they are encouraged to depict their understanding through one of many symbolic languages, including drawing, sculpture, dramatic play, and writing. They work together towards the resolution of problems that arise.

In Practice

Investigating education and care

1 Research the different ways in which Froebel, Montessori and Steiner would (a) introduce children to a set of wooden blocks and (b) help children to use the blocks.
2 Implement each approach with a group of children in three separate sessions.
3 Evaluate your observations, noting the way in which your role as an early years worker changed according to which approach you used.
4 Note the differences in the way in which the children responded, especially in relation to creativity, language and play. Which approaches encouraged the child to be a symbol-user? Evaluate your observations.

Forest Schools

The philosophy of Forest Schools, which started in Denmark in 1950, is to encourage and inspire individuals of any age through positive outdoor experiences. Forest Schools have demonstrated success with children of all ages who visit the same local woodlands on a regular basis and through play, have the opportunity to learn about the natural environment, how to handle risks and most importantly to use their own initiative to solve problems and cooperate with others. Forest School programmes run throughout the year for about 36 weeks, going to the woods in all weathers (except for high winds).

Forest Schools aim to develop:

- a greater understanding of their own natural and man-made environments
- a wide range of physical skills
- social communication skills
- independence
- a positive mental attitude, self-esteem and confidence.

Providing for children's developmental needs, indoors and outdoors

When children feel their efforts are appreciated and celebrated, they learn more effectively. If adults only praise and recognise results (**products of learning**), children are more likely to lose heart and become less motivated to learn.

Planning should therefore focus on process and the efforts children make (**processes of learning**) as much as product. An example would be finger-painting rather than hand-prints, so that children can freely make their own patterns in the paint. At the end, the paint is cleared away, with no pressure on children to produce a product. However, staff might photograph the processes involved in finger-painting and display these on the wall, to remind children of what they did. Children love to share process books later with interested adults, other children and their parents/carers.

Layout of indoor and outdoor learning environments

In an inclusive early childhood setting that embraces diversity, the layout and presentation of material provision offers a range of experiences and activities across the birth to five years framework. Increasingly, from the time they can walk, children are integrating with children in the Foundation years for parts of the day, which gives a more natural and family-group feeling. Children with special educational needs and disabilities are also included in settings. All of this means that the traditions of wide provision are of central importance.

Indoor learning environment

Given that children from birth to six years learn through the senses, the layout needs to support and extend this kind of learning. The layout from Reggio Emilia and Pistoia in Northern Italy has reminded practitioners in the UK of the importance of:

- an attractive and welcoming entrance area, where children and families are greeted, can find and share information, and feel part of a community
- natural light
- the feeling of space without clutter
- making spaces beautiful using natural materials.

The environment also needs to support and actively encourage and extend the symbolic life of the child, making one thing stand for another (for example, pretending a leaf is a plate in the outside playhouse). Understanding cause-and-effect relationships is also very important, and the learning environment needs to promote this (for example, kicking the ball hard makes it go a long distance, while tapping it with your toes makes it roll only a little way).

Figure 4.4 These photos give examples of messy play with paints

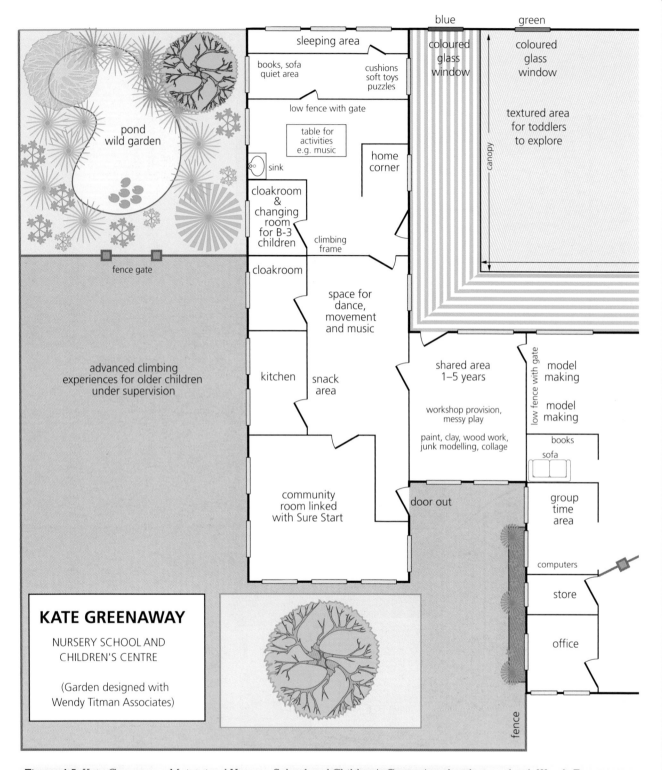

Figure 4.5 Kate Greenaway Maintained Nursery School and Children's Centre (garden designed with Wendy Titman Associates)

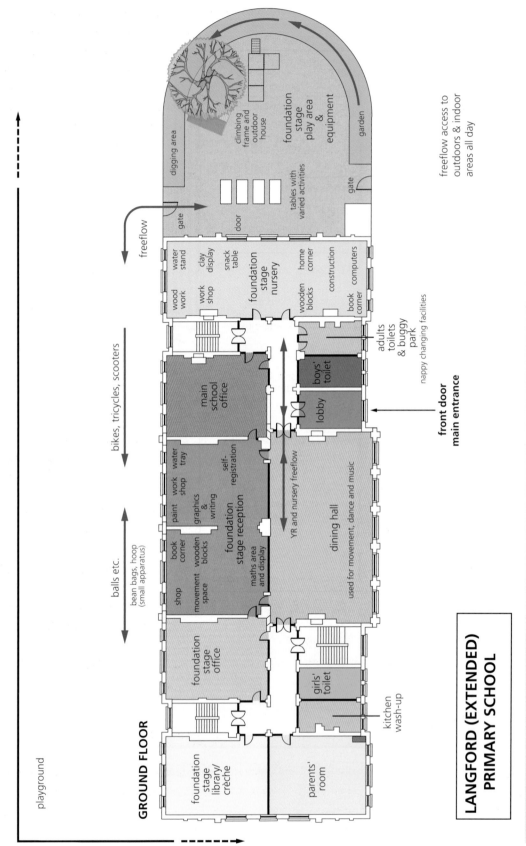

GROUND FLOOR

playground

balls etc.

bean bags, hoop
(small apparatus)

bikes, tricycles, scooters

foundation
stage
library/
crèche

parents'
room

foundation
stage office

shop

movement
space

book
corner

wooden
blocks

paint

work
shop

graphics
&
writing

water
tray

self-
registration

foundation
stage reception

maths area
and display

kitchen
wash-up

girls'
toilet

dining hall

used for movement, dance and music

YR and nursery freeflow

main
school
office

lobby

boys'
toilet

adults
toilets
& buggy
park

nappy changing facilities

**front door
main entrance**

wood
work

work
shop

water
stand

clay
display

snack
table

foundation
stage
nursery

wooden
blocks

home
corner

book
corner

construction

computers

freeflow

gate

door

digging area

tables with
varied activities

climbing
frame and
outdoor
house

foundation
stage
play area
& equipment

gate

garden

freeflow access to
outdoors & indoor
areas all day

**LANGFORD (EXTENDED)
PRIMARY SCHOOL**

Figure 4.6 Langford (extended) primary school has a Foundation Stage layout, with the nursery class and reception class working together

Tuning in to children, and responding to what you have observed

Sometimes, practitioners think that children are stuck in their play, because they stay doing something for ages; they might even call this obsessive. A child who stays at the workshop area for ages, dripping glue from a glue stick onto paper, and covering the paper until it is soggy, is not necessarily being obsessive. There will be reasons why the child does this, because human behaviour is not random. The following case studies look at three different children. When the practitioner tunes in to each one, we can see that they all have completely different needs. Responding to each child individually is part of creating a rich learning environment indoors and outdoors.

Case Study — Tuning in to children

Nadia (two years old) is exploring glue and its properties for the first time in her life. She might be interested in the way the glue falls off the glue stick, or in the soggy mound of glue on the paper. She does not seem to be interested in the function of glue – to join things together. So, does she need to be using this expensive glue? She might gain just as much satisfaction from flour and water glue, which is cheaper. Does she need expensive paper to drip the glue onto? She might learn just as much if the glue is dripped onto newspaper.

Activity

It is important to respond sensitively once you have tuned in to a child. Evaluate your practice in relation to the case study on tuning into children above. Discuss this in a small group, then take action and try out (implement) the ideas in your practice. In the example explored in the case study, you could consider the following points:

- Always have different kinds of glue available in the workshop. You could offer Nadia flour and water glue in an attractive pot, showing her how she can use it by demonstrating. Chat about the flour glue.

- When the paper is very soggy, and Nadia wants to continue but it is beginning to flow off the table, replace the paper with newspaper. Chat as you do so, saying you think this might help Nadia to carry out her idea of dripping the glue on the paper.

- Chatting is important in developing communication – not too much, not too little. Give Nadia key words, but in sentences, such as, 'This newspaper will be better, I think, for you to drip your flour glue onto. Let's try it out, shall we?' Nadia might well echo, 'Try it out, shall we'.

- Chatting is especially important for children with English as an additional language (EAL) and for children with special educational needs (SEN).

Case Study — Monty develops his expertise in the block play area

Some children spend a great deal of time in a particular area, every day. Monty has a favourite – block play. It is important to encourage this, so that he will be able to become a specialist in this area. You could support him to develop his skill, making bridges, roofs, walls, and so on. Monty is the opposite to the kind of child who flits from one thing to another.

Discussion point

Unless practitioners observe and tune in to children, they often find their actions and behaviour a worry, when all the child needs is the right kind of support to get the most out of the learning environment, indoors and outdoors. In a small group, discuss how you are helping children. What more can you do to support and extend their learning? Children do not know how to use glue, wooden blocks, and so on, unless they feel supported and are given the right sort of help, in the right way, at the right time.

Case Study | Is Hayley flitting from one thing to the next?

Hayley comes into the garden. She goes to the two-wheeler bikes with no pedals and rides one to the end of the garden. Then she runs to the watering can and picks it up. She walks around with it, drops it on the path and runs to the practitioner who is putting up the sun umbrella. She looks up at its spokes, standing underneath it. Then she goes to the outdoor sandpit, and chooses to play with the wheel, tipping dry sand in and flicking it with her hand as the sand spins round in it. She takes the sand-wheel to the water pump and puts it under the spout, pumping water into it and watching it turn.

Hayley seems to be flitting from one thing to the next, yet everything she has chosen to do has the same pattern in it: everything has a core and radials coming out of it – the spokes on the bicycle wheels, the spout on the watering can, the spokes on the umbrella, the sand-wheel, which becomes the waterwheel. The researcher Chris Athey would say that she is 'fitting', not 'flitting'.

Activity

How should the practitioner respond? Discuss this in a small group, then implement one of your ideas in your practice and evaluate your own practice. What do you need to remember next time?

- Perhaps Hayley would like to be offered similar objects with a core and radials, to broaden her experience.

- The practitioner could have a chat with her as she moves from one thing to another, helping her to build her vocabulary about core and radial objects and what they do (their function).

- The practitioner could take photos of all the objects and make a book of these, calling it 'Hayley's interesting objects'.

Children usually like to feel that an adult is nearby; it makes them feel safe and secure, especially when they are trying something new and unfamiliar. The first time glue is used or paint is mixed are good examples of this. It is important not to crowd, overwhelm or invade a child's thinking space, but it is vital to support a child's learning by being there for them, smiling and looking interested, and commenting on what they do from time to time; for example, 'You like red best, I think, because I've noticed that you have used it three times in your painting so far.'

We must never underestimate the important of early friendships. Children miss their friends when they are away or ill, and find it more difficult to get involved. A supportive adult is important at these times, offering companionship as the child chooses activities and experiences.

Planning a safe and predictable environment

Children need a safe and predictable environment. It is important for staff to work as a team so that different messages are not given by different people – for example, if one adult allows children to sit on tables and another does not, children will push the boundaries because they are confused. When children feel safe, they explore and enjoy stimulating provision that has been planned for them.

Providing risk and challenge in the environment

Children are biologically driven to make risk assessments, but only if they are constantly encouraged to use these processes – for example, toddlers can be encouraged to come down the stairs (under supervision) sliding on their tummies, feet first. They will pause and check where they are every few steps, making their own risk assessment. Children who are not supported to make their own risk assessments, by an adult sensitive and helpful to their needs, are more likely to have accidents.

The learning environment for babies

The importance of people – learning before sitting

It can be very boring to be a baby. This is because babies depend on adults to bring interesting experiences to them, because they cannot move about enough to reach for things when sitting, or crawl or walk to get them.

Bored, unhappy babies cannot learn much, and the important period of babyhood, when so much learning is possible, will then be lost. Studies of child development suggest that the first years of life are of great importance for development and learning, and also that this is the time when the child's willingness and ability for future learning are set.

Imagine what it would be like if you spent long periods on your back with only a ceiling to look at, or you were in a pram in the garden with a plastic cover hiding your view of the sky and trees, or you could hear voices, but could not see who was talking because they were standing behind you.

Material provision, equipment and resources for babies

Children from birth to three years enjoy and benefit from the companionship and stimulation of being with older children, but they also become exhausted if they do not have a safe base/haven/ nest to return to, where they can be quiet and calm.

Babies need to be cuddled, held on your knee so that they can see things, talked to and sung to, and bounced in time with music. They need things to look at, swipe at, grab and hold, chew, suck and mouth, smell, shake and listen to. Babies need objects and people.

Quiet times

Sometimes babies need to be quiet, but they still need to feel that people are near. Of course, it is important that the sun is not in their eyes, and that they are comfortable in temperature and with a clean nappy.

Babies need times to:

- look at a mobile
- listen to gentle music playing
- hear the birds singing as they lie in a pram under a tree, looking through the branches at the patterns of the leaves against the sky
- sit propped up in a specially designed chair and watch what is going on
- watch other children
- follow voices they know because they spend time with them and love them
- receive warmth and affection.

Floor time

Anyone who observes babies finds that they are exploring the environment using their senses and movement. They need plenty of opportunities to be on the floor so that they can do this. When lying on their backs, they can watch mobiles or leaves and branches swaying and fluttering in the trees above their pram, and swipe at objects above them with their arms, or kick at them with their legs. But they also need to feel their arms, legs and tummies against the ground. Experts in physical movement development (like JABADAO, the National Centre for Movement, Learning and Health in Leeds) are finding that children often do not spend enough time on the floor. They need to be given opportunities to crawl as well as to sit and lie down. It is exciting when children take their first steps, but they still need plenty of time down on the floor. This means that there should be plenty of spaces to do this when working with very young children in the first year of their life.

Babies need time to be on the floor, on their tummies, with interesting natural objects (not plastic all the time) placed in front of them, which they need to reach for. Adults can be very encouraging and help babies to have things in reach, and at the point where the baby is trying to crawl, keep frustration at bay by making sure there is enough success to keep them trying. It is very difficult for a baby when they are trying to crawl forwards to get something they want, and they find they are moving backwards. Having something to push against can be just the right help at the right time!

Are there objects a baby can put in his or her mouth, touch and handle, smell, carry about, look at and make sounds with? They will learn more if everything is not made of plastic. The floors will need to be clean, as a baby will stop to examine every piece of fluff, dropped crumb or spillage. When the baby crawls outside, he or she will need surfaces such as grass, and rougher surfaces. But remember, babies put everything in their mouths.

Sitting babies – treasure baskets
Elinor Goldschmied pioneered treasure baskets for sitting babies. These are now widely used in most settings. It is very important that they are presented to babies in the correct way or the baby will not get the full benefit of the learning the treasure basket offers. Make sure the basket is the correct shape, height and size. It is distressing for the baby if it tips as they lean on it, or if they are unable to reach the objects on the other side. It is uncomfortable to sit at a basket that is too high (like an adult sitting at a table when the chair is too low for the table height).

The baby needs the companionship of an adult who sits near them (usually on a chair that is near to the ground in height), but who does not join in – simply there as an anchor, smiling when shown objects, but saying nothing. When adults are concentrating (perhaps writing and thinking hard), it would interrupt the flow of thought and the deep focusing to have someone make suggestions or ask questions and try to make conversation with them. Ideally, the treasure basket experience will take place away from the hurly-burly of the main area, perhaps screened off with a clothes horses draped with material, to signal to other, older, more mobile children that this is a quiet area, set aside for sitting babies to concentrate and learn.

The objects should not be made of plastic, but of natural materials or metals that can be washed and kept clean. This is because plastic does not offer much to the range of senses through which babies learn. As objects become shabby they should be removed, and there should be new objects to keep the interest of the baby who has regular use of the basket. As your observations of a baby build, you will be able to select objects with that baby's interests in mind. The baby who loves to bang and bash objects will choose different ones to the baby who loves to dangle and shake objects. It is deeply satisfying to try to work out what a baby will particularly enjoy exploring, especially when you have built on your observations successfully.

Babies need sufficient objects to be able to select from, so the basket should be full enough to encourage this. Examples would be: a small wooden brush, a small cardboard box, a loofah, a wooden spoon, a small metal egg whisk, a bath plug and chain, a small bag of lavender, a large feather.

Of course, you will need to make a risk assessment based on your observations of what a baby needs. Never put an object in the treasure basket that makes you anxious about its safety for a baby, and remember that some babies have allergies. Remember also that some babies are less adventurous than others and will need more support and encouragement to enjoy the treasure basket.

Sleep is important for learning

Getting the right rest is crucial for the learning of babies and young children. Not all babies will need to sleep at the same time, and it is very worrying to find practice where all babies are expected to have their nappies changed at the same time and to sleep at the same time. These are very individual things.

It is important for babies to feel that they are near someone when they sleep. Some babies sleep best on a mat on the floor of a quiet area that is gated, with a cover to keep them warm; others sleep better in a darkened room, in a cot kept for them. This area should not be too full of stimulation. It is important to relax and let go when falling asleep. Neutral colouring is best, and the room should not be cluttered.

It is also important to keep to the sleep-time rituals and patterns that are familiar to the baby at home. Some babies need to have a cuddle, being lowered into their cot as they fall asleep. Others might never go to sleep on a lap, but need to be in a cot, in a quiet room with their teddy, in order to fall asleep.

Sleep is important for learning. It helps the memory to embed rich learning experiences with people, objects, events and places.

Eating together

The advantage of family groups in early childhood settings is that babies can easily be part of mealtimes. When a whole row of babies all need feeding together, there are often tears and staff become anxious and frustrated, because it seems impossible to get each baby fed quickly enough. Meals become times of stress instead of times of deep pleasure.

Babies learn more if they are given finger foods as soon as this is appropriate. A carrot stick is a wonderful learning experience, and makes a good contrast with a metal teaspoon. Observing a baby's learning at mealtimes is fascinating – for example, does the baby pass the spoon from one hand to the other? Is the spoon held with a palmar grip? Does the baby try to pick up the carrot stick with a pincer grip?

Case Study — Using everyday events for learning

At lunchtime, a group of sitting babies and toddlers were encouraged to choose their pudding. A plate of freshly prepared fruit was placed on the table. A tiny portion was given to the babies to try out. Several showed they wanted more through their movements. The key worker passed the plate to the babies, who were allowed to take more for themselves. This encouraged:

- learning that one portion of fruit is the same as the next
- physical coordination
- a feeling of control over what happens
- decision-making.

Case Study — Using everyday events for learning

When Joey (ten months) is changed, he dislikes the plastic changing mat – he tries to move off it. His key worker respects his feelings and puts a towel on the mat. She talks about what she is doing and why, and she sings 'Ten little toes' to help him relax. He giggles in anticipation of each toe being gently touched.

This everyday event has helped Joey to learn about:

- himself and where he ends
- affectionate and sensitive communication between people
- making sense of what someone says
- music, with its melody (tune) and pitch (loudness)
- eye contact when people talk to each other
- facial expressions
- having fun together.

Babies and toddlers learn better if they are not anxious. Laughing releases chemicals into the brain which open it up to learning. Anxiety closes the brain off to the possibility of learning.

Progress check

Material provision, equipment and resources for babies

Expensive equipment is not necessary to create a rich environment in which babies can develop and learn. Babies are helped to develop and learn when they are:

- introduced to treasure baskets
- offered homemade or commercial toys – for example, baby mirrors, which help their sense of identity (who it that? is that me?); rattles to hold and shake, with and without sounds; wobbly toys and pop-up toys; bath toys that sink and float; a soft toy, such as a teddy bear
- provided with opportunities to crawl on comfortable surfaces – a mixture of carpets and other surfaces to explore, including grass
- have suitable places to sleep – some babies sleep best in a cot, others in a basket on a floor away from draughts, some tightly tucked in, others with loose bedclothes covering them; babies should *never* be left to sleep unsupervised when in group care
- eat in a family group – this is best for babies, as they are part of the conversation, and they are talked to and given attention in a way that is impossible with a group of babies
- share a book with their key person, which can calm them (they love to look at patterns, grids and circles – see Figure 4.7); books will be chewed and sucked, as babies learn through all their senses.

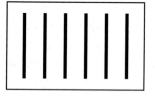
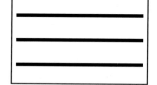
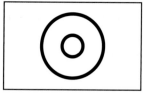

Figure 4.7 Babies to look at patterns, grids and circles (based on Murray and Andrews (2003) *The Social Baby*)

Discussion point

In a small group, discuss and evaluate how babies are helped to develop and learn, taking into account the areas explored in the Progress check above.

The learning environment for toddlers

The importance of people

Toddlers need adults who create a warm, affectionate atmosphere, support wellbeing, encourage children to try things, observe and tune in to their learning, and make individual plans to help them learn. Children need to feel valued, appreciated and respected.

When children feel their efforts are appreciated and valued, they develop a positive self-image and a good sense of wellbeing. This, more than anything else, helps them to learn. The key person in the setting is of great importance in this.

By this age, children are beginning to get a sense of the rhythms of time and passing time through the day as they become familiar with the early childhood setting. They are helped in knowing the shape of the day if there is a predictable environment. This does not mean rigid routines, but it does mean having a consistent shape to the day, or to outings, so that children can begin to participate fully in preparations, having experiences and a sense of closure as they join in clearing things up each day. This means that staff need to work together as a team to create consistent boundaries and ways of doing things, so that children feel safe and secure and able to develop their intellectual lives. Then they can be explorers and problem-solvers, and they can make and use symbols, with reasoning and enquiring minds.

Material provision, equipment and resources for toddlers

Becoming mobile changes the life of a baby. Crawling babies love to follow people and to find out about objects wherever they travel. They need stable furniture so that they can pull themselves up and cruise in between.

Heuristic play

This is a good time to offer crawling babies and toddlers heuristic play experiences, which were first developed by Elinor Goldschmied. The term 'heuristic' comes from the Greek word for 'to find' or 'to discover'.

Children need to be comfortable. Rather than a cold, draughty floor, they need a warm, inviting floor space, without lots of clutter to capture their attention. The space needs to be prepared in advance so that children come upon the carefully spaced piles of objects when they enter the area. All the objects are collected from everyday use, rather than toys.

One pile might include spheres, circular objects and cylinders, such as a cotton reel, a bobble from a hat, a bracelet. Another might be of metal objects, such as tins with smoothed edges, or a metal tea caddy. The adult sits quietly and provides a calm and concentrating atmosphere that supports the child's explorations without intervening, except to say something like, 'Yes, you have a lovely tin' – but only if the child brings it to them. Otherwise, a warm smile is sufficient and the child then returns to his or her explorations.

The session varies in length, but careful observation will signal to the adult when to draw things to a close. Often children stay concentrating for half an hour. A further ten minutes or so should be taken to clear up with the children, who are encouraged to put the collections into the right type of bag. This is then hung on the wall, with the children watching. As long as children's efforts are valued, they enjoy helping. They do not respond well when nagged or criticised for putting an object in the wrong bag. They need encouragement and positive, sensitive support.

Outdoor learning environment

Children should be able to learn outside for most of the day if they choose to do so. They need appropriate clothes (as do adults), so that everyone can be outside in all weathers. The idea that learning can only take place indoors is extraordinary when we stop to think about it.

There should be different surfaces – playground surfaces, grass, an earth patch to dig in, a large, drained sandpit, planted areas with trees and wild areas for butterflies. Settings that do not value the importance of the outdoor learning environment are only offering children half a curriculum.

Double provision

Through double provision (providing more than one activity at a time), the different needs and interests of children from birth to five years can be attended to with quality. There might be a workshop area, with carefully selected and presented found materials, such as boxes, tubes, dried flowers, moss, twigs, wool, string, masking tape, glue, scissors and card. Here, older children could become involved in making models and constructions, and adults can help them to carry out their ideas without losing track of them on the way or becoming frustrated. Children can be helped as they try to join things, and make decisions about whether a string knot would be better than masking tape or glue.

Nearby, on the floor, there might be a beautiful basket full of balls of wool and string, which younger and less experienced children can enjoy unravelling and finding out how these behave. Other children might like to return to this earlier way of using string too. Remember that careful supervision is essential to prevent accidents.

It is a good idea to try to offer everything at different levels of difficulty, so that there is something for everyone to find absorbing. Absorbed children behave better, on the whole.

EYFS 2012

The EYFS stipulates that the learning environment should provide opportunities for both indoor and outdoor play which will enable young children the chance to:

- select and use activities and resources with help as per own request

- take turns and share resources with appropriate support as required

- talk to other children when playing together, including initiate conversations

- play cooperatively in a group, for example, demonstrate friendly behaviour

- form positive relationships with peers and familiar adults

- move confidently in a range of ways, for example, safely negotiating space when playing racing and chasing games, adjusting speed or changing direction to avoid obstacles

- handle tools effectively for the purpose, including mark making.

Attractive presentation and tidy-up time indoors and outdoors

If an area is dirty, shabby or in a muddle, it is less attractive to children. Often a well-used area becomes cluttered and untidy halfway through a morning or afternoon, and the children leave it. It is important that adults do not neglect these abandoned areas. Children can be encouraged to help tidy it, but adults can role-model this mid-session if children are very involved in other areas. At the end of the session, everyone needs to tidy up though, unless there are good reasons for a child not to, such as being upset or unsettled. Children should never be nagged or made to feel bad, but they should be encouraged and given specific but appropriate tasks as members of the learning community. Even a toddler enjoys putting rubbish in the bin. It is a question of finding something suitable for each particular child. The important thing is not to overdo the requests for help in tidying, and to remember that it is discriminatory to expect only a few children to do all the tidying. (Look again at the section on tidying away at the end of the heuristic play session on page 193.)

Movement area

The most important play provision for toddlers and children up to at least five years is on the floor! Making a movement corner is as important as making a book corner for brain development, learning and wellbeing. The floor needs to be clean and carpets should not be scratchy. Penny Greenland at JABADAO (the National Centre for Movement, Learning and Health) emphasises the importance of movement in early childhood.

Having an interested person, sensitively supporting and mirroring is also important. Mirroring is another vital pattern for late learning, as research by Colwyn Trevarthen at Edinburgh University shows. Adults who make good play companions are a valuable resource as part of the play provision. The rough-and-tumble play traditional in mammals, including human children, just before sleeping, is often engaged in with adults in the family.

The importance of people in the lives of toddlers

Having read the sections in this chapter about the importance of people, what do you think are the key messages? Discuss this in a small group, and make a set of commitments to work on in your practice. Write them down and review them in a month's time. Evaluate your progress.

Guidelines for material provision, equipment and resources for working with toddlers

Children who are beginning to be confident walkers need:

Outdoors

- a range of surfaces to walk on, and to try to run
- a large, bouncy ball to kick and throw, bats, hoops, beanbags
- flowers (these are for picking as far as a toddler is concerned) – encourage children to pick daisies and dandelions rather than flowers from the flowerbed; they enjoy putting flowers in a vase of water to place on the meal table
- climbing opportunities, always carefully supervised: a small climbing frame or steps
- wheeled trucks to push and pull, pull-along toys, pushchairs for dolls and teddies and other soft toys
- plants and a growing area, and watering cans
- a well-drained sandpit
- a covered pond and fishing nets to use when supervised with an adult
- puddles to stamp in wearing wellies
- picnics
- mud pies and a digging area
- a sandpit.

Indoors

- stable furniture to pull themselves up on and cruise between
- heuristic play (see page 193)
- a designated space for vigorous movement, with cushions on which to leap and roll about
- wooden and natural material objects to feel, mouth and hold
- simple towers to make and knock down
- finger-painting
- non-toxic crayons and felt-tip pens and paper
- wet and dry silver sand (not builder's sand)
- play dough – find some good recipes for play dough (some involve cooking, which makes the dough last longer); check the dough is safe to put in the mouth and even to eat, as some children might do this
- opportunities for water play, carefully supervised, at bathtime, in paddling pools or with bowls of water – remember, children can drown in very shallow water, so always supervise these activities
- a tea set, toy cars and other play props to encourage pretend symbolic play with a willing adult
- objects to transport in trucks, bags, and so on
- boxes for children to put things into and take things out of
- blankets to cover teddies, dolls, and so on (enveloping)
- picture books and books with simple texts, and stories and rhymes, such as *Spot the Dog*
- simple dressing-up clothes – mainly hats, shoes and belts for toddlers
- action songs and finger rhymes.

Figure 4.8 Boys engaged in imaginative play

In Practice

Audit the provision in your setting/placement. If there are gaps in the provision, think about what would you introduce first, and why.

Case Study

Playing with an adult – interdependent relationships

The key worker sat on the floor, facing Rebecca (two years old), and sang 'Row, row, row the boat' with her. She sang the song and did the actions twice through and then stopped. Rebecca touched her on the thigh and the key worker responded, 'Again? You want to sing again?' The singing and moving were repeated, and Rebecca smiled with pleasure. In this play:

- Rebecca is helped to be imaginative
- her idea to repeat the song is taken up
- she is encouraged to use her initiative and not be passive
- she is learning the basis of drama, music and dance.

The learning environment for children from three to five years
The importance of people

Communication, skilful body movements, play and the use of cultural symbols and creative and imaginative making of symbols are all important aspects of a child's development during this period. Adults have a huge role in supporting children as these overarching aspects emerge and strengthen.

Just as babies and toddlers need plenty of time to be in the garden/outdoors, so too do children from three to five years. They also enjoy toddler experiences, alongside increasingly complex experiences. They are beginning to be able to take increasing responsibility for their own risk-assessing (at the woodwork bench, when cooking and gardening), but they need adult support or they will not manage to do so. Children benefit from discussions about safety, and taking care of themselves, others and equipment. They also need adults who give them help in caring for others, thinking of others, looking after the material provision and equipment and making decisions and choices which help their development and learning. Children do not respond well to being judged and chided by adults. They do respond well to being helped to take responsible decisions.

Figure 4.9 Dinosaurs could be the key for this child to learn many different things

Case Study — Supporting learning through nurturing a child's interest

See Figure 4.9: this little boy is showing through the gesture of holding up the dinosaur that he wants us to look at it. It is his favourite; his eyes coordinate when he looks at it. It is important for children to hold objects and look at them as they play, as this will help later tracking of print on the page of a book. It will also help him if the adult names the dinosaur. Often we use the general word (dinosaur) instead of giving children the word for the type (Tyrannosaurus rex). He is ready to be given this vocabulary and delights in using the correct description of his dinosaur. Language helps children to sort and classify things in the world: he will be able to establish that the class of dinosaurs contains different types. He will learn the difference between a Tyrannosaurus rex and a Brontosaurus, but only if he is in a language-rich, enabling environment. There need to be books of dinosaurs, people who help him look them up, show them to him and name them for him.

Material provision, equipment and resources for children from three to five years

Outdoors

The garden and outdoor areas offer children major learning opportunities. They help children to learn about nature and gardening. Children can try out their physical skills and become competent, adventurous and confident in their physical bodies. Parents enjoy joining their children in the outdoor area, for picnics and other enjoyable experiences that make them feel part of the community.

Children need challenging places to climb and swing, and to be taught how to stay safe and be responsible. Children are biologically driven to make risk assessments, but only if this is encouraged. They need places to run, jump, skip and wheel.

In her book, *Playing Outdoors: Spaces and Places, Risk and Challenge* (2007), Helen Tovey lists the following as important if children are to have a challenging and creative outdoor area. Children need:

- designated spaces (but children should be allowed to rearrange them and use them in a different way)
- connected spaces, which encourage children to join in (sand and water areas)
- elevated spaces (mounds, trees, ramps, steps, climbing frames)
- wild spaces, so that children do not only experience neat and trim tarmac areas
- spaces for exploring and investigating
- spaces for mystery and enchantment (dens)
- natural spaces (digging patches and opportunities to grow flowers and vegetables)
- space for the imagination (providing children with open-ended props, logs, and so on)
- spaces for movement and stillness (climbing, dragging, swinging on bars, jumping, balancing, and so on, as well as sitting in secluded, tucked-away places in peace and calm)
- social spaces (outdoor seats for chatting together)
- fluid places (flexible resources that can be moved about when needed).

It is important that resources are organised with a minimum of setting out equipment and arranging it – for example, making a den with a tea set in it. The children will want to change things about if they are thinking and using the environment well.

Research Activity

Investigate the different approaches to Forest Schools in the UK and in countries such as Germany, Denmark, Norway and Sweden.

Bikes, scooters and carts

Bikes need to be three-wheeled and two-wheeled, with some needing two or three children cooperating in order to make them work. Two-wheeler bikes with no pedals are excellent for children, as they can tilt and balance without having to perform a complex combination of actions. Scooters and carts to push and pull are also important, as are prams and pushchairs for dolls and teddies.

Different ways of doing similar things – indoors and outdoors

The outdoor learning environment should echo and mirror the indoor area, but both will offer different experiences. Indoors, children will use felt-tip pens and pencils, while outdoors they might chalk on the ground and make marks on a larger scale. Indoors, they might use paint and brushes on paper, but outdoors they may have buckets of water and large brushes, and paint on walls and the ground.

Hoses for warmer weather and a water pump give children opportunities for learning in many ways, from not splashing others to the science of pumping and spraying. Gardening equipment is needed for the planting areas. Buckets, spades, sieves, and so on, are needed in the sand area. They will make dens, play in tents and may wear dressing-up clothes indoors or outdoors.

It is very important that great care is taken of equipment in both environments, so that jigsaw pieces do not end up on a flowerbed, for example. Sets (puzzles, crockery from the home corner, sets of zoo animals, wooden blocks) should not be moved from the area where they belong. If children have made a den and want to have a pretend meal in it, then a picnic box can be taken into the garden, full of bits and bobs. This allows children to learn to care for equipment.

Open continuous provision indoors should be provided every day

Everything in the list for continuous, open-ended provision that is suitable for toddlers should also be provided for children aged three to five years.

Children need to be able to experience materials at different levels of complexity, since at times they are operating at their highest levels of possibility, and at other times they need a quieter, less exhausting day. None of us, adults or children, are at our best all day and every day.

It is always useful to move around the environment on your knees in order to see it from a child's-eye view (or crawl to gain a toddler or mobile baby's view). Lying on your back helps to understand a baby's view from a cot. In other words, what would a child see as they move about the learning environment?

Children from three to five years need access to the following every day:

- wet sand and dry sand (these are two entirely different learning experiences), with equipment nearby in boxes labelled with words and pictures for children to select
- clean water in a water tray or baby bath, with buckets, guttering, waterwheels, and so on, to make waterfalls, and boxes of equipment labelled with pictures and words
- found and recycled materials in a workshop area, with glue, scissors, masking tape, and so on
- book-making area, next to the workshop
- small world – dolls' house, train set, garage, cars, farms, zoos, dinosaurs
- paint/graphics materials in a mark-making area, with a variety of paper and different kinds of pencils, pens and chalks (this might be next to the workshop area)
- malleable clay or dough
- wooden set of free-standing blocks (not plastic, and not bits and pieces from different sets) – unit blocks, hollow blocks and mini hollow blocks (for example, from Community Playthings)
- construction kit (one or two carefully selected types, such as Duplo® or Brio®)
- book area, which is warm, light and cosy
- domestic play area
- dressing-up clothes (mainly hats and shoes)
- daily cookery with baking materials and equipment

- ICT, digital camera, computer – it is preferable to use computer programs that encourage children to use their imaginations, rather than responding to computer-led tasks
- nature table, with magnifiers, growing and living things, such as mustard and cress, hyacinths, wormery, fish tank
- woodwork bench, with glue to join things and tape to bind things together, saws, hammers and a vice
- a range of dolls and soft toys
- music and sounds area, with homemade and commercially produced instruments
- movement area (perhaps next to the music area)
- story props, poetry and song cards
- sewing table
- cooker/food preparation.

Displays and interest tables indoors

Issues of gender, culture and disability need to be thought through when it comes to setting up displays. Positive images and multicultural artefacts need to be discussed and planned by staff as a team. Seasonal and cultural festivals and educational visits across the year help children through special and one-off opportunities for exploration.

Displays should respect children's work – do not cut up children's paintings to make an adult's collage. The paintings children do should be mounted and displayed as they are.

Guidelines for displays and interest tables

- Adults should not draw or write on children's work without their permission. After all, adults do not allow children to draw or write on their records without permission.
- Any writing or notes about a painting should be mounted separately underneath the child's painting or drawing. The label should be discussed with the child, who should agree to the wording.

Guidelines for displays and interest tables (cont.)

- Any lettering should be done carefully on ruled lines so that it looks attractive. Your writing must project a good role model for children.
- Writing should not be at 'jaunty angles' on a display, as children are developing their understanding of which direction the print goes when reading.
- In English, writing goes from left to right; in Urdu it goes from right to left; and in Chinese it goes up and down.

Wall displays (such as photographs) for crawling babies should be at their eye height, along the floor, against the wall. Wall displays for older children should also be at their eye height, and not above. Remember not to clutter the walls. Leave some walls blank, and perhaps only put a display on one wall. Having too much on the walls is too exciting and colourful, and children become calmer when the walls are calmer, in natural shades.

Guidelines for making a display

- Use a piece of material that takes the eye to important parts of the display.
- Display the essential objects of the experience (for example, autumn leaves, conkers and tree bark).
- Include a non-fiction book on the subject (about autumn or seasonal rhythms).
- Include a book of literature, such as a poem or a story about autumn.
- Include photos/audiotape of sights/sounds of the garden in autumn and the children raking up leaves, to help children to link into the experience and reflect.

The Reggio Emilia approach reminds us that practitioners need to consider the following in setting up displays, which are seen as part of what they describe as the 'microclimate'. Consider:

- how different parts of the display relate to each other in the way they are presented
- how light shines and is part of the display
- the way in which colours and materials create different experiences
- that the display can smell as well as be touched
- that sounds are an aspect to be built in to the display.

Figure 4.10 A display about wood

Staying anchored and available to children

It is very difficult for children when adults flit about and do not stay in one place for long enough for children to engage with them in focused ways. It does not encourage children to focus either.

It is a good idea, as part of planning the curriculum framework in the learning environments indoors and outdoors, to see where there might need to be anchored adults working in depth with children. The following points are important:

- The anchored adult needs to sit at the child's height or on the floor, so as to give full attention to a child or children in one area, while retaining an overview of the rest of the room.
- The practitioner must be free to focus on what the children in a particular area are doing (for example, playing with wooden blocks or in the movement corner) and be able to have engaging conversations, listening to what children say and being sensitive to what they do, allowing them plenty of time (for example, cooking together or planting bulbs in the garden).
- Another adult must be free to help children generally – for example, to deal with children's toilet needs, to hang up a painting or comfort a tearful child, or simply to respond to children who ask for help.
- If each adult has a clear understanding of their role in the team, it helps each practitioner to focus on the children and reduces the temptation to chat with other adults instead of engaging with the children.

Planning the play environment (not making a plan)

Remember, you are planning the play environment: you are not planning the way in which children play in it. Children need to be able to initiate their own ideas in their play and to be spontaneous. This is only possible if the environment is set up to encourage play.

Case Study · Planning the play environment

Some of the children visited the market and found it fascinating. The staff set up a market in the garden, with stalls made of upturned cardboard boxes, and play props that were mainly boxes of stones, leaves, conkers, and so on. The children developed their own play, but the important thing was that they had materials such as paper bags to put stones and leaves into when they pretended to be customers or stallholders.

Research Activity

Research how play is timetabled in one or all of the following situations:

- an early childhood setting
- a Reception class in a primary school
- the first two years of statutory schooling in primary school.

Quality learning takes place when you are able to match what is offered in the curriculum to the interests and needs of individual children. Good teaching means helping children to learn, so that they make connections with what they already know, and at times are helped to extend this.

Bear these factors in mind when you plan – quality is more likely to result. If you can help children to enjoy learning, you will have given them a good start, which they will take with them through their lives. Both the adult and the child contribute actively when the curriculum is of high quality.

Discussion point

In a small group, discuss how:

- when an adult is directing all the learning, the learning is of poor quality
- when children lead their own learning all the time, the learning is of poor quality
- when children colour in outlines given by adults, the learning is of poor quality
- when adults and children take turns to lead and direct, the learning is of good quality.

Research in this book to read more about this and discuss what you find.

Section 4: How to develop age-appropriate routines which encourage children to care for themselves

The care needs of individuals from birth to 16 years

From the moment they are born, all children depend completely on an adult to meet all their needs, but the way in which these needs are met will vary considerably according to family circumstances, culture and the personalities of the child and the caring adult.

To achieve and maintain healthy growth and development (that is physical, intellectual, emotional and social development) certain basic needs must be fulfilled, as shown in Table 4.3.

At each developmental stage, children and young people will have different skills and abilities. Although children do not make significant progress in self-care until the toddler years, there are signs of growing independence much earlier.

- **At about eight months**, babies begin to understand how objects relate to one another and may begin using them for their intended function: for example, brushing their hair, 'chatting' on the play phone, etc.

Basic needs for healthy growth and development		
food	cleanliness	sleep, rest and activity
protection from infection and injury	intellectual stimulation	relationships and social contacts
shelter, warmth, clothing	fresh air and sunlight	love, and consistent and continuous affection
access to health care	appreciation, praise and recognition of effort or achievements	security and nurture

Table 4.3 Children need these basic needs to be fulfilled in order to develop

- **At around ten to eleven months**, babies start learning how to drink out of a cup, and will also begin to hold out their arms or legs to help when getting dressed.
- **By around 12 to 15 months**, babies are able to hold a cup in both hands and drink from it, and will recognise themselves in the mirror.
- **By 18 months**, most children go through a period of saying 'NO'; it is their way of asserting their new feelings of self-identity.
- Between **one and four years**, children can:
  - *Use a fork and spoon*: they may start wanting to use utensils as early as 13 months; most children have mastered this skill by 17 or 18 months.
  - *Take off their own clothes*: children usually learn to do it between 13 and 20 months.
  - *Brush their teeth*: they may start wanting to help with this task as early as 16 months, but probably will not be able to do it on their own until sometime between the third and fourth birthday.
  - *Wash and dry their hands*: this skill develops between 19 and 30 months and is something children should learn before or at the same time as using the toilet.
  - *Get dressed*: they may be able to put on loose clothing as early as 20 months, but will need a few more months before they can manage a T-shirt and another year or two months after that before they are able to get dressed all by themselves. By 27 months, they will probably be able to pull off their shoes.
  - *Use the toilet*: most children are not physically ready to start toilet training until they are at least 18 to 24 months old, and some will not be ready to begin for as much as a year after that. Two key signs of readiness include being able to pull their own pants up and down, and knowing when they have to go before it happens.
  - *Prepare their own breakfast*: children as young as three may be able to get themselves a bowl of cereal when they are hungry, and most can do it by the time they are four and half.

- **Children aged four to eight:** children aged four and five can eat skilfully with a knife and fork and can undress and dress themselves, except for laces, ties and back buttons. By six to seven years old, children are completely independent in washing, dressing and toileting skills.
- **Children aged eight to twelve:** children are competent at most self-caring tasks, although they may need reminding about washing regularly. The level of independence shown will depend on the individual child's past experiences and level of maturity; for example, when crossing roads alone.
- **Young people aged 12 to 16:** young people tend to identify more with friends and begin to separate from their parents. They are less dependent on family for emotional support and are becoming skilled at making decisions. Again, the level of independence will vary according to the young person's level of maturity and temperament. It will also depend on how much responsibility the young person has been given by his or her parents.

Culturally and ethnically appropriate care

Parents develop their own way of caring for their child which reflects their culture and personal preferences. It is important to consult parents and carers about these ideas and preferences. This involves respecting their decisions and acknowledging them as being the people who know their child best. Practitioners can then use this knowledge to plan individualised and culturally sensitive care.

How to meet the care needs of children in ways that maintain their security and respect their privacy

It is important that children have their rights to privacy respected when having their care needs met.

Intimate, personal care such as nappy changing, toileting, dressing and undressing should be coordinated by a key person. When developmentally appropriate, young children should be asked to *consent* to offers of intimate care. You might say, for example, to a toddler in the toilet: 'Would you like me to help pull your knickers down?' rather than just going ahead and doing it. Similarly, a child who has had a toileting accident should be encouraged sympathetically to help when changing his or her clothing.

How to assist daily living through practical activities

Children in early years settings can be encouraged to be independent by:

- providing wall pegs at child level, so that they can hang up their own coats
- having clearly marked areas, such as places to build with blocks, baskets with dress-up clothes, chairs and low tables with art supplies, to enable children to select activities and to use appropriate materials
- giving unobtrusive adult help, for example, by placing the shoe directly in front of the foot that matches when a child is struggling to learn how to dress herself
- teaching toddlers how to pull pants down themselves when being toilet-trained
- providing step stools so they can climb up and wash their own hands
- providing bean bag chairs, or comfortable mats so that young children can sit in comfort as they 'read' stories by themselves.

Caring for children's skin

Hand and face washing

Babies and toddlers need to have their hands washed frequently. This is because they are constantly picking things up and putting their hands in their mouths, and they may also pick up an infection. It is important to build regular hand washing into routine care – washing their hands before and after eating. Most young children dislike having their faces washed as they feel they are being suffocated. Always use a clean cloth and wipe each part of the face separately and gently. Dry thoroughly with a soft towel.

Protection from sun

Babies benefit from being outside in the fresh air for a while every day. When air is trapped in a building it becomes stale, the level of humidity rises and there is an increased risk of infections spreading. When working in nurseries, practitioners should ensure that rooms are well ventilated and that there are opportunities for babies to go outside. Sunlight is beneficial too, but care should be taken with babies and young children:

- Keep all children out of the sun when it is at its most dangerous, between 11 am and 3 pm; those caring for young children should plan outdoor activities to avoid this time unless children are well protected by hats and sun protection cream. Permission must be obtained from the child's parent or guardian before applying sunscreen creams.
- Specialists advise keeping babies up to nine months of age out of direct sunlight altogether to prevent the risk of developing skin cancer in later life.
- Use sun hats with a wide brim that will protect face, neck and shoulders on older babies.
- Use sun protection cream on all sun-exposed areas.
- Use sunshades or canopies on buggies and prams.

Hair

Most parents will style their own children's hair. If we need to care for their hair while they are in the setting, it is important to follow the parents' preferences; for example, using a wide-toothed comb, or using hair oil rather than shampoo.

Features of head lice	
They are tiny grey-brown insects with six legs, ending in claws.	Head lice only live in human scalp hair: they cannot be caught from animals.
They have mouths like small needles which they stick into the scalp and use to drink the blood.	They are unable to fly, hop or jump. They cling to hair shafts and climb swiftly between them.
Head lice are not the same as **nits**, which are the cases or shells of eggs laid by female lice, 'glued' on to the hair shafts. Nits remain glued in place after the lice hatch; they are pinhead sized and pearly white.	
Head lice are between 1 and 3 mm in size – from pinhead to match head length (see Figure 4.12).	Head lice generally remain close to the scalp, for warmth, food and cover, and do not wander down the hair shafts. They move away in response to disturbance.
Head lice do not discriminate between clean and dirty hair, but cease to move around in really wet hair.	They are caught just by head-to-head contact with someone who is infested. When heads touch, the lice simply get across by climbing through the dry hair.

Table 4.4 Features of head lice

Figure 4.11 How the Bug Buster kit works

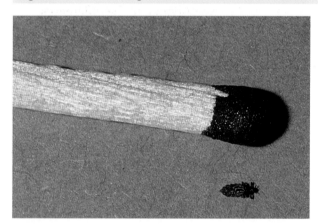

Figure 4.12 Head louse

Head lice

Head lice are a common affliction. Anybody can catch head lice, but they are particularly prevalent among young children, 3 to 11 years old, probably because they tend to put their heads together when playing.

See Table 4.4 for detailed information on head lice.

Many people only realise that they have head lice when the itching starts, usually after two to three months. The itching is due to an allergic reaction to the louse bites which takes time to develop. Sometimes a rash may be seen on the back of the neck where lice droppings (a black powder, like fine pepper) irritate the skin.

Treatment

The Community Hygiene Concern charity (www. chc.org) has developed the '**bug buster**' kit; this contains specially designed combs, which are used in wet hair to detect and cure head lice methodically, without having to subject children to chemical treatments. This method has been approved by the UK Department of Health. (See Figure 4.11.)

Prevention

The best way to prevent lice is for families to learn how to check their own heads reliably. National Bug Busting Days are educational days that many schools in the UK take part in. The aim is to inform children and their parents about the behaviour of head lice and how to detect and remove them. Co-ordinating Bug Busting Days across the country can help to prevent head lice circulating. See www.chc.org for more information about Bug Busting for schools.

Teeth

Although not yet visible, the teeth of a newborn baby are already developing inside the gums. A baby's first teeth are called milk teeth and these begin to appear at around six months. Dental care should begin as soon as the first tooth appears, with visits to the dentist starting in the child's second year. Teeth need cleaning *as soon as they appear*, because plaque sticks to the teeth and will cause decay if not removed. Caring for the first teeth, even though they are temporary, is important for the following reasons:

1 This develops a good hygiene habit which will continue throughout life.
2 Babies need their first teeth so that they can chew food properly.
3 First teeth guide the permanent teeth into position. If first teeth are missing, the permanent teeth may become crooked.
4 Painful teeth may prevent chewing and cause eating problems.
5 Clean, white shining teeth look good.

In Practice

Caring for teeth

1 Use a small amount (a smear) of baby toothpaste on a soft baby toothbrush or on a piece of fine cloth (such as muslin) to clean the plaque from the teeth. Gently smooth the paste onto the baby's teeth and rub lightly. Rinse the brush in clear water and clean her mouth.

2 Brush twice a day – after breakfast and before bed.

3 After their first birthday, children can be taught to brush their own teeth – but will need careful supervision.

4 They should be shown when and how to brush, that is, up and down away from the gum. They may need help to clean the back molars.

5 Avoid sugary drinks, sweets and snacks between feeds or mealtimes.

Research Activity

Caring for a baby's teeth

Prepare a leaflet for parents showing how teeth develop in a young baby and how to ensure their healthy development. Include tips for making caring for the teeth an enjoyable routine activity.

Nappy area

Young babies will need several changes of nappy each day, whenever the nappy is wet or soiled. As with any regular routine, have everything ready before you begin:

- a plastic-covered padded changing mat
- baby lotion
- nappy sacks for dirty nappies
- baby bath liquid
- a bowl of warm water (or baby wipes)
- barrier cream, such as zinc and castor oil cream
- cotton wool
- new, clean nappy.

It is important to pay attention to the differences between boys and girls when cleaning the nappy area – see the guidelines below. If you are using a special changing table or bed, make sure the baby cannot fall off.

Never leave the baby unattended on a high surface. As long as there are no draughts and the room is warm, the changing mat can be placed on the floor.

Guidelines for cleaning the nappy area

1 Wash your hands and put the baby on the changing mat.
2 Undo the clothing and open out the nappy. It is quite common for baby boys to urinate just as you remove the nappy, so pause for a few seconds with nappy held over the penis.
3 Clean off as much faeces as possible with the soiled nappy.

Guidelines for cleaning the nappy area (cont.)

4 Boys: moisten cotton wool with water or lotion and begin by wiping his tummy across, starting at his navel. Using fresh cotton wool or baby wipes, clean the creases at the top of his legs, working down towards his anus and back. Wipe all over the testicles, holding his penis out of the way. Clean under the penis. Never try to pull back the foreskin. Lift his legs using one hand (finger between his ankles) and wipe away from his anus, to buttocks and to back of thighs.

5 Girls: use wet cotton wool or baby wipes to clean inside all the skin creases at the top of her legs. Wipe down towards her bottom. Lift her legs using one hand (finger between her ankles) and clean her buttocks and thighs with fresh cotton wool, working inwards towards the anus. Keep clear of her vagina and never clean inside the lips of the vulva.

6 Dry the skin creases and the rest of the nappy area thoroughly. Let the baby kick freely and then apply barrier cream if required.

 In Practice

Procedure for changing nappies in a group setting

Nappy changing is an important time and you should ensure that the baby feels secure and happy. Singing and simple playful games should be incorporated into the procedure to make it an enjoyable experience. Every setting will have its own procedure for changing nappies. The following is an example:

❏ Nappies should be checked and changed at regular periods throughout the day.

❏ A baby should never knowingly be left in a soiled nappy.

❏ Collect the nappy and the cream needed. Put on apron and gloves. Ensure that you have warm water and wipes.

❏ Carefully put the baby on the changing mat, talking to them and reassuring them.

❏ Afterwards dispose of the nappy and discard the gloves.

❏ Thoroughly clean the nappy mat and the apron with an anti-bacterial spray.

❏ Wash your hands to avoid cross-contamination.

❏ Record the nappy change on the baby's **Nappy Chart**, noting the time, whether it was wet or dry or if there has been a bowel movement. Also note any change you have observed – such as in colour or consistency of the stools, or if the baby had difficulty in passing the stool. Also, note if there is any skin irritation or rash present.

❏ Check nappy mats for any tears or breaks in the fabric and replace if necessary.

Never leave a baby or toddler unsupervised on the changing mat.

For information on disposing of waste in the early years setting, see your setting's Health and Safety policy on disposal of waste.

Taking into account the preferences of parents and carers

Every setting will have its own policies and procedures concerning the physical care of babies and young children. However, it is also important to work in partnership with parents and carers, and this involves taking into account their preferences, whether cultural or personal. For example, parents may express a preference for:

● only using organic, environmentally-friendly products, including skin care products and foods

● practising baby-led weaning (see Chapter 10)

● using a dummy when their baby is put down for a sleep and at certain other times.

Provided that the parent's preference does not conflict with professional practice in the setting, their preferences should be noted and complied with.

Providing respectful and personalised physical care

Babies and young children need to form relationships with adults who are warm, responsive and respectful. When providing physical care, we should always be aware of the child's individual needs and preferences, and help them to enjoy care routines.

In Practice

Respectful care

1 Let a baby or child know in advance what you intend to do.

2 Use positive facial expressions and reassuring words.

3 Remember that physical touch reassures babies and toddlers.

4 Let them 'go' at their own pace. Do not hurry a baby or child when feeding or dressing them.

5 Give the baby or child your whole attention when carrying out a personal care activity.

6 Where possible, involve the baby or child in the care routine. A baby can hold the clean nappy for you; a toddler can be supervised washing her own face.

Procedures which protect babies, young children and practitioners

Early years settings keep babies and children safe by having good procedures for issues such as safe recruitment and general management. All settings are required to have a policy to deal with allegations made against staff. However, no system alone can protect children; in 2009, a nursery worker, Vanessa George, was jailed for a minimum of seven years after admitting abusing toddlers at the nursery and photographing the abuse. A review into the case concluded that the environment had enabled a culture to develop in which staff did not feel able to challenge some inappropriate behaviour by George. The review also found that an 'informal' recruitment process was partly to blame.

Routines for babies and young children that support their health and development

Good routines can provide valuable opportunities for promoting health and development, whether in a home or group setting. Everyday care routines for babies and children under three years provide opportunities for the promotion of:

- **intellectual and language skills**: talking to babies and children when carrying out routine care promotes communication skills and understanding.
- **emotional development**: babies and children feel secure when handled and treated in an affectionate and competent manner.
- **social skills**: young children see and understand that they are treated equally when routines are carried out, and will learn the concepts of sharing and taking turns. They will also experience a feeling of belonging, which is very important.
- **development of independence**: good routines allow time and space for toddlers to try to do things for themselves, rather than being rushed by the adult.

Daily and weekly routines

Routines should be planned and organised around the needs of individual babies and children. The routines should ensure that each baby or child has all his or her personal care needs met in a positive environment. Factors to take into consideration when planning and implementing routines include:

- sleep, rest and stimulation
- nappy changes
- stage of development.
- feeding
- play preferences

Sleep, rest and stimulation

Physical care routines should promote physical and sensory development, and provide babies and young children with stimulation. Outings and visits need to be planned in advance and will become part of the weekly routine. Babies and toddlers need periods of quiet and rest as well as regular opportunities for naps.

Feeding

Feeding routines also need to be planned; babies should not have to wait for their feeds. Recent research has suggested that babies should be weaned before six months to avoid developing allergies. This may lead to a change in the Department of Health guidelines, which currently recommends waiting until a baby is six months old before weaning. You need to keep up to date with the latest government guidelines.

Routines for meal and snack times for toddlers should include allowing time for them to feed themselves and planning to make the experience as enjoyable as possible. Special dietary needs and parental preferences must always be taken into account.

Nappy changes

Nappies must be changed regularly to avoid nappy rash, and should always be changed immediately after they have been soiled. Whenever possible, the baby's key person should change the baby's nappy as this helps to develop a close, trusting relationship and enables the key person to report any concerns to the parents.

Play preferences

It would be very boring if babies and children were all routinely offered the same activities every day – even when they appear to enjoy them. Planning routines for play should take account of their play preferences but it is important to introduce new activities in order to promote their learning and development.

Stage of development

Understanding about the sequence of development as well as the stage which each baby or child is going through will help you to plan for the future. For example, a seven-month-old baby who enjoys sitting can be helped to become more mobile if you place a few toys just out of his reach. Observations of the way in which a child is developing will help the planning process.

Showing respect and sensitivity during everyday care routines

The importance of showing respect when working with babies is discussed earlier in this chapter. The key worker system is fundamental to children's wellbeing; he or she gets to know the child and their family well, and is the best person to be able to plan for their needs in a sensitive way.

The principles of effective toilet training

Newborn babies pass the waste products of digestion automatically – in other words, although they may appear to be exerting a physical effort when passing a stool or motion, they have no conscious control over the action. Parents used to boast with pride that all their children were potty-trained at nine months, but the reality is that they were lucky in their timing! Up to the age of 18 months, emptying the bladder and bowel is still a totally automatic reaction – the child's central nervous system (CNS) is still not sufficiently mature to make the connection between the action and its results.

Recognising that a child is ready to move out of nappies

There is no point in attempting to start toilet training until the toddler shows that he or she is ready, and this rarely occurs before the age of 18 months. The usual signs are:

- increased interest when passing urine or a motion: the child may pretend-play on the potty with their toys
- they may tell the carer when they have passed urine or a bowel motion, or look very uncomfortable when they have done so
- they may start to be more regular with bowel motions, or wet nappies may become rarer; this is a sign that the bladder is developing
- they can stand on their feet and sit on potty seat or a toilet. Some experts assess a child's readiness by their ability to climb stairs using alternate feet, that is, one foot per step.

When to start toilet training

Toilet training should be approached in a relaxed, unhurried manner. If the potty is introduced too early or if a child is forced to sit on it for long periods of time, he or she may rebel and the whole issue of toilet training will become a battleground.

Toilet training can be over in a few days or may take some months. Becoming dry at night takes longer, but most children manage this before the age of five years. Before attempting to toilet train a child, make sure that he has shown that he is ready to be trained. Remember that, as with all developmental milestones, there is a wide variation in the age range at which children achieve bowel and bladder control.

Guidelines for toilet training

1 **Be positive and supportive to the child's efforts**: be relaxed about toilet training and be prepared for accidents.

2 **Structuring the physical environment to facilitate training**: have the potty close at hand so that the child becomes familiar with it and can include it in his or her play. It helps if the child sees other children using the toilet or potty. It is also helpful if children are dressed in clothes that are easy for them to manage by themselves, such as pull-up trousers rather than dungarees.

3 **Working in partnership with parents and carers**: it is important to work closely with parents so that we take a similar approach to toilet training, otherwise the child may become anxious. If a parent starts training their toddler when there is a new baby due, be prepared for some accidents. Many children react to a new arrival by regressing to baby behaviour.

4 **Encouraging and praising**: always praise the child when he or she succeeds and do not show anger or disapproval if the opposite occurs; the child may be upset by an accident. It is important not to over-encourage children as this can make them anxious about letting you down.

5 **Treating child with respect and avoiding guilt**: do not show any disgust for the child's faeces. He or she will regard using the potty as an achievement and will be proud of them. Children have no natural shame about their bodily functions (unless adults make them ashamed).

6 **Establishing a routine**: offer the potty regularly so that the child becomes used to the idea of a routine, and learn to read the signs that a child needs to use it. Cover the potty and flush the contents down the toilet. Always wear disposable gloves. Encourage good hygiene right from the start, by washing the child's hands after every use of the potty.

7 **Flexible personalised approach**: some children feel insecure when sitting on a potty with no nappy on – try it first still wearing a nappy or pants if the child shows reluctance. The child may prefer to try the 'big' toilet seat straightaway; a toddler seat fixed onto the normal seat makes this easier. Boys need to learn to stand in front of the toilet and aim at the bowl before passing any urine; you could put a piece of toilet paper in the bowl for him to aim at. Some children are frightened when the toilet is flushed; be tactful and sympathetic. You could wait until the child has left the room before you flush.

8 **Providing plenty of fluids and fibre to prevent hard stools**: children need to drink plenty of water or other drinks in order for them to learn what having a full bladder feels like. They also need to be given foods that contain fibre (such as fruit and vegetables) to prevent constipation.

Dealing with accidents

Even once a child has become used to using the potty or toilet, there will be occasions when they have an 'accident' – that is, they wet or soil themselves. This happens more often during the early stages of toilet training, as the child may lack the awareness and control needed to allow enough time to get to the potty. Older children may become so absorbed in their play that they simply forget to go to the toilet.

You can help children when they have an accident by:

- not appearing bothered; let the child know that it is not a big problem, just something that happens from time to time
- reassuring the child in a friendly tone of voice and offering a cuddle if he or she seems distressed
- being discreet – deal with the matter swiftly; wash and change the child out of view of others and with the minimum of fuss
- an older child could be supervised discreetly and encouraged to manage the incident themselves, if they wish to do so
- following safety procedures in the setting – for example, wear disposable gloves and deal appropriately with soiled clothing and waste.

Activity

Toilet training

1 Arrange to interview a parent or carer who has recently toilet-trained a child.

2 Try to find out the methods they used and any problems they encountered.

3 Write a report of the methods used.

In small groups, make a colourful, eye-catching wall display that provides tips for parents and carers on toilet training.

Discussion point

In class, discuss the problems that can arise with toilet training and compare the strategies used by different families.

Guidelines for encouraging independence

A sound knowledge of child development will help you to know how to encourage children to be independent. It is often easier – and certainly quicker – to rush a child who is learning to put on his own shoes, for example, so it pays to be patient and follow these guidelines:

- **Encouragement** is the most important factor in helping children towards independence.

- **Praise:** whenever children attempt a new skill, *whether they succeed or not*, praise them and urge them to try again.

- **Do not interfere**: try not to step in too quickly to help; it is essential that they have enough time to manage these things on their own, at their own pace. Never pressure children to try something before they are ready.

- **Be flexible**: put up with the experimentation even if it means a lot of mess and you could obviously do it a lot quicker yourself. The more they practise, the better they will be.

- **Set limits**: Keep a watchful eye on children as they begin to experiment with doing things on their own. Set limits and explain them: tell them why it is dangerous to turn on the oven or use the bread knife yet.

- **Promote independence at mealtimes**: As soon as the child can pick up tiny objects with finger and opposing thumb (at around six to nine months) encourage self-feeding with tiny sandwiches, little bits of banana, cooked carrot or grated apple. **NB** Always supervise because of the dangers of **choking**.

- Let babies hold their cup even though you control it: gradually pass the control over to them.

Guidelines for encouraging independence (cont.)

- **Encourage fine motor skills** by giving the child a fat crayon and a piece of card to scribble on.

- **Promote independence when dressing**: zips, buttons, and hooks are difficult for small children: choose clothing with elastic waistbands, velcro, or ones which slip on with zips and buttons partly closed. Lay out clothing so that children can lift it the right way round: trousers front up, jumpers and dresses front down; this is so that they can sit down and put them on. Help them to put their shoes on, but let them fasten them themselves whenever possible. (Children sit with their knees turned out and naturally put shoes on with the fastenings on the inside where they can see them; that is why they are often on the wrong feet.)

- **Promote independence in older children and young people**: as with all children, praise them for their efforts as well as their abilities. Encourage them to communicate, to voice their own opinions. Listen to their ideas and show respect for them.

Sources of support for practitioners to help deal with their own feelings

Throughout this chapter the emphasis has been on what *you* can do for the children in your care – how you can promote their development and give them a quality learning environment. It may sometimes feel as if you are less important than they are. This is far from the truth. Children need you to be strong and positive for them, but you also need to be strong and positive for yourself.

Stress caused by work is the second biggest occupational health problem in the UK (after back problems). Because there is still a stigma attached to mental health problems, employees are often reluctant to seek help in case they are seen as unable to cope.

Many situations can lead to stress at work. These include:

- poor relationships with colleagues
- an unsupportive boss
- lack of consultation and communication
- too much interference with your private, social or family life
- too much or too little to do
- too much pressure, with unrealistic deadlines
- work that is too difficult or not demanding enough
- lack of control over the way the work is done
- poor working conditions
- being in the wrong job
- feeling undervalued
- insecurity and the threat of unemployment.

Any one of these situations could leave you feeling low and lacking in confidence.

Case Study   A stressful situation

Marsha recently obtained a qualification in child care and education and has been employed as an early years practitioner at Meadlands Day Nursery for two weeks. She has just been called in to see her supervisor as her colleagues have reported that she is frequently tearful and unable to contribute to activities in the nursery. Carol, her supervisor, asks why she is unhappy, and Marsha says that she 'doesn't like the atmosphere in the nursery, that there is a lot of bickering between the staff, and she feels that one particular child is constantly being ridiculed by her colleagues'. Carol asks her to give more information about the complaints, but Marsha bursts into tears and asks if she can go home as she cannot cope anymore.

Case Study   A stressful situation (cont.)

1 Identify and write down the stressors (the factors producing stress) which Marsha mentions.

2 How should Carol deal with this situation?

3 Find out about the Type A and Type B personalities from psychology textbooks. Are some personalities more suited to working in early years settings?

Dealing with stress

If work-related stress is affecting you, it is important to deal with the problem as soon as possible. One of the most important factors in reducing stress levels is managing time effectively. When you are the 'junior' in a team, the amount you are expected to do can seem overwhelming. Remember, everyone has to go through this at the beginning. Try to remain calm while you consider different ways of dealing with your feelings:

- Discuss the problems with your manager or senior worker; make notes to help you to focus on what is bothering you and take them with you when you talk to your manager.
- Ask your tutor or teacher for advice. Remember, he or she will have seen many students through various practical placements and will have encountered most situations.

Assessment practice

Unit 4

- How would you plan the care of (a) a baby, and (b) a three-year-old child for a full day in the setting?
- Explain the importance of helping children to manage risk and challenge in their environment.
- How could you maintain the safety and privacy of children and respect their wishes.

Useful resources

Organisations and websites

British Red Cross – for information on first aid for children and how to become a qualified first-aider:
www.redcross.org.uk

Child Accident Prevention Trust is a UK charity, working to reduce the number of children and young people killed, disabled or seriously injured in accidents:
www.capt.org.uk

The **Food Standards Agency** carries out a range of work to make sure that food is safe to eat, including funding research on chemical, microbiological and radiological safety, and on food hygiene and allergy:
www.food.gov.uk

The **Foundation Stage Forum** shares information on all aspects of Foundation Stage education, from childminding to Reception and Year 1, and from practical to theoretical and research:
www.foundation-stage.info

Royal Society for the Prevention of Accidents – for all child safety advice and information:
www.rospa.com

Books and publications

Meggitt, C. (2003) *Food Hygiene and Safety*. Oxford. Heinemann Educational Publishers.
Nursery World, 4 February 2010, pages 19–22.

5 The principles underpinning the role of the practitioner working with children: Unit 5

Section 1: How to maintain professional relationships with children and adults

The range of professional relationships in multi-disciplinary teams

As an early years practitioner, you will work alongside other professionals – either in your own setting or in the wider early years community. Multi-agency working enables different services and professionals to join forces in order to prevent problems occurring in the first place. It is an effective way of supporting children, young people and families with additional needs, and helps to secure improved outcomes. Integrated working involves everyone who works with children and young people, whether part-time or full-time. Any member of the children and young people's workforce (such as an early years practitioner, a nurse, teacher, youth worker, sports coach or social worker) needs to understand the importance of working together in an integrated way and to build it into their everyday practice. Integrated and multi-agency working is also collectively known as partnership working.

Key terms

Integrated working – When everyone supporting children and young people works together effectively to put the child at the centre, meet their needs and improve their lives.

Multi-agency working – Practitioners from different sectors and professions within the workforce are brought together to provide integrated support to children and their families; for example a 'team around the child'.

The importance of multi-agency working and integrated working

Before multi-agency working became the accepted way of working, the parents of a child or young person with special or additional needs would probably face many different appointments with several different people, none of whom would have spoken to each other and all of whom would expect the parents to give a detailed breakdown of their child's disability. Multi-agency working and integrated working is designed to cut across this by bringing together professionals with a range of skills to work across their traditional service boundaries.

Every Child Matters

Multi-agency working is a holistic approach to child care and education and is an important feature of the government's *Every Child Matters* (ECM) framework:

As we have seen in Chapter 1, the five outcomes for ECM are to:

- be healthy
- be safe
- enjoy and achieve
- make a positive contribution
- achieve economic wellbeing.

The benefits of multi-agency working and integrated working

The key principles of multi-agency and integrated working are openness, trust and honesty, agreed shared goals and values, and regular communication between the different services, agencies and teams of professionals. When performed well, multi-agency working and integrated working enables agencies and professionals to do the following:

- **Maintain a focus on the child or young person** by putting them at the centre of everything they do and by involving them. This ensures that everyone communicates about the 'whole' child or young person.
- **Improve communication and information-sharing:** this involves developing strong partnership links with relevant agencies and within the community.
- **Support children, young people and families with additional needs:** this helps to secure improved outcomes.
- **Support the early intervention process:** early intervention helps to prevent problems occurring in the first place.
- **Work in an inclusive way:** the needs of every child and young person are valued and supported to ensure active participation in all areas of the setting or curriculum. It also means embedding processes of consultation and engagement with children and families in practice.
- **Reduce inappropriate referrals:** this involves being knowledgeable and well-informed about the roles and functions of other professionals, and understanding when and to whom they can make a referral.
- **Reduce duplication:** this is a key aspect of integrated working: 'Ensuring a child only tells their story once'.

- **Maintain confidentiality:** this means understanding that confidentiality is paramount in helping to build trust and confidence.

Professionals who may work together to support children and young people

There are many different services and professionals providing integrated support for children: see Figure 5.1.

Multi-agency panels, or the Team Around the Child (TAC)

Practitioners remain employed by their home agencies but meet on a regular basis to discuss children and young people with additional needs who would benefit from multi-agency input. An example of this type of working arrangement is a Youth Inclusion and Support Panel (YISP).

Multi-agency teams

These are made up of practitioners seconded or recruited into the team, making it a more formal arrangement than a multi-agency panel. The team works with universal services (those available to *every* child) to support families and schools, as well as individual children and young people.

Key term

Agency – In this context, this term covers the range of organisations, services and professional groups who provide services to children and their families.

Integrated working practices

Examples of integrated working include Sure Start children's centres and extended schools, which offer access to a range of integrated, multi-agency services. In Children's Centres for example, practitioners work in a coordinated way to address the needs of children, young people and families, providing services such as:

- integrated early learning and full daycare
- family support
- health services

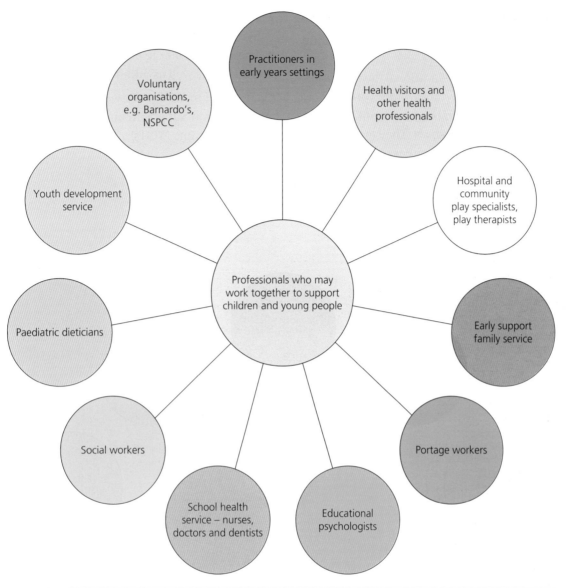

Figure 5.1 Professionals involved with integrated working

- outreach services to children and families not attending the centre
- access to training and employment advice.

Key term

Extended – A school which provides a range of services and activities, often beyond the school day, to help meet the needs of its pupils, their families and the wider community.

The functions of external agencies

How multi-agency teams work

Within multi-agency teams, practitioners share a sense of team identity and are generally line-managed by the team leader; they may however maintain links with their home agencies through supervision and training.

Features of multi-agency teams include the following:

- There is a dedicated team leader – also called the **lead professional**.
- There is a good mix of educational, health care, social care, youth justice and youth work staff.
- The people who work in the team think of themselves as team members. They are recruited or seconded into the team, either on a full- or part-time basis.
- The team works at a range of levels – not just with individual children and young people, but also small group, family and whole-school work.
- The team is likely to share a base, though some staff may continue to work from their home agencies.
- There are regular team meetings to discuss case working as well as administrative issues.

Examples of multi-agency working include Behaviour and Education Support Teams (BESTs) and Youth Offending Teams (YOTs).

Key term

Lead professional – The lead professional takes the lead to coordinate provision, and acts as a single point of contact for a child and their family when a TAC is required.

Figure 5.2 Professionals who may form a BEST

Behaviour and Education Support Teams (BESTs)

These are multi-agency teams bringing together a complementary mix of professionals from the fields of health care, social care and education. The aim of a BEST is to promote emotional wellbeing, positive behaviour and school attendance, by identifying and supporting those with, or at risk of developing, emotional and behavioural problems.

- BESTs work with children and young people aged five to eighteen years, their families and schools. A BEST will aim to intervene early and prevent problems from developing further, and works in targeted primary and secondary schools and in the community, alongside a range of other support structures and services.
- A BEST has a minimum of four to five staff members, who between them have a complementary mix of education, social care and health skills in order to meet the multi-faceted needs of children, young people and their parents.

Schools with BESTs include those with high proportions of pupils with (or at risk of developing) behavioural problems, usually demonstrated in levels of exclusions and attendance.

 **Progress check**

Multi-agency working and integrated working in your setting

Look at the lists of agencies and professionals in Table 5.1 and find out which of these work with (or have connections with) your own setting. (There may be other agencies connected to your setting which are not in this list.) List each agency or professional, and write a brief paragraph of their role in supporting children.

Children's setting	Agencies/professionals
Children's Centre Integrated local settings set up by Sure Start to provide holistic care to young children and their families	Family information services
	Play specialists
	Speech and language therapists
	Stay and Play Group
	Toy library
	Jobcentre
	Parenting classes, e.g. basic skills, English as an additional language (EAL)
	Child and family health service
	Family Support Team (FSP)
	Outreach and family support
Nursery school Local authority provision for young children	Early education
	Extended care
School Local authority provision for children aged 5 to 16	Education
	Extended care: breakfast and after-school clubs
	Education welfare officer
	Behaviour and Education Support Team (BEST)
	Counselling services

Table 5.1 Multi-agency work with children

The role and responsibilities of the practitioner in all professional relationships

There are many different settings for children, and each one will offer its own mix of benefits and drawbacks. This section makes some general comments about working in children's settings, but you should judge each setting on its own terms. Spend time there and watch how the children play, and how they seem when they arrive and leave. Talk to staff, and read the information provided (such as leaflets and booklets for parents and carers, and Ofsted reports). Effective practice as a team member will depend on liaising with others, and reporting on and reviewing your activities. Conflicts between team members often arise from poor communication – for example, an early childhood practitioner who fails to report, verbally or in writing, that a parent will be late collecting his or her child on a particular day may cause conflict if a colleague challenges the parent's conduct.

Your responsibilities as a professional early years practitioner are explored below under the following headings:

- Respect the principles of confidentiality
- Commitment to meeting the needs of the children
- Responsibility and accountability in the workplace (see page 225, the need for reliability and accountability in professional practice)
- Respect for parents and other adults
- Communicate effectively with team members
- Work effectively with professionals from other agencies.

Respect the principles of confidentiality

Confidentiality has also been examined in Chapters 1 and 3. It is the preservation of secret (or privileged) information concerning children and their families that is disclosed in the professional relationship. It is a complex issue, which has at its core the principle of trust. The giving or receiving of sensitive information should be subject to a careful consideration of the needs of the children and their families – for example, a child who is in need of protection has overriding needs which require that all relevant information be given to all the appropriate agencies, such as social workers or doctors. Within the child care and education setting, it might be appropriate to discuss sensitive issues, but such information must never be disclosed to anyone outside the setting.

Commitment to meeting the needs of the children

The needs and rights of all children should be paramount, and the early childhood practitioner must seek to meet these needs within the boundaries of the work role. Any personal preferences and prejudices must be put aside; all children should be treated with respect and dignity, irrespective of their ethnic origin, socio-economic group, religion or disability.

Respect for parents and other adults

The training you have received will have emphasised the richness and variety of child-rearing practices in the UK. It is an important part of your professional role that you respect the wishes and views of parents and other carers, even when you may disagree with them. You should also recognise that parents are usually the people who know their children best; and in all your dealings with parents and other adults, you must show that you respect their cultural values and religious beliefs.

Communicate effectively with team members

The training you have received will have emphasised the importance of effective communication in the workplace. You will also be aware of the need to plan in advance for your work with young children: a knowledge of children's needs in all developmental areas will enable you to fulfil these within your own structured role.

Work effectively with professionals from other agencies

Working in the early years is increasingly about coordinating services for the benefit of children and their families. This makes new demands on early years practitioners. It is very important that you are confident about your own training and expertise. For example, if you are a child's key person, you will know a great deal about his or her development, learning, and emotional wellbeing. You will need to communicate what you know in a concise and clear way. If an assessment of the child's development is needed, you could offer records in the form of observations and assessments for your setting or school. It will also be important that you are able to listen carefully and take note of what other professionals have to say; for example, a paediatric dietician may need you to keep an accurate record of what a child is eating in nursery, and may ask you to follow a particular approach to encourage a child to eat more healthily. It is important that families do not receive conflicting advice from different professionals, so you will need to follow the dietician's advice and avoid putting across your own personal views. If you feel there is a conflict between what you are being asked to do and what you see as good early years practice, it is important to discuss this with your manager, headteacher, or SENCO.

Key principles and codes of practice

You also need to understand the expectations about your own work role as expressed in relevant **standards**, including codes of practice, regulations, minimum standards or national occupational standards. There are ten principles that underpin most codes of practice:

1 The welfare of the child
2 Keeping children safe and maintaining a healthy and safe environment
3 Working in partnership with parents/families
4 Children's learning and development
5 Valuing diversity
6 Equality of opportunity
7 Anti-discrimination
8 Confidentiality
9 Working with other professionals
10 The reflective practitioner.

These principles reflect those rights and principles embodied in the United Nation's Convention on the Rights of the Child and along with relevant legislation, such as the Childcare Act 2006, underpin the codes of practice of all work in childcare and education. See Chapters 1 and 3 for more information on legislation to support children and their rights.

Establishing and maintaining relationships with parents

Parents and staff working together

The parent or carer is a deeply important person to the child, and the relationship between parent and child is always very emotional. Emotional relationships can be a source of great strength, but they can also be very unreasonable at times. It is important to recognise that parents and staff have different kinds of relationships with the children in their care.

Staff need to develop consistent, warm and affectionate relationships with children, especially babies, but they do not seek to replace the parents. Babies need to be with the same people each day to develop social relationships. This is why the EYFS requires all early years settings and schools to implement a key worker system.

Parents and staff have one thing in common which is very important: they all want the best for the child. The roles involved are not the same, but they are complementary:

- Staff have knowledge of general child development.
- Parents know their own child the best.

If the partnership between parents, staff and child is going to develop well, each needs to be able to trust and respect the other. The self-esteem and wellbeing of the people in the partnership – the parents, the staff members and the child – are important when they are working together. How we feel about ourselves influences how we relate to other people.

Parents may have had bad experiences at school, and when their child joins a group setting, all those past feelings may come rushing back to the surface. Parents may be anxious and suffer low self-esteem. They might expect your setting to be like the one they went to, and this will make them fear for their child. This is often so when parents are required to bring their child to the early years setting under a child protection order. Staff will need to be sensitive to the feelings of parents in this sort of situation.

Developing a partnership with parents

Hopefully an atmosphere of trust is initiated during the first meeting with parents. Remember that you are not trying to make *friends* with parents: this is a professional relationship only. Friendships are about choosing each other; they are based on being interested in the same things, such as the same sort of food, dancing or football. A professional relationship is one in which people do not choose each other. They come together because of the work they do together. Early childhood practitioners and parents come together because they each spend time with and work with the child. You do not have to like someone to have a good professional relationship with them. Early years practitioners need to bear in mind the following facts:

- Every family is different, with different needs and traditions.
- The great majority of parents are concerned to do their best for their children, even if they are not always sure what this might be.
- Each one of us only really knows what it is like to grow up in our own family. Parents almost always like some of the things about their own family and the way they were brought up; but they will just as certainly wish that other aspects of their upbringing had been different.
- Parents usually welcome help when trying out some alternative ways of doing things. They will not want to change too much though, and they will not want rapid changes forced on them by other people. Early childhood practitioners need to respect parents' wishes.

Guidelines for working with parents

- **Supporting parents:** begin by seeing yourself as a resource and support that can be used by parents to further their children's best interests.

- **Respect all parents:** the vast majority of parents, including those who abuse their children, love them. It is important not to judge parents, and to respect their good intentions. Almost every parent wants to do the job well, even if on the surface they do not seem to be interested or loving.

- **Recognise the good intentions of parents:** work positively, with this aim as a central focus. Concentrating on the good intentions of parents helps to give them a positive self-image. Just as children need positive images reflected about themselves, so do parents. The attitude of the staff must therefore be to show parents respect; bringing up a child can be hard.

- **Reinforce the parents' sense of dignity and self-esteem:** showing parents respect and reinforcing their dignity demonstrates to them that the child also needs respect and a sense of dignity.

- **Using your experience:** if you are not a parent, you will not have experienced some of the things that parents have. If you are a parent, you will only know about being a parent of your own children; you will not know what it is like to be a parent of other people's children.

Guidelines for communicating well with parents

- Maintaining eye contact helps you to give your full attention to a parent.
- Remember that your body language shows how you really feel.
- Try not to interrupt when someone is talking to you. Show positive attention and that you are listening.
- Every so often summarise the main points of a discussion, so that you are both clear about what has been said.
- If you do not know the answer to a parent's question, say so, and say that you will find out. Do not forget to do this!
- Remember that different cultures have different traditions. Touching and certain gestures might be seen as insulting by some parents, so be careful.
- If the parent speaks a different language from you, use photographs and visual aids. Talk slowly and clearly.
- If the parent has a hearing impairment, use sign language or visual aids.
- When you are talking together, bear in mind whether this is the parent's first child or whether they have had other children already.
- Remember that if the parents have a child with a disability, they may need to see you more often to discuss the child's progress.
- If the parent has a disability, make sure that when you sit together you are at the same level.
- Never gossip.

How to improve communication skills in your own professional practice

 Progress check

Relationships with parents

- What steps could a setting take to make parents feel welcome on arrival?
- How can information about early years education and care be shared with parents in an interesting and accessible way?
- What is the difference between a friendship and a professional relationship?
- What is a Children's Centre? How can Children's Centres support families with young children?

Assessment practice

Multi-agency working

1. How does multi-agency working operate in your area? Find out who would be the relevant 'partners' or agencies in your own work setting.

2. Try to visit one agency such as a Children's Centre of another department, and find out how referrals are made and how often the multi-agency team meets. Collect as much written information as possible from your visit, to help you when writing up the information required for this unit assessment.

Discussion point: Multi-agency working

A mother comes to pick up her child in the afternoon. She reads the weekly menu and looks angry and upset. You ask if anything is the matter, and she says, 'I've had enough. I've just been at the doctor's with Rhianna and been told to cut out cakes and puddings to help her weight. But I can see here that they have cake, custard and all sorts for pudding in nursery.' You try to explain that the nursery's menus have been checked with the dietician and that each meal is properly balanced, but she storms off.

Think about why early years practitioners should work closely with health care professionals in order to help in a situation like this. Discuss your ideas with another learner or in a group. Think together about how a CAF could help this child and her family (the CAF is examined at the end of this chapter, and also in Chapters 2 and 3).

Reflective practice: The need for clear and effective communication

Think about the examples below and reflect on why clear and effective communication between different professionals is important in providing for the needs of every child and young person:

- An eight-year-old child has sickle cell anaemia and attends school but is often in hospital for weeks at a time. Hospital play specialists, hospital teachers and the child's class teacher are all involved in the child's care and education.

- A child with a severe visual impairment attends a mainstream school and has daily support from a dedicated learning support assistant.

- A young child with special educational needs attends a Children's Centre and is also visited at home by a Portage worker.

Ongoing communication with parents

Ongoing communication with parents and carers is essential to meet the children's needs. For many parents there can be regular and informal communication when children are brought to or collected from the setting. However it is unusual for both parents to perform this task, and therefore it is often the same parent who has contact. The methods below can usually work for both parents and practitioners. Finding ways to communicate with parents can sometimes be difficult, especially when staff may not feel confident themselves.

- Regular contact with the same person: always meet and greet parents when they arrive. At the start, it is very important that parents meet the same practitioner – preferably their child's teacher or key person – on a daily basis.
- A meeting place for parents: ideally, there should be a room that parents can use to have a drink and a chat together.
- Information that applies in the longer term should ideally be given in writing; for example, information concerning food allergies or medical conditions, such as asthma or eczema.
- As well as informing staff members, notices may also need to be attached to a child's own equipment, lunchbox or displayed in particular areas such as food preparation or nappy-changing. In a school setting the class teacher should ensure that any other adults involved in the child's care receive information as appropriate.

Table 5.2 gives details of appropriate methods of communication.

Verbal information

Routine information can be exchanged verbally. This usually happens at the start and end of the session, when parents and their child's key person chat informally. (The role of the key person is discussed on page 150.)

Talking with parents

Always let parents know about their child's positive behaviour and take the opportunity to praise the child in front of their parents. Then if you need

Method of communication	Role of professional
Accident and incident report forms	To record information when a child or young person has been ill or is injured when at the setting.
	These reports are a statutory requirement in all settings.
Admission form	All parents fill in an admission form when registering their child.
	This is confidential information and must be kept in a safe place where only staff members have access to it.
Email	• To give information about an event
	• To respond to a request from parent or colleague
	• To arrange meetings and share documents.
	Ensure confidentiality is maintained by checking recipients and who is to be copied in.
Formal letters	• Welcome letter prior to admission to the setting
	• To give information about parents' evenings or meetings
	• To alert parents to the presence of an infectious disease within the setting
	• To advise parents about any change of policy or staff changes.
	Copies of all letters received and sent and a record of all communication be should kept for future reference.
Formal reports	These include the CAF and policy documents in the setting.
	(Preparing other formal reports is discussed below.)
Home books	To record information from both staff and parents. Home books travel between setting and the home, and record details of the child's progress, any medication given, how well they have eaten and slept, etc.
Newsletters	To give information about future events – fundraising fairs, open forums and visiting speakers, etc.
Notice boards Display boards	• To give general information about the setting, local events for parents, support group contact numbers, health and safety information, daily menus, etc.
	• To help parents and visitors feel welcome
	• To show the names of staff, with their photographs.
Personal records	To record your professional development, e.g. attendance at training sessions and certificates gained.
Policy and procedure documents	These official documents should be openly available, and parents, carers and young people should be able to discuss them with staff if they have any concerns.
Presentations Powerpoint Interactive whiteboard	• To present information and data on a range of topics, e.g. food hygiene, safety issues and risk assessment
	• To clarify new procedures
	• To explain roles and responsibilities in the setting.
Suggestions box	Some settings have a suggestions box where parents, carers and young people can contribute their own ideas for improving the service.
	Any comments received can be addressed in newsletters or on the notice board.

Method of communication	Role of professional
Telephone	• To share information with parents and professionals • To arrange meetings and visits • To order resources.
	Make sure that you communicate clearly and that your message has been understood. It is also good practice to make notes to provide a record of calls made and received.
Use of an interpreter	Use a language interpreter to support a person for whom English is an additional language.
	Use British/Irish Sign Language interpreters or visual aids as appropriate to communicate with a parent, child or young person with a hearing impairment.
Use of pictorial and design communication aids	Use photographs and visual aids to communicate with a parent who speaks a different language from you.
	Use Signalong, Makaton and/or PECS (Picture Exchange Communication System) to support children and young people with communication difficulties.
Video and DVD	• To share information in training sessions • To record children's development and learning.
	Remember to follow the rules of confidentiality that apply in your setting when displaying photographs of children.

Table 5.2 Appropriate methods of communication

to share a concern with them, they will already understand that you are interested in their child's welfare and are not being judgemental.

Communicating with children

See Chapters 1, 2 and 3 for more information on communication with children. As a recap, early years practitioners should develop effective communication skills in order to support children. These include:

- **Making eye contact and show that you are listening**: it is very difficult to have a conversation with someone who never looks at you! When talking with very young children, it is usually necessary to stoop down to their level or to sit at a table with them. (As noted earlier, it is important to be aware that, in certain cultures, mutual eye contact is considered impolite or disrespectful.)
- **Listen carefully** to the child's own spoken language and use it as a basis for conversation. Very young children tend to use one or two words to mean any of a number of things; for example, 'drink' can mean 'this is my drink', 'I want a drink', 'Where is my drink?' or 'You have got a drink'.

- **Repeat** a child's words in a correct form, or a complete sentence. This checks understanding and provides the child with an accurate model for the future. For example, young children often use speech such as 'feeded' instead of 'fed', 'runned' instead of 'ran'. In checking what they mean the adult should use the correct term, for example: Child: I feeded carrots to my rabbit. Adult: Oh, you fed your rabbit some carrots.
- **Be a positive role model**, speak clearly and use correct grammar and patterns of speech.
- **Use open-ended questions**: encourage children to speak by asking 'open' questions which require an answer in phrases and/or sentences, rather than a simple 'yes' or 'no'; for example, 'Tell me about your party,' instead of 'Did you have a good time at your party?' This opens up opportunities for the child to talk about a range of different things or one single event of his/her own choice. You can always ask more questions as the conversation progresses to check the information, supply additional vocabulary and correct grammar.

- **Use prompts**: these invite the child to say more, to share ideas and feelings. They also tell the child that you are properly listening and interested, that their ideas are important and that you accept them and respect what they are saying. Examples of prompts are: 'Oh, I see,' 'Tell me more,' 'That's interesting.'
- **Listen attentively**: get rid of distractions and pay attention to what the child is saying. It is difficult to pay close attention to what the child is saying if you are busy trying to read at the same time.
- **Respond sensitively**: remember the importance of non-verbal communication. Watch out for when a child seems upset or looks sad, and say, 'You seem upset; do you want to tell me about it?'
- **Say 'Please' and 'Thank you' to children**: children deserve the common courtesies that we as adults use with each other. Children will learn by imitating the speech and behaviour of adults.
- **Use appropriate language to help promote self-esteem**: kind words give children more self-confidence and help them to behave better, try harder and achieve more. They communicate love and respect, and also create an atmosphere in which problems can be discussed openly and understandings can be reached. For example: a child has spilt her orange juice on the floor. You could say, 'Don't be so clumsy! Just look at the mess you made.' But it would be better to say, 'Here's a cloth. Please wipe the juice up,' and later, 'Thank you for doing such a good job of cleaning the floor.'
- **Do not use inappropriate language that puts children down**: negative words make the child feel bad, and they prevent effective communication. Avoid words which:

  (a) ridicule: 'You are acting just like a baby.'
  (b) shame: 'I am so ashamed of you.'
  (c) label: 'You are a naughty boy.'

- **Do not use unkind words**, spoken without thinking of their results, make the child feel disliked, and result in low self-esteem. More importantly, unkind words do not help; they only make matters worse.
- **Always be positive**: tell children what to do instead of what not to do. For example, instead of 'Don't slam the door!' try 'Please shut the door quietly'; instead of 'Don't spill your drink!' say 'Try holding your beaker with both hands.'

The need for reliability and accountability in professional practice

The supervisor, line manager, teacher or parent will have certain expectations about your role, and your responsibilities should be detailed in the job contract. As a professional, you need to carry out all your duties willingly and to be answerable to others for your work. It is vital that you know who is your manager, and how you would raise any concerns or seek guidance or support. All staff need to know how to obtain clarification of their own role and responsibility, and to know how well they are carrying out their role. If you do not feel confident in carrying out a particular task, either because you do not fully understand it or because you have not been adequately trained, then you have a responsibility to state your concerns and ask for guidance. If you have a difficulty or disagreement with another member of staff, you must handle this in a professional manner. This means raising your concern directly with that person, or with the appropriate manager. You should not complain about colleagues in the staffroom, in front of parents, or outside work with friends or family.

Employment rights and responsibilities

The law in the UK requires that any employee who works for more than 16 hours a week should have a **contract of employment**. This document must contain the following information:

- the name of the employer and employee
- the title of the job
- the date when employment commenced
- the scale of pay
- the hours of work
- entitlement to holidays
- the length of notice required from employer and employee
- the procedures for disciplinary action or grievances
- sick-pay provision
- pensions and pension schemes.

Responsibility for paying income tax and National Insurance contributions will need to be decided; such payments are usually deducted from your gross pay. Those applying for jobs within the private sector may want to consider using a reputable nanny agency; such agencies are used to negotiating contracts designed to suit both employer and employee.

The Trade Union Voice has comprehensive advice for its members about contracts, terms and conditions and all other matters relating to the employment of early years practitioners for its members. If you are a member, log in and go to www.voicetheunion. org.uk and select 'downloads'; alternatively, search online for 'voice the union information packs'.

Grievance and complaints procedures

If a dispute arises in the workplace, either among employees or between employees and employers, it must be settled. Usually this is achieved at an early stage through discussion between colleagues or between the aggrieved person and his immediate superior. If the grievance is not easily settled, however, an official procedure is needed.

 In Practice

Complaints and grievances procedures

❑ All employees have a right to seek redress for grievances relating to their employment, and every employee must be told how to proceed on this matter.

❑ Except in very small establishments, there must be a formal procedure for settling grievances.

❑ The procedure should be in writing and should be simple and rapid in operation.

❑ The grievance should normally be discussed first between the employee and their immediate supervisor.

❑ The employee should be accompanied, at the next stage of the discussion with management, by their employee representative if they so wish.

❑ There should be a right of appeal.

Managers should always try to settle the grievance 'as near as possible to the point of origin', in the words of the Industrial Relations Code of Practice.

Section 2: The skills needed to become a reflective practitioner

The reflective cycle and the skills of reflective practice

What is a reflective practitioner?

A reflective practitioner is an individual who has developed the ability to gain self-knowledge – both of him- or herself and of his or her practice. Reflection allows the practitioner to learn about, evaluate, develop and take a position on his or her practice.

Reflective practice is associated with learning from experience; it is an important strategy for all who work in the caring field and is grounded in the individual's range of values, knowledge, theories and practice, which influence the judgements made about a particular situation.

Reflective practice requires a set of skills that the practitioner must use, such as:

- self-awareness
- the ability to view situations from multiple perspectives
- critical analysis and searching for alternative explanations
- the ability to use evidence in supporting or evaluating a decision or position.

Other skills include the ability to integrate new knowledge into existing knowledge, while making a judgement on the incident or situation. This is because evaluation is central to developing any new perspective.

The reflective cycle

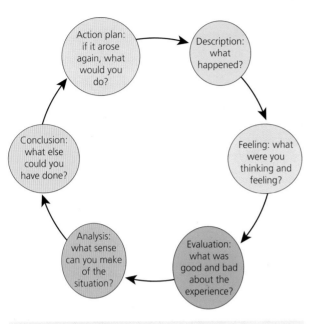

Figure 5.3 The reflective cycle

Using the reflective cycle

Description of experience: what happened?

Claire and I were supervising about 12 children aged three years who were using the outdoor play equipment. One of the children, Sasha, climbed to the top of the little slide and pushed Ben very hard so that he fell and bruised his knees. I picked Ben up to examine his knees and to comfort him. Claire – who is my room supervisor – rushed towards Sasha and gave her an angry shove, saying, 'You naughty girl – now you know what it feels like!' I then told Claire that I was taking Ben indoors to deal with his injury. By the time I came back outside, Sasha was playing happily on the trikes; Ben was no longer crying and he went off to play indoors at the water tray.

Feelings: how did it make you feel?

I was quite shaken. I felt that Claire had reacted instinctively and lashed out without thinking first. She has quite a short fuse, but I have never seen her do anything like that before. I was annoyed that I did not say anything to Claire about it.

Evaluation: what was good and what was bad about the experience?

The good part about the experience was that ultimately neither child was seriously hurt. The bad part was that I had not felt able to talk to Claire about it and felt that the opportunity for telling her how I felt was now lost.

Analysis: what sense can you make of the situation?

I lacked assertiveness. I felt ashamed that I had witnessed bad practice and done nothing about it. I think Claire has been under a lot of stress recently as her mother is in hospital. I think I was hesitant to challenge her because she is senior to me and because normally I would trust her judgement.

Conclusion: what else could you have done?

I could have told Claire that I would like to discuss her behaviour towards Sasha, and could have arranged to see her after work.

Action plan: what would you do if it arose again?

I would try to remember what I have learnt about being assertive without being aggressive. I would definitely speak to Claire about how I felt and hope that it could be discussed rationally.

Problem-solving in the workplace as a reflective practitioner

A problem occurs when there is a difference between what 'should be' and what 'is' – between the ideal and the actual situation. Problem-solving is important in childcare contexts, both for the children's learning and for the adult's practice. Problem-solving is:

- a tool, which helps you to achieve a goal
- a skill, because once learned, it stays with you for life, in the same way as being able to read and write
- a process, because it involves taking a number of steps.

Problem-solving is also the foundation of a young child's learning. Opportunities for problem-solving occur in the everyday context of a child's life; by observing the child closely, practitioners can use the child's social, cognitive, physical and emotional experiences to encourage problem-solving and to promote strategies which will be of lasting value.

One of the skills of being a reflective practitioner is to learn how to solve problems effectively.

A problem-solving cycle

There are different models of problem-solving cycles. Some are more suited to engineering problems where scientific investigation is important.

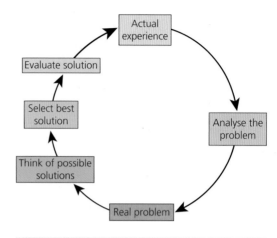

Figure 5.4 A problem-solving cycle

Case Study   A worked example

1 **Actual experience:** this is something which is identified as a problem – there is a difference between what 'should be' and what 'is'.

   Bethany, aged three and a half, attends a nursery four days a week. She is a very lively girl and her key person, Emma, has noticed a problem during story time. Bethany wriggles and fidgets throughout the story; she gets up and walks around. She picks toys up and 'whizzes' them through the air. Bethany sometimes copies the other children when they are responding to the adult, but usually whines when fetched back to sit in the group.

2 **Analyse the problem:** gather information about the problem, through observation and data from other sources.

   Emma observes Bethany, using an event-sampling observational technique. She discusses the problem with Bethany's mother and also tables it to be discussed at the next team meeting. Bethany's mother tells Emma that Bethany is always lively at home and does not even sit still at mealtimes. She has a new baby brother at home who is now three months old.

3 **Real problem:** after analysing the information obtained, the cause of the problem is decided.

Emma decides that the real problem is one of attention-seeking behaviour. Bethany did not have this problem until after the birth of her brother.

4 **Think of possible solutions:** brainstorm and analyse data; ensure that many possible ideas are explored and as much relevant data as possible is gathered.

   After discussion at the team meeting, Emma comes up with a range of possible solutions:

   ● Encourage Bethany to improve her listening skills by working one to one with her and reading.
   ● Encourage Bethany to choose a friend with whom to listen to a story read by an adult.
   ● Plan story times to include more opportunities for active movement.
   ● Set up a system of rewards – such as a star chart – which would apply to all the children at story time, rewarding wanted behaviour. Bethany's parents would be encouraged to continue this system at home.
   ● Encourage play with an infant doll – involving Bethany in feeding and caring for the doll.
   ● Choose books which promote discussion about young babies in the family.

5 **Select best solution:** make sure the solution is achievable within time and resource constraints.

It is decided to encourage Bethany to play with a doll and to read books about the birth of a new baby in the family, with one-to-one attention. If this does not work, Emma will introduce a reward system, with the parents' cooperation.

6 **Evaluate solution:** how effective was the solution? If the problem was not solved, you may need to start the whole process again.

Bethany responds well to both strategies. She begins to carry the doll around at home and 'care' for it just like Mummy is caring for her brother. She also enjoys sitting quietly while an adult reads to her. Story time behaviour is greatly improved. Emma plans to work with mothers who are expecting a baby to prepare the older sibling for the event, using books and dolls – both in the nursery and at home.

Observations, discussion and involving the parents were essential to solving the problem and also encouraged reflective practice.

Case Study   Tensions in the nursery

Helen is the manager of a day nursery in an inner-city area. There are six full-time members of staff at the nursery, caring for 34 children. Two newly qualified nursery nurses have recently been employed, and Helen has noticed new tensions within the nursery. One of the new workers, Sarah, has asked for three weeks' annual leave at Christmas, so that she can visit her family in Australia. Darren, who has worked there for eight years, always takes two weeks off at that time, to visit Ireland. The other new staff member, Dianne, has suggested a more positive approach to equal opportunities, with more emphasis on multicultural provision, the observance of festivals and more variety in the daily menu, etc. One of the more experienced members of staff claims that the nursery already offers equal opportunities and that any changes are both unnecessary and expensive; she also claims that parents are not in agreement with such plans.

In addition, another staff member, Pat, has had a great deal of time off work because her father has recently died; the rest of the staff feel that her absences have gone on for an unreasonable length of time, and they are tired of having to take on extra work.

Divide into groups and discuss the following questions:

1 How should Helen deal with these issues?

2 Do you think they are all equally important, or should any one issue be addressed before the others?

Feed back each group's answers into the whole group and summarise the strategies for solving the problems.

How to evaluate your own performance and receive feedback

Improving your own performance

There are many skills involved in working with and caring for children and young people which all adults need. These include:

- experience and the support to reflect and learn from experience
- confidence and the ability to respond in the best possible ways to individual children
- really knowing about the child, trusting your own knowledge and the judgements that are based on this
- being prepared to learn from the child, for example by listening to what a child tells you and observing what they do.

Working in the field of child care and education can be physically and emotionally exhausting, and professionals will need to consolidate their skills and to develop the ability to be reflective in their practice. You also need to be able to give and receive feedback; this is a skill which needs to be practised in order for it to be effective for both parties.

It is important to keep abreast of all the changes in childcare practices by reading the relevant journals such as *Nursery World*, *Early Years Educator* and *Infant Education*, and by being willing to attend training courses when available.

Evaluating your own performance

As an early years practitioner you need to know and understand the techniques of reflective analysis:

- questioning what, why and how
- seeking alternatives
- keeping an open mind
- viewing from different perspectives
- thinking about consequences
- testing ideas through comparing and contrasting
- asking 'what if?'
- synthesising ideas
- seeking, identifying and resolving problems.

Self-evaluation is needed to improve your own professional practice, and to develop your ability to reflect upon routines/activities and modify plans to meet the individual needs of the children you work with. When evaluating your own practice you should consider the following questions:

- Was your own particular contribution appropriate?
- Did you choose the right time, place and resources?
- Did you intervene enough or too much?
- Did you achieve your goals (such as objectives/outcomes for the child or children and yourself)? If not, why not? Were the goals too ambitious or unrealistic?
- What other strategies/methods could have been used? Suggest possible modifications.
- Who to ask for further advice (such as senior practitioner, setting manager, other professional)?

Giving and receiving feedback with colleagues, children and adults

Feedback is structured information that one person offers to another, about the impact of their actions or behaviour. It is vital to the success of most workplace tasks, and is an activity we engage in on a daily basis. Feedback should not be confused with criticism, which is often an unprepared reaction to people who are not behaving in the way you want them to; criticism can make the recipient feel undervalued or angry – both unproductive emotions.

Giving feedback

Feedback should be:

- **Balanced**: include a positive message to balance points about less effective behaviour.
- **Focused on performance**: concentrate on things which can be changed, and link your feedback to the task or role. Do not direct your comments to personality, character, attitude or things the person cannot change, such as their personal circumstances or something in the past.

- **Timely and regular**: talk to the person at an appropriate moment soon after the incident you want to talk about. Offer feedback often – as an everyday habit. Do not wait until the incident has gone stale, and do not save your remarks to deliver all at once. Good feedback needs to be practised regularly to be effective.
- **Clear and direct**: use plain, clear language. Choose phrases the person will understand. Be brief and to the point. Successful feedback is easy to understand.
- **Specific**: give an accurate description of the behaviour you are talking about, and about what you would like to see instead.
- **Solution-focused**: show that you are willing to give ideas about how the person can tackle the issues you have raised.

Feedback skills

Skilled people make feedback a positive experience, leaving everyone feeling valued, even if the feedback itself is difficult or negative. If feedback is delivered badly, or not at all, the impact can be demoralising and long-lasting.

Guidelines for developing effective feedback skills

- **Active listening:** listen attentively – be aware of your body language (see Chapter 1), in order to understand another person's viewpoint, perspective, needs and feelings.
- **Observation:** be aware of how people talk, speak, move, react. Try to describe this accurately.
- **Clear verbal expression:** use direct language and choose words appropriate to the listener.
- **Structure your message:** introduce the conversation; set the context; explain the issue; summarise the discussion; and end on a positive note.
- **Plan and prepare your message:** think in advance about the time, place and content of the conversation.
- **Timing:** be aware of the other person's needs and priorities. Always choose breaks or quiet moments to talk: this will allow them time to absorb and think.
- **Self-awareness:** be aware of your own feelings; aware of what you find difficult; aware of your limits; and be able to talk about these.
- **Resilience:** try not to take things personally: learn from the experience.
- **Assertiveness:** express your needs, feelings, and opinions in an honest, direct and appropriate manner. Show awareness that other people have different perspectives, while explaining your own position.

Receiving feedback

The information you hear when receiving feedback from others may be new – and even surprising. You may react with strong emotion. Effective feedback is an offer of information, not a diagnosis of your character or potential, so you should not react angrily or take it too personally. Hearing feedback can:

- help you become aware of how you are getting on – the good and the bad, what is working and what is not
- give you some ideas to help you plan your own development, in order to reach your full potential
- give you a 'reality check' – you can compare how you think you are with what other people tell you.

Feedback from a number of different people helps you make a balanced decision about the information you are hearing. Not everyone has good feedback skills; you are likely to get a mixed quality of feedback – some perceptive and supportive, some critical and unspecific.

Progress check

Receiving feedback

- **Ask questions**: state what you want feedback about. Be specific about what you want to know. Give them time to think about what they want to say.
- **Listen**: listen attentively. Do not interrupt or digress. Ask for clarification if you are not sure you have understood what you have heard. Try not to be defensive or to reject the information. You need to listen, but not necessarily to agree. Take notes of what is said.
- **Check**: check what you have heard. Repeat back what they have said and ask for examples of what the speaker means. Give your reactions to the feedback or ask for time to think about it if necessary. Ask for suggestions on what might work better.
- **Reflect**: feedback is information for you to use – it is not a requirement to change. If you are unsure about the soundness of the feedback, check it out with other people. Work out the options open to you and decide what you want to do. It is up to you to evaluate how accurate and how useful the feedback is.

Barriers to the feedback process

Feedback is sometimes difficult to give or receive. The giver and receiver both need to be open to receiving feedback and open to the possibility that the feedback being given may be based on incorrect assumptions. You may find it difficult to **give** feedback because you:

- believe that feedback is negative and unhelpful
- worry that the other person will not like you
- believe that the other person cannot handle the feedback
- have had previous experiences in which the receiver was hostile to feedback.

Receiving corrective feedback may be difficult because you:

- have the urge to rationalise, since the criticism can feel uncomfortable
- believe that your self-worth is diminished by suggestions for improvement
- have had previous experiences in which feedback was unhelpful or unjustified.

How to use feedback to set SMART targets to improve practice

Every member of a team needs to know exactly what is expected of them. These expectations are called targets or 'objectives'. The targets that are most likely to be achieved are those which are 'SMART'. **SMART** is an acronym for:

- **Specific**: they must be easy to understand and say exactly what you want to happen.
- **Measurable**: success can be measured by checking back carefully against the instructions that have been given.
- **Achievable**: the targets can be reached with reasonable effort in the time you are allowed.
- **Relevant**: the targets must be appropriate, building on previous strengths and skills.
- **Time-related**: the targets have clearly set deadlines and are reviewed frequently.

Activity

Using SMART targets

Look at the following scenarios and see how **SMART** targets can help individuals and teams to plan and to achieve their objectives:

- **Scenario 1**: Paula has been asked if she would organise a display for the nursery room. The only instructions she has been given are: 'Paula, can you put up a nice, colourful display in the nursery room, please?'

- **Scenario 2:** At a different nursery, Mark has also been asked to organise a display. On Wednesday, he was given these instructions: 'Next Monday we need to create an interactive display for the nursery room. It will be on the theme of autumn. We have already collected some pine cones and autumn leaves, and we also have some good posters, but I would like you to plan what else we need and let me have a list of resources by tomorrow lunchtime.'

Section 3: Differing principles and practices that underpin working with children of different ages

Principles and practices

As we have seen in Chapter 1, all early years practitioners should work within a framework which embodies sound values and principles. The EYFS builds on previous developments (Birth to Three Matters, Curriculum Guidance for the Foundation Stage, and the National Standards for Under 8s Daycare and Childminding). The EYFS framework uses the **KEEP** (Key Elements in Effective Practice) principles and the values are threaded throughout the EYFS in the commitment cards (Principles into Practice).

KEEP principles

Make sure you know, use and act on the KEEP principles:

1 Effective practice in the early years requires committed, enthusiastic and reflective practitioners with a breadth and depth of knowledge, skills and understanding.

2 Effective practitioners use their learning to improve their work with young children and their families in ways which are sensitive, positive and non-judgmental. Therefore, through initial and ongoing training and development, practitioners need to develop, demonstrate and continuously improve their:

- relationships with both children and adults
- understanding of the individual and diverse ways that children develop and learn
- knowledge and understanding in order to actively support and extend children's learning in and across all areas and aspects of learning
- practice in meeting all children's needs, learning styles and interests
- work with parents and carers and the wider community
- work with other professionals within and beyond the setting.

CACHE statement of values

The **CACHE Statement of Values** is also a useful tool for checking that you are upholding important childcare values. See Chapter 1 for a full examination of the CACHE values.

The implications of child-centred versus adult-led practice

What is child-centred practice?

A child-centred organisation focuses its practice on improving outcomes for children and young people;

it also works with others to promote and contribute to better outcomes for all children and their families. Child-centred practice involves more than focusing on the rights and responsibilities of the child or young person. In child-centred practice the intention is to try to keep the interests and the wellbeing of children central to the process; to do this, you have to engage with children and involve them wherever possible in the issues that concern them.

It will also:

- recognise that children are individuals in their own right, 'loaned and not owned' by the significant adults in their lives
- create opportunities for all children to reach their full potential
- recognise that educating children together is a truer reflection of the real world
- recognise the Foundation years as being important for learning
- provide an environment that positively promotes the wellbeing of children
- be inclusive of all abilities
- provide for an awareness and direct experience of a diversity of cultures and faiths

- involve children in decision-making processes in all aspects of their school life.

The advantages of child-centred practice

There are advantages to both children and adults in making your practice child-centred. These include the following points:

- Services are appropriate for their needs: insights gained from children can help adults work more effectively; it can also help to ensure that the services provided are relevant to children's needs.
- Taking into account the needs of others: children who learn to express their own needs also learn to consider the needs of others. They may develop skills of cooperation, negotiation and problem-solving.
- Respect and understanding: children and parents/carers often work together; this can make relationships stronger and promote greater understanding and respect.
- Promoting self-esteem and self-worth: when you involve children and you respect their ideas and their capabilities, they grow in confidence and self-esteem.

Case Study An after-school club for children aged between five and six

Practitioners wanted to find out how children felt about their after-school clubs. Although parents and carers had important views to contribute, they realised that children also had their own perspectives. When talking with the children, practitioners found that:

- they were unhappy about the lighting – it was too gloomy in some clubs
- some children said they grew hungry and wished there was some food provided
- some children felt tired and wished there was somewhere for them to have a quiet time, not just the structured activities

- they were also concerned about their environment – the paint on the walls, the lighting and their access to the garden, and so on.

These were all legitimate and important insights which affected how those children experienced their care, and which could have easily been overlooked by adults who may have a different set of concerns. By placing the child at the centre of their practice, the practitioners developed a greater understanding of the sorts of factors that might affect children's lives.

There are many factors which affect children – for example, the local environment, their opportunities for play and social interaction, the impact of traffic and noise pollution on their lives, the quality of the streets and housing for children. On each of these issues, children will have a view and a valid contribution to make.

Guidelines for child-centred practice

Practitioners should recognise the importance of:

- being aware of children at all times
- thinking about how your involvement with their families may affect them and being open to engaging with children, listening to them and realising the potential for them to participate and contribute to your work
- recognising (when working with very young children) that they may not be able to contribute in any obvious way, but we still need to be aware of them
- recognising the value of contributions from any older siblings who may have much to contribute
- engaging with children individually, or as little groups: you can talk with them, they can participate in discussions, community meetings, councils
- encourage children to make scrapbooks, videos, keep diaries, use disposable cameras, make drawings.

Adult-led practice

There will always be aspects of children's care and education which require practitioners to take the lead. This is called adult-led practice. In early years settings, practitioners lead activities which encourage children to use language, to practise skills and to develop thinking. Adult-led and adult-intensive activities may include:

- story and song times
- activities such as cooking with small groups
- trips into the local community

- a new game
- shared reading and writing
- scientific investigations
- new imaginative play settings.

The three areas of learning defined by the EYFS must be delivered through planned, purposeful play, with a balance of adult-led and child-initiated activities.

1 **Involvement**: all team members should be involved in planning, but their level of involvement will vary, depending on confidence, professional skills and organisation. (A staff member offering verbal input in a team meeting is involved in planning, but so too is an absent member who later comments on written plans.)

2 **Parents and carers**: planning must involve parents and carers, as they provide vital information about their children's interests, skills and needs that must be taken into account when planning the curriculum. Inform parents and carers also about what is going on in the setting, out of professional respect; doing this will also help them make links between experiences in the setting and at home.

3 **Children**: practitioners should find ways to seek children's opinions and to involve them in their learning. For example:

- brainstorm with small groups around topic themes and ask the children to suggest stories and activities
- ask children to suggest resources for a new imaginative play area
- ask children to think about what they would like and intend to do that day, the following day or week.

4 **Child-initiated learning**: this involves planning the learning environment to allow for children to take the initiative. Planning includes:

- how the environment (outside and inside) is organised
- the resources made available
- the routines
- the way in which practitioners respond to how children function in the environment.

There should be open-ended opportunities to encourage children to take the initiative. Children need to make use of the environment in different ways; by linking resources, people and play in creative ways, you are promoting child-initiated learning. (See the section on planning for play on page 288.)

5 **Adult-initiated learning**: this involves planning for what you will promote and encourage. Sometimes practitioners will encourage children to use resources that they, rather than the children, have chosen. There are various reasons for choosing to plan in this way:

- practitioners may have identified a learning need from their observations, made it a learning goal and identified specific experiences that will promote this learning
- children may lack the experience to set up the resources correctly, for example a new game
- practitioners may want the children to investigate a particular concept, for example forces, using cars in block play
- in response to their observations, practitioners may think that the resources will interest the children and encourage them to develop their ideas and skills
- more experienced children may be encouraged to pursue a line of investigation that may not otherwise have occurred to them, or to do independently what previously needed adult help.

Providing the environment for children to develop independence in learning

In order for children to develop independence in learning, practitioners need to:

- provide opportunities or challenges for them to be active, to take risks, to make mistakes and to learn from these
- provide broad and varied experiences which enable them to explore and investigate

- have a sound knowledge of child development and to be aware of the ways in which they learn
- provide appropriate levels of assistance for individual children
- be thoughtful and reflective practitioners who actively encourage them to become independent through giving them responsibility for their learning from a very early stage
- encourage children to explain key ideas in their own words. Tasks and activities involve them in learning through thinking and doing, rather than by rote
- help them to be able to show or explain it clearly to others in their own words, orally or in writing or pictures
- use technology to enable children to work more effectively
- encourage children to review their own learning strategies, achievements and future learning needs.

High/Scope is a comprehensive educational approach which strives to help children develop in all areas. High/Scope sets out its goals for young children:

- To learn through active involvement with people, materials, events, and ideas.
- To become independent, responsible, and confident – ready for school and ready for life.
- To learn to plan many of their own activities, carry them out, and talk with others about what they have done and what they have learned.
- To gain knowledge and skills in important academic, social, and physical areas.
- The emphasis of the High/Scope philosophy is that children are encouraged to make decisions about their own choice of activities on a 'Plan', 'Do' and 'Review' basis. There will still be some adult-led activities such as PE and other large and small group activities, but mostly the children will have a choice in planning activities.

Valuing children and young people's interests and experiences

Every child needs to be included – and to have full access to the curriculum, irrespective of their ethnic background, culture, language, gender or economic background. No child should be held back in their learning due to restricted access to learning opportunities.

In order to apply curriculum plans, it is important to work closely in partnership with the child's parents/carers. Practitioners sometimes talk about 'my children', but children belong to their parents. When parents and practitioners work well together, respecting what they each bring to the partnership, in a spirit of respect and trust, with a genuine exchange of information and knowledge, the child gains and so do the parents and staff.

Schemas

Schemas are observable patterns of repeat behaviour in children. Children often have a very strong drive to repeat actions, such as moving things from one place to another, covering things up and putting things into containers, or moving in circles or throwing things. These patterns can often be observed running through their play and vary between one child and another. If practitioners build on these interests, powerful learning can take place. (See Chapter 2 for more information on schemas.)

How to recognise the needs of the child as an individual

Within an effective learning environment, practitioners should be able to respond to a child's individual learning needs as they are observed and identified. Many early years settings now focus on particular children on particular days. This means that each child is observed regularly, and activities are planned in a differentiated way to provide for the interests and needs of individual babies and children.

Not all children learn in the same way; they make progress at different rates. For example, some children understand and remember well if they *see* something. Others need to be more actively involved to make good progress. Children can be taught in different ways: this is known as **differentiation**. In practice, this can mean:

- giving work at a more basic and simple level
- doing different activities
- using ways of teaching that match the child's way of learning
- using books that fit in better with the child's own experiences
- moving the child into a small group
- giving different support through a key person
- giving complicated information in small steps.

Key term

Differentiated – The adaptation of classroom learning to suit each student's individual needs, strengths, preferences, and pace, either by splitting the class into small groups, giving individual learning activities, or modifying the material.

The benefits of a multi-professional, multi-agency approach in maximising children's experiences and learning

Early Support

Early Support is a government programme for coordinated, family-focused services for young disabled children and their families in local authorities, hospitals and community-based health services across England. Families receive coordinated support through key person/worker systems, effective sharing of information between agencies, family support plans and family-held records.

Section 4: Current local and national initiatives and issues relevant to the sector

Government initiatives and local government and regional developments

Recent government initiatives include:

- the Children's National Service Framework (2004)

- the Common Assessment Framework for Children and Young People (CAF) (2006)
- the Common Core of skills and knowledge for the children's workforce (2005 and 2010).

(The Children's National Service Framework is described in Chapter 6.)

The Common Assessment Framework (CAF)

The Common Assessment Framework (CAF) is a key component of the Every Child Matters programme. It is usually used by practitioners to assess the additional needs of a child and his or her family, and to help to identify the services required to meet their needs. The lead professional will usually work with the parents and other agencies to draw up a CAF. It is not always necessary to undertake a CAF for a child – for example if a child is making good progress and the agencies are communicating well

---

Case Study — Max

Max is a three-year-old boy who has learning difficulties and has recently been diagnosed as having autism. Max has a baby sister, Zoe, who is four months old. Six months ago, Max's mother, Carol, was contacted by the local Early Support Team, who helped to find him a place in the nursery at her local Children's Centre. Max quickly settled in, and although he does not interact with other children he enjoys his time there and has built relationships with two key people. His favourite activity is playing in the sensory room with his mother or a staff member, and he particularly likes the bubble tubes.

Max's key person, Tom, describes Max as a lovely little boy who has difficulties with social and communication skills and who needs supervision at all times to keep him safe as he has very little understanding of danger. As a member of the Early Support Team, Tom coordinates services for Max and his family,

and ensures that the appropriate services are in place to support the family. He works closely with Max's parents and immediately made sure that they have access to information about autism in order to understand Max's needs. Tom also helps to coordinate appointments for Max, organises transport to appointments, and makes referrals to other services. For example, he arranged a referral to an occupational therapist to support the family in looking at safety, particularly in the home, and also arranged a referral to the Disability Nursing Team who supports the family in understanding Max's behaviour. Max also has a Portage worker who helps him to interact socially through play.

1 List the ways in which Early Support is helping to improve outcomes for Max.
2 Find out how Early Support (or its equivalent programme in Wales, Scotland and Northern Ireland) supports children and families in your own area.

together. The CAF begins with information-sharing and assessment of:

- **the child or young person's development**: this is the area in which early years practitioners can usually make the biggest contribution, looking at the child's progress within the framework of the EYFS, including health, and social and emotional development. For young people, the CAF helps to work out what support they might need. This could be a learning mentor for help with the young person's schoolwork, or a drugs worker for help with a drugs problem.
- **parents and carers**: this section looks at the care and support offered to the child or young person, including relationships, stimulation and responding to the child or young person's needs.
- **family and environment**: this takes a wider look at the overall family and environment, and the overall capacity of the parents to support the child or young person's development now and over time. Drawing on these assessments, the lead professional works with the parents and the TAC to put together an integrated plan to support the child's development.

The CAF recognises that a range of factors may affect children's development and vulnerability. A child with complex needs who has supportive parents and a supportive family environment, with good housing and family income, will be much less vulnerable than a child with a lower level of special need, but who lives in an overcrowded and potentially dangerous flat with a parent suffering from depression. Where a child does not make the expected progress, or where a child is at risk of significant harm, a referral may be made for safeguarding. (This is discussed further in Chapter 3.)

The CAF has three elements:

1 **A simple pre-assessment checklist:** to help practitioners identify children or young people who would benefit from a common assessment.
2 **A three-step process (prepare, discuss, deliver)** for undertaking a common assessment: this helps practitioners to collect and understand information about the needs and strengths of the child or young person, based on discussions with the child or young person, their family and other practitioners as appropriate.
3 **A standard form:** to help practitioners record and, where appropriate, share with others the findings from the assessment, in terms that are helpful in working with the family to find a response to unmet needs.

The Common Core of Skills and Knowledge for the Children's Workforce

The Common Core of Skills and Knowledge for the Children's Workforce is a document which sets out the basic skills and knowledge needed by people (including volunteers) whose work brings them into regular contact with children, young people and families. It will enable multi-disciplinary teams to work together more effectively in the interests of the child. The common core was first published in 2005 and refreshed in 2010.

The skills and knowledge are described under six main headings:

1 Effective communication and engagement with children, young people and families.
2 Child and young person development.
3 Safeguarding and promoting the welfare of the child.
4 Supporting transitions.
5 Multi-agency and integrated working.
6 Information sharing.

Over time, the aim is that everyone working with children, young people and families will be able to demonstrate a basic level of competence in the six areas of the Common Core. In the future, the Common Core will form part of qualifications for working with children, young people and families and it will act as a foundation for training and development programmes run by employers and training organisations.

The Common Core helps to improve life chances for all children and young people, including those who have disabilities and those who are most vulnerable. It provides more effective and integrated services, and also acknowledges the rights of children and young people. All those working with children and young people should know and understand how to demonstrate a commitment to treating everyone fairly. When working with children and young people you should be respectful by actively listening and avoiding stereotypical assumptions. You should ensure that your attitudes and actions support the equality, diversity and inclusion of all pupils. This includes recognising and respecting the rights and responsibilities of children, young people, their parents and carers (CWDC, 2010).

Local government and regional developments

Every local education authority (LEA) has certain duties to provide for children and young people in its area. The government sets out the national guidelines for each initiative and the local authority has a duty to implement them. (The main areas relevant to children and young people are described in Chapter 1.)

Sure Start

Under the government's Sure Start programme, LEAs have duties to:

- prepare, submit and publish plans on early years and child care
- ensure provision of nursery education places for three- and four-year-olds as well as disadvantaged two-year-olds from 2013
- convene and work with Early Years Development and Childcare Partnerships (EYDCPs)
- provide information and advice for childcare providers
- prepare an annual review of child care in their area
- maintain a children's information service.

Local social services departments have duties to provide child care for children in need.

New initiatives for early education, schools and youth employment

On 29 November 2011, the Chancellor of the Exchequer delivered his 2011 Autumn Statement to Parliament. Here is a summary of key points from the statement which relate specifically to children and young people:

- Free entitlement to early education is extended for two-year-olds. This will double the amount of children eligible to 15 hours free education and care a week: 260,000, rather than 130,000. Disadvantaged two-year-olds will have access to these places.
- The government will introduce a 'Youth Contract' scheme, to start in April 2012. The scheme will fund employment subsidies to private organisations to help place 160,000 young people in employment with businesses via the Work Programme. The scheme will provide support for 40,000 more apprentices and extra support from Job Centre Plus in the form of weekly rather than fortnightly, signing on meetings and more time to talk to an adviser.

Current issues relevant to the sector

There are hundreds of community-based activities for children and young people in the UK. Most of them are run by concerned individuals who want to make a difference for the children in their area and are voluntary organisations (or charities). Some receive funding from national and local government agencies or from the National Lottery. Others belong to a 'parent' organisation.

An example of an initiative which works in the community is **Play England** – formerly known as the Children's Play Council of the National Children's Bureau. It is supported by the Big Lottery Fund (BIG). Play England's aim is for all children and young people in England to have regular access to and opportunity for free, inclusive, local play provision and play space. Its objectives are to:

- create, improve and develop children and young people's free local play spaces and opportunities throughout England, according to need
- research and demonstrate the benefits of play
- promote equality and diversity in play provision
- raise awareness and promote standards

- support innovation and new ways of providing for children's play
- promote the long-term strategic and sustainable provision for play as a free public service to children
- ensure that local authorities work with other local stakeholders to develop children's play strategies and plans
- ensure that good, inclusive and accessible children's play services and facilities are provided locally.

Activity

Researching your local provision for children

1 Decide on an area to research, for example:

- the provision of play areas
- the provision of leisure activities for young people, such as youth clubs, arts activities, sports, music and volunteering projects
- support groups: for lone parents, for disabled children and their families or for young people with mental health problems.

2 Using the library or the internet, investigate the local provision for your chosen topic.

3 Write a short report, detailing the aims of the provider, the service available, and the benefits to the group served.

Reviewing current research and using professional literature

Using professional literature will help you to inform your practice and in turn promote professional development. Reviewing literature is carrying out an analysis of what others have said or found out about the research area in question.

The first step is to decide which literature is most relevant to you. In other words, what are you hoping to find out? Through the literature, you should

be able to confirm your concerns – discarding, modifying or adding to them as you read. As a result, you will identify a number of themes and sub-themes within your original topic which will provide the framework for your enquiry. You then need to focus on the themes you have identified.

1 **Be systematic**: keep a careful record of all you read, including exact bibliographic references. One useful method of keeping track of reading is to use a card index file (either a paper or digital version). Each time you find a book or an article which you think will be useful, note it down on a card, remembering to record a full note of the author, etc. You should include a few notes for each reference to remind you of the main issues raised by the author when you return to it. For example:

- **Quotes and references**: if you come across a statement which you might wish to quote, or one which you feel summarises the issues well and you might wish to refer to, make sure you write down a full reference, including the page number. This will help you to find it again and, if you use the quotation in writing up the study, you should cite the page number.
- **Reading in greater depth**: this allows you to identify competing perspectives within each sub-theme, to compare and contrast them and to identify strengths and weaknesses in the views given.

The search may include books, journals, policy statements, professional journals and other publications, including electronic ones. While books are important, journals tend to be more up to date in their treatment of the issues which you might be researching. Many of the articles available online through the internet are highly topical.

2 **Be critical of what you read**: most writers have a particular viewpoint on an issue and you should consider the validity and reliability of statements made, the authority of the author and the professional relevance of the issues raised. Some journals are more authoritative than others.

3 **Read reviews of books and reports in journals**, and follow up those which seem promising.

4 **Ask yourself questions** about what you read:

- Presentation: is the style appropriate, clear, readable?
- Authors: who are they and where are they from?
- Target audience: is it aimed at practitioners, academics, researchers?
- Relevance: does it raise significant issues?
- Evidence: what is the evidence for arguments made? Is it appropriate? Do you have enough information to know if they drew appropriate conclusions?
- Plausibility: does it convince you?

If the focus of your enquiry is the effectiveness of a new policy within your area, for example, on learning and teaching in schools, it will be important to understand and analyse policy documents as well as any other relevant official publications. However, government policy documents will always take a rather one-sided view of the issues, so you need to balance this by reading about aspects of, for example, philosophy (child-centred education), psychology (how children learn) and sociology (poverty and discrimination).

5 **Libraries** can be very useful in showing you the way to find appropriate information on a particular topic.

Assessment practice

Unit 5

- Explain the value of a multi-professional approach when working with children and parents
- Describe the benefits of developing reflective practice within the setting
- Describe two recent initiatives that have affected provision for children
- Explain the importance of reflective practice for improving your own performance.

Useful resources

National service framework for children, young people and maternity Services (2004): This ten-year programme is intended to stimulate long-term and sustained improvement in children's health. It aims to ensure fair, high quality and integrated health and social care from pregnancy, right through to adulthood:
http://www.dh.gov.uk/en/Publicationsandstatistics/Publications/PublicationsPolicyAndGuidance/DH_4089100

Play England (as discussed on page 240):
www.playengland.org.uk

The Common Assessment Framework for children and young people: Practitioners' guide (September 2007): This updated guide is for any practitioner who wants to know about the CAF for children and young people, and when to use it. It is for everyone who works with children, young people and families, whether they are employed or volunteers, and working in the public, private or voluntary sectors:
https://www.education.gov.uk/publications/standard/publicationDetail/Page1/DFES-0337-2006

The Common Core of Skills and Knowledge for the Children's Workforce (2010) describes the skills and knowledge that everyone who works with children and young people (including volunteers) is expected to have. The six areas of expertise offer a single framework to underpin, multi-agency and integrated working, professional standards, training and qualifications across the children's workforce:
http://www.cwdcouncil.org.uk/common-core

Section 1: The principles underpinning the rights of children to a healthy lifestyle and environment

How human rights legislation relates to the 'Being healthy' outcome

In Every Child Matters, the 'Being healthy' outcome is 'Enjoying good physical and mental health and living a healthy lifestyle'. In addition to the UN Convention on the Rights of the Child articles listed in Chapter 1, the following Articles relate specifically to the rights of children to enjoy good health:

- **Article 6**: All children have the right to life. Governments should ensure that children survive and develop healthily. All possible measures should be taken to:
  - improve **perinatal care** for mothers and babies
  - reduce infant and child mortality, and

- create conditions that promote the wellbeing of all young children during this critical phase of their lives.

- **Article 19**: Governments must do everything to protect children and young people from all forms of violence, abuse, neglect and mistreatment. All necessary measures should be taken to:
  - safeguard young children at risk and offer protection to victims of abuse, taking positive steps to support their recovery from trauma while avoiding stigmatisation for the violations they have suffered.

- **Article 23**: Every disabled child and young person has the right to a full life and to active participation in the community.

- **Article 24**: Every child and young person has the right to the best possible health and health services. All children should have access to the highest attainable standard of health care and nutrition during their early years, in order to reduce infant mortality and enable children to enjoy a healthy start in life. It recognises that the right to survival and development can only be implemented in a holistic manner, through the enforcement of all the other provisions of the Convention, including rights to:
  - health
  - adequate nutrition
  - social security
  - an adequate standard of living
  - a healthy and safe environment
  - education and play (Articles 24, 27, 28, 29 and 31).

- **Article 25**: Children and young people who are in care or live away from home for health reasons have the right to have their care reviewed regularly.

- **Article 27**: Children and young people have the right to a standard of living that helps them develop fully. Parents have the main responsibility for making sure children and young people get this right. All necessary measures should be taken to assist parents in providing living conditions necessary for the child's development – including 'material assistance and support programmes' for children and families.

- **Article 39**: Governments should help restore a child's health, self-respect and dignity after abuse or neglect.

For more information, see also the Children's Rights Alliance for England website: www.crae.org.uk.

Key term

Perinatal: Relating to the period from about three months before to one month after birth.

The role of the World Health Organization in public health

The World Health Organization (WHO) is responsible for providing leadership on global health matters, shaping the health research agenda, setting norms and standards, articulating evidence-based policy options, providing technical support to countries and monitoring and assessing health trends.

One of the main health problems affecting a large percentage of people worldwide is access to clean water. Save the Children runs regular campaigns to promote health and safety of children around the world.

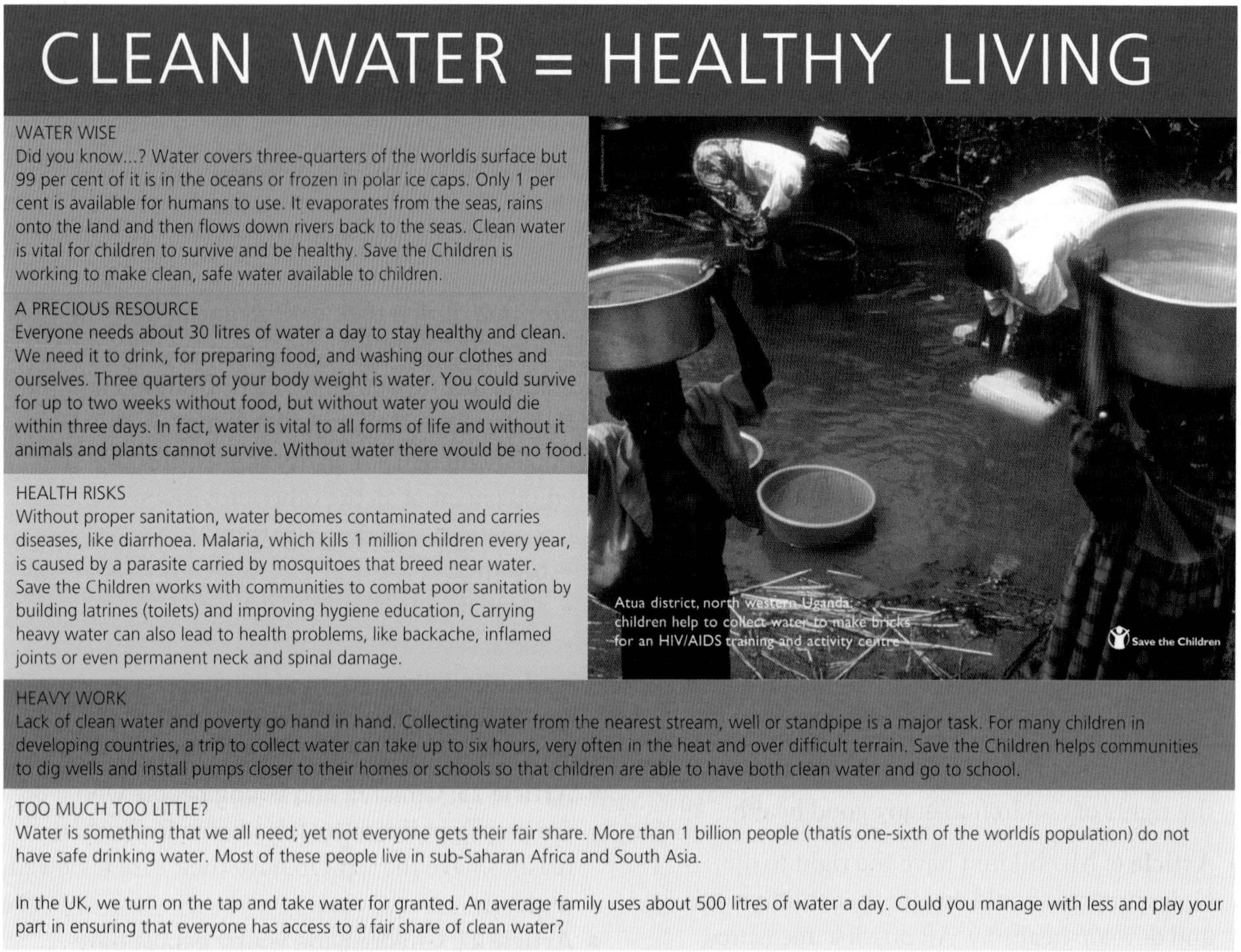

CLEAN WATER = HEALTHY LIVING

WATER WISE
Did you know...? Water covers three-quarters of the world's surface but 99 per cent of it is in the oceans or frozen in polar ice caps. Only 1 per cent is available for humans to use. It evaporates from the seas, rains onto the land and then flows down rivers back to the seas. Clean water is vital for children to survive and be healthy. Save the Children is working to make clean, safe water available to children.

A PRECIOUS RESOURCE
Everyone needs about 30 litres of water a day to stay healthy and clean. We need it to drink, for preparing food, and washing our clothes and ourselves. Three quarters of your body weight is water. You could survive for up to two weeks without food, but without water you would die within three days. In fact, water is vital to all forms of life and without it animals and plants cannot survive. Without water there would be no food.

HEALTH RISKS
Without proper sanitation, water becomes contaminated and carries diseases, like diarrhoea. Malaria, which kills 1 million children every year, is caused by a parasite carried by mosquitoes that breed near water. Save the Children works with communities to combat poor sanitation by building latrines (toilets) and improving hygiene education, Carrying heavy water can also lead to health problems, like backache, inflamed joints or even permanent neck and spinal damage.

Atua district, north western Uganda: children help to collect water to make bricks for an HIV/AIDS training and activity centre

Save the Children

HEAVY WORK
Lack of clean water and poverty go hand in hand. Collecting water from the nearest stream, well or standpipe is a major task. For many children in developing countries, a trip to collect water can take up to six hours, very often in the heat and over difficult terrain. Save the Children helps communities to dig wells and install pumps closer to their homes or schools so that children are able to have both clean water and go to school.

TOO MUCH TOO LITTLE?
Water is something that we all need; yet not everyone gets their fair share. More than 1 billion people (that's one-sixth of the world's population) do not have safe drinking water. Most of these people live in sub-Saharan Africa and South Asia.

In the UK, we turn on the tap and take water for granted. An average family uses about 500 litres of water a day. Could you manage with less and play your part in ensuring that everyone has access to a fair share of clean water?

Figure 6.1 A poster from one of Save the Children's campaigns to promote child health

Activity

Clean Water = Healthy Living

1 Read the information presented on the poster in Figure 6.1 and answer the following questions:
- What percentage of all the water on earth is available to humans in their environment?
- What percentage of the world's population does not have safe drinking water?
- How much water does each person need each day in order to stay healthy and clean?
- How many litres of water does the average family in the UK use each day?

2 List the main risks to health from contaminated water and a poor water supply.

3 Discuss ways in which you and your peer group could:
- help to conserve water; and
- raise awareness about the global health problem of unsafe water supplies.

The centrality of the public health environment in modern life

Public health is involved in helping people to stay healthy and avoid getting ill. This includes work on a whole range of policy areas including:

- immunisation
- nutrition
- tobacco and alcohol
- drugs recovery
- sexual health
- pregnancy
- children's health.

The National Service Framework for Children, Young People and Maternity Services

The National Service Framework was set up by the Department of Health in 2004 and has the following aims:

- To help parents find and stay in learning or work, including having high-quality, affordable child care (for both pre-school and school-aged children) and child-friendly working practices.
- To ensure that families are made aware of the Healthy Start Scheme, and encouraged to apply for it if they qualify. Healthy Start provides low-income pregnant women and young families with advice on diet and nutrition, local support to eat healthily, and vouchers to buy healthy food.
- To ensure that families with low incomes are supported to claim all benefits to which they are entitled.
- To provide support for groups especially likely to be living in poverty – for example, teenage parents, families with disabled children and those who are homeless.
- To ensure as far as possible that local authority accommodation for families with children is not damp or cold (in line with the cross-government fuel poverty strategy), has adequate space for play and privacy, and at least one working smoke alarm and a carbon monoxide detector, where appropriate.
- To minimise environmental pollution in residential areas and around nurseries and schools.

Legislation related to health issues

Alcohol and the law

The Licensing Act 2003 and The Licensing Act (Scotland) 2005

It is against the law:

- to give an alcoholic drink to a child under five except in certain circumstances, for example, under medical supervision
- to be drunk in charge of a child under seven in a public place or on licensed premises
- to sell alcohol to someone under 18, anywhere
- for an adult to buy or attempt to buy alcohol on behalf of someone under 18
- for someone under 18 to buy alcohol, attempt to buy alcohol or to be sold alcohol in any

circumstances (unless acting at the request of the police or a weights and measures inspector)

- for someone under 18 to drink alcohol in licensed premises, with one exception: 16- and 17-year-olds accompanied by an adult can drink but not buy beer, wine and cider with a table meal
- for an adult to buy alcohol for a person under 18 for consumption on licensed premises, except as above.

In Scotland, a person shall not knowingly act as an agent for a person under 18 in the purchase of alcoholic liquor. In Britain, some towns and cities have local by-laws banning the drinking of alcohol in public (on public transport, for example).

Smoking and the law

The Tobacco Advertising and Promotion (Display) (England) Regulations 2010; Tobacco and Primary Medical Services (Scotland) Act 2010

Since 2007, under-18s have been banned from buying cigarettes in England and Wales. In Scotland, the ban came into force in 2006. Shops that break these laws could lose their licence to sell tobacco for as long as a year. Lifting the legal age for buying tobacco from 16 to 18 brought the law into line with rules on the sale of alcohol. From 2012, cigarettes and other products will have to be kept under the counter for large stores and from 2015 for small shops.

The National Health Service

As we saw in Chapter 1, the government's Department of Health is responsible for providing health care through the National Health Service (NHS), which was set up in 1948 to provide free health care to the entire population. Some services are no longer free in all parts of the UK – for example, dental care, prescriptions and ophthalmic services (although free prescriptions have been reintroduced in Wales, Scotland and Northern Ireland). There are also exemptions to these

charges, so that certain groups of people are not disadvantaged by being on low incomes:

- children under 16 or in full-time education
- pregnant women or with a baby under one year
- families receiving income support or family credit.

The Primary Health Care Team (PHCT)

The PHCT, part of the National Health Service, is a team of professionals which generally includes one or more of the following:

- **General practitioner (GP) or family doctor**: cares for all members of the family and can refer for specialist services.
- **Health visitor**: carries out developmental checks and gives advice on all aspects of child care.
- **Practice nurse**: works with a particular GP; provides services such as immunisation and asthma and diabetes clinics.
- **Community midwife**: delivers antenatal care and cares for the mother and baby until 10 to 28 days after delivery.
- **District nurse**: cares for clients in their own homes.

Some health authorities also employ a community paediatric nurse: a district nurse with special training in paediatrics to care for sick children at home.

Services offered by the Primary Health Care Team

Services will include some or all of the following featured in Figure 6.2.

Child health clinics

Child health clinics are often held at the health centre or in a purpose-built centre. In rural areas, the clinic may take turns with other community groups in village halls or community centres. Depending on the population served, clinics may be weekly or fortnightly and are run by health visitors, health care assistants and nursery nurses. A doctor or community paediatrician is usually present at specified times. Services provided at a child health clinic include:

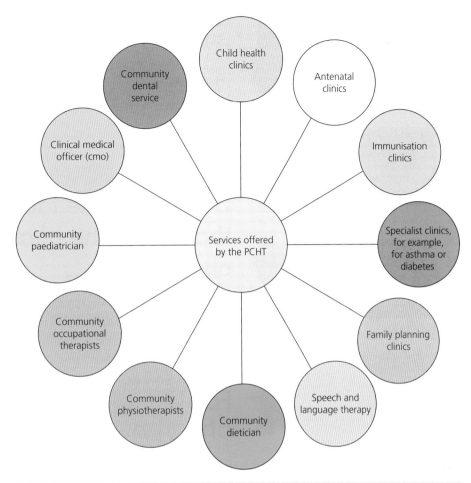

Figure 6.2 Services offered by the PCHT

- routine developmental surveillance (or reviews)
- medical examinations
- immunisations
- health promotion advice
- antenatal and parentcraft classes.

Health education initiatives

Recent health education campaigns – both by statutory authorities and by voluntary organisations – of particular relevance to children's health include the following:

Child weight management

The **National Child Measurement Programme (NCMP)** is an annual programme to measure the height and weight of all children in Reception and Year 6. The information is used to help the NHS and local authorities plan and provide better health services for children. Most areas are now sharing each child's individual results with parents, along with **Change4Life** (see below) tips and an invitation to parents to contact their local NHS if they want to discuss the results or get further advice. Sharing a child's results with the parents gives them the information they need to make the best possible decisions about their child's health.

Water is Cool in School Campaign

This publicity campaign aims to improve the quality of provision of and access to fresh drinking water for children in UK primary and secondary schools.

School Fruit and Vegetable Scheme (SFV)

Under the SFV Scheme, all four- to six-year-old children in LEA-maintained infant, primary and

1 medium apple	**2** broccoli florets	**2** halves of canned peaches
1 handful of grapes	**1** medium banana	**3** heaped tablespoons of peas
1 medium glass of orange juice	**7** strawberries	**3** whole dried apricots
Just Eat More (fruit & veg) / 5 A DAY	**3** heaped tablespoons of cooked kidney beans	**16** okra

Figure 6.3 A campaign to promote healthy eating

special schools are entitled to a free piece of fruit or vegetable each school day. That provides one of their **5 A DAY** portions, and the scheme also helps to increase awareness of the importance of eating fruit and vegetables, encouraging healthy eating habits that can be carried into later life.

Change4Life – Eat Well, Move More, Live Longer

Change4Life is a society-wide movement that aims to prevent people from becoming overweight by encouraging them to eat better and move more. It is the marketing component of the government's response to the rise in obesity.

'Sleep safe, sleep sound, share a room with me'

This is a recent campaign from the Foundation for the Study of Infant Deaths; leaflets and posters were distributed to all midwives and health visitors.

'Birth to Five'

Birth to Five is a comprehensive guide to parenthood and the first five years of a child's life. It covers child health, nutrition and safety and is given free to all first-time mothers in England.

Section 2: The factors that affect the health of children

There are very many factors which affect the healthy growth and development of children. These factors work in combination and so it is often difficult to estimate the impact of any single factor on child health.

Factors affecting children's health

See Figure 6.4 for a range of factors which affect children's health.

Poverty

The UK has a very high rate of child poverty: four million children (one in three) are currently affected. This is one of the highest rates in the industrialised world.

Poverty is the single greatest threat to the health and wellbeing of children in the UK. As we saw in Chapter 2, growing up in poverty can affect every area of a child's development: physical, intellectual, emotional, social and spiritual. Children growing up in poverty are significantly more likely to:

- live in poor, overcrowded housing
- have a disability, as parents may not be able to seek employment if they are full-time carers
- be looked-after children (in care)
- live in families where a necessary preoccupation with affording basic provisions can lead to high levels of stress and anxiety, reducing opportunities to enjoy family life

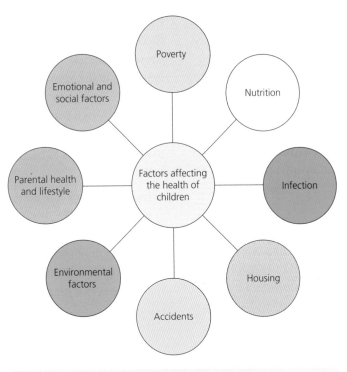

Figure 6.4 Factors affecting the health of children

live with parents from an ethnic minority: twice as many people in ethnic minority groups live in poverty compared with the indigenous population.

How poverty affects children's health

Poverty is linked with the health of children because:

- **Healthy eating costs more**: it costs more to provide a nutritionally balanced diet than one which is based on foods that tend to be high in sugar and fats.
- **Poor housing conditions**: low-income families tend to live in poorer housing, which may also be overcrowded, compared with those who are better off.
- **Unemployment**: parents who are unemployed have a higher incidence of mental health problems, long-term physical illness, disability and also higher mortality rates.

All these factors can have a lasting impact on the physical, emotional and social wellbeing of the child and family. Poverty is closely linked with social disadvantage; this means that families who have low incomes are likely to have fewer physical and personal resources to cope with illness. They will be at a disadvantage socially. They are also less likely to attend health clinics and, therefore, to receive adequate medical care, both preventative and in response to illness.

Key term

Child poverty – There is no single agreed definition for 'child poverty' in the UK. However, it is generally understood to describe a child living in a family which lacks the resources that would enable that child to participate in activities and have housing and material goods that are customary in the UK. Child poverty is not only defined by the lack of physical necessities, such as food and clothing.

Nutrition

Eating habits developed in childhood are likely to be continued in adult life. This means that children who eat mainly processed, convenience foods will tend to rely on these when they leave home. There are various conditions that may occur in childhood that are directly related to poor or unbalanced nutrition:

- **failure to thrive** (or faltering growth) – poor growth and physical development

- **dental caries or tooth decay** – associated with a high consumption of sugar in snacks and fizzy drinks
- **obesity** – children who are overweight are more likely to become obese adults
- **nutritional anaemia** – due to an insufficient intake of iron, folic acid and vitamin B12
- **increased susceptibility to infections** – particularly upper respiratory infections, such as colds and bronchitis.

Infection

During childhood there are many infectious illnesses that can affect children's health and development. Some of these infections can be controlled by childhood immunisations (see Chapter 9) – these are diphtheria, tetanus, polio, whooping cough, measles, meningitis, mumps and rubella. Other infections can also have long-lasting effects on children's health.

Housing

Poor housing is another factor which can affect children's health. Low-income families are more likely to live in:

- **homes which are damp and/or unheated**: this increases the risk of infection, particularly respiratory illnesses
- **neighbourhoods which are unattractive and densely populated**, with few communal areas and amenities – children without access to a safe garden or play area may suffer emotional and social problems
- **poorer neighbourhoods** – which are significantly more likely to have comparatively high levels of crime, especially violent crime
- **overcrowded conditions** – homeless families who are housed in 'hotels' or bed and breakfast accommodation often have poor access to cooking facilities and have to share bathrooms with several other families; often children's education is badly disrupted when families are moved from one place to another.

Homelessness

It is estimated that about 180,000 children become homeless in England each year. Most of them will be living in temporary hostel accommodation or 'bed and breakfast' housing. The vast majority of these children are in lone parent families, with very little financial or extended family support. Most of these families become homeless to escape from violence from a male partner or ex-partner, or from neighbours. The experience of homelessness causes many health problems for the children of such families:

- mental health problems, including delays in social or language development
- behavioural problems
- disruption of social relationships and difficulty in forming new friendships
- experience of marital conflict and domestic violence.

Accidents

Some childhood accidents have lasting effects on a child's healthy growth and development, and many are preventable (see Chapter 3).

Environmental factors

Pollution of the environment can have a marked effect on children's health and development. The three main threats to health are water pollution, air pollution and noise pollution.

Water pollution

As we saw on page 244, we all need clean, non-polluted water to prevent the spread of infectious diseases and poisoning. In the UK, water is purified before we use it. Although water treatment can remove bacterial contamination, it does not remove heavy chemical pollution. Examples of chemical pollutants in water that can affect children include:

- **lead**: this can enter into our bodies via air, food and water, concentrates in the liver, kidney and bones and can cause learning disability
- **nitrates**: these enter water from fertilisers that leach out of the soil; too much nitrate in drinking water has been found to cause a serious blood disorder in babies under three months, called 'blue baby syndrome'.

Air pollution

Children are particularly vulnerable to air pollution. This is partly because they have a large lung surface area in relation to their small body size, which means that they absorb toxic substances quicker than adults do and are slower to get rid of them. The effects of air pollution from factory chimneys, the use of chemical insecticides and car exhausts include:

- **lead poisoning**: children are particularly susceptible to lead poisoning, mostly caused by vehicle exhaust fumes. Even very low levels of lead in the blood can affect children's ability to learn. Higher levels are associated with damage to the kidneys, liver and reproductive system
- **asthma**: air pollution can act as a trigger for asthma and can make an existing condition worse. The incidence of asthma is much higher in traffic-polluted areas
- **cancer**: the use of insecticides and fertilisers by farmers has been linked with various childhood cancers. Radioactivity from nuclear power stations has also been found to cause cancer.

Noise pollution

Noise pollution can also be a hazard to child health. There is evidence to suggest that high levels of noise, mostly caused by heavy traffic, are responsible for medical and social problems. For example, it has been found that children living on noisy main roads had far fewer friends than those in quiet suburbs, and that traffic noise adversely affects children's progress at school.

Lifestyle factors

Parental substance misuse: smoking, alcohol and drugs

The health of children whose parents misuse substances is affected in a number of ways through physical and emotional neglect, exposure to harm and poor parenting. One of the main difficulties in assessing the harm to children of living with parental substance misuse is that – in the majority of cases – substance misuse is associated with a range of other factors, for example:

- poverty and deprivation
- poor physical and mental health
- poor housing
- debt
- offending
- unemployment.

There are a number of factors which have an impact – directly or indirectly – on the child's health and wellbeing.

- **Parents not available**: the addiction may mean that parents are often absent both physically (because they are out looking for drugs) and emotionally (because they are intoxicated). Either way, they are not available to the child.
- **Poor parenting skills**: substance use is often, but not always, associated with poor or inadequate parenting. This can show itself in a number of ways:
  - **physical neglect**: children are not kept clean, warm, or fed and there is a lack of care for the child's safety
  - **emotional neglect**: the parent shows little or no affection or nurture
  - **unpredictable parental behaviour**: for example, lurching between 'too much' or 'not enough' discipline and mood swings – being very affectionate or very remote. This leads to inconsistent parenting which can be confusing and damaging to the child.
- **Living conditions**: the child may be living in an unsafe environment because of the substance use: for example, through the people that come to the house, being left alone for long periods – because the parent is either intoxicated or out – or being taken out late at night to seek drugs or alcohol. Domestic abuse may be a factor in both circumstances although research shows that it is more often associated with alcohol misuse.

Emotional and social factors

A child who is miserable and unhappy is not healthy, although he or she may appear physically healthy. Children need to feel secure and to receive unconditional love from their primary carers. Child abuse, although not common, is bound to affect a child's health and wellbeing, and can have long-lasting health implications. See Chapter 3 for information about child abuse.

The range of factors that affect children at different times in their lives

Before the birth: pre-conception and antenatal factors

The first 12 weeks of life in the womb (or uterus) are the most crucial as this is the period during which all the essential organs are formed. The health of women pre-conception as well as during pregnancy has a real impact on the unborn child's later health. In addition to having a good diet during pregnancy, women who are pregnant should be aware of the risks of substance misuse and infection.

Drug and alcohol misuse during pregnancy

Most drugs taken by the mother during pregnancy will cross the placenta and enter the foetal circulation. Some of these may cause harm, particularly during the first three months after conception. Drugs that adversely affect the development of the foetus are known as **teratogenic**.

- **Prescription drugs** – drugs are sometimes prescribed by the woman's doctor to safeguard her health during pregnancy, for example antibiotics or anti-epilepsy treatment; they have to be very carefully monitored to minimise any possible effects on the unborn child.
- **Non-prescription drugs** such as aspirin and other painkillers should be checked for safety during pregnancy.
- **Alcohol** can harm the foetus if taken in excess. Babies born to mothers who drank large amounts of alcohol throughout the pregnancy may be born with **foetal alcohol syndrome**. These babies have characteristic facial deformities, stunted growth

and learning disability. Even moderate drinking may increase the risk of miscarriage.

- **Illegal drugs** such as cocaine, crack and heroin are teratogenic and may cause the foetus to grow more slowly. Babies born to heroin addicts are addicted themselves and suffer painful withdrawal symptoms. They are likely to be underweight and may even die.
- **Smoking** during pregnancy reduces placental blood flow and, therefore, the amount of oxygen the foetus receives. Babies born to mothers who smoke are more likely to be born prematurely or to have a low birth weight.

Key term

Teratogenic – a drug or other substance capable of interfering with the development of a foetus, causing birth defects.

For foetus sake, don't drink any alcohol when you're pregnant.

FASawareUK
For more information on Foetal Alcohol Spectrum Disorder go to fasaware.co.uk

Figure 6.5 Foetal alcohol syndrome carries significant danger to the baby's health

Infection

Viruses and small bacteria can cross the placenta from the mother to the foetus and may interfere with normal growth and development. During the **first three months** (the first trimester) of a pregnancy, the foetus is particularly vulnerable. The most common problematic infections are:

- **Rubella** (German measles) – this is a viral infection which is especially harmful to the developing foetus as it can cause congenital defects such as blindness, deafness and learning disability. All girls in the UK are now immunised against rubella before they reach childbearing age, and this measure has drastically reduced the incidence of rubella-damaged babies.
- **Cytomegalovirus** (CMV) – this virus causes vague aches and pains, and sometimes a fever. It poses similar risks to the rubella virus, that is, blindness, deafness and learning disability, but – as yet – there is no preventative vaccine. It is thought to infect as many as one per cent of unborn babies, and of those infected babies, about ten per cent may suffer permanent damage.
- **Toxoplasmosis** – this is an infection caused by a tiny parasite. It may be caught from eating anything infected with the parasite, including:
  - raw or undercooked meat, including raw cured meat such as Parma ham or salami
  - unwashed, uncooked fruit and vegetables
  - cat faeces and soil contaminated with cat faeces
  - unpasteurised goat's milk and dairy products made from it.

In about one-third of cases, toxoplasmosis is transmitted to the foetus and may cause blindness, hydrocephalus or learning disability. Infection in late pregnancy usually has no ill effects.

- **Syphilis** – this is a bacterial sexually transmitted disease (STD). It can only be transmitted across the placenta after the 20th week of pregnancy. It causes the baby to develop congenital syphilis, and can even lead to the death of the foetus. If the woman is diagnosed as having the disease at the beginning of pregnancy, it can be treated satisfactorily before the 20th week.

Research Activity

Foetal alcohol syndrome

'Foetal Alcohol Syndrome is the biggest cause of non-genetic mental handicap in the western world and the only one that is 100 per cent preventable.' (Foetal Alcohol Syndrome Aware UK)

Visit www.fasaware.co.uk to find out about foetal alcohol syndrome. In groups, prepare a poster that highlights the problems associated with heavy drinking during pregnancy.

Children aged from birth to four years

This age range spans a critical stage in a child's life. Physically, the child is vulnerable and totally dependent on others both before birth and for a significant period in the early years. When children experience **neglect** of their physical needs (such as through poor nutrition and poor housing), it can lead to failure to thrive and delayed development. The young child also has a need for stimulation and **attachment** in order to develop emotionally. Parents who use drugs are less likely to take advantage of services such as play schemes, trips and parenting groups than other vulnerable families. This may be because of stigma. There is then a further impact on the child who will have fewer opportunities for social experiences of the kind other children enjoy.

Children aged five to eleven years

Children in this age range still require physical care but their emotional needs and the development of social skills assume a greater importance. They need routine and consistency in their lives. They also need to have bonds of attachment. Children whose home life lacks routine and positive discipline as well as cleanliness, appropriate clothing, adequate food and 'normal' activities may be marked out as different; this leads to the child feeling isolated. They may also have problems with attendance at school, lateness, concentration and a lack of basic social skills. Over time, they may come to see substance use as the norm and start to engage in risky behaviour themselves, such as drug or alcohol use and offending.

The risks to child health (all ages) from passive smoking

When someone smokes, invisible particles from tobacco smoke mix with the surrounding air. This can be called passive smoke or second-hand smoke. Breathing in this air is called **passive smoking**. Unfortunately it is not just adults who are at risk to the adverse effects of passive smoking. Young children and toddlers are especially sensitive to the effects of second-hand smoke, due to the fact that their bodies are still growing and developing, and they breathe faster then adults and therefore may inhale more smoke.

Children **of all ages** who are exposed to second-hand smoke at home:

- are twice as likely to suffer from chest infections, such as bronchitis, pneumonia or **bronchiolitis**
- will have less-developed lungs which have a reduced ability to function well
- will suffer severe asthma attacks if they are already asthmatic and suffer frequent attacks
- have a higher risk of developing asthma if they were not born with it
- are more likely to be hospitalised before they reach their second birthday
- will suffer from more colds, coughs and sore throats
- are more likely to suffer ear infections, fluid in the ears, chronic middle ear disease or 'glue ear', which could lead to some loss of hearing. Many children will need to have the fluid from their ears surgically drained as a result of passive smoking
- could suffer from possible heart disorders
- will have a higher risk of developing cancer as an adult
- will suffer from some loss of sense of smell

- are more likely to have been born with a low birth weight (see Chapter 13 for more information on the problems associated with low birth weight)
- are more likely to die of cot death: infants of mothers who smoke are up to three times more likely to die from Sudden Infant Death Syndrome (SIDS) compared to those whose mothers do not smoke
- will be absent from school more often due to various illnesses caused from breathing in the tobacco smoke – and will take longer to recover from the above illnesses.

Key term

Bronchiolitis – Bronchiolitis is a breathing condition caused by a viral infection. Babies between three and six months are most commonly affected, though it can occur up to two years.

The importance of healthy eating

The National Diet and Nutrition Survey (2011) of children and young people showed that all age groups showed:

- a preference for high-fat-content diets, shown by the high consumption of chips, snack foods, biscuits, chocolate confectionery and soft drinks
- low consumption of fruits and vegetables
- that the prevalence of eating disorders such as anorexia nervosa and bulimia nervosa, which predominantly affect females, has increased in recent years. Bulimia nervosa was greatly increased among 10- to 19-year-old females.

The researchers concluded that the combination of an unhealthy diet and non-active lifestyle could have a significant impact on children's health and wellbeing. A well-balanced diet during childhood that ensures sufficient intakes of vitamins and minerals being consumed and non-sedentary behaviour will help to reduce the risk of developing diseases in adulthood.

Figure 6.6 It is essential to teach children about the importance of a healthy diet

Obesity and ill-health

Obesity (or fatness) results from taking in more energy from the diet than is used up by the body. Some children appear to inherit a tendency to put on weight very easily, and some parents and carers offer more high-calorie food than children need. Numbers of overweight and obese children and adolescents of secondary school age are on the increase. Factors that may be contributing to this trend are the high intake of food high in fat and an inactive lifestyle where more time is spent on sedentary activities outside school such as watching television or playing computer games. Another factor that should be taken into consideration is that fewer children walk to school.

Obesity can lead to emotional and social problems as well as the physical problem of being more prone to infections. An obese child is often the target for bullying, and if severely obese, the child will be unable to participate in the same vigorous play as their peers.

The importance of physical activity

Some children take no regular physical exercise, apart from at school, and this is often because of the family's attitude and habits. Taking regular exercise allows children to develop their motor skills and to 'run off' any pent-up feelings of frustration and aggression. Children who do not take much exercise tend to become inactive adults. Adults who are physically inactive have about double the chance of suffering from coronary heart disease, which is the greatest single risk to health in the UK. Obesity is also more common in children who take little exercise.

The importance of rest and sleep

Rest and sleep are important for our health and wellbeing. When we sleep, we rest and gain energy for a new day. But sleep does more than that. When we dream, we process all the events of our daily life. After a night without enough sleep we often feel exhausted and irritable, but after a good night's sleep we feel rested, refreshed and full of energy. It is important to parents and carers that their child sleeps through the night, as it influences the entire family's life and wellbeing. Children need more sleep than adults because the brain is developing and maturing and they are physically growing as well.

Sleep is important to child health for the following reasons:

- It rests and restores our bodies.
- It enables the brain and the body's metabolic processes to recover (these processes are responsible for producing energy and growth).
- During sleep, growth hormone is released; this renews tissues and produces new bone and red blood cells.
- Dreaming is believed to help the brain sort out information stored in the memory during waking hours.

Illness and disability

Children with a chronic physical illness are twice as likely to suffer from emotional problems or disturbed behaviour as those without. This is especially true of physical disorders which involve the brain, such as epilepsy and cerebral palsy. Serious illness or disability can cause a lot of work and stress for everyone in the family, especially the parents. Children who are ill – and frequently in hospital – experience more stressful situations than children without an illness.

Long-term effects on health

The affected child might:

- have fewer opportunities to learn everyday skills, and to develop their interests and hobbies
- have to miss a lot of school and have particular difficulties with learning
- see themselves as different from other children, when what they really want is to be just the same as their friends
- become depressed
- be vulnerable to bullying.

Children with a disability will experience similar effects on their health and wellbeing.

The inverse care law

The families who are most in need of child health surveillance are often those who are least likely to make use of the services provided. Although children in the UK today enjoy better health than at any other time, the provisions of a National Health Service have not led to equality of health experience. The following guidelines highlight people who might be seen as priority groups by health visitors and the primary health care team when organising caseloads and targeting resources. The health care of such priority groups is difficult and often involves a working partnership with other community services, such as social service departments or housing departments.

Guidelines to priority groups for health surveillance

- Very young or unsupported parents, particularly those with their first baby.
- Parents thought to be at particular risk of abusing their children.
- Parents who are socially isolated, due to mental-health problems or linguistic or cultural barriers.
- Families living in poor housing, including bed and breakfast accommodation or housing where there is overcrowding.
- Parents with low self-esteem or a lack of confidence.
- Parents with unrealistic expectations about the child, or with a poor understanding of the child's needs.
- Parents and/or children suffering significant bereavement (or separation as a result of a recent divorce).
- Parents who have experienced previous SIDS in the family.

Section 3: How to plan and implement routines and activities for children

There are many ways in which you can contribute to the promotion of health in childcare settings. The most important part of your role is to be a good role model for children.

Planning and implementing routines to support children's rights to a healthy lifestyle

There are a number of routines that can be planned in early years settings to support children's rights to a healthy lifestyle. The first thing to consider is the needs of the children. Although young children have the same basic needs, it is important to understand that babies and children are unique individuals – and that, within the routine, you should aim to meet children's needs in an *individual* way that supports the individual's development and learning. Even though the routines are part of a group setting's framework, routines should not adopt a 'one approach for all'; rather, each routine should allow for flexibility to take account of individual preferences.

For example: babies and children have the same basic needs for food, warmth, affection and stimulation. However, there will be many differences in the way that an individual baby likes to be fed and also variations in what they like to eat. Every baby will also have a unique preference for how an adult can comfort them and show them affection.

We saw in Chapter 4 how doing the same things in the same order helps children know what to expect when they are in the setting. For example, toddlers may know that when the practitioner says it is lunchtime, they need to put away their toys, go and wash their hands, sit down at their place at the table and wait for the practitioner to sit down. Most children who have been in the setting for a while remember the basic routines and are more comfortable when the routine is consistent.

When planning a routine, make sure that the routine follows the policies, procedures and codes of conduct in your own setting.

Case Study — Planning and implementing a self-service snack system

Background

The Nursery Manager has decided to introduce a different system for children's snack time. Having a rigidly defined group snack time inevitably interrupts many children's play at an inappropriate time. A self-service snack system – sometimes called a 'rolling' snack bar – would allow children to sit together in pairs or in small groups and also allow others to continue in their play.

Aim

To plan a flexible routine for snack time in a pre-school setting that will help young children to learn healthy eating habits and to develop positive attitudes toward food.

Rationale

Young children have small stomachs and high energy levels so they need nutritious snacks and meals frequently. A flexible self-service snack system will enable children to access snacks at a natural break in their play, or when they feel hungry.

Brainstorming

At a staff meeting, everyone was encouraged to put forward their ideas and concerns about the new system. These included concerns about:

- the supervision of hand-washing and of eating
- ensuring that every child participated
- responsibility for preparation and washing up
- children with food intolerances
- disruption to the nursery's normal routine.

The Plan

The snack bar was created from two small tables covered in colourful washable fabric in a corner of the room. This limited the number of children who could visit at any one time, and the four chairs around the table also served as a reminder to keep numbers low. The snack area would be available from 10 am to 10.50 am every day.

On the tabletop was a basket of name cards, a tray of milk cartons, plates with today's snack and plates or napkins for the children. Next to the table was a bucket for waste cartons. Each day, a photo of 'Today's snack' was displayed on the wall above the tables (these photos were taken

Case Study — Planning and implementing a self-service snack system (cont.)

by staff and printed on the computer). There were also photographs and captions showing the sequence to follow when the children arrived for their snack:

1 Find your name card.
2 Put your name card in the basket.
3 Choose your drink.
4 Sit at the table.
5 Put your milk carton in the bucket.

Children would be encouraged to be independent from the introduction of the scheme. Practitioners would be responsible for their 'key' children – supervising their hand-washing and use of the snack area. Any problems encountered when implementing the scheme should be reported on the same day to a designated staff member. It was agreed that the new system would run for at least three months and then staff would evaluate its success.

Reflective practice

What do you think are the advantages and disadvantages of a self-service snack system?

How is snack time managed in your setting? Could it be improved in any way?

Assessment practice

Choose two routines used in your setting.

Write a paragraph stating how each routine promotes development in **each** of the following areas: physical, cognitive, language and communication, emotional and social development.

A hand-washing routine

Hand-washing is an important skill that children need to learn. It can be made into a fun activity by teaching young children the Hand Washing Song, which uses the tune 'Row, Row, Row Your Boat' but with the following words:

Wash, wash, wash your hands

Play our handy game

Rub and scrub and scrub and rub

Germs go down the drain.

Teaching children when and how to wash their hands

Place these steps, with pictures, on the wall near the sink as a reminder.

1 Turn on warm water.
2 Wet your hands with water.
3 Apply liquid soap.
4 Rub your hands together under running water at least 20 seconds. Rub top and inside of hands, under nails and between fingers. Sing the 'Hand Washing Song' twice to be sure you have rubbed long enough.
5 Rinse your hands for at least ten seconds.
6 Dry your hands with clean, disposable paper towel.
7 Turn off the water using the paper towel instead of your bare hand.
8 Throw the paper towel away in the lined bin.

For more information on the importance of hand-washing, see Chapter 4, pages 169–70.

Other routines that could be used to promote and maintain a healthy lifestyle:

- mealtime routine
- rest and sleep routine
- outdoor play routine
- indoor physical activity routine.

Planning and implementing activities to promote and maintain a healthy lifestyle

As we have already seen, there is a great deal more to promoting and maintaining a healthy lifestyle than concentrating on physical health. Children need to have all their needs met in order to be healthy. The following activities should provide opportunities for different needs to be met, with the emphasis on holistic health needs.

Activity

A healthy eating activity for young children

You will need: paper and felt tip pens; food magazines; scissors; a chart or poster showing the healthy eating food pyramid or circle; paper plates – one for each child; paper glue.

- Ask the children to sit in a circle on the floor and close their eyes.

- Ask them to imagine that it is lunchtime and they are quite hungry.

- Ask the children what they would like to eat. What are their favourite foods? Then ask them to open their eyes.

- Write their favourite foods down on a chart. Ask them to describe what their favourite foods look like.

- Draw a picture of their favourite foods. (Some young children will choose junk food as their favourites, depending on their previous nutrition experiences.)

- Next, show the children a picture of the food pyramid. Ask them to find their favourite foods on this food pyramid. Point out the different foods recommended on the food pyramid.

- Pass out one paper plate to each child. Instruct them to cut out pictures of their favourite foods from the magazines. Then ask them to glue these pictures onto their paper plate to make a food collage. Encourage the children to pick nutritious food choices as well as their not-so-nutritious favourites.

Activity

Health awareness

1 In groups, plan an activity to use with a group of nursery or school-age children. Choose from the following topics:
   - accident prevention
   - care of the teeth
   - the importance of hand-washing.

2 Follow these guidelines when planning your activity:
   - decide how many children will be involved – their ages and stages of development
   - choose an appropriate activity: for example, a story-telling session, a puppet show, a board game, role-play session or creative activity
   - think about your aims and be specific: for example, 'My activity aims to help children understand the importance of cleaning your teeth'
   - design the activity and arrange to carry it out with a group of children in your setting(s).

3 After the activity, evaluate its success and suggest ways you could improve it in future.

Activity

Musical statues or freeze dancing

This activity can be carried out with any age group in an early years setting and allows children to engage in physical activity indoors. It is a simple one to carry out and children usually love it. It promotes physical activity, coordination and balancing skills and the ability to understand and follow instructions.

1 Play different types of music for short and long periods of time.

2 Stop the music at unpredictable times, asking the children to 'freeze' on the spot and stop whatever action they are doing when the music stops.

3 Involve the children in choosing different actions to do to the music: for example, dancing, jumping, hopping, skipping.

Figure 6.7 Freezing on the spot

More activities to promote and maintain a healthy lifestyle

- Choose books and displays which reinforce healthy lifestyles.
- Use drama and music sessions to encourage children to express their feelings in a safe environment.
- Create interesting board games with a healthy theme, such as how to avoid accidents when playing outside.
- Welcome visitors to talk about their work in health care, for example invite a health visitor or dentist to explain the importance of good hygiene routines.
- Demonstrate safety and hygiene routines, for example a road safety officer or police officer could visit the setting to teach children how to cross the road safely.
- Make the home area into a hospital ward and encourage role play as patients, nurses and

doctors. This would also be a good opportunity to talk about coughs and colds and how to prevent cross-infection.

- Play a game where children crawl on hands and knees – an obstacle course works well – to help children learn that they should creep and crawl to get under smoke in case of a fire in a building or home.

Assessment practice

Unit 6

For this assignment, you need to collate information about all aspects of children's health. You need to know about – and present information – on:

- a range of factors which may affect children's health and well-being at differing times in their lives
- examples of different routines for children that will maintain a healthy lifestyle
- an explanation of how routines and activities can promote and maintain a healthy lifestyle
- evidence of current and relevant research relating to child health
- the relevance of current legislation as it applies to supporting a healthy lifestyle for children.

Useful resources

Child Poverty Action Group: promotes action for the prevention and relief of poverty among children and families with children: www.cpag.org.uk

The Ten Steps for Healthy Toddlers poster from the Infant and Toddler Forum can be used as a planning tool when devising a healthy routine for toddlers: www.infantandtoddlerforum.org

Other useful websites include: http://www.readysteadytoddler.org.uk

http://www.contentedbaby.com/ BabyandToddlerRoutine.htm

http://www.nhs.uk/conditions/pregnancy-and-baby

7 Play and learning in children's education: Unit 7

Section 1: The relevant theoretical approaches in the field of play and education

The importance of play

Play is a word that is widely used in the field of early childhood, but it is very difficult to define. It is probably one of the least understood aspects of an early childhood practitioner's work, yet play is probably one of the most important elements of childhood.

A traditional way of talking about play has been to break it up into types of play. The problem with this is that people seem to add more and more types to the list.

Looking at play as a whole concept

Breaking play up into types can help to make play more tangible – that is, less abstract to understand. However, there is much to be said for looking at play as a whole, because it is so central to childhood. Play is one of the most important ways in which children develop and learn. The huge variety of types of play shows that play creeps into most areas of a child's life. A good childhood will involve children in play, wherever they live in the world. Play takes different forms in different families and in different cultures. Children who are sick or children with complex needs might have difficulty or face challenges in playing, but with support they can be helped to play.

Why is play important?

The more that neuroscientists and other experts studying the brain and human development find out, the more it seems that there are some mechanisms in the brain that are overarching in the way they influence a child's development, and consequently in the way they influence learning.

Communication and movement are examples of these, and so is play. Play helps children to become imaginative and to develop symbols (making one thing stand for another). These are important aspects of human development.

Play involving symbolic and imaginative aspects of development is a very powerful mechanism in the brain that allows children to begin to transform experiences and to make sense of them. Play helps children to apply their learning; it is not so much about the new things that children learn. It is about how children begin to try things out and make sense of what they have been learning and put it to use. Play helps children to:

Figure 7.1 These children are free to play with the dough as they need: one chooses to roll patterns onto the dough; the other makes a sandwich with the plates, with dough in between; both are deeply involved in their play. This continuous, open-ended provision ensures that each child learns in their own way. There is a serious problem when young children are given adult-directed activities with tasks to perform; they cannot develop their own ideas and thinking, and their play and creativity are seriously constrained – this can lead to behaviour problems

- reflect on life
- bring together and organise what they have been learning
- have opportunities to apply what they have been learning and to experiment safely, away from the dangers of the real world

- think flexibly
- transform what they know from the literal and real to the imagined and created.

EYFS 2012

As a result of the Tickell Review, the revised Early Years Foundation Stage (EYFS) includes a strong endorsement of the principles and themes of the original EYFS with support for play as the route through which the areas of learning should be delivered. There is also an increased focus on the characteristics of effective teaching and how children learn through developing the characteristics of learning:

- play and exploration
- creating and critically thinking
- active learning.

At the same time it is made clear that play alone does not lead to successful learning and the role of practitioners and parents in supporting learning through play is emphasised as fundamental in children's learning.

Figure 7.2

Figure 7.3

Figures 7.2, 7.3 and 7.4 At first, children literally imitate what they see adults doing; gradually they take on a character as they do so, and they create a story to go with this; the girl in this sequence of photographs is dressing her doll and then feeding her

The relationship between play and learning

It would be inaccurate to say that play is the only way in which children learn. However, play is a major part of learning, opening up possibilities to reflect on and apply ideas and imagination, relationships and feelings, to be physically coordinated, to be capable of flexible thinking, to be ethically thoughtful and to develop a sense of awe and wonder.

Discussion point

Discuss the following in a group:

- What are your memories of your childhood play? Did you play?
- Did you make dens in the garden, under a table or with your bedclothes?
- Did you pretend you were in outer space, on a boat, on a desert island, going shopping, keeping house?
- Did you feel you had hours and hours to play?
- Did you enjoy using inexpensive play props or were your favourite toys expensive, commercially produced toys?

Types of play

There are many types of play, and the number grows all the time, which makes this approach to analysing play less and less manageable. Examples are explored in Table 7.1.

Activity

Look at Table 7.1 on different types of play.

1 How many types of play can you identify?

2 Can you group the types of play so that they are clustered by similar characteristics?

3 Can you reduce the number of types?

4 How useful do you find this approach to looking at play? State your reasons, with advantages and disadvantages.

 In Practice

Observe a group of children at play. How many of the different types of play set out in Table 7.1 can you see in one play scenario? Evaluate your findings.

Type of play	What happens in this type of play
Role play	Children imitate the roles of adults. They pretend to be a doctor, nurse, vet, parent, postman or postwoman, builder, cook, and so on. At first, they tend to be very literal, imitating what they see adults do. Gradually, they are able to become a character, such as the grumpy cook, the parent in a rush, and so on.
Domestic play	The first signs of role play in toddlers are often about scenes of everyday life. We see children preparing food, washing up crockery, washing clothes, ironing, shopping, putting dolls to bed and taking them for walks in prams, and so on. The play is very literal at first, imitating what they see people do. Later, they assume different characters that are not straightforward imitations.
Fantasy play	Most role play is about imitating the people children see. They become babies, siblings and different kinds of adults, such as shopkeepers. Fantasy play is more future-looking. It is about roles the children do not know about, but might themselves take on one day – for example, going to the moon in a space rocket or diving in the sea with dolphins.
Phantasy play	Children role-play unreal events, often using characters from cartoons on television. Because it is not rooted in reality, this type of play is often rather lacking in a storyline or character development, so remains superficial and unfocused.
Play using props	Children sometimes use props that are very realistic in appearance, but often they prefer to make their own or to use 'found' objects. These usually have just a suggestion of what they are – for example, they might use a wooden block and pretend it is the iron; a stone might become a cake; they might make mud pies and pretend to cook them in a cardboard box that they pretend is the oven.
Water play, sand play, small-world play, messy play, natural materials play, den play, outdoor play, music play, dance play	The list of types of play that are linked to an area of material provision could go on forever. It shows that the environment adults create for children is of great importance, in order for a rich variety of play scenarios to emerge.
Pretend (or ludic) play	When children pretend, they transform reality and rearrange it – for example, a clothes peg is not really a door key, but they pretend it is.
Symbolic play	When something stands for something else, it is symbolic of the real thing – for example, a leaf can symbolise a plate; a pebble can symbolise a potato on the plate. Symbolic play involves children in making one thing stand for another.
Imaginative play	The imagination is fed by the real experiences children have. The way they play shops will be richer if they have visited supermarkets, corner shops, markets and car boot sales. When children play imaginatively, they use their experiences, rearranging and transforming them – for example, a group of children who went regularly to the swimming pool later made a swimming pool using large hollow blocks.
Creative play	This description is often used in relation to play with sand, dough, clay, paints, sensory materials, and so on. It tends to emphasise the artistic aspect of play. In fact, creative play is about the scientific and humanities aspects of play as much as the artistic. Children certainly create ideas and play with paint, but they also play with scientific ideas and create using these, e.g. finding the fulcrum as they play on a seesaw in the garden.

Type of play	What happens in this type of play
Dramatic (or narrative) play	Drama involves characters and a story. This kind of play prepares children in deep and important ways for later creative writing. It involves creative, imaginative and pretend play. It is more than simply retelling a story, because the children adapt the story and characters to meet the needs of the play scenario.
Socio-dramatic play	Dramatic play could take place alone. We often see this when children talk to themselves, assuming the different voices of their characters. Socio-dramatic play, on the other hand, involves several children, playing out characters and developing a story together.
Physical play: gross-motor play	This occurs when children celebrate their physical prowess – for example, by riding a two-wheeled bicycle or climbing to the top of the climbing frame.
Rough-and-tumble (or boisterous) play	This often involves chasing, catching, pretend fights and pillow fights. Unless children are sufficiently coordinated to manage their play with skill, it often ends in tears. Rough-and-tumble play requires great sensitivity to others in order not to hurt them physically. This form of play often occurs before going to sleep, and it bonds those playing emotionally and socially. It tends to be off-putting to those not taking part in it.
Dizzy play	This kind of play is rarely described in books about play in the UK. Marjatta Kalliala, who is Finnish, writes in detail about Callois's theory of dizzy play in her book, *Play Culture in a Changing World* (2006). Children sometimes just love to stand on the spot and spin round and round, making themselves dizzy on purpose. They tip and tilt and spin. Research is showing that this kind of play is important for brain development. Babies often lean sideways out of prams, or lean back to view the world upside down.
Manipulative play: fine motor play	Children use their hands, playing with small-world animals, the dolls' house or with construction kits such as Brio®. In the 1900s there was great emphasis on exercises to develop the hands, but it is now realised that a rich play environment encourages this without the need for uninteresting exercises.
Deep play: daring and adventure play	From an early age, children love to test their physical skills as they play and to perform feats of daring – for example, they walk on narrow walls, jump off the stairs, and so on. Rather than placing too much emphasis on safety, it is now becoming better understood that children need environments that are as safe as necessary. This requires risk assessments to be made by practitioners. Helen Tovey writes about this in her book, *Playing Outdoors: Spaces and Places, Risk and Challenge* (2008). It is the children who never engage in adventure play who are most likely to have accidents.
Exploratory (or heuristic) play	This kind of play was pioneered by Elinor Goldschmied, who died in 2009 at the age of 98. This kind of play encourages toddlers to explore natural objects, such as shells, stones and wooden objects, rather than manufactured plastic toys. There is more on this in Chapter 4.
Playful learning	Adults and children usually signal when they are changing from ordinary life into play mode. They exaggerate their movements, facial expressions and the way they speak, and they might announce, for example, 'We're playing the tiger who came to tea!' This is often described as playful.
Solitary play	Children often choose to play alone. It used to be thought that to begin with they always played in a solitary way, but because of the work of researchers such as Colwyn Trevarthen, it has become clear that from the start there are times when very young babies enjoy playing with an adult who is sensitive to them.

Type of play	What happens in this type of play
	The solitary play of babies at first is in gazing at a mobile, trying to reach it and bang it, realising they can make things happen, using the hand as something to look at, and the feet as something to play with.
	Sitting babies enjoy having objects to play with.
	Toddlers and young children begin to engage in pretend play and can often be heard talking to themselves as they do so.
	Children often play in very deep ways when they are alone. The idea that this is an early level of play is misleading – solitary play can be very rich.
Parallel (or companionship) play	From an early age, children enjoy the company of someone who plays alongside them, as babies and young children can be lonely; but they do not have to interact. When one child reaches for a wooden spoon, the other might do the same, but they do not take any notice of each other. This type of play helps children to be sensitive to and aware of others as they play.
Associative play	Two children might be pretending to be cooking. They are each in character, but do not take any notice of each other. They do not develop a narrative, storyline or dramatic story together. It does not seem to bother them that both of them are cooks, and that there are no customers in the café. This type of play is a rehearsal for full-blown cooperative play.
Cooperative play	In this type of play, children relate to each other in their characters. They agree what their play props symbolise (stand for). They develop a story together. They cooperate. The play becomes rich when it is sustained over a long period of time.

Table 7.1 Types of play

Activity

Look at the photographs in this chapter of children at play. For each image, decide which type of play they are involved in. Are any of the children involved in several types of play at the same time?

Developmental sequence of play

Nowadays, it is understood that children develop at very different rates, so the concept of age-related stages has been criticised. However, there are sequences of development in play that are useful to know about. It is important to remember that there will be cultural variations in the way children play, and some children with disabilities, complex needs or learning difficulties of different kinds will also be different in the way they develop their play.

Babies

Babies need safe opportunities to play in a way that allows them to do so through the senses and through their movements. The floor needs to be a safe place for babies to have tummy time and to crawl. Babies learn through the movements of their hands, coordinating with their vision and mouths. They learn through putting objects in their mouths, and need a range of objects that are safe enough for them to do this. When they crawl, they need floors that have different textures and surfaces, indoors and outdoors, and interesting things to move towards as they become more mobile.

They need to be able to heave themselves up on chairs, and so on, in ways that are safe, so that furniture does not topple on them or slide away, making them fall unnecessarily, and become frustrated. They will climb up on things as soon as they are able, so the room needs to be made safe enough for them to do this, with windows carefully fastened and bookcases firmly on the wall or cordoned off. Cupboards will need to be fastened shut, or perhaps some will be allowed to be opened and explored safely. What is put in these cupboards will need to be carefully monitored for safety.

Toddlers

Wobbly walkers have increased opportunities to play, because they are more mobile than lying-down babies, sitters and crawlers, so they can get about more easily and go where they want (but also where adults do not want them to go!). Usually, toddlers are beginning to talk and pretend in their play at the same time. All of the safety issues considered for babies, sitters and crawlers still apply.

Children who are beginning to walk still need to explore objects using their senses and feedback from their movements. But they are also imitating adults now, and their play is therefore very literal. They imitate drinking from a cup, stirring their tea, washing up, covering dolls with bedclothes and tucking them in to go to sleep. Researchers suggest that they are not yet 'becoming the person' they imitate (such as the mother with her baby or the doctor giving the injection). Instead, they imitate what the mother or the doctor does.

Developing play through pretend, imagination, symbols and a well-coordinated body: 18 months to seven years

As play develops, children become increasingly able to engage in a world of pretend. They can imagine things beyond the literal and real imitation of things. They can move from the present into the past and the future, and as they do so they transform things. In real life, they are not a mother or a driver of a car, but once they can go beyond simply imitating what they see people do and can actually imagine what it is like to be someone else, they 'become the person'. (Read the section on theory of mind in Chapter 2 to see how children begin to understand that other people do not necessarily think or feel about things exactly as they do.)

This is why we begin to see children experiment with ideas like 'You be unkind to me and I will cry', 'You

be the baddy and I will be the policeman', and so on. They want to explore what it is like to be good, bad, kind, unkind, and so on. Play gives them a safe 'space' to do this. They can decide not to play anymore if it becomes too much to explore evil and baddies, and they can escape from this imagined world of pretend back into the real world again. Play gives them opportunities to see how other people react when they have (pretend) temper tantrums, or (pretend) refuse to eat their lunch, or (pretend) will not go to sleep. Children need to reassure themselves and those they are with that this is a world of pretend, and is not real; they often make remarks while they play such as, 'I'm pretending'.

Although the development of this possibility to transform the real world through the ability to pretend, imagine and symbolise is a key part of the development of play (typically from about 18 months/two years until about five or six years), during this time children are also becoming increasingly coordinated physically and in their movements. This is why we begin to see pretend fights, in which they are learning not to really hurt one another. It is almost like a carefully choreographed dance as the drama unfolds. It is the reason why we see pirates climbing the rigging, children jumping off things and chasing each other without bumping into each other. They will often misjudge their movements at first, but the skills develop with practice over time. The play in the garden or at rural or urban forest school is of great importance in the development of this aspect of play.

Remember that play:

- helps children to move away from the here and now and to transform real life (pretend, imagine and symbolise), so that they make sense of their learning, reflect on what they have been learning, and apply what they know effectively and appropriately in relation to feelings, ideas, thoughts and relationships
- gives children opportunities to develop strong and well coordinated physical ('thinking') bodies
- helps children to be flexible thinkers.

By the end of the first classes of primary school, through their play, children should have developed both aspects of the sequence in the development of play.

The importance of play for children with learning difficulties, disabilities and complex needs

Not all children go through all the sequences outlined above in the development of their play. Some children with complex needs play using the senses and movement, rather than developing pretend play, involving the imagination and symbolic aspects of development. But it is important not to underestimate children with complex needs, because they are often challenged in their movements and ways of experiencing play through the senses. The important thing is to observe what the child enjoys. This gives a very positive approach and encourages the development of play.

Case Study — Dancing the developmental ladder

Jo is four years old, has autism and is fascinated by strips of material, which he loves to wave in front of his face and brush across his nose. The practitioner does not label this an obsession, but instead builds on his interest. She provides a variety of ribbon-like strips, and over several weeks he begins to experiment with a wider range. After a few months he is interested in eye contact with her, provided the ribbons are swaying in front of his face. One day, he parts the ribbons and looks her directly in the eye. He says, 'Boo.'

Children with special educational needs and disabilities often 'dance' the developmental ladder. They may do some things at the same time as most children their age, or they may have a different timescale for different aspects of their development.

Play therapy (therapeutic play)

This kind of play helps children who are in emotional pain to find out more about how they feel, to face their feelings and to deal with them, so that they gain control over their lives. Helping children through play therapy requires professional training, but every child can improve their emotional and mental wellbeing through the feeling of control that play gives. This happens quite naturally for most children, but some children need more help.

In some cases, children who do not play can be helped through play therapy. Play therapists undertake specialist training, and help children who are emotionally vulnerable to heal the hurt and emotional pain they are experiencing. Play therapists are often based in hospitals, special schools and Children's Centres.

Most children will begin to play if they are given sensitive adult help. Once children know how to play, there is usually no stopping them. Therefore, most children do not need the help of a play therapist. Their natural childhood play helps them to self-heal.

Children with English as an additional language

One of the powerful things about play is that it does not depend on language; but it does provide a relaxed context, with no pressure, and that is the ideal situation in which to learn a new language. Play gives children 'comprehensible input' because children make props, they mime and gesture as part of their play, and they create shared meaning as they play.

The features of play

Quite often, practitioners will observe children at play, and will have a sense that this is a rich play scenario, but this does not help the adult to say why this might be. The 12 features of play (Bruce, 1996, 2004, 2011a and b) are often used to help practitioners share the importance of their children's play with parents and with other practitioners. Play will have low status unless practitioners can help parents and colleagues to see how richly it helps children to develop and learn.

If seven or more of the 12 features are present, then it is probably a rich play scenario. If only a few of the features are present, it does not necessarily mean the child is not doing something worthwhile, but it may not be play.

Case Study   Comprehensible input through play

Noor (three years old) has only just arrived in England. She has been separated from most of her family, but her mother is reunited with three of her children after fleeing from a war zone. Noor is in the home corner. She finds a sheet from the doll's bed and wraps it round her body. She puts the doll into the sling she has made. She finds the broom and sweeps the floor. She finds the saucepan and puts it on the stove,

pretending to prepare the meal. The practitioner smiles when she catches her eye, and sits near her, but does not invade her focused play.

Noor is adjusting to her new surroundings. She does so by playing out familiar, everyday things, such as caring for the baby and preparing a meal. Learning to speak English can come later. Now what she needs is the sensitive encouragement of the practitioner.

The 12 features of play

1. Children use real, **first-hand experiences** in their play, such as going to the shops or preparing food.

2. Children have a sense of control when they play and they begin to make up **rules** – for example, the dog must be fed and his plate must be here, on the floor, because I say so. Children feel powerful when they play.

3. Children find, use and **make play props** when they play. This is creative, as they use things in flexible and new ways. It is imaginative, as they rearrange their experiences to suit the play, themselves and the characters.

4. Children **choose to play**. No one can make a child play.

5. When children play, they sometimes **rehearse the future** – for example, in their role play, when they pretend to be adults.

6. Children might **pretend** when they play – for example, that they are the goodies chasing the baddies. They organise their thinking, transforming it as they do so.

7. Children might choose to **play alone**, needing some personal space and time to

reflect and try out an idea they have – for example, with their small-world garage.

8. They might **play with other children**, in parallel, associatively or cooperatively.

9. When children play they have a **personal play agenda**. They might want to put pretend jam on all the pretend cakes, or bath the dog. They will find a way to carry this out. Adults are welcome to play with children, providing that everyone respects each other's personal play agenda.

10. Children involved in rich play become deeply **involved** and are difficult to distract. Children wallow in their play.

11. Children **show us their latest learning when they play**. They might have just mastered riding a bicycle, so in their play they keep riding their bike to post a letter, to go to the shops, to take their child to school – anything, as long as they are on their bike!

12. **Play brings together the learning** children do. It organises the learning, so that it becomes connected and an integrated whole.

(From Bruce, 2004, 2011a, b and c)

Activity

In Figures 7.5 and 7.6, try to identify some of the features of play that are present. Is this rich play?

Figures 7.5 and 7.6 Note the storage of the equipment: the transparent boxes allow children to see what is in them. The flooring is flat enough for building with wooden blocks. The children are allowed to fetch cars, planes, and so on, to use with the blocks because the two areas are next to each other. Perhaps these children are interested in up and under: the vehicle is under the bridge they have built; the plane is held up in the air – the boys are using their knowledge and experience of aeroplanes. They are very involved in their play (wallowing in it) and they are playing cooperatively. They have chosen to play and they have selected play props. They are pretending, and have created a play scenario using their ideas (their play agenda)

Creating environments that encourage and support play

Play does not just happen. It is true that babies and young children are biologically disposed to play, but they will not develop their play unless they meet people and experience situations that encourage the development of play. What adults provide has a direct impact on play. If adults encourage play and create an enabling environment that cultivates play, the quality of children's play will be deeper.

Continuous provision

There should always be a core of open-ended provision that is continuously offered – this means it is constantly available. Other experiences can be added in or changed, and may not be offered all day every day in the same way.

The following are considered to be open-ended continuous provision:

- malleable natural materials (clay, mud, dough)
- home corner for domestic play

Figure 7.8 It is quite a skill to avoid pouring the water over his feet – the child demonstrates this in his play. He also shows us that he is interested in pouring water on the concrete wall of the sandpit, as well as the sand inside the pit. He is noticing that the results are different: water seeps into sand; it splashes off concrete. He might enjoy discussing this later, if photos were taken and he shared them with his key person. Often children do not want to interrupt their play, but they do appreciate reflecting afterwards, and photos are an excellent way to do this in a relaxed way

Figure 7.7 The children are involved in parallel (companionship) play: both are digging in the sand and filling holes with water, watching it seep into the sand

- workshop area, with found and recycled material for model making and mark making, and including masking tape and scissors that cut (for left- and right-handed children)
- small-world play (dolls' house, farm, prehistoric animals, roads, trains)
- sand (wet and dry) and water.

Space and places to play indoors: room design

Freedom of movement is central to early childhood. Susan Isaacs, a pioneer in integrated early years provision, thought that children cannot learn if they are made to sit still.

It is hard for children to develop their play if the day is timetabled into rigid slots, with routines that break up the day. If children are allowed to move about freely between the indoor and outdoor areas, research suggests that their play is calmer and of deeper quality.

There is also the advantage that giving children greater choice of where and how they play gives adults more time and opportunity to support children's play and choices, rather than organising and directing adult-led 'activities' for most of the day.

Space and places to play outdoors: gardens, parks, forests, urban forests

Play does not happen to adult order. Challenging play helps children to play at their highest levels. Play outdoors gives children opportunities to consolidate and practise skills.

Settings now work hard to make their outdoor area an important part of the play environment. This is important, as it is a requirement of the Early Years Foundation Stage in England, the Foundation Phase in Wales, the Curriculum for Excellence in Scotland, and the 3–5 Framework in Northern Ireland.

Children need to interact with nature, so plants, trees, flowers and vegetables are part of this. This encourages bird and insect life. Ideally, children are

Figure 7.9 There is nothing as enjoyable as a book in a den, with dappled sunshine and a cosy cover

taken to forests, or to parks with copses of trees, so that they learn how to be in woodland and in open green spaces. To play in this situation strengthens the play and encourages creativity. Den-making is something children all over the world engage in. Dens, mud pies, hoops, beanbags and balls in zones all have a contribution to make to outdoor play.

Open-ended natural materials to play with

These encourage children to think, feel, imagine, socialise and concentrate deeply. This type of material encourages children to think about natural resources in the world ('Where does clay come from?'). Children will tend to use a range of fine motor skills with these materials, such as working at the woodwork bench or making a clay coil pot. Examples of open-ended materials are:

- found materials, such as those used in junk-modelling
- transforming raw materials, like clay and dough
- self-service areas
- dressing-up clothes and cookery items in the home area
- wooden blocks.

Carefully chosen and limited use of commercial toys and equipment

It is important to note that toys are often expensive and of doubtful quality in terms of educational experience. Pre-structured toys can only be used in one prescribed way, whereas open-ended material can be used as a prop for all kinds of play scenarios.

A set of wooden unit blocks has more potential for creative and imaginative play than one set of a plastic construction kit. It is best to keep adding to the wooden blocks, and to choose one construction kit that is as open-ended as possible, so that many different things can be constructed with it, and then to keep adding to that.

The role of the adult in play

There are different ways of supporting children's play. All of these have a place, but it is fascinating to see the differences and to be aware of them.

Janet Moyles's play spiral

This approach to play argues that children need play materials first (Moyles gives the example of a plastic construction kit) in order that they can explore freely. Then the adult demonstrates how to make a box with the materials, and discusses this with the children, who also make boxes. Children are then left free to use the kit without the adult; in Moyles's observations, they will use the adult's teaching in their free play. The adult is either directly teaching and showing, or leaving children without adult presence, to use materials in their own way.

Play tutoring

The adult might take a group of children to the shops, and on their return set up a shop for play. The adult will show the children how to play shops. It is important to remember that this is not play, because the adult is in complete control and leads all the time. But it is often an important way of helping children to learn how to play.

12 features of play

Both the play spiral and the play tutoring approaches give the adult a directing role when they join children in play. In this approach, the adult takes a partnership role, rather than a directing role. The adult tunes in to the child and builds the play with the child, more like a conversation (sometimes called coconstruction). The adult can initiate play, or the child can. The important thing is that the adult is not taking control and doing all the leading, but instead is supporting what the child initiates or takes up. The supporting might be through a conversation during the play, or it might be that the adult sees some prop that might be useful for the child to take their play agenda and ideas forward, so adds this to the play provision for the child to take up if they choose to do so.

Laissez-faire approach to play

Leaving children to play without any support leads to low-level play. This is especially the case when children are separated into age groups in settings. A group of two-year-olds is unlikely to be engaged in play scenarios as rich as a mixed age group of two-, three- and four-year-olds. The older children lead and the younger children enjoy participating under the leadership of the older children. In many countries, where there is no group provision and children play at home or outside with older children, this is the way that younger children learn how to play.

Of course, two-year-olds will not play for long in this way, as it is exhausting for them and intellectually stretching. But children love to be able to experience deep thinking, and this is a child's opportunity to do that.

Pioneers of play

Look back at Chapter 4 for information on the theories of play developed by Steiner, Montessori and other pioneers of play.

Jan Amos Comenius (1592–1670)

This Moravian educator and bishop anticipated some of the ideas of Friedrich Froebel by a century. He believed that children learn through the senses and through real, first-hand experiences. He thought that teachers should try to make learning interesting and enjoyable, and that learning by doing and helping children to play was part of this. He thought play was important because what children learned through their play they would use later in life. In his book, *The Great Didactic*, published in Amsterdam in 1649 (the year Charles I was executed in England), Comenius emphasised movement and exercise; he believed that giving children interesting, real and play experiences was the key to education, and that children should understand the reasons for rules.

Friedrich Froebel (1782–1852)

Before theories about play were established, Froebel pioneered the view that play acts as a way of bringing together and organising learning. (It is sometimes called an integrating mechanism.) Play helps children to use what they know, to apply their knowledge and understanding as they think, have ideas and feelings, relate to people and are confident in their physical bodies. He thought that play helps children to show their deepest possible levels of learning. Play helps children to understand themselves, others and the universe.

Karl Groos (1861–1946)

Groos wrote a book called *The Play of Animals* in 1898. He believed that play is a way for children to run off excess energy, but, more importantly, that play is preparation for later life, as it gives children opportunities to practise skills they will need later.

Johan Huizinga (1872–1945)

The Dutch cultural historian saw play within an evolutionary framework. This was because he said that animals inhabited the earth before humans did, and animals play, so this means that play is older than human culture. In 1938, Huizinga wrote a book called *Homo Ludens*, which translates as *Man the Player*. In it, he argues that play gives children freedom, experiences that are more than their ordinary, real lives, beyond their local space and time. He said that play gives children a sense of order. No financial profit is gained from play.

Susan Isaacs (1885–1948)

Susan Isaacs, like Margaret McMillan, was influenced by Froebel. She was also influenced by the theories of Melanie Klein, the psychoanalyst. Isaacs made detailed observations of children in her Malting House School in Cambridge during the 1930s.

A summary of Isaacs's ideas:

● Isaacs valued play because she believed that it gave children freedom to think, feel and relate to others.

- She looked at children's fears, their aggression and their anger. She believed that, through their play, children can move in and out of reality. This enables them to balance their ideas, feelings and relationships.
- She said of classrooms where young children have to sit at tables and write that they cannot learn in such places because they need to move just as they need to eat and sleep.
- Isaacs valued parents as the most important educators in a child's life. She spoke to them on the radio, and she wrote for parents in magazines. In her book *The Nursery Years*, she wrote:

If the child has ample opportunity for free play and bodily exercise, if this love of making and doing with his hands is met, if his interest in the world around him is encouraged by sympathy and understanding, if he is left free to make believe or think as his impulses take him, then his advances in skill and interest are but the welcome signs of mental health and vigour.

- Isaacs encouraged people to look at the inner feelings of children. She encouraged children to express their feelings. She thought it would be very damaging to bottle up feelings inside.
- She supported both Froebel's and McMillan's view that nurseries are an extension of the home and not a substitute for it, and she believed that children should remain in nursery-type education until they are seven years of age.
- She kept careful records of children, both for the period they spent in her nursery and for the period after they had left. She found that many of them regressed when they left her nursery and went on to formal infant schools. Modern researchers have found the same.

Anna Freud (1895–1982)

Anna was the daughter of Sigmund Freud, who pioneered the idea of psychoanalysis. She was a teacher and a trained therapist. Anna Freud thought it was important to observe children at play, and to see how they use play to move in and out of reality,

experimenting in this way with their feelings. Play is a self-healing process, and supports children in sorting out their feelings and learning to manage them. Anna Freud did not think that many children would need specialist therapeutic help, although some would. The most important thing is that children have a childhood in which they are loved, with clear boundaries and opportunities for natural play.

Lev Vygotsky (1896–1934)

Vygotsky thought that play creates a 'zone of potential development', in which children are able to function at their highest level of learning. He suggested that it is as if children become a 'head taller than they really are'. He valued imaginative play, so did not focus so much on play before the toddler age when that emerges. In his view, play creates a way of freeing children from the constraints of everyday life.

Donald Winnicott (1896–1971)

Winnicott developed his understanding of play through pioneering the idea of the transitional object. This can be a substitute for someone important to the child emotionally when that person is not present. Alternatively, it can help a child to enjoy the presence of someone they love who *is* present.

Transitional objects work in two ways: they make a healthy and natural link with those people the child loves – for example, teddy stands for the father who goes to work but returns; but teddy also has an imaginative life, taking meals with the child, sleeping together and having adventures together.

Jean Piaget (1896–1980)

For Piaget, play is about keeping balanced. He thought this had two aspects:

- accommodation – adapting to situation
- assimilation – confirming what you already know through your experiences.

Play is mainly to do with assimilation, using what is known, familiar and understood. It is about applying what has already been learned. Piaget thought there were two aspects to play, in a developmental sequence: sensory and movement play, and then imagination, pretend and symbolic play. In middle childhood, play increasingly turn into **games with rules**.

Erik Erikson (1902–1994)

Erikson was a student of Anna Freud. He thought that children are partners in their futures. In his view, children deal with difficult experiences by creating an ideal situation, which they then master and control. This helps them into their future lives.

Jerome Bruner (1915–)

Bruner suggests that children need a long childhood because there is so much for them to learn in preparation for their lives as adults. They learn about the technical aspects of life and about their culture. Play in early childhood is the main way in which they experiment freely and learn to do this, and through which they are initiated into the culture. Children play with objects provided and chosen by adults, and by 'doing' (Bruner calls this enactive learning). They learn the rules of games from people who teach them as they play together, and they become familiar with the rules of the culture through their play.

Discussion point

Now that you have read about the different pioneers and theories of play, choose the two theories that you most agree with. In a small group, discuss the different theories and say what attracts you to the two theories you have chosen. Can you find a key message about which all these pioneers and theorists agree?

Section 2: How to use appropriate tools to assess the learning needs of individual children

Every early years setting must work closely with other professionals and agencies to ensure that each child has the best possible opportunities in their learning. These professionals and agencies are discussed more fully in Chapter 11.

In order to plan a quality curriculum framework, the first step is to observe children *as individuals*. Observation helps adults tune in to what interests a child, and to see how to support and extend their interest. When children are interested in the experiences and activities they are offered, they learn more effectively, and adults can add to this and provide children with what they need.

Observation informs planning and practice

Giving children what they need means linking the child's interests with what is needed in the official curriculum framework documents of the country. The role of the practitioner is to observe, support and extend the child's learning.

Throughout, this book stresses the importance of observation and how it informs the way practitioners can become involved in:

- creating learning environments indoors and outdoors, based on what they have observed that children are interested in
- supporting the individual and group interests of children

- extending the interests of individual children, when appropriate
- meeting the needs of children as unique individuals
- sharing and exchanging through rich dialogue and observations with parents/carers.

The revised English Early Years Foundation Stage (from birth to five years of age) covers the year leading into Key Stage 1 with the Foundation Profile. This helps practitioners to assess the development, learning and wellbeing of children across the year, using observations which make formative assessments to plot progress. It is a holistic approach, covering the six areas of learning set out in the EYFS theme called 'Learning and Development'.

The early learning goals are not expectations, but aspirations. For example, more than half the children in England achieve the goals for personal, social and emotional development, but only about one-third reach the goals for communication, language and literacy because, against advice of early childhood experts, they were set too high. Children in other countries are not expected to reach this level as they turn five years of age, and yet they do better in the long term, despite being taught to read and write later (typically at six to seven years of age). Looking at the progress of children across the six areas of learning has proved important. For example, it has been shown that children who achieve well on the goals for physical development are achieving better in pencil control in the literacy goals. There are important messages here:

- Early is not best.
- Narrow approaches constrain rather than help development and learning.
- Learning with quality takes time to embed.
- Children learn through a variety of richly deserved experiences, and so it is often difficult to track down their exact learning journey. Indirect teaching is powerful.

Adult-led teaching needs to be very sensitive and be based on observation, tuning in to the child at the right time in the right way.

Observation informs assessment

See also Chapter 1 for information on assessment and observation.

- **Baseline assessment**: when we first meet a child we need to get to know them and their family/carers. We use our first observations as a way of doing this, along with what parents/carers know and understand.
- **Formative assessment**: as our observations build, we are able to gain a fuller picture of the child, and we quite literally *form* assessments as we accompany the child on their learning journey.
- **Summative assessment**: at regular points (depending on whether a child has special needs) or when the child is leaving the setting and moving on, we take stock and pause to reflect on an aspect of development and learning, or on the whole child's learning.

Observing children at play

When observing children at play, follow the four steps of narrative observation. See below for a sample observation sheet.

1 The observer writes briefly about the context of the observation. (Where is the child?)
2 The observer writes down as exact a description as possible of what the child says and does, and enough description of the conversations and actions of other children the child might be with, to give a clear picture of the child being observed.
3 The observation can then be analysed and interpreted.
4 The observation can be shared with the parents and other practitioners to further support and extend the development of play.

Narrative observation of play

Child's name: ....

Date of observation: ....

Time observation begins:.. ends: ....

Give a short description of the context in which the play is taking place:

....

....

Describe what is happening and any communication/language (both non-verbal and spoken):

....

....

....

Analysis of the play
Which features of play are present?
• Using first-hand experience? How?
• Using rules, making rules, changing rules? In control?
• Finding, making or miming play props?
• Choosing to play? In what way?
• Rehearsing the future? How?
• Pretending? Example?
• Playing alone? Talking to themselves?
• Children and adults playing together? How?
• What is the child's personal play agenda?
• Deeply involved? What makes you think so?
• Showing latest skills and learning in the play? What are these?
• Sustained, integrated ideas, feelings, relationships in free-flow play?

(Based on Bartholomew and Bruce, 1993; Bruce, 1991, 2004, 2011a)

In Practice

- ❏ Observe a child with special educational needs. Is the child playing according to the 12 features of play? Analyse and evaluate your observations.

- ❏ Observe children playing together in one of these areas: wooden block play, small-world (dolls' house, farm, road, and so on), home corner. What ages are the children? Using the 12 features of play, analyse your observations. Plan how you could add to the provision in light of your observations.

- ❏ Observe one or several children playing in the garden, or if you join children and adults (trained practitioners in forest school work) when they go to their forest school outing. Use the 12 features of play to do this, and analyse the observations you have gathered. In which ways does the play indoors differ from the play outdoors?

- ❏ Observe a child who is sick but is able to play – at home in bed or in a hospital. Identify which of the 12 features of free-flow play the child exhibits. Plan how to help the child by providing appropriate material to support the play.

Figure 7.10 Phones are an important part of modern life and children often use them in their play to represent their experience

Play and other aspects of the early childhood curriculum

First-hand experience

Play is part of a network of ways in which children develop and learn. These include the importance of real, first-hand experiences in which children actively participate. Taking children to the shops, or for a walk in the park or by the river; encouraging them to help to prepare meals, wash up, wash clothes and learn how to dry them; going out in the rain with boots and umbrellas and raincoats – all these contribute to children's development and learning.

Representing experiences

Children begin to find ways of representing their experiences so that they are not forgotten, but are kept in the brain as a resource to be used. Representation is therefore important in the development of learning. Children, when supported and encouraged by adults and older children, will represent visits to shops, parks, rivers and the sea, meals, pets, family, rain, snow, sun and so on.

Games and their rules

Games help children, in a different way, to take part in, make sense of and understand their families, communities and culture. Games involve rules. Whereas play is about the way that children experiment with what happens if they break, make or change rules, games teach children the rules themselves. There are different kinds of rules in different sorts of games:

- **Social and cultural games** – the rules of greetings and partings, thank-you games and taking-turns games. In different cultures, the rules will be different. 'Thank you' is a word only used in Gujarati when it is a heartfelt thing, but in English it is used more superficially – for example, when taking change from a shop assistant.
- **Mathematical games** – matching games, such as snap or snakes and ladders, involving counting.
- **Ring games and songs** – for example, 'Brown girl in a ring', and choosing partners, taking turns and joining in the chorus.

Play in relation to other aspects of the early childhood curriculum

Figure 7.11 shows how play connects with other aspects of the curriculum.

The 12 features of play emphasise the important contribution that play makes to children's mastery of their learning, and the way in which it helps them to concentrate deeply and to reflect on their learning. Through play, children are able to transform experiences and make them manageable, to be flexible enough to think through alternatives, imagine how things could be or might have been, and to work out important ways of relating to self and others. They begin to see the bigger picture, the wider world, and perhaps to think about the universe, and to have sense of awe and wonder. Play lifts learning to a higher level and shows children in their deepest ideas, feelings, relationships and using their physical limits.

Play is like a reservoir full of water. The deeper the reservoir, the more water can be stored in it and used during times of drought. The benefits of play are of lasting impact during adult life, through both good and bad times.

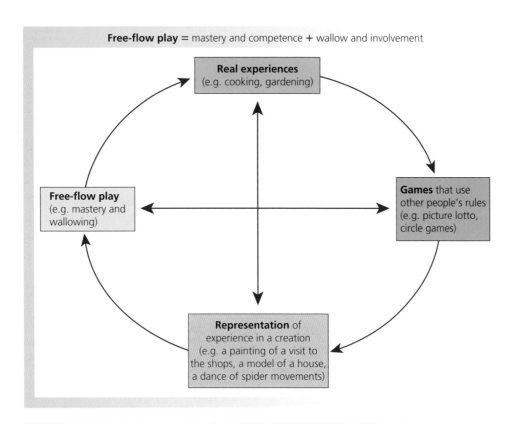

Free-flow play = mastery and competence + wallow and involvement

Real experiences
(e.g. cooking, gardening)

Free-flow play
(e.g. mastery and wallowing)

Games that use other people's rules
(e.g. picture lotto, circle games)

Representation of experience in a creation
(e.g. a painting of a visit to the shops, a model of a house, a dance of spider movements)

Figure 7.11 The network for learning

Section 3: How to plan and provide learning opportunities in consultation with others

The early childhood curriculum frameworks in UK countries

The Early Years Foundation Stage (EYFS) in England

The EYFS sets standards for the development, learning and care of young children at *birth to five years* when they attend a home learning environment (HLE) or group setting. It provides for equality of opportunity and anti-discriminatory practice and creates a framework in which parents and professionals can work in partnership. As seen in Chapter 1, the principles guide the EYFS through four themes:

1 Every child is a **unique child**, who begins learning at birth and can become resilient, capable, confident and self-assured.
2 Children learn to be strong and independent through **positive relationships** with their parents and carers and with others, including their key person at their early years setting.
3 **A positive environment** – in which children's experiences are planned to reflect their needs, and help build their confidence, and in which there is a strong partnership between early years practitioners, parents and other professionals – is crucial if children are to fulfil their potential and learn and develop well.
4 **Children develop and learn in different ways and at different rates**. All areas of learning and development are important and are inter-connected.

Evidence shows that the right foundations of early learning (from pregnancy until age five) make significant differences to outcomes for children and to future life chances. Physical and mental health and the establishment of positive attitudes to learning that will continue throughout the EYFS into the school years and beyond are all affected by what happens at the beginning of children's lives.

The learning and development requirements

There is an aspiration that by the end of the academic year during which a child reaches the age of five, a child will have reached the **early learning goals**. This is a very contentious area that continues to cause much debate, since few children, especially boys, reach several of the literacy goals. Many early childhood experts have formed the view that these goals are not appropriate for such young children.

The six interconnected areas of development and learning are:

- personal, social and emotional development
- communication, language and literacy
- problem-solving, reasoning and numeracy
- knowledge and understanding of the world
- physical development
- creative development.

Each area depends on the others.

Assessment

Assessment in the revised EYFS plays an important part in helping parents and practitioners to understand children's needs and plan activities to meet them, supporting children's progress. It is particularly important that parents are left in no doubt about their child's progress and development, and that learning and development needs are identified early and addressed in partnership with parents and other relevant practitioners.

Early years providers must assess young children's progress on an ongoing basis, and also complete assessments at two specific points, as described below.

The National Curriculum

The National Curriculum sets out the statutory requirements for the knowledge and skills that every child is expected to learn in schools. The National Curriculum framework enables teachers to provide all school-aged children with challenging learning experiences, taught in ways that are both balanced and manageable. It sets out the standards used to measure the progress and performance of pupils in each subject, to help teachers plan and implement learning activities that meet the individual learning needs of pupils.

The National Curriculum applies to children of compulsory school age (five to sixteen years) in schools in England. It sets out what pupils should study, what they should be taught and the standards that they should achieve, and is divided into four key stages:

- Key Stage 1: children aged between five and seven (Year groups: 1 and 2)
- Key Stage 2: children aged between seven and eleven (Year groups: 3, 4, 5 and 6)
- Key Stage 3: children aged between 11 and 14 (Year groups: 7, 8 and 9)
- Key Stage 4: children aged between 14 and 16 (Year groups: 10 and 11).

In Key Stage 1 of the National Curriculum, the compulsory subjects consist of: English, Mathematics, Science, Information and Communication Technology, Design and Technology, History, Geography, Art and Design, Music, Physical Education. In addition there is a non-statutory framework for Personal, Social and Health Education (PSHE) and Citizenship. Primary schools must also provide Religious Education and sex education, although parents may withdraw their children from these lessons if they wish to do so. For more information see: http://nationalstrategies. standards.dcsf.gov.uk/primary.

The early years framework in Scotland

The key documents are Birth to Three: Supporting Relationships, Responsive Care and Respect and the newly developing generic framework for the curriculum, known as the '3–18 framework', 'Excellence for All'.

Birth to Three

The document is based on principles summarised as:

- the best interests of children
- the central importance of relationships
- the need for all children to feel included
- an understanding of the ways in which children learn.

The document shares the belief (stated in the National Care Standards: Early Education and Care up to the Age of 16) that children have a right to:

- dignity
- privacy
- choice
- safety
- realising potential
- equality and diversity.

There is a strong emphasis on recognising and valuing the important role of parents. (This is so in all four countries of the UK.) Parents constantly ask for more information about their child's development and learning. Talking together with other parents and practitioners, including health visitors, empowers parents, along with television programmes and magazines aimed at supporting parents positively. This helps to ease anxieties which parents experience, for example about their child's behaviour, or eating and sleeping patterns.

Curriculum for Excellence: three to eighteen years

The Scottish curriculum framework (three to eighteen years) is underpinned by the values that appear on the ceremonial mace in the Scottish Parliament. These are:

- wisdom
- justice
- compassion
- integrity.

This new curriculum framework aims to be more flexible, delivering a coherent and enriched curriculum. The curriculum is defined as 'the totality of all that is planned for children and young people throughout their education'.

The framework is based on the following principles:

- challenge and enjoyment
- breadth
- progression
- depth
- personalisation and choice
- coherence
- relevance.

The purpose of the curriculum framework is captured in four capacities. It aims for every child to be:

- a successful learner
- a confident individual
- a responsible citizen
- an effective contributor.

There are eight areas of experience and outcomes:

- expressive arts
- health and wellbeing
- languages
- mathematics
- religious and moral education
- sciences
- social studies
- technologies.

Skills for learning, life and work are linked to literacy, numeracy, health and wellbeing.

Assessment is required to support the purposes of learning. This is sometimes described as 'assessment is for learning'.

The early years and early primary level (three to eight years) emphasises active learning, real-life and imaginary situations, and the importance of parents' and children's interests and experiences from home as the starting point from which to extend learning.

The early years framework in Wales

The Learning Country: Foundation Phase (three to seven years)

The basic message of the Foundation Phase in Wales is that it offers children a sound foundation for their future learning through a developmentally appropriate curriculum. It brings more consistency and continuity in a child's learning:

> 'Emphasis has been placed on developing children's knowledge, skills and understanding through experiential learning – learning by doing and by solving real-life problems both inside and outdoors.'

Key elements in the curriculum framework are:

- learning by doing
- the importance of first-hand experience (experiential learning)
- learning though play
- active involvement in learning (not exercises in books)
- time to develop speaking and listening
- time to develop confident readers and writers
- practical mathematical experiences through everyday problem-solving experiences
- emphasis on understanding how things work and finding different ways to solve problems.

In addition, the curriculum places more focus on:

- skills and understanding
- the whole child – personal, social, emotional, physical and intellectual wellbeing
- positive attitudes to learning (enjoying it and wanting to continue the learning)
- giving children high self-esteem and confidence so that they experiment, investigate, learn new things and make new relationships
- encouraging children's development as individuals through creative, expressive and observational skills, and recognising that different children have different ways of responding to experiences
- learning about conservation and sustainability through outdoor, first-hand experiences involving real-life problems.

There are seven areas of learning in the Welsh curriculum framework:

- personal and social development, wellbeing and cultural diversity
- knowledge and understanding of the world
- mathematical development

- language, literacy and communication skills
- Welsh language development
- physical development
- creative development.

Assessment: the Foundation Phase outcomes

At the end of the Foundation Phase when children are seven years old, there is a statutory teacher assessment of each child. Teachers are required to make rounded judgements of children, based on their knowledge of the way in which a child performs across a range of contexts. Strengths and weaknesses are identified. The child's progress is checked against adjacent outcomes to see which makes the best fit to the child's performance: the best possible match is made. This takes place in the following areas of learning:

- personal and social development, wellbeing and cultural diversity
- language, literacy and communication skills (in English or Welsh)
- mathematical development.

The early years framework in Northern Ireland

Curricular Guidance for Pre-School Education

All four countries of the UK have reviewed their early childhood curriculum frameworks recently, and Northern Ireland has developed Curricular Guidance for Pre-School Education. It states that:

'There is no place, at this stage, for the introduction of formal schooling in the sense of an established body of knowledge to be acquired, or a set of skills to be mastered'.

It emphasises that children (three- to four-year-olds) arrive in early years settings with experiences, and have developed in a number of ways already.

The curricular framework is designed to guide practitioners and settings, but there is an expectation that all will refer to it.

There are six areas of learning:

- the arts
- language development
- early mathematical experiences
- personal, social and emotional development
- physical development and movement
- the world around us.

Each area has a section on progress in learning. Throughout, the document is inclusive.

The Foundation Stage in primary schools is for children in Year 1 (aged four to five years) and Year 2 (aged five to six years). They begin the curriculum which goes through to Stage 4 in the secondary school.

Cross-curricular areas (which continue through the education stages) are:

- communication
- using mathematics
- using ICT.

Thinking skills are developed to enable the child to:

- think critically and creatively
- develop personal and interpersonal skills and dispositions
- effectively function in a changing world.

Personal capabilities aim to encourage:

- lifelong learning
- contributing effectively to society.

For Northern Ireland, the areas of learning are:

- language and literacy
- mathematics and numeracy
- the arts
- the world around us
- physical development and movement
- personal development and mutual understanding
- religious education (from which children may be withdrawn as this is defined by the Department for Education and the four main Christian Churches).

There is assessment for learning, and reporting to parents through a meeting and an annual report.

Key terms

Statutory framework – This means that a document is required by law to be followed and carried out in practice. It is not a matter of choice; it is a legal requirement.

Discussion point

1. Which country has a curriculum framework that includes children from birth? Discuss this with your colleagues. (There are useful websites and resources on page 314.)

2. Reflect on the advantages and disadvantages of curriculum frameworks with common themes throughout the different age phases. Discuss.

3. If you were a child, what would you find helpful in the different curriculum frameworks? As a practitioner, reflect on what is helpful in the different curriculum frameworks. Discuss with another learner or in a group. Think together about how a Common Assessment Framework (CAF) could help this child and his or her family. (See Chapter 5 for information on the CAF.)

EYFS 2012

The EYFS stipulates that every area of learning and development must be delivered through planned, purposeful play and through both adult-led and child-initiated activity. There should be a fluid interchange between activities initiated by children, and activities led or guided by adults.

In planning and guiding children's activities, practitioners should be guided by the different ways that children learn. Three characteristics of effective teaching and learning are:

• **playing and exploring** – children investigate and experience things, and 'have a go'

• **active learning** – children keep on trying if they encounter difficulties, and enjoy achievements

• **creating and thinking critically** – children have and develop their own ideas, make links between ideas, and develop strategies for doing things.

What do we mean by curriculum?

Children are biologically driven to seek out what they need for their development and learning. To do this, they need and depend on other people, and cultural influences are a key part of their development and learning. The curriculum framework has three aspects:

1 **Child** – the child's development and learning, including movement, communication, play, symbolic behaviour, emotional development and relationships (with self and others).

2 **Context** – the access which practitioners create so that every child is helped to develop and learn, and how learning builds on the child's social relationships, family and cultural experiences.

3 **Content** – what the child already knows and understands, together with what the child wants to know more about (the child's interests), and what society and community decide the child needs to know in order to participate and contribute to the community and the wider world. The content of the curriculum is different in every home nation in the UK.

This section explores the areas of learning and development in the early years frameworks of each UK home nation.

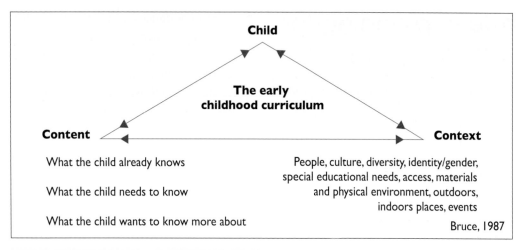

Child

The early childhood curriculum

Content

What the child already knows

What the child needs to know

What the child wants to know more about

Context

People, culture, diversity, identity/gender, special educational needs, access, materials and physical environment, outdoors, indoors places, events

Bruce, 1987

Figure 7.12 Framework for the early years curriculum

Principles influencing early childhood curriculum frameworks in the UK

1. The best way to prepare children for their adult life is to give them a good childhood that meets their needs and builds on their interests.

2. Children are whole people, who have feelings, ideas, relationships involving a sense of self and others, a sense of awe and wonder, and who need to be emotionally, physically and morally healthy.

3. Children do not learn in neat and tidy compartments. Everything new that they learn links with everything they have already learned.

4. Children learn best when they are respected and helped to be autonomous, active learners.

5. Self-discipline is emphasised as the only kind of discipline worth having. Children need their efforts to be valued in their own right.

6. There are times when children are especially able to learn particular things.

7. What children can do (rather than what children cannot do) is the starting point for a child's learning.

8. There are many different kinds of symbolic behaviour. These show the inner thoughts, feelings and ideas of the child, through the way they draw, paint, make things, dance, sing, talk/sign, and enjoy making stories, mark-make or pretend-play. The Italian educator Malaguzzi called this the 'hundred languages' of children.

9. Relationships with other people are central to a child's emotional and social wellbeing, and for opening up their possibilities for an intellectual life and a sense of fulfilment.

10. A good education is about the child, the context in which development and learning takes place, and the knowledge and understanding that evolves as part of the child's learning journey.

(Bruce, 1987, 2009b, 2011b; Bruce and Spratt, 2010)

Your role in planning for children's learning

Practitioners working directly with young children have an important role. Children remember and look back with pleasure and affection to those who supported and extended their learning in their earliest years. It is important to note that there is a shift from making curriculum plans (which are too rigid to meet the needs or develop the interests of individual children) to curriculum planning, which is flexible and ever-changing. The principles set out in the box above have a long tradition and have informed the curriculum frameworks of the four UK countries as they exist today. The principles inform the planning alongside observations of individual children. This means that the emphasis is on planning within an effective curriculum framework, rather than making a plan using a rigid and prescribed curriculum syllabus.

Types of planning

Rigid plans hold back learning: they do not meet the learning needs or develop the interests of individual children, and lead to an activity-based curriculum which does not help the group or individual children to develop and learn. Planning begins with the observation of the child as a unique, valued and respected individual, with their own interests and needs. We could say this is all about getting to know the child, but further general planning is also necessary, because there is only so much that children can learn on their own. They need an environment that has been carefully thought through, plus the right help from adults in using that environment. This aspect of planning ensures that the learning environment indoors and outdoors is balanced in what it offers, so that it helps all children in general, but also caters for individual children.

In this way, the curriculum:

- differentiates for individual children
- is inclusive and embraces diversity
- offers experiences and activities which are appropriate for most children of the age range (the group), because it considers the social and cultural context and the biological aspects of children developing in a community of learning links with the requirements of legally framed curriculum documents (which include the first three points).

You could use the following sources to plan work for children:

- the children's interests and preferences
- observations and assessments
- the children's mothers, fathers and carers
- your colleagues in the setting
- other professionals such as health visitors.

As appropriate to your particular role, you will need to plan, implement and evaluate curriculum plans according to the requirements of your setting. When planning, implementing and evaluating curriculum plans, your overall aims should be to:

- support all the children you work with
- ensure each child has full access to the relevant curriculum
- encourage participation by all children
- meet children's individual learning and development needs
- build on children's existing knowledge and skills
- help all children achieve their full potential.

Your planning should be flexible enough to allow for children's individual interests and unplanned, spontaneous opportunities for promoting children's development and learning. For example, an unexpected snowfall can provide a wonderful opportunity to talk about snow and for children to share their delight and fascination with this type of weather. A child might bring in their collection of postcards, prompting an unplanned discussion about the collections of other children; this could be developed into a 'mini-topic' on collections if the children are really interested. It is important that children have this freedom of choice to help represent their experiences, feelings and ideas.

Activity

Making a process book

Plan and make a process book, showing the sequence of steps needed for children to do finger-painting. This needs to include making the paint, using it and clearing away, with the children participating at each step. It is important to have tables at an appropriate height. Children like to stand or work on the floor. They need to be free to move, and often they do not want to sit on chairs (although these should be provided). It is important to offer experiences and activities that allow children to have a choice about this. It is best to use powder paint as it is more flexible and offers more possibilities than mixed paints, which are also much more expensive. There could be paints with lids on the pots for new painters; and children who are more experienced can mix their own and use pots without lids.

Long-term planning

Long-term planning focuses on the following:

- What is known about the general development and learning needs of most children between birth and five years of age.
- General provision arising from this first point, in considering what is planned indoors and outdoors.
- A general sense of direction, making everyone aware of the principles, values and philosophy that support the curriculum.
- A particular emphasis for a period of time (perhaps for several months); for example, the way in which children and adults communicate; how to get the most from the outdoor environment; how to support children settling in to the setting; creativity; play.

Medium-term planning

This is the way in which the principles and general framework set by the long-term planning are applied. The medium-term plan will need to be **adjusted constantly** because it will be influenced by the observations made of individual children.

For children from birth to three years, it needs to include reviews of care routines, key worker relationships and the way in which the day is organised to offer play and experiences, including materials and physical resources.

If short-term planning (see below) is effective, many settings find that medium-term planning becomes unnecessary. If the daily plans are good, they often extend over several weeks and become medium-term plans, which are adjusted slightly each day. This is especially so if the curriculum offers continuous open-ended materials, equipment and resources, indoors and outdoors.

Short-term planning

This is based on observation sheets of individual children's interests and needs. (If a medium-term plan is used, the observations will inform how to adjust and change the plan so that it is responsive to the individual child's interests and needs.)

One type of plan widely used is called PLOD (possible lines of direction). This was first developed with staff at Redford House Workplace nursery at Froebel College in Roehampton, and later developed with staff at Pen Green Children's Centre. These can be used for one child (as in Figure 7.13), or for several children with similar interests.

Individual Learning Plans

In many settings observations are recorded in the Individual Learning Plan, sometimes called the Individual Learning Journey. This plan usually shows the different activities, organised into the EYFS areas of learning, and charts the child's development and learning by recording when an activity was introduced. It may also record the child's continued interest in and repetition of the activity and the child's level of competence noting the skills or abilities demonstrated in each area of learning. Many early years settings now focus on particular children on particular days. This means that every child is observed regularly, and the curriculum is planned in a differentiated way to cater for the interests and needs of individual children.

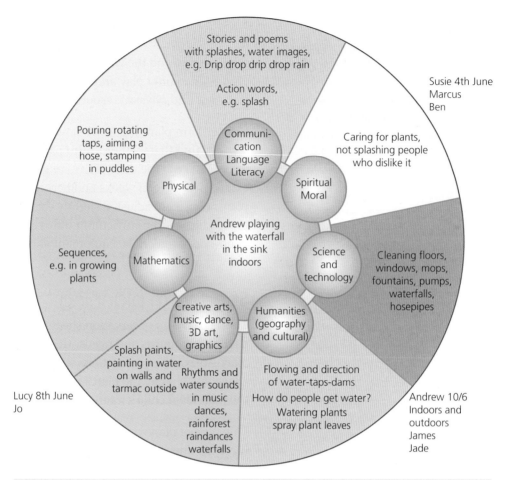

Figure 7.13 Planning PLOD (possible lines of development)

Case Study   Observation and planning

In one setting, observations of the target child (Andrew) over a week showed that a 'waterfall' consisting of three beakers of graded sizes was greatly used. Andrew lined them up next to the tap so that the water fell exactly as he wanted it to. He had a bowl of corks under the waterfall; he aimed the water at them one by one, to make them bob about.

When the tap was turned on, a waterfall was created, which led to much glee and discussion. The long-term plan identified science as a major area for attention.

The nursery practitioner reported this observation of Andrew to a group of staff. They decided to put the waterfall out again. In addition, they provided a bigger version in the outside area, using buckets and old water trays. They planned who will be in which areas, and aimed for Andrew to learn that water:

- flows
- splashes
- cascades in the outdoor waterfall more than the indoor waterfall
- flows downwards if it can
- makes a trajectory (a moving line)
- has the force to move things that are in its way.

To extend Andrew's interest, the staff planned a visit to the local shopping mall where there is a fountain. They also linked the short-term plans made for Andrew with the medium-term plan (see Figure 7.13) and the long-term plan, which had a focus on knowledge and understanding of the world (science).

Encouraging children to plan their own learning and activities

Chapter 4 gives detailed advice and information on planning the play environment for babies and young children; see pages 200–1.

Some of the richest learning comes from experiences of everyday living. Examples would be getting dressed, choosing what to do, going shopping, using what you have bought for cooking, using a recipe book, washing up, sharing a story or photographs of shared events (visiting the park), laying the table, eating together, sorting the washing and washing clothes. It is a challenge to find ways of making this manageable for children to take part in with independence, but careful planning makes this both possible and enjoyable, and makes for a deep learning experience.

Planning and providing learning opportunities in consultation with parents and others

Planning work also involves working with other people (for example, parents, carers, colleagues and other professionals) to deliver the appropriate curriculum for the children in your setting. You should regularly check and discuss the progress of children with parents, carers and colleagues. Seek additional support especially if children are not progressing as expected, for example by consulting other professionals as appropriate.

Remember to observe the children while they are involved in the learning activities and assess whether you need to change or extend these activities to meet their early learning and developmental needs more fully. Children's responses should also be considered when providing support for learning activities. Be sensitive to children's needs and preferences. You should take notice of non-verbal responses and

 Progress check

Planning for individual children

1. **Observe the child** at different times, in different places, indoors and outdoors, at mealtimes, home time, with different people. What does the child choose to do? What interests the child?

2. **Support the learning**. Are there plenty of opportunities to repeat the experiences which the child has chosen? Is there open and continuous material provision, rather than closed and prescribed activities? Do children have plenty of choice about how they spend their time? What kind of help do the children need? Do adults recognise when help is needed, and do they join children as companions and sensitively engage them in conversations? Do adults know not to interfere when the children are deeply involved?

3. **Extend the learning**. Learning can be extended in two ways:

   • **broadening and deepening the learning** – it is important not to automatically think that children constantly need new experiences. They might need to play with the same dinosaurs for several weeks. If they do, this is an opportunity to help them learn the names of different dinosaurs, what they ate and the habitat they lived in. Dinosaur scenarios could be built with sand and water and plants in seed trays, so that children create their own small worlds about dinosaurs. This is often the best way to extend learning.

   • **onwards and upwards** – it is important not to rush children into new learning when what they really need is to consolidate what they know. A child might have enjoyed cooking roti or bread rolls. Making a carrot cake is a similar experience, but it involves adding eggs and the mixture is stirred and beaten rather than pummelled. These differences could be talked about, but children will need to make the roti and the carrot cakes so that the conversation will be possible. A book of recipes with pictures is helpful – you could make these and laminate them.

preferences demonstrated by the children; these are just as important as what they say. Remember to give the children positive encouragement and feedback to reinforce and sustain their interest and efforts in the learning process. You can use children's positive or negative responses to modify or extend activities to meet each child's needs more effectively. For example, if the learning intentions prove too easy or too difficult, you may have to set new goals. By breaking down learning activities into smaller tasks, you may help individual children to achieve success more quickly. In modifying plans, you are continuing a cycle of planning and implementing activities. After the learning activities, you should use all the available relevant information to evaluate the effectiveness of your planning and implementation of the activity; this might include responses from parents, carers, colleagues and other professionals.

Supporting the planning cycle for children's learning

Following your observation and assessment of a child's development, learning and/or behaviour, your recommendations can provide the basis for planning appropriate routines and/or activities to encourage and extend the child's skills in specific areas. Effective planning is based on children's individual needs, abilities and interests, hence the importance of accurate and reliable child observations and assessments. Depending on the type of setting, you will also need to plan provision based on the requirements for curriculum frameworks for early learning (see above).

When planning care routines, play opportunities and learning activities, your overall aims should be to:

- support the care and development of all the children you work with
- ensure that every child has full access to the appropriate curriculum
- meet children's individual developmental and learning needs
- build on each child's existing knowledge, understanding and skills.

Activity

Describe how you plan provision to promote children's learning and development in your setting. Include examples of any planning sheets you use.

 Progress check

Participating in the planning cycle

It is important to be an active member of staff, participating in the planning cycle.

- Take your carefully gathered observations of children to meetings.
- Be an advocate for the child's developing learning.
- Make sure you are aware of lines of accountability and reporting.

Promoting children's learning

Although it can seem a daunting task to provide a quality learning environment for children from birth to seven years, remember that the things that matter most are:

- your relationship and communication with children, their families and the team of staff (that is, people)
- how you support the children in using core experiences and open-ended, continuous material provision, equipment and resources, both indoors and outdoors.

Children need:

- people who give them interesting and engaging experiences
- carefully considered and organised materials for indoors and outdoors
- to be greeted and made to feel welcome with their parent/carer as they arrive
- to be connected with their key person when they part from their parent/carer

- to feel physically, socially and emotionally safe, so that their intellectual lives open up as they relax and enjoy learning.

It is very difficult for children when adults do not stay in one place for long enough for children to engage with them in focused ways.

 Progress check

Supporting learning

- **The role of the adult** in supporting children's development and learning through developmentally appropriate materials provision, equipment and resources is central. The environment (people and provision) needs to support all children, including those with special educational needs, disabilities, both genders, children from diverse backgrounds and different cultures, or with English as an additional language.
- **Clutter confuses children**. There should be nothing in a learning environment, indoors or outdoors, that has not been carefully thought through and well organised. Children need to know what they are allowed to do, and what they are not allowed to do, and the environment needs to signal to children how it should be used and kept. When children feel insecure, they test boundaries.
- **The space indoors and outdoors should be flexible**, so that it can be set up and transformed for different uses in a variety of ways. Attention should be given to light, because the way that it shines into a building changes the atmosphere. If the sun is shining onto a child's face during story time, it will be difficult for the child to become engaged.
- **The temperature is important**. Being too hot or too cold makes it difficult to learn. Outdoors, children need suitable clothing, for all weathers (and so do the adults!), and indoors, the rooms should have good air circulation to encourage concentration and reduce the spread of infection.

Promoting activities and experiences which encourage learning and development in each area of the early years framework

Personal, social and emotional development

Promoting young children's personal, social and emotional development involves helping them to develop social and emotional skills such as:

- attachments to other people
- positive social interactions
- positive self-image and identity
- socialisation (including behaving in socially appropriate ways)
- sharing and cooperating
- independence and self-reliance (including self-help skills, such as feeding, toileting, dressing)
- understanding moral concepts.

Developing attachments to other people

Babies develop an awareness of others in relation to themselves; for example, people who fulfil their needs for food and drink, warmth and shelter, sleep, physical comfort and entertainment. The security of early attachments is essential to babies and young children because they provide a firm foundation for promoting:

- emotional wellbeing
- positive relationships with other people
- confidence in exploring the environment.

These early attachments enable children to feel secure about their relationships and to develop trust in others. Security and trust are important elements in the young child's ability to separate from their parents and carers in order to develop their own independence and ideas.

Encouraging positive social interactions

Having at least one secure personal relationship with a parent or carer enables children to form other relationships. Consistent, loving care from a parent or carer who is sensitive to the child's particular needs enables the child to feel secure and to develop self-worth. Children observe the behaviour of parents, carers and other significant adults (such as early years practitioners, play workers, teachers, and teaching assistants) and their observations affect children's own behaviour, including how they relate to others. A child's ability to relate to others may also be affected by:

- special needs, for example communication and/or social interaction difficulties
- family circumstances such as separation or divorce
- death, abandonment or other permanent separation from parent or main carer.

All children need affection, security, acceptance, encouragement, patience and a stimulating environment. Children deprived of these in the first five to six years of life may find it difficult to relate to other people throughout childhood (and even adulthood). However, children are amazingly resilient and subsequent sustained relationships with caring adults in a supportive environment can help children to overcome early parental separation, rejection or neglect.

Adults who provide inconsistent or inappropriate care may unwittingly encourage inappropriate behaviour in children, which can lead to adults spending less time interacting with the child, resulting in the child having ineffective communication skills as well as difficulties in establishing and maintaining positive relationships with other people. Appropriate social interactions with adults (and other children) in various settings will lead to children being able to demonstrate positive ways of relating to others and using appropriate social skills.

Activity

Which early social interactions can you remember? (For example, at playgroup, nursery, school, clubs; hobbies, on holiday, early friendships.)

How do you think these early social interactions influenced your attitudes and actions? For example, did they have positive or negative influences?

Encouraging children's positive self-esteem

See Chapter 3 for more information on supporting a child's self-esteem. A person's self-esteem is changeable; sometimes we feel more positive about ourselves than at other times. Even if we have had past experiences that resulted in negative or low self-esteem, we can overcome this and learn to feel more positive about ourselves.

Activity

Think of positive words to describe yourself using the same initial as your first name, for example caring, creative Carlton; magnificent, marvellous Miriam; sensitive, sharing Shazia; terrific, tremendous Tom.

You could also try this with friends, colleagues or a group of children.

Encouraging children's positive self-image and identity

Children develop their self-image through interactions with others, starting with family members and gradually including carers, teachers, friends and classmates. Through positive interactions, children learn to value themselves and their abilities, if they receive approval, respect and empathy. Early childhood experiences and relationships may have positive or negative influences on children's self-image.

Some children may experience particular difficulties in developing a positive self-image – for example, children with special needs; children from ethnic minorities; children who are or have been abused. These children may be experiencing prejudice and/or discrimination on a regular basis, which affects their ability to maintain a positive self-image. By praising all children and encouraging them to feel good about themselves and their achievements, adults can help all children to establish and maintain a positive self-image. Developing and implementing inclusive policies, procedures and strategies will also help.

Guidelines: ten ways to encourage children's positive self-esteem and self-image

1 Treat every child as an individual; every child has unique abilities and needs.

2 Be positive by using praise and encouragement to help children and young people to focus on what they are good at.

3 Help children and young people to maximise their individual potential.

4 Encourage children to measure their achievements by comparing them to their own efforts.

5 Have high but realistic expectations of all children and young people.

6 Take an interest in each child's efforts as well as their achievements.

7 Encourage positive participation during play activities, for example, sharing resources, helping others and contributing ideas.

8 Give children and young people opportunities to make decisions and choices.

9 Promote equality of opportunity by providing positive images of children, young people and adults through books, stories and songs.

10 Remember to label the behaviour, not the child, as this is less damaging to their self-esteem. For example, say 'That was an unkind thing to say' rather than 'You are unkind'.

Socialisation

Socialisation involves how children relate socially (and emotionally) to other people. Children need to learn how to deal appropriately with a whole range of emotions, including anger and frustration, within a supportive environment. Socialisation occurs through the observation, identification, imitation and assimilation of the behaviour of other people. Children model their attitudes and actions on the behaviour of others. You need to be aware of the significant impact you make on children's social (and emotional) development, and ensure that you provide a positive role model.

An essential aspect of socialisation involves getting young children to behave in socially acceptable ways without damaging their self-esteem: that is, rejecting the children's unacceptable behaviour, not the children themselves. Socialisation begins from birth, as babies interact with the people around them and respond to their environment.

Developing independence

Children need the freedom to develop their independence in ways that are appropriate to their overall development. Some children may need more encouragement than others to become increasingly independent and less reliant on other people.

Adults caring for children should avoid inhibiting the child's need for independence as this can lead to either emotional dependence, excessive shyness and an over-cautious nature or emotional detachment, anti-social behaviour and a rebellious nature. Adults should also avoid unrestricted independence as the child may be exposed to danger and physical harm (for example, from fire, boiling water, traffic) and/or the child may become selfish and unable to recognise the needs and rights of others. Adults should strike a balance between allowing for the individual child's need for independence, and providing supervision with guidelines for socially appropriate behaviour which takes into account the needs of everyone in the early years setting.

Encouraging children's self-reliance

Encouraging children's self-reliance is an important part of helping them to develop the independence and resilience which will enable them to face life's demands and challenges in preparation for their adult lives. Encouraging self-reliance involves helping children to develop:

- independence – the ability to think and act for themselves
- dependence on their own capabilities and personal resources
- competence in looking after themselves
- trust in their own judgement and actions
- confidence in their own abilities and actions.

Guidelines: eight ways to encourage children's self-reliance

You can encourage children's self-reliance in the following ways:

1 Provide freedom for children to become more independent.

2 Be patient and provide time for children to do things for themselves. For example, let younger children dress themselves; although it takes longer, it is an essential self-help skill. Children with physical disabilities may need sensitive support in this area.

3 Praise and encourage children's efforts at becoming more independent.

4 Be aware of children's individual needs for independence; every child is different and will require encouragement relevant to their particular level of development. Do not insist that children be more independent in a particular area until they are ready.

5 Be sensitive to children's changing needs for independence. Remember that a child who is tired, distressed or unwell may require more adult assistance than usual.

6 Offer choices to make children feel more in control. As they develop and mature, increase the scope of choices. Involve the children in decision-making within the childcare setting.

7 Provide play opportunities that encourage independence; for example, dressing-up is a fun way to help younger children learn to dress independently.

8 Use technology to encourage independence, for example, specialist play equipment, voice-activated word processing, motorised wheelchairs.

Developing moral concepts

As part of their social development, children gradually develop moral concepts including:

- knowing the difference between right and wrong, and understanding what is and is not appropriate behaviour
- developing an awareness of fairness and justice, and understanding that goodness is not always rewarded, but that we still need to do what is right
- helping others, including recognising the needs and feelings of others
- sharing, including understanding the importance of turn-taking and cooperation
- developing empathy for others and their beliefs even if we disagree with them, including freedom of speech.

Encouraging children to share and cooperate

Encouraging children to take turns is an essential element of helping them to interact appropriately with other children. From about the age of three, young children begin to cooperate with other children in play activities. By about five, they should be quite adept at playing cooperatively with other children. Gradually children should be able to participate in more complex cooperative play, including games with rules as their understanding of abstract ideas increases.

We live in a highly competitive society; we all want to be the best, fastest, strongest or cleverest. The media (television, magazines and newspapers) focus our attention on being the best. Most sports and games have only one winner, which means that all the other participants are losers. Winning makes the individual feel good, confident and successful; losing makes the individual feel bad, inadequate and unsuccessful. Competitive games can prepare children for the competitiveness of real life. However, competition can also contribute to:

- negative self-image and low self-esteem
- aggressive behaviour
- lack of compassion for others
- overwhelming desire to win at any cost.

Competitive sports and games can be beneficial to children's social development as long as they emphasise:

- cooperation and working as a team
- mutual respect
- agreeing on rules and following them
- participation and the pleasure of taking part are more important than winning
- everyone doing their personal best.

As well as being competitive, people can also be sociable and cooperative; we like to be part of a group or groups. Cooperative activities encourage children to:

- be self-confident
- have high self-esteem
- relate positively to others
- work together and help others
- make joint decisions

- participate fully (no one is left out or eliminated)
- have a sense of belonging.

In Practice

1. Observe a group of children during a play activity or a game. Focus on one child's social and emotional development.
2. In your assessment comment on: the child's level of social interaction; the child's ability to make choices or decisions; the child's use of language to express needs and/or feelings; the child's behaviour during the activity; the role of the adult in promoting the child's social and emotional development; suggestions for further activities to encourage or extend the child's social and emotional development including appropriate resources.

Guidelines: ten ways to promote young children's social and emotional development

As an early years practitioner, you need to provide appropriate activities and experiences to promote young children's social and emotional development. You can help to promote children's social and emotional development by:

1 Using praise and encouragement to help the children focus on what they are good at. Treat every child in the childcare setting as an individual. Each child has unique abilities and needs. Help the children to maximise their individual potential.

2 Taking an interest in the children's efforts as well as their achievements. Remember that the way children participate in activities is more important than the end results – for example, sharing resources, helping others and contributing ideas. Encourage the children to measure any achievements by comparing these to their own efforts. Foster cooperation, rather than competition, between children.

3 Giving the children opportunities to make decisions and choices. Letting children and young people participate in decision-making, even in a small way, helps them to feel positive and important; it also prepares them for making appropriate judgements and sensible decisions later on.

4 Promoting equal opportunities by providing positive images of children and adults through: sharing books and stories about real-life situations showing children (and adults) the children can identify with; providing opportunities for imaginative play that encourage the children to explore different roles in positive ways, such as dressing-up clothes, cooking utensils, dolls and puppets.

5 Being consistent about rules and discipline. All children need consistency and a clearly structured framework for behaviour so that they know what is expected of them. Remember to label the behaviour, not the children, as this is less damaging to their emotional wellbeing.

6 Setting goals and boundaries to encourage socially appropriate behaviour, as suitable to the children's ages and levels of development. Using appropriate praise and rewards can help.

Guidelines: ten ways to promote young children's social and emotional development (cont.)

7 Encouraging the children's self-help skills. Be patient and provide time for the child to do things independently, for example choosing play activities and selecting their own materials; helping to tidy up; dressing independently during dressing-up.

8 Providing opportunities for the children to participate in social play; for example encourage children to join in team games, sports and other cooperative activities.

9 Using books, stories, puppets and play people to help the children understand ideas about fairness, jealousy, growing up and dealing with conflict situations.

10 Encouraging the children to take turns, for example sharing toys and other play equipment. Emphasise cooperation and sharing rather than competition.

 In Practice

Plan, implement and evaluate a play activity which encourages or extends a child's social and emotional development. Use the assessment from your previous observation of the child's social and emotional development as the basis for your planning.

Encourage the child to use a variety of social skills and emotional abilities. For example: positive behaviour; independence (such as using self-help skills or making choices); effective communication skills; sharing resources; expressing needs and/ or feelings; understanding the needs and feelings of others.

Consider how you could meet the needs of children with behavioural difficulties with this activity.

Communication, language and literacy

The aim of the early years practitioner is to support children to develop a love of books, so that they will want to read for pleasure and understanding, information and knowledge, and not just out of duty or under direction.

The areas of the brain that are for movement, gestures, sound and language are close to each other, and form interactive networks.

Using music to support reading

● Ring games and traditional songs and dances help the brain form connections in a natural way, and this helps children learn to read, and later to write. If you sing, 'Dinner-time, it's dinner-time' to children – especially children with special needs, complex needs or who are learning English as an additional language – you will probably find they understand more easily what you are saying. It helps children to segment the sounds, and to identify and pronounce them.

● The sound of words is important in learning to read, but we have to remember that saying or singing certain words varies in different regions of the same country; for example, 'bath' in the north of England is pronounced differently from in the south. The context is very important too, especially when words are spelt the same but pronounced differently; for example, 'When you have read this book, you might like to read another one.'

● Singing helps children because many of the words rhyme, and this makes the text predictable; it is also more manageable because the poetry is in a verse or small chunk. Clapping the rhythm or dancing to the song while singing also helps the brain to understand the shape of the song.

Listening to stories

It is important to remember that stories are not always in written form: stories can be told (the

Gallic, Celtic and Maori traditions use storytelling powerfully) or told in pictures. Stories have a special way of using language called book language, such as, 'Once upon a time …'. Children need a wealth of experience of book language before they can read well and become enthusiastic readers. They need many different forms (genres) of stories.

In Practice

Select a book for a small group time, based on your observations of a child. Use the guidelines for selecting appropriate books below to help you.

Think about issues of gender, ethnicity, culture and disability, and be sure that all children see positive images of themselves in the stories you tell and in the books that you offer.

Children need one-to-one stories. These are called bedtime-type stories. The child can interact with the reader and become deeply involved. The adult and child can pause, chat, go back and revisit, and read at their own pace.

Small-group stories, with two to four children, are more difficult for children because the adult needs to keep the story going, so cannot allow constant interruptions. Skilled adults are able to welcome many of the children's contributions, but the larger the group, the more important it becomes for children to be able to listen. Large groups, with four to eight children, are less sensitive to the individual needs of children, so these need to be more of a theatre show or performance by the adult, in order to maintain the attention of the children; they cannot be so interactive.

It is better to use poetry cards and action songs with very large groups (eight or more children). This gives children the rhythm, intonation and pace, and small, manageable chunks of text in a song. This makes for a good community experience of reading

Guidelines for selecting appropriate books

1 Everyday events – these help children to recognise common events and feelings. They help children to heighten their awareness of words that describe everyday situations.

2 Poems – these help rhyming and rhythm, and the chorus often gives a predictable element; the repetition helps children. This is also true of many stories, but poems are an enjoyable experience for young children, who may not be able to concentrate on a whole story in the early stages.

3 Folk stories – these introduce children to different cultures. However, avoid stories in which animals behave as if they were humans, or in which animals behave in a way that is out of character (such as a spider saving the life of a fly in an act of bravery). These are called anthropomorphic stories. They can confuse young children, who are trying to sort out what is and is not true.

4 True stories – these lead to an understanding of non-fiction books, which are full of information on different topics and subjects.

5 Make-believe stories – these lead to an understanding of fiction. Avoid stories of witches and fairies for very young children (under four years); children need to be clear about the distinction between reality and imagination, otherwise they may be fearful and have nightmares. Bear in mind that it is one thing for a four-year-old child to make up their own stories about monsters, witches or ghosts (in which the child has control), but if an adult introduces these characters, the child may be scared.

6 Action rhymes and finger rhymes – these help children to predict what is in a text. Predicting is a very large part of learning to read; knowing what comes next is important.

7 Repeating stories – knowing a story well helps children begin to read. Sometimes adults say, 'Oh, but he is not reading, he just knows it off by heart.' Knowing what comes next is probably one of the most important parts of learning to read.

Figure 7.14 Sharing a story

together. Poetry cards can be made out of cardboard boxes, and can be large and rather like theatre props. Children enjoy playing with them afterwards if they are left near the book corner.

Encouraging children to share stories together, whether or not they can read fluently, is very helpful. This encourages emergent readers to approximate-read, and to pick out the words they know with confidence. Being able to have a go and to do so with confidence and pleasure is crucial.

Helping children to read

You can help children to read by enjoying a book or poetry card together, without any pressure. Children can see how a book is used, where to begin, how to turn a page and the direction of print, using pictures as clues, finding familiar words and guessing. Being able to guess and predict what the print says is important. Children are usually fascinated by guesses that go wrong, as they learn to link what they read with meaning, and to work out the words using their increasing ability to segment and blend the graphemes and phonemes. It is important to say, 'What do you think he says next?' Show the child any patterns – for example, a phrase that is repeated – and talk about the letters, words and sentences as you

go. Picture cues are very important when learning to read, so talk about these and the clues they give.

Alphabet books and friezes are important as they help children to segment words, while offering a meaningful picture to help the child along. Regularly singing the alphabet is helpful too. Pointing out children with the same letter at the beginning of their names helps, and there can be fascinating discussions about why George is pronounced with a 'J' sound, while Gary is with a 'G' sound.

Decide as a team which books you will introduce as core texts, to help children become familiar with them. Note which books are favourites of particular children, and use these with the child in the same way. Above all, remember that learning to read should be fun, and it should hold meaning for the child.

In Practice

Stages of reading

Observe children aged three to seven years. Identify which children are emergent, beginner and fluent readers. What are the factors that you use to decide this? What can you do to support each child in their enjoyment of books?

Sounds and how words look

Children need to learn to segment (break down) sounds and print. They also need to learn to blend (join) sounds and print. They need to begin to see that what they have segmented can be blended back into a word. The ideal age to do this is between six and seven years of age. Using nursery rhymes encourages this; for example, 'Humpty Dumpty':

> **'Humpty Dumpty sat on a wall,**
>
> Humpty Dumpty had a great fall…'

Children quickly begin to see that the last chunk is the same (-all), while the beginnings are different ('w' and 'f').

Studies of the brain suggest that the brain loves complexity, and that singing, dancing, moving, doing action songs and seeing print in meaningful patterns are all part of the interconnectedness of different parts of the brain.

For information on helping children to write, see page 491.

In Practice

Select one of the bullet points from the Progress check on Encouraging creative writing later in life. Carry out the idea and evaluate your findings. How does this work in your setting?

Reasoning, problem-solving and numeracy

Mathematics involves problem-solving and reasoning in particular ways. Problem-solving is part of the whole curriculum, not just mathematics.

Progress check

Encouraging creative writing later in life

- Learning about different roles, characters and themes is essential if children are going to learn to write stories.
- Having dressing-up clothes to act out stories helps children to create narratives – a skill needed for later writing.
- Ask children to act out a story you have told.
- Encourage children to act out stories that they have made up and which you have written down for them. Vivian Gussin-Paley, in her school in Chicago, did this as a daily part of the curriculum.
- Act out stories in an atmosphere of sharing. This should not involve a performance of the story. The idea is to help children to understand how stories are made. This will help them later when they want to write their own stories.
- Young children should not be expected to perform stories in school assemblies or in situations with audiences full of strangers (such as for the summer or Christmas show). It is not effective practice to encourage children to perform before they have gone through the sequence: make – share – show. They need to be able to make their own stories and to share these with friends and adults whom they know well, before they perform.
- To perform becomes appropriate only in junior school. Any earlier, and some children begin overacting and playing to the audience rather than becoming involved in the story; other children are put off for ever because of the stress of being made to perform. Waving at people in the audience during a performance may be very sweet for adults to see, but it is a clear sign that the child is not involved in what they are doing and is not ready to perform. The exercise is a failure in terms of involving a child in a story.
- Research suggests that if children are encouraged to play in the early years, they will be better at creative writing at seven years of age.

Children learn about topological space (on/off, over/ under, in/out, surrounding, across, near/far) before they learn about Euclidian space (circles, squares, and so on).

Number

Number has several different aspects:

- matching – this looks like this (two identical cups in the home corner)
- sorting – this looks different from this (the cup and the saucer)
- one-to-one correspondence – one biscuit for you, one biscuit for me
- cardinal numbers – the two cups remain two cups, however they are arranged (this means that the child understands the number, such as two)
- ordinal numbers – this is first, second, third (for example, the sequence in cooking: first, I wash my hands; second, I put on my apron…).

Children learn about number in the following ways:

- reciting – number songs
- nominal understanding – they pick out numbers on house doors, buses, in shops, on shoe sizes, and so on
- subitising – remembering number patterns to recognise how many – for example, four dots, one on each corner of a square, or on a domino (chimpanzees can do this with numbers up to seven)
- counting backwards – 5, 4, 3, 2, 1, lift-off!

There are three counting principles:

1 A number word is needed for every object that is counted. This is the one-to-one correspondence principle.
2 The numbers always have the same order, 1, 2, 3 (not 1, 3, 2). This is called the stable-order principle.
3 When children count, they have grasped the cardinal number principle if they understand

the three-ness of three. Three objects are the same number if they are spread out or if they are together.

 Progress check

Number

- Do not do exercises or tasks with young children that are isolated from their experience.
- Remember that children learn mathematics through cooking, tidy-up time, playing in the home area, painting and being in the garden. Mathematics is everywhere.
- Numbers are found on rulers, calibrated cooking jugs, the doors of houses, and so on.
- Counting is only one part of exploring numbers. It is one thing for children to be curious about numbers on calibrated jugs, weights and measures, but they need to be free to experiment and explore. This is very different from formally teaching them numbers through adult-led tasks, unrelated to real life.

 In Practice

Evaluate the learning environment and list the opportunities which children have to see, experience and interact with number situations.

Understanding time

Time has two aspects:

- Personal time: it feels like a long time before a car journey ends – it might be an hour, but it feels like a day.
- Universal time, including:
  - Succession: Monday, Tuesday, Wednesday…
  - Duration: day, night, an hour, a minute…

Shape and size

Children need adults to describe things that are 'bigger than' and 'smaller than' in order to learn that these things are relative, not absolute sizes. Something is 'big' only in relation to something else. Always use relative terms with children.

Introduce words like 'cylinder' and 'sphere' before 'oblong' and 'circle'. Use everyday things, like tins of food or a football to explain what a cylinder and a sphere look like.

Length

Use words such as 'longer than' or 'shorter than'. Children need to have rulers and tapes in their environment so that they become aware that things can be measured. Which is the tallest plant? Who has the longest foot? Gradually, they develop an understanding of the exactness of absolute measurements.

Volume and capacity

'This glass is full.' 'This bucket is nearly empty.' Listen to yourself speak and you will be surprised at how often you use mathematical language in everyday situations.

Area

You can introduce the concept of area using an example of a blanket that covers the bed mattress. Another example would be a pancake covered with lemon and sugar – the lemon and sugar cover the area of the pancake. Children often explore area in their block play.

Weight

Introduce the concept of weight using relative ideas: 'This tin of soup is heavier than that apple.' Rather than using a weighing machine, use a balance, so that children see this. Remember that young children need to experience weight physically. They love to carry heavy things. They love to lift each other up, and often carry bags around.

Case Study — Exploring weight

Kit (aged three years) picked up a large piece of ice while out for a walk in the winter. He enjoyed throwing it and watching it skim across an icy stream. He kept saying, 'This is heavy.' His parents helped him to make comparisons: 'Is it heavier than this stone?' 'Is it heavier than this twig?' The natural outdoor environment was an ideal place for Kit to learn about weight.

Computers

The most appropriate computer programs invite children to be interactive. Children benefit from using a word processor and printer, as well as using digital cameras. They enjoy picking out letters and punctuation marks, and through this kind of play they learn about important aspects of reading, writing and numbers, which will be used in a more elaborate way as they get older.

Creative development

Creative development is important in the following areas:

- arts (dance, music, drama, the visual arts, including sculpture, ceramics and pottery, painting and drawing, collage)
- sciences (biology, chemistry, physics, applied engineering, environmental studies, industry)
- humanities (history, geography, cultural aspects).

In Practice

Promoting children's creativity in the arts

Drawing, painting, weaving, collage, sewing, woodwork, sculpture and model-making, and pottery are examples of arts and crafts. Organise art materials for the children to select and use in their own way.

Guidelines for promoting children's creativity in the arts

Adults often use children's art lessons as a chance to do art for themselves! Therefore:

Do not:

- draw for children
- use templates
- ask children to trace
- ask children to colour in
- ask children to copy your model step by step.

Figure 7.15 A boy and a girl work side by side, taking care of the tools and of each other's safety

Guidelines for promoting children's creativity in the arts (cont.)

Do:

- give children real, first-hand experiences, such as looking at plants or mini beasts in the pond
- give children opportunities to represent things, and to keep hold of their experiences (for example, by making a model of the plant out of clay)
- encourage lots of different ideas: it is best when every child in a group has made a different model. This means that children are doing their own thinking and are not dependent on adults for ideas
- remember that children are creative in lots of different ways: arts and crafts are only one area in which children are creative. Children can be creative scientists, creative mathematicians, creative writers, and so on.

Creativity in the arts and crafts

Children need experiences such as using clay and paint and woodwork. Representing a dog is quite different when using clay, wood at the woodwork bench, paint, or pretending to be a dog in the home corner. Teach children skills when the need arises. Adults need to be effective observers and tune in to these situations.

Children can make models with clay, wet sand, wax, soap-carving, wood, dough, junk and recycled materials. This will involve them in using sticky tape, scissors, rolling pins, string, wire and other materials. Most of the time, these materials can be offered as general areas of provision, available all the time. Clearly, the woodwork can only be used when an adult joins the children, in order to maintain a safe environment.

Drawing and painting

For drawing, it is best to use plain white paper of varied sizes, plus pencils, wax crayons, felt-tip pens, chalks and slates, and charcoal.

For painting, there should be powder paints and different thicknesses of brushes. Materials should be stored carefully so that children can take and access what they need when they need it. Children should be offered pots of basic coloured paints, but they should also be able to mix paints, provided they are taught to do so. They simply need the basic colours – red, yellow, blue – and white and black for light and dark shades of colour.

Book-making

Children love to make books, but need help to do so initially. If they see that you have made recipe books, books of stories and poems, and books for display with information, they will want to do the same. They need to learn how to fold and cut the paper. An adult may need to be with them so that they do not give up.

Collage and workshop area

This requires glue, found materials, junk and recycled materials, and scissors. Materials can be set out in attractive baskets or boxes covered in wallpaper. Glue should always be non-toxic.

Music

Recent studies in neuroscience show that music is important in helping language and memory to develop. Adults naturally sing, 'Up we go', when they lift a baby or toddler out of a pram. Music helps children to remember words, but music is important in its own right. Everyday sounds have rhythm, such as the tick-tock of an alarm clock, tearing paper, shaking a salt cellar, jangling a bunch of keys, fire engines, and so on. Children love to go on listening walks, and to make the sounds they have heard using homemade musical instruments you can help them to make. The importance of singing and listening to a wide range of music from different cultures cannot be overemphasised.

Music is about hearing and making sounds by:

- singing
- making a melody
- clapping rhythms
- making loud and soft sounds (the dynamic)
- making sounds going up and down (the pitch)

- using instruments, to pluck, blow, bow, bang
- singing and dancing action songs and ring games.

You can use what children do naturally – spinning, running, jumping, stamping – to make up a dance. A 'Singing in the Rain' dance was made up by a group of five-year-old children in Year 1 Key Stage 1, helped by their teacher, Dee De Wet. The children watched a video extract from the film, Singing in the Rain, then they experimented with moving about:

- with fancy feet
- by jumping in puddles
- by swishing through puddles
- by dashing about under an umbrella.

They made a dance sequence. Every child had an umbrella and a raincoat, and used the above sequences in line with the traditional music from the film. Every child made up his or her own dance, yet they all danced at the same time, and were sensitive to each other's movement and ideas.

Progress check

Helping children to make dances

- Use an action phrase – for example, 'shiver and freeze'. Ask the children to move like the words in the phrase.
- Show different objects, perhaps something spiky. Ask the children to move in a spiky way and make a dance.
- Take an idea from nature or everyday life: rush and roar like the wind; be a machine or a clock; dance like shadows moving or fish in an aquarium.
- For inspiration only, use experiences that the children have had very recently.

The book by Mollie Davies (2003), *Movement and Dance in Early Childhood*, offers more ideas on how to help young children dance, both boys and girls.

Drama

In their play, children experiment with goodies and baddies, friendship and foes, kindness and unkindness. Penny Holland's work shows how adults can help children to explore these major themes of what it is to be human. Telling children stories and sharing poetry cards with them also helps. Retelling stories with props is beneficial. The adult might help children to act out the story of Pegasus using a toy horse, with paper wings attached with sticky tape. Children might wear dressing-up clothes to retell the story of *Where The Wild Things Are* by Maurice Sendak, including the rumpus dance.

Scientific knowledge and understanding

The physical sciences

- **Electricity**: electrical circuits are easy to make with children and can be used to make a light for the doll's house or the train tracks.
- **Heat**: remember, heat is not just about temperature. Heat is energy; temperature is a measure of how much energy. Cookery is the best way to help children understand about temperature. Making a jelly or ice cream is a good way of looking at coldness. Making something that needs to be cooked in the oven shows children about high temperatures. Look at a central-heating system and the radiators. Think about the sun and how it makes the tarmac on the playground feel warm on a sunny day in the summer. Look at the fridge. Play with ice cubes in the water tray. Again, talk about relative heat. Is this hotter than that? Describe what is happening, think about the cause and effect, why things happen as they do. Metal feels colder than wood, but why? They are both at room temperature. Does the metal conduct the heat out of your hand?

Figure 7.16 This is an example of problem-solving, as well as the satisfaction and engagement which a fulfilled intellectual life brings

- **Sound**: listen to the sounds around you. Help children to be aware of them. Children love to record sounds and find ways to imitate sounds they hear. Some sounds are quieter and some are noisier than others. Children are not very concerned about how many decibels a sound is, but they are interested that a shout is louder than a whisper.

- **Light**: use torches and lanterns; make rainbows with prisms; put on puppet shows and have lighting effects; use cellophane® to make different colours of light. Children in Key Stage 1 enthusiastically make light effects for stories they have made up or enjoyed from books. Experiment with shadows and shadow puppets.

- **Gravity**: use parachutes or drop objects from heights.

- **Floating and sinking**: this is a difficult concept. Young children benefit from a waterwheel and different experiments with boats, but true understanding takes time.

Guidelines for looking at animals

There are reasons why animals, birds and insects have developed as they have done. The following points will give children an introduction to the evolution of the animal world in ways they can understand.

1 Where do animals live? You can find ants, spiders and birds and look at their habitats. Remember, never kill animals, and always return them to their habitat; make a point of explaining this to the children. You could provide pots containing magnifying glasses, which makes it easier to look at these creatures without squashing them accidentally.

2 What do animals eat? Study cats, birds and fish, and talk about their diets.

3 How do animals eat? Talk about claws, type of feet, mouths, beaks, types of teeth, jaws that chew (cows) and jaws that gnash. Study dogs, cats and humans. A bird that eats nuts needs a beak which is a good nutcracker. A bird that catches fish needs a long beak.

4 How do animals protect themselves? Look at camouflage, claws, tusks, fur for warmth, oil on ducks' feathers to make them waterproof.

Figure 7.17 The adult is supportive by encouraging the child to water the plants; helping and guiding, but not taking over

Guidelines for looking at plants

1 Why do plants have leaves? Do all plants have leaves?

2 Why is a tree trunk like it is? Do all trees have exactly the same sort of trunk? Make some bark rubbings. Hug trees to see if you can reach all the way round them with your arms.

3 Why do flowers have colours? Insects are important for plant life.

4 Why do some flowers have scent and nectar? Plants might need to attract insects and birds to visit them.

The natural sciences

Use mixtures to demonstrate how materials can be changed and recovered (salt and water, sugar and water, earth and water, flour and water, mud pies, and mud and straw to make bricks). All these mixtures have properties that children can explore:

- Salt and sugar dissolve in water. When the water evaporates, the salt or sugar can be seen again.
- Flour and mud do not dissolve. They become suspended in water.
- You can look at transformations using water, ice and steam. You can reverse these, and turn steam into water again.
- Study what happens when you cook an egg. You cannot reverse this transformation.
- Low technology can be explored by looking at activities such as weaving. If you have a frame with string going up and down and from side to side, near the entrance, then children and families will enjoy the in-and-out movement of threading pieces of material, wool, ribbon, and so on. These weavings often become attractive wall hangings in the office or entrance hall of the setting.
- It is important to use technology that is easy for children to understand. Examples would be a tin opener, an egg whisk or scissors. Encourage children to use wooden blocks and construction kits.

High technology includes digital cameras, tape recorders or CD players for music and stories, computers, word processors and printers, and telephones for conversations. Nowadays, children are able to use these from an early age.

Knowledge and understanding of the world

Young children are interested in people, families and homes. They like to learn about what people in the community do. They show this in their role play, and by visiting offices, shops, clinics, the vet, the train station, and so on, they can learn about different communities and develop a sense of geography.

Figure 7.18 Woodwork is a form of low technology; other forms are egg whisks, waterwheels and bicycles

They are also interested in old objects, in what things were like when they were babies or when their parents were babies, and what sort of childhood their grandparents had. Collecting artefacts of bygone days and inviting older people to share and talk about their lives, often with the help of photographs, helps children to develop a sense of history. Having a timeline helps too – again, using photos to show the order and sequence of events.

Physical development

Children need to move as much as they need to eat and sleep. They learn through action and language that gives it meaning. They need to be skilled in

Figure 7.19 The boy uses fine physical control to place the cylinders and the lion on the top, encouraged by his key person

a range of movements, using both fine and gross motor skills. They need repetition to consolidate. Movement needs to be appropriate – stroke a dog gently, but throw hard to make a splash with a pebble in a puddle.

Large apparatus

Large apparatus includes climbing frame, ropes to swing on, planks to walk on with ladders and things to jump off. Children need to be encouraged to become generally skilled in movement.

Small apparatus

Small apparatus includes bats, balls, hoops, beanbags, ropes and pushcarts. It is very important to encourage turn-taking and cooperation.

Floor work

Floor work enables children to explore:

- weight transfer from one part of the body to another
- travel from one spot to another
- flight: the five basic jumps are on two legs, from one leg to the other, on the left leg, on the right leg, from two legs to one leg.

Guidelines for floor work

1 Give children (aged between four and seven years) a general theme to investigate through floor work – for example, starting low and getting higher.

2 Do not make children do just one thing, such as a handstand. There are lots of different ways of changing your balance.

3 To help children enjoy creating and solving problems about weight transfer, you can say, 'Can you start on your feet and stop with another bit of you touching the floor?' In this way, you are helping children with reasoning and problem-solving as they think about their own movements.

Research Activity

Find photographs in the different chapters of this book which show the importance of one area of the curriculum. Do these also demonstrate other areas of development and learning? Evaluate this.

Working alongside children to support their learning and engaging with them to support sustained shared thinking

It is very difficult for children when adults do not stay in one place for long enough for children to engage with them in focused ways. It does not encourage children to focus either. It is a good idea, as part of planning the curriculum framework in the learning environments indoors and outdoors, to see where there might need to be anchored adults working in depth with children. The following points are important:

- The **anchored adult** needs to sit at the child's height or on the floor, so as to give full attention to a child or children in one area, while retaining an overview of the rest of the room.
- The practitioner must be free to focus on what the children in a particular area are doing (such as playing with wooden blocks or in the movement corner) and be able to have engaging conversations: listening to what children say and being sensitive to what they do, allowing them plenty of time (such as when cooking together or planting bulbs in the garden).
- Another adult must be free to help children generally – for example, to deal with children's toilet needs, to hang up a painting or comfort a tearful child, or simply to respond to children who ask for help.
- If every adult has a clear understanding of their role in the team, it helps every practitioner to focus on the children and reduces the temptation to chat with other adults instead of engaging with the children.

See Chapter 13, Unit 18 for more information on engaging with babies.

See Chapter 13, Unit 18 for more information on engaging with babies.

Research Activity

Research the *Core Experiences for the Early Years Foundation Stage* booklet, which shows progression of experiences through the materials provided for children from birth to five years.
This was developed by staff at Kate Greenaway Nursery School and Children's Centre, building on a Froebelian approach to the curriculum established at Southway Early Childhood Centre and Nursery School (Bedford) and linked to the English EYFS.

Section 4: How to record and evaluate the planning and assessment cycle

We need to link our assessments of the child's individual progress with the way we evaluate what we provide for children. This means that *observations need to inform planning*, and how we evaluate our planning to see how it worked. Then we can change, modify, consolidate, support and extend each child's personal learning. This will help us to see if what we are providing is appropriate, and whether it is helping or constraining a child's development and learning.

The purpose of assessment is to provide useful information about children's learning and development which can be shared with other staff, with parents and the child, and which will be helpful in informing future planning. Every child will develop and make progress at his or her own pace, and as we have seen, observations are vital to the planning and assessment cycle. Effective assessment is important because it helps adults to match learning activities and experiences to the needs of the child.

Assessment should be an integral part of the daily routine in an early years setting. It occurs when adults listen, watch and interact with a child or group of children.

- **observational assessment**, in everyday situations, informs the planning process – this is sometimes called 'assessment for learning'
- **planning – or setting targets** – for learning will draw attention to aspects for observation and assessment during play
- **recording or record-keeping** will draw together the bits of information needed for effective reporting
- **evaluation** of learning and teaching will influence future planning.

Planning

Effective planning establishes clear goals for learning which are designed to match the needs and the achievements of children. Planning, whether long or short term, should leave staff feeling enabled and also well prepared in their contributions to children's learning. Sharing this information with children and parents will support the learning partnership.

Although staff in early years settings should plan a broad set of learning opportunities throughout the year, there may be times when there is particular emphasis on certain aspects of the curriculum, for example on music making and dance, or exploration of living things. Alternatively, a set of learning experiences may be grouped around seasonal or other themes, or local events, festivals or outings.

- **Long-term planning** gives a picture of how these activities are providing children with a broad and balanced range of learning experiences over a period.
- **Short-term planning** allows observations and assessments of children's development and learning to inform the weekly or daily programme. In setting out a range of learning opportunities, plans therefore need to take account of what individual children and small groups of children have recently learned and of their current needs and interests.

Planning should also be flexible so that it can take account of children's ideas and responses to learning experiences and allow learning to develop. When there has been a need to alter a plan, future plans should be reviewed and adjusted to ensure that a broad and balanced range of learning continues to be provided or that goals for learning are revised. In this way the learning opportunities provided should be influenced by and responsive to children's interests within an overall long-term plan.

Staff interaction

It is from observation and assessment of children at play that we learn how and what they learn. Of course, it is not possible to observe everything where large numbers of children are involved in a range of play. This means that observation and assessment should be focused and selective. It should have purpose.

Observation and assessment must influence the learning situation, to be of true value; for example:

- to recognise where additional support or challenge is required for individuals or groups of children. In this case observation and assessment should lead to prompt action as a result of the observation
- to use the evaluation of observations to inform planning, for example, to practise a skill or offer a new learning experience
- to direct staff support for the following day or week.

Observation is also useful in helping staff to evaluate the effectiveness of their provision and of their interactions during learning.

Recording

Day-to-day records of observations and assessments help staff to plan learning experiences which take account of children's needs and development. Records should also provide a profile of each child's progress in different aspects of their development and learning. Profiles will provide the information necessary to report to parents, colleagues and other professionals.

Record-keeping should be kept manageable; if it is too detailed it takes valuable time away from interacting with children. It should concentrate on what is significant in children's learning rather than attempt to record everything that happens. Staff in some settings use notebooks, diaries or post-its to record observations which are then used in making plans to develop children's learning. This recognises a link between planning and recording. Planning helps to focus what is recorded and the observations made during learning influence future planning, setting out the next steps in learning.

Such records can be used to build up a full picture of each child's progress in learning. Alternatively, from time to time during the year, staff may complete parts of a record as a way of taking stock of children's progress.

The record should:

- cover each of the key aspects of children's development and learning;
- include brief comments on significant strengths and development needs observed during a child's learning.

They can also include photographs and examples of children's work.

Reporting

Reporting is a means of:

- promoting partnership with parents,
- sharing information with children, colleagues and other professionals, and
- shaping the next steps in learning.

Records begin when a child is preparing to start the early years setting. Parents and children complete statements such as 'I can …' and 'I enjoy …', with pictures or photographs and statements. This helps to involve children in recognising their capabilities and also values the learning which they have already achieved.

Reporting to parents informally

There are many opportunities for informal reporting to parents during day-to-day contacts; sending home examples of children's work will continue this process. Children can be involved in self-assessment, for example by discussing photographs or examples of work which might be included in profiles. Information from parents about learning at home can also be included. Records (see above) may provide evidence for making oral and written reports to parents.

This information will also be shared with primary schools and other professionals.

Evaluating

Reflecting on observations and assessment is an important part of staff development. It involves:

- thinking about what has worked well in providing learning experiences and in interacting with children;
- thinking about improvements that could have been made to help learning take place more effectively, for example by asking a question in a different way, providing a different resource, or challenging children more during an interaction.

Evaluating aspects of children's learning over time will help in judging whether the learning experiences and interactions are helping them to make good progress. Discussing all of this with other staff will help in promoting children's learning effectively.

 Progress check

Evaluating plans

- A medium-term plan can be used to check the balance of the long-term plan. Is science being developed so that it reaches every child? Not all children will learn exactly the same science, but they should all have appropriate opportunities.
- How does science link with the official documents? What science are children supposed to have learned about at this stage in their education?
- Are the medium-term planning resources working well for this group of children in their learning? Most experts agree that if there are good plans for individual children, the whole group tends to benefit.
- Are the adults using observation of children to inform their planning?
- Are the adults giving support to individual children's learning as well as to the group?
- Are adults able to extend the learning to add knowledge that children did not previously have (for example, Andrew might be interested in water pumps – see page 290)?
- Are children learning about areas other than science? Is there a good balance in this curriculum?

Evaluating the planning and assessment cycle

As you discuss your work with colleagues, you will be able to make realistic, honest and forward-looking self-evaluations, which will empower you in your professional development. Research shows that children develop and learn through their play and the first-hand experiences they are offered by adults who are interested in what they do, and who support and extend their learning. Children benefit from the relationships and companionship they find with other children. However, none of this can happen if the conditions are not favourable: the role of the adult is crucial in creating, maintaining and planning the general environment.

Margaret Carr, a Professor of Early Childhood Studies in New Zealand, has developed *Teaching Stories* to help practitioners assess and evaluate their work with children and families. You can use these to help you evaluate your practice through thinking about how it feels to be a child in your setting. Here are Carr's thoughts on what a child asks of a practitioner:

BELONGING: DO YOU KNOW ME?

How do you appreciate and understand my interests and abilities and those of my family?

WELLBEING: CAN I TRUST YOU?

How do you meet my daily needs with care and consideration?

EXPLORATION: DO YOU LET ME FLY?

How do you engage my mind, offer challenges and extend my world?

COMMUNICATION: DO YOU HEAR ME?

How do you invite me to listen and communicate, and respond to my own particular efforts?

CONTRIBUTION: IS THIS THE PLACE FOR US?

How do you encourage and facilitate my endeavours to be part of the group?

Assessment practice

Unit 7

For this assignment, you need to collate information about all aspects of play and learning in children's education. You need to know about – and present information – on a wide variety of topics, which include:

- the current influences on the planning and provision of learning opportunities
- examples of different theoretical models of how children play and learn
- the importance of consulting with parents and others when planning and providing learning opportunities
- a reflective account of the role of the practitioner in supporting the learning needs of children.

 Useful resources

Organisations and websites

Book Trust Children's Books encourages children and parents to enjoy reading for pleasure and information; it support adults in reading to young children, recommending a wide range of books, rhymes and stories:
www.booktrustchildrensbooks.org.uk

Books for Keeps promotes the use of diverse texts about different cultures, disabilities, gender and age:
www.booksforkeeps.co.uk

Useful resources (Cont.)

Centre for Literacy in Primary Education has undertaken pioneering work in supporting and training practitioners to enjoy helping children to love stories and books. It offers excellent training for those working with children in Reception and Key Stage 1:
www.clpe.co.uk

Early Education – the booklet on Core Experiences for the Early Years Foundation Stage from Kate Greenaway Nursery School and Children's Centre can be ordered from this website:
www.early-education.org.uk

Siren Films produces high-quality DVDs covering a wide range of topics, such as the first year of life, two-year-olds, play, attachment and key person, three- and four-year-olds, early literacy and schemas in toddlers:
www.sirenfilms.co.uk

Books

Bartholomew, L. and Bruce, T. (1993) *Getting to know you*. London: Hodder and Stoughton Educational.

Brooker, E. (2002) *Starting School: Young Children Learning Cultures*. Maidenhead: Open University Press.

Bruce, T. (1996) *Helping Young Children to Play*. London: Hodder & Stoughton.

Bruce, T. (2004b) *Developing Learning in Early Childhood*. London: Paul Chapman Publishing.

Bruce, T. (2009b) 'Learning through Play: Froebelian Principles and their Practice Today', *Early Childhood Practice: The Journal for Multi-professional Partnerships* 10(2): 58–73.

Bruce, T. (ed.) (2010) *Early Childhood: A Guide for Students* (2nd edn). London: Sage.

Bruce, T. and Spratt, J. (2010) *The Essentials of Communication, Language and Literacy* (2nd edn). London: Sage.

Bruce, T. (2011a) *Learning Through Play* (2nd edn). London: Hodder Education.

Bruce, T. (2011b) *Early Childhood Education* (4th edn). London: Hodder Education.

Bruce, T. (2011c) *Cultivating Creativity: Babies, Toddlers and Young Children* (2nd edn). London: Hodder Education.

Community Playthings. *Foundations* (CD-ROM illustrating the value of block play, available at www.communityplaythings.co.uk/resources/request-literature.html).

Community Playthings. *Spaces; Creating places; I made a Unicorn!* (Educational booklets, available at www.communityplaythings.co.uk/resources/request-literature.html).

Davies, M. (2003) *Movement and Dance in Early Childhood*. London: Paul Chapman Publishing Ltd.

Department for Children, Schools and Families (2008) *Mark Making Matters: Young Children Making Meaning in All Areas of Learning and Development*. Nottingham: DCSF Publications.

Department for Education and Skills (2005) *Celebrating Young Children and Those Who Live and Work with Them* (DVD).

Department for Education and Skills (2007) *Primary National Strategy: Creating the Picture*. London: DfES, available at http://publications.teachernet.gov.uk/eOrderingDownload/fs_creating_pic_0028307.pdf

Drury, R. (2007) Young Bilingual Learners at Home and School: Researching Multilingual Voices. Stoke-on-Trent: Trentham Books.

Edgington, M. (2004) The Foundation Stage Teacher in Action. Teaching 3, 4 and 5 year olds (3rd edn). London: Sage.

Useful resources (Cont.)

Edwards, C., Gandini, L. and Forman, G. (1998) *The Hundred Languages of Children*. Westport, CT and London: Ablex Publishing.

Greenland, P. (2009) *Physical Development. Early Childhood: A Guide for Students* (ed. T. Bruce) (2nd edn). London: Sage.

Gura, P. (ed.) (1990) *Exploring Learning: Young Children and Blockplay*. London: Paul Chapman Publishing.

Kalliala, M. (2006) *Play Culture in a Changing World*. Oxford: Oxford University Press.

Langer, E. (1997) *The Power of Mindful Learning*. Harlow: Addison-Wesley.

Matthews, J. (2003) *Drawing and Painting: Children and Visual Representation* (2nd edn). London: Paul Chapman Publishing Ltd.

National Assessment Agency. *Early Years Foundation Stage* (DVD, available online by searching for 'early years foundation stage profile exemplification videos').

Nursery World, 4 February 2010, pp. 19–22.

Ockelford, A. (1996) *All Join In: A Framework for Making Music with Children and Young People Who are Visually Impaired and Have Learning Difficulties*. Peterborough: RNIB. This inclusive book, containing music, is also invaluable for all children from birth to seven years of age.

Ouvry, M. (2004) *Sounds like Playing: Music in the Early Years Curriculum*. London: BAECE/Early Education.

Sylva, K., Melhuish, E., Sammons, P., Siraj-Blatchford, I. and Taggart, B. (2004) *The Effective Provision of Pre-School Education (EPPE) Project: Final Report*. London: DfES/Institute of Education, University of London, available at www.dcsf.gov.uk/research/data/uploadfiles/SSU_FR_2004_01.pdf

Tovey, H. (2007) *Playing Outdoors: Spaces and Places, Risk and Challenge*. Maidenhead: Open University Press.

Worthington, M. and Carruthers, E. (2003) *Children's Mathematics: Making Marks, Making Meaning*. London: Paul Chapman Publishing Ltd.

Ziegler, J. and Goswami, U. (2006) 'Becoming literate in different languages: similar problems, different solutions', *Developmental Science* 9(5): 429–53.

Section 1: The range of settings which provide care for children

Children, families and the outside world

The Children Act 1989 states that: 'Children are best looked after within the family, with support if necessary.' Parents want the best for their children and have hopes and aspirations for them. They want them to feel safe and loved, have people around them who are constant and show they care about them, and they want them to achieve and enjoy life. The same principles apply when children are 'looked after' by social services. Because of these children's experiences, they may have a lot of needs and hopes that are more difficult for professionals to help them with.

Family life

Family life in the United Kingdom has changed dramatically in recent decades. The speed of this change, and the different opinions held by people about how the family, make this an area of much controversy.

Different family structures

Children arriving in early years settings and schools are now likely to come from a range of family structures, including those:

- whose parents are **married**
- whose parents live together, but are not married (**cohabiting** parents)
- being brought up by a **lone parent** (usually, but not always, a mother) following a relationship breakdown or through being widowed
- with a **single parent** who has chosen this family structure as a lifestyle choice (for example, never intending to have a relationship with the biological father, or using a sperm donor service to become pregnant)
- in **reconstituted families** (where only one adult is a biological parent to the child, and where there may be children living together who have different biological parents): one of the parents in a family like this may be called a **step–parent**
- in families headed by a **gay or lesbian couple**
- who are looked after, living with **foster parents** (usually children are taken into care by the local authority for safeguarding reasons, and placed in the short or medium term with a foster parent or parents)
- living in a family in a **private fostering** arrangement (when a child under the age of 16 is cared for by someone who is not their parent or a close relative for more than 28 days, as part of a private arrangement made between the parent and the carer).

In the UK, marriage levels are at an all-time low. Two in every three marriages ends in a divorce – the highest rate in Europe. Almost half of all children are born to unmarried parents, and a quarter of all children now live in a family headed by a lone parent – the highest proportion in Europe.

Discussion point

Many people are very concerned by family breakdown and the loss of the traditional childhood. The writer Sue Palmer refers to 'toxic childhood syndrome' and a 2007 UNICEF report found that children in the UK were the unhappiest in the developed world. The Labour Government's Children's Plan, launched in December 2007, says it would make Britain 'the best place in the world for children and young people to grow up'. How happy do you think family life is today for young children?

The importance of parents and primary carers

In all family set-ups, parents and primary carers have a central role in their children's lives. They:

- are the first and most enduring carers and educators of their children
- know and understand their own child best
- have specific legal responsibilities towards their children
- give their children a strong sense of identity and belonging
- have skills and experience which can be of value to the early years setting
- are partners with early childhood practitioners in the care and education of their children.

Parental responsibility

The Children Act 1989 replaced the term 'parental rights' with 'parental responsibility'. Parents have responsibility for all aspects of a child's upbringing and welfare. While the law does not define in detail what parental responsibility is, the list below covers the key roles:

- Physical and emotional care of the child.
- Naming the child and agreeing to any change of name.
- Ensuring that the child receives an efficient, full-time education suited to his or her needs and abilities.
- Maintaining the child and providing a home.
- Disciplining the child.

Figure 8.1 Children benefit greatly from spending leisure time with their parents or primary carers

- Consenting to the child being medically examined or receiving medical treatment.
- Accompanying the child on visits outside the UK and agreeing to the child's emigration, if that issue arises.
- Responsibility for the child's property.
- Appointing a guardian for the child, if necessary.
- Consenting to a private fostering arrangement (in which the child is cared for by a person who is not a close relative).
- Allowing confidential information about the child to be shared and discussed by others.

Some aspects of parental responsibility require the consent of both parents of the child. These include the authority to:

- agree to the child being adopted
- remove the child from the UK.

How parental responsibility is acquired

- The mother always has automatic parental responsibility.
- The father has parental responsibility if he was married to the mother at the time of the birth of the child.
- An unmarried father has parental responsibility if the birth was jointly registered by both parents (from December 2003), or if he is named on a parental responsibility agreement made by a court.
- The Children Act 1989 does not create any rights of consultation between a child's parents before action is taken in respect of a child. On the contrary, the Act says that each person with parental responsibility may act independently in meeting that responsibility, except where the law requires consent (for example, adoption).

Because of this, parental responsibility is no guarantee of cooperation. If the child is living with the mother for example, a father with parental responsibility may find it very frustrating that he does not have to be involved in decisions regarding the child. If he disagrees very strongly with what

the mother is doing, he has to apply to the court for either a 'prohibited steps order' or a 'specific issue order'.

Can parental responsibility be lost or given away?

- Parental responsibility is not lost as a result of separation or divorce.
- Parental responsibility cannot be surrendered or transferred. It can, however, be temporarily delegated or entrusted to someone else.
- Parental responsibility is not lost when another person acquires it; rather, parental responsibility is then shared. This is so even when a local authority acquires parental responsibility under a care order.
- Parental responsibility is lost when an adoption order is made; otherwise, it is lost only in exceptional circumstances.

All parents, including adoptive parents, are legally required to support their child financially, whether they have parental responsibility or not.

Different parenting styles

Early years practitioners need to bear in mind the following facts:

- Every family is different, with different needs and traditions.
- The great majority of parents are concerned to do their best for their children, even if they are not always sure what this might be.
- Each one of us only really knows what it is like to grow up in our own family. Parents almost always like some of the things about their own family and the way they were brought up; but they will just as certainly wish that other aspects of their upbringing had been different.
- Parents usually welcome help when trying out some alternative ways of doing things. They will not want to change too much, though, and they will not want rapid changes forced on them by other people. Early childhood practitioners need to respect parents' wishes.

Progress check

- What is parental responsibility? Who can have it, and what does it mean?
- Why is it important to engage parents, and local communities, as partners rather than seeing them as problems?

The diverse groups that care for children in a variety of environments

Young children need both education and care. Children are not made up of separate parts: a child is a whole person. It is inappropriate to talk about either the education of or caring for young children. Instead, the term 'integrated early years settings' is used to describe places which provide education *and* care for young children. Children need good physical and health care as much as they need new, interesting and stimulating experiences.

A wide range of organisations exists to provide services for young children and their families. These include statutory services, voluntary services, self-help agencies and private services.

The differing roles of the statutory, private, voluntary and independent settings that provide care for children

Statutory provision of services

A statutory service is one that is provided by the state. Some statutory services are provided by central government and funded from central taxation, such as the National Health Service (NHS).

Others are provided by local government and funded by a combination of local and central taxation, such as education and social service departments.

The statutory sector comprises the following:

- **Central government departments** in which policy is devised by a Secretary of State (who is an MP), helped by Ministers of State (also MPs) and managed by the Permanent Secretary (a civil servant); for example:
  - The National Health Service (NHS)
  - Department for Education (DfE)
- **Executive agencies** (such as the Benefits Agency which issues social security payments) contracted by central government departments to deliver services.
- **Local government departments** chaired by an elected member of the local council and administered by a paid officer; for example:
  - housing department
  - local education authority
  - children and young people's services.
- **Local health authorities and trusts**, led by a chairperson and managed by a chief executive.

These are largely funded through **local taxation** (Council Tax) and from grants made by central government.

Health services for children

The government's Department of Health is responsible for providing health care through the National Health Service (NHS), which was set up in 1948 to provide free health care to the entire population.

The National Service Framework for Children, Young People and Maternity Services was set up by the Department of Health in 2004 and has the following aims:

- To help parents find and stay in learning or work (including having **high quality, affordable child care** for both pre-school and school age children) and child-friendly working practices.
- To ensure that families are made aware of the **Healthy Start Scheme**, and encouraged to apply

for it if they qualify. Healthy Start will provide low-income pregnant women and young families with advice on diet and nutrition, local support to eat healthily, and vouchers to buy healthy food.

- To ensure that families with low incomes are supported to claim all **benefits** to which they are entitled.
- To **provide support** for groups especially likely to be living in poverty, for example, teenage parents and families with disabled children and those who are homeless.
- To ensure as far as possible that **local authority accommodation** for families with children is not damp or cold (in line with the cross-government fuel poverty strategy), has adequate space for play and privacy, and at least one working smoke alarm and a carbon monoxide detector, where appropriate.
- To minimise **environmental pollution**, in residential areas and around nurseries and schools.

See also Chapter 6 for information on health care provision.

Social services for children

From 2006, education and social care services for children have been brought together under a **director of children's services** in each local authority.

Social services provide a range of care and support for children and families, including:

- families where children are assessed as **being in need** (including disabled children)
- children who may be suffering 'significant harm' – for example, from violence in the home or from some form of child abuse. (This aspect of social work is known as **child protection**.)
- children who require **looking after** by the local authority (through fostering or residential care)
- children who are placed for **adoption**.

Social workers with responsibilities for children and families may work in the following areas:

Safeguarding and promoting the welfare of children

In the great majority of cases, children are safeguarded while remaining at home by social services working with their parents, family members and other significant adults in the child's life to make the child safe, and to promote his or her development within the family setting. (See Chapter 3 for more detail on safeguarding children.)

Supporting disabled children

Social workers must provide a range of services to families with disabled children to minimise the impact of any disabilities and enable them to live as normal a life as possible. Typically they provide short-term breaks in foster families or residential units, support services in the home and, increasingly, assistance for disabled children to participate in out-of-school and leisure activities in the community alongside their non-disabled peers.

Supporting looked-after children

Where the local authority looks after a child following the imposition of a care order, or accommodates a child with the agreement of their parents, it is the role of the social worker to ensure that adequate arrangements are made for the child's care and that a plan is made, in partnership with the child, their parents and other agencies, so that the child's future is secure.

Children are generally looked after in foster care. A minority will be cared for in children's homes and some by prospective adoptive parents. *All* looked-after children will have a social worker and carers (for example, foster carers, residential care staff) responsible for their day-to-day care, who should be involved in making plans or decisions about the young person.

Education services for children

The **Department for Education (DfE)** is headed by the Secretary of State for Education and is responsible for deciding the policies and the funding to the local education authorities.

All three- and four-year-olds are now entitled to free early education for 15 hours per week for 38 weeks of the year. From the term after their third birthday children under the age of five may attend any of the following:

- maintained (or state) nursery schools
- **nursery classes** attached to primary schools
- playgroups or pre-schools in the voluntary sector
- privately run nurseries
- infant schools
- Children's Centres
- **home learning environment (HLE)**: many young children are cared for by childminders (in the childminder's home) or by nannies or grandparents.

Research Activity

Investigating education and care

Research the age at which children start compulsory schooling in six countries, including one country in Africa, Asia, Europe and Australia/New Zealand. You can use the internet or telephone the relevant embassies, who will help you track down this information.

Maintained nursery schools

These are part of the provision made by some local education authorities.

Figure 8.2 A private day nursery

Maintained nursery schools offer either full-time or part-time places for children from the term after their third birthday. Most children will leave to join the reception class in a primary or infant school in the September of the school year in which they will be five years old. By law, all children must start school the term after their fifth birthday. Some nursery schools offer places for two-year-olds, under the 'Early Learning for Disadvantaged Two-Year-Olds' scheme.

There is a headteacher who has specialist training in the age group, and graduate trained teachers working with qualified nursery nurses.

Adult to child ratios are 1:13 in England, Wales and Northern Ireland, but 1:8 in Scotland (full-time).

Nursery classes and nursery units
Nursery classes are attached to primary schools. The headteacher of the primary school may or may not be an expert in early years education.

The class teacher will be a graduate trained teacher who will work alongside a fully qualified nursery nurse.

Nursery units are usually in a separate building with a separate coordinator.

They are larger than a nursery class but will have the same adult to child ratio as the nursery class – which is 1:13. Like the nursery class, these units come under the management of the headteacher, who again may or may not be trained to work with this age group.

Infant schools
In England and Wales children start at infant school between the ages of four and five in a Reception class. They sometimes attend part-time (mornings only or afternoons only) for the first term or two. Reception is the final part of the Foundation Stage. Pupils then transfer to Year One in the September following their fifth birthday, and to Year Two the following year. These two years form Key Stage 1 in the English and Welsh education system. At the end of this time, pupils will move to a linked junior school.

Extended services
In June 2005 the government launched *Extended schools: Access to opportunities and services for all*, a prospectus outlining the vision of extended schools, to feature the following:

- high quality 'wraparound' child care provided by the schools site or through other local providers, available 8am to 6pm all year round
- a varied menu of activities to be on offer such as homework clubs and study support, sport, music tuition, special interest clubs and volunteering
- parenting support including information sessions for parents at key transition points, parenting programmes and family learning sessions
- swift and easy referral to a wide range of specialist support services such as speech and language therapy, family support services and behaviour support
- providing wider community access to ICT, sports and arts facilities, including adult learning.

Integrated care and education for children
Recent legislation has led to a number of reforms in the delivery of care and education to children. While the school system remains largely unchanged, the statutory services for children from birth to five years old are becoming increasingly integrated. This involves a new structure for the delivery of an integrated service, to include:

- Children's Trusts
- The Early Years Foundation Stage
- Sure Start programmes
- Children's Centres
- Local Authority day nurseries (see above for information).

Children's Trusts
Children's trusts are new organisations which bring together health, education and social services for children, young people and families. Some take on responsibility for *all* children's services, from child protection to speech therapy, while others will focus on particularly vulnerable children, such as those

with disabilities. At first most trusts will commission *local* children's services. The trusts will employ a range of professionals – for example:

- social workers
- family support workers
- health visitors
- school nurses
- educational psychologists
- speech and language therapists
- child and adolescent mental health professionals.

Children's Trusts are underpinned by the Children Act 2004 duty to cooperate and to focus on improving outcomes for all children and young people. Trusts can also include Sure Start local programmes. Other local partners may include: housing, leisure services, the police, youth justice, independent sector organisations such as voluntary organisations, and community sector organisations such as churches. They will be led by local 'children's champions', whose role is to advocate the interests of children across different services.

 Progress check

Integrated early childhood services must include:

- early years provision (integrated child care and early education)
- social services
- relevant health services, for example health visitors, antenatal, postnatal care
- services provided by Jobcentre Plus to assist parents to obtain work
- information services.

The Early Years Foundation Stage (from birth to five years old)

All schools and early years providers have to follow a structure of learning, development and care for children. This is called The Early Years Foundation Stage (EYFS) and it enables children to learn through a range of activities. The main principles of the EYFS are as follows:

- children learn through play
- providers work closely with parents

- the child's learning at home is taken into account
- parents and guardians are kept up-to-date on the child's progress
- it is **inclusive** – it ensures the welfare, learning and all-round development of children with different backgrounds and levels of ability, including those with special educational needs and disabilities.

The EYFS applies to all schools and registered early years providers in the maintained, private, voluntary and independent sectors attended by children from birth to five years. This includes:

- reception and nursery classes in maintained and independent schools
- day nurseries
- childminders
- playgroups
- after-school and breakfast clubs
- holiday play schemes
- Children's Centres.

The following groups do not have to use the EYFS:

- mother and toddler groups
- nannies
- short-term, occasional care (such as crèches).

Research Activity

What kind of provision?

Research the early years provision made by your local authority. What proportion of four-year-olds are in reception classes? What kind of provision are most three-year-olds and their families offered?

Sure Start

Sure Start is an extensive government programme launched in the late 1990s as a cornerstone of the then Labour Government's drive to eradicate child poverty in 20 years, and to halve it within a decade. The first Sure Start local programmes were established in 1999, with the aim of improving the health and wellbeing of families and children from before birth to age four, so that they can flourish at home and when they begin

Figure 8.3 Supporting learning and social development

school. They started in the most disadvantaged areas in the UK.

Sure Start local programmes are delivered by local partnerships and work with parents-to-be, parents and children to promote the physical, intellectual and social development of babies and young children. All Sure Start local programmes are now called Sure Start Children's Centres, and have these four key objectives:

1 **Improving social and emotional development** – by supporting early bonding between parents and their children, helping families function and enabling early identification and support of children with emotional and behavioural difficulties.

2 **Improving health** – by supporting parents in caring for their children to promote healthy development before and after birth.

3 **Improving children's ability to learn** – by providing high quality environments and child care that promote early learning and provide stimulating and enjoyable play, improve language skills and ensure early identification of children with special needs.

4 **Strengthening families and communities** – by involving families in building the community's capacity to sustain the programme and create pathways out of **social exclusion**.

The emphasis is on prevention in order to reduce social exclusion later on, and to improve the chances of younger children through early access to education, health services, family support and advice on nurturing. These projects include support for:

- special educational needs
- outreach services and home visiting
- families and parents
- good quality play, learning and child care
- primary and community health care
- advice about child health and development
- advice about parent health.

Children's Centres

The majority of Children's Centres are developed from Sure Start local programmes, Neighbourhood

Nurseries and Early Excellence Centres. Sure Start Children's Centres are places where children under five years old and their families can receive seamless holistic integrated services and information, and where they can access help from multi-disciplinary teams of professionals. Children's Centres serve children and their families from the antenatal period, through until children start in Reception or Year One at primary school. They also offer a base within the community, linking to other providers of day care – such as childminder networks and out-of-school clubs.

Each centre offers the following services to families with babies and pre-school children:

- good quality early learning integrated with full daycare provision (a minimum of ten hours a day, five days a week, 48 weeks a year)
- family support services
- a base for a childminder network
- child and family health services, including antenatal services
- support for children and parents with special needs
- links with Jobcentre Plus, local training providers and further and higher education institutions.

Children's Centres may also offer other services, including:

- training for parents (such as parenting classes, basic skills, English as an additional language)
- benefits advice and information
- toy libraries.

Local authority day nurseries

Local authority day nurseries are funded by social services and offer full-time provision for children under school age. They cater mainly for families who may be facing many challenges and who need support. They provide care from 8 am often until 7 pm and are registered and inspected every year. Staffing levels are high, the usual ratio being one staff member for every four children. Some local authority day nurseries also operate as family centres, providing advice, guidance and counselling to the families with difficulties.

Progress check

- Integrated early years settings are places that provide both education and care for young children.
- The Early Years Foundation Stage (EYFS) enables children to learn through a range of activities and emphasises the importance of learning through play.
- All three-and four-year-olds are entitled to free early education for 12 and a half hours per week for 38 weeks of the year.
- Sure Start Children's Centres provide early education integrated with health and family support services, and child care from 8 am to 6 pm.

Voluntary services and self-help agencies for children and families

These are health, education and social care services which are set up by **charities** to provide services which local authorities can buy in and benefit from their expertise. Voluntary organisations are:

- non-profit making
- non-statutory
- dependent on donations, fundraising and government grants.

Example: **Children England** is an organisation whose members are all registered charities that work with children, young people and their families. They range from very large national organisations (such as **Barnardo's**) to small locally based charities.

Voluntary organisations often arise because:

- there is a gap in services – for example, the Salvation Army provides hostels for homeless people
- there is a need for a campaign both to alert the public to an issue and to push for action to be taken – for example, Shelter, a pressure group for the homeless.

Within any local authority in the UK there are child care and education settings which come into the category of voluntary or self-help provision. Two examples are community nurseries and Pre-School Learning Alliance Community Pre-Schools.

Community nurseries

Community nurseries exist to provide a service to local children and their families. They are run by local community organisations – often with financial assistance from the local authority – or by charities such as Barnardo's and Save the Children. Most of these nurseries are open long enough to suit working parents or those at college. Many centres also provide or act as a venue for other services, including:

- parent and toddler groups,
- drop-in crèches,
- toy libraries, and
- after-school clubs.

Pre-School Learning Alliance Community Pre-Schools

Pre-School Learning Alliance Community Pre-Schools (playgroups) offer children aged between three and five years an opportunity to learn through play:

- They usually operate on a part-time sessional basis. Sessions are normally two-and-a-half hours each morning or afternoon.
- Staff plan a varied curriculum that takes into account children's previous experiences and developing needs.
- The Early Years Foundation Stage is adapted by each group to meet the needs of their own children and to allow them to make the most of a variety of learning opportunities that arise spontaneously through play.
- At many pre-school playgroups, parents and carers are encouraged to be involved, and there are often parent and toddler groups meeting at the same sites.

Leisure activities and recreation services

These services provide children and their families with activities and opportunities for recreation and sport. Some of these are provided by the local authority and are either provided free or at a subsidised cost; others are privately owned and run. They include:

- sports centres, children's gyms
- music groups
- parks
- adventure playgrounds and soft play areas
- holiday schemes and activities
- lessons such as dance and drama
- clubs, for example, Beavers, Cubs and Scouts; Rainbows, Brownies and Guides; Woodcraft Folk
- libraries.

Local provision for children

Most local authorities have a special department to coordinate all the services to children within their locality. These departments are often called Early Years Services and deal exclusively with the needs of young children and their families. The range of services which is provided varies greatly from one local authority to

Figure 8.4 Good local authority provision can really enhance children's physical development

another, but typically will include the following services (those marked with an asterisk* must be provided by law):

- **Housing***: children and their families in need, for example homeless families and those seeking refuge are a priority. Services include providing bed and breakfast accommodation or council housing.
- **After-school clubs***: these offer supervised play opportunities in a safe, supportive and friendly environment. They usually cater for children from five to 11 years, but some centres have facilities for children under five.
- **Nursery education**: most authorities are not able to offer full nursery education to all children within the borough. Nursery classes are usually attached to maintained primary schools. Nursery schools are separate.
- **Community places for families with low incomes**: most local authorities keep a number of full day nursery places at Children's Centres, specifically for children in families with low incomes.
- **Regulation and registration of services*** such as childminders, private fostering and private or voluntary-run daycare and family centres.

- **Social workers***: work with families where children are assessed as being *in need*; they give practical support and advice on a wide range of issues including adoption and foster care.
- **Infant or primary education***: children must attend full-time school from the age of five – and must follow the National Curriculum.
- **Residential holidays**: provide opportunities for children to develop self-reliance, as well as providing a break for many children who otherwise would not have the chance of a holiday.
- **Holiday play schemes**: full-day programmes of activities during the school holidays.
- **Advice, information and counselling***: local authorities have a duty to provide information and counselling to families where there is a child in need.
- **Children's centres***: these include early learning, parent information services and support for children and parents with special needs.
- **Respite care***: families where a child has special needs may be offered a residential holiday for their child so that they can have a break – or respite – from caring full-time for them.

These services are usually listed and coordinated by a local **Council for Voluntary Service**. Voluntary organisations sometimes also provide some of the statutory services and will receive payment from the local authority or government for these services; for example, after-school clubs.

Key terms

Statutory service – Any service provided and managed by the state or government – such as the NHS or a local authority day nursery.

Voluntary organisation – An association or society which has been created by its members rather than having been created by the state, such as a charity.

The UK private sector

This sector comprises businesses that make profits. In education, this includes private nurseries. In social services, the private sector includes old peoples' homes run by big chains and by individuals. In health, there are private hospitals.

Private nurseries, hospitals and schools are legally required to be registered and inspected, and to follow guidelines laid down in laws and by local authorities.

Private day nurseries, private nursery schools, preparatory schools and kindergartens

- Private nursery schools and private day nurseries are available for those parents who can afford them, and some financial support is available to parents through government schemes. In addition, there are workplace nurseries which subsidise places in order that staff and students in institutions can take up this form of care.
- These are required to appoint qualified staff, and to meet the National Daycare Standards.

Childminders, nannies and grandparents: Home Learning Environment (HLE)

- Children are looked after in their own homes by grandparents or nannies, or in the childminder's home.

- Childminders are offered training through the National Childminding Association and CACHE.
- Nannies sometimes live with a family, but not always. Sometimes, they look after children from several different families.

Research Activity

Imagine you want to register as a childminder. What must you do? Research this, and make a plan.

The regulatory framework and its impact on the care given to children

The main pieces of legislation underpinning social services for children are the Children Act 1989, the Children Act 2004, and the Childcare Act 2006.

Children Act 1989

Local authorities have specific legal duties in respect of children under the Children Act 1989, including:

- To safeguard and promote the welfare of children in their area who are in need.
- Provided that this is consistent with the child's safety and welfare, to promote the upbringing of such children by their families, by providing services appropriate to the child's needs.
- To make enquiries if they have reasonable cause to suspect that a child in their area is suffering, or likely to suffer significant harm, to enable them to decide whether they should take any action to safeguard or promote the child's welfare.

Children Act 2004

The Children Act 2004 requires all local areas to produce a single, strategic, comprehensive plan for all services affecting children and young people in their area. A Children and Young People's Plan has the five wellbeing outcomes set out in the Children Act at its heart. These are to:

1 Be healthy.
2 Stay safe.

3 Enjoy and achieve.

4 Make a positive contribution.

5 Achieve economic wellbeing.

Local authorities work together with families who need help and support to promote the welfare and safety of their children. To do this they work closely with other services such as health, education, housing, police and probation, as well as with voluntary organisations.

The Early Years Foundation Stage has also had a great impact on the way in which care and education is organised. The EYFS principles are stated in Chapter 7, page 282.

The Childcare Act 2006

Section 41 of the Childcare Act 2006 contains the duty to implement the EYFS which is mandatory for the following providers:

- Providers registered on the Early Years Register (maintained by Ofsted).
- Providers exempt from registration on the Early Years Register in relation to provision for children aged three and older, where the provision is part of the school's activities, is provided by the school proprietor or their employee, and at least one child is a registered pupil at the school. This includes maintained schools, independent schools, and non-maintained special schools.

The Childcare Act 2006 requires the Secretary of State to specify learning and development requirements and welfare requirements. The learning and development requirements are given legal force by an Order made under Section 39(1)(a) of the Childcare Act 2006. The safeguarding and welfare requirements are given legal force by Regulations made under Section 39(1)(b) of the Childcare Act 2006. Together, the Order, the Regulations and the Statutory Framework document make up the legal basis of the EYFS.

The EYFS requirements sit alongside other legal obligations and do not supersede or replace any other legislation which providers must still meet. For example, where provision is taking place in maintained schools there is a range of education legislation in place with which headteachers, teachers and others must comply. Providers must comply with the requirements of the Safeguarding Vulnerable Groups Act 2006 (which creates offences) and take into account any guidance issued in relation to the scheme set out in that Act. The requirements under the Act include a duty not to engage a barred person in regulated activity, to carry out 'barred list checks' and, in certain circumstances, to refer individuals to the body responsible for barring persons from working with children or vulnerable adults. It is an offence under the Act to allow a barred person to engage in regulated activity.

- Providers must also be aware of other legal duties, such as employment law, equality legislation, health and safety legislation, data collection legislation, data protection legislation and common law duties such as confidentiality and the law of negligence (DfE, 2011).

Section 2: The diverse care needs of children

From the moment they are born, all children depend completely on an adult to meet all their needs, but the way in which these needs are met will vary considerably according to family circumstances, culture and the personalities of the child and the caring adult/s.

To achieve and maintain healthy growth and development (that is physical, intellectual, communication and language, and emotional and social development) certain basic needs must be fulfilled:

- food
- cleanliness
- sleep, rest and activity
- protection from infection and injury
- intellectual stimulation
- relationships and social contacts
- shelter, warmth, clothing
- fresh air and sunlight
- love, and consistent and continuous affection
- access to health care
- appreciation, praise and recognition of effort or achievements
- security and nurture.

It is difficult to separate these basic needs from practical care, as they all contribute to the **holistic** development of a healthy child.

How to use your knowledge of child development to recognise children's care needs

As children grow and develop, different care needs come into focus; this is particularly true when a child differs from the developmental norm. Maslow's hierarchy of needs is a useful tool for considering these needs in a developmental framework. For example, at the basic level of physiological needs, a child who is cold or hungry will be unable to respond to planned activities – and will not be able to develop healthily.

Note: The following care needs are dealt with more fully in Chapter 4.

Children's care needs

Food and clean water

All children need a healthy diet consisting of a wide variety of foods to help the body to grow and to provide energy. It must include enough of these nutrients: proteins, fats, carbohydrates, vitamins, minerals, and fibre – as well as water, to fuel and maintain the body's vital functions. For babies, nutrients are provided entirely by milk, but as children grow and develop their energy needs also change.

Cleanliness

Both the environment and children need to be kept clean. Practising good hygiene routines (personal hygiene routines and hygiene routines in the setting) will help to prevent infection and to maintain children's and adult's health.

Sleep and rest

Getting the right amount of rest is very important for the learning of babies and young children. Not all babies will need to sleep at the same time, and it is inappropriate practice for a setting to expect all babies to have their nappies changed at the same time and to sleep at the same time. These are very individual things.

It is important for babies to feel that they are near someone when they sleep. All early years practice must take into account any cultural preferences, such as later bedtimes and family circumstances.

Figure 8.5 Sleep is essential for healthy development

Figure 8.6 Children should be allowed to enjoy physical activity outdoors

Physical activity

Physical play promotes a child's health and links with all other areas of a child's development. The brain works better if children have plenty of fresh air and exercise. This is why both indoor and outdoor play are very important.

Protection from infection and injury

Infections are very common in childhood and are responsible for the majority of illnesses that occur in babies and children under the age of five years. A particular concern for early years settings is that young children often lack basic hygiene skills and must rely on others for their care. Repeated close physical contact with other children, adults and at-risk areas of the environment (such as toilet facilities) increases the risk of acquiring infections. To protect children from injury, you should assess for the following hazards: choking and suffocation (especially in babies and toddlers), and accidents such as falls, burns and scalds, poisoning, and road accidents. The necessary precautions must be taken to prevent accidents.

Shelter and suitable clothing

Babies, especially newborns, lose heat very quickly, especially through the head, and this can quickly become a life-threatening situation. The room temperature in the setting should be maintained at between 18–21 °C. Babies need to be kept warm but not too hot, especially when sleeping. Rooms for sleeping babies should be kept at a temperature between 16–20 °C. Daytime clothes should be adapted to the stage of mobility and independence of the child: for example, a dress will hinder a young girl trying to crawl; dungarees may prove difficult for a toddler to manage when being toilet-trained. Clothes which are appropriate for the weather should be chosen: for example, children need to be protected from the sun and should wear wide brimmed-hats with neck shields; they need warm gloves, scarves and woolly or fleece hats in cold, windy weather and waterproof coats and footwear when out in the rain.

Fresh air and sunlight

Children benefit from being outside in the fresh air for a while every day. When air is trapped in a building it becomes stale, the level of humidity rises and there is an increased risk of infections spreading. Adequate ventilation within the setting is important to disperse bacteria or viruses transmitted through sneezing or coughing. Make sure that windows are opened to let in fresh air to the setting, but ensure that there are no draughts.

Follow the rules for sun safety and protection in Chapter 4, page 163.

How to identify individual care needs

Mia Kellmer Pringle (1920–1983) has suggested that there are four **significant developmental needs** which have to be met from birth. These are the need for love and security, new experiences, praise and recognition, and responsibility.

The need for love and security

This is probably the most important need as it provides the basis for all later relationships. The young child instinctively wants to move away and become more independent, but separating from the parent figure may be difficult. Each child deals with this challenge in his or her own way.

- **Security**: in their first year, their need for security may be met by having a comfort blanket or a favourite toy – Winnicott called this a transitional object (see Chapter 2).
- **Routine**: another aspect of the child's need for love and security is the need for routine and predictability. This is why having daily routines is so important in child care. By meeting children's need for routine, carers are helping the child to feel acknowledged and independent, and this increases their self-esteem.
- **Attachment**: like Bowlby, Pringle recognised the child's need to have a steady, durable and caring relationship with empathetic adults. A continuous, reliable, loving relationship, first within the family unit, then with a growing number of others, can meet this need. It can give the child a sense of self-worth and identity. In early years settings, the key worker system helps to meet this need.

The need for new experiences

New experiences are a fundamental requirement for cognitive development. Children learn from their experiences. In early life it is largely through play and language that the child explores the world and learns to cope with it. As children pass through each stage of development they often return and work on a previous level in a new way. For experiences to be meaningful, they must extend what children have already learned; they should present children with social, intellectual and physical challenges.

The need for praise and recognition

Growing up requires an enormous amount of learning – emotional, social and intellectual. Consequently, strong incentives are necessary for children to continue through the difficulties and conflicts that they will inevitably encounter. The most effective incentives are praise and recognition sustained over time.

- **Self-fulfilling prophecy**: children feel like failures when they cannot live up to the unrealistic hopes of their parents and are less likely to repeat their efforts. The lower the expectation of the carer, the lower the level of effort and achievement of the child – sometimes called the self-fulfilling prophecy.
- **Intrinsic motivation**: if you make children feel anxious when they have not succeeded, they will avoid activities likely to lead to failure. It is important to praise children appropriately when they try hard or have achieved something new, however small it might seem. This will motivate children to greater effort and lead to the desire to achieve something for its own sake; this is called intrinsic motivation.

The need for responsibility

Being responsible involves knowing what is to be done and how to do it. Children have different levels of understanding at different ages. Your role is to structure the environment to provide challenging tasks according to their different interests and ability levels. The need for responsibility is met by allowing children to gain personal independence, first through learning to look after themselves in matters of everyday care; then through a gradual extension of responsibility over other areas until they have the freedom and ability to decide on their own actions. Cooperation rather than competition allows children more freedom to accept and exercise responsibility. You can help by building group work into your planning activities.

Case Study   Assessing needs

Jack is an only child who lives with his young mother, Samantha, in a small flat in an inner-city area. Jack's mother is at her wit's end with the daily effort of coping with Jack's behaviour. Every weekday, Samantha drops Jack off at his childminder's house at 8.15 am and goes to a department store where she works as a catering assistant. She picks him up again at 5.45 pm and rushes home to prepare the evening meal. Jack always watches television while she cooks and then they eat their meal together. As soon as he has finished, Jack starts demanding attention.

Case Study | Assessing needs (cont.)

First he wants a story, then he wants to play a space adventure game that his grandma gave him; and then he starts throwing his toys around. Samantha usually reacts to his demands by shutting him in his room and telling him that he can only come out again when he has learned how to behave. At other times she threatens to cancel the Sunday outings with his father. Weekends are usually taken up with household chores. Jack's father takes him to the park or to his grandparents' house on Sundays. Jack loves these visits, but Samantha finds that he demands even more of her attention when he comes home.

1 Look at the four needs described above. For each need, list the possible consequences of failure to meet that need – in terms of the effects on the child.

2 Identify any needs which are not being met for Jack's healthy development. Try to think of ways in which all the needs could be met, both for Jack and for his mother, Samantha.

Activities that support and maintain daily living for children

Activities should be planned and organised around the needs of individual babies and children. They should ensure that the personal care needs of every baby or child are met in a positive environment.

Factors to take into consideration when planning and implementing routines include:

- sleep, rest and stimulation
- feeding
- nappy changes
- play preferences
- stage of development.

For more information on these, see page 208.

Figure 8.7 Young children like to take control over their own daily routines

Promoting and supporting children's independence and self-care

It is important to provide physical care for children which is appropriate to their individual needs and their stage of development. The routine care of children's skin, hair and teeth is discussed in Chapter 4.

As they grow and develop, young children should be encouraged to develop self-care skills in their personal care routines. These skills include being able to:

- wash their hands
- use the toilet independently
- dress themselves
- brush their hair
- pour drinks and to feed themselves.

Many of these skills are learned through children copying adult behaviour.

Supporting independence and self-care

Children like to feel independent, but sometimes they need an adult's encouragement to feel that they are capable and that adults believe that they can do it. Teaching independence with self-care skills such as hand-washing, brushing teeth, and dressing and undressing is an important step in development that can be achieved when children are supported in a positive and encouraging way.

Hand-washing

Hand-washing is an important skill that children need to learn. It can be made into a fun activity by singing 'This is the way we wash/dry our hands … on a cold/hot and frosty/sunny morning'. Children soon learn that hand-washing is a routine task that must always be done after going to the toilet, before meals and after playing outdoors.

Dressing and undressing

Children need plenty of time and support to learn how to dress and undress themselves. You can help by breaking the process down into steps and encouraging them when they have mastered the first step by offering descriptive praise.

Toileting

It is important to encourage self-care skills when children are using the toilet independently. They should be encouraged to pull their own pants down and shown how to wipe their bottoms – for example, showing girls how to wipe from the front to the back. You also need children to learn that going to the toilet is a private activity and to withdraw by partially closing the door while remaining nearby in case help is needed.

Brushing teeth

It is essential to establish a tooth-brushing routine. Children should brush after meals, after snacks, and before bedtime, so that it becomes a lifelong habit. Offering children a choice during routines increases the likelihood that they will do the activity and gives them a sense of control. So for example, when brushing teeth, you could say, 'Do you want to use the minty toothpaste or the strawberry toothpaste?'

Engaging with children during care routines to support their learning and development

Encourage

It is very important that you encourage *all* attempts when the child is first learning how to do a routine. If you discourage children because it was not done *quite* right, their attempts at trying might stop.

Practice makes perfect

Remember that young children need a lot of practice (and support) before they are able to carry out new tasks independently. As children gain the skills required for the task, we need to slow down the routine and expect that it might take extra time to complete.

Step by step

Break down activities and tasks and activities into easy, manageable steps; for example:

- Cut food up into bite-size pieces.
- Have well-defined places to pack away toys.
- Use a non-slip mat under a baby's bowl when feeding.
- Use child-size cutlery and a drinking cup with a lid to avoid spills.
- Use a footstool to reach the bathroom basin.
- Use small steps and a toilet seat to make the child feel more secure when going to the 'big' toilet.
- Choose clothing with bigger buttons and shoes with velcro fastenings.

Support

It is important to let children know that you understand their feelings when they are becoming frustrated, and that you will support them so that they feel successful. For example: 'I know it's hard to get your hands really dry; let me help'.

Praise

Praise every little attempt to do any step. Attention to a child's use of a new skill will strengthen that skill. Effective praise is **descriptive praise**; for example, 'Thank you for putting your cup on the side there – it stopped it from being knocked over,' or 'Putting your shoes on all by yourself so quickly was great as now we have more time to play outside'. Children will learn that when you offer descriptive praise (rather than just saying 'Clever boy'), you are teaching them what you like and why you liked it. They are more likely to do it again.

Modelling

First, model how to do the first step and then say, 'Now you show me'. Show one step at a time, allowing time for the child to process the information and imitate what you did before moving to the next step.

Guidelines for promoting self-reliance skills throughout childhood

Babies:

- Encourage babies to cooperate when getting them dressed and undressed – for example, by pushing their arms through sleeves and pulling off their socks.
- Provide finger foods from about eight months and tolerate mess when babies are feeding themselves.
- Set out a variety of toys to encourage them to make choices.

Children aged between two and four years:

- Provide a range of activities – both indoors and outdoors.
- Encourage children to help tidy away toys.
- Allow children to have a free choice in their play.
- Encourage children in self-care skills – washing hands, brushing hair and getting dressed; be patient and provide them with adequate time.
- Build choice into routines such as meal and snack times.
- Encourage children to enjoy simple cooking activities.

Children aged between five and eight years:

- Provide activities which promote problem-solving skills, such as investigating volume and capacity in sand or water play.
- Allow children to take responsibility for set tasks – such as wiping the tables, caring for plants, etc.
- Encourage them to learn specific skills – such as using scissors and threading large needles.
- Allow children the opportunity to make choices and encourage them to assess risks when supervised.

Section 3: How to work effectively in multi-professional teams to support the care of children

How to work with colleagues in multi-professional teams

Practitioners working in early years settings liaise with members of different teams. These include professionals from:

- **health**: health visitors, speech therapists, physiotherapists, play specialists, school nurses, etc.
- **education**: teachers, specialist teachers, educational psychologists, educational welfare officers, governors, etc.
- **social services**: social workers, outreach workers, etc.

Children's Trusts comprise multi-professional teams of social workers, early years practitioners, learning mentors, education welfare officers, and nurses.

The Sure Start projects for children under five years and their parents are organised on a multi-professional basis, with social workers, health visitors, outreach workers, and early years workers sharing their perceptions and skills.

Supportive and effective relationships need to be developed with all these professionals and with parents too.

The importance of valuing and respecting families, colleagues and other professionals

We all have different views about how we conduct our lives. It is inevitable that every practitioner will encounter colleagues with different backgrounds, beliefs and outlooks on life. Regardless of your own view, you should always respect the views of others. This involves:

- not passing judgement on the way in which other people live
- avoiding stereotyping people on the basis of age, sex or ethnicity (or colour) (see Chapter 1)
- not trying to impose your views on others.

Only if people feel that their individual values and beliefs are respected will they develop the confidence to express themselves freely and to make choices.

Procedures and working methods in a variety of settings

Practitioners need to be able to work independently, as well as in a team. Positive feedback about their role and contribution to the setting is important in order to develop an *effective team approach* and for each individual to be seen as a valued member of the team. Clear communication and expectations, particularly about behaviour management, are necessary in order to provide a consistent approach. In working with other multidisciplinary professionals, it is important to define your role and responsibilities, together with those of others within the team and other agencies.

How communication and confidentiality are managed within the team

In working with other professionals, practitioners must:

- understand what information other organisations can offer and share with individuals, families, carers, groups and communities
- work effectively with others to improve services offered to individuals, families, carers, groups and communities.

Supportive and effective relationships need to be developed with all these professionals and with parents too. The need for each practitioner to have effective communication and teamwork skills is therefore important. (See Chapter 1 for information on developing effective communication skills.)

Confidentiality in a multi-professional team

It is essential to maintain confidentiality when working with children and young people, as it imposes a boundary on the amount of personal information and data that can be disclosed without consent. Confidentiality arises where a person disclosing personal information reasonably expects his or her privacy to be protected, such as in a relationship of trust. It is useful to understand fully the meaning of the terms 'consent', 'disclosure' ('allegation') and 'privacy'.

Consent

Consent means agreement to an action based on knowledge of what the action involves and its likely consequences. For example, information on a child should only be collected and stored with the consent of the child's parents or carers – and they should have free access to this information on request. The only exceptions to the rule of consent are the very small number of cases where the child might otherwise be at risk of immediate and significant harm if you shared a piece of information with the parent.

Disclosure (allegation)

A safeguarding allegation means the giving out of information that might commonly be kept secret, usually voluntarily or to be in compliance with legal regulations or workplace rules. Allegation used to be known as disclosure. For example, a child tells an adult something that causes him or her to be concerned about the child's safety and wellbeing.

Privacy

Privacy refers to the right of an individual or group to stop information about themselves from becoming known to people other than those to whom they choose to give the information. For example, when former Prime Minister Tony Blair's ex-nanny wrote a book about life at Number 10 Downing Street, the Blairs took swift legal action to prevent details being leaked to the press. Tony Blair stated, 'We will do whatever it takes to protect our children's privacy.'

The right to confidentiality is not absolute

When working within a multi-professional team, private information about the child or young person may often be shared with other professional persons within the team. The obligation to preserve the child's confidentiality then binds *all* professionals equally. Records should only show information which is essential to provide the service, and in many instances should be available to the scrutiny of the child and his or her family (for example, patients have the right to see their medical records).

The roles and responsibilities of other professionals

Working in the early years is increasingly about coordinating services for the benefit of children and their families. This makes new demands on early years practitioners. It is very important that you are confident about your own training and expertise. For example, if you are a child's key person, you will know a great deal about the child's development, learning, and emotional wellbeing. You will need to communicate what you know in a concise and clear way. If an assessment of the child's development is needed, you could offer records in the form of observations and assessments for your setting or school. It will also be important that you are able to listen carefully and take note of what other professionals have to say; for example, a paediatric dietician may need you to keep an accurate record of what a child is eating in nursery, and may ask you to follow a particular approach to encourage a child to eat more healthily. It is important that families do not get conflicting advice from different professionals, so you will need to follow the dietician's advice and avoid putting across your own personal views. If you feel there is a conflict between what you are being asked to do, and what you see as good early years practice, it is important to discuss this with your manager, headteacher, or SENCO.

Assessment practice

Unit 8

Collate evidence and information relating to the care of children in different settings, including:

- the role of the practitioner in caring for children

- how care for children may be provided within families and society

- a summary of the main regulations that govern the care of children in different types of settings

- the daily care needs of children of different ages

- the key issues which enable multi-professional teams to work together

- an evaluation of ways to work effectively in multi-professional teams to support the care of children.

 Useful resources

Organisations and websites

The **National Children's Bureau** works to advance the wellbeing of all children and young people across every aspect of their lives: **www.ncb.org.uk**

Child Care is a monthly magazine for all childminders, nannies and child carers: **www.professionalchildcare.co.uk**

Directgov: For information on statutory care provision: **www.direct.gov.uk**

Every Child Matters: This is a framework in England designed to ensure quality provision of children's play and learning.

Book
Bruce, T. (2011) *Early Childhood Education* (fourth edition). London: Hodder Education.

9 Care of sick children: Unit 11

Learning outcomes

In this chapter, you will learn:

1. The principles of promotion and maintenance of health.
2. The causes and prevention of ill health.
3. The effects of ill health on children and families.
4. The responses to childhood illness.
5. The role of the adult in supporting children and their families suffering from childhood illnesses.

Section 1: The principles of promotion and maintenance of health

The key factors in the promotion of community health and health education

What is health?

The World Health Organization (WHO) defines health as a 'state of complete physical, mental, and social wellbeing, and not merely the absence of disease or infirmity'. Health and social wellbeing can best be viewed as a holistic concept, encompassing the different aspects of a person's health needs.

Aspects of health

- **Physical health**: this is the easiest aspect of health to measure, and is concerned with the physical functioning of the body.
- **Emotional health**: how we express emotions such as joy, grief, frustration and fear; this includes coping strategies for anxiety and stress.
- **Mental health**: this relates to our ability to organise our thoughts coherently, and is closely linked to emotional and social health.
- **Social health**: how we relate to others and form relationships.
- **Spiritual health**: this includes religious beliefs and practices, as well as personal codes of conduct and the quest for inner peace.
- **Environmental health**: an individual's health depends also on the health of the society in which they live; for example in famine areas health is denied to the inhabitants, and unemployed people cannot be healthy in a society which only values those who work.

The promotion of community health

Health education is a method of self-empowerment; it enables people to take more control over their own health and that of their children. Health education can be divided into primary, secondary and tertiary categories.

Primary health education is directed at healthy people. It is a prophylactic (or preventative) measure that aims to prevent ill health from arising in the first instance. The areas of primary prevention in children are:

- sound nutrition and diet, that is, healthy eating
- immunisation
- the prevention of emotional and behavioural problems
- dental prophylaxis, that is, the prevention of tooth decay
- the prevention of childhood accidents
- basic hygiene.

Secondary health education is directed at people with a health problem or a reversible condition.

It emphasises the importance of the early detection of defects and ways in which people can make lifestyle changes to improve their condition.

Screening: by routinely examining apparently healthy people, screening aims to detect either those who are likely to develop a particular disease or those in whom the disease is already present but has not yet produced symptoms. Screening may detect a problem with hearing, sight, or physical, emotional or behavioural development.

Reducing behaviours likely to damage health: for example, overweight people can be encouraged to change their dietary habits, or a smoker to quit smoking.

Tertiary health education is directed at those whose ill health has not been, or could not be, prevented and who cannot be completely cured. However, the quality of their lives can still be influenced; for example:

- Children with brain damage can achieve their own potential with good support in communication and structured play.
- Patients dying of cancer can do so with dignity if their pain is kept under control.

Rehabilitation programmes are chiefly concerned with tertiary health education.

The aims of health education

- To provide information and to raise awareness.
- To change people's behaviour and attitudes.
- To meet national and local health targets, for example, promoting self-examination of the breasts to aid in the early detection of breast cancer.

Five approaches to health education

1 **The medical approach**: this approach promotes medical intervention to prevent or improve ill-health; it uses a persuasive and authoritarian method – for example, persuading parents to bring their children for immunisation.

2 **The behaviour change approach**: this approach aims to change people's attitudes and behaviour, so that they adopt a healthy lifestyle – for example, teaching people how to give up smoking.

3 **The educational approach**: this approach aims to give information and to ensure understanding of health issues. Information is presented in as value-free a way as possible, so that the people targeted feel free to make their own decisions; for example, clients are given information about the effects of smoking and can then make a choice to stop smoking if they want to.

4 **The client-directed approach**: this approach aims to work with clients so that they can identify what they want to know about, and make their own decisions and choices; for example, the anti-smoking issue is only considered if the clients identify it as a concern.

5 **The social change approach**: this approach aims to change the environment to facilitate the choice of healthier lifestyles; for example, the change taking place in school dinners (see page 414) and the no-smoking policy implemented in all restaurants, bars and workplaces in the UK.

Advertisers often use scare tactics to get the message across; this has been called the **fear creation approach**.

Health education campaigns

Recent health education campaigns of particular relevance to children include:

- **The Water is Cool in School Campaign** aims to improve the quality of provision and access to fresh drinking water for children in UK primary and secondary schools.
- **The School Fruit and Vegetable Scheme (SFV)** is part of the **5 A DAY** programme to increase fruit and vegetable consumption. Under the **SFV** Scheme, all four- to six-year-old children in LEA-maintained infant, primary and special schools are entitled to a free piece of fruit or vegetable each school day.
- **'Sleep safe, sleep sound, share a room with me'** is the latest campaign from the Foundation for the Study of Infant Deaths; leaflets and posters have been sent to all midwives and health visitors.

Figure 9.1 A poster campaign

- **Birth to Five** is a comprehensive guide to parenthood and the first five years of a child's life. It covers child health, nutrition and safety and is given free to all first-time mothers in England.

Health education by private companies

Manufacturers of 'healthy' products such as wholemeal bread or high-protein-balanced foods for babies often promote their products both by advertising and by using educational leaflets. Such leaflets are offered free in health clinics, postnatal wards and supermarkets. Examples of this type of health promotion are:

- booklets on 'feeding your baby' published by formula milk manufacturers
- leaflets on child safety on the roads produced by manufacturers of child car seats and harnesses
- the promotion of herbal remedies to encourage a stress-free lifestyle.

There are strict controls over the claims that manufacturers can make about the health-giving properties of their product.

Health education by the voluntary sector

Voluntary organisations are in a strong position to enhance the health of the population. They use a variety of methods:

- **Self-help** – some organisations bring people together to share common problems and to help them to gain more confidence and control over their own health.
- **Direct service provision** – the British Red Cross has a network of shops for the rental of equipment in the home (including walking frames, commodes and chairs).
- **Community health** – voluntary organisations work with local people to identify and solve problems affecting their health. GASP – Group Against Smoking in Public – is a Bristol-based group that campaigned for an increase in the provision of no-smoking areas in public areas and has a range of programmes to help people to quit smoking.
- **Health education and promotion** – some organisations undertake fund-raising to provide support for research. The Wellcome Trust is a medical research charity that provides funding for research in the biomedical sciences.

Health education leading to preventative action

All **immunisation** programmes are an attempt to prevent disease and, therefore, to promote health – both in the individual and in the general population. The campaign to prevent **sudden infant death syndrome** is another example of an important health message reaching those who need it.

Research Activity

Health product advertising

1 Collect advertisements from magazines and newspapers for any product that claims to promote better health. Discuss their aims and objectives:

   • Which groups are they targeting?

   • Do they give any useful information on healthy living, in addition to information on using their product?

2 Find out about the advertising standards which apply to health product advertising.

3 Which television advertising campaigns for such products are memorable? Why?

Discussion point

In small groups, discuss a serial on television or radio. List all the health promotion messages you can remember that have been contained within the storylines.

1 Do you think that television or radio programmes are a good way of getting a health message across?

2 Does the inclusion of a telephone helpline number detract from or enhance the impact of a health problem in a storyline?

3 Does the programme mirror real life or is it viewed as escapism?

Your role in child health education

There are many ways in which you can contribute to health education programmes in early years settings. The most important part of your role is to be a **good role model** for children. Opportunities for teaching children about health and safety are covered in the guidelines box below.

Guidelines for teaching children about health and safety

• Provide healthy meals and snacks.

• Practise good hygiene routines, such as hand-washing and teeth-brushing.

• Choose books and displays which reinforce healthy lifestyles.

• Use drama and music sessions to encourage children to express their feelings in a safe environment.

• Create interesting board games with a healthy theme, such as how to avoid accidents when playing outside.

• Welcome visitors to talk about their work in health care, for example, invite a health visitor or dentist to explain the importance of good hygiene routines.

• Demonstrate safety and hygiene routines, for example, a road safety officer or police officer could visit the setting to teach children how to cross the road safely.

• Make the home area into a hospital ward and encourage role play as patients, nurses and doctors.

Preventing ill health through immunisation

Immunisation is a way of protecting children against serious disease. Once children have been immunised, their bodies can fight those diseases if they come into contact with them.

If a child is not immunised they will be at risk from catching the disease and will rely on other people immunising their children to avoid becoming infected.

An immunisation programme protects people against specific diseases by reducing the number of people getting the disease and preventing it being passed on. With some diseases – like smallpox or polio – it is possible to eliminate them completely.

Reasons for immunisation against disease

Not every disease that affects children can be immunised against. There is no routine vaccination for chicken pox or scarlet fever in the UK, although the chicken pox vaccine is offered with the MMR in some other countries. The following diseases are all included in the NHS programme of routine immunisation.

Diphtheria

A bacterial infection which starts with a sore throat but can rapidly get worse, leading to severe breathing difficulties. It can also damage the heart and nervous system.

Pertussis (or whooping cough)

A bacterial infection that can cause long bouts of coughing and choking, making it hard to breathe. It is not usually serious in older children, but it can be very serious and can kill babies under one year old. It can last for up to ten weeks.

Hib

Hib (*Haemophilus influenzae type b*) is an infection that can cause a number of major illnesses like blood poisoning, pneumonia and meningitis. All of these illnesses can kill if not treated quickly. The Hib vaccine protects the child against only *one* type of **meningitis** (Hib). It does not protect against any other type of meningitis.

Measles

The measles virus is highly contagious and causes a high fever and rash. Around one in 15 of all children who get measles are at risk of complications including chest infections, fits and brain damage. In very serious cases, measles kills. In the year before

Routine childhood immunisation programme		
When to immunise	**What vaccine is given**	**How it is given**
2, 3 and 4 months old	Diphtheria, tetanus, pertussis (whooping cough), polio and Hib(DTaP/IPV/Hib)	One injection
	MenC	One injection
Around 13 months	Measles, mumps and rubella (MMR)	One injection
3 years 4 months old or soon after	Diphtheria, tetanus, pertussis and polio (dTaP/IPV or DTaP/IPV)	One injection
	Measles, mumps and rubella (MMR)	One injection
10 to 14 years old (and sometimes shortly after birth)	BCG (against tuberculosis)	Skin test then, if needed, one injection
13 to 18 years old	Tetanus, diphtheria and polio (Td/IPV)	One injection

Table 9.1 Recommended immunisation schedule

the MMR vaccine was introduced in the UK (1988), 16 children died from measles.

Pneumococcal disease

This is the term used to describe infections caused by the bacterium *Streptococcus pneumoniae*. It can pneumonia, septicaemia (blood poisoning) and meningitis, and is also one of the most common bacterial causes of ear infections. The bacterium is becoming increasingly resistant to antibiotics in the UK and worldwide.

Tetanus

A bacterial infection caused when germs found in soil and manure get into the body through open cuts and burns. Tetanus is a painful disease which affects the muscles and can cause breathing problems.

Polio

It is a highly infectious viral disease spread mainly through close contact with an infected person. The polio virus attacks the nervous system and can paralyse muscles permanently. If it attacks the muscles in the chest, or those that control swallowing, it can be fatal.

Meningococcal disease

This is one of the serious causes of **meningitis** – an inflammation of the lining of the brain – and serious blood infections in children. Although fairly rare now, before the introduction of the vaccine it was the most common killer in the one to five-year age group. The Men C vaccine protects the child against only *one* type of meningitis (meningococcal).

Mumps

Mumps is caused by a virus which can lead to fever, headache, and painful, swollen glands in the face, neck and jaw. It can result in permanent deafness, viral meningitis (swelling of the lining of the brain) and encephalitis. Rarely, it causes painful swelling of the testicles in males and the ovaries in females.

Rubella

(German measles) is caused by a virus. In children it is usually mild and can go unnoticed. Rubella infection in the first three months of pregnancy causes damage to the unborn baby in nine out of ten cases; it can seriously damage their sight, hearing, heart and brain. In the five years before the MMR vaccine was introduced, about 43 babies a year were born in the UK with congenital rubella syndrome.

Carrying out immunisations

Immunisations are usually carried out in child health clinics. The doctor will discuss any fears the parents may have about particular vaccines. No vaccine is completely risk-free, and parents are asked to sign a consent form prior to immunisations being given. Immunisations are only given if the child is well, and may be postponed if the child has had a reaction to any previous immunisation or if the child is taking any medication that might interfere with their ability to fight infection. The effects of the disease are usually far worse than any side effects of a vaccine.

The advantages of immunisation	The disadvantages of immunisation
Having children immunised at an early age means they are well protected by the time they start playgroup or school, where they are in contact with many children.	Immunisation always includes the possibility of **side effects**.
Children who are not immunised run a risk of catching diseases and having serious complications.	The possible risks that follow certain childhood immunisations must be weighed up against the possible risks of complications of the childhood illness. For example, with the MMR vaccine there is a risk of one in 1,000 of febrile convulsions (fits). However, if a child catches the measles disease, the risk of convulsions is one in 200 people with the disease.
Immunisation also protects those children who are unable to receive immunisation, by providing what is called **herd immunity**.	

Care of children after immunisations

Children should be observed closely after any immunisation:

- If fever occurs, keep the child cool, offer plenty to drink and give children's paracetamol.
- If the temperature remains high or if there are any other symptoms, such as convulsions, call a doctor immediately.

Note: take care when changing the baby's nappy after the 5-in-1 vaccine. The **polio vaccine** is passed into a child's nappies for up to six weeks after the vaccine is given. If someone who has not been immunised against polio changes the child's nappy, it is possible for them to be affected by the polio virus. Carers should be careful to wash their hands thoroughly, and the child should not be taken swimming during this time.

How immunity to disease and infection can be acquired

Babies are born with some **natural immunity.** They are:

- able to make their own infection-fighting cells
- further protected by **antibodies** and other substances found in breast milk.

A child's own experiences of infection boost his or her immunity. For some infections (for example, measles) immunity is lifelong, while for others it is short-lived. Certain illnesses such as the common cold are caused by one of several strains of virus, which is why having one cold does not automatically prevent another one later. Sometimes the immune system does not work properly, as in the case of **HIV/AIDS** infection and some other rare conditions. Sometimes it *over*-works and causes **allergy**. It can also be affected by emotional distress and physical exhaustion.

There are two types of immunity: **active immunity** and **passive immunity**. As discussed above, immunity can be induced by contact with an infection. It can also be induced by **immunisation** against certain infective agents.

Active immunity

Active immunity is when a vaccine triggers the **immune system** to produce **antibodies** against the disease as though the body had been infected with it. This also teaches the body's immune system how to produce the appropriate antibodies quickly. If the immunised person then comes into contact with the disease itself, their immune system will recognise it and immediately produce the antibodies needed to fight it.

Passive immunity

Passive immunity is provided when the body is given **antibodies** rather than producing them itself. A newborn baby has passive immunity to several diseases, such as measles, mumps and rubella, from antibodies passed from its mother via the placenta. Passive immunity only lasts for a few weeks or months. In the case of measles, mumps and rubella it may last up to one year in infants; this is why MMR is given just after a child's first birthday.

Herd immunity

If enough people in a community are immunised against certain diseases, then it is more difficult for that disease to get passed between those who are not immunised; this is known as herd immunity. Herd immunity does not apply to all diseases because they are not all passed on from person to person. For example, tetanus can only be caught from spores in the ground.

> ### ✓ Progress check
>
> - Babies are born with some natural immunity and are further protected by antibodies and other substances found in breast milk.
> - Active immunity is when the immune system produces antibodies against a disease as though the body had been infected with it.
> - Passive immunity occurs when the body is given antibodies rather than producing them itself.
> - Herd immunity occurs when enough people in a community are immunised against certain diseases to prevent the spread of infection.

Key terms

Antibodies Antibodies are proteins made by the body's immune system.

Immunisation Immunisation protects children (and adults) against harmful infections before they come into contact with them in the community.

Immunity A condition of being able to resist a particular infectious disease.

Vaccine A substance that stimulates the body's immune response in order to prevent or control an infection.

Activity

Information on immunisation

1 Read through the section on common childhood diseases and the information on immunisation.

2 Prepare a booklet for parents on those childhood diseases for which there is immunisation. Include the following information:
   - the causes, signs and symptoms of the diseases
   - possible complications and treatment
   - the immunisation schedule
   - contra-indications to immunisation
   - where to go for further advice and help on immunisation.

Make the booklet as eye-catching as possible, using illustrations.

Child health surveillance

Surveillance is defined as close supervision or observation, and its primary purpose is to detect any abnormality in development so that the child can be offered treatment. For example, early detection of a hearing impairment gives the young child a better chance of receiving appropriate treatment and/or specialist education.

Personal Child Health Record

All parents are issued with a Personal Child Health Record that enables them to keep a record of their child's development (see Figure 9.2). This form is completed by doctors, health visitors and parents, and is a useful source of information if the child is admitted to hospital or is taken ill when the family are away from home.

Developmental reviews

Parents will want to know if their child has problems as soon as possible: it is easier to come to terms with a serious problem in a young baby than in an older child. Health professionals should always take the parent's worries seriously and never assume that parents are fussy, neurotic or over-anxious. Early childhood practitioners are usually very astute in recognising abnormalities in development because of their experience with a wide variety of children.

Developmental reviews give parents an opportunity to say what they have noticed about their child. They can also discuss anything that concerns them about their child's health and behaviour. Child development is reviewed by doctors and health visitors, either in the child's home or in health clinics. The areas that are looked at are:

- **gross motor skills** – sitting, standing, walking, running
- **fine motor skills** – handling toys, stacking bricks, doing up buttons and tying shoelaces (gross and fine manipulative skills)
- **speech and language** – including hearing
- **vision** – including squint
- **social behaviour** – how the child interacts with others, such as family and friends.

Early detection is important as:

- early treatment may reduce or even avoid permanent damage in some conditions
- an early diagnosis (of an inherited condition) may allow genetic counselling and so avoid the birth of another child with a disabling condition.

Screening as part of surveillance

The aim of a screening programme is to examine all children at risk from a certain condition; the term **screening** refers to the examination of apparently healthy children to distinguish those who probably have a condition from those who probably do not.

6–8 WEEK REVIEW

This review is done by your health visitor or a doctor. Below are some things you may want to talk about when you see them. However, if you are worried about your child's health, growth or development you can contact you health visitor or doctor at any time.

Do you feel well yourself?	yes ☐	no ☐	not sure ☐
Do you have any worries about feeding your baby?	yes ☐	no ☐	not sure ☐
Do you have any concerns about your baby's weight gain?	yes ☐	no ☐	not sure ☐
Does your baby watch your face and follow with his/her eyes?	yes ☐	no ☐	not sure ☐
Does your baby turn towards the light?	yes ☐	no ☐	not sure ☐
Does your baby smile at you?	yes ☐	no ☐	not sure ☐
Do your think your baby can hear you?	yes ☐	no ☐	not sure ☐
Is your baby startled by loud noises?	yes ☐	no ☐	not sure ☐
Are there any problems in looking after your baby?	yes ☐	no ☐	not sure ☐
Do you have any worries about your baby?	yes ☐	no ☐	not sure ☐

Any other issues you would like to discuss? ....
....
....

Results of newborn bloodspot screening

Condition	Results received? yes / no / not done	Follow up required? no / yes & reason	If follow up, outcome of follow up
PKU			
Hypothyroidism			
Sickle Cell			
Cystic Fibrosis			
Other			

24

Figure 9.2 Sample page from a Personal Child Health Record

Hearing defects are often detected in this way at one of the routine checks carried out at the Child Surveillance Clinic (see below).

Screening for hearing impairment

The Otoacoustic Emissions Test

Newborn babies are usually screened using the otoacoustic emissions (OAE) test. A tiny earpiece is placed in the baby's outer ear and quiet clicking sounds are played through it. This should produce reaction sounds in a part of the ear called the cochlea, and the computer can record and analyse these. It is painless and can be done while the baby is asleep. Sometimes clear results are not obtained from the OAE test. Then a different method can be used, called:

The Automated Auditory Brainstem Response (AABR)

Small sensors are placed on the baby's head and neck, and soft headphones are placed over the ears. Quiet clicking sounds are played through the earphones and a computer analyses the response in the brain, using information from the sensors.

The Hearing 'Sweep' Test

At school age (between four and five) all children should have the hearing 'sweep' test. This is an audiogram test across the main speech frequencies (high and low pitches) and using sounds of different volumes (loudness), which are played through earphones. The child has to indicate whether they have heard them, or perform various actions depending on the type of noise.

Screening for visual disorders

Screening tests for visual problems are carried out on all children at: the newborn examination, the six-to-eight week review, and the pre-school (or school-entry) vision check.

The newborn examination and six-to-eight week review

The eyes of newborn babies are examined for any obvious physical defects, include cross-eyes, cloudiness (a sign of cataracts), and redness. This includes:

- **The red reflex**: this test uses an **ophthalmoscope**. Light is directed into the baby's eyes and a red reflection should be seen as the light is reflected back. If the reflection is white instead, the child will be referred to a specialist immediately, as it can be a sign of a cataract or other eye condition.
- The **pupil reflex** is checked by shining a light into each eye from a distance of 10 cm. The pupils should automatically shrink in response to brightness.

General inspection of the eyes may suggest other conditions. For example, one eye larger than the other may indicate glaucoma.

A **specialist examination** is indicated in babies who:

- have an abnormality detected in the above routine examinations, *or*
- have a known higher risk of visual disorders. For example, low birth weight babies at risk of retinopathy of prematurity; babies who have a close relative with an inheritable eye disorder; and babies with known hearing impairment.

Pre-school vision screening

This takes place when the child is aged between four and five years. The school entry vision check which was carried out by school nurses is being replaced by a vision check carried out by an **orthoptist**. The main aim is to detect amblyopia. **Amblyopia**, sometimes known as 'lazy eye', is reduced visual acuity, not correctable with glasses, in an otherwise 'healthy' eye. The brain has suppressed, or failed to develop, the ability to see properly with the affected eye. The most common cause is a manifest **squint** (strabismus) where there are two competing images, so one is suppressed.

Key terms

Genetic counselling Guidance given (usually by a doctor with experience in genetics) to individuals who are considering having a child but who are concerned because there is a blood relative with an inherited disorder.

Orthoptist A professional who investigates, diagnoses and treats defects of vision and abnormalities of eye movement.

Retinopathy of prematurity An abnormal growth of blood vessels in the retina at the back of a premature baby's eye; when severe it can cause loss of vision.

When do developmental reviews take place?

Parents are usually invited to developmental reviews when their child is:

- six to eight weeks old
- six to nine months old
- 18 to 24 months old
- three to three-and-a-half years old
- four-and-a-half to five-and-a-half years old (before or just after the child starts school).

In some parts of the UK, the age that children are reviewed may vary slightly from those given above, especially after the age of three. During a developmental review some health visitors may ask parents or carers questions about their baby; others may ask the child to do simple tasks such as building with blocks or identifying pictures; others may simply watch the child playing or drawing, getting an idea from this observation and from the adult's comments of how the child is doing. If the child's first language is not English, parents may need to ask if development reviews can be carried out with the help of someone who can speak their child's language.

After the child has started school, the **school health service** takes over these reviews.

Neonatal examination

All babies are examined as soon as possible after birth. Both a doctor and a midwife carry out routine examinations: see Figure 9.3.

The face is examined for cleft palate – a gap in the roof of the mouth, and facial paralysis – temporary paralysis after compression of the facial nerve, usually after forceps delivery

Eyes are checked for cataract (a cloudiness of the lens)

Hands are checked for webbing (fingers are joined together at the base) and creases – a single unbroken crease from one side of the palm to the other is a feature of Down's syndrome

The head is checked for size and shape: any marks from forceps delivery are noted

The heart and lungs are checked using a stethoscope; any abnormal findings will be investigated

The neck is examined for any obvious injury to the neck muscles after a difficult delivery

Feet are checked for webbing and talipes (club foot), which needs early treatment

Genitalia and anus are checked for any malformation

Skin – vernix and lanugo may still be present, milia may show on the baby's nose; black babies appear lighter in the first week of life as the pigment, melanin, is not yet at full concentration

The spine is checked for any evidence of spina bifida

Hips are tested for cogenital dislocation using Barlow's test

The abdomen is checked for any abnormality, e.g. pyloric stenosis, where there may be obstruction of the passage of food from the stomach; the umbilical cord is checked for infection

Figure 9.3 Examination of the newborn baby

Key terms

Anterior fontanelle – A diamond-shaped, soft area at the front of the head, just above the brow. It is covered by a tough membrane; you can often see the baby's pulse beating there under the skin. The fontanelle closes between 12 and 18 months of age.

Posterior fontanelle – A small, triangular-shaped soft area near the crown of the head; it is much smaller and less noticeable than the anterior fontanelle.

 ## Progress check

Developmental reviews look at the following areas of development:

- gross and fine motor skills
- communication: speech and language, including hearing
- visual development
- social behaviour.

Early detection of any problems or delays may reduce or even avoid permanent damage in some conditions.

Research Activity

Investigating child health surveillance

Arrange to visit a child health clinic and find out the following information:

1 What surveillance programmes are routinely carried out, and by whom?

2 If further tests are necessary, to whom is the child referred?

3 What records do health visitors maintain?

4 How do health personnel try to ensure equality of access to health surveillance?

The influences on health and access to health care

The environmental factors influencing child health are discussed in Chapter 6.

6- to 8-week check

Parental concerns	Observation	Measurement	Examination
The doctor will ask the parent about: • feeding • bowel actions • sleeping • micturition (passing urine).	While the parent is undressing the baby for examination, the doctor will look out for: • the responsiveness of the baby – smiles, eye contact, attentiveness to parent's voice, etc. • any difficulties the parent has holding the baby – which may indicate maternal depression • jaundice and anaemia. The general appearance of the baby will give an indication of whether he or she is well nourished.	• The baby is weighed naked and the weight is plotted on the growth chart (see Chapter 3). • The head circumference is measured and plotted on the growth chart.	• The eyes are inspected using a light – the baby will turn his or her head and follow a small light beam. An ophthalmoscope is used to check for a cataract. • The heart is auscultated (i.e. listened to with a stethoscope) to exclude any congenital defect. • The hips are manipulated, again to exclude the presence of congenital dislocation of the hips. • The baby is placed prone and will turn his or her head to one side; hands are held with the thumbs inwards and the fingers wrapped around them. • The **posterior fontanelle** is usually closed by now; the **anterior fontanelle** does not close until around 18 months.

Hearing

Most babies will have been screened soon after birth. There is no specific test at this age. The parent is asked if he or she thinks the baby can hear. A baby may startle to a sudden noise or freeze for some sounds.

Health education points

The doctor will discuss the following health topics, give the first immunisation and complete the personal child health record.

• Nutrition: breastfeeding, preparation of formula feeds, specific feeding difficulties.
• Immunisation: discuss any concerns and initiate a programme of vaccinations.
• Passive smoking: babies are at risk of respiratory infections and middle ear disease.
• Illness in babies: how to recognise symptoms.
• Crying: coping with frustration and tiredness.
• Reducing the risk of cot death (SIDS: sudden infant death syndrome).

6- to 9-month check (cont.)

Parental concerns	Observation	Measurement	Examination
The doctor or health visitor will enquire again about any parental concerns.	The doctor will look out for: • socialisation and attachment behaviour • visual behaviour • communication – sounds, expressions and gestures • motor development – sitting, balance, use of hands, any abnormal movement patterns.	Head circumference and weight are plotted on the growth chart.	• Manipulation of the hips is carried out. • The heart is listened to with a stethoscope. • The testes are checked in boys. • The eyes are checked for a squint – if this is present, the child is referred to an ophthalmologist (eye specialist); visual behaviour is checked. • Hearing is *sometimes* tested by the distraction test.

Health education points

- Nutrition: weaning; control of sugar intake.
- Immunisations: check they are up-to-date.
- Teeth: regular brushing once teeth appear; information on fluoride; visit the dentist.
- The need for play and language stimulation.
- Accident prevention.

2-year check

This check is similar to the previous tests. It is often easier for the health visitor to carry out the check during a home visit. The parent is asked about any general concerns. A physical examination is not normally carried out at this age.

- The height is measured if the child is cooperative.
- Weight is only checked if there is reason for concern.
- The parent is asked if there are any concerns about vision and hearing, and the child is referred to a specialist if necessary.
- A check is made that the child is walking and that the gait (manner of walking) is normal.
- Behaviour and any associated problems are discussed (e.g. tantrums, sleep disturbance, poor appetite or food fads).
- The possibility of iron deficiency is considered. It is common at this age and may be a cause of irritability and developmental and behavioural problems, as well as anaemia.

Health education points

- Nutrition and dental care: the child will be referred to the dentist if teeth are obviously decayed.
- Immunisation: check they are up-to-date.
- Common behavioural difficulties, such as temper tantrums, sleep disturbance, toilet training.
- Social behaviour: learning to play with other children and to share possessions.
- Accident prevention.

4- to 5-year check for 'school readiness' (cont.)

Parental concerns	Observation	Measurement	Examination
This check is usually carried out by the GP and the health visitor. The parent is asked if there are any general concerns about the child's progress and development, or any behavioural or emotional problems.	• Motor skills – Can the child walk, run and climb stairs? Does the child tire more quickly compared with other children? • Fine manipulative skills – Can the child control pencils and paintbrushes? • Behaviour – Parents are asked about the child's ability to concentrate, to play with others and to separate from his or her parents without distress. • Vision, language and hearing – Observation and discussion with the parent will determine any problems that may need specialist assessment.	Height and weight are measured and plotted on the growth chart.	• The heart is listened to for any abnormal sounds. • The lungs are listened to for wheezing. • In a boy, the testes will be checked again; if still not descended, he will be referred to a surgeon. • The spine is inspected for signs of curvature or spina bifida occulta. • Blood pressure is usually measured only if the child has a history of renal disease or growth problems.

Health education points

- Immunisation: pre-school booster.
- Dental care: diet – danger of sweets and snacks; brushing teeth; dental decay; visits to the dentist.
- The child's needs for play, conversation and social learning.
- The recognition and management of minor ailments.
- Accident prevention.

8-year check

This is carried out by the school nurse, and parents are encouraged to attend the sessions at school. It involves the following:

- a general review of progress and development; the parent may voice concerns such as bedwetting (enuresis) or food fads
- height and weight are measured
- vision is tested and, if a problem is found, the child is referred to an ophthalmologist or optician.

Health education points

- Accident prevention: particularly safety on the roads and awareness of 'stranger danger'
- Diet
- Exercise
- Dental health.

Hearing

Parents who are concerned that their child is not hearing properly should have access to hearing testing. This is particularly important if the child has had:

- meningitis
- measles
- mumps
- recurrent ear infections or glue ear.

4- to 5-year check for 'school readiness' (cont.)
Speech discrimination test
Any child who is suspected of having any hearing loss or whose language development is delayed may have the speech discrimination test. This involves using a set of toys, each with a single-syllable name – for example, dog, horse, key, tree, spoon, house, cup – which will test the child's ability to hear different consonants – for example, d, g, p, m, s, f and b. The child is gently encouraged to cooperate with the tester and together they name the toys using a normal voice. The child is then asked to find the toys with decreasing voice intensity – for example, 'Show me the house', 'Put the duck in the box'. Each ear is tested through the complete range of sounds.

Table 9.2 Developmental reviews

Access to health care

The families who are most in need of child health surveillance are often those who are least likely to make use of the services provided – this is known as the **inverse care law**. Although children in the UK today enjoy better health than at any other time, the provisions of a National Health Service have not led to equality of health experience. The list below outlines people who might be seen as priority groups by health visitors and the primary health care team when organising caseloads and targeting resources. The health care of such priority groups is difficult and often involves a working partnership with other community services, such as social service departments or housing departments.

Priority groups for health surveillance

- Very young or unsupported parents, particularly those with their first baby.
- Parents thought to be at particular risk of abusing their children.
- Parents who are socially isolated, due to mental-health problems or linguistic or cultural barriers.
- Families living in poor housing, including bed and breakfast accommodation or housing where there is overcrowding.
- Parents with low self-esteem or a lack of confidence.
- Parents with unrealistic expectations about the child, or with a poor understanding of the child's needs.
- Parents and/or children suffering significant bereavement (or separation as a result of a recent divorce).
- Parents who have experienced previous SIDS (sudden infant death syndrome) in the family.

The role of the adult and other professionals in supporting children and their families' health

- **Primary care services** are provided at the first stage of treatment when you are ill: by family doctors, dentists, pharmacists, optometrists and ophthalmic medical practitioners, together with district nurses and health visitors.
- **Secondary care** is the second stage of treatment when you are ill and usually provided by a hospital.
- **Tertiary care** is the third and highly specialised stage of treatment, usually provided in a specialist hospital centre.

The Primary Health Care Team (PHCT)

The PHCT is made up of a team of professionals which generally includes one or more of the following:

- **General practitioner (GP)** or family doctor: cares for all members of the family and can refer for specialist services.
- **Health visitor**: carries out developmental checks and gives advice on all aspects of child care.
- **Practice nurse**: works with particular GP; provides services such as immunisation and asthma and diabetes clinics.
- **Community midwife**: delivers antenatal care and cares for the mother and baby until 10 to 28 days after delivery.
- **District nurse**: cares for clients in their own homes.

Some health authorities also employ a **community paediatric nurse**: a district nurse with special training in paediatrics to care for sick children at home.

Services offered by the Primary Health Care Team

Services will include some or all of the following:

- Child health clinics
- Immunisation clinics
- Family planning clinics
- Community dietician
- Community occupational therapists
- Clinical medical officer (CMO)
- Antenatal clinics
- Specialist clinics, for example, for asthma, diabetes, etc.
- Speech and language therapy
- Community physiotherapists
- Community paediatrician
- Community dental service.

Child health clinics

Child health clinics are often held at the health centre or in a purpose-built centre. In rural areas, the clinic may take turns with other community groups in village halls or community centres. Depending on the population served, clinics may be weekly or fortnightly and are run by health visitors, health care assistants and nursery nurses. A doctor or community paediatrician is usually present at specified times. Services provided at a child health clinic include:

- routine developmental surveillance (or reviews)
- medical examinations
- immunisations
- health promotion advice
- antenatal and parent craft classes.

The School Health Service

The School Health Service is part of the community Child Health Service and has direct links with those who carry out health checks on children before they start school. The aims of the school health service are to:

- ensure that children are physically and emotionally fit so that they can benefit fully from their education and achieve their potential
- prepare them for adult life and to help them achieve the best possible health during the school years and beyond.

Your role in child health screening and surveillance

Throughout your training, you will have learnt about child development and about the importance of knowing what to expect from children at each developmental stage. When working with children, you can use this knowledge and your powers of **skilled observation** to detect any developmental or health problems. Increasingly, trained early years practitioners are being employed in child health clinics to assist doctors and health visitors in carrying out routine screening tests and to offer parents advice on all aspects of child health and development.

Services provided by the School Health Service

The service provides **routine testing for vision, hearing or speech** – to discover which children may need further tests or treatment. If treatment is thought to be required, the child's parents will be informed and consent requested.

The school nurse may work with one or more schools, and provides an important link between the school and health services. School nurses provide the following services:

- growth measurements – height and weight
- advice on management of health conditions; for example, if a child has a long-term illness or special need, they will discuss possible strategies with the child's teacher
- enuresis (bedwetting) support and advice, including providing an enuresis alarm
- immunisation
- advice on health and hygiene, sometimes running workshops or similar sessions
- advice for parents on specific health issues, for example, treating head lice or coping with asthma
- eyesight tests from time to time
- liaison with the school doctor.

The attention of the school doctor is drawn to any possible problems, and parents and the GP or family doctor are informed if any further action is considered necessary. The school doctor visits the school regularly and meets with the school nurse (or health visitor) and with teachers to find out whether any pupils need medical attention. In addition, the doctor reviews the medical notes of all children in Year 1 and of all new pupils transferring to the school.

Parents or carers are usually requested to complete a **health questionnaire** about their child at certain stages and are asked if they would like their child to have a full medical examination. In addition, the school doctor may ask for parental consent to examine a child if his or her medical records are incomplete or if the doctor particularly wishes to check on the child's progress. Parents are invited to be present at any medical examination and kept informed if the school doctor wishes to see their child again or thinks that they should be seen by the family doctor or a specialist.

The **audiometry team** checks children's hearing on a number of occasions before the age of 13 or 14 years. The school doctor will be told if a child seems to have a hearing problem. The doctor will then examine the child and let the family doctor know the result.

The **speech and language therapist** can provide assessment and treatment if the parent, a teacher or the school doctor feels that a child may have a speech or language problem.

Section 2: The causes and prevention of ill health

The causes of ill health

Every aspect of our lives can have an effect on our health and wellbeing. Health is not just a *personal* matter. It is affected by the people around us, by *where* we live and by *how* we live.

Genetic factors

Growth and development of the embryo and foetus are controlled by **genes**. The influence of our genes determine everything from eye colour to body shape, and even affect intelligence and personality. Certain conditions and rare disorders are inherited through the genes, for example, **sickle cell anaemia** or a tendency to heart disease or asthma. **Down's syndrome** results from a chromosomal abnormality and may be associated with health problems, such as heart defects and a tendency to chest infections.

Infection

Infectious diseases are still a major cause of illness in children; they range from a mild attack of the common cold to a life-threatening illness such as meningitis. Children are particularly vulnerable to infection because their immune systems have not yet built up resistance. Most common childhood infections are not serious and clear up quickly. Some serious viral infections, such as rubella and measles, are less common now because of routine immunisation. Bacterial infections are usually cured rapidly by the administration of antibiotics.

Allergies

An allergy is a negative physical reaction to a particular substance, called an allergen. The most common allergens are:

- pets – usually cats or dogs
- house dust mites
- eggs
- pollen
- milk
- peanuts
- grass.

Symptoms range from very mild through to extremely serious – for example, anaphylaxis. Asthma is often 'triggered' by one of these common allergens, often in association with other factors such as weather or emotional upset.

Environmental factors

The three main diseases directly influenced by poor environments worldwide are:

- diarrhoea: from unsafe water, sanitation and hygiene
- chest infections (lower respiratory tract infections): from air pollution, indoor and outdoor
- malaria: as a result of poor water quality, housing and land use management which fails to curb the mosquito population effectively.

In the UK, poor housing, overcrowding and air pollution are all contributory to ill health.

The signs and symptoms of common childhood illnesses

Recognising general signs of illness in babies and children

Small children are not always able to explain their symptoms, and may display non-specific complaints such as headache, sleeplessness, vomiting or an inability to stand up. Babies have even less certain means of communication, and may simply cry in a different way, refuse feeds or become listless and lethargic. In most infectious illnesses, there will be **fever**.

Key terms

Signs of illness – Those that can be observed directly, for example, a change in skin colour, a rash or a swelling.

Symptoms of illness – Those experienced by the child, for example, pain, discomfort or generally feeling unwell. Detection of symptoms relies on the child being able to describe how they are feeling.

Identifying signs of illness in children with different skin tones

Both within and between different ethnic groups there is a wide variety of skin tones and colours affecting the way skin looks during illness. When dark-skinned children are ill, they may show the following signs:

- **Skin appearance**: normal skin tone and sheen may be lost; the skin may appear dull and paler or greyer than usual. You must pay attention to those parts of the body with less pigmentation – the palms, the tongue, the nail beds and the **conjunctiva** (the insides of the bottom eyelids), all of which will be paler than usual.
- **Rashes**: in children with very dark skin, raised rashes are more obvious than flat rashes.
- **Bruising**: the discolouration that is obvious in pale skin may not be easily observed in darker-skinned children. When bruised, the skin may appear darker or more purple when compared with surrounding skin.
- **Jaundice**: in a fair-skinned child, gently press your finger to his forehead, nose, or chest, and look for a yellow tinge to the skin as the pressure is released. In a darker-skinned child, check for yellowness in his gums or the whites of his eyes.

Recognising illness in babies

The responsibility of caring for a baby who becomes ill is enormous; it is vital that carers should know the signs and symptoms of illness and when to seek medical aid. You should:

- **Observe the baby carefully** and note any changes; record his or her temperature and take steps to reduce a high temperature (see pages 361–2).
- **Give extra fluids** if possible and carry out routine skin care. The baby may want extra physical attention or prefer to rest in his or her cot.

Meningitis in babies

Meningitis is an inflammation of the lining of the brain. It is a very serious illness, but if it is detected and treated early, most children make a full recovery. The early symptoms of meningitis – such as fever, irritability, restlessness, vomiting and refusing feeds – are also common with colds and 'flu. However, a baby with meningitis can become seriously ill within hours, so it is important to act quickly if meningitis is suspected.

In babies under 12 months

- Tense or bulging fontanelles.
- A stiffening body with involuntary movements, or a floppy body.
- Blotchy or pale skin.
- A high-pitched, moaning cry.
- High temperature.
- The baby may be difficult to wake.
- The baby may refuse to feed.
- Red or purple spots (anywhere on the body) that do not fade under pressure – do the glass test (see below).

In older children

- Headache.
- Inability to tolerate light.
- Neck stiffness and joint pains – the child may arch the neck backwards because of the rigidity of the neck muscles.
- Fever.

Table 9.3 Symptoms of meningitis

In babies under 12 months, perform the 'glass test':

Press the side or bottom of a glass firmly against the rash – you will be able to see if the rash fades and loses colour under the pressure. **If it does not change colour, summon medical aid immediately.** If spots are appearing on the child's body, this could be septicaemia, a very serious bacterial infection described as the 'meningitis rash'.

General signs and symptoms of illness in children

When children feel generally unwell, you should ask them if they have any pain or discomfort and treat it appropriately. Take their temperature and look for other signs of illness, such as a rash or swollen glands. Often, feeling generally unwell is the first sign that the child is developing an **infectious disease**. Some children can also show general signs of illness if they are anxious or worried about something, either at home or at school.

Children react in certain characteristic ways when they are unwell. Some of the more common **emotional and behavioural changes** include:

- being quieter than usual
- becoming more clingy to their parents or primary carer
- attention-seeking behaviour

Figure 9.4 The 'glass test' for meningitis

- changed sleeping patterns; some children sleep more than usual, others less
- lack of energy

Condition (and cause)	Signs and symptoms	Role of the carer
Colic	This occurs in the first 12 weeks. It causes sharp, spasmodic pain in the stomach, and is often at its worst in the late evening. Symptoms include inconsolable high-pitched crying, drawing his or her legs up to his or her chest, and growing red in the face.	Try to stay calm! Gently massage his or her abdomen in a clockwise direction, using the tips of your middle fingers. Sucrose solution (3 x 5 ml teaspoons of sugar in a cup of boiling water and left to cool) is said to have a mild painkilling effect on small babies. Dribble 2 ml of this solution into the corner of the baby's mouth twice a day. If the problem persists, contact the doctor.
Diarrhoea	Frequent loose or watery stools. Can be very serious in young babies, especially when combined with vomiting, as it can lead to severe dehydration.	Give frequent small drinks of cooled, boiled water containing glucose and salt or a made-up sachet of rehydration fluid. If the baby is unable to take the fluid orally, he or she must be taken to hospital urgently and fed intravenously, by a 'drip'. If anal area becomes sore, treat with a barrier cream.
Gastroenteritis (virus or bacteria)	The baby may vomit and usually has diarrhoea as well; often has a raised temperature and loss of appetite. May show signs of abdominal pain, i.e. drawing up of legs to chest and crying.	Reassure baby. Observe strict hygiene rules. Watch out for signs of dehydration. Offer frequent small amounts of fluid, and possibly rehydration salts.
Neonatal cold injury – or hypothermia	The baby is cold to the touch. Face may be pale or flushed. Lethargic, with runny nose, swollen hands and feet. Pre-term infants and babies under 4 months are at particular risk.	Prevention. Warm *slowly* by covering with several light layers of blankets and by cuddling. No direct heat. Offer feeds high in sugar and seek medical help urgently.
Reflux	Also known as gastro-intestinal reflux (GIR) or gastro-oesophageal reflux (GOR). The opening to the stomach is not yet efficient enough to allow a large liquid feed through. Symptoms include grizzly crying and excessive possetting after feeds.	Try feeding the baby in a more upright position and bring up wind by gently rubbing their back. After feeding leave the baby in a semi-sitting position. Some doctors prescribe a paediatric reflux suppressant or antacid mixture to be given before the feed.
Tonsillitis (virus or bacteria)	Very sore throat, which looks bright red. There is usually fever and the baby will show signs of distress from pain on swallowing and general aches and pains. May vomit.	Encourage plenty of fluids – older babies may have ice lollies to suck. Give pain relief, e.g. paracetamol. Seek medical aid if no improvement and if fever persists.
Cough (usually virus)	Often follows on from a cold; may be a symptom of other illness, e.g. measles.	Keep air moist. Check the baby has not inhaled an object. Give medicine if prescribed.

Condition (and cause)	Signs and symptoms	Role of the carer
Croup (virus)	Croup is an infection of the voice box or larynx, which becomes narrowed and inflamed. Barking cough (like sea lions), noisy breathing, distressed; usually occurs at night.	If severe, seek medical help. Reassure them and sit them up. Keep calm and reassure the baby. Inhaling steam may also benefit some babies. You can produce steam by boiling a kettle, running the hot taps in the bathroom, using a room humidifier or putting wet towels over the radiator. If using steam, take care to avoid scalding.
Bronchiolitis (virus)	A harsh dry cough which later becomes wet and chesty; runny nose, raised temperature, wheezing, breathing problems, poor feeding or vomiting. May develop a blue tinge around the lips and on the fingernails (known as cyanosis).	Observe closely. Seek medical help if condition worsens. Increase fluids. Give small regular feeds. Give prescribed medicine. Comfort and reassure.
Febrile convulsions (high temperature)	Convulsions caused by a high temperature (over 39° C, 102° F) or fever are called febrile convulsions. Baby will become rigid, then the body may twitch and jerk for one or two minutes.	Try not to panic. Move potentially harmful objects out of the way and place the baby in the recovery position. Loosen clothing. Call doctor. Give tepid sponging. Comfort and reassure.
Otitis media (virus or bacteria)	Will appear unwell; may have raised temperature. May vomit, may cry with pain. May have discharge from ear.	Take to doctor, give antibiotics and analgesics (or painkillers). Increase fluids; comfort and reassure.
Conjunctivitis (virus or bacteria)	Inflammation of the thin, delicate membrane that covers the eyeball and forms the lining of the eyelids. Symptoms include a painful red eye, with watering and sometimes sticky pus.	Take to doctor who may prescribe antibiotic eye drops or ointment. Bathe a sticky eye gently with cool boiled water and clean cotton wool swabs. Always bathe the eye from the inside corner to the outside to avoid spreading infection.
Common cold (coryza) (virus)	Runny nose, sneeze; tiny babies may have breathing problems.	Keep nose clear. Give small frequent feeds. Nasal drops if prescribed.
Meningitis (virus or bacteria)	Raised temperature, may have a blotchy rash. May refuse feeds, have a stiff neck, have a seizure. Bulging fontanelles; may have a shrill, high-pitched cry.	Seek medical help urgently. Reduce temperature. Reassure.

Table 9.4 Illness in babies

- crying: babies cry for a variety of reasons (see Chapter 13). Older children who cry more than usual may be physically unwell or you may need to explore the reasons for their unhappiness
- regression: children who are unwell often regress in their development and behaviour. They may:
  - want to be carried everywhere instead of walking independently
  - go back to nappies after being toilet-trained
  - start to wet the bed
  - play with familiar, previously outgrown toys.

The following are common signs and symptoms of illness in children:

- **Loss of appetite** – the child may not want to eat or drink; this could be because of a sore, painful throat or a sign of a developing infection.
- **Lacking interest in play** – he or she may not want to join in play, without being able to explain why.
- **Abdominal pain** – the child may rub his or her tummy and say that it hurts; this could be a sign of gastro-enteritis.
- **Raised temperature (fever)** – a fever (a temperature above 38 °C) is usually an indication of viral or bacterial infection, but can also result from over-heating.
- **Diarrhoea and vomiting** – attacks of diarrhoea and/or vomiting are usually a sign of gastro-enteritis.
- **Lethargy or listlessness** – the child may be drowsy and prefer to sit quietly with a favourite toy or comfort blanket.
- **Irritability and fretfulness** – the child may have a change in behaviour, being easily upset and tearful.
- **Pallor** – the child will look paler than usual and may have dark shadows under the eyes; a black child may have a paler area around the lips and the conjunctiva may be pale pink instead of the normal dark pink.
- **Rash** – any rash appearing on the child's body should be investigated; it is usually a sign of an infectious disease.

High temperature (fever)

The normal body temperature is between 36–7 °C. A temperature of above 37.5 °C means that the child has a fever. Common sense, and using the back of your hand to feel the forehead of an ill child, is almost as reliable in detecting a fever as using a thermometer.

A child with a fever may:

- look hot and flushed; the child may complain of feeling cold and might shiver. This is a natural reflex due to the increased heat loss and a temporary disabling of the usual internal temperature control of the brain
- be either irritable or subdued
- be unusually sleepy
- go off their food
- complain of thirst.

Children can develop high temperatures very quickly. You need to know how to bring their temperature down (see below) to avoid complications, such as dehydration and febrile convulsions.

Guidelines for bringing down a high temperature

- Offer cool drinks: encourage the child to take small, frequent sips of anything he or she will drink (though preferably clear fluids like water or squash, rather than milky drinks). Do this even if the child is vomiting because, even then, some water will be absorbed.
- Remove clothes: keep the child as undressed as possible to allow heat to be lost.
- Reduce bedclothes: use a cotton sheet if the child is in bed.
- Sponge the child down: use tepid water (see tepid sponging below).
- Give the correct dose of children's paracetamol: make sure you have written consent from the parents or carers to use it in case of emergency. If not, contact the parents and try to obtain consent.
- Cool the air in the child's room: use an electric fan or open the window.
- Reassure the child: they may be very frightened. Remain calm yourself and try to stop a baby from crying as this will tend to push the temperature higher still.

If the temperature will not come down, call the doctor. Always consult a doctor if a high fever

Guidelines for bringing down a high temperature (cont.)

is accompanied by symptoms such as severe headache with stiff neck, abdominal pain or pain when passing urine.

Note: medicines should not be given unless the written permission of the parent or next-of-kin is obtained.

Guidelines for tepid sponging to reduce a temperature

- Make sure the air in the room is comfortably warm – not hot, cold or draughty.
- Lay the child on a towel on your knee or on the bed and gently remove their clothes; reassure them by talking gently.
- Sponge the child's body, limbs and face with tepid or lukewarm water – not cold; as the water evaporates from the skin, it absorbs heat from the blood and so cools the system.
- As the child cools down, pat the skin dry with a soft towel and dress only in a nappy or pants; cover them with a light cotton sheet.
- Keep checking the child's condition to make sure that he does not become cold or shivery; put more light covers over the child if he is shivering or obviously chilled.
- If the temperature rises again, repeat sponging every ten minutes.

✓ Progress check

The normal body temperature is between 36–7 °C.

- A high temperature is anything above 37.5 °C.
- All family and workplace first aid kits should contain a thermometer, and you need to know how to take a temperature.
- Children can develop high temperatures very quickly, which can lead to complications, such as dehydration and febrile convulsions.
- To bring a child's temperature down, offer cool drinks, reduce clothing worn and try tepid sponging.

Common infectious childhood illnesses

Everyone concerned with the care of babies and young children should be aware of the signs and symptoms of the common infectious diseases, and should know when to summon medical aid. (See Chapter 4.)

Disorders of the digestive tract

One of the most common signs that something is wrong with the digestive system is diarrhoea, when the bowel movements are abnormally runny and frequent. Other symptoms of infection or illness are vomiting and abdominal pain. Although these symptoms are often distressing both to the child and his carer, they are rarely a serious threat to health.

Vomiting

Vomiting is the violent expulsion of the contents of the stomach through the mouth. A single episode of vomiting without other symptoms happens frequently in childhood. It could be a result of over-eating or too much excitement. Vomiting has many causes, but in most cases there is little warning and after a single bout the child recovers and quickly gets back to normal. Table 9.6 details possible causes of vomiting in children over one year old and what to do about it.

Guidelines for helping a child who is vomiting

- Reassure the child, who may be very frightened.
- Stay with the child and support their head by putting your hand on their forehead.
- Keep the child cool by wiping the face with a cool, damp cloth.
- Offer mouthwash or sips of water after vomiting.
- Give frequent small drinks of cold water with a pinch of salt and a teaspoon of glucose added – or you can buy special rehydrating powders.
- Encourage the child to rest lying down with a bowl by their side. Do not leave them until they have fallen asleep – and stay within call in case they vomit again.

Disease and cause	Spread	Incubation	Signs and symptoms	Rash or specific sign	Treatment	Complications
COMMON COLD (coryza) Virus	Airborne/droplet, hand-to-hand contact	1–3 days	Sneeze, sore throat, running nose, headache, slight fever, irritable, partial deafness		Treat symptoms Vaseline to nostrils	Bronchitis, sinusitis, laryngitis
CHICKENPOX (varicella) Virus	Airborne/droplet, direct contact	10–14 days	Slight fever, itchy rash, mild onset, child feels ill, often with severe headache	Red spots with white centre on trunk and limbs at first; blisters and pustules	Rest, fluids, calamine to rash, cut child's nails to prevent secondary infection	Impetigo, scarring, secondary infection from scratching
DYSENTERY Bacillus or amoeba	Indirect: flies, infected food, poor hygiene	1–7 days	Vomiting, diarrhoea, blood and mucus in stool, abdominal pain, fever, headache		Replace fluids, rest, medical aid, strict hygiene measures	Dehydration from loss of body salts, shock; can be fatal
FOOD POISONING Bacteria or virus	Indirect: infected food or drink	½ hour to 36 hours	Vomiting, diarrhoea, abdominal pain		Fluids only for 24 hours; medical aid if no better	Dehydration – can be fatal
GASTROENTERITIS Bacteria or virus	Direct contact. Indirect: infected food/drink	Bacterial: 7–14 days Viral: 1 hour to 36 hours	Vomiting, diarrhoea, signs of dehydration		Replace fluids – water or Dioralyte; medical aid urgently	Dehydration, weight loss – death
MEASLES (morbilli) Virus	Airborne/droplet	7–15 days	High fever, fretful, heavy cold – running nose and discharge from eyes; *later* cough	Day 1: Koplik's spots, white inside mouth. Day 4: blotchy rash starts on face and spreads down to body	Rest, fluids, tepid sponging. Shade room if photophobic (disliking bright light)	Otitis media, eye infection, pneumonia, encephalitis (rare)
MENINGITIS (inflammation of meninges which cover the brain) Bacteria or virus	Airborne/droplet	Variable – usually 2–10 days	Fever, headache, drowsiness, confusion, photophobia, arching of neck	Can have small red spots or bruises	Take to hospital; antibiotics and observation	Deafness, brain damage, death

Disease and cause	Spread	Incubation	Signs and symptoms	Rash or specific sign	Treatment	Complications
MUMPS (epidemic parotitis)	Airborne/droplet	14–21 days	Pain, swelling of jaw in front of ears, fever, eating and drinking painful	Swollen face	Fluids: give via straw, hot compresses, oral hygiene	Meningitis (1 in 400), orchitis (infection of testes) in young men
PERTUSSIS (Whooping cough) Bacteria	Airborne/droplet; direct contact	7–21 days	Starts with a snuffly cold, slight cough, mild fever	Spasmodic cough with whoop sound, vomiting	Rest and reassurance; feed after coughing attack; support during attack; inhalations	Convulsions, pneumonia, brain damage, hernia, debility
RUBELLA (German measles) Virus	Airborne/droplet; direct contact	14–21 days	Slight cold, sore throat, mild fever, swollen glands behind ears, pain in small joints	Slight pink rash starts behind ears and on forehead. Not itchy	Rest if necessary. Treat symptoms	Only if contracted by woman in first 3 months of pregnancy – can cause serious defects in unborn baby
SCARLET FEVER (or Scarlatina) Bacteria	Droplet	2–4 days	Sudden fever, loss of appetite, sore throat, pallor around mouth, 'strawberry' tongue	Bright red pinpoint rash over face and body – may peel	Rest, fluids, observe for complications, antibiotics	Kidney infection, otitis media, rheumatic fever (rare)
TONSILLITIS Bacteria or virus	Direct infection, droplet		Very sore throat, fever, headache, pain on swallowing, aches and pains in back and limbs		Rest, fluids, medical aid – antibiotics, iced drinks relieve pain	Quinsy (abscess on tonsils), otitis media, kidney infection, temporary deafness

Table 9.5 Common infectious illnesses

Possible causes of vomiting with accompanying symptoms	What to do
Gastroenteritis The child also has diarrhoea.	See the doctor within 24 hours. Prevent dehydration (see page 401).
Intestinal obstruction The child's vomit is greenish-yellow.	**Call an ambulance.** Do not give the child anything to eat or drink.
Meningitis The child has a fever, a stiff neck or flat, purplish spots that do not disappear when pressed.	**Call an ambulance.**
Head injury The child has recently suffered a blow to the head.	**Call an ambulance.** Do not give the child anything to eat or drink.
Appendicitis The child has continuous abdominal pain around the navel and to the right side of the abdomen.	**Call an ambulance.** Do not give the child anything to eat or drink.
Infection The child seems unwell, looks flushed and feels hot.	Reduce the fever. See the doctor within 24 hours.
Hepatitis The child has pale faeces and dark urine.	See the doctor within 24 hours.
Travel sickness When travelling, the child seems pale and quiet and complains of nausea.	Give the child a travel sickness remedy before starting journey. Take plenty of drinks to prevent dehydration.
Migraine The child complains of a severe headache on one side of the forehead.	See the doctor if accompanied by severe abdominal pain – it could be appendicitis.
Whooping cough (pertussis) The child vomits after a bout of coughing.	See the doctor within 24 hours.

Table 9.6 Possible causes of vomiting and what to do

Diarrhoea

Most children have diarrhoea at some time, usually after an infection involving the digestive tract – for example, **gastro-enteritis**. If the fluid lost through passing frequent, loose, watery stools is not replaced, there is a danger the child will become **dehydrated**. Babies become dehydrated very quickly and can become seriously ill as the result of diarrhoea. Diarrhoea can also be caused by:

- emotional factors – over-tiredness, excitement and anxiety
- allergy
- reaction to certain drugs and medicines.

Toddler's diarrhoea

Toddler's diarrhoea occurs when an otherwise healthy child (between the ages of one and three) passes loose, watery faeces. The cause is uncertain, but it is thought to be the result of poor chewing of food. Signs and symptoms are:

- loose, watery faeces often containing recognisable pieces of food – such as raisins, corn, carrots and peas
- nappy rash if the child is in nappies.

What to do:

- Consult a doctor to exclude other causes of diarrhoea, such as an infection.

- Encourage the child to chew foods thoroughly.
- Mash or liquidise foods which are difficult to chew and digest.

Children generally grow out of toddler's diarrhoea by three years of age. As it is not an infectious condition, there is no need for the child to be kept away from friends or from nursery.

Guidelines for caring for a child with diarrhoea

- Reassure the child, who may be very distressed.
- Prevent dehydration by giving regular drinks of water.
- Keep a potty nearby.
- Be sympathetic when changing soiled underwear; soak any soiled clothing in a nappy sterilising solution before washing.
- Maintain a high standard of hygiene; hand washing by both you and the child is vital in preventing the spread of infection.
- Unless it is toddler diarrhoea, keep child away from other children; early years settings will have an exclusion policy in the case of infectious illness, such as gastro-enteritis.

Dehydration

Children can lose large amounts of body water through fever, diarrhoea, vomiting or exercise; this is called **dehydration**. In severe cases, they may not be able to replace this water simply by drinking and eating as usual. This is especially true if an illness stops them taking fluids by mouth or if they have a high fever.

Signs of dehydration in babies are:

- sunken fontanelles: these are the areas where the bones of the skull have not yet fused together; they are covered by a tough membrane and a pulse may usually be seen beating under the anterior fontanelle in a baby without much hair
- fretfulness
- refusing feeds
- dry nappies – because the amount of urine being produced is very small.

See Table 9.7 for signs of dehydration in children.

If you think a baby or child might have dehydration, do not try to treat them at home or in the setting. Call the doctor immediately, or take the child to the nearest Accident and Emergency Department. The doctor will prescribe oral rehydrating fluid to restore the body salts lost.

Infestations of the digestive tract

Threadworms

Threadworms are tiny white worms that infest the bowel. People of any age can get threadworms, but they are most common in children aged between five and twelve years old. They *cannot* be caught from animals.

Signs of dehydration in children	
Mild to moderate dehydration	**Severe dehydration**
Dry mouth	Very dry mouth
No tears when crying	Sunken eyes and dry, wrinkled skin
Refusing drinks	No urination for several hours
At first thirsty, then irritable – then becomes still and quiet	Sleepy and disorientated
Inactive and lethargic	Deep, rapid breathing
Increased heart rate	Fast, weak pulse
Restlessness	Cool and blotchy hands and feet

Table 9.7 Signs of dehydration in children

- They are highly contagious, and pass easily from one person to another.
- The eggs are usually picked up by the hands and then transferred to the mouth.
- The eggs hatch in the small intestine, and the worms migrate downwards to the rectum where they emerge at night.
- They cause intense itching: the child will then scratch, eggs will be caught under the nails and the cycle may repeat itself.

The whole family will need take medication prescribed by the doctor.

Strict hygiene measures help to prevent infestation: scrubbing the nails after a bowel movement, the use of separate flannels and towels, and daily baths.

Toxocariasis

This is an infection of the roundworms that usually live in the gut of dogs and cats. The eggs of the worm are excreted in the faeces of the animal, and young children may pick them up and transfer them to their mouths. Infection can occasionally be serious, leading to epilepsy or blindness. Prevention is through public awareness: all dog and cat owners must regularly worm their pets, and dogs should not be allowed in areas where young children play.

Skin disorders

Up to three million micro-organisms exist on each square centimetre of skin. Most of these are **commensals** (literally 'table companions' from the Latin) and are harmless to their host. These commensals have become adapted through evolution to live off human skin scales and the slightly acid secretions produced by the skin. Some important points to note regarding skin conditions are:

- Newborn babies are particularly prone to skin infection.
- Micro-organisms thrive in moist conditions, such as at the axillae (the armpits) and the groin.
- Washing and bathing increase the number of bacteria released from the skin for up to ten hours.
- The skin can never be sterilised. Iodine preparations used to prepare skin for surgical

operations kill a large percentage of organisms but cannot remove the bacteria that colonise the hair follicles.

- To provide a defence against infection, the skin must be intact (unbroken).
- There are two main reasons why the skin should be kept clean:
  - to prevent infection by micro-organisms via the sweat pores
  - to prevent the accumulation of oil, sweat and micro-organisms, which will encourage insect parasites.

Parasitic skin infections

The two most common causes of parasitic skin infection in the western world are:

- the head louse, and
- the scabies mite.

Head louse

See Chapter 4, page 204 for detailed information on head lice.

Scabies

Scabies is largely a disease of families and young children. The scabies mite differs from the louse in that it does not have a recognisable head, thorax and abdomen. It has a tortoise-like body, with four pairs of legs, and is about 0.3 mm in size.

- The scabies mite lives in burrows in the outer skin. These can be mistaken for the tracks made by a hypodermic needle.
- It is usually found in the finger webs, wrists, palms and soles.
- Transmission is mainly by body contact, which must last for at least 20 minutes.
- Cleanliness does not prevent infestation.
- A widespread itchy rash appears, which is most irritating at night.
- If untreated, secondary sepsis may occur, with boils and impetigo.

Treatment

Insecticide lotion is applied to the whole body below the neck; treatment is usually repeated after 24 hours. Calamine lotion may be used to soothe the itch that often lasts after treatment.

Key terms

Head lice Head lice are tiny grey/brown insects that live on the scalp and neck. Although they may be embarrassing and sometimes itchy and uncomfortable, head lice do not usually cause illness.

Scabies Scabies is an itchy rash caused by the human scabies mite. It is spread easily through close physical contact.

Eczema – an allergic skin condition

Eczema (from the Greek 'to boil over') is an itchy and often unsightly skin condition that affects millions of people to some degree. The most common type which affects children is **atopic eczema**. About one in eight of all children will show symptoms at some time, ranging from a mild rash lasting a few months, to severe symptoms that persist over years.

- Eczema is *not* infectious.
- It often starts as an irritating red patch in the creases of the elbows or knees, or on the face.
- It can spread quickly to surrounding skin that becomes cracked, moist and red.
- In severe cases it can blister and weep clear fluid if scratched.
- Later, the skin becomes thickened and scaly.
- Skin damaged by eczema is more likely to become infected, particularly by a bacterium called staphylococcus aureus that produces yellow crusts or pus-filled spots.

Causes

There is no single known cause, but certain factors predispose a child to suffer from eczema:

- an allergy to certain foods, such as cows' milk
- an allergy to airborne substances like pollen, house dust, scales from animal hair or feathers, or fungus spores
- environmental factors, such as humidity or cold weather
- a family history of allergy
- emotional or physical stress.

Guidelines for managing eczema

In mild cases where the child's life is not disrupted, the following measures are usually advised:

- **Do not let the child's skin become dry**: apply a moisturising cream or emollient to the skin several times a day. Aqueous cream is a good moisturiser and can also be used for washing instead of soap. Apply the cream with downward strokes – do not rub it up and down. (Try to put some cream on when you feed the baby or change a nappy.)

- **Identify triggers**: identify and avoid anything that irritates the skin or makes the problem worse; for example, soap powder, pets and other animals, chemical sprays, cigarette smoke or some clothing.

- **Avoid irritants**: avoid substances that dry or irritate the baby's skin, such as soap, baby bath, bubble bath or detergents; bathe the child in lukewarm water with a suitable skin oil added. Avoid wool and synthetics – cotton clothing is best.

- **Prevent scratching**: use cotton mittens for small children at night; keep the child's nails short.

- **Foods to avoid**: do not cut out important foods, such as milk, dairy products, wheat or eggs, without consulting the GP or health visitor. However, citrus fruits, tomatoes and juice can be avoided if they cause a reaction.

- **House dust mite**: the faeces of the house dust mite can sometimes make eczema worse. If the child has fluffy or furry toys in the bedroom, the house dust mite collects on them. Limit these toys to one or two favourites, and either wash them weekly at 60 °C or put them in a plastic bag in the freezer for 24 hours to kill the house dust mite.

- **Apply steroid creams** as prescribed by the GP: these must be used sparingly as overuse can harm the skin.

In severe cases, the GP will refer the child to a skin specialist (dermatologist).

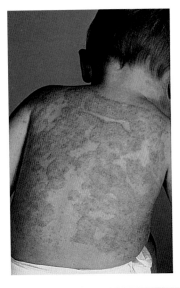
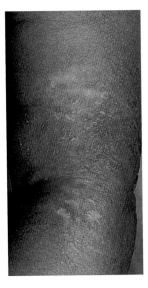

Figure 9.5 Eczema appears as a dry, scaly rash which becomes red and may start to 'weep'

Caring for a child with eczema in the early years setting

- **Food allergies** can create problems with school lunches; the cook must monitor carefully what the child eats.
- **Clothing**: wearing woolly jumpers, school uniforms (especially if not cotton) and football kits can all make the eczema worse.
- **A special cleaner** may be needed rather than the school soap; they may also need to use cotton towels as paper towels can cause a problem.
- **Extra time and privacy** may be needed for applying creams at school; children may need to wear bandages or cotton gloves to protect their skin.
- **Changes in temperature** can exacerbate the condition: getting too hot (sitting by a sunny window) or too cold (during PE in the playground).
- **Difficulty holding a pen**: if the eczema cracks, they may not be able to hold a pen.
- **Pain and tiredness**: eczema may become so bad that the child is in pain or needs to miss school, due to lack of sleep, pain or hospital visits.
- **Irritability and lack of concentration** can result due to tiredness: sleep problems are very common as a warm, cosy bed can lead to itching and therefore lack of sleep.

- **Using play dough, clay and sand**: some children with eczema may have flare-ups when handling these materials.

Early years practitioners should find out from the child's parents or specialist nurse which activities are suitable and which should be avoided; you should also provide alternatives so that the child is not excluded from the normal daily activities in the setting.

Other common skin disorders

Impetigo

Impetigo is a highly contagious bacterial infection of the skin; the rash commonly appears on the face but can affect the rest of the body. The rash consists of yellowish crusts on top of a reddened area of skin. The child should not mix with others until the condition is treated. Impetigo is easily spread by contact with infected flannels and towels, so scrupulous attention to hygiene is necessary. Treatment is with antibiotic medicines and creams.

Warts

Warts are the most common viral infection of the skin. They appear as raised lumps on the skin and are quite harmless. Most warts occur in children between the ages of six and twelve and disappear without treatment. If they become painful, the local hospital's outpatient department will arrange for their removal, usually by freezing with liquid nitrogen (a form of cryosurgery).

Verrucae

Verrucae (or plantar warts) are warts on the sole of the foot, and may hurt because of pressure. They are picked up easily in the warm, moist atmosphere of swimming baths. Treatment is by the application of lotions or by freezing. Tincture of thuja is an effective homeopathic remedy.

Molluscum contagiosum

This is a viral infection which consists of clusters of small whitish-yellow, pearl-like spots on any part of the body. The skin should be kept moist using E45 creams and bath oils, as the virus flourishes on dry skin. The bath towel should be changed after every use. The spots normally disappear within a few months, but can last longer.

Pytiriasis rosea

This is an unidentified viral infection that affects mainly school-age children. The rash is scaly, consisting of beige-coloured oval patches that appear on the chest, back and limbs. Sometimes the rash will cause irritation and can be controlled by use of a mild steroid cream.

Ringworm

This is not due to a worm at all: it is a **fungal** infection, often acquired from an animal. On the body it forms a reddish patch with a ring of small pimples at the edge. Usually it affects the scalp, causing the hair to break and sore bald patches to appear. Treatment is by medicine (griseofulvin), and the hair does grow again.

Athlete's foot

This is the name for ringworm that grows on the skin of the feet. It appears as a pink, flaky rash, particularly between the toes, and is intensely irritating. Treatment is by powder or cream; and the child should not walk barefoot around the house as the condition can easily spread to others.

Cold sores

These are small painful blisters that develop on or around the lips. They are caused by the herpes simplex virus and are caught by close contact with an infected person; they can be triggered by illness, cold winds, bright sunlight and emotional upset. Treatment is by an anti-viral cream.

Asthma – a respiratory disorder

Asthma is a condition that affects the airways, the small tubes that carry air in and out of the lungs. If you have asthma, your airways are almost always sensitive and inflamed. When you come into contact with something you are allergic to, or something that irritates your airways (a trigger), your airways will become narrower, making it harder to breathe. The muscles around the walls of your airways tighten.

The lining of the airways becomes inflamed and starts to swell; often sticky mucus or phlegm is produced.

Asthma in children

About one in ten children will have an asthma attack (or episode) at some time. There are 1.2 million children in Britain who are currently receiving treatment for asthma. In general, children who have mild asthma are more likely to be free of symptoms once they grow up, but this is not guaranteed. Some people find that their asthma goes away when they are teenagers but comes back again when they are adults.

Although there is no guarantee that symptoms will go away, they can usually be controlled with **medication**. Asthma should never be left untreated in the hope that a child may grow out of it.

Causes and symptoms of asthma

There is no single cause of asthma. Most children who develop asthma have several **triggers**, or predisposing factors, and these vary from one child to another. Triggers include the following:

- colds and viruses
- pollen – from grass
- pet hairs and feathers
- tobacco smoke
- stress and excitement
- weather changes
- exercise
- mould
- dust and house dust mites
- certain types of medication
- chemicals and fumes, for example, from car exhausts, paints and cleaning fluids
- certain foods, such as peanuts or eggs.

It is important to try and identify possible triggers, so that they can be avoided. Generally, the more triggers present, the worse the attack. Typically, a child's first attack will follow one or two days after the onset of a respiratory illness, such as a cold.

Common symptoms of asthma are:

- wheezing (although not all children experience this)

- elevated breathing rate (the normal rate is under 25 breaths per minute; over 40 is cause for calling the doctor)
- coughing, especially in the early morning
- longer expiration (breathing out) than inspiration (breathing in)
- sweating
- the child may appear very frightened
- the child becomes pale; a darker-skinned child may also appear drained of colour, particularly around the mouth.

Attacks may build over days or occur within seconds. There are two types of asthma:

- **Acute asthma** (or an asthma attack or episode) – this may require medical stabilisation within a hospital setting.
- **Chronic asthma** – this produces symptoms on a continual basis, and is characterised by persistent, often severe symptoms, requiring regular oral steroid medication.

What to do when a child has an acute asthmatic attack

Not all asthma attacks can be prevented. When the child is having an acute attack of wheezing – the difficulty is in breathing **out** rather than in, catching one's breath – he or she needs a reliever drug (a bronchodilator, usually in a blue inhaler case). Most children will have been shown how to

Figure 9.6 Using a reliever inhaler during an asthma attack

deliver the drug by an aerosol inhaler, a spinhaler or a nebuliser.

Prevention of asthma

Where possible, avoid likely triggers of asthma – see above.

Preventer inhalers are usually brown and contain corticosteroids. These have to be taken regularly everyday, even when the child is feeling well; they act by reducing the inflammation and swelling in the airways. Corticosteroid drugs should not be confused with the anabolic steroids taken by athletes to improve their performance.

Guidelines for helping a child who is having an asthmatic attack

- If the attack is the child's *first*, then **call a doctor** and the parents.
- Stay calm and **reassure the child**, who may be very frightened.
- Encourage the child to sit up to increase lung capacity.
- If the child has a **reliever inhaler** or nebuliser, then supervise him while using it.
- Never leave the child alone during an attack.
- Try not to let other children crowd around.
- If these measures do not stop the wheezing and the child is exhausted by the attack, call a doctor. He or she will either give an injection of a bronchodilator drug or arrange admission to hospital.

Activity

Promoting awareness about asthma

Design a poster for use in a nursery or primary school, which presents the following information in a lively style:

- the main factors known to trigger an asthma attack
- what to do when a child has an asthma attack
- how preventers and relievers – via inhalers – work.

Policies and procedures for infection control

There are some general rules about excluding children from childcare settings:

- Children who are ill should *not* attend child care. If a child becomes ill while in child care, a parent or guardian should be asked to take the child home as soon as possible.
- Children with diarrhoea or vomiting illnesses should not be in childcare settings. Parents should contact their GP for advice regarding the child's illness and possible need for collection of samples. The exclusion period should last until at least 48 hours after the last episode of diarrhoea or vomiting.
- Parents should be advised if there are known cases of infection within the childcare setting. It is particularly important that the parents of children whose immunity may be impaired due to illness or treatment (such as leukaemia or HIV) are given this information. It is also important that mothers who are pregnant are made aware of the following infections: chicken pox/shingles, rubella, slapped cheek syndrome and measles.
- It is good practice that a child requiring antibiotics does not come into the childcare setting for 48 hours after they have begun treatment. This is so that the child's condition has an opportunity to improve, and that in the unlikely event of a reaction to antibiotics, the parent or carer can be with the child and is able to seek further help or advice from the GP. It is possible that some infections may take the child much longer to recover from and feel well enough to attend childcare. Other infections are subject to specific exclusions advice.

Exclusion policies

The **2010 Health Protection Agency (HPA)** orange poster *Guidance on Infection Control in Schools and other Child Care Settings* details the current guidelines for if – and when – to exclude a child with an infectious disease from the setting. Every early years setting must have an **exclusion policy** for infectious diseases, and parents should be informed of their responsibilities. The exclusion criteria for some of the more common infections are given in Table 9.8.

Vulnerable children

Some medical conditions make children vulnerable to infections that would rarely be serious in most children; for example, children:

- being treated for leukaemia or other cancers
- on high dose steroids and with conditions which seriously reduce immunity.

Some of these children may require additional pneumococcal and influenza vaccinations.

Female staff and pregnancy

If a pregnant woman develops a rash or is in contact with someone with a potentially infectious rash, this should be investigated by a doctor. Pregnant women are at risk from such infections from their own children at home as well as in the workplace.

- **Chickenpox** may affect the pregnancy if a woman has not already had chickenpox. If exposed early in pregnancy (first 20 weeks) or very late (the last three weeks), the GP and antenatal carers should be informed so that investigations and any treatment that may be indicated can be initiated; for example, a blood sample may be taken to check immunity.
- **Shingles** is caused by the same virus as chickenpox: anyone who has not had chickenpox is potentially vulnerable to the infection if they have close contact with a case of shingles.
- **Rubella (German measles)**: if a pregnant woman comes into contact with German measles she should inform her GP and antenatal carers immediately so that investigations and treatment can be initiated. This infection may affect the developing baby if a non-immune woman is exposed in early pregnancy.
- **Slapped cheek syndrome** (Parvovirus B19/ Fifth disease) can occasionally affect the

Infectious illness	Recommended period for exclusion from the setting
Chicken pox	For 5 days from onset of rash. (See also section on female staff and pregnancy below.)
Diarrhoea and/or vomiting	For 48 hours from last episode of diarrhoea or vomiting. Exclusion from swimming should be for 2 weeks following last episode of diarrhoea.
Hand, foot and mouth	None. Exclusion is ineffective as transmission takes place before the child becomes unwell.
Impetigo	Until lesions are crusted or healed, or 48 hours after commencing antibiotic treatment.
Measles*	For 4 days from onset of rash.
Meningococcal meningitis*	The local Health Protection Unit (HPU) will give advice on any action needed. There is no reason to exclude from school siblings and other close contacts of a case.
Non-meningococcal meningitis*	None. Once the child is well, infection risk is minimal. Meningitis C is preventable by vaccination.
Meningitis due to other bacteria*	Exclude until recovered. There is no reason to exclude from school siblings and other close contacts of a case. Hib meningitis and pneumococcal meningitis are preventable by vaccination.
Mumps*	For 5 days from onset of swelling.
Rubella* German measles	For 6 days from onset of rash. (See section on female staff and pregnancy below.)
Shingles	Exclude only if rash is weeping and cannot be covered. (See section on Female staff and pregnancy above.)
Scabies	Child can return after first treatment has commenced.
Slapped cheek disease (Fifth Disease/Parvovirus)	None. Exclusion is ineffective as nearly all transmission takes place before the child becomes unwell. (But see section on female staff and pregnancy below.)
Whooping cough*	For 5 days from commencing antibiotic treatment.

Table 9.8 Exclusion recommendations following infectious illness

Note: the diseases marked* are **notifiable**. This means that under the Public Health (Infectious Diseases) Regulations 1988, these infections and all cases of food poisoning must be reported to the Local Authority Proper Officers.

baby. If exposed during the first 20 weeks of pregnancy, inform GP and antenatal carers immediately for investigation and management.

- **Measles**: if a pregnant woman is exposed to measles, she should immediately contact her GP and antenatal carers for investigation and treatment.

Female staff should ensure they are immune to measles, mumps and rubella.

Research Activity

Find out about your setting's policy relating to excluding children when they have an infectious illness.

Section 3: The effects of ill health on children and families

The possible effects of chronic and acute illnesses, hospital admission and care

Chronic illness

A chronic illness tends to last a long time – as contrasted with acute illness (those of sudden onset and of short duration). A child with a chronic illness shows little change in symptoms from day to day and may still be able – though possibly with some difficulty – to carry out normal daily activities. The disease process is continuous with progressive deterioration, sometimes in spite of treatment. The child may experience an acute exacerbation (flare-up) of symptoms from time to time.

Some examples of chronic illness in children are:

- juvenile rheumatoid arthritis
- psoriasis – a skin disorder which usually develops after age 11
- diabetes mellitus (Type 1)
- thalassaemia major – an inherited blood disorder
- chronic renal failure
- atopic eczema
- sickle-cell disorders (sickle-cell-anaemia).

Long-term illness may mean that the child's ability to exercise freedom of choice in daily activities is curtailed. Frequent periods of hospitalisation disrupt family and social life, and impose strain on all members of the family; siblings often resent the extra attention given to the sick child, and the parents themselves may also need financial support. Social workers based at hospitals will give advice on any benefits and can provide a counselling service. They may also be able to put parents in touch with a voluntary organisation for the parents of children with similar conditions. Most children's units in hospitals have a separate playroom with trained staff who provide the sick child with an opportunity for a choice of play activities.

Cystic fibrosis (CF)

Cystic fibrosis is caused by a faulty recessive gene that *must* be inherited from both parents – the parents are **carriers** even if they do not display any symptoms. In people with CF, the abnormal gene causes unusually sticky secretions of mucus that clog the airways, leading to chest infections. The gene also affects food digestion, leading to an inability to absorb nutrients from the intestines. Although cystic fibrosis is present from birth, the condition may not become apparent for many months or years. By the time it is detected, damage to the lungs may have already begun. Among West—Europeans and white Americans, one child in 2,000 is born with CF and one person in 25 is a carrier of the faulty gene.

Features of cystic fibrosis

- Failure to grow normally, due to **malabsorption** of nutrients (failure to thrive).
- A cough that gradually gets worse.
- Recurrent chest infections.
- Severe diarrhoea with pale, foul-smelling faeces.

Children with cystic fibrosis have a higher concentration of salt in their sweat; therefore, a sample of the child's sweat can be taken and analysed for diagnosis. Genetic tests will also be carried out. Recent research has succeeded in locating the gene that causes cystic fibrosis. This means that it is now possible to detect the carrier state, and also to test for cystic fibrosis before birth. Once cystic fibrosis is suspected in the young baby, simple laboratory tests will confirm or refute the diagnosis. Early treatment can limit lung damage and can help to ensure that failure to thrive is averted.

Treatment and care

- Vitamin supplements and pancreatin (a replacement enzyme) will be prescribed for the child to take with meals; this helps in the proper digestion of food.
- A high energy diet (a diet high in calories) will be recommended.
- Parents and carers will be shown how to give physiotherapy (postural drainage) to clear mucus or phlegm from the lungs.

- Children with this condition are susceptible to lung infections and antibiotic treatment is very important in protecting the lungs.
- There is no cure for cystic fibrosis but, due to earlier diagnosis and new methods of treatment, most people survive into adulthood.

Guidelines for working with children who have cystic fibrosis

- Children with CF can join in with whatever the other children are doing, but they have to remember to carry out their physiotherapy, enzymes and exercise programmes.

- The lungs of a child with CF must be kept clear to prevent infection. If appropriate, learn how to perform the necessary postural drainage and physiotherapy techniques. Always obtain permission from the child's parents or guardians before performing any of these techniques.

- Children with CF can eat a normal diet but also need to take enzyme and vitamin supplements; and they may also need salt tablets if they are undertaking strenuous exercise in hot weather.

- A child with CF may tire easily but should be encouraged to take lots of exercise to keep healthy. Good exercises are running, swimming, cycling and skipping.

Sickle cell disorders (SCD)

Sickle cell disorder is an inherited blood condition caused by abnormal haemoglobin. Under certain conditions the red blood cells that contain the haemoglobin and are normally round become sickle- or crescent-shaped. They clump together and lodge in the smaller blood vessels, preventing normal blood flow and resulting in **anaemia** (a lack of haemoglobin).

In the UK the disorder is most common in people of African or Caribbean descent, but may also occur in people from India, Pakistan, the Middle East and the East Mediterranean. It affects about one in 2,500 babies born each year.

The features of sickle cell disorders

Children with a sickle cell disorder can almost always attend a mainstream school but are subject to *crises* that may involve the following:

- pain – often severe, occurring in the arms, legs, back and stomach, and due to the blockage of normal blood flow
- infection – these children are more susceptible to coughs, cold, sore throats, fever and other infectious diseases
- anaemia – most sufferers are anaemic; only if the anaemia is severe, however, will they also feel lethargic and ill
- jaundice – this may show as a yellow staining of the whites of the eyes.

Treatment and care

Blood transfusions may be necessary. Infections should be treated promptly, and immunisation against all the normal childhood diseases is recommended.

Guidelines for working with children who have a sickle cell disorder

- Know how to recognise a crisis. If the child suddenly becomes unwell or complains of severe abdominal or chest pain, headache, neck stiffness or drowsiness, contact the parents without delay: the child needs urgent hospital treatment.

- Make sure the child is always warm and dry. Never let a child get chilled after PE or swimming.

- Make sure the child does not become dehydrated. Allow them to drink more often and much more than normal.

- Advise parents that the child should be fully immunised against infectious illnesses and ensure that any prescribed medicines (such as vitamins and antibiotics) are given.

- Give support. The child may find it difficult to come to terms with their condition; make allowances when necessary.

- Talk to the parents to find out how the illness is affecting the child.

- Help with schoolwork. If badly anaemic, the child may find it difficult to concentrate, and regular visits to the GP or hospital may entail many days off school.

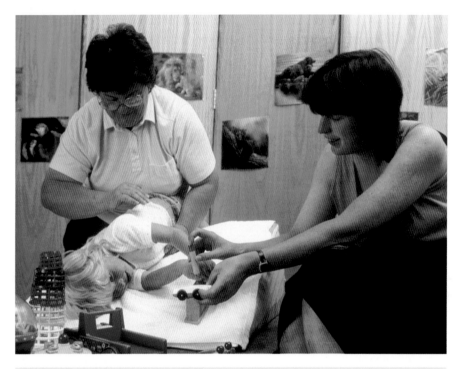

Figure 9.7 Physiotherapy for a young child

Diabetes mellitus

Diabetes mellitus is a condition in which the amount of glucose (sugar) in the blood is too high because the body is not able to use it properly. Normally the amount of glucose in our blood is carefully controlled by the hormone insulin, which helps the glucose to enter the cells where it is used as fuel by the body. Most children will have Type 1 diabetes, meaning they can no longer produce insulin because the cells in the pancreas that produce it have been destroyed – and without insulin, the body cannot use glucose.

Signs and symptoms

Children may display some or all of these symptoms:

- increased thirst
- breath smells of pear drops (acetone)
- frequent passing of urine – especially at night (children who have previously been dry at night might start to wet the bed (enuresis); this is caused by the body trying to rid itself of excess glucose)
- genital itching – sometimes leading to thrush, a yeast infection
- extreme tiredness and lack of energy
- loss of appetite

- blurred vision
- loss of weight: the amount of weight lost can be quite dramatic – up to ten per cent of the child's total body weight can be lost in as little as two months, caused by the body breaking down protein and fat stores as an alternative source of energy.

Treatment and care

Diabetes cannot be cured, but it can be treated effectively. The aim of the treatment is to keep the blood glucose level close to the normal range, so it is neither too high (hyperglycaemia) nor too low (hypoglycaemia, also known as a hypo). Most children with diabetes will be treated by a combination of insulin and a balanced diet, with the recommendation of regular physical activity.

Insulin has to be injected – it is a protein that would be broken down in the stomach if it were swallowed like a medicine. The majority of children will take two injections of insulin a day, one before breakfast and one before the evening meal. They are unlikely to need to inject insulin at school, unless on a school trip. In most cases the equipment will be

Figure 9.8 An insulin pen and insulin

an insulin 'pen' rather than a syringe. The child's parents, carers or a Diabetes Specialist Nurse can demonstrate the device used and discuss where the pen and insulin should be kept while the child is in school.

Hypoglycaemia (hypo)

Hypoglycaemia is the most common complication in diabetes where there is not enough sugar in the blood – usually because of too much insulin. It must be treated promptly to avoid possible brain damage from prolonged low blood sugar levels. Hypoglycaemic attacks (hypos) are especially likely to happen before meals. They can also happen as a result of:

- too much insulin
- not enough food to fuel an activity
- too little food at any stage of the day
- a missed meal or delayed meal or snack
- cold weather
- the child vomiting.

Recognising a hypo

Hypos happen quickly, but most children will have **warning signs** that will alert them, or people around them, to a hypo. Signs include:

- weakness or hunger
- confused or aggressive behaviour
- loss of concentration or coordination
- rapid, shallow breathing
- sweating
- dizziness
- glazed eyes and pallor
- headache
- trembling or shakiness.

How to manage a hypo

- Stay with the child – never leave them alone or expect them to go and get their own food or drink.
- Sit the child down and reassure him or her.
- Give the child a sugary drink (such as a fizzy non-diet drink) or sweet food.
- If the child recovers quickly after a sweet drink or food, give some more and allow the child to rest.
- If the child does not recover quickly or becomes unconscious, call an ambulance immediately and place the child in the recovery position. Always inform the parents of any hypoglycaemic attack, so that adjustments can be made to the treatment.

Guidelines for meeting the needs of a child with diabetes in an early years setting

Children with diabetes should be treated as any other child. Diabetes is *not* an illness and children should be encouraged to take part in all the activities and daily routine.

- Make sure that all contact details are up to date – home contact numbers, GP, diabetic specialist nurse, etc.

- Always contact parents immediately if the child becomes unwell and keep them informed of the child's progress.

- Ensure there is always a supply of glucose tablets or sweet drinks in the setting.

- When on outings, take a supply of sweet drinks or glucose tablets with you.

- Allow the child to take glucose tablets or snacks when required – most children with diabetes carry glucose tablets with them.

- Make sure you and all other members of staff know how to recognise and deal promptly with a child who has a hypoglycaemic attack.

- Always stay with the child if he or she feels unwell, and allow privacy if blood glucose testing is necessary during the day.

- Observe the child carefully during any vigorous exercise, such as swimming or climbing.

- Be understanding if the child shows emotional or behavioural problems caused by the necessary restrictions to their routine.

- Inform the child's parents if you are planning an activity which might involve extra strains and excitement.

- Make sure that the child eats regularly and that cooks are consulted about the child's dietary needs.

Epilepsy

Epilepsy is a condition of the nervous system affecting 150,000 children in the UK. It is not a mental illness and cannot be 'caught'. A person with epilepsy experiences seizures or fits. A **seizure** is caused by a sudden burst of excess electrical activity in the brain, causing a temporary disruption in the normal message passing between brain cells. This results in the brain's messages becoming temporarily halted or mixed up. Seizures can happen at any time and they generally only last a matter of seconds or minutes, after which the brain usually returns to normal.

The type of seizure a child has depends on which area of the brain is affected. Some seizures involve convulsions, or strange and confused behaviour, but others, such as absences, may be harder to recognise. Some may be unnoticeable to everyone except the child experiencing the seizure.

Note: some very young children have convulsions when there is a sudden rise in their body temperature, and this is called a febrile convulsion. This is *not* classified as epilepsy.

Causes

In most cases of epilepsy there is no known cause, but sometimes a structural abnormality of the brain is found. In some children, individual attacks may be brought on by a trigger, for example, a flashing light; in others, the attacks have no trigger.

Treatment

The aim of medical treatment is to control the child's tendency to have seizures, so that they can get on with life with as little disruption from epilepsy as possible. Avoiding the things which may trigger seizures and taking **anti-epileptic drugs** are the main treatment methods. Different anti-epileptic drugs are best for different seizures so each drug is selected according to the type of seizures that the child is experiencing. Although each drug has a slightly different way of acting, they all act on the brain to suppress seizures. They do not treat the underlying cause and do not 'cure' epilepsy.

Guidelines for meeting the needs of a child with epilepsy in an early years setting

- Children with epilepsy should be treated as any other child. Epilepsy is *not* an illness and children should be encouraged to take part in all the activities and daily routine, unless otherwise advised by the child's parents or doctor.

- Teachers and nursery managers should be aware of the child's **individual needs** and what is best for them should they have a **seizure** – for example, what kind of seizure the child has. Are there any know triggers? How long does the seizure usually last? Does the child need to sleep after a seizure? Do they need to go home? Are they usually confused afterwards? Does the setting have a medical room where the child can recover before going back to class? Is there a school nurse to advise or help if needed?

- Make sure that all contact details are up to date – home contact numbers, GP, etc.

- Record exactly what happened during a seizure; this will help in an initial diagnosis and also to build up a picture of the child's condition.

- Always contact parents immediately if the child has a seizure and keep them informed of the child's progress.

- Record any seizure in the appropriate record book.

- Make sure that you and all other members of staff know what to do when a child has a seizure.

- Try to minimise embarrassment for the child; if the child has been incontinent during the seizure, deal with it discreetly.

- Always stay with the child during a seizure and until they have recovered completely.

- Supervise activities such as swimming and climbing.

- Try to deal with seizures in a matter-of-fact way. Your attitude will influence the attitude of other children towards the child with epilepsy.

Research Activity

Find out about the different kinds of seizure experienced by a child with epilepsy. Make a simple chart detailing the signs and symptoms of the seizure and how you should respond to each one.

Acute illness

An acute illness is one that occurs suddenly, and often without warning. It is usually of short duration. Examples are:

- gastro-enteritis
- otitis media (inflammation of the middle ear)
- appendicitis
- tonsillitis
- an acute asthmatic attack.

Symptoms of acute illness in a child

Signs of such illness in a child include:

- loss of appetite
- a lack of interest in play
- unusual crying or screaming bouts
- diarrhoea and vomiting
- abdominal pain – babies with colic or abdominal pains will draw their knees up to their chest in an instinctive effort to relieve the pain
- lethargy or listlessness
- fever
- irritability and fretfulness
- pallor – a black child may have a paler area around the lips, and the conjunctiva may be pale pink instead of red
- dehydration – any illness involving fever or loss of fluid through vomiting or diarrhoea may result in dehydration; the mouth and tongue become dry and parched, and cracks may appear on the lips.

The first sign in a baby is a sunken anterior fontanelle: see page 366.

Hospital admission and care

Every year one in four children under five years old goes into hospital, and over two million children are seen in accident and emergency units. How a child reacts to a hospital visit depends on:

- their age
- the reason for hospitalisation
- the tests and treatment needed
- the ambience of the ward
- their personality
- their previous experience of hospitals
- the attitude and manner of the doctors, nurses and other staff
- the carer's own anxieties and perceived ability to cope with what is often a very stressful situation.

When a child has to be admitted to hospital, either for medical treatment or for a surgical operation, it is best if possible to prepare them in advance. Often, the experience is stressful for parents, particularly if they have their own negative childhood memories of hospitalisation. In the event, the majority of children do enjoy their hospital stay, but adverse reactions can be avoided in younger children by careful preparation and complete honesty in all information given.

Isolation

Some conditions (such as **leukaemia**) result in damage to the child's immune system, and hospital care in such cases may involve **reverse barrier nursing**. This technique provides the child with protection from infection that could be introduced by those people who have regular contact:

- A separate cubicle is used.
- Gowns and masks must be worn by any person who is in contact with the child.
- Gloves and theatre caps may be worn during certain procedures.
- Items – such as toys and clothes – cannot be freely taken in or out.

Children in isolation need a parent or carer to stay with them to an even greater extent than do those on an open ward, because of the strain of loneliness or boredom. Parents, in turn, need support from friends and relatives as they are having to cope with many stressful events: the anxiety over their child's illness and treatment; the unnaturalness of being confined with their child; the lack of privacy because of the need for continuous observation by nursing staff. Some hospitals provide a parents' room where they can go to have a cup of tea and share problems with others in similar situations.

Guidelines for preparing children for hospitalisation

- If possible, arrange to visit the ward a few days before admission – most wards welcome such visits and are happy to talk with carers. (This helps to overcome fear of the unknown.)
- Encourage children to talk about their feelings so that you know how to help them.
- Always be honest – never say that something will not hurt if it might, and only tell them that you will be there all the time if that is your plan.
- Keep explanations simple – reading a book about a child going to hospital may help to allay fears.
- If the child is going to have an operation, explain that they will have a 'special hospital sleep' that will stop them from feeling any pain.
- Do not let the child see your own worry, as this will make him or her feel frightened.
- Play hospital games using toys to help the child act out any fears.
- Try to be involved in the child's care as fully as possible.
- Take the child's favourite toy or 'comforter' as a link with home – the child could even help to pack their case.
- Tell the ward staff about the child's eating and sleeping patterns, and about particular preferences or special words that may be used for the toilet, etc.
- If the child is of school age, the hospital school will provide educational activities. Play specialists, nursery nurses or teachers will provide play activities for younger children.

Learning about hospital play

Invite a hospital play specialist or nursery nurse working in hospital to come and talk about their job. Prepare a list of questions beforehand and collect as much information as you can about the needs of the child in hospital.

The impact on parents and other family members when children are ill

Having a child with a serious or chronic illness is bound to have an effect on the whole family. Family members will be worried and under considerable stress. While a child is being treated in hospital it is best for everyone if life continues as normally as possible. Parents are often tempted to spoil their child and relax the usual rules, but this can cause more problems in the long run. The child will feel more secure if discipline is as usual. Each family is unique in the way that it will react initially and adjust in the long term. Parents whose baby or child develops a chronic or life-threatening illness may react in the following ways, which are part of what is known as the grieving process:

- **Disbelief, shock, numbness, pain and withdrawal**: even when parents suspect that there is something seriously wrong with their child, having their suspicions confirmed may still produce feelings of shock and panic. Explanations from health professionals may be impossible to fully comprehend, and they may feel numb and withdraw initially from others while they try to take in what has happened.
- **Despair and anger**: there may be powerful feelings of resentment and anger: 'Why is this happening to us?' Some of this anger may be directed towards professionals who are responsible both for breaking the bad news and for providing treatment and care.

- **Guilt**: parents may feel that they could have prevented the illness or disability. 'If only we had noticed sooner that something was wrong earlier …' is a common reaction as parents make a great effort to come to terms with a child's serious or life-threatening illness.
- **Confusion**: parents may be unable to understand what is happening, begin to question their ability to be good parents and worry about how they will cope in the future.
- **Isolation and feeling a loss of control**: parents may feel an increasing sense of isolation and feel that they have no control over events. They may feel that nobody else can fully appreciate what they are feeling and nothing can take away their pain.
- **Missing social life**: parents may have less time for each other and for social activities outside the home. Plans for dinners or holidays may have to be cancelled.

The reactions of brothers and sisters

Just as there are variations in the way parents react to a child's illness, the way in which the sick child's brothers and sisters react will differ greatly. Their reaction will depend upon their age and stage of development – and particularly on their level of understanding. Common reactions include:

- **Jealousy**: children may feel jealous of all the attention the sick child is getting. Parents and other relatives appear to be focusing all their attention on the ill child, with disruption of previous routines. Some children regress and develop attention-seeking behaviour in an effort to claim more of their parents' time.
- **Guilt and fear**: siblings may feel guilty that they are well and able to play and do things that their sick brother or sister cannot. They may be frightened at the strength and power of their parents' feelings of sadness and may even be afraid that they too could develop the same illness.
- **Neglect**: siblings can feel unloved and neglected by parents and others, whose loving attention may seem exclusively reserved for the sick child. They feel somehow very different from their friends, for whom life seems to go on as normal.

- **Grief**: children may go through a similar grieving process as do adults. They may feel overpowering feelings of sadness and loss; these feelings can result in:
  - loss of appetite and lack of energy
  - mood swings – one minute seeming full of energy and optimism, and the next seeming withdrawn and uncommunicative
  - sleeping problems.

The impact of ill health on the development of the child

Physical development

Physical development will almost always be affected when a child has a chronic illness. Depending on the nature and course of the condition, children may experience:

- **Delay in gross motor and fine motor skills development**: this could be because their treatment takes place mostly in a bed or chair, or because the illness itself prevents full mobility. The child may feel constantly tired and lacking in energy.
- **Faltering growth**: this may occur when a child's condition causes an inability to take in the nutrients necessary for growth and development.

Communication and language development

Although children who are away from their peers for long periods of time lack the normal conditions for communication, many children develop very good communication skills because of the increased attention from adults communicating with them.

Intellectual development

Children of school age will be able to have school lessons in hospital, but this has to be fitted in around treatments and care procedures. Also the child may lack the ability or energy to concentrate, and so may fall behind in all aspects of learning.

Emotional and social development

Chronic illnesses can interfere with children's happiness and how they feel about themselves. This can make treatment difficult, as when children are distressed or unhappy their illness may be harder to control.

Increased physical symptoms caused by the illness can also have an effect on a child's emotional development. Other effects include:

- **Poor self-esteem**: feeling unable to do the normal things his or her peers can do because of missing school may cause the child to have poor self-esteem.
- **Feelings of frustration**: children may develop attention-seeking behaviour or become aggressive when they see others doing things they want to do.
- **Regression**: babies and younger children particularly may revert to behaviour typical of a younger age group by becoming clingy, lethargic, tearful, or withdrawn.

Section 4: The responses to childhood illness

Children who are sick should not be at school or nursery; playgroups and schools are not appropriate places in which to care for sick children. However, it is often at a daycare setting that the child first shows signs and symptoms of an illness. Childminders and nannies working in the family home also need to know how to act to safeguard children's health.

How to report and record illness and seek help

Nannies and childminders should always contact the child's parents directly in case of accident or illness. In schools or nurseries, you should notify a senior member of staff if you notice that a child is unwell;

that person will then decide if and when to contact the child's parents.

Keeping records

Every child's record should contain the following information:

- child's full name
- address and telephone number of child's home
- address and telephone number of child's GP and health visitor
- date of birth
- address and telephone number of parent or carer's place(s) of work
- names and addresses of child's primary carers
- additional emergency contact telephone number, possibly a relative.

Recording illness

Records of a child's illness should be kept so that the child's parents and doctor can be informed; as with the Accident Report Book (see page 177), these records should include:

- when the child first showed signs of illness
- the signs and symptoms
- any action taken (for example, taking the temperature)
- progress of the illness since first noticing it (such as any further symptoms).

How to record and monitor children's health

Staff in schools and nurseries should offer support and reassurance to a child who may have to wait a while to be taken home. Any incident of vomiting or diarrhoea should be dealt with swiftly and sympathetically to minimise the child's distress and to preserve their dignity.

A member of staff should remain with the child at all times and keep them as comfortable as possible.

All early years settings should have a written policy on when to exclude children for childhood infections.

Responding to a child's needs in a home setting

Wherever possible, children should stay at home when ill, within the secure environment of their family and usual surroundings. The child will want their primary carer available at all times. The parents may need advice on how to care for their child, and this is provided by the family GP and primary health care team – some health authorities also have specialist paediatric nursing visiting services.

If the illness is infectious, advice may be needed on how it spreads; visits from friends and relatives may have to be reduced. The most infectious time is during the incubation period, but the dangers of infecting others remain until the main signs and symptoms (such as a rash) have disappeared. A child attending nursery or school will usually be kept at home until the GP says he is clear of infection.

The needs of sick children

Children who are sick have:

- physical needs – food and drink, rest and sleep, temperature control, exercise and fresh air, safety, hygiene and medical care
- intellectual and language needs – stimulation, appropriate activities
- emotional and social needs – love, security, play and contact with others.

The most important part of caring for sick children is to show that you care for them and to respond to all their needs. If a child is going to be nursed for some weeks, it is often useful to draw up a **plan of care**, just as nurses do in hospital. This has the following benefits:

- It helps you to keep a record of any changes in the child's condition and to ask for outside help if necessary.
- It reassures you that you are providing for all the child's needs.
- It enables you to plan a simple programme of activities to keep the child entertained and occupied.

- It enables another family member or colleague to assist in the general care, allowing you a break.

Meeting physical needs

Bed rest

Children usually dislike being confined to bed and will only stay there if feeling very unwell. There is no need to keep a child with a fever in bed; take your lead from the child. Making a bed on a sofa in the main living room will save carers the expense of extra heating and of tiring trips up and down stairs. The child will also feel more included in family life and less isolated. The room does not have to be particularly hot – just a comfortable temperature for you. If the child *does* stay in bed in his or her own room, remember to visit him or her often so that he or she does not feel neglected.

Hygiene

All children benefit from having a routine to meet their hygiene needs, and this need not be altered drastically during illness.

Temperature control

If the child has a fever, you will need to take their temperature regularly and use tepid sponging to reduce it (see page 361).

Feeding a sick child and providing drinks

Children who are ill often have poor appetites – a few days without food will not harm the child but fluid intake should be increased as a general rule.

Drinks should be offered at frequent intervals to prevent dehydration – the child will not necessarily request drinks.

Safety when caring for a child at home

- Keep all medicines safely locked away in a secure cupboard.

- Supervise the child at all times; watch out for any sudden changes in their condition.
- Be aware of any potential complications of the child's condition and watch for warning signs.

Guidelines for caring for a child in bed

- Use cotton sheets – they are more comfortable for a child with a temperature.

- Change the sheets daily if possible – clean sheets feel better.

- Leave a box of tissues on a table next to the bed.

- If the child has bouts of vomiting, pillows should be protected and a container should be kept close to the bed. This should be emptied and rinsed with an antiseptic or disinfectant, such as Savlon®, after use.

- Wet or soiled bed linen should be changed to prevent discomfort. Paper tissues that can be disposed of either by burning or by sealing in disposal bags are useful for minor accidents.

- A plastic mattress cover is useful as a sick child's behaviour may change and cause him or her to wet the bed.

Basic hygiene routines in caring for children who are sick

Children who play closely together for long periods of time are more likely than others to develop an infection – and any infection can spread very quickly from one child to another. All settings should have set routines for tidying up and for cleaning the floors, walls and furniture. Good hygiene routines will help to prevent infection. Children will take their cue from you, so you need to ensure that you are a good role model by setting a good example of a high standard of personal hygiene.

Guidelines for keeping the setting clean and hygienic

- Keep a window open to ventilate rooms, but avoid draughts.
- All surfaces should be damp dusted daily.
- Teach children *when* and *how* to wash their hands properly, and supervise them.
- Clean up any spills and accidents straightaway. Use a bleach solution and disposable towels to clean up any spillage (or treat according to your own setting's policy).
- Check the toilet area for cleanliness on a regular basis.
- Use paper towels and tissues and dispose of them in covered bins.
- Use antiseptic solutions such as Savlon® to disinfect toys and play equipment regularly; toys used by babies under one year should be disinfected daily.
- Encourage children to cover their nose and mouth when coughing or sneezing.
- Discourage parents from bringing their child into the nursery or school if they have a high temperature or other signs of infection.
- Keep sand trays clean by sieving and washing the sand regularly.

Disposing of waste

Every setting must have a written policy which explains how waste should be disposed of safely and hygienically. You should always do the following:

- Protect yourself from infection by wearing protective apron and gloves.
- Protect children by keeping them away from spillages at all times.
- Dispose of waste safely and hygienically – in separate covered bins in designated areas; food waste should be kept well away from toilet waste.
- Clean up spillages which could cause infection – using special solutions. If children are likely to come near the affected area, ask another member of staff to keep them away while you deal with the incident.

- Wrap children's soiled clothes in a polythene bag and give them to the parents when they arrive.
- When a child uses a potty, make sure that it is emptied straightaway after use and cleaned appropriately.

Guidelines for a hygiene routine for a sick child at home

- The child's room should be well ventilated and uncluttered. Open a window to prevent stuffiness but protect the child from draughts.
- Provide a potty to avoid trips to the lavatory.
- Protect the mattress with a rubber or plastic sheet.
- A daily bath or shower is important. During an acute phase of illness, this can be done in the form of a bed bath – an all-over wash in bed.
- Brush hair daily.
- Clean teeth after meals and apply vaseline to sore, cracked lips.
- Keep the child's nails short and clean, and prevent scratching of any spots.
- Dress the child in cool, cotton clothing; put a jumper and socks or slippers over pyjamas if the child does not want to stay in bed the whole time.

Guidelines for encouraging sick children to drink

- Provide a covered jug of fruit juice or water; any fluid is acceptable according to the child's tastes, for example, milk, meaty drinks or soups.
- If the child has mumps, do not give fruit drinks because the acid causes pain to the tender parotid glands.
- A sick toddler who has recently given up his bottle may regress. Allow him to drink from a bottle until he is feeling better.
- Try using an interesting curly straw.
- Give the child an 'adult' glass to make them feel special.

Guidelines for encouraging sick children to drink (cont.)

- Try offering drinks in a tiny glass or eggcup, which makes the quantities look smaller.

- Offer fresh fruit juices, such as pear, apple or mango; dilute them with fizzy water to make them more interesting, but avoid giving more than one fizzy drink a day; vary the drinks as much as possible.

- If the child does not like milk, add a milkshake mix or ice cream.

Guidelines for encouraging a sick child to eat

- Most children with a fever do not want to eat, so while you should offer food, you should never force a child to eat.

- Allow the child to choose their favourite foods.

- Give the child smaller meals but more often than you would normally.

- If the child has a sore throat, give ice cream or an iced lolly made with fruit juice or yoghurt.

- If the child is feeling slightly sick, offer mashed potato.

- Offer snacks regularly and always keep the child company while they eat.

- Most children who are sick do not find ordinary food very appetising, but may be tempted to eat with 'soldiers' of fresh bread and butter, slices of fruit or their favourite yoghurt.

- Try to make food as attractive as possible; do not put too much on the plate at once and remember that sick children often cope better with foods that do not require too much chewing, such as egg custard, milk pudding, thick soups, chicken and ice cream.

Helping children who are in pain

Very young children or children who are very sick are not always able to express how they are feeling. Parents know their child's usual reactions and behaviour and so may be able to tell if their child is in pain, but it is often difficult for adults to know how much pain a young child is in. Signs that a young child is in pain include:

- crying or screaming
- facial changes or pulling a face
- changes in their sleeping or eating patterns
- becoming quiet and withdrawn
- refusing to move.

Often a child with acute earache will not be able to describe where they are hurting, but may pull or rub at their ear lobes. Hospitals and clinics use a scale such as the Faces Pain Scale: see Figure 9.9. This involves asking the child to point to the face that shows how much hurt they are feeling from 'no pain' on the left through to 'hurts worst' on the right.

Pain can cause acute distress to the affected child. Distraction techniques can help with minor pain – for example, blowing bubbles, playing with puppets, etc. Children's ibuprofen or paracetamol can be administered with parental permission.

How to take a temperature

All family first aid kits should contain a thermometer. There are many types, but the most widely used in the home are digital thermometers and temperature strips:

- **Digital thermometer**: this is battery-operated and consists of a safe narrow probe with a tip sensitive to temperature. It is placed in the mouth and is easy to read via a display panel.
  1 Place the narrow tip of the thermometer under the child's armpit – or for older children, place under their tongue.
  2 Read the temperature when it stops rising; some models beep when this point is reached.
- **Forehead temperature strip**: this is a rectangular strip of thin plastic which contains temperature-sensitive crystals that change colour according to the temperature measured. It is placed on the child's forehead. It is not as accurate as other thermometers but is a useful check.
  1 Hold the plastic strip firmly against the child's forehead for about 30 seconds.
  2 Record the temperature revealed by the colour change.

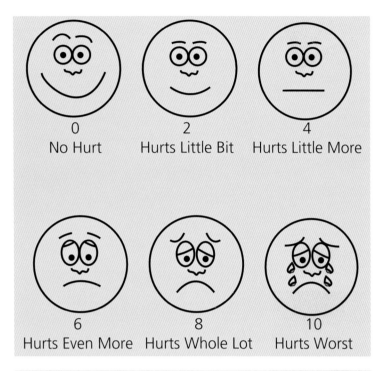

Figure 9.9 Wong-Baker FACES™ Pain Rating Scale © Wong-Baker FACES Foundation 1983, www.WongBakerFACES.org

Whatever the cause of a high temperature, it is important to try to reduce it (see Figure 9.10). There is always the risk a fever could lead to convulsions or fits.

Health and safety policies for dealing with children

The main legislation on health and safety is outlined in Chapter 4. Most early years settings will have a range of policies and procedures dealing with:

- the administration and storage of medicines
- infectious diseases and exclusion guidelines
- moving and handling
- infection control
- reporting and recording illness and accidents
- safety on trips away from the setting
- first aid.

Regulations for the storage and administration of medicines

Some children have illnesses or chronic medical conditions which are controlled by medication.

Children with asthma or allergies will require the medication to be kept in the setting in case it is needed. Procedures to follow for the storage and administration of any medicines must comply with the regulations of your home country.

In England, the EYFS issued a guidance document, *Managing Medicines in Schools and Early Years Settings*. This requires settings to do the following:

1 **Policy**: have a policy about the management and administration of medicines.
2 **Written record**: every medicine given to children must be written down, and this record is shared with the child's parents or carers.
3 **Parent consent forms**: ensure that parent consent forms have been completed, giving permission for each and every medicine prior to it being administered. The consent form must be very precise and contain the following information:
    - full name of child and date of birth
    - name of medication and strength
    - who prescribed it
    - dosage to be given in the setting
    - how the medication should be stored (such as in the fridge) and the expiry date

Figure 9.10 Forehead temperature strip and digital thermometer

• any possible side effects that may be expected
• signature, printed name of parent and date.

If the administration of the medicine requires any technical or medical knowledge, individual training should be provided for the staff team from a suitably qualified health professional. The manager will decide who administers the medication in your setting. It might be on a voluntary basis; often the child's key person takes the responsibility, or the task could form part of an employee's contract.

It is good practice for two members of staff to be present when administering medication, and for each of them to sign the record sheet, which should include date, time, dosage, and space for the parent's or carer's signature when he or she collects the child.

The Control of Substances Hazardous to Health Regulations 2002 (COSHH) states that medicines should be kept in a safe place, preferably in a locked cupboard, clearly **labelled** with the child's name. The exception to this rule is the use of inhalers for children with asthma. The inhaler should be kept nearby for the child, in a place easily reached by an adult yet out of reach of other children (for example, a high shelf).

Guidelines for giving medicines to children

Here is a list of essential points to bear in mind when medicines are prescribed for a child:

• Store all medicines out of reach of children and in childproof containers.

• Ask the doctor for as much information as possible about the medicines; for example, if there are likely to be side effects, or if certain foods should be avoided.

• Measure doses of medicine accurately, using a marked medicine spoon for liquid; teaspoons are not equivalent to a 5 ml spoon.

• Always follow instructions carefully.

• Most medicines for young children are made up in a sweetened syrup to make them more palatable.

• Remember that your attitude is important – if you show anxiety when giving medicine to a child, they will be anxious too.

• Store medicines at the correct temperature, in the fridge or away from direct heat if that is the direction on the bottle.

• Make sure you understand the instructions for giving the medicine before leaving the chemist, such as how much, how often and when; check whether it should be given before or after meals.

• Make sure that all the medicine is swallowed – this can be difficult with babies, see tips below.

• Throw away any leftover prescribed medicines on completion of treatment.

Guidelines for giving medicines to children (cont.)

- If a child needs to take medicine contained in syrup regularly, remember to brush her teeth afterwards to prevent tooth decay.
- Never put medicines into a child's drink or food as the child may not take it all. If necessary, tablets can be crushed and added to a teaspoon of jam or honey. Follow this with a drink.
- **DO NOT** give aspirin to any child under the age of ten years, because of the risk of **Reye's syndrome**.
- Always obtain **written consent** from the child's parents before giving any medicines.

Key term

Reye's syndrome – A very rare condition that causes serious liver and brain damage. Many children who developed Reye's syndrome had previously taken the painkiller aspirin to treat their symptoms. It is recommended that no child under 16 years should be given aspirin.

Appropriate responses in emergency situations

First aid is an important skill. By performing simple procedures and following certain guidelines, it may be possible to **save lives** by giving basic treatment until professional medical help arrives. Practice of first aid skills is vital; in an emergency there is no time to read instructions. If you have memorised some of the most basic procedures, it will help you to react quickly and efficiently.

All those who work with children should take a recognised First Aid Course, such as those run by the St. John's Ambulance Association or the British Red Cross Society. You should also take refresher courses periodically, so that you feel competent to deal with any medical emergency.

The following pages explain first aid techniques to use with babies and children. They should not be used as a substitute for attending a first aid course with a trained instructor.

How to give CPR (cardiopulmonary resuscitation)

A child's heart or breathing can stop as a result of lack of oxygen (such as choking), drowning, electric shock, heart attack or other serious injury. The basic principle of giving CPR is to do the work of the child's heart and lungs. If a baby or child has collapsed, you need to find out if he or she is conscious or unconscious.

1. **Can you get a response?** Check if he or she is conscious. Call their name and try tapping them gently on the sole of their foot. If there is no response you need to **check for breathing**.
2. **Open the airway**: place one hand on the forehead and gently tilt the head back. Then using your other hand, lift the child's chin. Take a quick look and remove any visible obstructions from the mouth and nose.
3. **Look, listen and feel** for normal breathing: place your face next to the child's face and listen for breathing. You can do this while looking along the child's chest and abdomen for any movement. You may also be able to feel the child's breath on your cheek. Allow up to ten seconds to check if the child is breathing or not.
4. **If the child is not breathing**: if another person is present ask them to **call an ambulance** straight away.
5. If you are alone give **one minute of CPR** *then* call an ambulance. If the casualty is under one year old, take the baby with you call an ambulance.

Below are instructions on how to administer CPR to babies and children. Anyone untrained or unable to administer rescue breaths should give chest compressions only.

CPR: resuscitation for a baby who is not breathing (from birth to approximately one year)

1 Open the airway by gently tilting the baby's head back and lifting the chin.

2 Give FIVE rescue breaths by placing your mouth over their mouth and nose, and blow gently for about one second, until you see the chest rise.

3 Place two fingers on the centre of the baby's chest, and give 30 chest compressions by pressing down about a third of the depth.

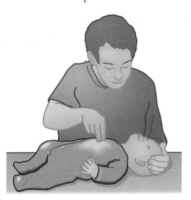

4 Then give TWO rescue breaths, followed by 30 chest compressions.
5 Continue this cycle of breaths and compressions for one minute.
6 If not already done, call for an ambulance now and continue the above cycle until help arrives or the baby starts to breathe.

CPR: resuscitation for a child who is not breathing (from one year onwards)

1 Open the airway by gently tilting the child's head back and lifting the chin.

2 Pinch the child's nose. Give FIVE rescue breaths by placing your mouth over their mouth and blow steadily until you see the chest rise.

3 Place one hand on the centre of the child's chest and lean over the child. Give 30 chest compressions by pressing down about a third of the depth of the chest.

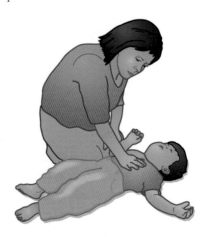

4 Then give TWO rescue breaths, followed by 30 chest compressions.

5 Continue this cycle of breaths and compressions for one minute.

6 If not already done, call for an ambulance now and continue the above cycle until help arrives or the child starts to breathe.

The recovery position

If a child is unconscious this means that they have no muscle control; if lying on their back, their tongue is floppy and may fall back, partially obstructing the airway. Any child who is breathing and who has a pulse should be placed in the recovery position while you wait for medical assistance. This safe position allows fluid and vomit to drain out of the child's mouth so that they are not inhaled into the lungs.

Recovery position for a baby (from birth to approximately one year)

Hold the baby with the head tilted downwards.

Recovery position for a child (from one year onwards)

1 Place arm nearest to you at a right angle, with palm facing up.

2 Move other arm towards you, keeping the back of their hand against their cheek.

3 Get hold of the knee furthest from you and pull up until foot is flat on the floor.

4 Pull the knee towards you, keeping the child's hand pressed against their cheek.

5 Position the leg at a right angle.

6 Make sure that the airway remains open by tilting the head back, then check breathing by feeling and listening for breath.

In Practice

The recovery position

In pairs, practise placing each other in the recovery position.

Choking

Choking is when a child struggles to breathe because of a blockage in the airway. Children under three years are particularly vulnerable to choking because their airways are small and they have not yet developed full control of the muscles of their mouth and throat.

Causes of choking

Usually, choking in small children is caused by a small foreign object blocking one of the major airways. This may be a small toy put in the mouth and inadvertently 'swallowed', or a small piece of food they have not chewed properly.

Symptoms

Choking often begins with small coughs or gasps as the child tries to draw in breath around the

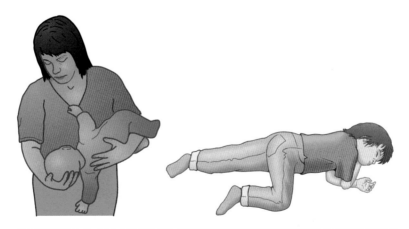

Figure 9.11 (g) The recovery position for a baby (h) The recovery position for a child

obstruction or clear it out. This may be followed by a struggling sound or squeaking whispers as the child tries to communicate their distress. The child may thrash around and drool and their eyes may water. They may flush red and then turn blue. However if a small item gets stuck in the throat of a baby or toddler, you may not even *hear* them choking – they could be silently suffocating as the object fills their airway and prevents them from coughing or breathing.

How to treat choking

For a baby who is choking:

1 First check inside the baby's mouth. If you can **see** the obstruction, try to hook it out with your finger, but do not dig around or do a finger sweep of the mouth in the hope of finding it as you risk pushing it further down. If this does not work, **act quickly**:
2 Lay the baby down along your forearm, supporting her head and neck with your hand. The baby's head should be lower than her bottom.
3 Give up to **five back blows**, between the shoulder blades with the heel of your hand.
4 Check the baby's mouth and pick out any obstructions.
5 If the baby is still choking, give up to five **chest thrusts** (as for CPR), pushing inwards and upwards.
6 Check the mouth again. If still choking, give three full cycles of back blows and chest thrusts, checking the mouth after each cycle.
7 Call an ambulance if the baby is still choking and repeat cycles of back blows and chest thrusts until medical aid arrives. If the baby loses consciousness, start CPR.

For a toddler or older child who is choking:

1 **First check inside the child's mouth**. If you can **see** the obstruction, try to hook it out with your finger, but do not dig around in the hope of finding it as you risk pushing it further down. If this does not work, **act quickly**:
2 Sit down and put child face down across your knees with head and arms hanging down (or **stand** an older child leaning forward). Keep the child's head lower than the chest.
3 Give up to **five sharp back blows** between the shoulder blades with the heel of your hand.

4 Check the mouth again and remove any obstruction. If the child is still choking, give **abdominal thrusts:** place a clenched fist above the belly button. Grasp your fist with your other hand. Pull upwards and inwards up to five times.
5 Check the mouth again. If the child is still choking, give three full cycles of back blows and abdominal thrusts, checking the mouth after each cycle.
6 Call an ambulance if the child is still choking and repeat cycles of back blows and abdominal thrusts until medical aid arrives. If the child loses consciousness, start CPR.

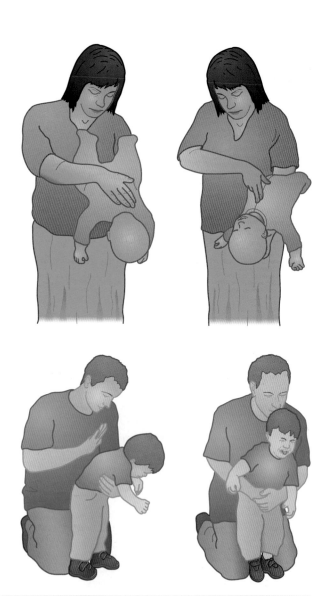

Figure 9.12 How to treat an infant or child who is choking

Dealing with common minor injuries

All injuries which require some sort of treatment – however minor they may seem – must be recorded in the **Accident Report Book,** and the child's parents or guardian must also be informed.

Minor cuts and grazes

1 Sit or lie the child down and reassure them.
2 Clean the injured area with cold water, using cotton wool or gauze.
3 Apply a dressing if necessary.
4 Do not attempt to pick out pieces of gravel or grit from a graze; just clean gently and cover with a light dressing.

Record the injury and treatment in the **Accident Report Book** and make sure the parents/carers of the child are informed.

Severe bleeding

1 Summon medical help: dial 999 or 112, or call a doctor.
2 Try to stop the bleeding:
   • apply direct pressure to the wound; wear gloves and use a dressing or a non-fluffy material, such as a clean tea towel
   • elevate the affected part if possible.
3 Apply a dressing. If the blood soaks through, *do not* remove the dressing, apply another on top, and so on.
4 Keep the child warm and reassure them.
5 Do *not* give anything to eat or drink.
6 Contact the child's parents or carers.
7 If the child loses consciousness, follow the procedure for resuscitation.

Note: always record the incident, and the treatment given, in the Accident Report Book. Always wear disposable gloves if in an early years setting, to prevent cross-infection.

Nosebleeds

1 Sit the child down with his or her head well forward.
2 Ask him or her to breathe through their mouth.
3 Pinch the fleshy part of his or her nose, just below the bridge.
4 Reassure the child, and tell him or her not to try to speak, cough or sniff as this may disturb blood clots.

5 After ten minutes, release the pressure. If the nose is still bleeding, reapply the pressure for further periods of ten minutes.
6 If the nosebleed persists beyond 30 minutes, seek medical aid.

Minor burns and scalds

1 Place the injured part under slowly running cold water, or soak in cold water for ten minutes.
2 Gently remove any constricting articles from the injured area before it begins to swell.
3 Dress with clean, sterile non-fluffy material:
   • DO NOT use adhesive dressings.
   • DO NOT apply lotions, ointments or grease to burn or scald.
   • DO NOT break blisters or otherwise interfere.

Sprains and strains

Follow the **RICE** procedure:

• R – rest the injured part
• I – apply ice or a cold compress
• C – compress the injury
• E – elevate the injured part.

1 Rest, steady and support the injured part in the most comfortable position for the child.
2 Cool the area by applying an ice pack or a cold compress. (This could be a pack of frozen peas wrapped in cloth.)
3 Apply gentle, even pressure by surrounding the area with a thick layer of foam or cotton wool, secured with a bandage.
4 Raise and support the injured limb, to reduce blood flow to the injury and to minimise bruising.

How to get emergency help

• Assess the situation: stay calm and do not panic.
• Minimise any danger to yourself and to others; for example, make sure someone takes charge of other children at the scene.
• Send for help. Notify a doctor, hospital and parents etc, as appropriate. If in any doubt, call an ambulance: **dial 999 or 112.**

Calling an ambulance

Be ready to assist the emergency services by answering some simple questions:

- Give your name and the telephone number you are calling from.
- Tell the operator the location of the accident. Try to give as much information as possible, for example, are there any familiar landmarks, such as churches or pubs nearby?
- Explain briefly what has happened: this helps the paramedics to act speedily when they arrive.
- Tell the operator what you have done so far to treat the casualty.

In Practice

First aid boxes and safety information

The contents of a first aid box in the workplace are determined by the Health and Safety at Work Act. See Chapter 4, page 172 for the statutory contents of the box.

Accident Report Book

Every early years setting is required by law to have an **Accident Report Book** and to maintain a record of accidents. Record the injury and treatment in the Accident Report Book and make sure the parents/carers of the child are informed. Information may be recorded in the format below:

> Name of person injured: Bethany Taylor
>
> Date and time of injury: Thursday 10th May 2012, 10.40 am
>
> Where: Play area
>
> What exactly happened: Bethany fell in the outdoor area and grazed her knee
>
> What injuries occurred: a graze
>
> What treatment was given: graze was bathed and an adhesive dressing applied
>
> Name and signature of person dealing with the accident: LUCY COWELL *Lucy Cowell*
>
> Signature of witness to the report: *Paul Hammond*
>
> Signature of parent or guardian: *Janet Taylor*

Section 5: The role of the adult in supporting children who are ill and their families

Identifying and supporting the range of responses from children and their families when children are unwell

It is important that support given to the child and family is family-centred. This means that the child's parents have a key role in making decisions about the sort of care their child receives, where the care takes place and how they can establish networks of support.

Professional carers, such as doctors, nurses, social workers and early years workers should recognise the needs of the child and the whole family and aim to meet those needs in an honest, caring and supportive manner.

Parents should be involved in every aspect of their child's illness and be encouraged to make decisions about the care their child will receive, for example how much they will be involved in practical care. Parents should never feel pressurised to undertake nursing tasks, such as changing dressings, unless they feel comfortable about them.

Information about the child's illness and the care and treatment involved must be given in a way that is easy to understand, and professionals should operate an 'open door' policy which encourages parents to ask about any aspect of care they are unsure about.

Care plans should be drawn up with the parents' involvement, and should take account of the physical, emotional and social needs of the whole family. Parents who are caring for a sick child at home may feel isolated, and many parents will experience stress and tension within their marital relationships. Support groups can help enormously, by putting parents in touch with others who are going through the same difficulties.

Financial help should be available for all parents caring for a chronically ill child at home or in hospital. Extra costs incurred as a direct result of their circumstances include:

- transport costs to get to the hospital or assessment centre
- increased household bills for heating, lighting and laundry
- one parent having to give up work to look after the sick child
- increased telephone bills as parents have to keep in touch with hospital staff, family and friends.

The Benefits Agency can advise parents about the different allowances payable in individual circumstances.

Providing support in the child's early years setting

Whether you are working in the family home as a nanny, in a nursery or in a school, you will need to keep well informed about the family's situation and to offer appropriate support. You will need to be aware of:

- the child's needs and their stage of development
- how they may be feeling
- any behaviour changes.

How you can help

- You need to offer practical and emotional support to the child and to his or her family.
- Key persons can develop a strong emotional bond with the child and provide a safe, trusting relationship which will help the child and the parents; there should always be a back-up person to help when the child's key person is away.
- Always find time to listen to the child.
- Observe the child closely and try to see if the child is experiencing any areas of difficulty.

- Allow the child to express his or her feelings; encourage children to use play as a form of therapy to release feelings of tension, frustration and sadness; you could offer activities such as playing with dough, bubble-blowing, water play, small world play and home corner play.
- Reassure them that they are very much loved by their family and their carers.

The role of play and specific activities in meeting individual needs of children who are ill

For children, play is at the very centre of their lives. Play can make a real difference to children who are ill, whether in hospital or at home. This is when children are at their most vulnerable – ill, separated from their friends and often in an unfamiliar setting or routine. Play is important because it:

- creates an environment where stress and anxiety are lessened
- helps the child to regain self-confidence and self-esteem
- helps the child to understand what is going to happen to them – for example, hospital play specialists explain procedures and treatments using play
- speeds recovery and rehabilitation.

Children who are ill often regress and may want to play with toys that they have long since outgrown. They may have a short attention span and tire quickly, so toys and materials should be changed frequently.

You will need to be understanding and tolerant of these changes in behaviour. Never put pressure on a child to take part in an activity if they do not want to. If a child is ill for some time, you can achieve variation in toys and games by borrowing them from a local toy library.

Play activities for sick children

- Jigsaw puzzles: the child could start with simple puzzles and progress to more challenging ones, perhaps with family help.
- Board games such as Lotto, Ludo and Halma.
- Card games such as Uno, Snap and Happy Families.
- Making a scrapbook: provide magazines, photos, flowers, scissors and glue to make a personal record.
- Drawing and painting: provide poster paints, lining paper and a protective plastic apron; children also love to paint with water in 'magic' painting books.
- Play dough: either bought or homemade; playing with dough is creative and provides an outlet for feelings of frustration.
- Making models with Duplo® or Lego®.
- Playing with small-world objects, such as toy farms, zoos and Playmobil®.
- French knitting or sewing cards can be used with older children.
- Crayons, felt tip pens and a pad of paper.
- Books to be read alone or with an adult.
- Audio tapes of songs, rhymes and favourite stories.
- Videos, cartoons and computer games.
- Encourage other children and adults to visit once the child is over the infectious stage.

If the child wishes to draw or paint, or do some other messy activity, use protective sheets to protect the bed covers. Many activities are easier to manage if you supply a steady surface such as a tray with legs or a special bean-bag tray.

The role of other professionals in the support of children who are ill and their families

In hospital, the child and family are helped and supported by a multidisciplinary team of professionals, which includes:

- paediatric nurses
- doctors
- social workers
- play leaders and nursery nurses
- play therapists and hospital play specialists: they may hold a Level 3 qualification in child care and education, the Hospital Play Specialist Board Certificate, a psychotherapy qualification or other child care qualification
- teachers: hospital-based teachers provide lessons for children of school age who are in hospital for longer than a week
- counsellors
- representatives of different religious faiths.

Other professionals who may help the child in hospital include physiotherapists, occupational therapists, speech and language therapists, medical social workers and dieticians.

In the community, support is offered by:

- the primary health care team: the GP, district nurse, health visitor and practice nurse
- paediatric specialist nurses: some health authorities operate a 'hospital at home' service
- Macmillan nurses – trained district nurses who specialise in caring for people with life-threatening conditions.

Multi-agency working and the sharing of information

As with all multi-agency working, the child is the central focus. Members of the primary health care team (the PHCT) will work together in the best interests of the sick child and his or her family. The GP will be responsible for arranging the services and professional help necessary in each individual case. Hospital staff will keep the GP informed of treatment and progress. If a child is of school age, the school nurse will liaise with both the hospital and the GP so that the relevant educational support is put in place.

The support for parents and families who are looking after children who are ill

There are a number of local support groups for the families of children who are ill. Parents can find out about the general and specialist support groups in their area from:

- the Reference section in the local public library
- Health visitors and GP centres.

There are also a number of useful organisations at national level, most of which have local branches to support families in their own neighbourhood. These include the following:

- **Action for Sick Children**: the UK's leading health charity, specially formed to ensure that sick children always receive the highest standard of care possible. Provides useful information for parents and professionals on all aspects of health care for children: www.actionforsickchildren.org
- **Contact a Family**: this website is for families who have a disabled child and those who work with disabled children or who are interested to find out more about their needs: www.cafamily.org.uk
- **National Association of Hospital Play Staff**: aims to promote the physical and mental wellbeing of children and young people who are patients in hospital, hospice or receiving medical care at home: www.nahps.org.uk

10 Nutrition and healthy food for children: Unit 12

Section 1: The essential food groups and a balanced diet for children

Good nutrition, or healthy eating, is one of the most important ways we can help ourselves to feel well and be well. We need food:

- to provide **energy** for physical activity and to maintain body temperature
- to provide material for the **growth** of body cells
- for the **repair and replacement** of damaged body tissues.

The substances in food that fulfil these functions are called **nutrients**.

Food and energy requirements

Food requirements vary according to age, gender, size, occupation or lifestyle, and climate. Different foods contain different amounts of energy per unit of weight; foods that contain a lot of fat and sugar have high energy values. An excess of calories will result in weight gain, as the surplus 'energy' is stored as fat; an insufficient intake of calories will result in weight loss, as the body has to draw on fat reserves to meet energy requirements. Babies and young children have relatively high energy requirements in relation to their size.

Food groups

Types of food can be arranged into five groups, based on the **nutrients** they provide. To ensure a balanced, healthy diet, some foods from each group should be included in a child's diet every day (see Table 10.1). The easiest way to monitor our nutrition is to keep in mind the **five food groups**; eating a variety of foods from each of these food groups every day automatically balances our diet. The Eatwell plate (Figure 10.1) shows how much of what you eat should come from each food group.

Figure 10.1 The Eatwell plate

The balanced nutritional needs of young children and appropriate daily portion intake

Table 10.1 below shows how to provide young children with a nutritionally balanced diet. It also outlines the daily portions recommended by the British Nutrition Foundation.

Food groups	Main nutrients	Types to choose	Portions per day	Suggestions for meals and snacks
1. Bread, other cereals and potatoes All types of bread, rice, breakfast cereals, pasta, noodles, and potatoes (beans and lentils can be eaten as part of this group)	Carbohydrates (starch), fibre, some calcium and iron, B-group vitamins	Wholemeal, brown wholegrain or high-fibre versions of bread; avoid fried foods too often (e.g. chips). Use butter and other spreads sparingly	FIVE All meals of the day should include foods from this group	One portion = • 1 bowl of breakfast cereal • 2 tbsp pasta or rice • 1 small potato Snack meals include bread or pizza base
2. Fruit and vegetables Fresh, frozen and canned fruit and vegetables, dried fruit, fruit juice (beans and lentils can be eaten as part of this group)	Vitamin C, carotenes, iron, calcium folate, fibre and some carbohydrate	Eat a wide variety of fruit and vegetables; avoid adding rich sauces to vegetables, and sugar to fruit	FOUR/FIVE Include 1 fruit or vegetable daily high in vitamin C, e.g. tomato, sweet pepper, orange or kiwi fruit	One portion = • 1 glass of pure fruit juice • 1 piece of fruit • 1 sliced tomato • 2 tabsp of cooked vegetables • 1 tbsp of dried fruit, e.g. raisins
3. Milk and dairy foods Milk, cheese, yoghurt and fromage frais (this group does not contain butter, eggs and cream)	Calcium, protein, B-group vitamins (particularly B12), vitamins A and D	Milk is a very good source of calcium, but calcium can also be obtained from cheese, flavoured or plain yoghurts and fromage frais	THREE Children require the equivalent of one pint of milk each day to ensure an adequate intake of calcium	One portion = • 1 glass of milk • 1 pot of yoghurt or fromage frais • 1 tbsp of grated cheese, e.g. on a pizza Under 2s – do not give reduced-fat milks, e.g. semi-skimmed – they do not supply enough energy

Food groups	Main nutrients	Types to choose	Portions per day	Suggestions for meals and snacks (cont.)
4. Meat, fish and alternatives Lean meat, poultry, fish, eggs, tofu, quorn, pulses – peas, beans, lentils, nuts and seeds	Iron, protein, B-group vitamins (particularly B12), zinc and magnesium	Lower-fat versions – meat with fat cut off, chicken without skin etc. Beans and lentils are good alternatives, being low in fat and high in fibre	TWO Vegetarians will need to have grains, pulses and seeds; vegans avoid all food associated with animals	One portion = • 2 fish fingers (for a 3-year-old) • 4 fish fingers (for a 7-year-old) • baked beans • a small piece of chicken
5. Fatty and sugary foods Margarine, low-fat spread, butter, ghee, cream, chocolate, crisps, biscuits, sweets and sugar, fizzy soft drinks, puddings	Vitamins and essential fatty acids, but also a lot of fat, sugar and salt	Only offer small amounts of sugary and fatty foods. Fats and oils are found in all the other food groups	NONE Only eat fatty and sugary foods sparingly, e.g. crisps, sweets and chocolate	Children may be offered foods with extra fat or sugar – biscuits, cakes or chocolate – as long as they are not replacing food from the four main food groups

Table 10.1 The balanced nutritional needs of young children

The dangers of too much salt

Salt (sodium chloride) should be avoided as far as possible in the diets of young children, as their kidneys are not mature enough to cope with large amounts of salt. Be aware that many common foods, such as cheese, manufactured soups, packet meals and bread, are already quite high in added salt. Children will receive sufficient salt for their dietary needs from a normal balanced diet, without adding any salt to food as it is cooked or at the table.

Guidelines for reducing salt in children's diets

- Cut down gradually on the amount of salt used in cooking, so that children become used to less salty foods.
- If preparing baby food at home, do not add salt, even if it tastes bland. Manufactured baby food is tightly regulated to limit the salt content to a trace.
- Try using a low-salt substitute, such as LoSalt®, Solo® or a supermarket's own brand low-sodium salt, in cooking or at the table. These products substitute up to 70 per cent of the sodium chloride with potassium chloride.

Dietary fibre

Dietary fibre – or roughage – is found in cereals, fruits and vegetables. Fibre is made up of the indigestible parts or compounds of plants, which pass relatively unchanged through the stomach and intestines. Fibre is needed to provide roughage to help keep the food moving through the gut. A small amount of fibre is important for health in pre-school children, but too much can cause problems, as their digestive system is still immature. It could also reduce energy intake by 'bulking up' the diet. Providing a mixture of white bread and refined cereals, white rice and pasta, as well as a few wholegrain varieties occasionally, helps to maintain a healthy balance between fibre and nutrient intakes.

Providing drinks for children

An adequate fluid intake will prevent dehydration and reduce the risk of constipation. Milk and water are the best drinks to give between meals and snacks, as they do not harm teeth when taken from a cup or beaker. You should offer children something to drink several times during the day. The best drinks for young children are **water** and **milk**:

- **Water** is a very underrated drink for the whole family. It quenches thirst without spoiling the appetite; if bottled water is preferred, it should be still, not carbonated (fizzy), as this is acidic. More water should be given in hot weather in order to prevent **dehydration**. Research into how the brain develops has found that water is beneficial. Many early years settings now make water available for children to help themselves.
- **Milk** is an excellent, nourishing drink which provides valuable nutrients.

All drinks that contain sugar can be harmful to teeth and can also take the edge off children's appetites. Examples are:

- flavoured milks
- fruit squashes
- flavoured fizzy drinks
- fruit juices (containing natural sugar).

Unsweetened, *diluted* fruit juice is a reasonable option for children; however it is not as good as water or milk, and ideally should only be offered at mealtimes. Low-sugar and diet fruit drinks contain artificial sweeteners and are best avoided. Tea and coffee should *not* be given to children under five years, as these prevent the absorption of iron from foods. They also tend to fill children up without providing any nourishment.

Children aged one to five years

Offer around six to eight drinks per day from a beaker or cup (although more may be needed in very hot weather or when the child is very active). One drink for this age group will be about 100–150 ml.

Sweetened drinks, including diluted fruit juice, should only be consumed *with*, rather than between, meals, to lessen the risk of dental decay. Consumption of sugar-free, fizzy or fruit-based drinks, although not recommended, should also be confined to mealtimes, because the high acidity level of these drinks can cause dental decay.

How much food should children be given?

Children's appetites vary enormously, so common sense is a good guide on how big a portion should be. Always be guided by the individual child:

- Do not force a child to eat when he or she no longer wishes to.
- Do not refuse to give the child more if he or she is really hungry.

Some children always feel hungry at one particular mealtime. Others require food little and often. You should always offer food that is nourishing, as well as satisfying the child's hunger.

Vitamins and minerals in children's diets

Iron

Iron is essential for children's health. Iron deficiency can lead to **anaemia**, which can hold back both physical and mental development. Children who are poor eaters or who are on restricted diets are most at risk.

Iron comes in two forms:

- in foods from **animal sources** (especially meat) – this form is easily absorbed by the body
- in **plant foods** – this is not quite so easy for the body to absorb.

If possible, children should be given a portion of meat or fish every day, and kidney or liver once a week. Even a small portion of meat or fish is useful, because it also helps the body to absorb iron from other food sources.

Note: If children do not eat meat or fish, they must be offered plenty of iron-rich alternatives, such as egg yolks, dried fruit, beans and lentils, and green, leafy vegetables. It is also a good idea to give foods or drinks that are high in vitamin C at mealtimes, as this helps the absorption of iron from non-meat sources.

Calcium and vitamin D

Children need **calcium** for maintaining and repairing bones and teeth. Calcium is:

- found in milk, cheese, yoghurt and other dairy products
- only absorbed by the body if it is taken with **vitamin D**.

The skin can make all the vitamin D that a body needs, when it is exposed to gentle sunlight. People with darker skin are at greater risk of vitamin D deficiencies, such as **rickets**, because increased pigmentation reduces the capacity of the skin to manufacture the vitamin from sunlight. Additional sources of vitamin D include:

- milk
- oily fish
- fortified margarine
- tahini paste (but note that tahini is made from sesame seeds, which may cause an allergic reaction in a small number of children)
- fortified breakfast cereals
- meat
- soya mince and soya drinks
- tofu.

Vitamins A and C

Vitamin A keeps skin and bones healthy, helps prevent nose and throat infections, and is necessary for vision in dim light. It is found in carrots, fish liver oils and green vegetables.

Vitamin C is important for the immune system and growth. It also helps in the absorption of iron, especially iron from non-meat sources. Vitamin C

intakes are often low in children who eat little fruit and vegetables.

Young children can be given extra A, C and D vitamins in tablet or drop form. These can be obtained from local health centres and should be given as instructed on the bottle.

Key terms

Anaemia – A condition in which the concentration of the oxygen-carrying pigment (haemoglobin) in the blood is below normal.

Nutrients – Nutrients are the essential components of food which provide the individual with the necessary requirements for bodily functions.

Nutrition – The study of the food process in terms of the way that it is received and utilised by the body to promote healthy growth and development.

How to provide healthy snacks

Some children really do need to eat between meals. Their stomachs are relatively small, so they fill up and empty faster than adult stomachs. Sugary foods should not be given as a snack, because sugar is an appetite depressant and may spoil the child's appetite for the main meal to follow. Healthy snack foods include:

- pieces of fruit – banana, orange, pear, kiwi fruit, apple or satsuma
- fruit bread or wholemeal bread, with a slice of cheese
- milk or homemade milkshake
- sticks of carrot, celery, parsnip, red pepper, cauliflower
- dried fruit and diluted fruit juices
- wholegrain biscuits, oatcakes or sesame seed crackers.

Breakfast	Orange juice Weetabix® + milk	Milk	Apple juice	Milk	Yoghurt Porridge
	1 slice of buttered toast	Cereal, e.g. corn or wheat flakes	1 slice of toast with butter or jam	Cereal with slice of banana, or scrambled egg on toast	Slices of apple
		Toast and jam			
Morning snack	Diluted apple juice	Blackcurrant and apple drink	1 glass fruit squash	Peeled apple slices	Diluted apple juice
	1 packet raisins	Cheese straws	1 biscuit	Wholemeal toast fingers with cheese spread	Chapatti or pitta bread fingers
Lunch	Chicken or macaroni cheese	Thick bean soup or chicken salad sandwich	Vegetable soup or fish fingers/ cakes	Sweet potato casserole	Bean casserole (or chicken drumstick) with noodles
	Broccoli	Green beans	Sticks of raw carrot	Sweetcorn	Peas or broad beans
	Fruit yoghurt	Fresh fruit salad		Spinach leaves	
	Water	Water	Kiwi fruit	Chocolate mousse	Fruit yoghurt
			Water	Water	Water
Afternoon snack	Diluted fruit juice	Milkshake	Diluted fruit juice	Hot or cold chocolate drink	Lassi (yoghurt drink)
	Cubes of cheese with savoury biscuit	Fruit cake or chocolate biscuit	Thin-cut sandwiches cut into small pieces	1 small packed dried fruit mix, e.g. apricots, sultanas	1 banana
					1 small biscuit

Table 10.2 Providing a balanced diet

Activity

The balanced daily diet

Look at the following daily diet, as suggested for a 4-year-old:

- **Breakfast** – a boiled egg, toast; a glass of milk
- **Mid-morning** – a packet of crisps; a glass of orange squash
- **Lunch** – a cheese and egg flan, chips, baked beans; apple fritters and ice cream; a glass of apple juice
- **Snack** – chocolate mini roll; a glass of orange squash
- **Tea** – fish fingers, mashed potatoes, peas; a glass of strawberry milkshake.

Arrange the servings in five columns – that is, one each for the four food groups and one extra column for extra fat and sugar. Count the number of servings from each food group and assess the nutritional adequacy of the diet.

How could you improve the menu to ensure a healthy balanced diet?

Section 2: Nutrition and the growing child

The nutritional needs of babies

The way in which babies are fed involves more than simply providing enough food to meet nutritional requirements; for the newborn baby, sucking milk is a great source of pleasure and is also rewarding and enjoyable for the mother. The *ideal* food for babies to start life with is breast milk, and **breastfeeding** should always be encouraged as the first choice in infant feeding; however, mothers should not be made to feel guilty or inadequate if they choose not to breastfeed their babies.

Breastfeeding

During pregnancy, the breasts produce **colostrum**, a creamy, yellowish fluid, low in fat and sugar, which is uniquely designed to feed the newborn baby. Colostrum also has higher levels of antibodies than mature milk and plays an important part in protecting the baby from infection. Mature milk is present in the breasts from around the third day after birth. Hormonal changes in the mother's bloodstream cause the milk to be produced, and the sucking of the baby stimulates a steady supply.

Advantages of breastfeeding

- Human breast milk provides food constituents in the correct balance for human growth. There is no trial and error to find the right formula to suit the baby.
- The milk is sterile and at the correct temperature; there is no need for bottles and sterilising equipment.
- Breast milk initially provides the infant with maternal **antibodies** and helps protect the child from infection – for example, against illnesses such as diarrhoea, vomiting, chest, ear and urine infections, eczema and nappy rash.
- The child is less likely to become overweight, as overfeeding by concentrating the formula is not

possible, and the infant has more freedom of choice as to how much milk he or she will suckle.
- Generally, breast milk is considered cheaper, despite the extra calorific requirement of the mother.
- Research indicates that the brains of children who are breastfed develop better.
- Sometimes it is easier to promote mother–infant bonding by breastfeeding, although this is certainly not always the case.
- Some babies have an intolerance to the protein in cows' milk (which is the basis of formula milk).
- The mother's uterus returns to its pre-pregnancy state more quickly, as a result of the action of oxytocin, which is released when the baby suckles.
- It will help the mother to lose weight, by getting rid of any excess fat stored while she was pregnant.

The **UNICEF UK Baby Friendly Initiative** offers a range of assessment, training and information services to help the health services to promote and support breastfeeding. The initiative was started after research found that:

- breastfed babies are less likely to suffer many serious illnesses – gastroenteritis, respiratory and ear infections are much less common in breastfed babies
- breastfed babies are less likely to suffer from eczema, wheezing and asthma as children, particularly if there is a family history of these conditions.

Adults who were breastfed as babies are less likely to have risk factors for heart disease, such as obesity, high blood pressure and high cholesterol levels.

Disadvantages of breastfeeding

- In rare cases (about two per cent), the mother may not be able to produce enough breast milk to feed her baby.
- She may feel uncomfortable about breastfeeding her baby in public.
- If employed, the mother may need to arrange to breastfeed the baby during working hours, or may need to extend her maternity leave, which could have financial implications.

- The mother can become very tired, as breastfeeding tends to be more frequent than bottle-feeding.
- The mother may suffer from sore or cracked nipples, which makes breastfeeding painful.

Bottle-feeding

Expressed breast milk can be used for bottle-feeding. If formula milk is used for bottle-feeding, it *must* be commercially modified baby milk. Any other type of milk, such as cows' milk or goats' milk, will not satisfy a baby's nutritional needs, and should not be given to babies under one year of age. A young baby's digestive system is unable to cope with the high protein and salt content of cows' milk, and it is likely to cause an adverse reaction. Soya-based milks can be used if the baby develops an intolerance to modified cows' milks (this happens very rarely). For the first four to six months, the baby will be given infant formula milk as a substitute for breast milk; he or she may then progress to **follow-on milk**, which should be offered until the age of one year.

Advantages of bottle-feeding

- The mother knows exactly how much milk the baby has taken.
- The milk is in no way affected by the mother's state of health, while anxiety, tiredness, illness or menstruation may reduce the quantity of breast milk produced.
- The infant is unaffected by such factors as maternal medication – laxatives, antibiotics, alcohol and drugs affecting the central nervous system can affect the quality of breast milk.
- Other members of the family can feed the infant. In this way, the father can feel equally involved with the child's care, and during the night could take over one of the feeds so that the mother can get more sleep.
- There is no fear of embarrassment while feeding.
- The mother is physically unaffected by feeding the infant, avoiding such problems as sore nipples.
- It is useful for mothers who want to return to work before the baby is weaned.

Disadvantages of bottle-feeding

- Babies who are bottle-fed using formula milk do not have the same protection against allergies and infections as breastfed babies.
- When making formula milk, it is possible to get the mixture wrong and make it too strong, too weak or too hot.
- Babies tend to swallow more air when bottle-fed and need to be 'winded' more often.
- Babies may bring up feeds more often – this is known as **possetting**.
- Babies who are bottle-fed tend to suffer more from constipation.
- There is a lot of work involved in thoroughly washing and sterilising all the equipment that is needed for bottle-feeding.
- Studies indicate that bottle-fed babies were found to have an increased risk of obesity until at least six years of age.
- Using formula milk can be expensive. It has been estimated that it costs at least £450 a year to feed a baby using formula milk.
- There is a greater risk of the baby developing **gastroenteritis** – usually when equipment is not sterilised properly, or when the milk is incorrectly stored or becomes contaminated.

Figure 10.2 Bottle-feeding

Making the choice between breastfeeding and bottle-feeding

A range of factors influences the mother's decision on how to feed her newborn baby:

- Breastfeeding is harder for some mothers than others – for example, if a new mother does not receive the support she needs to establish breastfeeding, it is more difficult to stimulate the 'let-down' reflex (when milk flows from the ducts towards the nipple).

- Some babies may have medical conditions that make breastfeeding difficult – for example, they may be tongue-tied or may have been born prematurely.
- The mother may have to return to work and find that bottle-feeding is more convenient when leaving her baby in the care of others.
- Many new mothers feel that there is a bottle-feeding culture in the UK. Breastfeeding is often seen as an embarrassing activity when carried out in front of others.

The important thing is that a mother makes her own choice and is happy that her baby is feeding properly.

Guidelines for bottle-feeding a baby

- Collect all the necessary equipment before picking up the baby. The bottle may be warmed in a jug of hot water. Have a muslin square or bib and tissues to hand.
- Check the temperature and flow of the milk by dripping it on to the inside of your wrist (it should feel warm – not hot or cold).
- Make yourself comfortable with the baby. Do not rush the feed – babies always sense if you are not relaxed and it can make them edgy too.
- Try to hold the baby in a similar position to that for breastfeeding and maintain eye contact – this is a time for cuddling and talking to the baby.
- Stimulate the rooting reflex by placing the teat at the corner of the baby's mouth; then put the teat fully into his or her mouth and feed by tilting the bottle so that the hole in the teat is always covered with milk.
- After about ten minutes, the baby may need to be helped to bring up wind; this can be done by leaning him or her forwards on your lap and gently rubbing his or her back or holding him or her against your shoulder. Unless the baby is showing discomfort, do not insist on trying to produce a 'burp' – the baby may pass the wind out in the nappy.

The National Children's Bureau states that:

Babies who are bottle-fed should be held and have warm physical contact with an attentive adult whilst being fed. It is strongly recommended that a baby [in a childcare setting] is fed by the same staff member at each feed. Babies should never be left propped up with bottles, as it is dangerous and inappropriate to babies' emotional needs.

Key terms

Colostrum – Colostrum is the first 'milk' that the breasts produce, as a precursor to breast milk. It is rich in fats, protein and antibodies, which protect the baby against infection and kick-start the immune system.

Lactation – Production of milk by the breasts.

The principles of weaning and its importance to the baby's development

Weaning is the gradual introduction of solid food to the baby's diet. The reasons for weaning are to:

- meet the baby's nutritional needs – from about six months of age, milk alone will not satisfy the baby's increased nutritional requirements, especially for iron
- satisfy increasing appetite
- develop new skills – for example, use of feeding beaker, cup and cutlery
- develop the chewing mechanism – the muscular movement of the mouth and jaw also aids the development of speech
- introduce new tastes and textures – this enables the baby to join in family meals, thus promoting cognitive and social development.

When to start weaning

Department of Health guidelines advise parents to wait until their baby is around six months before starting him or her on solid food. When the following three key signs are present together, it means that the baby is ready for solid food:

- The baby can stay in a sitting position while holding his or her head steady.
- The baby can coordinate his or her eyes, hands and mouth – that is, look at food, grab it and put it in his or her mouth him- or herself.
- The baby can swallow his or her food – if the baby is not ready, most of it will be pushed back out.

Babies who are born prematurely should not be introduced to solid foods just because they have reached a certain age or weight. They will need individual assessment before weaning.

Giving solids too early – often in the mistaken belief that the baby might sleep through the night – places a strain on the baby's immature digestive system.

If parents do choose to introduce solid foods before 26 weeks, they should consult their health visitor or GP first. There are also some foods they should avoid giving their baby. These include:

- foods containing gluten, which is in wheat, rye, barley, oats
- eggs
- fish and shellfish
- liver
- citrus fruit juices
- nuts and seeds.

Note: Babies under one year old should not be given honey, because it is not pasteurised and can cause infant botulism – a rare, but very serious illness, which occurs when Clostridium botulinum or related bacteria produce toxins in the intestines of babies under one year old.

Stages of weaning

Every baby is different. Some enjoy trying new tastes and textures, moving through weaning quickly and easily, while others need a little more time to get used to new foods.

Stage 1 (around six months)

Give puréed vegetables, puréed fruit, baby rice and finely puréed dhal or lentils. Milk continues to be the most important food.

Stage 2 (about six to eight months)

Increase variety; introduce puréed or minced meat, chicken, liver, fish, lentils and beans. Raw eggs should not be used, but cooked egg yolk can be introduced from six months, along with wheat-based foods – for example, mashed Weetabix® and pieces of bread. Milk feeds decrease as more solids rich in protein are offered.

Stage 3 (about nine to twelve months)

Cows' milk can safely be used at about 12 months, along with lumpier foods such as pasta, pieces of cooked meat, soft cooked beans, pieces of cheese and a variety of breads. Additional fluids can be given –

for example, diluted unsweetened fruit juice or water. Three regular meals should be taken, as well as drinks.

Methods of weaning

Some babies take to solid food very quickly; others appear not to be interested at all. The baby's demands are a good guide for weaning – mealtimes should never become a battleground. Even very young children have definite food preferences and should never be forced to eat a particular food, however much thought and effort has gone into the preparation. Table 10.3 offers guidelines on introducing new solids to babies.

The best baby food is homemade from simple ingredients, with no sugar, salt or spices. Any leftovers can be frozen in ice cube trays. Puréed, cooked vegetables, fruit and ground cereals such as rice are ideal to start weaning. Chewing usually starts at around the age of six months, whether or not the baby has teeth, and slightly coarser textures can then be offered. The baby should be fed in a bouncing cradle or high chair – not in the usual feeding position in the carer's arms.

Food can be puréed by:

- rubbing it through a sieve using a large spoon
- mashing it with a fork (for soft foods such as banana or cooked potato)
- using a mouli-sieve or hand-blender
- using an electric blender (useful for larger amounts).

	4–6 months	6–8 months	9–12 months
You can give or add	Puréed fruit Puréed veeetables Thin porridge made from oat or rice flakes or cornmeal Finely puréed dhal or lentils	A wider range of puréed fruits and vegetables Purées which include chicken, fish and liver Wheat-based foods, e.g. mashed Weetabix® Egg yolk, well cooked Small-sized beans such as aduki beans, cooked soft Pieces of ripe banana Cooked rice Citrus fruits Soft summer fruits Pieces of bread	An increasingly wide range of foods with a variety of textures and flavours Cow's milk Pieces of cheese Fromage frais or yoghurt Pieces of fish Soft cooked beans Pasta A variety of breads Pieces of meat from a casserole Well-cooked egg white Almost anything that is wholesome and that the child can swallow
How	Offer the food on the tip of a clean finger or on the tip of a clean (plastic or horn) teaspoon	On a teaspoon	On a spoon or as finger food
When	A very tiny amount at first, during or after a milk feed	At the end of a milk feed	At established mealtimes
Why	The start of transition from milk to solids	To introduce other foods when the child is hungry	To encourage full independence

	4–6 months	6–8 months	9–12 months
Not yet	Cow's milk – or any except breast or formula milk Citrus fruit Soft summer fruits Wheat (cereals, flour, bread, etc.) Spices Spinach, swede, turnip, beetroot Eggs Nuts Salt Sugar Fatty food	Cow's milk, except in small quantities mixed with other food Chillies or chilli powder Egg whites Nuts Salt Sugar Fatty food	Whole nuts Salt Sugar Fatty food

Table 10.3 Introducing new solids to babies

Guidelines for weaning

- Try to encourage a liking for savoury foods.
- Only introduce one new food at a time.
- Be patient if the baby does not take the food – feed at the baby's pace, not yours.
- Do not add salt or sugar to feeds.
- Make sure that food is the right temperature.
- Avoid giving sweet foods or drinks between meals.
- Never leave a baby alone when he or she is eating.
- Limit the use of commercially prepared foods – they are of poorer quality and will not allow the baby to become used to home cooking.
- Select foods approved by the baby's parents or primary carers.

Finger foods

Finger foods are any foods that can be given to a baby to manage by him- or herself. After weaning, encourage the baby to chew – even if there are no teeth – by giving finger foods or foods that have a few lumps. Examples of finger foods include:

- wholemeal toast
- pitta bread
- banana or peeled apple slices
- cubes of hard cheese – for example, Cheddar
- chapatti
- breadsticks
- cooked carrots or green beans.

Always stay near to the baby during feeding to make sure he or she does not choke and to offer encouragement.

Baby-led weaning

Some parents use a technique for weaning their babies called baby-led weaning. This involves letting the baby select those items of food that can be held or grasped by the baby and taken to his or her mouth. Starter foods may include pieces of broccoli, carrot or fruit cut into 'chip' shapes and offered to the baby on a tray. The use of bowls and weaning spoons is discouraged. The principles behind this way of feeding babies are that baby-led weaning:

- offers the baby the opportunity to discover what other foods have to offer, as part of finding out about the world around him or her
- utilises the baby's desire to explore and experiment, and to mimic the activities of others
- enables the transition to solid foods to take place as naturally as possible – by allowing the baby

to set the pace of each meal, and maintaining an emphasis on play and exploration rather than on eating.

For more information, visit this website: http://babyledweaning.com

 Progress check

- Weaning is the gradual introduction of solid food to the baby's diet.
- Giving solids too early places a strain on the baby's immature digestive system.
- The Department of Health recommends that babies be started on solid food at around six months.
- Babies usually start chewing food at around the age of six months, whether or not they have teeth.

Research Activity

The cost of weaning

1 Visit a pharmacy or supermarket to find out about the wide variety of foods for weaning babies.

2 Draw up a week's menu for a baby of nine months, using a variety of commercially prepared foods in jars and packets.

3 Work out how much it would cost to provide your menu for one week.

The social and educational role of food and mealtimes

Eating patterns may be influenced by various factors:

- religious beliefs or strong ethical principles
- cultural background and ethnic origin
- the availability of different foods
- time and money constraints
- preferences and tastes that are shaped during early infancy.

Food is part of every child's culture, and eating rituals vary with different cultures.

The role of mealtimes

Mealtimes can provide a valuable opportunity to further the child's **social development** by promoting:

- **listening** and other conversation skills
- **independence** in eating and serving food, and in taking responsibility
- **courtesy** towards others and turn-taking
- a **shared experience**, which provides a social focus in the child's day
- **self-esteem** – the child's family and cultural background are valued through their mealtime traditions
- **self-confidence** – through learning social skills, taking turns and saying 'please' and 'thank you', the child gains confidence as a valued and unique member of their social situation.

Cognitive development is supported by mealtimes by:

- promoting **hand–eye coordination** through the use of cutlery and other tools
- stimulating the **senses** of taste, touch, sight and smell
- **enjoyment** of interesting conversations
- promoting **language development** and increasing vocabulary
- developing the **mathematical** concepts of shape and size, using foods as examples
- creating opportunities for **learning through linked activities** – for example, stories about food, origins of food, preparation and cookery
- experiencing **cultural variation** in foods and mealtime traditions.

As an early years practitioner, you are ideally placed to ensure that **stereotyping** in relation to eating habits is not practised. Mealtimes and the choice of food can be used in a positive sense to affirm a feeling of cultural identity.

The presentation and preparation of food with children

Preparing food with children

Almost all children have some experience of cooking, or at the very least food preparation, in their own homes. This experience can range from watching tins being opened and the contents heated, seeing fruit being peeled and cut, or bread being put in a toaster and then spread, to a full meal being cooked. Food preparation and cooking activities are also useful in raising children's awareness of healthy and nutritious foods, educating them about diet and choice. For example, by discussing the need for an ingredient to sweeten food, children can be introduced to the variety available and be made aware of healthy options, such as using honey instead of sugar.

Children learn through active involvement so any cooking activity must be chosen carefully to ensure that children can participate. There is very limited value in them watching an adult carry out the instructions and occasionally letting them have a stir!

When selecting a cooking activity, remember:

- that parental wishes must always be respected
- to check that all children can eat the food to be cooked
- to check that there are no problems regarding allergies or religious dietary restrictions
- to follow the basic food safety and hygiene guidelines on pages 423–28.

Food presentation and children's preferences

Many children go through phases of refusing to eat certain foods, or may refuse to eat anything at all. This is particularly common for children up to the age of five years, and it is a normal part of growing up and asserting independence. Children will not harm themselves if they do not eat for a short while. Try the following strategies to encourage eating:

- Offer regular meals and snacks rather than allowing a child to 'pick.'
- Make mealtimes fun. Use brightly coloured plates and present the food in an attractive way.
- Remain calm and relaxed.

If the problem shows no sign of improving, seek advice from a health visitor, doctor or dietician.

Figure 10.3 Cooking activities for children can be educational and fun

How to prevent food dislikes and minor eating problems

The early years setting is an ideal place to provide meal and snack times that make eating an enjoyable social event. When children positively enjoy their food-related experiences, they are less likely to develop food-related problems. Also, children are more likely to try new foods if they see their friends trying them in a relaxed and happy atmosphere. There will be opportunities to talk about food, their likes and dislikes and the texture, colour and smell of different foods.

Introducing new foods

When introducing children to new foods, the following points are important:

- They should have the chance to try the same food on more than one occasion. The first time they try a food it can be the fact that it is new or that they do not like the texture that makes them not want to eat it. The second time they try it, it is not so unfamiliar and their preferences may change.
- When trying new foods, children need to know that they do not have to swallow the food. If they know they can spit it into a tissue, they are less likely to be worried about putting a new type of food into their mouth.

The role of the adult in promoting healthy eating

Every child is unique; they gradually develop a whole catalogue of likes, strong dislikes and mild preferences regarding food and mealtimes:

- Some like their food bathed in sauces, while others prefer it dry.
- Some like every food kept separate from the others on the plate.
- Many do not like 'tough' meat or foods that are difficult to chew.

It is important to **respect** a child's likes and dislikes and offer alternative foods from the same food group where necessary.

Guidelines: the role of the adult in promoting healthy eating

1 **Set an example**: children will imitate both what you eat and how you eat it. It will be easier to encourage a child to eat a stick of raw celery if you eat one too! If you show disgust at certain foods, young children will notice and copy you.

2 **Offer a wide variety of different foods**: give babies and toddlers an opportunity to try a new food more than once; any refusal on first tasting may be due to dislike of the new rather than of the food itself.

3 **Be prepared for messy mealtimes**: present the food in a form that is fairly easy for children to manage by themselves (for example, not difficult to chew).

4 **Do not use food as a punishment, reward, bribe or threat**: for example, do not give sweets or chocolates as a reward for finishing savoury foods. To a child this is like saying 'Here's something nice after eating those nasty greens'. Give healthy foods as treats, such as raisins and raw carrots, rather than sweets or cakes.

5 **Introduce new foods in stages**: for example, if switching to wholemeal bread, try a soft-grain white bread first. Always involve the children in making choices as far as possible.

6 **Teach children to eat mainly at mealtimes** and avoid giving them high-calorie snacks (such as biscuits and sugary drinks) which might take the edge off their appetite for more nutritious food. Most young children need three small meals and three snacks a day.

7 **Presentation is important**: food manufacturers use a variety of techniques to make their children's food products exciting – colours, shapes, themes and characters. Using these tactics can make mealtimes more fun.

Guidelines: the role of the adult in promoting healthy eating (cont.)

8 **Avoid adding salt to any food**: too much salt can cause dehydration in babies and may predispose certain people to hypertension (high blood pressure) if taken over a lifetime.

9 **Allow children to follow their own individual appetites** when deciding how much they want to eat. If a child rejects food, never force-feed him. Simply remove the food without comment. Give smaller portions next time and praise the child for eating even a little.

10 **Never give a young child whole nuts to eat** – particularly peanuts. Children can very easily choke on a small piece of the nut or even inhale it, which can cause a severe type of pneumonia. Rarely, a child may have a serious allergic reaction to nuts.

Figure 10.4 Mealtimes can be fun and sociable

The effects of poor eating on the overall health of the child

Healthy eating – or good nutrition – during childhood makes it easier to maintain a healthy weight, and has been shown to improve children's concentration and behaviour. It can also help to reduce the risk of developing many common diseases including heart disease, cancer, diabetes, obesity, osteoporosis and dental decay.

Malnutrition and under-nutrition

In recent years there has been increasing public concern about the quality of children's diets, rapidly increasing rates of **child obesity**, diet-related disorders, and low consumption of fruit and vegetables by children. There are various conditions that may occur in childhood that are directly related to a poor or unbalanced diet; these are a result of either **malnutrition** or **under-nutrition** and include:

● **failure to thrive*** (or faltering growth): poor growth and physical development

- **dental caries** or tooth decay: associated with a high consumption of sugar in snacks and fizzy drinks
- **obesity**: children who are overweight are more likely to become obese adults (see also page 255)
- **nutritional anaemia**: due to an insufficient intake of iron, folic acid and vitamin B12
- **increased susceptibility to infections**: particularly upper respiratory infections, such as colds and bronchitis.

(*Failure to thrive can also result from child abuse: physical abuse, emotional abuse, neglect and sexual abuse. This complex subject is discussed in Chapter 3.)

Key terms

Under-nutrition – This occurs when people do not get enough to eat.

Malnutrition – A person's diet is lacking the necessary amounts of certain elements that are essential to growth, such as vitamins, salts and proteins.

Section 3: Influences on food and diet

The effects of the food industry, media and healthy eating campaigns

The majority of people in the UK do their food shopping in supermarkets, so it is easy to see how much influence the supermarket owners and buyers can have on people's tastes and buying habits. Most large supermarket chains now have shelves displaying foods that are classified as:

- healthy eating foods: low-fat, low-sugar, etc.
- organic: free-range eggs, chickens, etc.
- gluten-free flour and bakery products
- dairy free, nut-free foods
- suitable for diabetics, vegetarians or vegans, etc.

Many manufacturers have responded to recent campaigns to reduce the salt and fat content in processed food. All foods must be labelled according to the current legislation.

The influence of the media

Adverts for food appear in most magazines and almost all commercial television programmes. The principal means of advertising to children is television, and the watchdog Ofcom recently phased in new regulations banning the advertising of 'junk' foods or foods high in fat, salt or sugar.

Case Study | The power of advertising

Following concerns about child obesity, UK regulations were introduced in 2007 banning the advertising of foods high in fat, salt or sugar during any children's programming on television. However, researchers from the University of Newcastle said that the number of junk food ads seen by children actually *increased* after the ban, from 6.1 per cent to 7 per cent. After linking the data to how many people saw the adverts, the researchers discovered that 14.6 per cent of commercials were for food, and half of those were for less healthy items such as crisps, sugared breakfast cereals and drinks containing large amounts of sugar. The research, published in 2012, found that although nearly all the ads shown during children's programmes adhered to the rules, children were not only watching programmes intended for them.

Healthy eating campaigns

The Children's Food Campaign

Sustain (the alliance for better food and farming) launched the Children's Food Campaign. It wants to improve young people's health and wellbeing through:

- good food and real food education in every school
- protecting children from junk food marketing
- clear food labelling that everyone, including children, can understand.

Jamie Oliver's Feed Me Even Better campaign

Following his success with improving school meals and his Feed Me Better campaign, Jamie Oliver has now launched the Feed Me Even Better campaign. Jamie's eight-point plan wants:

1 More money for school food: financially reward schools that increase school meal take-up with the School Food Premium.
2 Nutritional standards made mandatory for all schools.
3 Cooking classes made compulsory in all schools, with a minimum of 24 hours of practical lessons during every key stage.
4 Train teachers so that they can teach cooking.
5 Every school should grow some food with the involvement of the pupils.
6 Capital funding used to improve school canteens and kitchens.
7 Ofsted inspections to include the assessment of the nutritional content of school food.
8 Use the pupil premium to give poorer pupils access to healthy food.

Cool Milk

Cool Milk works in partnership with local authorities and early years groups to supply free and subsidised school milk to children in pre-schools, nurseries and primary schools. Cool Milk aims to make the provision of milk easier for schools, nurseries, local authorities and parents, while promoting the important health benefits and learning opportunities that school milk offers.

The role of poverty and economy on food choices

In the UK today, food poverty differs from the way in which people in Victorian times would have perceived it – that is, with large sections of the population unable to afford to eat. Food poverty today is as much concerned with dietary imbalance as it is with undernourishment. Food poverty today is caused by:

- an overabundance of processed food
- a lack of balance in the diet
- poor access to available food
- people suffering from obesity and diabetes (Type 2).

There are many reasons why families may suffer from lack of access to healthy food:

- The big supermarket groups, which provide the widest range of goods at the cheapest prices, have withdrawn from deprived areas. They now concentrate their businesses in out-of-town locations, which favour the car-owning consumer.
- If people have to rely on small corner stores, they may have to pay anything from six to thirteen per cent more for a nutritionally adequate diet than they would if they shopped in a big supermarket.
- The poorest communities suffer from high unemployment and inadequate housing. There is a north–south divide in the UK, with the north and Scotland having the greatest concentration of poorer areas and thus food poverty.
- There is also some evidence that healthier foods cost more. Replacing white bread with wholemeal and high-fat products with low-fat products means more expense.
- It is estimated that up to 300,000 children are not taking up free school meals because of stigma and the fear of attracting the attention of bullies.

Some facts about food poverty:

- Five per cent of adults cannot afford fresh fruit daily.
- One in 20 mothers go without food to meet the needs of their children.
- People suffering food poverty are more likely to be overweight due to consumption of high-fat and sugary foods.
- Living in food poverty increases the likelihood of dying of heart disease or cancer.
- Babies born to poorer families are more likely to be premature and be underweight.
- Pregnant teenagers often have nutritionally inadequate diets, thus posing a risk to their own and their children's health.

Different religious and cultural requirements

The UK is home to a multicultural and multi-ethnic society. The main ethnic minority groups are situated near large cities; many people came to the UK from the West Indies and Asia in the 1950s and

Muslims	Hindus	Sikhs
Muslims practise the Islamic religion, and their holy book, the Koran, provides them with their food laws.	Wheat is the main staple food eaten by Hindus in the UK; it is used to make types of bread called chapattis, puris and parathas. Orthodox Hindus are strict vegetarians as they believe in Ahimsa – non-violence towards all living beings – and a minority practise veganism. Some will eat dairy products and eggs, while others will refuse eggs on the grounds that they are a potential source of life.	Most Sikhs will not eat pork or beef or any meat that is killed by the halal method. Some Sikhs are vegetarian, but many eat chicken, lamb and fish. Wheat and rice are staple foods
Unlawful foods (called haram) are: pork, all meat which has not been rendered lawful (halal), alcohol and fish without scales.		Fasting: devout Sikhs will fast once or twice a week, and most will fast on the first day of the Punjabi month or when there is a full moon.
Wheat, in the form of chapattis, and rice are the staple foods.		
The Koran dictates that children should be breastfed up to the age of 2 years.		**Rastafarians**
Fasting: during the lunar month of Ramadan Muslims fast between sunrise and sunset; fasting involves abstinence from all food and drink, so many Muslims rise early to eat before dawn in order to maintain their energy levels. Children under 12 years and the elderly are exempt from fasting.	Even non-vegetarians do not eat beef as the cow is considered a sacred animal, and it is unusual for pork to be eaten as the pig is considered unclean. Ghee (clarified butter) and vegetable oil are used in cooking. Fasting: common for certain festivals, such as Mahshivrati (the birthday of Lord Shiva).	Dietary practices are based on laws laid down by Moses in the Book of Genesis in the Bible. These laws state that certain types of meat should be avoided. The majority of followers will only eat Ital foods, which are foods considered to be in a whole or natural state. Most Rastafarians are vegetarians and will not consume processed or preserved foods. No added salt; no coffee.

Afro-Caribbean diets	Jewish diets	Festivals from different cultures	
The Afro-Caribbean community is the second largest ethnic minority group in the UK. Dietary practices within the community vary widely. Many people include a wide variety of European foods in their diet alongside the traditional foods of cornmeal, coconut, green banana, plantain, okra and yam. Although Afro-Caribbean people are generally Christian, a minority are Rastafarians.	Jewish people observe dietary laws which state that animals and birds must be slaughtered by the Jewish method to render them kosher (acceptable). Milk and meat must never be cooked or eaten together, and pork in any form is forbidden.	Shichi-go-san (Japanese festival for young children)	November 15
		Chinese New year	Late January/ early February
	Shellfish are not allowed as they are thought to harbour disease. Only fish with fins and scales may be eaten.	Shrove Tuesday (Mardi Gras)	40 days before Easter
		Rosh Hoshanah (Jewish New Year)	Usually September
	Fasting: The most holy day of the Jewish calendar is Yom Kippur (the Day of Atonement), when Jewish people fast for 25 hours.	Holi (Hindu Spring festival)	February or March
		Id Al Fitir (major Muslim festival)	At end of Ramadan
		Divali (Hindu New Year)	October or November
		Rastafarian New Year	January 7

Table 10.4 Multicultural provision and dietary implications

1960s, in response to labour shortages. The Asian community represents the largest ethnic minority in the UK – about 1.25 million people. Asian dietary customs are mainly related to the beliefs of the three main religious groups: Muslims, Hindus and Sikhs.

Food and festivals from different cultures

There are particular foods that are associated with certain religious festivals – for example, in the Christian tradition, mince pies at Christmas and pancakes on Shrove Tuesday; and in the Hindu tradition, poori are eaten at Diwali. Providing foods from different cultures within an early years setting is a very good way of celebrating these festivals. Parents of children from ethnic minority groups are usually very pleased to be asked for advice on how to celebrate festivals with food, and may even be prepared to contribute some samples.

Research Activity

Different traditions

Find out about the dietary requirements and restrictions in *one* cultural or religious group different from your own. Choose from:

- Jewish
- Muslim (Islamic)
- Hindu
- Rastafarian.

Discussion point

The nursery school where you are working has 22 white British children and one child from Turkey. The nursery teacher says, 'We only offer English food here because we do not have any children from ethnic minorities.' Discuss this statement and decide what your approach would be if you were in charge of the nursery.

Children on vegetarian diets

Children who are on a vegetarian diet need an alternative to meat, fish and chicken as the main sources of protein. Alternatives might include:

- milk
- cheese and eggs
- pulses (lentils and beans).

They also need enough **iron**. As iron is more difficult to absorb from vegetable sources than from meat, a young child needs to obtain iron from sources such as:

- leafy green vegetables – such as spinach and watercress
- pulses (beans, lentils and chick peas)
- dried fruit (such as apricots, raisins and sultanas) – although some dentists believe that dried fruit contributes to dental decay, and so it should be given sparingly
- some breakfast cereals.

It is easier to absorb iron from our food if it is eaten with foods containing vitamin C, such as fruit and vegetables, or with diluted fruit juices at mealtimes. Do not give young children tea or coffee, especially at mealtimes, because this reduces the amount of iron they can absorb.

The vegan diet

A vegan diet completely excludes all foods of animal origin; that is, animal flesh, milk and milk products, eggs, honey and all additives which may be of animal origin. A vegan diet is based on cereals and cereal products, pulses, fruits, vegetables, nuts and seeds. Human breast milk is acceptable for vegan babies.

The role of school meals in promoting the health of children

As we have seen, what children eat not only affects their health and wellbeing, but also their ability to concentrate and perform well at school.

Figure 10.5 Eating food from a different culture can broaden young children's horizons

Change4life

The School Food Trust supports the NHS Change4life programme by ensuring that as many children as possible are eating healthy school food. All school lunches must now meet *nutrient-based standards* to ensure that they provide children with the fuel they need to lead a healthy, active lifestyle. Change4life also provides guidance and resources on the following:

- healthier breakfast clubs
- healthier tuck shops
- water provision
- healthier vending machines
- healthier lunchboxes
- dining room environment
- healthier cookery clubs.

The Nursery Milk Scheme

The Nursery Milk Scheme enables:

- Children under five to receive free of charge 189 ml (one-third of a pint) of milk for every day they attend approved day care facilities for two hours or more.

- Babies aged under 12 months may instead receive dried baby milk made up to 189ml (one-third of a pint).

Daycare providers who have been approved to supply milk under the scheme can be reimbursed for the cost of the milk they supply.

Government initiatives to promote healthy eating

Campaigns such as **School Fruit and Vegetable Scheme** (SFV) have made a real difference to the diets of children in the UK. See Chapter 6, page 247 for more information.

Eat Smart, Play Smart

Eat Smart, Play Smart is a **Food Standards Agency** teaching resource developed for primary school teachers throughout the UK to use with children aged five to seven years. The materials have been designed to engage children's interest in healthy food choices and in keeping active – giving them important guidance to promote healthier lifestyles.

Eat Smart, Play Smart has been developed to:

- help children to understand the need for healthy diets and to choose appropriately from different food groups for their meals
- encourage children to be more active in their everyday lives and to understand the benefits of being active. Ways of increasing activity in the home and at school are suggested in fun, energetic and easy-to-follow ways.

Section 4: Disorders requiring special diets

Food intolerances and food allergies

Food intolerance

Food intolerance is an adverse reaction to some sort of food or ingredient that occurs *every time* the food is eaten, but particularly if larger quantities are consumed. Food intolerance is **not** the same as

- a **food allergy** because the **immune system** is not activated
- **food poisoning**, in which toxic substances would cause symptoms in anyone who ate the food.

Food intolerance does not include *psychological* reactions to food; it is much more common than food allergy.

Some babies develop an intolerance to cows' milk protein; the most common symptoms are vomiting, diarrhoea and failure to thrive. After weaning, foods most likely to cause an adverse reaction in babies are:

- hen's eggs
- fish
- citrus fruits
- wheat and other cereals
- pork.

Sometimes an adverse reaction will be temporary, perhaps following an illness, but the offending food should always be removed from the baby's diet. Dietetic advice should be sought before any changes to a balanced diet are made.

Food allergies

A food allergy is an abnormal response (an allergic reaction) of the immune system to otherwise harmless foods. Up to five per cent of children have food allergies. Most children outgrow their allergy, although an allergy to peanuts and some other tree nuts is considered lifelong.

There are eight foods that cause 90 per cent of all food allergic reactions. These are:

- peanuts
- soy
- tree nuts (such as almonds, walnuts, pecans, etc.)
- wheat
- milk
- shellfish
- eggs
- fish.

Milk is the most common cause of food allergies in children, but peanuts, nuts, fish and shellfish commonly cause the most severe reactions.

What are the symptoms of an allergic reaction?

Symptoms of an allergic response can include:

- vomiting
- hives (or urticaria) – an itchy raised rash usually found on the trunk or limbs
- itching or tightness in the throat
- diarrhoea
- eczema
- difficulty breathing
- cramps
- itching or swelling of the lips, tongue or mouth
- wheezing.

Allergic symptoms can begin within minutes to one hour after ingesting the food.

Anaphylaxis

In rare cases of food allergy, just *one bite* of food can bring on **anaphylaxis**. This is a severe reaction that involves various areas of the body simultaneously. In extreme cases, it can cause death.

Anaphylaxis is a sudden and severe potentially life-threatening allergic reaction. It can be caused by insect stings or medications, as well as by a food allergy. Although potentially any food can cause anaphylaxis, **peanuts**, **nuts**, **shellfish**, **fish** and **eggs** are foods that most commonly cause this reaction.

Symptoms of anaphylaxis may include all those listed above for food allergies. In addition, the child's breathing is seriously impaired and the pulse rate becomes rapid. Anaphylaxis is fortunately very rare, but is also very dangerous:

- Symptoms can occur in as little as five to 15 minutes.
- As little as half a peanut can cause a fatal reaction in severely allergic individuals.
- Some severely allergic children can have a reaction if milk is splashed on their skin.
- Being kissed by somebody who has eaten peanuts, for example, can cause a reaction in severely allergic individuals.

Emergency treatment of anaphylaxis

1 **Summon medical help immediately**. The child will need oxygen and a life-saving injection of adrenaline.
2 **Place the child in a sitting position** to help relieve any breathing difficulty.
3 **Be prepared to resuscitate** if necessary.

In some settings attended by a child or children known to be at risk from anaphylaxis, the staff may be trained to give the adrenaline injection.

How can food allergies be managed?

The only way to manage food allergies is strictly to avoid the foods to which the child is allergic. It is important to learn how to interpret ingredients on food labels and how to spot high-risk foods. Many children outgrow earlier food-allergic symptoms as they get older, but parents will need professional support and advice to ensure that their child is receiving a safe, balanced diet.

Key terms

Allergy – Abnormal sensitivity reaction of the body to substances that are usually harmless.

Anaphylaxis – An immediate and severe allergic response; a shock reaction to a substance.

Recording and reporting allergies and intolerances in a range of settings

All staff in early years settings should be aware of the identities of children who have food allergies, and should have clear instructions on how to deal with each case. In particular, lunchtime supervisors need to be kept informed. Most settings display a photograph of any child with a special dietary requirement or allergy in the food preparation area to ensure that permanent and supply staff are aware of each individual child's needs.

When a child has been diagnosed as having a **severe allergy** to a particular food, staff *may* decide to minimise the risk of exposure by avoiding having the food or ingredient in the setting. In severe cases it is essential that there is regular access to up-to-date advice from a registered dietician because ingredients in processed foods change frequently. Everybody involved in the care of children with known allergies should know:

- how to recognise the symptoms of a food allergy or intolerance
- how to avoid the foods he or she is sensitive to
- what to do if they have an allergic reaction
- how to use their adrenaline injector or EpiPen®, if they have one
- when and how to record and report any suspicion of food allergy or intolerance.

Progress check

Allergies and intolerances

- All staff should be aware of which children suffer from an allergy and to which food, and of the policy regarding first aid and administering medication.
- All staff involved in the care of that child must be aware of the foods and ingredients being offered to the child.
- Care must be taken in the preparation and serving of food not to cross-contaminate food being served to a child with an allergy.
- If you ever notice swelling of a child's mouth or face or breathing difficulties when eating, seek medical advice immediately. Symptoms such as a rash or vomiting after eating may also suggest that there has been a reaction to a food. Always inform the parent or carer.
- To lessen the risk of peanut allergies, peanut-containing foods should not be given to children under three years of age if the child has a parent or sibling with a diagnosed allergy. Whole nuts should not be given to any child under the age of five years because of the risk of choking.

In Practice

In your setting:

- ❏ Find out how many children have food allergies or intolerances.
- ❏ How is information displayed about children's allergies?
- ❏ Is there a policy document relating to reporting and recording allergies and intolerances?

Ways to deal with emergencies

Emergencies in early years settings related to food and mealtimes include severe food allergy (anaphylaxis), choking and a diabetic child having a hypo (hypoglycaemic) episode. Chapter 9 (Unit 11) gives guidance on the appropriate first aid measures required.

Supporting children and their families who have special diets

Any child who has to follow a special diet for health reasons will occasionally feel like an outsider. Every health condition that requires a special diet has a support organisation where parents and carers can find information and often join in discussion forums on the internet.

Contact a Family is a UK-wide charity providing advice, information and support to the parents of all disabled children – no matter what their disability or health condition. Its internet address is: www. cafamily.org.uk.

The diet for coeliac condition

Coeliac disease is a condition in which the lining of the small intestine is damaged by gluten, a protein found in wheat and rye. In babies, it is usually diagnosed about three months after weaning onto solids containing gluten, but some children do not show any symptoms until they are older. Treatment for coeliac disease is by gluten-free diet and has to be for the rest of the person's life. All formula milks available in the UK are gluten-free, and many manufactured baby foods are also gluten-free. Any cakes, bread and biscuits should be made from gluten-free flour, and labels on processed foods should be read carefully to ensure that there is no 'hidden' wheat product in the ingredients list.

Note: Commercially available 'Play-doh' is made from 40 per cent ordinary flour, as is the homemade variety used in nurseries and playgroups. Extra vigilance is needed by staff to stop children with coeliac disease putting it in their mouth, or safer still, dough can always be made using gluten-free flour.

The diet for cystic fibrosis

The majority of children with cystic fibrosis (see Chapter 9, page 374) have difficulty in absorbing fats; they need to eat 20 per cent more protein and more calories than children without the disease, and so require a diet high in fats and carbohydrates. They are also given daily vitamin supplements and pancreatic enzymes.

The diet for galactosaemia

Galactosaemia is a very rare genetic disorder leading to liver disease, eye cataracts and learning difficulties; it is caused by an inability to absorb galactose (a nutrient found in milk). The child with galactosaemia cannot digest or use galactose – which, together with glucose, forms lactose, the natural sugar of milk. A list of 'safe foods' with a low galactose content will be issued by the dietician, and food labels should be checked for the presence of milk solids and powdered lactose which contain large amounts of this sugar.

The diet for children who have difficulties with chewing and swallowing

Children with cerebral palsy can experience difficulties with either or both of these aspects of eating. Food has to be liquidised, but this should be done in separate batches so that the end result is not a pool of greyish sludge. Presentation should be imaginative. Try to follow the general principle of making the difference in the meal as unobtrusive as possible.

Insulin dependency in children

Diabetes mellitus occurs in one in every 500 children under the age of about 16 years, and results in difficulty in converting carbohydrate into energy due to underproduction of insulin. Insulin is usually given by daily injection and a diet sheet will be devised by the hospital dietician. It is important that mealtimes be *regular* and that some carbohydrate be included at every meal. Children with diabetes should be advised to carry glucose sweets whenever they are away from home, in case of hypoglycaemia (low blood sugar).

Information about dealing with emergencies related to diabetes and to choking can be found in Chapter 9.

The issues of overweight children and obesity

Obesity (fatness) results from taking in more energy from the diet than is used up by the body. Some children appear to inherit a tendency to put on weight very easily, and some parents and carers offer more high-calorie food than children need. Some associated dietary problems are:

- **Changing lifestyles** – fast food is overtaking traditionally prepared meals. Many convenience meals involve coating the food with fatty sauces or batters.
- **Foods high in sugar and fat**: children eat more sweets and crisps and drink more fizzy drinks – this is partly because of advertising, but also because such foods are more widely available.
- **Poor fruit and vegetable consumption**: despite it being more readily available, many children do not eat enough fresh fruit or vegetables, preferring processed varieties that often contain added sugar and fat.

Obesity can lead to emotional problems as well as to the physical problem of being more prone to infections: an obese child may be taunted by others, and will be unable to participate in the same vigorous play as their peers.

A child who is diagnosed as being overweight will usually be prescribed a diet low in fat and sugar;

high-fibre carbohydrates are encouraged, such as wholemeal bread and other cereals. The child who has to go without crisps, chips and snacks between meals will need a lot of support and encouragement from parents and carers.

Activity

Childhood obesity

As a group, prepare a fact file for your school or college on childhood obesity. Include the following information:

- What is obesity? What causes it? What are the problems associated with it?
- Find out the prevalence of obesity in children and young people in the UK. Present the information in chart form (pie charts, bar graphs, etc.), showing your results by gender and age group.
- Research the latest government initiatives into tackling childhood obesity.
- Useful websites are www.mendprogramme. org and www.nutrition.org.uk (British Nutrition Foundation).

Activity

Special dietary requirements

Find out about the policy in your work setting covering special dietary requirements. In particular, find out about:

- special diets (which have been medically advised)
- preference diets (where there is no degree of risk attached)
- food allergies.

How does your setting ensure that any special dietary requirements are identified, and that every child is offered the appropriate food and drink?

Section 5: Safe food preparation

Basic food hygiene

The term 'food hygiene' refers to the practices which should be followed to ensure that food is safe and wholesome throughout all the stages of production to the point of sale or consumption.

Food hygiene is important to everyone. The food we eat is one of the key factors in good health. If you are working with children and young people you will almost always be involved in handling food in some way. Examples include:

- preparing and serving snacks or meals for children in a nursery or other setting
- preparing and serving snacks or meals in the child's own home
- supervising mealtimes in a school.

The causes of food poisoning

Any infectious disease which results from consuming food or drink is known as food poisoning. The term is most often used to describe the illness, usually diarrhoea and/or vomiting, caused by bacteria, viruses or parasites.

Most cases of food poisoning result from eating large numbers of pathogenic (or harmful) bacteria which are living on the food. Most food poisoning is preventable, although it is not possible to eliminate the risk completely. The prevention of food poisoning is described in Chapter 4, page 168. You will need to look again at this information to complete this Unit.

Good working practices

If you handle food as part of your job, you are responsible for ensuring that food does not become

contaminated. You need to understand how current legislation affects your work (see Chapter 4) and to follow good working practices. These include the following:

- Keep yourself clean by following rules of personal hygiene.
- Know how to store and prepare food safely and hygienically.
- Ensure that areas for serving food are clean and safe.
- Protect food from anything which could cause harm.
- Be alert to food safety hazards.
- Ensure that children are given the opportunity to wash their hands before a meal.

General principles of food storage

Storing food properly is an important factor in the prevention of food poisoning. Correct storage – when food is kept at the correct temperature for the appropriate time – helps to:

- prevent food poisoning
- avoid spoilage
- preserve the food's qualities – of taste, appearance and nutritional value.

Some foods may be stored at room temperature, including:

- flour
- beans and pulses
- canned foods
- bottled food
- cereals
- tea, coffee and spices.

However, even these dried and canned foods have limits on their storage time.

Storage of canned foods

- Most canned foods have been sterilised during processing, which means any contaminating organisms originally present on the food have been destroyed and the cans need only be stored in a cool place.

- Unopened canned foods can be stored in a cool, dry place (21–24 °C) for at least 12 months. Many canned foods will keep longer but because of uncertainty as to the true age of the food, a 12-month maximum should be set.
- Canned rhubarb, fruit juices, soft drinks and some baby foods are exceptions and have a maximum storage life of about six months.
- Products such as canned ham which are marked 'Store below 4 °C' must be stored in the fridge. (This is because the ham has not been fully sterilised as prolonged heating adversely affects the texture of the meat.) The same applies to some imported canned meats and fish products.
- Read all labels carefully before the food is stored.
- Watch for swollen or leaking cans. This indicates some failure in processing, and the contents of the can should not be tasted.

Storing the contents of canned food once opened

- Adopt the same storage precautions for the contents of a can as you would for fresh food of the same kind. This is because contamination is possible as soon as the can is opened and some of the contents removed.
- Throw out the contents of any cans which have any unusual odour.
- Do not store the foods in the opened cans. They should be transferred to a glass or plastic container before refrigerating. This is because some preserved foods do not store well in cans; for example, highly acid or salted foods such as fruit juices or tomato products will attack tin plate in the presence of air.

Storage of dehydrated or dried foods

- Dehydrated foods do not readily go bad while dry, but they are deteriorating slowly all the time, particularly once the packets are open to the air. Dehydration inhibits the growth of microbes by removing water, but it does not make foods sterile and these foods may carry a high level of contaminating micro-organisms which become active again in the presence of water.

- Store in a cool place, away from obvious sources of heat such as a stove or direct sunlight. Dried foods will keep in an unopened container for about six months at 21–24 °C.
- Inspect regularly for insect infestation, as this can be a problem.
- If possible, store opened packages or dried fruits in the fridge, to maintain quality for a longer period.
- Rehydrated dried foods – those to which water has been added – need to be treated as highly perishable and kept in the fridge. This includes stocks, gravies and soups which have been made from dehydrated ingredients. Once these mixes are combined with other moist ingredients, conditions are right for the growth of bacteria.

Principles of temperature control for safe storage of foods

The temperature at which a food is kept for any time is extremely important. Between 5° and 63 °C is the **temperature danger zone** because this is the temperature range in which food poisoning bacteria may grow.

It is easy to reduce the risk of food poisoning by keeping the time spent by food in the temperature danger zone of rapid microbial growth as short as possible.

Remember: the shorter the time foods, including cooked foods, spend between 5° and 63 °C, the less are the chances of food poisoning.

High-risk and perishable foods

No food will last forever – however well it is packaged and stored. High-risk and perishable foods must be refrigerated because most food poisoning and spoilage bacteria do not multiply – or at least multiply only slowly – at temperatures 0–5 °C. They include the following:

- raw meat, poultry and fish
- cooked meat, cooked poultry, fish and seafood
- products made from meat, poultry and fish, such as pies, pasties and pâtés.

Guidelines to good practice: safe refrigeration

- Throw out food which is going off, because putting it in a colder part of the fridge will not stop it from deteriorating further. It could also taint other food.
- Store food you want to keep for a long time (or items like seafoods which are quite susceptible to spoilage) in the coldest part of the fridge.
- Cover all cooked foods and store them on a shelf above uncooked goods. This minimises the risk of food-poisoning organisms being transferred from uncooked to cooked foods through drip (cross-contamination).
- Never put hot food in a fridge. It raises the temperature of the fridge and may cause condensation; this can drip onto other foods and contaminate them.
- Cool down hot foods to room temperature as quickly as possible before putting them in the fridge – and use within two days.
- Foods with strong odours, such as seafoods and some cheeses, should be wrapped, and you should avoid storing them for long periods near foods, such as milk and cream, which are susceptible to tainting.
- Stack the shelves so that cold air can circulate and you can easily check the contents and rotate the stock as necessary.
- Do not leave fridge doors open any longer than necessary, because the temperature inside will rise.
- Cling-wrap films can prevent the transmission of odours and are useful in the short term and to stop spillages. However, closed glass or plastic containers are preferable.

Labelling on food
Date marks

In most countries food must (by law) be labelled with a date indicating the period when the food is safe to eat. Date marks have to be put on most packaged food. The two most important date marks are the 'use-by date' and the 'best-before date'.

'Use-by' date

This mark is found on highly perishable packaged food (those that 'go off' quite quickly) such as:

- cooked meats
- chilled ham
- sausages
- fish and dairy products.

The 'use-by' date means that the food has a short shelf-life and could become a health risk if stored incorrectly or for too long. Any food that is past the 'use-by' date is likely to be unfit to eat, even if it looks and smells alright.

'Best before' date

This is used for food that can safely be kept for longer, and is found on foods including:

- frozen food
- dried fruit
- flour, cakes and cereals
- canned food.

If eaten by the 'best before' date, you can be confident that the food is at its best quality. After that date food may not be dangerous to eat, but it may not taste (or perhaps smell) as good.

'Display until' marks

Supermarkets also use 'display until' date marks. This helps them to plan their stock rotation – that is, making sure that the oldest products are displayed at the front of the shelf and therefore sold first.

Storage instructions label

Packaged foods also have to display a storage instructions label. It is important to take notice of these instructions, as some less obvious foods – bottled sauces and preserves, for example – are recommended to be stored in the fridge once open.

Figure 10.6 Example food label

Protecting food from airborne hazards

Air and dust carry millions of microscopic particles of dead skin. Food left out before serving should be kept covered at all times. Other hazards include flies (especially blue- and green-bottle), which contaminate food by directly landing on it and by dropping their eggs and faeces.

Hygienic food preparation

The main hazards (risks) when preparing food are:

- cross-contamination
- multiplying bacteria.

Both carry a serious risk of food poisoning.

There are four basic rules to follow to ensure that the food you prepare is safe and hygienic:

1 CLEAN
2 SEPARATE
3 COOK
4 CHILL.

1 Clean

Be clean yourself: bacteria can be present throughout the kitchen, so you will need to be very clean.

Wash your hands thoroughly with hot soapy water frequently, but always:

- before handling food
- after handling raw meat, poultry or fish
- after using the toilet
- after gardening or handling rubbish
- after handling a pet or other animal
- after smoking
- after sneezing or coughing.

Keep the work area clean: wash surfaces and utensils frequently. After preparing each food item and before you go on to the next food, you should always clean:

- all preparation and eating surfaces, using hot soapy water
- chopping boards, knives and other utensils
- cloths and towels – if not using single-use cloths.

Wash raw fruit and vegetables: raw fruit and vegetables should be washed in cold running water.

2 Separate

Prevent cross-contamination: cross-contamination is when ready-to-eat food is contaminated with bacteria:

- directly: by contact with raw meat, poultry, fish or unwashed vegetables
- indirectly: by contact with hands, utensils or work surfaces which harbour harmful bacteria.

To prevent cross-contamination, you need to take these precautions:

- Always store raw meat by itself on the bottom shelf or in the drawer of the fridge so that juices cannot drip onto other food.
- Never place other food in direct contact with raw meat, poultry, fish or unwashed vegetables.
- Pack raw meat, poultry and fish separately at the supermarket. Make sure that other meat products, such as cooked ham, are never packed in the same bag.
- Use a different cutting board and utensils for raw meat products.
- Always wash hands, cutting boards, utensils and dishes after they come into contact with raw meat, poultry, eggs, seafood and unwashed fruit and vegetables.

3 Cook

Cook to proper temperatures: foods are cooked properly when they are heated to a high enough temperature and for long enough to kill the harmful bacteria which can cause food poisoning. To be safe, follow these precautions:

- Follow a recipe or the cooking advice label on the packet.
- Always cook food to a high temperature for the correct amount of time to kill any bacteria. Food should be cooked to a core temperature of 75 °C.
- Buy and use a meat thermometer. If you do not have one, be sure to cook burgers, chicken and pork until the juices run clear.
- If you are reheating food, such as a fish pie, do so only once. Make sure you reheat to piping hot (82 °C), to kill any bacteria which have survived in the food during cooling and refrigeration.
- Never pour hot gravy or sauce onto cold food.

4 Chill

Refrigerate foods quickly: the reason we refrigerate foods such as meats, dairy products and certain vegetables and fruits is that most bacteria do not multiply below 6 °C. The correct temperature for a fridge is between 0 and 5 °C. At this temperature the food remains ready for cooking or eating. For this reason, you need to:

- Store chilled foods in the fridge immediately after you return from shopping.
- Refrigerate perishable foods as soon as possible after cooking.
- Chill or freeze cooked food in shallow pans to allow for speedy cooling.
- Allow plenty of time to thaw frozen meat and poultry.

Legal requirements for safe food preparation

The Food Safety Act 1990 lays out your legal responsibilities when handling food in the workplace. (There are extra laws which apply to anyone working in an organisation whose main business is preparing and serving food.)

Guidelines for good practice when handling food

- Wear clean clothing and, where appropriate, protective clothing such as gloves and aprons.
- Follow good personal hygiene.
- Regularly wash your hands when handling food.
- Never smoke in food-handling areas.
- Keep the workplace clean.
- Do not bring outdoor clothing into food areas.
- Report any illness (such as infected wounds, skin infections, diarrhoea or vomiting) to your supervisor or manager immediately.
- You must not work with food if you have food poisoning or similar symptoms until your employer or doctor says it is safe to do so.

Guidelines for good practice when handling food (cont.)

- Protect food and ingredients against contamination which is likely to make them unfit to eat or a health hazard. For example, uncooked poultry should not contaminate ready-to-eat foods, either through direct contact or through work surfaces or equipment.
- Report any faults, problems or possible food hazards to your manager.

Employers and the law

There are two key food safety laws and regulations in Britain:

- the Food Safety Act 1990
- the Food Hygiene Regulations 2006

Similar laws apply in Northern Ireland.

Recognising and reporting personal illness

If you have – or have recently had – any illness which may cause food contamination, you must report it to your manager or employer. You should also report specific symptoms of food poisoning to your family or close personal contacts. The following symptoms should always be reported:

- diarrhoea
- vomiting
- nausea
- ear, eye or nose discharge
- septic cuts and boils
- any skin infection.

The reasons for reporting these symptoms are:

- If you have suffered from food poisoning you will have high numbers of pathogens (disease-causing organisms) in your gut which will be passed out of your body in your faeces. These bacteria can be easily transferred to lavatory seats, flush handles and of course to your hands.

- You could be a carrier and could contaminate food or other people with pathogenic bacteria without having any symptoms yourself; for example, if you have had Salmonella poisoning, you may harbour the bacteria for a long time after the symptoms have disappeared and you are feeling well.

Case Study — Reporting personal illness

Lorna works at Acorns Nursery as a nursery assistant. One day, she comes in for her day shift with a terrible cold. She has a constant runny nose and frequently sneezes. Her supervisor notices that Lorna is unable to control the sneezing and is using tissues to wipe her nose and then discarding them in the room's waste bin. When it is time to serve the midday meal, the supervisor insists that Lorna goes home and returns only when she has recovered.

1 What are the risks to the children in the nursery room if Lorna stays at work?
2 Why does Lorna's supervisor ensure that Lorna does not help with the serving of meals?
3 What particular risks do food handlers pose when they have an infection?

Activity

Food safety

1 In your workplace, find out what rules and instructions apply to food safety.

2 What particular precautions should you take if:
- you have a cut or sore on your finger
- you have a runny nose and cough
- you have experienced diarrhoea and sickness?

Assessment practice

- Describe the main food groups that are essential to meet the basic needs of the body.

- What is meant by a balanced nutritious diet for the growing child?

- Explain the possible effects of poor eating on the health and wellbeing of children.

- Discuss the factors that may influence the diet of young children and their families, and the types of food provided.

- Describe the policies and procedures of the setting that promote safe and healthy eating for children.

 Useful resources

Websites

For information on the **NHS Healthy Living campaign**:
www.nhs.uk/change4life

British Nutrition Foundation: for information on healthy eating and the Balance of Health pictorial guide:
www.nutrition.org.uk

Cool Milk: www.coolmilk.com

Feed Me Even Better:
www.jamieoliver.com/media/jamiesmanifesto.pdf

Sustain: for information about the Children's Food Campaign:
www.sustainweb.org

Book

Meggitt, C. (2003) *Food Hygiene and Safety*. Oxford: Heinemann Educational Publishers.

11 Working with children with special needs: Unit 14

Learning outcomes

In this chapter, you will learn:

1. The concept of special needs and current attitudes and values.

2. The range of factors affecting children's ability to learn.

3. The provision for children with special educational needs.

4. The roles and responsibilities of professionals working with children with special educational needs.

Section 1: The concept of special needs and current attitudes and values

What are special needs?

Children with special needs and disabilities are not an easily defined group. Some have a disability that is clear to see and is well-researched, such as Down's syndrome or cerebral palsy; others may have a specific learning need – for example, because of dyslexia or hearing impairment. Some people have lifelong special needs, such as people who have an autistic spectrum disorder. On the other hand, a child might have a special need for a short period of time – for example, a child who has periods of hearing loss caused by glue ear, when fluid builds up in the middle ear.

Every child is an individual

It is important think of each child as an individual, rather than making an assumption based on a label. Children are more alike than they are different. *Every* child needs to:

- feel welcome
- feel safe, both physically and emotionally
- have friends and to feel as if he or she belongs
- be encouraged to live up to his or her potential
- be celebrated for his or her uniqueness.

In other words, **children are always children first** – the special need is secondary.

Key terms

Disability – Any condition, impairment or disfigurement that is long-term and has significant, adverse effects on a person's ability to carry out day-to-day activities.

Special educational need – A learning difficulty, a behavioural, emotional or social difficulty, or a disability. It can be short-term or long-term. A child with a special educational need finds learning or accessing education more difficult than most children of the same age.

Other terminology for describing disability

Impairment

Impairment is the loss or limitation of physical, mental or sensory function on a long-term or permanent basis. Often children are described as having a hearing impairment rather than a hearing disability.

Figure 11.1 Jacob loves to climb and swing; he has Down's syndrome and he really enjoys outdoor play

Learning disability

People who have a learning disability have difficulties learning and find it particularly hard to understand new and complex information, and to develop new skills. A learning disability is a *lifelong* condition that is usually present from birth, although it may not become apparent until a child fails to reach particular developmental milestones.

Learning difficulty

Learning difficulty is a term used to describe any one of a number of barriers to learning that a child may experience. It is a broad term that covers a wide range of needs and problems – including dyslexia and behavioural problems – and the full range of ability. Children with learning difficulties may find activities that involve thinking and understanding particularly difficult, and many need support in their everyday lives as well as at school. According to the **Special Educational Needs and Disability Act 2001**, a child has a learning difficulty if he or she:

- has significantly greater difficulty learning than the majority of children of his or her age
- has a disability that prevents or hinders him or her from making use of educational facilities of a kind generally provided for children of his or her age in schools within the area of the Local Education Authority.

Theories and models of special needs

The difference between the social model and medical model of disability

The **medical model of disability** sees disabled people with disabilities as having the problem. Disabled people have to adapt to fit into the world as it is. If this is not possible, then they are excluded in specialised institutions or isolated in their homes. The medical model of disability emphasises the person's impairment and provides support for stereotypical views of disability that evoke pity, fear

Medical model thinking	Social model thinking
Child or young person is faulty	Child or young person is valued
Diagnosis	Strengths and needs defined by self and others
Labelling	Identify barriers and develop solutions
Impairment becomes focus of attention	Outcome-based programme design
Assessment, monitoring, programmes of therapy imposed	Resources are made available to ordinary services
Segregation and alternative services	Training for parents and professionals
Ordinary needs are put on hold	Relationships nurtured
Re-entry if normal enough *or* permanent exclusion	Diversity welcomed: child is included
Society remains unchanged	Society evolves

Table 11.1 The differences between the medical and social models of disability (From the Disability Equality in Education website)

and patronising attitudes towards disabled people. The medical model creates a cycle of dependency and exclusion. In addition, the design of the physical environment (for example, play, leisure, school and work facilities) presents disabled people with many barriers, making it very difficult or sometimes impossible for their needs to be met and limiting their day-to-day activities.

The **social model of disability** views the barriers that prevent disabled people from participating in any situation as what disables them. The social model suggests that disabled people are individually and collectively disadvantaged by a complex form of institutional discrimination as fundamental to our society as sexism and racism. Disabled people are often made to feel that it is their fault that they are different. The only difference is that they have an impairment that limits their physical, mental or sensory functions. Restructuring physical environments and accepting people with disabilities for who they are without fear, ignorance and prejudice benefits everyone.

The human rights model

The human rights model of disability can be seen as the most recent development of the social model. It states that:

- All human beings are equal and have rights that should be respected without distinction of any kind.

- People with disabilities are citizens and, as such, have the same rights as those without impairments.
- All actions to support people with disabilities should be 'rights-based'; for example, the demand for equal access to services and opportunities as a human right.

The human rights model is similar to the social model, as it places responsibility for addressing the problems of disability on society rather than on the person with disabilities.

Attitudes, perceptions and beliefs and their effect on the care and education of children

Anyone with a disability forms part of a minority group whose particular needs may not be adequately recognised or taken into account. Having a different appearance often leads to disabled people being treated differently and unequally. Of course, not all disabilities are recognisable from a person's external appearance – for example, deafness, epilepsy, autism or diabetes.

Discussion point

Like many other minority groups, disabled people suffer disproportionate levels of discrimination, including violence. The following headlines are taken from the BBC News website:

A 50-year-old disabled woman from Hartlepool is subjected to taunts and bullying as she lies dying.

Two men are attacked as they help their disabled brother into a car on Plymouth Hoe in Devon.

Two boys kill a partially-sighted man by kicking and stamping on him at a tram stop in Sheffield.

Three men and a youth launch a cowardly attack on a disabled man in Staffordshire for no obvious motive.

1. Could negative and discriminatory attitudes be one of the causes of violence against disabled people?

2. How might early years settings and schools change attitudes towards disability?

Talk about your ideas in a small group, or with another learner.

Activity

Enabling the child with a disability

1 Look at the layout of your own work placement. What physical changes would be necessary to include a child in a wheelchair or a partially-sighted child?

2 Try to write a story in which a child with a disability is the hero or heroine, but their heroism does not involve bravely enduring or overcoming their disability.

Key terms

Discrimination – Actions or behaviours that lead to a person or a group of people being treated less favourably. It is illegal to discriminate against people on the grounds of sex, race, disability, sexuality or age.

Inclusion – An approach to education and care that emphasises the child's right to participate in all aspects of the curriculum and daily life. Schools and early years settings are understood to have a duty to include the child.

In Practice

Making reasonable adjustments to ensure that children (and adults) with special needs and disabilities can participate in all activities and aspects of life:

If a child were coming into your setting who has difficulty walking and uses a standing frame, you would need to:

❑ think about whether there is enough space between the tables and equipment

❑ consider where you will store the frame when it is not being used

❑ consider how you will help the child to access any activities that are normally at floor-level – for example, block play or a train set.

Good early years practice includes offering children a broad and balanced curriculum, with both indoor and outdoor play opportunities. You need to think about how you can help all children to access this broad curriculum.

The use of appropriate and sensitive language and terminology

Avoiding stereotyping and labelling

As we have seen in Chapter 1, stereotyping often leads to discrimination. It matters a great deal how we 'label' people who are different from us. Many years ago, people who were obviously different – that is, they were perhaps unable to walk or talk or slow to learn – were believed to be in some way evil; some were even burned to death as witches. Now, we are much more aware of individual differences and have a great deal more knowledge about diverse needs and abilities. It is still very important that we do not apply labels to anyone.

Use of appropriate and sensitive terminology

As with other minorities, disabled people have developed preferred terminology; this is not political correctness – it is an important factor in avoiding the stereotypes and assumptions that result in discrimination. If in doubt about how to refer to someone's disability, ask them – or in the case of a child, ask their parents how they would like you to refer to it.

Discussion point

It has been argued that many children's films and stories equate being disabled with being wicked – for example, the witch who captures and tries to kill Hansel and Gretel is blind and stooped. On the other hand, goodness is often represented by an ideal of physical perfection and beauty – for example, Snow White.

What do you think? Are people's attitudes towards disabilities affected by the stories they hear in childhood? Discuss your ideas with another learner, or in a group.

Case Study — Harry, my son

When I first met Harry, he was my son. A year later he was epileptic and developmentally delayed. By 18 months he had special needs and he was a 'special' child. I was told not to think about his future.

My husband and I struggled with all this. By the time he was four, Harry had special educational needs and was a 'statemented' child. He was dyspraxic, epileptic, developmentally delayed and had severe and complex communication problems. Two years later – age six – he was severely epileptic, had cerebral palsy and had communication difficulties. At eight, he had severe epilepsy with associated communication problems; he was showing a marked developmental regression, and he had severe learning difficulties. At nine he came out of segregated schooling and he slowly became my son again. Never again will he be anything but Harry – a son, a brother, a friend, a pupil, a teacher, a person.

(Adapted from a true account – names have been changed.)

1 How many different labels can you identify in this short account?

2 Why do you think Harry's mother felt she had 'lost' her son?

Section 2: The range of factors affecting children's ability to learn

There are three main causes of disability that may affect a child's ability to learn:

- **genetic causes** – when a faulty gene leads to a disabling condition
- **developmental causes** – something goes wrong when the foetus is growing in the womb
- **illness and accident** – these can affect individuals who are born with no disability.

We will consider the first two types of causes in this section.

Genetic factors

The growth and development of the embryo and foetus are controlled by genes. Abnormal genes can cause abnormal growth and development (see Table 11.2).

Dominant gene defects

A parent with a dominant gene defect has a 50 per cent chance of passing the defect on to each of their children. Examples of dominant gene defects are:

- tuberous sclerosis (a disorder affecting the skin and nervous system)
- achondroplasia (once called dwarfism)
- Huntington's chorea (a disorder of the central nervous system).

Recessive gene defects

These defects are only inherited if two recessive genes meet. Therefore, if both parents carry a single recessive gene defect, each of their children has one in four (25 per cent) chance of being affected. Examples of defects transmitted this way are:

- cystic fibrosis (detailed in Chapter 9)
- sickle-cell anaemia (detailed in Chapter 9)
- phenylketonuria (a defective enzyme disorder)
- thalassaemia (a blood disorder)
- Tay-Sachs disease (a disorder of the nervous system)
- Friedreich's ataxia (a disorder of the spinal cord).

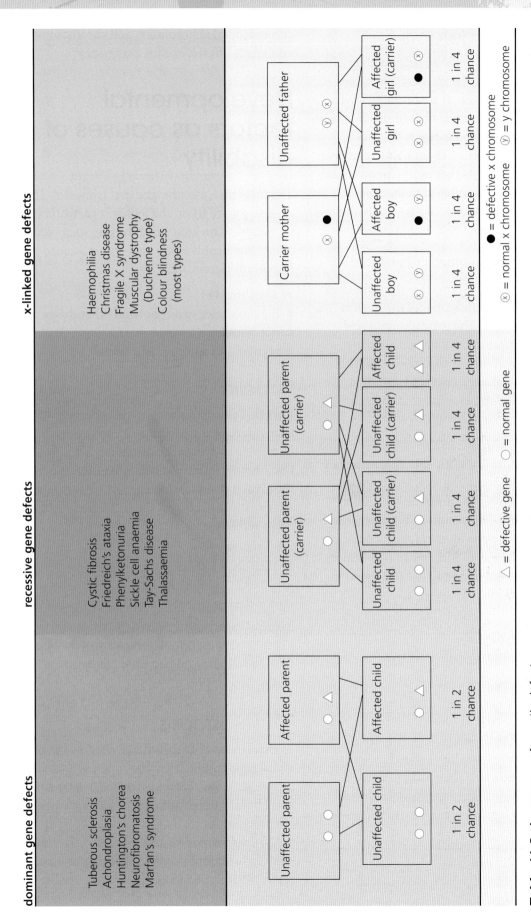

Table 11.2 A summary of genetic defects

Chromosomal defects

These vary considerably in the severity of their effect on the individual. About one in every 200 babies born alive has a chromosomal abnormality – which means that the structure or number of chromosomes varies from normal. Among foetuses that have been spontaneously aborted, about half has such an abnormality. This suggests that most chromosomal abnormalities are incompatible with life, and that those seen in babies born alive are generally the less serious ones.

Examples of defects transmitted this way are:

- **Down's syndrome**: Trisomy 21 is the term used for the chromosomal abnormality that results in Down's syndrome. The extra chromosome is number 21; affected individuals have three, instead of two, number 21 chromosomes. This results in short stature, as well as learning difficulties and an increased susceptibility to infection.

- **Klinefelter's syndrome**: 47XXY is the term used for the chromosomal abnormality that results in Klinefelter's syndrome. The affected male has one or more extra X-chromosomes (normally the pattern is XY). This results in boys who are very tall, with hypogonadism. Hypogonadism is when the sex glands produce few or no hormones. In men, these glands (gonads) are the testes; in women, they are the ovaries.

- **Turner's syndrome**: 45XO is the term used for the chromosomal abnormality which results in Turner's syndrome. Most affected females have only 45 chromosomes instead of 46; they have a missing or defective X-chromosome. This results in girls with non-functioning ovaries, a webbed neck and a broad chest; they may also have cardiac malfunctions.

- **Cri du chat syndrome**: this is a very rare condition in which a portion of one particular chromosome is missing in each of the affected individual's cells.

Genetic counselling is available for anyone with a child or other member of the family with a chromosomal abnormality, and chromosome analysis is offered in early pregnancy.

Developmental factors as causes of disability

The first three months (the first trimester) of a pregnancy are when the foetus is particularly vulnerable. The lifestyle of the pregnant woman affects the health of the baby in her womb. Important factors are:

- a healthy diet
- the avoidance of alcohol and other drugs
- not smoking
- regular and appropriate exercise.

Rubella

Rubella ('German measles') is especially harmful to the developing foetus as it can cause deafness, blindness and learning disability. All girls in the UK are now immunised against rubella before they reach childbearing age, and this measure has drastically reduced the incidence of rubella-damaged babies.

Thalidomide

A drug called Thalidomide was widely prescribed in the early 1960s, to alleviate morning sickness in pregnant women. Unfortunately, it was found to cause limb deformities in many of the babies born to women who had used the drug, and it was withdrawn in 1961.

Toxoplasmosis

Toxoplasmosis is an infection caused by the protozoan toxoplasma gondii. It may be contracted when pregnant women eat undercooked meat (usually pork) from infected animals, or by poor hygiene after handling cats or their faeces. In about one-third of cases, toxoplasmosis is transmitted to the child and may cause blindness, hydro-cephalus or learning difficulty. Infection in late pregnancy usually has no ill effects.

Irradiation

If a woman has X-rays in early pregnancy or receives radiotherapy for the treatment of cancer, the embryo may suffer abnormalities. Radiation damage may also result from atomic radiation or radioactive fall-out (following a nuclear explosion or a leak from a nuclear reactor). There is also an increased risk of the child developing leukaemia in later life after exposure to radiation.

The characteristics of common conditions and impairments in children

Cerebral palsy

This is the general term for disorders of movement and posture resulting from damage to a child's developing brain in the later months of pregnancy, during birth, in the neonatal period or in early childhood. The injury does not damage the child's muscles or the nerves that connect them to the spinal cord – only the brain's ability to control the muscles. (Palsy literally means 'paralysis'.)

Cerebral palsy affects two to three children in every thousand. In the UK, about 1,500 babies either are born with or develop the condition each year. It can affect boys and girls, and people from all races and social backgrounds.

Types of cerebral palsy

Cerebral palsy jumbles messages between the brain and muscles. There are three main types of cerebral palsy which correspond to the different parts of the brain affected:

- spastic cerebral palsy: affected children find that some muscles become very stiff and weak, especially under effort, which can affect their control of movement. This is the most common type of cerebral palsy and it affects different areas of the body.
- athetoid cerebral palsy: affected children have some loss of control of their posture, and tend to make involuntary movements. Their speech can be hard to understand, and hearing problems are also common.
- ataxic cerebral palsy: affected children usually have problems with balance. They may also have shaky hand movements and irregular speech.
- often, children will have a mixture of the different types of cerebral palsy. In some children, the condition is barely noticeable; others will be more severely affected. No two children will be affected in quite the same way.

Causes of cerebral palsy

Cerebral palsy is most commonly the result of a failure of part of the brain to develop, either before birth or in early childhood. Occasionally, it is due to an inherited disorder. It is sometimes possible to identify the cause of cerebral palsy, but not always.

The effects of cerebral palsy

Cerebral palsy may not be recognised until the child is several months old. A child with cerebral palsy may have some or most of the following features, in varying degrees of severity:

- slow, awkward or jerky movements
- stiffness of the arms and legs when being picked up
- delayed sitting or walking
- feeding difficulties
- muscle spasms
- floppiness
- unwanted (involuntary) movements.

Some children with cerebral palsy do have learning difficulties, but this is by no means always the case. Some have higher than average intelligence and some have average intelligence. Some children have difficulty in learning to do certain tasks (for example, reading, drawing or arithmetic), because a particular part of the brain is affected; it is termed a 'specific learning difficulty' and should not be confused with the child's general intelligence.

Care of children with cerebral palsy

There is no cure for cerebral palsy. It is a non-progressive condition; this means that it does not become more severe as the child gets older, but some difficulties may become more noticeable.

Therapy can help children with cerebral palsy. Physiotherapists, occupational therapists and speech therapists often work very closely together to devise a treatment programme that will meet the needs of both the child and the family. As the nature of cerebral palsy varies immensely, the therapy is adapted to the needs of the individual child.

Research Activity

Find out more about cerebral palsy at www.scope.org.uk or search online for Scope.

Blindness and partial sight (visual impairment)

The picture of total darkness conjured up by the word 'blindness' is inaccurate: only about 18 per cent of blind people in the UK are affected to this degree; the other 82 per cent all have some remaining sight. In the UK, there are just over one million blind and partially-sighted people, of whom 40 per cent are blind and 60 per cent are partially-sighted (or have a visual impairment).

Causes of visual impairment

The main causes of visual impairment in children are:

- abnormalities of the eyes from birth, such as cataracts (cloudiness of the lens)
- nystagmus (involuntary jerkiness of the eyes)
- optic atrophy (damage to the optic nerve)
- retinopathy of prematurity (abnormal development of retinas in premature babies)
- hereditary factors such as retinoblastoma, a tumour of the retina which is often inherited.

Childhood glaucoma and diabetic retinopathy are quite rare in children, but are common causes of visual impairment in adults.

Treatment of visual impairment

Some conditions that cause visual impairment are treatable, particularly if detected at an early stage, for example:

- glaucoma can be halted by medical or surgical means
- a cataract may be removed by removal of the lens
- laser therapy is also now being used to correct various visual defects.

Education for children with visual impairment

More than 55 per cent of visually impaired children in education attend mainstream schools along with sighted children. Most will have a Statement of Special Educational Needs (see page 454) which details the support and special equipment they need.

Deafness and partial hearing (hearing impairment)

Deafness is often called 'the hidden disability' as it may not be outwardly apparent that a person is deaf. As with total blindness, total deafness is rare and is usually congenital (present from birth). Partial deafness is generally the result of an ear disease, injury or degeneration associated with the ageing process.

There are two types of hearing loss:

- conductive: when there is faulty transmission of sound from the outer ear to the inner ear

Case Study — Mothers' response to blind babies

Research by Selma Fraiberg from 1974 to 1977 showed that blind babies begin to smile at about the same age as sighted babies (roughly four weeks), but that they smile less often. The blind infant's smile is also less intense and more fleeting than the sighted baby's smile. In addition, blind babies do not enter into a mutual gaze, which is an important factor in the formation of a deep attachment or bond between parents and their baby. Fraiberg's research found that most mothers of blind babies gradually withdrew from their infants. They needed help in learning to 'read' their baby's other signals, such as body movements and gestures. This help led to an improved interaction between mothers and their babies.

In Practice

Promoting an awareness of visual impairment

Tutors or learners – or both – may wish to send away for copies of the booklet produced by the RNIB (see Useful resources section on page 472) to enable them to carry out the first of the following activities.

Plan and mount a display on 'Children with visual impairment': using the booklets as a guide, each small group should plan and mount a display on one of the following topics:

❏ developing the senses

❏ establishing routines

❏ movement games

❏ play and toys.

When the displays are up, the groups should evaluate each other's displays, using a set of criteria agreed beforehand: Is the information presented in an easy-to-understand format? Does the material used illustrate the points effectively?

Try to contact a local group of parents of visually impaired children and invite them to view the display; health visitors or social services departments may be able to make the first contact for you here.

- sensori-neural: when sounds that do reach the inner ear fail to be transmitted to the brain (often referred to as 'nerve' deafness).

Causes of conductive hearing loss

The most common causes of this kind of deafness in children are:

- otitis media: infection of the middle ear
- glue ear: a build-up of sticky fluid in the middle ear, usually affecting children under eight years.

Causes of sensori-neural hearing loss

- **Heredity**: there may be an inherited fault in a chromosome.

- **Birth injury**: this may cause nerve or brain damage.
- **Severe jaundice**: in the newborn baby with severe jaundice, there may be damage to the inner ear.
- **Rubella**: there may be damage to the developing foetus if the mother is infected with the rubella (German measles) virus during pregnancy.
- **Ménière's disease**: this is a rare disorder in which deafness, vertigo and tinnitus result from an accumulation of fluid within the labyrinth in the inner ear.
- **Damage to the cochlea or labyrinth (or both)**: this can result from an injury, viral infection or prolonged exposure to loud noise.

Diagnosis of hearing impairment

Hearing tests are performed as part of a routine assessment of child development. The early detection of any hearing defect is vital in order that the best possible help can be offered at the time when development is at its fastest.

Treatment of hearing impairment

For conductive hearing loss, treatment is usually a hearing aid or surgical correction of the defect.

For sensori-neural hearing loss, treatment is also a hearing aid, but also special training, for example in language acquisition, speech therapy or perceptual motor training; a bilingual approach using British Sign Language (BSL) and verbal speech is often recommended.

Hearing aids

Almost all children with sensori-neural hearing loss will benefit from a hearing aid; and they can also be helpful for children with conductive hearing loss – for example, while they are waiting to be admitted to hospital for corrective surgery.

There are three types of hearing aid (see Figure 11.2):

1 **A body-worn hearing aid**: this is often strapped to the child's waist, with a wire connecting it to the earpiece; this type of aid is used for profound hearing loss as it enables greater amplification of sound than in the smaller devices.

2 **A post-aural hearing aid**: this fits comfortably behind the ear; it can be used even with small babies.

3 **An in-the-ear hearing aid**: this is generally reserved for use with older children.

The aim of all hearing aids is to amplify sounds. In children whose hearing is not helped by such aids, a cochlear implant may be considered instead.

Problems associated with hearing impairment

- **Communication**: if possible, children should learn to express themselves through a recognisable speech pattern (language acquisition). Isolation may result from the deaf child's inability to hear the familiar voices and household noises that a hearing child takes for granted.
- **A lack of auditory stimulation**: this may lead to delayed development.
- **A potential for injury**: this is related to a failure to detect warning sounds, such as traffic or warning shouts.
- **Anxiety and coping difficulties**: this is related to reduced social interaction and loneliness.
- **Parental anxiety**: this is related to having a child with impaired hearing.

See page 13 for information on how to help a child with a hearing impairment.

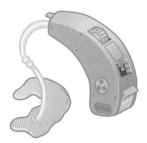

Figure 11.2 Different types of hearing aid

Carla, a baby of 15 months, has just been diagnosed with a severe hearing impairment. When she has her nappy changed, Mary, the baby room supervisor, notices that Laura, one of the early years practitioners, changes her nappy in silence, although she always smiles, chats and plays with the other babies during nappy-changing routines. When Mary asked her why she does not do the same with Carla, Laura replied that she did not see the point because Carla cannot hear anything.

1. Why is Mary concerned about Laura's childcare practice?

2. Discuss ways in which practitioners could promote Carla's development and meet her holistic needs.

Autism/autistic spectrum disorder

Autism is a disability that disrupts the development of social interaction and communication. Children are affected in many different ways by autism, which is why we use the term 'autistic spectrum'. The most seriously affected children have profound learning disabilities and delayed language, and will need intensive support and care. At the other end of the spectrum, children with Asperger's syndrome may manage the intellectual demands of schooling very well, although they will still find aspects of social interaction and communication difficult.

Causes of autism

Research suggests that there is no single cause, but that there may be a physical problem affecting those parts of the brain that integrate language and information from the senses. The condition is not caused by emotional problems in families or emotional deprivation. The onset of autism is almost always before the age of three years. It affects four times as many boys as girls.

Features of autism

The degree to which children with an autistic spectrum disorder are affected varies, but all those affected have what is known as the 'triad of impairments' or the 'three impairments'. The Early Support guide to autistic spectrum disorders describes these as follows:

- Social interaction – difficulty understanding social 'rules', behaviour and relationships; for example, appearing indifferent to other people or not understanding how to take turns.
- Social communication – difficulty with verbal and non-verbal communication; for example, not fully understanding the meaning of common gestures, facial expressions or tone of voice.
- Rigidity of thinking and difficulties with social imagination – difficulty in the development of interpersonal play and imagination; for example, having a limited range of imaginative activities, possibly copied and pursued rigidly and repetitively.

Read the Early Support guides at www.education.gov.uk and search for 'Early Support'.

Working with a child who has an autistic spectrum disorder

There is a great deal of controversy about the different interventions that may help a child with an autistic spectrum disorder (ASD), ranging from behavioural interventions to dietary and medical programmes. It is not advisable to attempt to implement any approach without careful consideration of how well it would suit a particular child, and review of the independent research evidence for its effectiveness. The best starting point for information is the National Autistic Society (www.nas.org.uk).

However, there is wide agreement that early years settings and schools can be difficult places for children with an ASD. A lot of early learning is based on language and play, two areas of great difficulty for a

Figure 11.3 Some characteristics of a child with autism

child with an ASD. The noise and amount of visual stimulation from displays and boxes of equipment can quickly become overwhelming. In this context, a child with an ASD might gain some feeling of security by rigidly following the same sequences of activity, or repeating the same action over again. While it is important not to deprive a child under stress of actions that provide some comfort, constant repetition is not the basis for successful development and learning, and the child will need skilled and sensitive support to interact with others and to extend his or her interests.

How you can help a child with an autistic spectrum disorder

- Visual learning is stronger than language-based learning or learning through exploratory play – putting things into symbols really helps children with an ASD. A visual timetable, showing the main sequence of events and routines in the day, can help the child to understand what is going to happen next. Symbols that the child can pick up or point to, in order to make choices and express preferences, will aid early communication.

- Reduce visual stimulation – keep displays and labels orderly: pictures all over the windows and labels at jaunty angles can be visually overwhelming. Have some places with blank walls, which can be calming.
- Keep everything as clear and consistent as you can – while for most children a sudden announcement of a trip or a special activity is fun, for many children with an ASD such changes in routine are very scary. As far as possible, keep routines consistent and alert the child when something is about to happen by using symbols or the visual timetable. When something new is coming up, try to prepare the child as much as you can. You might have a symbol that means 'a change', or be able to use a photograph to signal what is going to happen. Use as few words and as few symbols as possible: communicate clearly and briefly.
- Show how things work – a child with an ASD can be helped when adults show, step-by-step, how to put Lego® bricks together, or model pretending to eat in the home corner. Allow plenty of time and encourage the child to copy.
- Introduce new things slowly – sensory play can be very difficult. Start with just a very brief attempt, and introduce materials in small amounts in areas of low distraction. To encourage sand play, for example, start in a quiet zone, without any children, and encourage the child to touch a small amount of sand on a tabletop or on the floor.

Research Activity

Find out more about people with autistic spectrum disorders at www.nas.org.uk or search online for 'NAS'.

Speech and language difficulties

More than one million schoolchildren in the UK have a speech and language difficulty of some sort. For some, this is a delay – their language is developing, but more slowly than usual. In other cases, this may be connected with a hearing impairment such as 'glue ear' in early childhood. For other children with a language disorder, the difficulty may be more complex. They may know lots of words, but may get words in the wrong order and have difficulties understanding and taking part in conversations. Often, speech and language disorders are associated with other special needs, like autism.

Yet another group of children has a specific difficulty with language, sometimes called **dysphasia**. These children do not stammer or lisp; they are not autistic; their general intelligence is often average or above. Their language impairment is specific or primary – not the result of any other disability.

Children with a speech and language impairment have difficulties with:

- talking (expressive language)
- understanding (receptive language)
- both of the above.

Generally, the cause of delayed speech and language is environmental – to do with the amount of opportunities the child has had to communicate and talk with others from an early age. But there are also many children whose speech and language difficulties are caused by a health problem or by delayed physical development. This can be due to **dyspraxia** (difficulty planning and making the movements which produce speech) or delayed muscle development in the mouth, lips, tongue and palate.

Research suggests that the number of children with a speech and language delay has increased substantially in recent years, and that this is mainly the result of environmental and cultural factors, including:

- **Front-facing buggies** – most babies and toddlers now spend a considerable period of time in front-facing buggies; prams and back-facing buggies were more popular in the past. When a child cannot see his or her parent's face from the buggy, the child cannot communicate or develop language.
- **Increased use of mobile phones and devices such as the Apple iPod®** – when parents have

headphones in or are on the phone, they are not able to communicate with their children.

- **Increased watching of television by children**: while television can be stimulating to children's imagination and language, this is only the case in small amounts, and when there are opportunities to talk or play later. Watching the film *Toy Story* and then playing at being Buzz Lightyear for example, will stimulate a child's communication, as will watching a programme about dinosaurs and talking about what you can see. On the other hand, sitting quietly in front of the television for many hours will cause a child to miss out on opportunities to talk, listen and play.
- The Every Child a Talker (ECAT) programme seeks to support language development for all children, with an emphasis on those who may be at risk of language delay. This delay may result from environmental factors, or when a child has a longer-term special need, disability or health problem.
- When professionals and parents work together in a spirit of cooperation and mutual respect, many children can make very rapid progress in their language. As learning becomes increasingly language-based, it is important to offer this help soon as children move through primary schools.

But remember that the following are not signs of a language delay or communication difficulty:

- speaking little in nursery, because the child is learning English as an additional language
- speaking in a different accent or using a different dialect to most other children or adults in the early years setting or school
- having a different pattern of communication from that which is expected or usually valued by staff and other professionals. Remember that some children are not good at answering direct questions for example, because the pattern of communication in their home is more about discussing things together.

Some children have other difficulties which affect the development of language. These include:

- difficulties with listening and attention skills
- behaviour difficulties, due to the frustration of not understanding or being understood

- difficulties with written language (**dyslexia**)
- difficulties understanding abstract ideas, like time, emotions or make-believe – these children have trouble connecting ideas and using language socially
- profound difficulties relating to the outside world – many of these will be described as being on the autistic spectrum.

Some of these children benefit from learning signs, such as Makaton or British Sign Language (BSL), and others may benefit from using visual symbols to communicate, like the Picture Exchange System (PECS).

Makaton

Makaton is a set of signs which are used to support spoken language. Unlike British Sign Language (BSL), it is not a language in itself. The Makaton vocabulary is a list of over 400 items with corresponding signs and symbols, with an additional resource vocabulary for the UK National Curriculum. The Makaton Project publishes a book of illustrations of the Makaton vocabulary (see Figure 11.4). Most signs rely on movement as well as position, so you cannot really learn the signs from the illustrations. Also in many signs *facial expression* is important. If a child at a school or nursery is learning Makaton, the parents should be invited to learn too. The Makaton Project will support schools and parents in this, as they know that everyone involved with the child must use the same signs.

Picture Exchange Communication System (PECS)

PECS begins with teaching children to exchange a picture of a desired item with a teacher, who immediately honours the request. For example, if they want a drink, they will give a picture of 'drink' to an adult, who directly hands them a drink. Verbal prompts are not used, thus encouraging spontaneity and avoiding prompt dependency. The system goes on to teach discrimination of symbols and how to construct simple 'sentences'. Ideas for teaching commenting and other language structures, such as asking and answering questions, are also incorporated. It has been reported that both

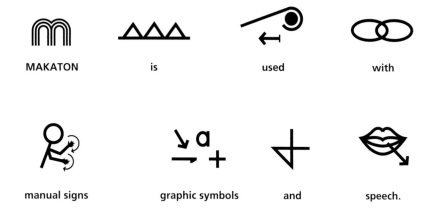

MAKATON   **is**   **used**   **with**

manual signs   **graphic symbols**   **and**   **speech.**

Figure 11.4 Makaton

In Practice

Support children with delayed speech, language and communication

❏ **Evaluating your early years setting or school classroom**: find out where the most communication takes place. Which are the areas of least communication? Think about how you could act on your findings – for example, if there is almost no talk in the computer area, you might need to think about programs and activities that require children to collaborate and talk together. If it is too noisy to talk in the block area because it is right by the door, you could move it or make it quieter by using curtains or other sound-absorbing barriers. ECAT can help you here, with the section on assessing the environment to identify what they call 'talking hotspots'. Remember that some children communicate best when outdoors, or when you take them out to the shop or on the bus – it does not all happen indoors.

❏ **Careful observation and assessment**: regularly record children's language and include what they say in your observations, or use audio or video recordings. Compare what they are saying with the expected levels of development (see Chapter 2). Identify which children need extra help with communication from you and the other staff.

❏ **Work closely with your local speech and language therapy service and early years advisory team**: often they are only too pleased to come and offer training and development.

❏ **Observing each other**: what strategies encourage children to talk? How can the whole team build on the good practice you observe? If there is a high level of trust among staff, you could video each other listening to and talking with children. There is more guidance on this in the ECAT programme, together with some helpful case studies.

❏ **If you are concerned about a child's development in this area, talk to the parent about your worries**: sometimes children are very quiet and uncommunicative in nursery or school, but good communicators at home with family and friends. Think about how you can make the child feel more confident. If the difficulties are similar, recommend a referral to speech and language therapy for further checking.

pre-school and older children have begun to develop speech when using PECS. The system is often used as a communication aid for children and adults who have an autistic spectrum disorder.

Objects of reference

Some children are unable to associate a symbol (picture or sign, for example) with a real thing in the world. In order to help their communication, adults can use **objects of reference**. This will often start with encouraging the child to make a choice between two real objects. For example, you might ask a child, 'Do you want an orange?' and show the orange; then withdraw the orange from sight and ask, 'Do you want an apple?', showing an apple. You would then repeat and follow up an indication of choice – for example, pointing or looking. So if a child made a movement when you showed the 'apple', you would then give a child a piece of apple. It is important to follow through consistently, so that the child experiences their communication leading to a choice. In time, this will allow the child to start expressing choices.

Objects of reference may be developed into a larger system. For example, you might have a display which shows a small amount of sand in a jar (sand play), a cup (drink/snack), a Lego® brick (construction play) and some grass (outdoor play). By pointing to the appropriate object, the child can make a choice of what she or he wishes to do next.

Research Activity

To find out more about speech and language difficulties, visit www.education.gov.uk and search for 'National Strategies Every Child a Talker'.

Developmental dyspraxia

Dyspraxia is a developmental disorder of the brain resulting in messages not being properly transmitted to the body. It affects at least two per cent of the population in varying degrees, and 70 per cent of those affected are male. Dyspraxia is a specific learning difficulty; this means that it does not affect a person's overall intelligence or ability in general, only specific aspects. Children with dyspraxia can be of average or above intelligence, but are often behaviourally immature. They try hard to fit in with the range of socially accepted behaviour when at school but often throw tantrums when at home. They may find it difficult to understand logic and reason. Dyspraxia is a disability but, as with autism, those affected do not look disabled. This is both an advantage and a disadvantage. Sometimes children with dyspraxia are labelled as 'clumsy' children. Such labelling is very unhelpful. There are many early indications – in the child's first three years – that he or she has dyspraxia (see below). Not all of these will apply to every child with dyspraxia, and many of these problems can be overcome in time.

Early indications of dyspraxia

In the first three years, the child may:

- be irritable and difficult to comfort from birth
- have delayed early motor skill development; problems sitting unaided, rolling from side to side, and may not crawl
- be delayed in toilet training
- have feeding difficulties including colic, milk allergies and so on
- have sleeping difficulties
- have delayed language development; single words not obvious until the age of three
- avoid simple construction toys, such as jigsaws and Lego®
- constantly move arms and legs
- be sensitive to loud noises
- be highly emotional and easily upset.

Later indications of dyspraxia

Older children are usually very verbally adept and converse well with adults, but they may be ostracised by their own peer group because they do not fit in. They may cleverly avoid doing those tasks that are difficult or even impossible for them. The child may:

- be clumsy, constantly bumping into objects and falling over
- often flap their hands when running or jumping
- be messy eaters; preferring to use fingers to eat and often spilling liquid from the drinking cup
- be unable to hold a pen or pencil properly and be confused about which hand to use
- have difficulties throwing and catching a ball
- be slow to learn to dress or to feed themselves
- be very excitable, becoming easily distressed and having frequent temper tantrums

- prefer adult company, feeling isolated in their peer group
- have speech problems, being slow to learn to speak or the speech may be incoherent
- may be unable to hop, skip or ride a bike
- have very high levels of motor activity, always swinging and tapping feet when seated, clapping hands and unable to sit still
- be sensitive to touch, finding some clothes uncomfortable
- dislike high levels of noise
- have reading and writing difficulties
- have poor short-term memory, often forgetting tasks learned the previous day
- be unable to answer simple questions even though they know the answers
- show a lack of imaginative play (for example, not enjoying dressing up, or playing inappropriately in the home corner)
- have phobias or show obsessive behaviour
- have a poor sense of direction
- be intolerant to having hair or teeth brushed, or nails and hair cut
- have no sense of danger (for example, jumping from an inappropriate height).

Assessment of dyspraxia

Assessment involves obtaining a detailed developmental history of the child, and using developmental tests or scales to build up a learning ability profile. Occupational therapists, physiotherapists and extra support at school can all help a child with dyspraxia to cope or to overcome many difficulties.

Dyslexia

Dyslexia is another specific learning difficulty, with particular impact on the child's language. The British Dyslexia Association (BDA) describes the following indications of dyslexia in the young child:

- has persistent jumbled phrases – for example, 'cobbler's club' for 'toddler's club'
- use of substitute words – for example, 'lampshade' for 'lamp post'
- inability to remember the label for known objects – for example, 'table', 'chair'

- difficulty learning nursery rhymes and rhyming words – for example, 'cat', 'mat', 'sat'
- later than expected speech development.

The BDA also describes some non-language indicators that a young child could be dyslexic:

- may have walked early but did not crawl – was a 'bottom–shuffler' or 'tummy-wriggler'
- persistent difficulties in getting dressed efficiently and putting shoes on the correct feet
- enjoys being read to but shows no interest in letters or words
- is often accused of not listening or paying attention
- excessive tripping, bumping into things and falling over
- difficulty with catching, kicking or throwing a ball, with hopping and/or skipping
- difficulty with clapping a simple rhythm.

(www.bdadyslexia.org.uk)

There are many children who will fit into some, or most of these categories. It is important to offer children continued support, to observe closely, to work with parents and to involve a specialist (for example, an educational psychologist) if necessary. Early years practitioners should avoid jumping to conclusions or applying a label to a child prematurely.

Attention deficit hyperactivity disorder

Attention deficit hyperactivity disorder (ADHD) is another specific learning difficulty. Children with ADHD show problems with focusing their attention and, at the same time, hyperactivity. If the difficulties generally present on their own, the child probably does not have ADHD. Some children may appear hyperactive in early years settings and schools because they need to move around to learn: in response to long carpet times and circle times, they may become fidgety and frustrated. Others may have poor capacity to direct their attention because they have experienced neglect in early childhood – for example, no one has interacted with them regularly, so they have not become used to focusing their attention.

The cause of ADHD is not known, but there is some evidence to suggest that a pattern of hyperactivity is inherited. There may also be a biological cause, perhaps due to a slower metabolism of glucose by the brain. Treatment may be by a stimulant medication (usually Ritalin), which often has an immediate improving effect on the child's behaviour but is a controversial treatment. Arriving at the correct dosage for the individual takes time and a high degree of cooperation between the parents and other professionals. It is generally agreed that medical treatment on its own is not an appropriate response to ADHD, and should be combined with:

- therapeutic input – for example, art therapy, occupational therapy or counselling for older children
- a programme to help with managing behaviour, setting clear limits, helping children anticipate difficulties and find their own ways of coping – for example, taking a moment or two out, or engaging in something calming
- sometimes lifestyle changes – for example, watching less television, spending less time on computers and electronic games, taking more exercise, and eating more healthily.

Characteristics of ADHD

The following are common characteristics found in children with ADHD:

- difficulty in remaining seated when asked to do so
- difficulty in sharing and taking turns in group situations
- excessive talking
- easily distracted by extraneous stimuli
- appearing not to be listening when being spoken to
- appearing restless, often fidgeting with hands or feet
- difficulty in playing quietly
- often losing things necessary for tasks or activities at school or at home – for example, books, pencils

- difficulty in sustaining attention in tasks or play activities interrupting others – for example, pushing into other children's games
- often engaging in physically dangerous activities without considering possible consequences – for example, running across the road without looking
- unable to focus attention on relevant detail at an age when such control is expected.

Behavioural, emotional and social difficulty

Behavioural, emotional and social difficulty (BESD) is classed as a special educational need; in many cases, a child with a BESD will also be considered to fall within the remit of the Equality Act 2010. This means that the child must not be treated less favourably than others, and that reasonable adaptations must be made to support the child's inclusion in an early years setting or school. BESD covers a very wide range of special needs, including:

- **conduct disorders** – where a child has difficulties in following instructions and keeping to rules
- **hyperkinetic disorders** – for example, attention deficit disorder or attention deficit hyperactivity disorder (ADD/ADHD)
- **other syndromes** – for example, Tourette's, which can cause a child to have vocal tics (repeating the same words, echoing words, or compulsive swearing) and physical tics (continual eye-blinking and throat-clearing, for example)
- **other disorders** – for example, anxiety, school phobia (being afraid to go to school), self-harming or depression.

Some children will have a medical diagnosis, but this is not necessarily the case.

As with many special needs, BESD can be largely prompted by a difficulty that is within a child, and equally can be prompted by environmental, cultural or family factors. For example, a child who has been shouted at and physically hurt by his parents may respond by behaving in an aggressive way towards others, and may have little self-control and resort swiftly to violence. A child may present with a severe conduct disorder in an early years setting where there is a degree of structure which the child is not developmentally ready for. The difficulties might then recede in a setting where there is a clear and firm management of behaviour, together with opportunities for children to play, make choices, and to move freely inside and outside.

There are more children with BESD in socially deprived areas, and there are many more boys with BESD than girls. BESD which results in difficult or aggressive behaviour is the most likely to be noticed, so it is important for practitioners also to consider the needs of anxious and withdrawn children, and those who are nervous or phobic about coming into early years settings and schools.

Research Activity

Find out more about helping children in the EYFS with behavioural, emotional and social difficulties; search online for 'Inclusion Development Programme: Supporting children with Behavioural, Emotional and Social Difficulties'.

Other factors affecting children's ability to learn

There are a number of factors – apart from the conditions described above – which can affect a child's ability to learn, including the following:

In Practice

How you can help a child with BESD

❑ Develop a positive relationship with the child, following the principles of the key person approach (see Chapter 5).

❑ Ensure that your policy and practice in managing children's behaviour combines an approach which takes account of children's different rates of development, while setting clear boundaries for all children and helping them to learn self-discipline.

❑ Think about how you can reduce the number of people who intervene when the child's behaviour is difficult. If a child is constantly told off all day by a range of staff, behaviour is unlikely to improve. The child is likely to respond with further negativity and difficult behaviour. Behaviour management should be coordinated by the key person, in the context of a positive relationship.

❑ As a team, decide together what behaviour you can ignore, and what behaviour is unsafe or unacceptable in all cases. Work consistently, and remember that improvement is likely to be in small steps.

❑ Help other children to be assertive in the face of aggressive or bullying behaviour, but remember it is ultimately the adult's responsibility to ensure that children feel safe and secure.

❑ Develop a positive relationship with the child's parents. By working together, you can help the child effectively. Parents will have valuable information and ideas to share with you, regarding the triggers and causes of their child's difficult behaviour and emotional outbursts. But if they feel 'told off' for the child's behaviour, then the relationship will quickly deteriorate. If you are giving the parent feedback on the child's day, carefully consider time and place. No parent wants to be told of their child's difficult behaviour in the corridor, or in public; and remember you are giving feedback and seeking the parent's cooperation, not offloading the stresses of a difficult day.

❑ Work closely with specialist services – educational psychology and CAMHS (Child and Adolescent Mental Health Services). You cannot meet the child's needs on your own.

❑ If the child's difficulties arise in part, or mainly, from family or environmental circumstances, then you will need to work collaboratively with a range of professionals using the CAF, and you may need to make a referral to Children's Social Care if you think the child is in immediate danger (see Chapter 3).

❑ All staff need time to talk about the difficulties presented by the child, and the child's key person will need particular support.

- **emotional**: the effects of trauma, such as bereavement or abuse
- **environmental**: the effects of poverty, lack of stimulation, poor provision for play
- **cultural**: different cultural expectations and experience
- **social**: lack of a stable relationship with adults, poor role models.

Each of these factors may prevent or delay a child's development; for example, lack of stimulation will prevent the child from experiencing early learning activities, which help in the development of concepts.

Loss and separation

There are many ways in which children and young people can experience loss and separation. Refugee children arriving in the UK, for example, face huge disruption to their lives and are usually separated from their wider family members and their familiar cultural context. Children of parents who are separated or divorced also face temporary upheaval. Bereavement is one extreme form of loss, especially if the child's parent dies. How children respond to the death of an important person in their life depends on a number of factors:

- their age and stage of development and consequently their understanding of death
- the nature of their relationship with the person who has died
- the circumstances of the death
- the reaction of other family members to the death
- the overall effect on the family unit
- their culture and family's spiritual beliefs
- their self-esteem and feelings of self-worth.

Children's reactions can vary from deep despair to denial or active protest. Whatever their reaction, it is important that they are allowed to express their feelings without being stopped or urged to 'be brave'. Children suffering bereavement through violent death (for example, murder or suicide) are more likely to need specialist professional help, both at the time of the death and also in the years to come, as they mature and reflect on the death and why it happened.

Normal signs of grief in young children include:

- bed wetting
- loss of appetite
- tummy upsets
- restlessness
- disturbed sleep
- nightmares
- crying: a tendency to tears at the least little thing, over a number of weeks
- attention-seeking behaviour
- increased anxiety and clinginess
- difficulty in concentrating.

These only become a cause for concern when they persist over a prolonged period of time.
Normal signs of grief in older children include:

- changes in personality; some may experience a depressed mood
- mood swings
- rudeness
- learning difficulties
- lack of concentration
- refusal to go to school
- sleep and appetite disturbances
- poor school work – although other children will throw themselves into their school work and end up by overworking.

These changes may not occur immediately after the bereavement but could show themselves months or even years after the event – as we have seen in Chapter 2, children return to grief at different stages of their development. Teachers and early years practitioners need to be aware of the date when the death occurred and be sensitive by not avoiding the reality of the special days which may be difficult for the child; these include the anniversary of the death, Father's Day or Mother's Day, Christmas and birthdays.

The Child Bereavement Trust (a charity) has a training programme for primary, secondary and special schools. The courses are designed to provide managers, teachers and support staff with information and resources to enable them to better understand how to support pupils experiencing a loss. Guidance is given on introducing the subject into the classroom.

The emotional and social impact of illness on children's ability to learn

Any child with an illness or disability may have a problem in developing a positive self-concept. Children need to feel confident and successful in order to learn effectively. Children's **self-esteem** may be adversely affected because they:

- **feel different from others**: they may notice that they are different from their peers; their siblings may resent them, seeing them as the brother or sister child who is spoilt or never punished.
- **are over-protected**: parents who try to cocoon their child can find that this is counter-productive. Children need to be equipped for life and can only learn by making mistakes.
- **lack freedom of choice**: parents may take freedom of choice away from the child (for example in trying new activities), thereby so disempowering them.
- **miss out on social opportunities**: friendships may be affected as parents often dictate where and with whom the child plays; in this way, they are depriving them of an opportunity for valuable social learning.
- **may be bullied**: differences are often seen as weaknesses by other children, who might tease or reject the child.

Deprivation and abuse

As we have seen in Chapter 3, there are many forms of child abuse and neglect. All such deprivation will affect the child's ability to learn and to form relationships with adults and other children.

Physically abused children may be:

- watchful, cautious or wary of adults
- unable to play and be spontaneous
- bullying other children or being bullied themselves
- unable to concentrate, underachieving at school and avoiding activities that involve removal of clothes (such as sports).

Emotionally abused or neglected children may:

- be slow to learn to walk and talk
- find it hard to develop close relationships
- get on badly with other children of the same age
- be unable to play imaginatively
- think badly of themselves; have low self-esteem
- be easily distracted and underachieve at school.

Medical conditions

Some medical conditions can affect children's learning. The child's condition may cause him to become quickly tired, or may lead to frequent absences for treatment. Examples of this include childhood leukaemia or chronic lung disease. Other medical conditions, like asthma or diabetes, may be adequately managed by taking medication and do not need to cause significant interference in the child's development and learning.

Section 3: The provision for children with special educational needs

The principles and values of equality, diversity and inclusion should underpin all work with children and young people. As a practitioner, you must know and understand the articles of the United Nations Convention on the Rights of the Child (see Chapter 5). The articles cover rights for all children (up to the age of 18 years). However, Article 23 refers to disabled children specifically:

'Children who have any kind of disability should have special care and support so that they can lead full and independent lives'.

The legal requirements for working with children with special needs in a range of settings

The term **'Special Educational Needs'**, or SEN, has a legal definition. The government's Department for Education (DfE) defines children with Special Educational Needs as having:

> 'learning difficulties or disabilities which make it harder for them to learn or access education than most other children of the same age.'

A child with **special needs** may need extra or different help at school or home because of:

- physical difficulties or disability
- communication problems
- a visual or hearing impairment
- emotional, social and behavioural difficulties
- a serious medical condition
- **OR** a combination of any of these.

The main **Acts** which have shaped the way in which children with special needs are cared for and educated today are:

- The Education Act 1996
- The Children Act 2004
- The Education (Additional Support for Learning) (Scotland) Act 2004
- The Disability Discrimination Act 2005
- The Special Needs and Disability Act (SENDA) 2001.

The Education Act 1996 states that children have **special educational needs** if they have a **learning difficulty** which calls for special educational provision to be made for them. Children have a learning difficulty if they:

- have a significantly greater difficulty in learning than the majority of children of the same age; or
- have a **disability** which prevents or hinders them from making use of educational facilities of a kind generally provided for children of the same age in schools within the area of the LEA;
- are under compulsory school age and fall within the definitions above or would do so if special educational provision were not made for them.

The Children Act 2004 defines learning disability as:

> 'a state of arrested or incomplete development of mind which induces significant impairment of intelligence and social functioning'.

The guidance to the **Education (Additional Support for Learning) (Scotland) Act 2004** stresses that additional support needs are *not* the same as special needs. At any point in their lives children and young people may need extra help in school. This may be for any reason, at any time and for any length of time. This is often referred to as additional support for learning or having additional support needs.

The Disability Discrimination Act 2005 placed new responsibilities on local authorities; these include the requirement to:

- eliminate unlawful discrimination against disabled children and adults
- eliminate harassment and bullying of disabled children and adults
- promote equality of opportunity and positive attitudes towards disabled children
- take steps to take account of disabled children's and adults' impairments, even if this results in more favourable treatment.

The **Special Needs and Disability Act (SENDA) 2001** strengthened the right of children with disabilities to attend mainstream educational facilities. It was supported by the SEN Code of Practice 2002 – see below.

- SEN and Disability Green Paper (2011): the Coalition Government proposes changing the system through which families of children and young people with SEN and disabilities receive their support. In particular, it proposes to simplify the assessment process and to replace the categories of early years/school action and early years/school action plus with *one* SEN category that will cover both early years settings and schools. (This Bill is still passing through Parliament at the time of writing.)
- The Special Educational Needs Code of Practice 2002 **includes the following principles**:
  - The special needs of children will be met in mainstream schools – wherever possible.
  - Children with special educational needs should be offered full access to a broad, balanced and relevant education, including an appropriate curriculum for the EYFS (in England) and the National Curriculum.

Figure 11.5 Children with some disabilities have a statutory right to attend mainstream educational facilities

The Equality Act 2010. See page 119 for more information on this Act.

Every registered early years setting must have a **Special Educational Needs Coordinator** or **SENCO** who takes responsibility for special education needs. The SENCO is responsible for:

- making sure that all children with special educational needs are being helped appropriately, ensuring liaison with parents and other professionals
- talking to and advising any member of staff who is concerned about a child
- coordinating provision for children with special needs
- making sure all written records are completed and appropriate Individual Education Plans are in place
- ensuring relevant background information about individual children is collected, recorded and updated
- contacting the relevant Area SENCO at the earliest possible stage where there is a concern.

Special Educational Needs policy

Every setting must have a Special Educational Needs policy. This should include information about:

- how they identify and make provision for children with special educational needs
- the facilities they have, including those which increase access for pupils who are disabled, including access to the curriculum
- how resources are allocated to and among pupils with special educational needs
- how they enable pupils with special educational needs to engage in activities of the school together with pupils who do not have additional needs
- how the governing body evaluates the success of the schools' work with pupils with special educational needs
- their arrangements for dealing with complaints from parents.

The identification and assessment process and the principles of inclusion

The benefits of early recognition and intervention

Sometimes parents are unaware that their child's development is delayed compared with other children of the same age, especially in the case of their first or oldest child. On other occasions, parents may have felt that 'something is not quite right', but have either been anxious about sharing their worries, or have talked to other professionals but not been fully understood. Sometimes a child can appear to be developing well during a check-up, but have difficulties in less structured environments or in the company of other children. The range of special needs is enormous, from severe to relatively minor, from temporary or short-lived to permanent. Young children with a disability will often arrive in an early years setting or school with difficulties that have not yet been understood or assessed. Sometimes parents have not noticed the difficulties, but it is more usual that there is a general anxiety or sense that all is not well with the child. Early years practitioners need to actively seek out information about a possible underlying disability. When you have worked with many children in a particular age group, your experience will help you to notice those children who appear to have specific difficulties which lie outside the range of ordinary child development. By working closely with the parents and other specialist professionals, you may be able to help identify that a child has a disability. The early support that can follow early identification can make a real difference to a child's wellbeing, quality of life, and later achievement and enjoyment in school.

The assessment process

In the UK about 17 per cent of all schoolchildren have a special educational need. Most (around 60 per cent) are taught in **mainstream** schools, where they receive additional help from a range of services. Children with special educational needs but *without* a statement will have their needs met through Early Years Action or Early Years Action Plus. (When children reach school age these are called School Action and School Action Plus.)

The framework in England that enables assessment to be carried out of the development and progress of all young children is the EYFS. As we have seen in earlier chapters, the EYFS focuses on six areas of learning and development:

- personal, social and emotional development
- communication, language and literacy
- problem-solving, reasoning and numeracy
- knowledge and understanding of the world
- physical development
- creative development.

Practitioners help to assess each child's development using the EYFS Profile.

The Statement of Special Educational Needs

The Statement of Special Educational Needs is a legal document produced by LEAs following multi-professional assessment and contributions from parents or carers. It specifies the precise nature of the child's assessed difficulties and educational needs, and the special or additional provision that should be made in order to meet that pupil's needs. Statements must then be reviewed at least annually.

An assessment must take account of the following five factors:

1 **Physical factors**: the child's particular illness or condition.
2 **Psychological and emotional factors**: the child's intellectual ability and levels of anxiety or depression will lead to different needs and priorities (for example, severe anxiety may adversely affect all daily activities, and its alleviation will therefore assume top priority).

3 **Sociocultural factors**: whether or not the child is part of a family, the family's background and the relationships within the family will all influence needs. Similarly, the individual's wider community and the social class to which they belong are also influential.

4 **Environmental factors**: a child living in a cold, damp house with an outside toilet will have different needs from someone who is more comfortably housed.

5 **Political and economic factors**: poverty or belonging to a disadvantaged group leads to reduced choice in day-to-day living.

The Early Support programme

Early Support is an integral part of the delivery of the EYFS for babies and young children under five with disabilities or emerging special educational needs. It helps staff in early years settings to identify impairments early and to work in partnership with families and other services to provide the best possible care and support for young disabled children. An important part of the Early Support programme is the **Family File**, which the family holds. The Family File:

- is used by the professionals and the family together, to plan appropriate support to be provided for the child
- informs the family about the different professionals they may meet and what their role is
- explains how the different health, education and social services can provide support
- allows parents and carers to share information about their child with the professionals they meet, without having to say the same things to every new person
- provides information about sources of financial support and child care.

Key term

Assessment – Through observing children and by making notes when necessary, practitioners can make professional judgements about children's achievements and decide on the next steps in learning. They can also exchange information with parents about how children are progressing.

Common Assessment Framework (CAF)

The Common Assessment Framework was introduced in 2005 as an assessment tool that can be used by the whole children's workforce to assess the additional needs of children and young people at the first signs of difficulties. See Chapter 5 for more details on the CAF.

Individual Education Plans

Every child with special educational needs should have an Individual Education Plan (IEP). The IEP's purpose is to detail the ways in which an individual child will be helped; for example:

- what special help is being given
- who will provide the help
- how often the child will receive the help
- targets for the child
- how and when the child's progress will be checked
- what help parents can give their child at home.

The child's teacher is responsible for the planning and should discuss the IEP with the parents or carers and with their child, whenever possible. IEPs are usually linked to the main areas of language, literacy, mathematics and behaviour and social skills. Sometimes the school or early education setting will not write an IEP but will record how they are meeting the child's needs in a different way, perhaps as part of the whole class lesson plans. They will record the child's progress in the same way as they do for all the other children.

In addition, practitioners should:

- assess how accessible the setting is for children who use wheelchairs or walking frames or who are learning English as an additional language, and take appropriate action to include a wider range of children
- work together with professionals from other agencies, such as local and community health services, to provide the best learning opportunities for individual children.

Discussion point

IEPs set out targets which can be described as SMART (Specific, Measurable, Achievable, Relevant, Time-limited). Here is an example of a SMART IEP target:

Target	Who will support	When and for how long?	Review
For James to use four Makaton signs while playing: *hello, me, yes, no*.	Vicky to model every day. All staff to use these signs with James. Teach all children the signs at group time.	Vicky to plan a 5-minute play session every morning. All staff throughout the session. James's parents to organise 5 minutes playing time every day at home with just James, using the signs.	6 weeks: evidence that James can use the signs in 5-minute sessions with Vicky. Evidence he uses the signs freely with other children.

Here is an example of a target which is not SMART: 'For all staff to help James to improve his language.'

In a small group, or with another learner, look at the targets set out below. Which targets do you think are SMART, and why?

- To help James to play in the sand.
- To help James to lift both feet off the ground with a daily 10-minute trampoline session.
- To encourage James's familiarity with other children by pointing to a photo card of each child in turn at group time and saying their names.
- To encourage James to play for one minute with messy materials, by providing a daily five-minute session using wet sand, play dough or paint.
- Stop James from pushing and hitting other children by teaching him the Makaton for 'no' and 'me'.

 In Practice

Outline your setting's procedures for ensuring that IEPs for children are in place and regularly reviewed. Provide examples of the relevant forms: an individual education plan; review sheets for child's comments, parents' comments and staff comments; record of review. Remember confidentiality.

The principles of inclusion

'Inclusion' (or 'inclusive education', 'inclusive schooling' or 'educational inclusion') is a term used within education to describe the process of ensuring equality of learning opportunities for all children and young people, whatever their disabilities or disadvantages. This means that all children have the right to have their needs met in the best way for them. They are seen as being part of the community, even if they need particular help to live a full life within the community. So, while integration is about bringing people who are different together, inclusion is about providing the support that is needed to enable different people to be together in a community. Despite the moves towards inclusion, there are arguments for keeping a minority of children in special schools.

Inclusion is about the child's right to:

- attend the local mainstream setting
- be valued as an individual
- be provided with all the support needed to thrive in a mainstream setting.

Individual Education Plan: Autumn Term 2012

Name: Lucas Year Group: 2 Pastoral Teacher: Maggie Conran

Targets to be achieved by: Feb 2013	Method/Resources	Outcome (tick best descriptor)
		Date:
Independence: For L to collect milk from the fridge and come back without needing an adult to shadow him.	Give L this job frequently. Begin with shadowing him and gradually reduce the support as he improves.	Achieved Ongoing Partially Not achieved
Communication: For L to use his communication book to request an activity he enjoys in the classroom, in addition to using it at snack times.	Provide L with photos of favoured activities in class. Introduce them to him and how to exchange them to receive the activity. Encourage L to get his book out of his drawer if he wants a specific activity.	Achieved Ongoing Partially Not achieved
PSRN (Maths) & CLL: To sort coloured objects into pots of the same colours (up to 3 colours).	Structured session with L in his chair (helps him focus). Model what is required and then encourage him to do the same. Plenty of repetition.	Achieved Ongoing Partially Not achieved
CLL: To select his own name from a choice of 2 in a variety of places such as on a name card and on the whiteboard screen.	Frequent use of name card and name on other games etc., and contrast with longer/different names for him to choose from.	Achieved Ongoing Partially Not achieved
Physical: To stand up from the floor from a half kneel to standing using support of a person or object.	Encourage L to stand in this way as often as possible. Model it and also encourage him to get to his knees before asking him to get up.	Achieved Ongoing Partially Not achieved

Parent's contribution: To help Lucas become more independent at home, e.g. fetching and pouring own drinks and using his communication book to express his preferences.

Parent's signature

Date

Teacher's signature

Date

Table 11.3 A sample IEP

Inclusive provision should be seen as an extension of the childcare setting's equal opportunities policy and practice. It requires a commitment from the entire staff, parents and children, to include the full diversity of children in the local community. This may require planned restructuring of the whole childcare environment to ensure equality of access.

Key term

Inclusion – 'Inclusion is a process of identifying, understanding and breaking down barriers to participation and belonging' (Early Childhood Forum).

Discussion point

The nursery manager at a private nursery explains to a child's parents that their son, Thomas, will not be able to join the rest of his group on a visit to a local children's theatre production of 'The Gruffalo's Child'. Thomas has Down's syndrome and learning difficulties. The nursery staff had met to discuss the problem and had concluded that there was no point in Thomas going as he would not appreciate the show and would probably disrupt the other children. Thomas's mother is very unhappy with their decision and has accused the nursery of discriminating against Thomas on account of his disability.

Discuss the following questions in a group:

1. Do you think the nursery staff were justified in their decision?

2. What could the nursery staff have done in order to enable Thomas to join the others?

3. Do you believe the nursery has discriminated against Thomas?

The range of provision available to children and families

There are many different statutory and voluntary services involved in the care and education of children with special needs. For information about these services, such as Children's Centres, see Chapter 8.

Education for children with special educational needs in mainstream settings

The Children Act 1989 promotes the integration of disabled children in mainstream settings such as nursery schools, day nurseries, schools and family centres. Some children have permanent one-to-one help from a special needs or learning support assistant. Others may have regular support from an assistant teacher.

Special schools

There will always be some children whose learning needs are not appropriately met in a mainstream classroom setting and who will require specialised education and resources to provide the level of support they require.

A special school is a school for children who have special educational needs due to severe learning difficulties, physical disabilities or behavioural problems. This includes children with complex needs. Children attending special schools generally do not attend any classes in mainstream schools. Special schools have many advantages for this group of children, including:

- specialist staff who are trained and experienced to provide individualised education, addressing specific needs
- low child:teacher ratios – often 6:1 or lower depending upon the needs of the children
- specialist facilities – such as soft play areas, sensory rooms, or swimming pools, which are essential for the therapy of certain conditions.

Children in residential care

The Children Act 1989 emphasised that the best place for children to be brought up is within their own families, and statistics show that the vast majority of disabled children are living at home. Some residential special schools offer weekly or termly boarding facilities; children may be in residential care for medical reasons or because the family cannot manage the care involved. All homes must be registered and inspected by social services departments to safeguard the interests of this particularly vulnerable group.

Foster placements

The Foster Placement (Children) Regulations 1991 apply safeguards to any child in foster care. Some voluntary organisations provide specialist training programmes for carers who foster disabled children, and the carer's active involvement in the child's education is encouraged.

Respite care

Ideally, this would be renamed 'natural break' or 'short-stay' care, as 'respite care' implies that carers need relief from an unwanted burden. However, the aim of such care is to provide support and encouragement so that parents and carers are able to continue caring for their child within the family. There are four types of respite care:

- care in a foster placement
- residential care, in a home or sometimes in a hospital unit
- holiday schemes (such as diabetic camps)
- care within the child's own home.

The latter is often the best provision of care if the right substitute carer can be found. Provision is patchy and is only worthwhile if the child derives as much benefit from the break as the carers.

Discussion point

Think of ways in which parents and carers of able-bodied children get respite from full-time care. Why can the same avenues not be opened to all carers? Discuss the possible problems for parents of disabled children in obtaining respite care, and then list their possible solutions.

The adaptation of curricula and techniques for supporting learning in a range of settings

Many children with learning difficulties will have personal priority needs which are central to their learning and quality of life. Some children may need the provision of a specific therapy or may require paramedical care. Others need to have existing equipment or activities modified or adapted to suit their particular needs. This might involve:

- adapting standard equipment, for example by having a tray on the table so that objects stay on the table, and a child with a visual impairment does not 'lose' objects that fall off

- providing the opportunity to learn sign languages, for example Makaton or PECS (see page 444)
- helping children to maintain good posture, appropriate muscle tone and ease of movement, and promoting skills in independent mobility
- helping children to manage eating and drinking; there is a wide range of specialist aids for eating and drinking, such as angled spoons and suction plates
- promoting relaxation and support to help children manage stress and anxiety; some settings use a sensory room, but a quiet, comfortable area will benefit all children
- providing palliative treatments for painful or degenerative conditions to ensure children's health and wellbeing
- promoting children's autonomy and independence through the use of specialist aids and equipment, for example non-slip table mats and specially designed cutlery for eating
- developing children's self-esteem (by encouraging and praising effort as well as achievement)
- allowing children's behaviour and alternative ways of communicating to be acknowledged and understood
- providing appropriate therapies, for example speech and language, occupational or physiotherapy (support from health services is generally set out as non-educational provision in a child's statement, but speech and language therapy may be regarded as either educational or non-educational provision)
- planning the use of music, art, drama or movement therapy: these therapies may play a complementary role in the curriculum for individual children and will need to be planned as part of the whole curriculum
- using specialist environments, for example ball pools, warm-water pools or light and sound stimulation rooms
- providing ramps for wheelchair users
- providing thick pencils and brushes for children with poor fine motor skills
- positioning children so that they learn effectively, for example by making sure the light falls on the adult's face, so that a child wearing a hearing aid is able to lip-read and a child with a visual impairment can use any residual eyesight to see facial expressions.

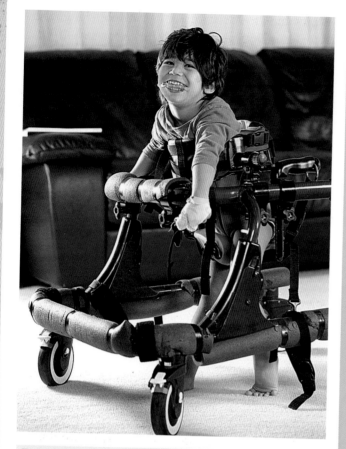

Figure 11.6 Using a walking frame or rollator

The use of a sensory curriculum for profound needs

The multisensory curriculum

All teachers differentiate the curriculum (that is, they provide different learning experiences) in order to meet the range of learning needs in their class. Children who are multisensory-impaired are likely to need the curriculum differentiated individually, because each child's combination of hearing impairment, visual impairment, other disabilities and learning characteristics will be different. Some settings have a multisensory room which provides opportunities for children with a wide range of special needs. This room features a variety of lights, smells, sounds and touch sensations which help to stimulate each sense. Staff need to be trained in the use of a sensory room so that it works optimally for each child.

 In Practice

Providing for Holly's needs

When Holly, a partially-sighted baby, joined the nursery, her key person Simon discussed her needs with her parents and contacted the RNIB for information about ways of supporting her development. Simon decided to plan a set of activities that could be used by Holly – and by sighted babies too – based on his research, which found that for profoundly blind and partially-sighted babies it is important to do the following:

1. Offer as wide a range of **tactile experiences** as possible right from the beginning. Simon started collecting tactile objects, such as:

   • a foil survival blanket to scrunch and reflect

   • a flat silky cushion containing polystyrene beads

   • pan scourer, lemon reamer, pasta strainer, dishwashing brush.

2. **Encourage movement:** helping babies to become aware of whole body movements and to learn to tolerate different positions, such as being placed on their stomach. Simon:

   • provided some brightly-lit and sound-producing toys to provide the motivation to roll and reach

   • rearranged the nursery furniture to provide a logical sequence to support the baby when moving – and to help 'mental mapping' of her environment.

3. Encourage exploration of **sound, rhythm and timing**. Simon provided:

   • tactile nursery rhyme prompt cards: he made these using A4 cards and stuck on different fabrics to link touch to a particular song; for example, a piece of fur fabric stuck on card to make a link with 'Round and Round the Garden like a Teddy Bear', or a single shiny silver star stuck onto dark blue card to make a link with 'Twinkle, twinkle little star'

   • a handbell, rolling chime ball, musical xylophone and a drum.

Simon used some of the tactile objects in a treasure basket that could be enjoyed by all the babies in the setting.

Cultural and social influences on the care and education of children with special educational needs

Everyone comes from a culture; not only a national culture and a religious culture, but a family culture as well. A child's family may be agnostic or atheist, Catholic or Church of England, Muslim or Jewish, Hindu or Sikh. Each group will have its own traditions that need to be respected. It is important to recognise also that adolescence is a time of questioning and challenging, and young people may not share the same beliefs as their parents. The context in which each child is brought up will influence the way in which he or she is able to learn. As we saw in Chapter 1, all education and care settings must work within an equal opportunities framework to ensure that every child receives equality of opportunity, and that specific cultural factors are valued.

Section 4: The roles and responsibilities of professionals working with children with special educational needs

Establishing partnerships with parents and carers

Working in partnerships with families is particularly important when a child person has additional support needs. Each parent or carer should be made to feel welcome and valued as an expert on their child, playing a vital role in helping practitioners to enable their child to participate and learn.

Where factors that impact on a child's ability to learn and develop are just starting to become apparent, partnership-working involving all the adults in a child's life becomes very important. The earlier a need for additional support is identified, the more likely it is that early intervention can prevent certain aspects of a child's development or behaviour developing into a persistent difficulty.

Parents and carers find that getting a diagnosis for their child is important. Being given a name for their child's condition or special need enables them to discuss their child's development needs with health, social services and education professionals. Getting information about what they and their children are entitled to, as early as possible, is very important. This applies to the benefits they are entitled to as well as the services.

Parents and carers often find that the most helpful sources of information and advice come from others with shared experiences. There are many organisations which exist to provide support and answer questions. For example, Contact a Family, The Down's Syndrome Association, Mencap and The Royal Society for the Blind; there are many more – most with their own website and helpline.

Communicating with parents and carers

The principles of effective communication are discussed in Chapter 5. One of the main purposes of communicating with parents and carers is to provide and to share information about the child and about the setting – both about the early years setting and the home. Practitioners need to build up a partnership with parents and carers, and to do this they need to promote a feeling of trust.

Providing flexible support

- Parents and carers want support which is flexible enough to respond to their particular families' needs, and which is both available in an emergency and can also be planned in advance.

- Children and young people want support which enables them to do the kinds of things their peers do: this can vary from going swimming with their siblings to spending time away from home with their friends. The most popular services are generally those developed by parents or carers themselves, or by local disability organisations.

Parent partnership services

The Parent Partnership Scheme (PPS) is a statutory service that offers the following support:

- information, advice and support for parents or carers of children with SEN
- putting parents or carers in touch with other local organisations
- making sure that the views of the parent or carer are heard and understood, and that these views inform local policy and practice.

Some parent partnerships are based in the voluntary sector although the majority of them remain based in their LEA or Children's Trust. All parent partnerships, wherever they are based, work separately and independently from the LEA; this means that they are able to provide impartial advice and support to parents and carers.

For more information, visit the NPPN (National Parent Partnership Network) website at: www. parentpartnership.org.uk.

Reflective practice: Supporting children with special needs

- How well does your setting provide for the special needs of children?

- Is there effective communication between the child's parents or carers and the setting?

- Do the play experiences and activities avoid stereotyping and ensure that each child has an equal opportunity to take part in activities?

The role of observation and assessment in producing individual learning plans in a variety of settings

Throughout this book, the importance of observing children is emphasised. In particular, see Chapter 2 for information. There is, by law, an assessment procedure that must be followed by the LEA if a child has been referred to them as having special educational needs by either the parent or carer, the child's school, or health or social services. This is the final step which occurs after observation and discussion when it is felt by the parent or the child's teacher that the child may need extra support. A detailed examination is carried out to ascertain the child's special educational needs and the special help he or she may need.

Activity

Extension work

- **A time sample observation.** Observe a child in your work placement whom you or the teacher has identified as being shy or withdrawn. Choose a day when you can observe the child at regular intervals, say every 10 or 15 minutes, and display the information obtained on a prepared chart.

- **Evaluate your observation.** Do you think the child has special needs, and if so, what is the nature of those needs? How could you help meet them?

- **A talking/listening game.** Plan a talking/ listening game that could be adapted to allow full participation by a child with a hearing impairment.

Recording, reporting and record-keeping

The principles of record-keeping and reporting are discussed in Chapter 5.

All observations and assessments must be in line with the setting's policy for record-keeping and relevant to the learning activities of the children you work with. Only the appropriate people should have access to confidential records. Practitioners should refer to their setting's policy on confidentiality and the sharing of information.

Any child with special educational needs will be placed on the setting's special needs register. An IEP addressing the individual child's needs and focusing on the key areas of concern is drawn up and reviewed at least every six months. The plan will be linked to the relevant curriculum. Individual confidential records are kept; these include information from other agencies or professionals, where appropriate, and dated notes of discussions with parents.

The needs and rights of individuals, parents/ carers and families

Parents' needs, rights and responsibilities are discussed in Chapter 8. The following needs may apply to any parent or carer in relation to their child with special needs:

- **Status**: carers need recognition of their own contribution to society, of their own needs as individuals, and of the fact that they are the people who know their child best.
- **Services**: these should be tailored to the carer's individual circumstances and planned in response to the needs of the child within the family.
- **An awareness of cultural diversity**: every effort should be made to provide services which recognise that people from different backgrounds may well have different requirements. The obvious example is dietary differences, but there are also other issues (such as touch by members of the opposite sex).
- **Leisure**: parents must have opportunities for a break – both to relax and to have some 'personal space'. Respite care or child-sitting can prove vital.

- **Practical help**: domestic help, adaptations to the home, incontinence services and help with transport may provide invaluable help to the carer.
- **Support**: parents often want someone to talk to, with whom they can share their problems and frustrations; parents may also need help in finding pleasure in their child.
- **Information**: the specific needs of the child being cared for must be detailed, and knowledge of the available benefits and services is also important.
- **Finance**: an income is needed which covers the costs of caring and which allows the carer to take employment or to share the care with other people. Accommodation may need to be adapted and special equipment purchased.
- **Planning**: carers should have the opportunities to explore alternatives to family care, for both the immediate and the long-term future.
- **Consultation**: services should be designed through consultation with carers at all levels of policy planning. This is particularly important when a child is the subject of a statement (see page 454).

The role of specialist professionals and how to work in a team with other professionals

Under the Children Act 1989, all local authorities have to keep a register of local disabled children. This is to help the local authority plan services more effectively. Registration is not compulsory and failure to register does not affect a child's right to services.

The professionals listed in Table 11.4 are all involved in the care and education of children with special needs. Please see Chapter 8 for guidelines for working in a multi-professional team.

Professionals involved in the care and education of children with special educational needs

Family doctors (GPs)

Family doctors are independent professionals who are under contract to the National Health Service (NHS), but who are not employed by it. They are the most available of the medical profession, and are also able to refer carers on to specialist doctors and paramedical services.

Physiotherapists

The majority of 'physios' are employed in hospitals, but some work in special schools or residential facilities. Physiotherapists assess children's motor development and skills, and provide activities and exercises that parents and carers can use to encourage better mobility and coordination.

Community nurses

Most community nurses work closely with family doctors and provide nursing care in the home. They also advise the parent or carer on specialist techniques (e.g. on how to lift, catheter care and so on).

Speech and language therapists

Speech and language therapists may be employed in schools, in hospitals or in the community. They assess a child's speech, tongue and mouth movements, and the effects of these on eating and swallowing. They provide exercises and activities both to develop all aspects of children's expressive and receptive communication skills and to encourage language development.

Play therapists

Play therapists also work in hospitals and have undertaken specialist training. They use play to enable children with special needs to feel more secure emotionally in potentially threatening situations.

Dieticians

Most dieticians work in hospitals and can advise on a range of special diets (e.g. for diabetics or those with cystic fibrosis or coeliac disease).

Health visitors

Health visitors are qualified nurses who have done further training, including midwifery experience. They work exclusively in the community, and can be approached either directly or via the family doctor. They work primarily with children up to the age of five years; this obviously includes all children with disabilities. Health visitors carry out a wide range of developmental checks.

Occupational therapists

Occupational therapists ('OTs') work in hospitals, schools and other residential establishments. Some OTs specialise in working with children (paediatric occupational therapists) and will assess a child's practical abilities and advise on the most appropriate activities and specialist equipment to encourage independent life skills.

School nurses

School nurses may visit a number of mainstream schools in their health district to monitor child health and development – by checking weight, height, eyesight and hearing, and by giving advice on common problems such as head lice. They may also be employed in special schools to supervise the routine medical care of disabled children.

Play specialists

Play specialists are employed in hospitals and in the community. They are often qualified nursery nurses who have additional training. They may prepare a child for hospitalisation and provide play opportunities for children confined to bed or in a hospital playroom.

Clinical psychologists

Clinical psychologists usually work in hospitals. They assess children's emotional, social and intellectual development and advise on appropriate activities to promote development.

Orthoptists

An orthoptist works with people who have visual problems and abnormal eye movements.

Professionals involved in the care and education of children with special educational needs (cont.)

Social workers

Most social workers now work in specialised teams dealing with a specific client group (e.g. a disability and learning difficulties team). They are employed by social services departments ('social work departments' in Scotland) and initially their role is to assess the needs of the child. They may refer the family to other departments, such as the Department of Social Security (DSS), the NHS or voluntary organisations. A social worker may also act as an advocate on behalf of disabled children, ensuring that they receive all the benefits and services to which they are entitled.

Nursery officers

Nursery officers are trained nursery nurses who work in day nurseries and family centres. Such staff are involved in shift work, and they care for children under five years when it is not possible for those children to remain at home.

The Special Educational Needs Coordinator (SENCO)

The special educational needs coordinator liaises both with colleagues in special schools and with the parents of children with special needs. They are responsible for coordinating provision for children with special educational needs, for keeping the school's SEN register and for working with external agencies (e.g. educational psychology services, social service departments and voluntary organisations).

Portage workers

Portage is an educational programme for children who have difficulty in learning basic skills due to either physical or behavioural problems. Home Portage Advisers are specially trained in understanding child development and come from a variety of professions, ranging from nurses or other health professionals to schoolteachers.

Technical officers

Technical officers usually work with people with specific disorders (e.g. audio technicians or audiologists monitor the level of hearing in children as a developmental check; and sign-language interpreters translate speech into sign language for deaf and hearing-impaired people).

Family aids

Family aids (or home care assistants) used to be called 'home helps'; they provide practical support for families in their own homes – shopping, cooking, looking after children and so on.

Educational psychologists

Educational psychologists are involved in the educational assessment of children with special needs, and in preparing the statement of special educational needs. They act as advisers to professionals working directly with children with a range of special needs, particularly those with emotional and behavioural difficulties.

Special needs teachers

Special needs teachers are qualified teachers with additional training and experience in teaching children with special needs. Children are supported by:

- special needs support teachers or specialist teachers who are often peripatetic (they visit disabled children in different mainstream schools), and who may specialise in a particular disorder (e.g. vision or hearing impairment)

- special needs support assistants who may be qualified early years practitioners and who often work with individual 'statemented' children under the direction of the specialist teacher.

Educational welfare officers

As in mainstream education, educational welfare officers will be involved with children whose school attendance is irregular; they may also arrange school transport for disabled children.

Table 11.4 Professionals involved in the care and education of children with special educational needs

Strategies to develop and encourage independence and promote self-esteem

We have already seen how children with special needs may have difficulties in developing a robust self-concept or self-esteem. The following strategies will help you to focus on promoting children's independence and self-esteem:

- **Value each child**: regard each child as an individual with unique strengths, needs, interests and skills. Respond to each child's individual needs.
- **Focus on the child's strengths**: demonstrate a genuine interest in their activities and hobbies. Praise and encourage children's attempts at activities, not just the end result. Show an interest in children's personal qualities such as kindness or temperament, rather than just focusing on their academic skills.
- **Set realistic, achievable goals**: always anticipate success.
- **Promote independence and self-reliance**: help the child develop decision-making and problem-solving skills.

- **Use mistakes as an opportunity to teach and assist**: understand that mistakes are an inevitable – and valuable – part of any learning experience.
- **Divide large tasks into smaller, manageable ones**: this will help to ensure success and so promote self-esteem.
- **Be a good role model**: by being a positive role model, you will increase your own self-esteem and this will be reflected in your work.

The promotion of appropriate behaviour of children with special educational needs (including establishing boundaries)

All children need to know what is appropriate behaviour, and what is inappropriate. They also need to know the boundaries for behaviour. By promoting their independence and self-esteem, children are less likely to feel frustrated and out of control.

Figure 11.7 Attending an early years setting can boost the self-esteem of a disabled child

Guidelines for promoting appropriate behaviour

- **Reinforce good behaviour**: tell the child what sort of behaviour is appropriate; reinforce positive behaviour with statements like 'I know it was difficult for you to wait your turn, and I'm pleased that you could do it'; 'You worked hard on that project, and I admire your effort'.

- **Ignore inappropriate behaviour that can be tolerated**: certain behaviour (particularly attention-seeking) may be ignored. The child should never be ignored – only the behaviour. Even though this behaviour may be tolerated, the child must understand that it is inappropriate.

- **Provide alternatives**: it is vital for children to have opportunities for physical exercise and movement, both at home and at school.

- **Be interested and involved**: very young children (and children who are emotionally deprived) often need much more adult involvement in their interests. A child about to use a toy or tool in a destructive way is sometimes easily stopped by an adult who expresses interest in having it shown to him. An angry outburst from an older child who is struggling with a difficult reading task may be prevented by a caring adult who moves close to the child to offer practical support.

- **Be ready to show affection**: an angry child may find it easier to regain control by a sudden hug or other impulsive show of affection. (However, children with serious emotional problems often have trouble accepting affection.)

- **Explain situations**: help the child to understand the cause of a stressed situation. We often fail to realise how easily young children can begin to react properly once they understand the cause of their frustration.

(See also Chapters 2 and 3 for more strategies for promoting positive behaviour.)

Working with children who have language, hearing or visual difficulties or limited attention span

When working with children with learning difficulties, always find out as much as you can about the particular problem. Observe how the teacher or manager structures activities, and never be afraid to ask how you can best support the individual child in their learning. Parents usually appreciate being asked for advice, and there are a number of voluntary organisations which provide specialist advice and information. See the Useful resources section on page 472.

Above all, be a good role model; other children see how you behave and will copy you. If you develop effective communication strategies, other children will, too. For example, it would be bad to ignore a child with a hearing impairment as other children may do the same thing.

Guidelines for working with children with hearing impairment

- **Face the child** when you speak: a child with a hearing loss needs to see as well as hear what you say to him. There is no need to exaggerate lip movements but you must speak clearly. When you show a child with a hearing impairment how to do something, use more demonstrations and gestures than you might with other children, but do not overdo it.

- **Reduce noise in the environment**: for a child with a mild hearing loss, make sure that background noise levels and loud music do not compete with conversation. Carpets, area rugs, and soft wall

Guidelines for working with children with hearing impairment (cont.)

coverings help make a childcare environment less noisy. Noisy environments also can be a problem for children who wear hearing aids, especially in understanding conversation.

- Use **non-verbal cues** to communicate: one way to get the attention of a child with a hearing impairment is to tap or thump on the table (if it is not too distracting for other children). He or she will respond to the vibration. You also can touch him or her on the shoulder or arm to get his or her attention if he or she is busy playing. Depending on the child's age, the child with a hearing impairment can show other children what method works best.

- Know **how to care for hearing aids**: find out from the child's parents how to care for the hearing aid (older children usually know how to take care of them). A common problem for young children is that they lose their hearing aids. Organise with the child a suitable place to keep the aid when it is not being worn.

- **Promote language development**: follow whatever communication methods a child's parents have decided to use. If sign language is part of the child's communication strategy, then it is a useful opportunity for all the children to learn some signs.

Guidelines for working with children with visual impairment

- **Create a safe environment**: find out from the child's parents how the child uses the vision available. For example, should things be positioned to the right or left of the child? Does she use vision to get around or avoid large objects? Does she need to touch things to avoid them?

- **Provide plenty of cues**: during dressing, eating, or any other daily activity, use lots of communication so that the child knows what will be happening. Try to be consistent. For example, if you are putting on a young child's shoes, always put the right one on first, to make things easier for her. You can say 'Let's put your shoes on now. First, the right one. You help me by holding up your right foot'.

- **Promote independence**: do not be too quick to 'rescue' a child. Try to give a child the least amount of assistance possible. Ask the child if he needs help instead of rushing to his aid.

- **Communicate**: use your voice to communicate feelings and meaning. Tone and volume can communicate many different emotions – such as happiness, anger, excitement.

- **Using touch**: ask parents if their child likes to be touched. Some children with visual impairments do not, but most do. A simple touch on the shoulder can be very reassuring.

- **Use names**: a child with a visual impairment may not be able to see the facial expressions or body language that show others which person is being spoken to, such as which child you have turned your head toward. Speak to each child by name, especially when there are other people in the room.

- **Provide activities with sensory experiences**: children with visual impairment learn through hearing and touch. Sand and water play, collages, play dough, and finger-painting are good learning activities.

Guidelines for working with children with a language difficulty

- **Simplify your language**: slow down the rate of your speech, simplify your language and repeat new words and ideas often. Try to reduce the number of questions you ask and emphasise the important words in the sentence – the ones that carry the information.

- **Use silence as a strategy**: do not feel you have to fill in silence with lots of talking – some children need more time to think before they speak. Make sure you leave gaps for them to fill in.

Guidelines for working with children with a language difficulty (cont.)

- **Provide positive cues**: try to cue children in to what you are doing – say their name, wait for them to look at you. You may need to 'model' language for them by giving them a choice – for example: 'Would you like orange juice or milk?'

- **Use simple repetitive language**: use simple, clear instructions, simple sentences, and repeat important information, giving the child time to think about what has been said. Comment on what children are doing in their free play sessions and try to expand what they say by adding a few words; for example, child says 'bus'. Adult: 'Yes, that's right – a big red bus'.

- **Involve the child's parents or carers**: they can provide valuable information which will help staff develop their child's communication skills. They can tell you if the child has special words or gestures for things. By discussing the work you are doing with their child, you offer the opportunity for the parents to help them to practise at home.

Guidelines for working with children with a limited attention span

- **Minimise distractions**: provide a quiet area for activities which require more concentration and special quiet times when noisy activities are not allowed.

- **Vary methods of instruction**: use a mix of verbal and visual methods to boost attention. Make frequent shifts between discussion, reading, and hands-on group activities.

- **Emphasise important information**: let children know when important information is about to be presented. Do this by slowing the pace of speech, include pauses, and highlight – by intonation and gesture – what is most important. Important points need to be summarised.

- **Use positive feedback**: children need plenty of praise and encouragement for completing tasks.

- **Encourage discussion**: encourage children to talk to each other about their learning, such as what strategies they are using to complete an activity.

- **Use memory games**: play games such as Kim's game – where children have to memorise objects on a tray and, as one is secretly removed, remember which object is no longer there.

- **Promote listening skills**: reading or telling stories will encourage the development of listening skills. Choose stories which will engage their attention – for example, by focusing on their particular interests. Ask children to identify sounds – using a CD with everyday sounds or listening for sounds outside the classroom. They will have to concentrate to identify particular sounds.

- **Use names**: using children's names when directly talking to them will alert them and help to maintain attention.

The practitioner's responsibilities in caring for bodily needs

Intimate care can be defined as care tasks associated with bodily functions, body products and personal hygiene which demand direct or indirect contact with or exposure of the genitals.

Staff who work with young children who have special needs and may need intimate care should have an understanding of what boundaries and behaviour can be expected in this area. Most schools will have an intimate care policy which describes best practice.

Guidelines for providing for intimate care needs

- **Respect and dignity**: all children who require intimate care are treated respectfully at all times; the child's welfare and dignity are of paramount importance.

- **Training**: staff members who provide intimate care should be trained to do so (including child protection and health and safety training in moving and handling) and be fully aware of best practice.

- **Apparatus**: equipment, such as a hoist or special toilet seat, should be provided to assist with children who need special arrangements following assessment from a physiotherapist or occupational therapist as required.

- **Developmental awareness**: staff should be supported to adapt their practice in relation to the needs of individual children taking into account developmental changes (such as the onset of puberty and menstruation in older children).

- **Communication**: there should be careful communication with each child who needs help with intimate care in line with their preferred means of communication (verbal, symbolic and so on) to discuss the child's needs and preferences. The child should be aware of each procedure that is carried out and the reasons for it.

- **Autonomy and independence**: as a basic principle children should be supported to achieve the highest level of independence that is possible given their age and abilities. Staff will encourage each child to do as much for themselves as they can. This may mean, for example, giving the child responsibility for washing themselves.

- **Planning for each individual**: individual intimate care plans should be drawn up for particular children as appropriate to suit the circumstances of the child. These plans include a full risk assessment to address issues such as moving and handling, personal safety of the child and the carer and health.

- **Privacy**: each child's right to privacy should be respected. Careful consideration should be given to each child's situation to determine how many carers might need to be present when a child needs help with intimate care. Where possible, one child will be cared for by one adult unless there is a sound reason for having two adults present. If this is the case, the reasons should be clearly documented.

- **Avoiding over-familiarity**: wherever possible, the same child should not be cared for by the same adult on a regular basis; there should be a rota of carers known to the child who will take turns in providing care. This will ensure, as far as possible, that over-familiar relationships are discouraged from developing, while at the same time guarding against the care being carried out by a succession of completely different carers.

- **Involving parents and carers**: parents and carers should be involved with their child's intimate care arrangements on a regular basis; a clear account of the agreed arrangements should be recorded on the child's care plan. The needs and wishes of children and parents should be carefully considered alongside any possible constraints (such as staffing and equal opportunities legislation).

- **Advocacy**: each child should have an assigned senior member of staff to act as an advocate to whom they can communicate any issues or concerns that they may have about the quality of care they receive.

Developing a sensitive, non-judgmental approach

In all your dealings with children and young people with special needs and their families, it is vital that you:

- **show respect** for the child and the family. You may disagree strongly with the way the parents tackle certain aspects of their child's care and education; however, you must remember that parents are the child's primary educators and that every parent needs support and understanding
- **are sensitive** to the child's and the family's needs, and ensure that your practice reflects this sensitivity
- **are non-judgmental**: it is easy to criticise others and to believe that you would approach things in a better way. However, parents can only learn to trust you if they know that you are not judging their actions.

Guidelines for developing a sensitive, non-judgemental approach when caring for children with special needs

- **Self-empowerment**: always encourage independence. Ask how the child wants to do things – let them make as many choices as possible.

- **Empathy**: try to imagine yourself in the child's situation. How would you like to be helped? (This is not to be confused with unwanted sympathy.)

- **Patience**: always be patient with children, particularly if communication is difficult or time-consuming.

- **Sensitivity**: try to anticipate the child's feelings. Having one's most intimate needs attended to by a stranger can be embarrassing.

- **Respect**: show awareness of a child's personal rights, dignity and privacy; never allow other children to poke fun at a child with a disability.

- **Communication and interpersonal skills**: develop good listening skills. Non-verbal communication is just as important as what you say.

- **Attitude**: an open-minded and non-judgemental attitude is important, as is a warm, friendly manner.

- **Be positive**: praise effort rather than achievement. Provide activities that are appropriate to the child's ability so that they have a chance of achieving.

- **Integration and inclusion**: make an effort to involve the child with other children. Integration emphasises the ways in which a child can be brought into the community, whereas inclusion sees the child already as part of the community, but needing additional help within it.

- **Set guidelines for behaviour**: these should be the same as for all children: do not make exceptions for the child with a disability.

- **Be a good role model**: support the child's carers or parents to enable them to provide a lifestyle that is as normal as possible.

The emotional needs of staff

It is important that the professionals involved with children with special needs and their families work as a team and are able to offer each other support and understanding. This need for support is not a sign of professional inadequacy or personal weakness, but rather a sign of maturity, recognising that you need help to do this work well. Most professional carers are very good at caring for others, but far less good at caring for themselves or for each other. If you know that one of your colleagues is involved in some stressful work, try to find the time to listen to them and how they feel afterwards. It can make an enormous difference to have a colleague who cares about you. Support for practitioners will vary from setting to setting, but the first person to talk to is your line manager or teacher.

Assessment practice

Working with children with special needs

1 Describe the medical model of disability and contrast it with the social model.
2 What types of provision are available to support children with special needs and their families?
3 Describe the factors that may affect a child's ability to learn.
4 What is meant by inclusion? What are the benefits of an inclusive approach for children with special needs?

Useful resources

Organisations and websites

British Dyslexia Association (BDA) – a national charity working for a 'dyslexia-friendly society' that enables dyslexic people of all ages to reach their full potential:
www.bdadyslexia.org.uk

Early Support – a national programme to help families with a disabled child to identify services that can help them, and to ensure that the services work together in a coordinated way:
www.education.gov.uk and search for 'early support'

Equality Act 2010 – brings together all the legislation which makes it illegal to discriminate on the grounds of sex, gender, race, sexuality, age or disability:
http://homeoffice.gov.uk/equalities/equality-act/

Every Child a Talker (ECAT) – this programme supports children's communication and language by focusing on developing an enabling environment and encouraging early years practitioners to listen to children and engage in conversation with them. The programme specifically helps children at risk of language delay:
www.education.gov.uk/schools/toolsandinitiatives/nationalstrategies

National Autistic Society (NAS) – aims to champion the rights and interests of all people with autism, and to provide individuals with autism and their families with help, support and services:
www.nas.org.uk

Royal National Institute of Blind People (RNIB) – this charity has produced an excellent booklet, **Focus on Foundation**, which offers practical advice on the inclusion in early years settings of children who are bland and partially-sighted:
www.rnib.org.uk

Royal National Institute for Deaf People (RNID) – the largest charity in the UK, offering a range of services for people who are deaf or have a hearing impairment, and providing information and support on all aspects of deafness, hearing loss and tinnitus:
www.rnid.org.uk

Scope – a charity that supports disabled people and their families. Its vision is a world where disabled people have the same opportunities as everyone else. Scope specialises in working with people who have cerebral palsy:
www.scope.org.uk

Books
Finlay, L. (2009) *Dandylion*. London: Red Fox.
Gerhardt, S. (2004) *Why Love Matters: How Affection Shapes a Baby's Brain*. East Sussex: Brunner-Routledge.
Shonkoff, J.P and Phillips, D.A. (2000) *From Neurons to Neighbourhoods*. Washington, DC: National Academy Press.
Smith, C. and Teasdale, S. (2003) *Let's Sign Early Years: BSL Child and Carer Guide*. Bolton: Cosign Communications.

12 Developing children's (three to eight years) communication, language and literacy skills: Unit 16

Learning outcomes

In this chapter, you will learn:

1. The stages of development of children's communication, language and literacy aged from three to eight years.

2. How to help children develop their communication, language and literacy skills.

3. The role of the adult in supporting communication, language and literacy.

Section 1: The stages of development of communication, language and literacy aged from three to eight years

The principal characteristics of the stages of development of communication, language and literacy

Children come into early years settings with a variety of language skills, having had different linguistic and cultural experiences. These experiences will influence their development in the language skills of speaking, listening and communicating. In Chapter 2, you will have learned about the sequence of language development, and in Section 2 of this chapter, you will learn more about the development of reading and writing skills.

The importance of context and a rich-language environment

The brain develops important interconnecting networks, which include movement, communication, play, symbol use, problem-solving and understanding why things happen (cause and effect). These become more complex, coordinated and sophisticated as the networks for learning in the brain develop. Before five years of age, the language system is not yet mature. Reading and writing develop most easily and enjoyably once language is well developed.

Many experts believe that removing the meaningful context and teaching letter–sound relationships in isolation and separately, although systematic to those adult readers devising the system, actually makes reading and writing more difficult for many children. This is particularly so for children who have low incidence disabilities, such as visual or hearing impairments, or children with English as an additional language.

National and local frameworks and policies

EYFS 2012

The learning and development requirements of the EYFS define what early years providers must do to promote the learning and development of all children in their care, ensuring they are 'school ready'.

There are seven different areas of learning and development that must shape educational programmes in early years settings. These are divided into three *prime areas*:

- personal, social and emotional development
- physical development
- communication and language.

There are four *specific areas* of learning and development, through which the three prime areas are applied. These are:

- literacy
- mathematics
- understanding the world
- expressive arts and design.

Educational programmes for developing young children's communication, language and literacy skills must encompass the following key issues:

- Communication and language development that involves giving children opportunities to speak and listen in a range of situations and to develop their confidence and skills in expressing themselves.
- Literacy development that involves encouraging children to read and write, both through listening to others read, and being encouraged to begin to read and write themselves. Children have to be given access to a wide range of reading materials, including books, poems, and other written materials, to inspire their interest.
- All practitioners must consider the individual needs, interests, and stage of development of each child in their care, and must use this information to plan a challenging and enjoyable experience for each child in all of the areas of learning and development.

Communication, language and literacy (as for **all** the areas of learning and development) must be delivered through planned, purposeful play, adult-led activity and child-initiated activity. There should be a fluid interchange between activities initiated by children, and activities led or guided by adults. This will move increasingly towards adult-led learning as children start to prepare for Reception class.

Six aspects of communication for EYFS

1 **Language for communication** is about how children become communicators. Learning to listen and speak emerges out of non-verbal communication, which includes facial expression, eye contact and hand gesture. *Aims*: children listen with enjoyment, and respond to stories, songs and other music, rhymes and poems and make up their own stories, songs, rhymes and poems. They speak clearly and audibly with confidence and control, and show awareness of the listener; for example, the use of convention such as greetings, 'please' and 'thank you'.

2 **Language for thinking** is about how children learn to use language to clarify their thinking and ideas or to refer to events they have observed. *Aims*: children use talk to organise, sequence and clarify thinking, ideas, feelings and events. They use language to imagine and recreate roles and experiences.

3 **Linking sounds and letters** is about how children develop the ability to distinguish between sounds and become familiar with rhyme, rhythm and **alliteration**. *Aims:* children link sounds to letters, naming and sounding the letters of the alphabet. They use their *phonic* knowledge to write simple regular words and make phonetically plausible attempts at more complex words.

4 **Reading** is about children understanding and enjoying stories, books and rhymes. *Aims*: children explore and experiment with sounds, words and texts. They read a range of familiar and common words and simple sentences independently, and know that print carries meaning and, in English, is read from left to right and top to bottom.

5 **Writing** is about how children build an understanding of the relationship between the spoken and written word, and how through making marks, drawing and personal writing, children ascribe meaning to text and attempt to write for various purposes. *Aims*: children attempt writing for

different purposes, using features of different forms such as lists, stories and instructions. They write their own names and other things such as labels and captions, and begin to form simple sentences, sometimes using punctuation.

6 **Handwriting** is about the ways in which children's random marks, lines and drawings develop and form the basis of recognisable letters. *Aims*: children use a pencil and hold it effectively to form recognisable letters, most of which are correctly formed.

Key term

Alliteration – When two or more words in a poem begin with the same letter or sound; for example, **R**abbits **R**unning over **R**oses.

Local frameworks

There are a number of projects and networks which work with a range of professionals to provide support for the development of children's communication, language and literacy skills. For example:

Bookstart

Bookstart is the national early intervention and cultural access programme for every child. It gives away free book packs to every child in the four UK home nations. In their baby's first year parents receive a free *Bookstart Baby Pack* from their health visitor or other health professional. The pack has been chosen to include everything parents need to get started sharing stories, rhymes and songs with their baby: canvas shoulder bag for carrying books, two board books and a guidance leaflet 'Babies Love Books' on sharing books.

My Bookstart Treasure Chest is a pack for pre-school children aged three to four years which is usually gifted by the child's nursery, playgroup or other early years setting. It includes two books chosen especially for pre-schoolers, a list of handy book recommendations, tips for reading to pre-schoolers and more. For more information visit: http://www. bookstart.org.uk

Booktime

Booktime is the free books programme that follows on from Bookstart. A book pack is given to every Reception-aged child during the autumn term. Packs include a book, selected by an expert panel, and guidance for parents and carers on shared reading. Additional interactive resources are also available to libraries, and many use them to support special events and activities that promote libraries and reading to families. For more information visit: www. booktime.org.uk

Talk To Your Baby

Talking to young children helps them become good communicators, which is essential if they are to do well at school and lead happy, fulfilled and successful lives. The *Talk To Your Baby Community of Research and Practice* is an online network open to everyone who shares an interest in the development of young children's speech, language, and communication. It brings together researchers and academics who are particularly interested in the development of theory, investigation and enquiry, with practitioners who are working with children and families to promote high-quality practice at home, in early years settings, and across local communities. For more information visit: http://www.literacytrust.org.uk/talk_to_your_baby

Every Child a Talker

Every Child a Talker (ECaT) was a national project to develop the language and communication of children from birth to five years of age. The project was set up after concern about the high levels of 'language impoverishment' in the UK, and how this affects children's progress in school and chances in life. For more information visit: http://www. talkformeaning.co.uk/everychild.php

The Young Readers Programme

The Young Readers Programme is the national programme that the National Literacy Trust uses to motivate disadvantaged children and young people to read for pleasure. The programme helps children and young people to acquire the skills they need to develop as readers, from knowing how to choose a book that engages them, to where they can find books once the project is over. All schools and children's centres are now able to participate in Young Readers Programme by purchasing a resource pack. For more information visit: http://www.literacytrust.org.uk/nyrp

London Literacy Champions

London Literacy Champions improves children's literacy by training local volunteers to support parents in disadvantaged areas. This Team London project is funded by the Mayor of London and the Reuben Foundation, and is delivered by the National Literacy Trust in partnership with 12 local authorities. For more information visit: http://www.literacytrust.org.uk/london_literacy_champions

Schools Network

The National Literacy Trust Schools Network supports schools to raise literacy attainment across the whole school, specifically by improving pupils' attitudes and behaviour towards literacy. For more information visit: http://www.literacytrust.org.uk/schools_network

Communities and local areas

The National Literacy Trust work focuses on families, helps local areas to target support to those with the greatest need, and helps communities to improve literacy levels and life chances. For more information visit: http://www.literacytrust.org.uk/communities

Policies and procedures which support the development of communication, language and literacy skills

You must know and understand the setting's policy and procedures for developing children's communication, language and literacy, including how this relates to the relevant national framework and curriculum guidelines for teaching English.

The setting should have a clear and agreed policy on how they will deliver the EYFS's requirements for communication, language and literacy to meet the needs of individual children, their circumstances and the local community. The setting's policy and procedures for communication, language and literacy should include:

1 **Policy statement:** a short statement about the setting's values and approaches to the development of children's communication, language and literacy skills.
2 **Aims:** the setting's aims for managing, organising and developing children's communication and language skills; the setting's view on partnerships with parents.
3 **Curriculum content:** the EYFS; curriculum planning and organisation including long-, medium- and short-term planning strategies and formats.
4 **Roles and responsibilities of staff:** all staff members should have clear documents that outline their roles and responsibilities.
5 **Teaching and learning:** planning and organisation; teaching styles and methods; matching children's learning needs and learning styles; the setting's policies and approaches for reading, writing, handwriting and spelling.
6 **Equal opportunities:** equality of access to the curriculum; inclusion; supporting children with English as an additional language; promoting positive images; appropriate resources.
7 **Special educational needs:** inclusion; differentiation; identification of children with special language and/or literacy needs; support programmes; special resources; involvement of outside agencies.
8 **Resources:** books; reading schemes; spelling and handwriting schemes; writing tools; ICT; teaching resources including 'big' books and white boards; displays; book corner and/or library.
9 **Assessment:** ongoing assessment; Early Years Foundation Stage Profile; end of key stage target setting; end of year group target setting; marking policy; rewards; recording progress; reviewing targets with children and parents; reporting to parents.

10 **Parent partnerships:** reading at home; reports and reviews; information to support parents; family literacy projects; parent helpers in school.

11 **Professional development:** staff training; sharing good practice within the setting; learning from and with other practitioners outside the school (networks).

12 **Monitor and review:** monitoring teaching, standards and resources for developing children's communication, language and literacy skills; roles and responsibilities; recording; review dates.

Obtaining information about individual children's progress and planning appropriate activities

Assessment plays an important part in helping parents and practitioners to understand children's needs and plan activities to meet them. The EYFS requirement is that providers must assess children's progress on an ongoing basis, and complete assessments at two specific points:

1 When a child is aged between 24 and 36 months, practitioners must review progress in the prime areas, and supply parents or carers with a short written summary of their child's development.

2 A report on progress is required is the final term of the year in which the child reaches age five, and no later than 30 June in that term. At this point, the EYFS Profile must be completed for each child.

Assessment

Ongoing assessment (known sometimes as **formative assessment**) is an integral part of the learning and development process. It involves practitioners observing children on an ongoing basis, understanding their level of achievement, interests and learning styles, shaping learning experiences for each child and reflecting on their observations. Assessment should happen as part of practitioners'

ongoing interaction with children, informed by feedback from parents, and other adults who interact with the child. Assessment must not entail prolonged breaks from interaction with children, nor does it require excessive paperwork. Key achievements and any concerns should be recorded periodically. Practitioners must give parents and carers regular updates on children's progress and achievements as part of their ongoing dialogue with families (DfE, 2011).

The Early Years Foundation Stage Profile

Assessment at the end of the EYFS is called the Early Years Foundation Stage Profile and provides parents, practitioners and teachers with a well-rounded picture of a child's knowledge, understanding and abilities, their progress against expected levels, and their readiness for school. The Profile should help teachers to plan activities for children starting Key Stage 1. Providers must make arrangements for each child to be assessed throughout the final year. The Profile report must reflect ongoing observation and should also take into account all relevant records held by the setting, and of any discussions with parents and/or carers.

Each child's level of development must be assessed (and recorded) against the 17 early learning goals. Practitioners must indicate whether children are not yet reaching, meeting, or exceeding, expected levels ('emerging', 'expected' or 'exceeding'). The **early learning goals** for communication, language and literacy are:

- **Listening and attention** – children listen attentively in a range of situations. They listen to stories, accurately anticipating key events and respond to what they hear with relevant comments, questions or actions. They can give their attention to what is being said to them and respond appropriately, while remaining involved in an activity.
- **Understanding** – children can follow instructions involving several ideas or actions. They answer 'how' and 'why' questions about their experiences and in response to stories or events.

- **Speaking** – children express themselves effectively, showing awareness of listeners' needs. They use past, present and future forms accurately when talking about events that have happened or are to happen in the future. They develop their own narratives and explanations by connecting ideas or events.
- **Reading** – children read and understand simple sentences in stories and information books, using phonic knowledge to decode regular words and read them aloud accurately. They demonstrate understanding when talking with others about what they have read, or what has been read to them.
- **Writing** – children write their own labels, captions, messages and simple stories which can be read by themselves and others. They use their phonic knowledge to spell words in ways which match their spoken sounds. They make use of letter patterns and sequences found in many words.

Aspect	Emerging	Expected (ELGs)	Exceeding
Listening and Attention	Children listen to others one-to-one or in small groups when the conversation interests them. When listening to familiar stories and rhymes children can join in at relevant points with repeated refrains and phrases and can anticipate key events. They can focus their attention by shifting between an activity and listening.	Children listen attentively in a range of situations. They listen to stories, accurately anticipating key events and respond to what they hear with relevant comments, questions or actions. They can give their attention to what is being said to them and respond appropriately, while remaining involved in an activity.	Children listen to instructions and follow them accurately, asking for clarification if necessary. They listen attentively with sustained concentration to follow a story without pictures or props. They can listen in a larger group, for example, at assembly.
Understanding	Children respond to instructions when, for example, they are asked to get an item or put it away. They can understand the meaning of words such as 'on', 'under'. They can identify familiar objects by the way in which they are used.	Children can follow instructions involving several ideas or actions. They answer 'how' and 'why' questions about their experiences and in response to stories or events.	After listening to stories children can express views about the events or characters in the story and answer questions about why things happened. They can carry out instructions which contain several parts in a sequence.
Speaking	Children can connect ideas using talk, actions or objects and can retell a simple past event in correct order. They question why things happen and give simple explanations.	Children express themselves effectively showing awareness of listeners' needs. They use past, present and future forms accurately when talking about events that have happened or are to happen in the future. They develop their own narratives and explanations by connecting ideas or events.	Children show some awareness of the listener by making changes to language and non-verbal features. They recount experiences and imagine possibilities, often connecting ideas. They use a range of vocabulary in imaginative ways to add information, express ideas or to explain or justify actions or events.

Aspect	Emerging	Expected (ELGs)	Exceeding
Reading	Children know that print carries meaning. They show interest in books and can suggest how a story might end. They can segment the sounds in simple words and blend them together, and join in with rhyming and rhythmic activities.	Children read and understand simple sentences in stories and information books, using phonic knowledge to decode regular words and read them aloud accurately. They demonstrate understanding when talking with others about what they have read, or what has been read to them.	Children can read phonically regular words of more than one syllable as well as many irregular but high frequency words. They use phonic, semantic and syntactic knowledge to understand unfamiliar vocabulary. They can describe the main events in the simple stories they have read.
Writing	Children give meaning to marks they make as they draw, write and paint. They can segment words orally, and use some clearly identifiable letters to communicate meaning, representing some sounds correctly and in sequence.	Children write their own labels, captions, messages and simple stories which can be read by themselves and others. They use their phonic knowledge to spell words in ways which match their spoken sounds, and make use of high frequency spellings.	Children can spell phonically regular words of more than one syllable as well as many irregular but high frequency words. They use key features of narrative in their own writing.

Table 12.1 Early Learning Goals (ELGs) for communication, language and literacy

Providers must supplement the Profile assessment with a *short commentary* on each child's skills and abilities in relation to the three key characteristics of effective learning which are:

1 **Playing and exploring:** children investigate and experience things, and 'have a go'.
2 **Active learning:** children keep on trying if they encounter difficulties, and enjoy achievements.
3 **Creating and thinking critically:** children have and develop their own ideas, make links between ideas, and develop strategies for doing things.

This commentary will give Year 1 teachers helpful background and context when considering every child's stage of development and learning needs.

The Profile must be completed for all children, including those with special educational needs and disabilities. Children will have differing levels of skills and abilities across the Profile and it is important that there is a full assessment of all areas of their development to inform plans for future activities.

Supporting children with special needs

If a child's progress in developing communication, language and literacy skills gives cause for concern, practitioners must discuss this with the child's parents and continue to provide focused support in that area, reducing the risk that the child will struggle when starting Key Stage 1. Practitioners should consider whether a child may have a disability or special educational need, which requires specialist support, and should link with and/or help families to access relevant services as appropriate.

Supporting children whose home language is not English

For children whose home language is not English, practitioners must provide opportunities to develop and use the child's home language in play and learning, supporting their language development at home. Providers must also ensure that children have sufficient opportunities to learn and reach a good standard in English language during the EYFS, ensuring children are ready begin Key Stage 1. When conducting assessments in communication, language and literacy, practitioners must assess children's skills in English. However if a child is not reaching the expected level in English, practitioners should discuss with parents the child's skills in the home language before reaching a conclusion on whether there is a language delay.

Section 2: How to help children develop their communication, language and literacy skills

The stages of development of reading and writing skills

Babies and toddlers (birth to age two to three years)

General stages:

- looking at patterns, fluttering leaves on trees, or in books for newborns
- sharing a focus, as you follow the baby/toddler's gaze at a picture or object
- talking about what you see together: position chairs so that adult and child face each other to encourage talking about what you see together
- finger rhymes
- action songs.

Sharing books:

- describing pictures, especially photographs of familiar people and objects
- pausing to let the child respond
- encouraging the child to turn the page (thick card or cloth pages are helpful)
- encouraging the child to make sounds in the story, or complete repetitious phrases
- enjoying the rhythms of the phrases and rhymes
- emphasising key words as they are said.

Two to three years, and five to six years

In general:

- singing finger rhymes and action songs becomes easier, and children begin to anticipate the movements and actions while singing or chanting the words
- they engage with the sounds of the rhyming
- they engage with the rhythms
- they engage with alliteration (repetition of initial sounds)
- they play spontaneously with sounds
- they are interested in sounds around them, such as police sirens, ambulances, animals and birdsong, or the rhythmic sounds of machinery; in London, children are often heard chanting on tube trains, 'Mind the Gap'
- they make nonsense rhymes, or repeat sounds in a string
- they enjoy games with sounds, led by adults
- children like to dictate shopping lists or messages on a card for someone they love. They often want to read these back, and do so with pride and a sense of achievement.

Activity

Observe a small group (two or three) of young children interacting together.

List the different methods of communication they use (verbal and non-verbal) and note the intention of the communication.

Arrange the different methods of communication used into various types: for example, body posture, eye contact, touch, hand gestures, facial expressions, and vocalisations or speech.

From five to six years, to eight years

- Children learn how texts work, and how to build words and break them up, so that they develop word recognition and understanding. They do so without understanding what they read; at this stage children do not read for meaning (this is often called barking at print).

- By the end of this part of childhood, most (but by no means all) children are becoming fluent readers and confident writers.
- Almost all children can learn to read and most really want to learn. The majority of children learn to read between the ages of four-and-a-half and six years old. Research shows that pre-school children who are exposed to plenty of language (books and conversation) tend to do better at school.

The importance of books

Children need to find out that what people say, think, feel and do can be written down, or printed in a book, which may then be read by someone else. They need to work out where the text begins and where it ends, and have to learn which direction they have to read the text in (left to right in English). Bilingual children need to learn to switch direction if reading a language that is presented in a different way. If they speak Urdu and English equally well, they need to learn to read from left to right in English, and right to left in Urdu. A close partnership with parents is important in helping children to achieve this.

Enjoying looking at books

Children use 'reading-like' behaviour; this is a rehearsal for the fluent reading which comes later. They pretend to 'read' in their role play. They memorise texts of books that are favourites. Many settings now introduce core texts, chosen carefully by the staff, and favourite texts that children consistently select from the book area.

Enjoying listening to stories

Though not all children will be read to at bedtime, they will benefit from spending some time every day sharing a book with an adult, while sitting on a sofa; this activity, which may take place either on a one-to-one basis or with two children and an adult, is one of the most important early reading experiences adults can give to children.

Children love to talk about what is being read to them, as they listen. This is why it is important for adults to share books with children in very small groups, or one-to-one. Children relate the stories that are read to them to their own experiences of people and the world they live in. They bring their own ideas, thoughts and feelings to the book. This is what adults do when they read, but they do not do

Figure 12.1 Sharing stories is important

this out loud in the way that young children need to do. It is therefore important to be clear that in small groups, or one-to-one, children can literally share the text as an active 'reader' would do silently.

In larger groups (and with this age group it is usually wise not to have more than six to ten children in a large group) children can be introduced to the core texts chosen by staff, with the expectation that they listen to the whole story without interruption. This helps them to focus on the music, rhythms, rhymes, alliteration and sounds as the story unfolds. It also gives children the sense of a complete narrative/story with its characters.

Reflective practice

What are the key communication skills (verbal and non-verbal) that a young child has?

How could you more effectively support the development of these skills?

How to use constructive feedback to support children

Practitioners should find opportunities, wherever possible, to discuss the learning with the children, giving them feedback and identifying next steps. This should all form part of the 'assessment *for* learning' process, and should be done, when possible, without interrupting children's play.

Practitioners should always recognise young children's competence, and appreciate their efforts when they show their understanding of new words and phrases. Make sure that children understand what they are being praised for by responding immediately; saying, for example, 'Well done, Daniel, you told that story very well'. It is important to use encouraging words when a child is putting in a lot of effort, even if he has not managed to achieve his aim.

Children need to receive positive feedback in order to develop confidence and good self-esteem. Then, they will be more likely to try again and to persevere until they succeed.

✓ Progress check

Giving positive feedback

- **Be specific**: make sure that the child knows what you are referring to when you say: 'Well done!' or 'I really liked that …'

- **Be positive and constructive**: comment on particular ideas the child expressed in writing. *First*, praise the child for what he or she has achieved and emphasise the good points. *Next*, focus on what you feel the child needs to learn. *Then*, suggest ways the child can improve – and end on a positive note.

- **Ask open-ended questions**: engage the child's interest by showing interest yourself: 'Why did he or she include the dog in the story …?' 'What sort of dog is your dog in the story?'

- **Be reassuring**: adapt the feedback to the developmental stage of the individual, taking account of the child's self-confidence. Always end on a positive note, reassuring the child that however difficult they may find it, it will soon seem much easier.

The barriers to learning how to read and write

Poor levels of attainment in reading and writing at primary school are associated strongly with later low achievement. There are various factors which create barriers for children when learning to read and write – both inside and outside their own homes. These include:

- **social and cultural attitudes** to the importance of reading and writing in everyday life: this will affect children's interest and motivation to learn literacy skills.
- **socio-economic status**: this may affect access to books and often influences how much time is available for reading and being read to.

- **access to pre-school provision**: effective pre-school provision promotes children's language development through a rich variety of activities involving talking and listening, including reading stories, singing songs, so familiarising them with the value of written text.
- **lack of familiarity with the sounds of language**: children who are learning a second language or who have a language delay will have difficulties in both reading and writing. Children from minority ethnic groups, particularly those whose first language is not English, and Traveller children may require additional support.
- **access to public libraries**: this includes parental knowledge of what materials are available within them; and parental attitudes from their own success or failure at reading.

Factors which impact on a child's ability to communicate effectively

These include:

- **any hearing impairments** – permanent or temporary
- **physical impairments** such as cleft palate and hare lip
- **speech dysfluency**: many children have some degree of dysfluency when they are learning to talk, repeating words and sounds, and stopping and starting again. This is especially common when a child is excited or agitated. Children may have episodes of dysfluency during the years of rapid language development between two and five years of age, and at other times speak quite normally
- other **medical conditions** which affect other aspects of development and, as a consequence, a child's confidence or self-esteem
- disorders which affect learning such as **autism**
- **an additional language** – children's home language must be valued; see below on bilingualism
- **lack of language input** (conversations) with an interested adult or positive role model
- **emotional factors** which can result in shyness, low self-esteem and a lack of confidence.

Key term

Speech dysfluency – The use of hesitators (sounds such as 'erm', 'ur'), pauses and repetitions which reflect the difficulty of mental planning at speed. Stammering (or stuttering) is a form of speech dysfluency.

How to work with children with English as a second language

Advantages of bilingualism

Children need to feel a sense of belonging in an early childhood setting. It has been known for children to be labelled as having 'no' language, when in fact they simply speak a different language from English.

It is important that children feel their bilingualism is valued and that they see it as the advantage that it is. In most parts of the world, it is common to speak three or four languages fluently. Bilingualism is a positive advantage for all sorts of reasons:

- Learning a language means learning about a culture.
- Knowing about different cultures through living the language means that children who are bilingual experience cultural diversity in rich and important ways. For example, in Gujarati, 'thank you' is only used for special situations as an expression of deep gratitude; in English, people thank each other often, and it is just a form of everyday politeness.
- Bilingual speakers come at an idea from several directions, because different languages emphasise different things. This makes their thinking flexible and analytic. Recent studies in neuroscience provide evidence to support this.
- Children can think in different ways about the same thing when they speak different languages. For example, the Inuit language has several words for 'snow', which makes it possible to think about snow in greater detail than is possible in English.
- Children who are bilingual grow up understanding different ways of thinking. This helps them to respect and value differences between people.

- Children find it easier to understand that names for objects can be changed.
- Children who are bilingual are often more sensitive to the emotional aspects of intonation. They can interpret situations more easily.

Promoting bilingualism

Allow for a period of silence

Before children speak a language, they need to listen to it and tune in. They will make intonational sounds as they try out the sounds of the language. Look at a baby to see this process. It takes about two or three years before the baby turns into a talking toddler. In order to learn to speak a language, it is also important to see the shapes the mouth makes. The mouth looks different when the sound 'oo' is made compared with the sound 'ee'.

Comprehensible input

The researcher Stephen Krashen suggests that children need to make sense of what is being said. If an adult picks up a cup, points at the jug of orange juice and asks, 'Would you like a drink of orange juice?' the meaning is clear. If the adult just says the words, without the actions or objects being visible, the meaning is not at all clear. The adult could be saying anything.

Transitional bilingualism

In some early childhood settings the child's home language has been valued only as a bridge into learning English. This is transitional (sometimes called **subtractive**) bilingualism. It is assumed that the child will no longer need to speak their home language once English begins to take over. For example, a child who speaks Punjabi at home might be expected to speak English at school and gradually to speak English rather than Punjabi at home.

In fact, children will need to continue their home language to help them transfer later on to reading and writing in English. If the child's home language is not valued alongside English, the opportunities for bilingualism and the advantages that bilingualism brings will be wasted. The home language is important for children to express their feelings and for thinking.

Additive and successful bilingualism

The home language (L1) is the language of thinking and feelings. English as an additional language (L2) is only useful if the home language is strong. Then children think and manage feelings with deeper skill and understanding. This is called **additive bilingualism**.

> **Key term**
>
> **Balanced bilingualism** – This is when a child speaks more than one language, each with equal fluency. In fact, the child's home language is usually more fluent than English. Very few children are completely balanced across two languages. For most, one language is more developed than the other.

 In Practice

> Describe how you have provided (or could provide) support for children with special language needs in your setting. Include examples for children with additional communication and/or interaction needs.

Section 3: The role of the adult in supporting communication, language and literacy

Working with colleagues, parents and families

Effective teamwork with your colleagues and with other professionals involves careful planning and organisation. Practitioners are expected to follow the guidelines in their own setting for ways in which to support children's language and literacy. This includes methods of promoting reading skills. Some settings use core texts that they have selected themselves, while others may use a reading scheme. There also needs to be a consistent approach to the promotion of writing skills.

Children need secure and loving relationships with their parents and/or a key person so that they become strong and autonomous readers and writers, conversationalists and listeners. They do not flourish when adults sit in judgement over them and use their power to control everything they do through adult-set and adult-led tasks, which are tightly structured and focused. But they blossom when they feel adults are alongside them, sensitive to their feelings and thoughts, and helping them to put these into words/signs.

When adults spend time engaging with children one-to-one or in small groups sharing non-fiction and fiction books, this:

- builds the feeling that reading is fascinating
- gives information about experiences
- deepens knowledge and understanding (for example, a book about pond dipping after an outing).

A wide range of fiction that includes stories, poems, rhymes, songs and music may introduce children to diversity and cultural differences, and help them to understand others through empathy with different characters and situations.

Parents play a vital role in all aspects of their children's development, but particularly in the development of communication skills. Being told stories promotes language and, by feeding the child's imagination, develops abstract thought. An international study by OECD (2011) found that children whose parents frequently read with them in their first year of school are still showing the benefit when they are 15. Throughout this book, the importance of developing a partnership with parents is emphasised. There are several ways in which parents can be involved in their child's learning journey. These include:

- **information sharing** – sharing information with parents about their child's learning and preferences, and encouraging parents to share information about their child's interests and needs

- **setting up a library in the setting** – this could double as an opportunity for parents to borrow books to share with their child at home and also for parents and practitioners to interact in a relaxed atmosphere
- **involving parents** in assessments of their child.

In Practice

Describe how you have contributed to maintaining a positive environment that supports children's speech, language and communication. Include information on: the physical environment; staff roles and responsibilities; training needs and opportunities; views of the child; appropriate involvement of parents or carers.

Meeting the individual needs of children to promote their communication skills

Adults working with young children need to be able to look and to listen attentively to how children communicate. By observing carefully, you can discover the range and variety of language used by the children in your setting and improve your own skills in providing appropriate opportunities for encouraging and extending children's speech, language and communication development. Regular observations are also helpful in identifying any potential problems children may have with their speech, language and communication skills. The observing adult can identify the ways in which each child communicates, how the child interacts with others, the child's social skills, and any difficulties the child has in communicating. You need to be able to demonstrate methods of providing support for speech, language and communication development, taking into account the following factors that apply to the children in your setting:

- the age
- specific needs
- abilities and interests, and
- home language (where this is different to that of the setting).

You can observe children's language in a variety of situations. Remember we all use language in some form in everything we do. For example, you could observe the following situations:

- a child talking with another child or an adult
- an adult talking with a small group of children
- a small group of children engaged in a role play activity
- a child playing alone
- small or large group discussions such as news time or circle time
- an adult reading or telling a story to a child or group of children
- a child or group of children participating in a creative activity such as painting or drawing
- a child or children playing outside
- a child involved in a literacy activity such as writing news, a story or a poem.

Research Activity

Find out about the policies in your setting with regard to child observations, language assessments, record keeping and confidentiality. Remember to keep this information in mind when doing your own observations of children within the setting.

In Practice

Plan, implement and evaluate a language activity for a small group of children, such as news time, circle time, discussion, story time or phonics session.

You could use your suggestions from the previous observation as the starting point for planning this activity.

The activity should encourage the children's active participation, including attentive listening and communicating with others during the activity, as well as supervising and maintaining the children's interest throughout the activity.

Activity

Observe a small group of three or four children with an adult. Note examples of turn-taking and any of the things you would expect to find in a conversation that have been identified in this chapter. Was there a difference in the number of times individual children spoke in the group? In what way? Evaluate the pros and cons of small groups and large groups.

Figure 12.2 Using non-verbal communication is essential when working with young children

Planning appropriate activities to develop and extend language and literacy

Activities to develop speaking and listening skills

These activities can be divided into five basic categories:

- exploration
- description
- conversation
- discussion
- instruction.

Exploration

- Toys and other interesting objects to look at and play with such as household objects (remember safety).
- Sounds to listen to including voices, music, songs and rhymes.
- Noise-makers such as commercial and homemade musical instruments.
- Bath toys and books.
- Construction materials including wooden bricks, plastic bricks and 'junk' modelling.
- Natural materials such as water, sand, clay, dough and cooking ingredients.
- Creative materials such as paint, paper and glue.
- Outdoor activities and outings including gardening, visits to parks and museums, swimming.
- Animals including visits to farms and wildlife centres, looking after small pets.

Description

- News time, circle time.
- Recording events, outings, visits and visitors.
- Books and stories appropriate to age/level of development including cloth books, board books, activity books, pop-up books, picture books, audio books, textbooks, novels, encyclopaedia.

Conversation

- Talking about their day, experiences and interests in a variety of settings with other children and adults, such as playgroup, nursery, school, after-school clubs, youth clubs.
- Talking during imaginative play activities such as playing with pretend/role play equipment; for example, dressing up clothes, home corner, play shop, puppets; playing with dolls, teddies and other cuddly toys; playing with small scale toys such as toy cars, garages and road systems, train set, dolls' houses.
- Talking about special events such as birthdays, new baby, religious festivals.
- Talking while doing activities – not necessarily related to the task!

Discussion

- Problem-solving during activities such as mathematics, science and technology.
- Follow-up discussion after an activity or event, such as watching DVD/television or live performance, listening to a story or recorded music.
- Cooperative group work.
- Games and puzzles.

Instruction

- Preparation before an activity.
- Explanation of what to do – verbal and/or written on a board.
- Instructions during an activity to keep the children on task.
- Extra support for individuals.
- Introducing or extending knowledge on a specific skill.
- Step-by-step instructions.
- Worksheets, workbooks and work cards.
- Delivering verbal and/or written messages, carrying out errands.

Activity

Describe an example activity for *each* of the five categories, based on your own experiences of working with children.

Activities to develop early reading skills

In order to learn to read, children must recognise that a certain pattern of letters represents a particular sound. They need to build up a set of skills that will help them to make sense of words, signs and symbols.

Please see page 300 for information on helping children to read.

Phonics

English is an irregular language, which makes it particularly hard to learn to read and write in English. Some argue that we should get children off to an early start for just this reason. Most early childhood experts take the view that the human brain needs to be sufficiently mature to tackle the fine detail of discriminating the sounds and look of English print. Even in countries where the language is very regular, such as Finland and Sweden, this is the approach. However, the brain does function easily and without stress in relation to learning about communication (both non-verbal and spoken/ signed language) and music, gesture and movement. This means that singing and dancing, and talking with and listening to children, all have a huge contribution to make in helping children towards reading and writing at six or seven years of age. This age is generally regarded, throughout the world, as the best time to learn to read and write, because the structures dealing with this level of symbolic functioning are present.

These rhyming strings of words nearly sound the same: 'pot', 'dot', 'got'; 'mess', 'cress', 'dress'; 'mum', 'chum', 'drum'. The last chunk rhymes, but the first chunk is different in each case. This is an aspect of **analytic phonics**. Many early childhood reading and writing experts consider that learning about rhyming through poems, songs, action rhymes, poetry cards and books are more powerful ways of helping young children to read in English than teaching isolated sounds, using flashcards (**synthetic phonics**) as the main strategy. A fierce debate about this seems to arise roughly every ten years. Most experts argue that the more strategies we have to offer children as they learn to read, the more we can find the ones that suit each child best. One size does not fit all children.

There is great opposition by early childhood experts to the suggestion that young children should be directly taught synthetic phonics through daily drill in large groups. However, daily group time (remember, large groups are four to eight children), with song, dance and rhyme, and encouragement, helps children become:

- phonologically aware
- able to discriminate sounds with increasing ease
- able to link these with the print in the rhymes using poetry cards.

Key terms

Analytic phonics – Children are taught whole words and later analyse their constituent parts, such as c-at or str-eet.

Synthetic phonics – Children are taught the sounds of letters and letter combinations first, then combine those to form words: c-a-t or s-t-r-ee-t.

Early reading skill	Activities to promote the skill
Shape recognition and matching: the ability to recognise shapes and to differentiate between them is important. Children learn to match shapes and patterns first and this helps them to match letters and, finally, words.	Snap Shape sorter Picture pairs Lotto Jigsaws Dominoes
Rhyming: research shows that children who can understand about rhyming words have a head start in learning to read and, even more, to spell.	Rhyming games such as 'I Spy with my little eye, something that rhymes with cat' (hat or mat). Leave off the end of rhymes for the child to complete, e.g. 'Humpty Dumpty sat on a wall, Humpty Dumpty had a great …?' Reading simple poetry.
Language skills: the more experience children have of language, the more easily they will learn to read. Children need to hear and join in conversations (with adults and children), and to listen to stories and poetry of all sorts.	Talking. Reading stories. Encouraging children to talk. Share their favourite stories again and again: repeating phrases helps to build children's language.
Concepts of print: this means 'how we look at books' and includes following print the right way (from left to right), turning the pages, looking at pictures.	Children need to learn practical skills: • how to hold a book (the right way up!) • how to turn pages singly • let the child see your finger following the print when reading.
Letter skills: children need to learn what sounds the letters can make.	Begin with letters with an interesting shape that makes them easy to recognise or a letter which is important to the child, such as their own initial. Use the letter sounds rather than letter names; e.g. 'a for ant', not 'ay for ape'. Try a letter hunt: looking for objects which begin with a particular letter.
Motor skills: since reading and writing are best taught together, pencil control is important.	Encourage creativity: drawing and painting with lots of different tools and materials to encourage pencil and brush control. Playing with small toys, especially construction sets, help to develop fine motor skills.
Looking at a variety of **printed materials:** newspapers, magazines, packaging, street and shop names etc.	Point out words in the environment: e.g. 'Push' 'Pull' 'Open' 'Closed' etc. Visit the library to encourage familiarity with the idea of books for everyone.
Memory skills: words are made up of sequences of letters and sounds, and children need to remember this before they can read.	Memory games: such as 'I went to the shops and I bought a …' and pairs (pelmanism) all help to improve children's memory skills and to increase their attention span. Sequencing: book page layout can be reinforced by, for example, laying out the child's clothes to be selected first from left then to the right: vest, pants, top, trousers, socks, shoes.

Table 12.2 Activities to promote early reading skills

Sounds and how words look

Children need to learn to segment (break down) sounds and print. They also need to learn to blend (join) sounds and print. The smallest sounds are phonemes and the smallest print is a grapheme. Children need to make grapho-phonic relationships. They need to begin to see that what they have segmented can be blended back into a word. The ideal age to do this, experts in most countries say, is between six and seven years of age.

Methods of teaching writing

Writing has two aspects:

1 what it says – the construction of meaning
2 the look of it – the handwriting and letter shapes (transcription).

When children begin to write, they are constructing a code. Most languages have a written code. Writing develops when children begin to use symbols. Often they begin by putting letter-type shapes into their drawings. This is known as meaningful mark-making. These gradually get pushed out to the edges of the drawing, to look more like words and sentences. This is called emergent writing. Practitioners need to observe the shapes, sizes and numbers that children experiment with. Children need to be free to experiment, without criticism or pressure. Left-handed children must never be encouraged to write with the right hand. Young children find capital letters, which are more linear, easier to write than lower-case letters, which have more curves, so they tend to experiment with capitals first. It is when children begin to experiment with curves that they are indicating they have more pencil control, so can begin to form letters more easily.

Children need:

● to manipulate and try out different ways of 'writing', using their own personal code – tracing or copying letters undermines this because their own movement patterns and laying down of neural pathways are an important part of the process
● to explore what writing is
● adults who point out print in books and in the environment – for example, on notices and street signs.

It is important to talk with children about environmental print, and to pick out their favourite letters (often those in their name). A child's own name is important to them, and they often write the names of people they love, plus the words 'love from'.

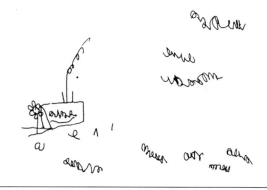

MARIANO PO
IEAOAO
AMAM AO

RIOA

OAIR
AROI
OIRA

Figure 12.3 Children's writing

Figure 12.4 Boys writing on whiteboards

Mark-making

If you respect the feelings of a child, you will be better able to support them on their journey into mark-making and personal symbols to show 'writing'.

Scribing

Sitting down with children at the mark-making table, at their level, and scribing their messages for them are all important aspects of working sensitively with children. Children do not offer adults their writing for it to be judged and found wanting. They give their effortful early attempts at writing with love, and trust that the adult will appreciate and value them. Then they begin to share with the adult those aspects they found difficult, and accept help that is proffered willingly.

Reasons for writing

Children are attracted to activities such as writing labels for the photograph album, as they engage with talking about what they were doing, or their friends and family. Writing messages such as 'closed' and 'open' for the shop helps children to see the reasons for writing.

Remember, you cannot plan the next steps for a child unless you first observe what interests the child and what engages them in learning. Observation helps practitioners to create a learning environment, indoors and outdoors, which supports the development of writing.

The methods and techniques used to support children with speaking and listening

Supporting the development of speaking skills

Practitioners need to be good role models, to listen to children and to involve them in discussions. In this way, children can develop their thinking and understanding of their experiences, and also develop a wide and varied vocabulary. Before planning any activities you need to consider the developmental needs of the children you are working with. Ways to promote the development of speech could include the following:

- telling stories and encouraging children to share information about celebrations and events that are important to them
- joining in with singing popular nursery rhymes and action songs
- providing opportunities for children to speak and listen to others' ideas, feelings, emotions and events
- encouraging imaginative play and activities that encourage children to talk to each other
- sharing greetings in daily routines
- using ICT, such as recording children's conversations and playing them back to them for discussion.

Supporting the development of listening skills

There are many activities that support the development of listening skills. Through participating in listening activities, children should be able to differentiate between sounds and discriminate sounds from each other. Activities should be differentiated to ensure children make progress. Some of the activities to support the development of listening skills could include the following:

- listening to and joining in with action songs and rhymes
- taking children on 'sound' walks both indoors and outdoors, to allow children opportunities to listen to a wide variety of sounds and to identify them
- encouraging children to listen to short pieces of music, in a variety of styles
- playing sound lotto
- playing the game 'I went to the market and I bought … (name an item)'; each child repeats the previous object and adds another item beginning with the same initial sound
- using circle time to provide opportunities for children to listen to others, both adults and their peers.

The use of story and rhyme in supporting communication, language and listening

Storytelling

There is a difference between reading stories from a book and storytelling. A love of stories is common to all young children, and by telling stories, rather than reading them, a storyteller can really bring the story to life and make it a more interactive experience for the children. To enhance the experience of storytelling, you can use:

- visual aids or props – objects related to the story
- sound effects – children could be encouraged to make appropriate sounds
- pictures or photographs
- children's drawings and paintings.

When telling (or reading) a story to a group of children, it is important to arrange seating comfortably, and to ensure that all children can see and hear both you and the book or visual aids. Practitioners should also find opportunities to read or tell stories to individual children or very small groups. Having extra attention at story time allows children to point, to comment and to help with page-turning.

Rhyme

Sharing rhymes with young children helps them listen to the patterns of language. Children first begin to notice that certain words have the same sounds at the end (rhyme). Later they notice that many words share a pattern in the way they are spelled. Understanding these links makes learning to read much easier.

Rhyming words helps children appreciate beginning and ending sounds – for example, 'cat', 'pat' and 'mat'. Rhyming activities suggested in the EYFS include:

- Share, recite and encourage joining in with rhymes, action songs and games. For example, as the children come to join the circle for group time, say the rhyme: 'I know a name which rhymes with hen, he's sitting in the group and his name is …' and encourage the children to provide the name (for example, Ben). For children whose names do not lend themselves to rhyme, say for example, 'I know a girl whose name I can sing, Jodie's coming next and she's in the ring'.
- Encourage repetition, rhythm and rhyme by using tone and intonation. Use rhymes from a variety of cultures, including those shared by parents from home. Increase children's repertoire of familiar and traditional rhymes.
- Encourage the children to use a microphone and recording equipment to record their own rhymes.

The use of technology to support language and literacy

The use of technology in the EYFS is based on the needs of the children, the focus of the curriculum, and whether the technology will add to children's educational opportunities and experiences.

The use of computers

Fine and gross motor skills develop at varying rates, and learning to write can be tedious and difficult as children struggle to form letters. A word processor allows them to compose and revise text without being distracted by the fine motor aspects of letter formation. If computers are used with children in kindergarten, pre-school, or other early years settings, the computer should be one of many activity choices they can explore.

Three- to five-year-olds generally spend about the same amount of time at a computer as they do on other activities such as playing with blocks or drawing. Most children of this age are limited to icons and pictures on the screen for understanding. They are also more interested and less frustrated when an adult is present; their computer use is usually facilitated by the teacher or practitioner.

Five- to eight-year-olds: as they mature, children use computers more independently, and the teacher's role moves from guidance towards monitoring and active support. Software programs for this age group should be limited in number and appropriate for children's skill level and the intended use. More opportunities for independent use become available with increasing language and literacy skills. For example, simple word processors become important educational tools as children experiment with written language.

Recording equipment

Tape recorders and MP3 players support early literacy experiences by integrating all aspects of literacy: speaking, listening, reading, and writing. They allow children to listen to recorded stories or songs, or to follow along in a book as they hear it being read on tape. Children can record family stories, their own made-up stories, poems, and songs, or themselves reading aloud. When adults write down children's stories from children's dictated words or from the recording equipment, children see how the spoken word can turn into the written word. They can also help children develop their own storytelling ability and an understanding of how sound translates to print.

Cameras

Cameras (film, video, or digital) can record children's activities while they are working, as well as performances and special events. Children can tell a story in pictures and write or dictate captions. Photos can be used to share the learning with other children and with parents. Photos can also introduce teachers and staff members to new students and families during home visits.

How to work with children whose progress may be causing concern

A continuous record of a child who is having difficulties with communication, language and literacy (for example, in a diary format) can help the practitioner to identify specific problems. Working with parents, colleagues and specialist advisers (if necessary), the early years practitioner can then plan a suitable programme to enable the child to overcome these difficulties. Observations can provide a check that children's language and literacy is progressing in the expected ways.

How to monitor progress and keep appropriate records

The Primary Framework and the EYFS are linked and have been developed alongside each other. Each framework outlines:

- the ways in which practitioners and teachers monitor children's progress
- when and how to keep records
- when and how to refer a child for specialist help (for example, the local speech and language team).

But although they match, it is important that schools use the EYFS to build on with children in Year 1 as well as those in Reception classes. The EYFS and the Primary Framework help nursery, reception and Key Stage 1 (years 1 and 2) teachers to see how the six area of the EYFS link to literacy in Key Stage 1. This is not about getting children ready for the next class. It is about building on what children know and can do, supporting them in this, and using what they know to help them into the less familiar. Then they continue their learning journey with high wellbeing, eager to learn more.

Assessment practice

Unit 16

1. Describe the different areas of communication, language and literacy development for children aged from three to eight years.

2. Find out about the different frameworks and policies relating to your home country which guide provision for children's learning in communication, language and literacy from three to eight years.

3. Describe three activities that support children's learning to promote:

   - speaking skills

   - listening skills

   - reading skills.

4. Identify three barriers to learning how to read and write.

How to provide and prepare resources to support learning and development

The British Association for Early Childhood Education (www.early-education.org.uk) produces a wide range of publications and resources to support early childhood practitioners and parents to support young children to learn effectively. The booklet on *Core Experiences for the EYFS* from Kate Greenaway Nursery School and Children's Centre can also be ordered from this website.

Centre for Literacy in Primary Education has undertaken pioneering work in supporting and training practitioners to enjoy helping children to love stories and books. It offers excellent training for those working with children in Reception and Key Stage 1: www.clpe.co.uk

The National Literacy Trust (www.literacytrust. org.uk) provides information relating to early years provision and literacy, including news, research, events, policy, resources and further information about their work in this area.

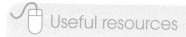 Useful resources

Conteh, J. (ed.) (2006) *Promoting Learning for Bilingual Pupils 3–11: Opening Doors to Success*. London: Sage.

Nyland, B., Ferris, J. and Dunn, L. (2008) 'Mindful hands, gestures as language: Listening to children', *Early Years* 28(1): 73–80.

Palmer, S. and Bayley, R. (2004) *Foundations of Literacy: A Balanced Approach to Language, Listening and Literacy Skills in the Early Years*. Edinburgh: Network Educational Press.

Trevarthen, C. (2004) *Learning about ourselves from children: Why a growing human brain needs interesting companions*. Perception-in-Action Laboratories, University of Edinburgh.

Whitehead, M. (2010) *Language and Literacy in the Early Years 0–7* (4th edn). London: Sage.

13 Working with babies from birth to 12 months: Unit 18

Section 1: The progress of development from birth to 12 months

The newborn baby

The importance of reflex responses to child development

Newborn babies display a number of reflex actions. A reflex action is one made automatically, without needing a conscious message from the brain – such as swallowing, sneezing or blinking. The presence of some of the newborn's primitive reflexes is essential to survival. The most important of these reflexes is breathing, closely followed by the 'rooting' and 'sucking' reflexes that help them to search out the breast and to feed successfully. The reflexes are replaced by *voluntary* responses as the brain takes control of behaviour; for example, the grasp reflex has to fade before the baby learns to hold (and let go of) objects which are placed in her hand. Doctors check for some of these reflexes during the baby's first examination. If the reflexes persist beyond an expected time it may indicate a delay in development.

These are the reflex responses:

- **The swallowing and sucking reflexes**: when something is put in the mouth, the baby at once sucks and swallows; some babies make their fingers sore by sucking them while still in the womb.
- **The rooting reflex**: if one side of the baby's cheek or mouth is gently touched, the baby's head turns towards the touch and the mouth purses as if in search of the nipple (Figure 13.1(a)).
- **The grasp reflex**: when an object or finger touches the palm of the baby's hand, it is automatically grasped (Figure 13.1(b)).
- **The stepping or walking reflex**: when held upright and tilting slightly forward, with feet placed on a firm surface, the baby will make forward-stepping movements (Figure 13.1(c)).
- **The startle reflex**: when the baby is startled by a sudden noise or bright light, she will move her arms outwards with elbows and hands clenched (Figure 13.1(d)).
- **The asymmetric tonic neck reflex**: if the baby's head is turned to one side, she will straighten the arm and leg on that side and bend the arm and leg on the opposite side (Figure 13.1(e)).
- **The falling reflex** (Moro reflex): any sudden movement which affects the neck gives the baby the feeling that he or she may be dropped; the baby will fling out their arms and open their hands before bringing them back over the chest as if to catch hold of something.

Activity

The skills of the newborn baby

1. Make a list of all the things a newborn baby is able to do.

2. What is the name given to movements, which are automatic and inborn? Describe four such movements and explain their importance in the study of child development.

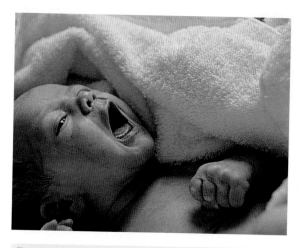

Figure 13.1a The rooting reflex

Figure 13.1b The grasp reflex

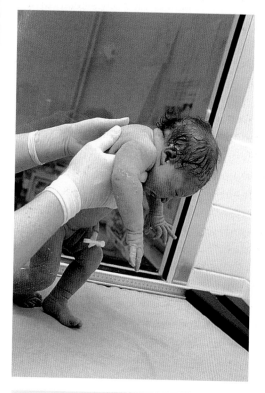

Figure 13.1c The stepping or walking reflex

Figure 13.1d The startle reflex

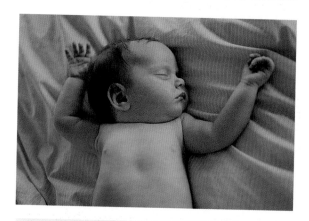

Figure 13.1e The asymmetric tonic neck reflex

Sequence of holistic development from birth to one year

From birth to four weeks

Babies:

- will turn their head towards the light and stare at bright shiny objects
- are fascinated by human faces and gaze attentively at their carer's face when being fed or cuddled
- enjoy feeding and cuddling
- often imitate facial expressions
- respond to things that they see, hear and feel.

Figure 13.2a

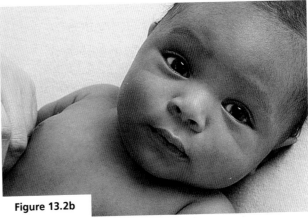

Figure 13.2b

Role of the adult

- Meet the baby's primary needs for milk, warmth and hygiene.
- Provide plenty of physical contact and maintain eye contact.
- Talk lovingly to babies and give them the opportunity to respond.
- Feed on demand, and talk and sing to them.

Equipment, toys and activities

- Pram or cot and bedclothes for sleeping.
- Nappy changing mat and equipment.
- Bathing equipment.
- Clothes and laundry facilities.
- Light rattles and toys strung over the pram or cot will encourage focusing and coordination.
- Mobile hung over the nappy changing area or cot.
- Use bright colours in furnishings.
- Try sticking out your tongue and opening your mouth wide; the baby may copy you.
- Try showing babies brightly coloured woolly pompoms, balloons, shiny objects and black and white patterns. Hold them directly in front of the baby's face and give him time to focus before slowly moving them.
- Talk with babies; if you talk closely to a baby and leave time for a response, you will find that very young babies react with a concentrated expression, and later with smiles and excited leg kicking.

Safety points

- When playing with a baby, always support the head as the neck muscles are not strong enough to control movement.

- Always place babies on their back to sleep.
- Keep the temperature in a baby's room at around 20 °C (68 °F).

From four to eight weeks

Babies:

- can turn from their side to their back
- make jerky and uncontrolled arm and leg movements
- are beginning to take their fist to their mouth
- open their hands to grasp an adult's finger
- show that they recognise their primary carers by responding to them with a combination of excited movements, coos and smiles
- love to watch movement: trees in the wind, bright contrasting objects placed within their field of vision, etc.
- enjoy listening to the sound of bells, music, voices and rhythmic sounds
- love to look at shapes – particularly circles and stripes.

Role of the adult

- Meet the baby's primary needs for milk, warmth and hygiene.
- Massage the baby's body and limbs during or after bathing.
- Talk to and smile with the baby.
- Sing while feeding or bathing the baby – allowing time for the baby to respond.
- Learn to differentiate between the baby's cries and respond to them appropriately.
- Encourage laughter by tickling the baby.
- Hold the baby close to promote a feeling of security.

Equipment, toys and activities

- Pushchair or combination pram/pushchair.
- Safety car seat.
- Use a special supporting infant chair so that babies can see adult activity.
- Light rattles and toys strung over their pram or cot will encourage focusing and coordination.
- Let them kick freely without nappies on.

Safety points

- Never leave rattles or similar toys in the baby's cot or pram as they can become wedged in the baby's mouth and cause suffocation.
- Do not leave a baby unattended on a table, work surface, bed or sofa; lay them on the floor instead.

Activity

Designing a mobile

1. Think of two or more designs for making a mobile.

2. Compare your ideas, considering the following factors:
   - availability of resources and materials
   - skills and time required
   - costs of materials
   - appropriateness of the design for its purpose
   - safety of the design.

3. Select one of the designs; if possible use a computer graphics program to prepare patterns and a word program to write a set of instructions for making the mobile.

4. Follow your written instructions and make the mobile. Evaluate both the instructions – were they easy to follow or did you have to modify the plan? – and the mobile. If appropriate, offer the mobile as a gift to a baby known to you (perhaps in family placement) and conduct a detailed observation on the baby's reaction to the mobile and his or her associated behaviour.

Babies at around three months

Babies:

- can now lift both head and chest off the bed in the prone position, supported on forearms

- kick vigorously with legs alternating or occasionally together
- watch their hands and play with their fingers
- can hold a rattle for a brief time before dropping it
- are becoming conversational by cooing, gurgling and chuckling; they love to exchange coos with a familiar person
- enjoy exploring different textures, for example on an activity mat.

Role of the adult

- Meet the baby's primary needs for milk, warmth and hygiene.
- Provide brightly coloured mobiles and wind chimes to encourage focusing at 20 cm.
- Place some toys on a blanket or play mat on the floor so that babies can lie on their tummies and play with them for short periods.
- Give babies a rattle to hold.
- Attach objects above the cot that make a noise when touched.
- Change their position frequently so that they have different things to look at and to experience.

Equipment, toys and activities

- Rattles.
- Chiming balls.
- Cradle 'gym' to encourage focusing and reaching skills.
- Wind chimes.
- Imitate the sounds made by babies to encourage repetition.
- Sing nursery rhymes.

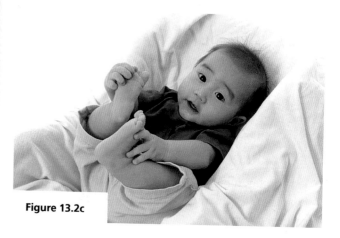

Figure 13.2c

- Encourage contact with other adults and children.
- Try action rhymes with the baby on your lap, such as 'This little piggy went to market ...'
- Respond to their needs and show enjoyment in caring for them.

Safety points

- Always protect babies of all skin tones from exposure to sunlight. Use a special sun protection cream, a sun hat to protect face and neck, and a pram canopy.
- Never leave small objects within reach as everything finds its way to a baby's mouth.
- Always buy goods displaying an appropriate safety symbol.

Babies at around six months

Babies:

- when lying on their backs, can roll over – moving from back to stomach
- can sit with support; sometimes without support
- bounce their feet up and down when held on the floor
- move arms purposefully and hold them up to be lifted
- reach and grab when a small toy is offered
- explore objects by putting them in the mouth
- enjoy playing with stacking beakers and bricks
- play with a rolling ball when in sitting position
- understand 'up' and 'down' and make appropriate gestures
- show interest in the edges of mats on the floor.

Figure 13.2d

Role of the adult

- Meet the baby's primary needs for milk, warmth and hygiene.
- Encourage confidence and balance by placing toys around the sitting baby.
- Provide rattles and toys that can be hung over the cot to encourage the baby to reach and grab.
- Encourage mobility by placing toys just out of the baby's reach.
- Provide safe toys for babies to transfer to their mouths.
- Look at picture books together and encourage the baby to point at objects with you.

Equipment, toys and activities

- Highchair with safety harness.
- Stacking beakers and nesting toys.
- Suction toys on tabletops.
- Provide cardboard boxes to put things into and take things out of.
- Build a tower of bricks with the baby and watch the delight when it topples over.
- Simple musical instruments, such as a xylophone or wooden spoon and saucepan.
- Safety mirror to develop the baby's recognition of self.

Safety points

- Make sure that furniture is stable and has no sharp corners.
- Always supervise a baby when trying 'finger foods' and at mealtimes.
- Always supervise water play.

Babies at around nine months

Babies:

- sit alone without support
- stand, holding on to furniture
- find ways of moving about the floor – for example, by rolling, wriggling, or crawling on stomach
- grasp objects between finger and thumb in a pincer grip
- understand their daily routine and will follow simple instructions, such as 'kiss teddy'

- may drink from a cup with help
- enjoy making noises by banging toys.

Role of the adult

- Meet the baby's primary needs for milk, warmth and hygiene.
- Allow plenty of time for play.
- Encourage mobility by placing toys just out of reach.
- Provide small objects for babies to pick up; choose objects that are safe when chewed, such as pieces of biscuit, but always supervise.
- Play peek-a-boo games, and hiding and seeking.
- Roll balls for the baby to bring back to you.

Equipment, toys and activities

- Highchair with safety harness.
- Bath toys – beakers, sponges and funnels, etc.
- Stacking and nesting toys.
- Picture books.
- Soft balls for rolling.
- Pop-up toys.
- Encourage self-feeding and tolerate messes.
- Talk constantly to babies and continue with rhymes and action songs.

Safety points

- Always supervise eating and drinking. Never leave babies alone with finger foods such as bananas, carrots, cheese, etc.
- Use childproof containers for tablets and vitamins, and ensure that they are closed properly.
- Use a locked cupboard for storing dangerous household chemicals, such as bleach, disinfectant and white spirit.

Babies at around one year

Babies:

- crawl on hands and knees, bottom-shuffle or 'bear-walk' rapidly about the floor
- stand alone for a few moments
- 'cruise' along using furniture as a support
- point with index finger at objects of interest
- understand simple instructions associated with a gesture, such as 'come to Daddy', 'clap hands' and 'wave bye-bye'
- help with daily routines, such as getting washed and dressed
- enjoy playing with bricks and containers – for putting toys into and taking them out
- love to play with toys that they can move along with their feet
- enjoy looking at picture books.

Role of the adult

- Meet the baby's primary needs for milk, warmth and hygiene.
- Read picture books with simple rhymes.
- Arrange a corner of the kitchen or garden for messy play, involving the use of water, play dough or paint.
- Talk to the baby about everyday activities, and always allow time for a response.

Figure 13.2e

Figure 13.2f

Equipment, toys and activities

- Push-and-pull toys to promote confidence in walking.
- Stacking toys and bricks.
- Shape sorters.
- Baby swing.
- Cardboard boxes.
- Encourage creative skills by providing thick crayons and paintbrushes, and large sheets of paper (such as wall lining paper).
- Join in games of 'let's pretend' to encourage imaginative skills; for example, pretending to be animals or to drive a bus.
- Think about attending a parent and toddler group.

Safety points

- As babies become more mobile, you need to be vigilant at all times. This is a very high-risk age for accidents.
- Always supervise sand and water play.
- Use safety equipment, such as safety catches for cupboards and stair gates, ideally at top and bottom of stairs.

Factors influencing development in the first year of life

The factors affecting development pre-conceptually and during pregnancy are discussed in Chapter 6.

Factors influencing development around the time of the birth

The majority of babies are born safely, usually in hospital, but sometimes in a special midwife-led unit or at home. Most women give birth vaginally, but sometimes the delivery is **assisted** medically, using forceps, vacuum delivery or a Caesarean section. Usually, women expecting twins or more babies are admitted to hospital for the birth; twins may be delivered vaginally provided both babies are in the head-down position, but triplets and quadruplets are usually born by Caesarean section.

Birth trauma

Occasionally, a baby may suffer from foetal distress during the birth process. This is usually caused by a lack of oxygen to the baby's brain (anoxia). During labour, midwives and doctors look out for signs of foetal distress and will often accelerate the delivery by using forceps (forceps are like tongs that fit around the baby's head to form a protective 'cage').

Premature and multiple births: potential effects on development

Babies who are born before the 37th week of pregnancy are premature babies. Around ten per cent of babies are born before 38 weeks of pregnancy, and most of them weigh less than 2,500g. The main problems for premature babies are as follows:

- **Temperature control** – heat production is low and heat loss is high, because the surface area is large in proportion to the baby's weight, and there is little insulation from subcutaneous fat.
- **Breathing** – the respiratory system is immature and the baby may have difficulty breathing by him or herself; this condition is called respiratory distress syndrome (RDS). This is caused by a deficiency in surfactant, a fatty substance that coats the baby's lungs and is only produced from about 22 weeks of pregnancy.
- **Infection** – resistance to infection is poor because the baby has not had enough time in the uterus to acquire antibodies from the mother to protect against infection.
- **Jaundice** – caused by immaturity of the liver function.

Key term

Premature (or preterm) baby – A premature baby is one who is born before 37 weeks of gestation.

The extent to which prematurity and multiple births affect the healthy development of the foetus and baby varies a great deal and is linked to how *early* a baby or babies are born. Babies born earlier than 34 weeks may need extra help in breathing, feeding and keeping warm. The earlier they are born, the more they are likely to need help in these areas.

Advances in the medical and nursing care of babies born prematurely have meant that many babies born after 35 weeks are able to breathe and feed independently, and their healthy development is not usually affected. However, babies who are born very early – such as around 25 weeks – require intensive neonatal care, which means being nursed in incubators (to maintain their body temperature) and receiving medical assistance with breathing and feeding. These vulnerable babies have a higher risk of developing hearing and sight problems and learning difficulties, than those who are born at full term.

Post-term babies

Post-term babies are those born after the expected date of delivery, after 40 weeks of pregnancy. These babies may also experience problems with breathing, feeding and keeping warm. This is because the placenta stops functioning after about 42 weeks, and so fails to provide the larger baby with enough oxygenated blood.

Factors influencing development in the first year of a child's life

Many factors affect the healthy growth and development of children. These include personal factors such as genetic influences and health status, and external factors such as poverty and deprivation. These are discussed in Chapter 2, Section 1.

The principles of promoting development and learning

The normative development of babies is discussed in Chapter 2. You need to have a thorough knowledge of these norms of development in order to:

- be reassured that babies are developing normally
- identify those babies and children who, for some reason, may not be following these normative stages
- build up a picture of a child's progress over time
- anticipate – and respond appropriately to – certain types of age-related behaviour
- guide you in providing for the baby's developmental needs.

As well as knowing about babies' developmental milestones, you need to know how to promote a baby's development in a wider, holistic sense.

Theoretical perspectives on development

The way in which humans develop is of great interest to scientists and psychologists. The main theorists in the area of child development (for example, Bowlby, Piaget, Chomsky, etc.) are discussed in Chapter 2. Current research into the development and learning of babies focuses on neuroscience.

Current research: studies in brain development and learning

In the past, some scientists thought the brain's development was determined genetically, and that brain growth followed a biologically predetermined path. Now neuroscientists believe that most of the brain's cells are formed *before* birth, but most of the connections among cells are made during infancy and early childhood. They refer to the 'plasticity' of the brain and believe that:

- early experiences are vital to healthy brain development
- the outside world shapes the development of a baby's brain through experiences that a child's senses (vision, hearing, smell, touch and taste) take in.

It is estimated that at birth, a baby's brain contains thousands of millions of neurons, or nerve cells, and that almost all the neurons that the brain will ever have are present. Babies start to learn in the womb, particularly in the last three months. When they are born, babies are able to recognise familiar sounds and they have already developed some taste preferences. The brain continues to grow for a few years after birth, and by the age of two years, the brain is about 80 per cent of the adult size.

The neurons are connected together to form even more billions of different neural pathways. Whenever we have a new experience, a new neural pathway in the brain is used. Every new experience changes our behaviour – this is called **learning**. If the experience is repeated, or the stimulus is very strong, more nerve impulses are sent along the new pathway. This reinforces the learning process and explains why repetition helps us to learn new things. Repetition strengthens the connections between neurons and makes it easier for impulses to travel along the pathway. This process is commonly known as hard wiring, and 90 per cent of the hard-wired connections will be complete by the age of three. It is very important to our understanding of brain development in early childhood, and explains and illustrates the long-lasting impact of early experiences.

Key term

Neuroscience – Studies of the brain which provide evidence to help early years specialists working with young children.

The importance of Bowlby's work on attachment

John Bowlby's work was important because it led to the introduction of key worker systems in institutions. Children no longer had a series of different nurses looking after them as each work shift changed. They were placed in smaller 'family' groups and were consistently looked after by the same team of staff. Also, increasing numbers of children began to be fostered in family homes rather than placed in large institutions. This helped children to form good attachments with a limited number of people who cared for them. Children could develop warm, physical, loving relationships, and found it easier to communicate with their carers. Much importance is given to the role of the key person in the EYFS – see page 510 onwards for more information on the key worker system.

Theories of attachment and bonding are also discussed in Chapter 2.

Case Study   Leaving baby to cry could damage brain development

'It is not an opinion but a fact that it's potentially damaging to leave babies to cry,' says parenting guru Penelope Leach. Using saliva swab tests, scientists have been able to measure high levels of the stress hormone cortisol in distraught babies whose cries elicit no response from parent or carer. Neurobiologists say that high cortisol levels are 'toxic' to the developing brain. Leach is not saying it is bad for babies to cry, but that crying, in the first year or so, is the only way a baby can gain a response. Denying a response, she argues, can have long-term emotional consequences.

By contrast, Gina Ford, author of best-selling parenting manual, *The Contented Little Baby Book*, advises that parents can leave a baby to cry for a while if he or she is clean and fed and burped. When they put a baby down to sleep at night, they can return if he or she cries but must not make eye contact.

Penelope Leach has codirected the UK's largest research project into different forms of child care for children aged under five years. Her own research work, she says, has shown that having a mother, father or carer who responds to the baby is a crucial factor in their development, outweighing the effects of poverty and disadvantage. Acknowledging that it is contentious, Leach says: 'If you really, really don't want a baby to make any difference, you could try not having one.' She is not talking about the mother who cannot reach the cot for five minutes after the baby has started to cry; 'But you can tell by sound and, quite frankly, by sight whether a baby is working herself into a lather,' she says.

Adapted from an article in *The Guardian*, April 2010

1 Discuss the issues raised in the case study.
2 How important do you think it is to be able to refer to scientific research in your practice?

James and Joyce Robertson: attachment and substitute care

James and Joyce Robertson made a series of films in the 1950s that showed Bowlby's theory about maternal deprivation in action. The films were of young children who were separated from their parents and showed that they went through various stages in their loss and grief:

- They *protested*: they cried out but were able to be comforted.
- They *despaired* about what was happening – and were inconsolable.
- They showed *denial* – and became detached in the way that they related to others. Superficially, they seemed unconcerned about the separation, but denied any affection or response to the mother when eventually reunited.

Robertson's research shows that maternal deprivation does seem to cause emotional difficulties for children. However, further research showed that long-term effects on development could be prevented by providing high quality **substitute emotional care** with a single substitute caregiver.

The importance of attachment between infant and parent/carer

When children receive warm, responsive care, they feel safe and secure. Secure attachments are the basis of *all* the child's future relationships. Because babies experience relationships through their senses, it is the expression of love that affects how a young child develops and helps to shape later learning and behaviour. They will grow to be more curious, get along better with other children, and perform better in school than children who are less securely attached. All parents find separation difficult, whether or not they have formed a strong attachment with their child.

Key term

Attachment – A warm, affectionate and supportive bond between child and carer that enables the child to develop secure relationships.

The importance of loving, secure relationships

Babies learn and begin to make sense of the world through responsive care and loving, secure relationships. These relationships are equally important with their primary carer(s) and with their key person in the setting.

Babies and children who do not have loving, secure relationships with the important people in their lives are likely to find it difficult to settle and to enjoy being in the setting. This in turn may lead to difficulties with concentration, with engaging with others and with their general ability to learn.

The possible effects of poor quality attachments

When babies learn that they can rely completely on at least one person for their physical and emotional needs, they form what is known as a **secure attachment**. A baby or child who has internalised a strong attachment figure is then able to separate from that attachment figure and make relationships with other important adults in their lives. Recent research has shown that settings that do not provide for a strong attachment figure can cause harm to babies and children.

Emotional security

Babies and children need to be able to trust others in order to feel emotionally secure. When there has been insecure or poor attachment – whether it is with their primary carer or parent, with adults in a setting, or both – they begin to show anti-social behaviour and aggression towards others.

Effects on mental health

Babies and young children with poor quality attachments may show less interest in exploring their environment than those with secure attachments. They may also display anxiety and even depression later on in life, although it is difficult to predict the cause and effect relationship as there are many other factors at work.

Effects on relationships with parents and professional carers

A baby's primary attachment is at its most intense between the ages of six months and one year, and it is then that the baby is likely to be acutely distressed when being left with a new carer. Babies who have experienced poor attachments at home may not feel able to trust the new carer enough to be able to form an attachment relationship. This is an unconscious self-defence mechanism – the baby does not want to experience emotional distress again.

Case Study — Attachments

Maya is 11 months old and has recently started attending a local Children's Centre. Jennie, her key person, has observed that she appears uninterested in the adults in the centre, and also does not seem to notice a difference between regular staff and strangers who visit. Maya shows no anxiety or distress when her mother leaves her everyday, and Jennie is worried that there does not seem to be a close relationship between Maya and her mother. She has also observed that Maya does not seem to engage properly with play activities – she appears listless and apathetic, but rarely cries.

What should Jennie do in this situation to ensure that Maya's needs are being met?

Temperament

Temperament is the term used to describe the different styles of behaviour in infancy; it interacts with experience to produce **personality**. The individual baby's temperament may have an influence on the quality of **attachment** to the main carer:

- A mother who is unresponsive and shows little sensitivity to her baby will undoubtedly affect her baby's behaviour.
- A baby who likes to be cuddled and obviously wants plenty of contact with their primary carer tends to be more placid and easy to look after.

- A baby who actively resists being hugged or held tight even when ill or tired tends to be much more active and restless generally.

Treating each baby as a unique individual

Although it is important to understand about differences in temperament and about how personality and temperament 'clashes' occur, we should always be wary of applying labels to children (and adults) as this leads to stereotyping and loss of self-esteem. It is very important that adults working with young children do not favour those with less challenging temperaments; and it is equally important that they do not discriminate against children with more challenging temperaments.

Section 2: The role of the professional in promoting development

Working in partnership with parents/carers and families

Parents choose child care for many different reasons:

- Many parents need personal space away from their child for part of the day. This may be while the family adjusts to a new baby, or while the parent catches up with chores or simply relaxes.
- Some parents want full-time nursery places so that they can work, because they positively *want* to work; other parents want full-time nursery places because they *have* to work, for economic reasons.
- Some parents will be required to bring their child to the nursery as a matter of child protection – they will have no choice in the matter.
- Other parents only want part-time nursery places. This might facilitate part-time work, or they may want their child to move in a wider social circle and to have new and interesting experiences.

- Some parents think it is important for their child to have some experiences away from them. Other parents will want to join in with their child – perhaps not every day, but regularly.

Parents and staff working together

See Chapter 5, pages 219–21 for guidance on working with parents.

Sharing information

Practitioners will need a certain amount of information from the baby's parents or carers. They record information about the baby's routines, interests and preferences; also they need to know about any medical conditions, allergies or special needs. Parents need to know about:

- how the key worker system works
- how their baby will be helped if he or she becomes upset or needs a change of clothes
- how they can be updated with their baby's development and progress.

Information about the individual baby's progress will be communicated to the parents or carers in the form of a daily or weekly diary, or a similar system.

The role of play in development when working with babies

Play is important because it helps babies to:

- learn about and to understand the world around them
- socialise and form relationships with their primary carers.

From a very early age babies learn best by exploring the world through their senses – touch, sight, hearing, taste and smell – and through their movements. In other words they learn by:

- doing
- seeing
- listening

- tasting
- smelling
- touching.

During the first year of life, babies mostly play with objects, with someone they love, or by themselves (**solitary play**). There are many ways in which you can play with a baby; babies do not need a room full of expensive toys in order to play. The most important part of a baby's development is to experience **continuous attention** and **affection** from their parents, caregivers, relations and other significant adults.

Supporting play with communication and language

Talking to babies is easier for some people than for others; this applies to the baby's parents as well as to carers. Some people are naturally chatty; others are naturally quiet and may feel silly talking to a baby who cannot 'talk' back to them. While you cannot change your personality, there are a number of ways in which you can communicate effectively with babies:

- Always listen to babies; when they smile at you or make cooing sounds, try to answer in words. You do not have to keep up a running commentary – you just have to be responsive to the baby's efforts to communicate.
- Try to talk normally, without trying to simplify your language, so that it feels natural and like a real conversation with a friend.
- Tell babies what you are doing whenever you are handling them; for example, if you are feeding a baby, talk about the food and about what the next course will be.
- Ask questions, such as 'Was that nice?' and 'Where's it gone?' The baby will answer with a gesture or a facial expression that speaks as clearly as any words.
- Bath time is a good time to talk to babies; talk to them and tell them what you are doing: 'I'm just going to put some soap on your tummy now.'
- Read picture books to babies; point to the pictures and name them. Even though young babies cannot understand what is going on in the book, they will be very responsive and will enjoy taking part in the experience.

- Learn some simple nursery rhymes and action songs; babies love to hear old favourites. Try to find out some simple rhymes or songs from other cultures too.

Playful activities with babies

Playing alongside babies helps them to learn in many ways – including the social skills they need to play with other children. It is useful to use a range of games and activities, so that you can follow the interests and preferences of individual children. Many babies develop favourite play activities, which they want to repeat many times. The following examples are popular with babies (and with toddlers):

- **Peek-a-boo**: sit close in front of the baby and cover your face with your hands, then open them and gently say: 'Boo!' You can vary the game by peeping round the side of your hands or moving to different parts of the room.
- **Hand and finger puppets**: have one puppet for yourself and one for the baby. Create your own stories, using funny voices and allow time for a response.
- **Water play**: fill a low, wide container with a few centimetres of water and place it on the ground. Float small objects such as flowers or corks in the water and let the baby reach and splash. Always supervise children when playing with water.
- **Hide and seek**: show the baby a toy, then hide it under a towel or small blanket and help the baby to find it.
- **Stacking beakers and blocks**: with the baby watching, build a tower and then show how to knock it down. After a few demonstrations, the baby will probably want to knock it down him- or herself.
- **Action rhymes**: make a language game for toddlers from the song, 'Here we go round the mulberry bush'. Touch various body parts and sing, 'This is the way we touch our nose … head … hand …' and so on.

Treasure basket play

The use of treasure baskets for sitting babies is discussed in Chapter 4, page 194. In this type of play,

the adult stays close to the baby for reassurance, but does not interact or initiate conversations. This is an ideal time to observe the baby (see below).

In Practice

Playing with babies

❏ Observe the baby's current interests and plan an appropriate activity.

❏ Do not rush the baby – allow them to play for as long as they like in their chosen way.

❏ Encourage the baby with friendly gestures, smiles and words.

❏ Allow the baby to repeat actions and games.

❏ Encourage 'conversations', talking and then waiting for a response.

Any toys and activities that you use with the babies in your care should be chosen carefully (see guidelines below).

Guidelines for selecting toys for small babies

1 Is the toy or plaything clean and safe?
   - no rough or broken edges
   - no small parts which could become loose and swallowed, for example check the eyes on a soft toy
   - no strings to become tangled around a baby's neck
   - not so heavy that a young baby could be injured
   - no toxic paint
   - complies with safety standards (if a bought toy, see Chapter 4, page 166).

2 Is the toy or activity appropriate for the child's developmental stage?
   - If using household objects – wooden spoons, saucepans, keys or empty plastic containers – check that the baby is closely supervised.
   - Once the baby is able to walk, even if 'cruising' by holding onto furniture, new safety checks will need to be made.

Using observation methods to assess development

The importance of regular observation has been emphasised throughout this book. You can use a variety of the methods and techniques for observations shown in Chapter 2 (Section 2). The observations can then be used to help you plan for the individual baby's development, and also to evaluate the success of any particular activities.

In Practice

Observation of a baby with a treasure basket

By observing closely while a baby is exploring the objects in a treasure basket, you will be able to learn a great deal about his or her interests, skills and preferences. You can use these observations to build up a picture of the baby as an individual. Share your observations with the baby's parents and use the knowledge you have gained to plan what to offer the baby next to engage his or her curiosity and extend his or her learning and development. Photographs of the baby handling the various objects will help to illustrate the baby's learning and enjoyment of the activity. (Remember to ask for parental permission before taking photographs.)

Planning care and activities to promote development and support the welfare of the child

Babies in a group setting need a carefully planned care and learning environment. The provision of a safe, secure and stimulating environment is discussed in Chapter 4, and Chapter 7 gives guidelines for providing learning activities in the child's first year.

All babies depend completely on an adult to meet all their needs, but how these needs are met will vary considerably according to family circumstances, culture and the personalities of the baby and the caring adult. To achieve and maintain healthy growth and all-round (holistic) development, certain basic needs must be fulfilled: see Figure 13.4.

The **key worker system** is particularly important for providing continuity of care. Babies need to be cared for by just one person most of the time, so that they can form a close relationship. This also helps to minimise the difficulty of separation for babies from their parents or primary carers.

The importance of routines

Routines around mealtimes and bedtimes can be very useful in helping babies and toddlers to adapt both physically and emotionally to a daily pattern, which suits both them *and* those caring for them. This is especially helpful during times of transition

Figure 13.4 The needs of babies and children

and change in their lives, such as starting nursery or moving house. If certain parts of the day remain familiar, they can cope better with new experiences. Having routines for everyday activities also ensures that care is consistent and of a high quality. This does not mean that caring for babies is, or should be, in itself a routine activity. Anyone looking after babies should be able to adapt to their individual needs, which will change from day to day. Therefore, you need to be flexible in your approach and allow, whenever feasible, the individual baby to set the pattern for the day – as long as all the baby's needs are met.

Routines for feeding babies in their first year are discussed in Chapter 11: Food and Nutrition. Routines for the care needs of babies and young children appear in Chapter 4, Section 4.

Care for a baby's skin

A baby's skin is soft and delicate, yet forms a tough pliant covering for the body. The skin has many important functions:

- Protection – it protects underlying organs and, when unbroken, prevents germs entering the body.
- Sensation – each square centimetre of skin contains up to 250 nerve endings called receptors. These detect different feelings, such as touch, cold, warmth, pressure, pain and hair movement.
- Secretion of oil (sebum) – this lubricates the skin and gives hair its shine.

- Manufacture of vitamin D – vitamin D is made when the skin is exposed to sunlight and is essential for healthy bones and teeth. Black skin protects against sunburn but is less efficient at making vitamin D, and black children may need a supplement of vitamin D in the winter.
- Excretion – the skin excretes waste products in sweat.
- Temperature regulation – the hypothalamus in the brain controls body temperature by causing the skin to release sweat. This evaporates from the skin's surface, cooling the body.

A young baby does not have to be bathed every day because only the bottom, face and neck, and skin creases get dirty, and the skin may tend to dryness. If a bath is not given daily, the baby should have the important body parts cleansed thoroughly – a process known as 'topping and tailing'. This process limits the amount of undressing and helps to maintain good skin condition. Whatever routine is followed, the newborn baby needs to be handled gently but firmly, and with confidence. Most babies learn to enjoy the sensation of water and are greatly affected by your attitude. The more relaxed and unhurried you are, the more enjoyable the whole experience will be.

Topping and tailing

Babies do not like having their skin exposed to the air, so should be undressed for the shortest possible time. Always ensure the room is warm, no less than 20 °C (68 °F) and that there are no draughts. Warm a large, soft towel on a not-too-hot radiator and have it ready to wrap the baby afterwards.

Collect all the equipment you will need before you start:

- changing mat
- water that has been boiled and allowed to cool

- cotton-wool swabs
- lidded buckets for soiled nappies and used swabs, and clothes
- bowl of warm water
- protective cream such as Vaseline
- clean clothes and a nappy.

Guidelines: a topping and tailing routine

- Wash your hands.
- Remove the baby's outer clothes, leaving on her vest and nappy.
- Wrap the baby in the towel, keeping his or her arms inside.
- Using two separate pieces of cotton wool (one for each eye; this will prevent any infection passing from one eye to the other), squeezed in the boiled water, gently wipe the baby's eyes in one movement from the inner corner outwards.
- Gently wipe all around the face and behind the ears. Lift the chin and wipe gently under the folds of skin. Dry each area thoroughly by patting with a soft towel or dry cotton wool.
- Unwrap the towel and take the baby's vest off, raise each arm separately and wipe the armpit carefully as the folds of skin rub together here and can become quite sore – again dry thoroughly and dust with baby powder if used.
- Until the cord has dropped off, make sure that it is kept clean and dry.
- Wipe and dry the baby's hands.
- Take the nappy off and place in lidded bucket.
- Clean the baby's bottom with moist swabs, then wash with soap and water; rinse well with flannel or sponge, pat dry and apply protective cream if necessary.
- Put on clean nappy and clothes.

Bathing the baby

When the bath is given will depend on family routines, but it is best not to bath the baby immediately after a feed, as she may be sick. Some babies love being bathed; others dislike even being undressed. Bath time has several benefits for babies, as it provides:

- the opportunity to kick and exercise
- the opportunity to clean and refresh the skin and hair
- the opportunity for the carer to observe any skin problems, such as rashes, bruises, etc.
- a valuable time for communication between the baby and the carer
- a time for relaxation and enjoyment.

Before you start ensure the room is warm and draught-free, and collect all necessary equipment:

- small bowl of boiled water and cotton swabs (as for 'topping and tailing' procedure)
- changing mat
- two warmed towels
- brush and comb
- baby bath filled with warm water – test temperature with your elbow, not with hands as these are insensitive to high temperatures; the water should feel warm but not hot
- lidded buckets
- clean nappy and clothes
- toiletries and nail scissors.

Guidelines for a bathing routine

- Undress the baby except for their nappy and wrap him or her in a towel while you clean their face, as for 'topping and tailing'.
- Wash the baby's hair before putting him or her in the bath: support their head and neck with one hand, hold them over the bath and wash their head with baby shampoo or soap; rinse their head thoroughly and dry with second towel.
- Unwrap the towel around their body, remove the nappy and place it in bucket.
- Remove any soiling from the baby's bottom with cotton wool; remember to clean baby girls from front to back to avoid germs from faeces entering the urethra or vagina.
- Lay the baby in the crook of one arm and gently soap his or her body front and back with baby soap. (If preferred, use baby bath liquid added to the bath beforehand.)
- Lift the baby off the towel and gently lower him or her into the water, holding them with one arm around the back of the neck and shoulders and holding the far arm to stop him or her slipping.
- Talk to the baby and gently swish the water to rinse off the soap, paying particular attention to all skin creases – under arms, between legs and behind knees. Allow time for the baby to splash and kick, but avoid chilling.
- Lift the baby out and wrap in a warm towel; dry him or her thoroughly by patting, not rubbing.
- Baby oil or moisturiser may now be applied to the skin; do not use talcum powder with oils as it will form lumps and cause irritation.
- Check if fingernails and toenails need cutting. Always use blunt-ended nail scissors and avoid cutting nails too short.
- Dress the baby in clean nappy and clothes.

Additional guidelines on keeping babies clean

- Cultural preferences in skin care should be observed; cocoa butter or special moisturisers are usually applied to babies with black skin and their bodies may be massaged with oil after bathing.
- Always put cold water in the bath before adding hot – many babies have been severely scalded by contact with the hot surface of the bath.
- Do not wear dangling earrings or sharp brooches and keep your own nails short and clean.
- Never leave a baby or child under ten years alone in the bath, even for a few seconds.
- Do not top up with hot water while the baby is in the bath; make sure that taps are turned off tightly as even small drops of hot water can cause scalds.
- From a few months old, babies may be bathed in the big bath, keeping the water shallow and following the same guidelines regarding temperature and safety. A non-slip mat placed in the bottom of the bath will prevent slipping.
- Avoid talcum powder because of the risk of inhalation or allergy; if it is used, place on your hands first and then gently smooth it on to completely dry skin.
- Do not use cotton-wool buds – they are not necessary and can be dangerous when poked inside a baby's ears or nose, which are self-cleansing anyway.
- Nail care should be included in the bathing routine. A young baby's nails should be cut when necessary. Do this after a bath when they are soft. Some parents use their own teeth to bite them gently off.
- Hair should be washed daily in the first few months, but shampoo is not necessary every day. A little bath lotion added to the bath water could be gradually worked into the baby's scalp until a lather forms and may then be rinsed off using a wrung-out flannel.

- If the baby dislikes having his or her hair washed, try to keep hair washing separate from bath time so that the two are not associated as unpleasant events.

Care for a baby's bottom

Excretion

The first 'stool' a newborn baby passes is **meconium** – a greenish-black, treacle-like substance which is present in the baby's bowels before birth and is usually passed within 48 hours of birth. Once the baby starts to feed on milk, the stools change:

- A breast-fed baby has fluid, yellow mustard-coloured stools which do not smell unpleasant.
- A bottle-fed baby has more formed stools which may smell slightly.

Babies pass urine very frequently; bottle-fed babies tend to pass stools less often than breast-fed babies. Constipation can occur in bottle-fed babies but can be relieved by giving extra boiled water to drink.

Nappies

The choice of nappies will depend on several factors: convenience, cost, personal preference and concern for the environment. There are two main types of nappy:

1. **Fabric nappies** – these are made from cotton terry towelling and come in different qualities and thickness. Fabric nappies may be squares or shaped to fit. The latest style is similar in shape to the disposable nappy and has popper fastenings. If using fabric squares, you will also need special nappy safety pins and six pairs of plastic pants. Disposable one-way liners may be used with towelling nappies to keep wetness away from the baby's skin and to make solid matter easier to dispose of, by flushing down the toilet.
2. **Disposable nappies** – these are nappy, liner and plastic pants all in one and are available in a wide range of designs. Some have more padding at the front for boys and there are different absorbencies for day and night time use. Some makes have resealable tapes so that you can check if the nappy is clean.

Research Activity

What sort of nappies?

Research the advantages and disadvantages of terry towelling and disposable nappies, including the following information:

- costs – initial outlay for purchase of nappies, liners, pants and continuing costs of laundry
- the effects of each method on the environment – chemicals used in laundering; disposal in landfill sites
- convenience and suitability for the purpose.

Changing a nappy

Young babies will need several changes of nappy each day – whenever the nappy is wet or soiled. See Chapter 4, pages 205–6 for guidelines on nappy changing.

Nappy rash

Almost all babies have occasional bouts of redness and soreness in the nappy area. This may be caused by leaving wet and dirty nappies on too long, poor washing techniques, infections, skin disorders such as eczema or seborrhoeic dermatitis, or reaction to creams or detergents.

For information on disposing of waste in the early years setting, see Chapter 4.

Care of the feet

- Feet should always be washed and dried thoroughly, especially between the toes, and clean socks should be put on every day.
- All-in-one baby suits must be large enough not to cramp the baby's growing feet.
- Toenails should be cut straight across, not down into the corners.

Care for a baby's teeth

See Chapter 4, page 205 for detailed information and guidance on caring for a baby's teeth.

Type	Causes	Treatment
Candidiasis or thrush dermatitis – The rash is pink and pimply and is seen in the folds of the groin, around the anus and in the genital area.	• Caused by an organism called candida albicans, a yeast fungus which lives naturally in many parts of the body. • In breastfed babies, it is sometimes caused by the mother taking a course of antibiotics. • In bottle-fed babies, it is sometimes caused by the teats not being inadequately cleaned and sterilised.	• Use a special antifungal cream at each nappy change (this is prescribed by the doctor). • Do not use zinc and castor oil cream until the infection has cleared, as the thrush organism thrives on it. • If oral thrush is also present, a prescribed ointment may be used.
Ammonia dermatitis – This produces the most severe type of nappy rash; the rash is bright red, may be ulcerated and covers the genital area; the ammonia smells very strongly and causes the baby a lot of burning pain.	• Caused when the ammonia present in the baby's urine and stools reacts with the baby's skin. • It is more common in bottle-fed babies because their stools are more alkaline, which allows the organisms to thrive.	• Wash with mild soap and water, and dry gently. • Expose the baby's bottom to fresh air as much as possible. • Only use creams if advised to do so, and leave plastic pants off. • If using towelling nappies, a solution of 30 ml vinegar to 2.5 litres of warm water should be used as a final rinsing solution to neutralise the ammonia.

Table 13.1 The most common types of nappy rash

Teething

Some babies cut their teeth with no ill effects; others may experience:

- general fretfulness (they may rub the mouth or ears)
- red or sore patches around the mouth
- diarrhoea
- a bright red flush on one or both cheeks, and on the chin
- dribbling.

Teething should not be treated as an illness, but babies will need comforting if in pain. Teething rings and hard rusks usually provide relief. Teething powders and gels are not advised, as they are dangerous if given in large quantities. Infant paracetamol may be helpful in relieving pain but is unsuitable for babies under three months unless advised by the doctor.

Fresh air and sunlight

Babies benefit from being outside in the fresh air for a while each day. See Chapter 4 for guidance and information on how fresh air benefits babies.

Sleep and rest

Everyone needs sleep, but the amount that babies sleep varies enormously, and will depend on the maturity of the brain (the pre-term baby may sleep for long periods) and on the need for food. Sleep is divided into two distinct states:

1 **Rapid eye movement (REM)**, which is termed active sleep
2 **Non-rapid eye movement (NREM)**, which is termed quiet sleep.

In REM sleep the mind is active and is processing daytime emotional experiences. In NREM sleep the body rests and restoration occurs. In babies under one year, more of the sleep is active (REM). It is important not to wake babies during deep sleep, as it plays a vital part in restoring energy levels.

Few aspects of parenthood are more stressful than months of broken nights. Carers could try the following strategies to encourage babies to adopt different sleep patterns for day and night.

Guidelines for encouraging a sleeping routine

- Allow the baby time to settle alone so that he or she begins to develop his or her own way of going to sleep. Some babies do cry for a short period as they settle; leave the baby but stay within hearing distance and check after five minutes to see if he or she is comfortable.

- Give the baby plenty of stimulation during the day by talking and playing with him or her when she is awake.

- Try to make night time feeds as unstimulating as possible; feed, change and settle the baby in his or her cot.

- Make bedtime at night into a routine; by repeating the same process each night, the baby is made to feel secure and comfortable. These are both good aids to sleep.

Discussion point

Two parents in your nursery are following the advice given in *The Contented Little Baby Book* by Gina Ford. One of the pieces of advice is that all babies should be placed in a darkened room to have a sleep at 11 am each day. They have each asked their baby's key worker to make sure that this happens every day. Discuss the following:

1. Do you think the nursery could or should accommodate the parents' wishes?

2. What would happen in your own setting if such a request were made?

Guidelines for establishing a bedtime routine

Between three and five months, most babies are ready to settle into a bedtime routine:

- Give the baby a bath or wash and put on a clean nappy and nightwear.

- Take him or her to say goodnight to other members of the household.

- Carry the baby into his or her room, telling him or her in a gentle voice that it is time for bed.

- Give the last breast- or bottle-feed in the room where the baby sleeps.

- Sing a song or lullaby to help settle the baby, while gently rocking him or her in your arms.

- Wrap the baby securely and settle him or her into the cot or cradle, saying goodnight.

- If the baby likes it, gently 'pat' him or her to sleep.

- The routine can be adapted as the baby grows. Advice from FSID (The Foundation for the Study of Infant Deaths) is that the safest place for a baby to sleep is in a cot in the parents' room for the first six months. After 6 months, the baby can be safely left in his or her own room.

How to recognise developmental delay or sensory impairment

Most babies and children reach important 'milestones' within the expected timeframes, but in some cases developmental delays can occur. It is important to recognise when a baby may not be developing at an average pace, so that appropriate support and possible treatment can be provided. By familiarising yourself with the **normative development** of babies (see Chapter 2), you will be able to observe babies in your care and to recognise if there are any signs of delay. Parents are usually the first to notice if there appears to be something wrong with their baby.

Signs of general developmental delay include:

- late smiling
- lack of curiosity in their environment
- lack of responsiveness
- difficulties with chewing.

Children who are **blind** or who have **visual difficulties** may show delay in the following areas:

- Delayed exploration skills, and they may take longer to walk (usually between 18 to 24 months).
- Their first smile may be delayed.
- Language skills may be normal, but there could be a delayed understanding of 'I' and 'you'. They find it difficult to understand the properties of objects and shapes.
- Difficulty in following objects or people with her eyes.

Children who are **deaf** or who have **hearing difficulties** may show delay in the following areas:

- does not startle to loud noises
- does not develop sounds or words that would be appropriate for the age.

Babies who were born **pre-term** or were **light-for-dates** may take longer to reach some of the milestones than otherwise, although this only applies in the first year.

How to provide a safe, hygienic environment in a variety of settings

There are many safety issues that must be addressed in any setting caring for babies. These are mostly concerned with prevention of accidents and are discussed in Chapter 4.

Sudden infant death syndrome (SIDS)

Sudden infant death syndrome is often called 'cot death'. It is the term applied to the sudden unexplained and unexpected death of an infant. The reasons for cot deaths are complicated and the cause is still unknown. Although cot death is the commonest cause of death in babies up to one year old, it is still very rare, occurring in approximately two out of every 1,000 babies. Recent research has identified various risk factors, and the Foundation for the Study of Infant Deaths has written the following guidelines.

Guidelines for parents from the Foundation for the Study of Infant Deaths

- Cut smoking in pregnancy – fathers too!
- Do not let anyone smoke in the same room as your baby.
- Place your baby on the back to sleep.
- Do not let your baby get too hot.
- Keep baby's head uncovered: place your baby with their feet to the foot of the cot, to prevent wriggling down under the covers.
- If your baby is unwell, seek medical advice promptly.
- The safest place for your baby to sleep is in a cot in your room for the first six months.
- It is dangerous to share a bed with your baby if you or your partner:
  - are smokers (no matter where or when you smoke)
  - have been drinking alcohol
  - take drugs or medication that makes you drowsy
  - feel very tired.

It is very dangerous to sleep together on a sofa, armchair or settee.

Guidelines for reducing the risk of cot death

- The room where an infant sleeps should be at a temperature that is comfortable for lightly clothed adults (16–20°C).
- If the baby is a natural tummy-sleeper, keep turning him or her over and tuck in securely with blankets (as long as the weather is not too hot); a musical mobile may help to keep him or her happy while lying on his or her back.
- Always invest in a brand new mattress if the baby's cot is second-hand.
- A pillow should never be used for sleeping; if the baby is snuffly or has a blocked nose, place a small pillow **under** the mattress, but make sure he or she does not slide down to the end of his or her cot.
- Never allow the baby to come into contact with smoky rooms; ask visitors not to smoke in the house. The risk factor increases with the number of cigarettes smoked.
- Learn to recognise the signs and symptoms of illness and know how to respond.
- Use a room thermometer if necessary and check the baby's temperature by feeling his or her tummy, making sure your hands are warm beforehand.
- Babies over one month of age should never wear hats indoors, as small babies gain and lose heat very quickly through their heads.
- Learn and practise on a special baby resuscitation mannequin how to perform artificial ventilation and cardiac massage. This should always be practised under the supervision of a qualified first-aider.

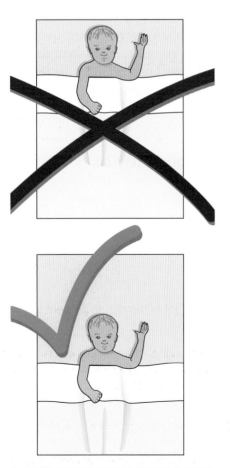

Figure 13.5 Preventing SIDS: the feet-to-foot position

Research Activity

Sudden infant death syndrome (SIDS)

In groups, prepare a display that details the risk factors implicated in sudden infant death syndrome. Using the information provided, make a poster for each risk factor and state clearly the precautions that should be taken to prevent cot death.

Exercise

Exercise strengthens and develops muscles. It also helps to promote sleep, as the body needs to relax after physical activity. Carers of young babies can provide opportunities for exercise in the following ways:

- Give plenty of opportunities for the baby to practise each new aspect of physical development as she becomes capable of it.
- Allow times for wriggling on the floor without being hindered by nappy or clothes.
- Allow freedom to look around, to reach and to grasp.
- Give opportunities to roll, crawl and eventually walk around the furniture safely.
- Provide objects and toys to exercise hand–eye coordination.

- After she has had her first 5-in-1 vaccination, the baby can be taken to special baby sessions at the local swimming pool.

Crying in young babies

Crying is a baby's way of expressing her needs. Finding out why a baby is crying is often a matter of elimination, so it is important that all carers should understand the physical and emotional needs of a baby at each stage of development (see Table 13.2).

Persistent crying

Some babies do cry a great deal more than others, and are difficult to soothe and comfort. Parents and carers can feel quite desperate through lack of sleep and may develop personal problems; they may suffer guilt at not being able to make their baby happy, or lack confidence in caring for her. Such feelings of desperation and exhaustion can unfortunately result in physical violence to the baby – throwing him or her into the cot, shaking or even hitting him or her. Parents experiencing such stress need a great deal of support.

Help and advice

Often just talking to others helps the carer to feel less isolated. Self-help groups such as Cry-sis or the National Childbirth Trust Postnatal Support System can help by offering support from someone who has been through the same problem. Talking to the health visitor or GP may help, and some areas run clinics with a programme to stop the 'spiral' of helplessness.

Guidelines for helping a crying baby

- Make sure the baby is not hungry or thirsty.
- Check that the baby is not too hot or cold.
- Check that the baby is not physically ill (see pages 357–8 for signs of illness in babies).
- Check if the baby's nappy needs changing.
- Treat colic or teething problems.
- Cuddle the baby and try rocking gently in your arms (the most effective rate of rocking is at least 60 rocks a minute; the easiest way to achieve this rapid and soothing rocking without getting exhausted is to walk while rocking her from side to side).
- Rock the baby in a cradle or pram.
- Talk and sing to the baby.
- Take the baby for a walk or a car ride.
- Leave the baby with someone else and take a break.
- Play soothing music or a womb-sounds recording.
- Talk to a health visitor, GP or a parent's helpline.
- Accept that some babies will cry whatever you do.
- Remember that this phase will soon pass.

If the crying ever feels too much to bear:

- Take a deep breath and let it out slowly. Put the baby down in a safe place, like a cot or a pram. Go into another room and sit quietly for a few minutes, perhaps with a cup of tea and the television or radio on to help take your mind off the crying. When you feel calmer, go back to the baby.
- Ask a friend or relative to take over for a while.
- Try not to get angry with the baby. He or she will instinctively recognise your displeasure and will probably cry even more.
- Never let things get so bad that you feel desperate. There are lots of organisations that can help at the end of a telephone line.

Hunger:

This is the most common cause of crying. It is quite likely unless the baby has just been fed. Breast-fed and bottle-fed babies should be fed on demand in the early weeks. By the age of six months, the baby will probably need solid foods.

Being undressed

Most new babies hate being undressed and bathed, because they miss the contact between fabric and bare skin. One solution is to place a towel or shawl across the baby's chest and tummy when he or she is naked.

Discomfort:

Until they can turn themselves over, babies rely on an adult to change their position; babies show marked preferences for sleeping positions.

Nappy needs changing:

Some babies dislike being in a wet or dirty nappy and there may be nappy rash.

Twitches and jerks:

Most new babies make small twitching and jerking movements as they are dropping off to sleep. Some babies are startled awake and find it difficult to settle to sleep because of these twitches. Wrapping a baby up firmly – or swaddling – usually solves the problem.

Over-tired or over-stimulated:

Some babies can refuse to settle if there is too much bustle going on around them, e.g. loud noises, too much bouncing or bright lights in a shopping centre; take him or her somewhere quiet and try rhythmical rocking, patting, and generally soothing him or her.

Pain or illness:

A baby might have a cold or snuffles and be generally fretful or may have an itchy rash, such as eczema. (For signs and symptoms of illness in babies, see Chapter 9.)

Allergy:

An intolerance of cow's milk could cause crying; seek medical advice.

Thirst:

In particularly hot weather, babies may be thirsty and can be given cool boiled water. Breastfed babies may be offered an extra feed as breast milk is a good thirst-quencher.

Feeling too hot or too cold:

Temperature control is not well-developed in the young baby; if too hot, he or she will look red in the face, feel very warm and may be sweaty around the neck folds; loosen clothes and wrappings and remove some layers of bedding, but watch for signs of chilling. If too cold, he or she may also have a red face or may be pale; to check, feel the hands, feet, tummy and the back of the neck; cuddle the baby, wrap a blanket around him or her and try a warm feed.

Boredom/need for physical contact:

Babies find being cuddled or carried reassuring; talk to him or her and provide interesting objects for them to look at and a mobile; put pram under a tree or near a washing line so that he or she can see movements (NB: remember to fix a cat net to prevent insects and other unwanted visitors).

Colic:

If the baby cries after being fed or has long bouts of crying, especially in the evening, he or she may be suffering from colic.

Child abuse:

A baby who has been abused in any way may cry and the carer should seek help from appropriate professionals.

Table 13.2 Causes of crying

Clothing and footwear

The layette

The layette is the baby's first set of clothes. Many shops specialising in baby goods supply complete layettes, and there is a vast range of clothing available. Baby clothes should be:

- loose and comfortable to allow for ease of movement; as babies grow rapidly, care should be taken that all-in-one stretch suits do not cramp tiny feet – there should always be growing space at the feet to avoid pressure on the soft bones
- easy to wash and dry, as babies need changing often; natural fibres (such as cotton and wool mixtures) are more comfortable; any garment for babies up to three months old must carry a permanent label showing that it has passed the low flammability test for slow burning
- easy to put on and take off – avoid ribbons, bows and lacy-knit fabrics which can trap small fingers and toes
- non-irritant – clothes should be lightweight, soft and warm; some synthetic fibres can be too cold in winter as they do not retain body heat, and too hot in the summer as they do not absorb sweat or allow the skin pores to 'breathe'.

Note also that:

- several layers of clothing are warmer than one thick garment
- clothing needs will vary according to the season, and the baby will need protective clothes such as a pram suit, bonnet or sun hat, mittens and booties.

Footwear for babies

Babies' feet are very soft and pliable. When choosing footwear bear the following in mind:

- There must be room for the baby to wiggle his or her toes in a baby stretch suit or in socks or tights.
- Socks should have a high cotton content so that moisture from the feet can escape; make sure that socks are not too loose as the friction can cause blisters.

- Soft corduroy shoes called padders keep a baby's feet warm when crawling or walking, but should not be worn if the soles become slippery.
- Outside shoes should not be worn until the baby has learnt to walk unaided, and then should be fitted properly by a trained shoe fitter.

Activity

Clothing a new baby

You have been asked to advise on the purchase of a layette for a newborn baby.

- Make a list of the items you consider to be essential, excluding nappies and waterproof pants.

- Visit several shops (or catalogues) and find out the cost of all the items on your list.

- Evaluate your selection, checking:
  - the ease of washing and drying
  - the design and colours used – are you reinforcing the stereotypes of pink for girls or blue for boys?
  - the safety aspects – no fancy bows, ties etc.
  - the suitability of the fabrics used
  - the quantity of clothes needed
  - the final cost of the layette.

✓ Progress check

- Several layers of clothing are warmer than one thick garment.
- Clothing needs will vary according to the season, and the baby will need protective clothes, such as a pram suit, bonnet or sun hat, mittens and booties.
- Natural fibres – such as cotton or cotton and wool mixtures – are more comfortable and allow the skin pores to 'breathe'.
- All-in-one baby stretch suits, tights and socks must always have growing space at the feet to avoid pressure on the soft bones.

Equipment for a young baby

Babies need somewhere to sleep, to be bathed, to feed, to sit, to play and to be transported.

For sleeping

Cradles and '**Moses baskets**' (wicker baskets with carrying handles) can be used as beds for a young baby, but are unsuitable for transporting the baby outside or in a car.

Prams and **carrycots** come in a wide variety of designs; safety mattresses are available which are ventilated at the head section to prevent the risk of suffocation. Prams can be bought second-hand or hired for the first year of a baby's life; they must meet the following safety requirements:

- Brakes should be efficient and tested regularly.
- A shopping basket should be positioned underneath to prevent shopping bags being hung on the handles and causing overbalancing.
- There must be anchor points for a safety harness.
- The vehicle must be stable, easy to steer and the right height for the carer to be able to push easily without stooping.
- The mattress must be firm enough to support the baby's back.

Often a baby will move into a **cot** for sleeping when he or she has outgrown his carrycot, but cots are also suitable for newborn babies. Cots usually have slatted sides – which allow the baby to see out – with one side able to be lowered and secured by safety catches. Safety requirements are as follows:

- Bars must be no more than 7 cm apart.
- Safety catches must be child-proof.
- The mattress should fit snugly with no gaps.
- Cot bumpers (foam padded screens tied at the head end of the cot) are widely used but not recommended by safety experts.
- If the cot has been painted, check that lead-free paint has been used.

A **travel cot** is a folding cot with fabric sides, suitable for temporary use only; it is especially useful if the family travels away from home and it can double as a playpen when the mattress is removed.

Blankets and sheets

These should be easy to wash and dry as they will need frequent laundering. The ideal fabric for sheets is brushed cotton; blankets are often made from cellular acrylic fabric, which is lightweight, warm and easily washable.

Figure 13.6 A traditional cot

For bathing

Baby baths are easily transportable (when empty) plastic basins that can be used with the fixed base bought for a carrycot, or within the adult bath. After a few months, the baby can be bathed in the adult bath; carers should guard against back strain, cover hot taps because of the risk of burns and always use a non-slip rubber mat in the base of the bath.

Note: Never leave a baby alone in any bath, even for a few seconds.

For feeding

If the baby is being bottle-fed, eight to ten bottles and teats, sterilising equipment and formula milk will be required. If he or she is being breast-fed, one bottle and teat is useful to provide extra water or fruit juice. A **highchair**, with fixed safety harness, is useful for the older baby.

For sitting

A **bouncing cradle** is a soft fabric seat which can be used from birth to about six months; it is generally enjoyed by babies and their carers as it is easily transported from room to room, encouraging the baby's full involvement in everyday activities. It should always be placed on the floor, never on a worktop or bed, as even young babies can 'bounce' themselves off these surfaces and fall.

For playing

Babies like to be held where they can see faces clearly, especially the carer's face; they prefer toys which are brightly coloured and which make a noise. In the first three months, provide:

- mobiles, musical toys and rattles
- soft balls and foam bricks
- toys to string over the cot or pram.

From about three months, provide:

- cradle gym, bath toys and activity mat
- chiming ball and stacking beakers
- saucepans and spoons
- building bricks
- rag books.

See also Chapter 2 for ideas about providing playthings and activities to promote holistic development.

For transport

Baby slings

Baby slings, used on the front of the carer's body, enable close physical contact between carer and baby, but can cause back strain if used with heavy babies; child 'back carriers' which fit on a frame like a rucksack are suitable for larger babies.

Pram or buggy

A newborn baby can be transported in a special buggy with a tilting seat (the baby must be able to lie flat). This can then be used for as long as the baby needs a pushchair; the buggy has the advantage of being easier to handle than a pram, easier to store at home and to take on public transport. It is not possible to carry heavy loads of shopping on a buggy, and lightweight buggies are not recommended for long periods of sleeping.

Car seats

A baby should never be carried on an adult's lap on the front seat of a car. Small babies must be transported in a rearward-facing baby car seat. If the car has a passenger airbag, the baby seat should always be fitted in the back seat; for babies under 10 kg, these seats can be used also as a first seat in the home.

Figure 13.7 A travel system

Parenting and child-rearing practices including social, cultural and religious influences

Different parenting styles and attitudes

See Chapter 5, pages 218–221 for guidance on appreciating different parenting styles and attitudes.

The diversity of child-rearing practices

Child-rearing practices vary across different cultures, and can also differ within cultural groups. Respecting cultural values and practices as they relate to the care of young children is not just a matter of having appropriate insight and a positive attitude toward diverse cultural practices. It may also demand a willingness to modify the routines in an early years setting in order to accommodate the needs of a particular child and their family. Examples of different customs around the birth of a baby include:

- 'wetting the baby's head' (a euphemism for having an alcoholic drink to celebrate the birth)
- baby 'showers' and the giving of gifts and cards

- restricted visiting by male members for the family for up to ten days following the birth
- preparing special foods for the mother to eat
- a Christian family may wish to have the baby baptised
- a Hindu family may wish to write the mantra 'Om' on the baby's tongue with honey
- a Muslim family may wish that a male relative whisper the Islamic call to prayer into the baby's ear and perhaps attach an amulet round the baby's neck or wrist.

Weaning is also an important milestone in many cultures and the progression from milk feeds to solids may be marked by specific ceremonies:

- For Hindus, there is a rice feeding ceremony at six months of age when various members of the family, usually starting with the grandparents, feed the baby its first rice.
- Congee, a traditional Chinese weaning food of rice boiled in watery meat broth, is introduced at six to ten months.

Section 3: The roles and responsibilities of professionals working with babies

The importance of the key worker system

The way in which babies are cared for has a huge impact on how they will respond to difficulties and relationships later in life. Babies are totally dependent on our ability to be responsive to their needs. If they learn to feel and enjoy their parents' love, care, comfort and protection, they will start to feel secure and understood. Being in warm, loving surroundings, with plenty of physical contact, is the single most important factor for improving a baby's physical and emotional wellbeing. Babies and toddlers are more likely to feel safe and loved when the same familiar people are looking after them each day. As early childhood practitioners, you need,

above all, to have '**empathy**': to be able to appreciate the world from a baby's point of view.

Young babies who spend much of their time in group settings and domestic care, being looked after by people other than their parents, have particular requirements. The most important factor in any early years setting for babies is the people who are doing the caring – in other words, *you*. Obviously, the physical environment should be attractive and planned to provide a safe and stimulating environment. Babies should be in rooms containing groups of no more than six children and two adults. Staff working with babies in group care or in a childminder's home should be adequately trained and supported in their work.

The **key worker role** benefits the baby or child, the parents or carers and the key worker. The benefits for **babies** are that:

- within the day-to-day demands of a nursery, each child feels special and individual, cherished and thought about by someone in particular while they are away from home
- the baby will experience a close relationship that is affectionate and reliable in the nursery as well as at home.

The benefits for **parents** are that:

- there is an opportunity to build a personal relationship with 'just one person' rather than 'all of them' in the nursery
- there is the possibility of building a partnership with professional staff who may share with them the pleasures and stresses of child-rearing. It is liaising with someone else who loves your baby or child too.

The benefits for the **key worker** are that:

- you feel that you really matter to a child and to their family
- you will probably have a profound influence on the baby's wellbeing, their mental health, and their opportunities to learn.

The key worker approach is very demanding physically and emotionally on the individual, as the relationship formed is intense. However, it also has benefits for the nursery as an organisation, with more satisfied staff and fewer absences; better care and learning for the babies and children; and a parent clientele who are likely to develop a more trusting confidence in the abilities, qualities and dedication of professional staff.

The organisation of care in a variety of settings

Providing consistent, individual care

In nursery and crèche settings, each baby should be allocated to a **key worker**, who, ideally, is responsible for:

- the routine daily hands-on care, such as feeding, washing, changing
- observing the baby's development
- encouraging a wide range of play activities tailored to the baby's individual needs
- recording and reporting any areas of concern
- liaising with the baby's primary carers or parents and establishing a relationship that promotes mutual understanding.

Any setting that uses the key worker system should have a strategy for dealing with staff absence or holidays.

Respecting differences

All babies need respectful and individual care. Within the early years setting, physical care arrangements should allow for individual differences; for example:

- **food**: provide a variety of foods – do not expect each child to eat the same thing

- **sleep**: allow babies to sleep when they need to, rather than having a set group time
- **anti-discriminatory practice**: books, toys and ceremonies should reflect the cultural diversity of the nursery and should be positively non-sexist and against violence (see Chapter 5)
- **stereotyping**: staff must avoid stereotyping language.

Attachment and separation
Separation anxiety

A baby may show signs of separation anxiety – typically at around six months; this may happen even when the primary carer, usually the mother, leaves the baby just for a few moments. The baby does not have a certain feeling that the parent will return and can become very distressed in a short space of time. They might become tearful, uneasy or even filled with panic.

Your role in supporting parents

Most parents are understandably anxious when they decide to leave their baby with a stranger. Unless their baby has had some experience of being left for long periods of time with anyone other than the primary carers, the parents will not be certain of their reaction. Some common worries include:

- What will happen if my baby will not stop crying?
- Will my baby settle to sleep immediately but then be panic-stricken when he or she wakes up and finds that his or her parent or primary carer is not there?
- How will the key worker handle such a situation?
- Will the staff get annoyed with me if I want to know everything that has gone on in my baby's life since I left this morning?

Guidelines for supporting parents

It takes time for staff to get to know a parent but you can help to alleviate some of their concerns, and to provide quality care and education for babies by doing the following:

- Show empathy – try to put yourself in the parent's shoes and follow the guidelines on page 149 for settling in new children.
- Welcome parents and make time for them – make friendly contact with the child's parents. You need to be approachable. Try not to appear rushed even when you have a really busy nursery.

Guidelines for supporting parents (cont.)

- Help **parents to separate from their baby** – when a baby is handed from the parent to a new carer, it is best if:
    - you approach slowly
    - you talk gently before picking up and taking the baby from the parent
    - the baby is held looking at the parent during the hand-over.
- Explain how you will be caring for the baby – for example, describe the daily routines and the layout of the setting.
- Be aware of your particular situation and your responsibilities – you need to maintain a professional relationship with parents (even if they also happen to be your friends) and work as a team member in an early years setting.
- Show that you enjoy being with the baby – physical contact is important; encourage 'conversations' with babies; smile and talk to them.
- Always act in the interests of the baby – use your knowledge of holistic development and your powers of observation to enable you to tailor the care you give to the individual baby's needs.
- Keep parents and other staff members informed – you need to know how and when to pass on information to parents about their baby's care; and to observe the rules of confidentiality.

Providing information for parents

When caring for babies, whether as a nanny in their home or in a nursery, you need to ensure that parents have information about their baby on a daily basis; most settings provide a **daily record chart** which helps to make sure the parents are involved in their child's care. Information includes:

- **Feeding**: what, when and how much their baby has consumed.
- **Excretion**: nappy changing information.
- **Health**: any concerns – such as nappy rash, unexplained rashes, teething symptoms, etc.
- **Holistic development**: all aspects of development should be noted – physical, intellectual, language, emotional and social.
- **Behaviour**: what the baby has been doing during the session; how happy; any problems, etc.

You need to be available to discuss any concerns a parent may have about their baby – ideally each key person will hand over to 'their' baby's parent or carer at the end of each session.

Policies and procedures for the care of babies and legal and ethical responsibilities

Every setting has policy and procedure documents that aim to keep babies and children safe from harm. These include policies and procedures for:

- nappy changing
- settling in
- safeguarding
- rest and sleep
- preparing food and feeding babies
- reporting illness and accidents
- health and safety.

Safeguarding

All babies, children and young people have the right to be protected from harm. If you are working in a nursery setting, you will need to know the lines of reporting if you suspect that a baby in your care is being abused in any way. For practitioners who work in isolation, such as nannies and childminders, you may not have a senior practitioner to consult. In this case, you should contact either your Early Years Development and Childcare Partnership (EYDCP) or the Pre-School Advisory Group in Northern Ireland. The NSPCC has a useful helpline if you need to voice a concern in total confidence. Foster carers will have established lines of support, as they are already known to be working with vulnerable children.

Reporting and recording illness in early years settings

- Nannies and childminders should always contact the baby's parents directly in the case of accident or illness.
- In schools and nurseries, you should notify a senior member of staff, who will then decide if and when to contact the baby's parents.

Recording procedures in early years settings are discussed in Chapter 2. The legal and ethical responsibilities that practitioners have towards babies, children and their parents are described in Chapter 5.

Good practice in non-group settings

Some early years practitioners choose to work as a nanny in the child's own home; others choose to be foster carers or childminders. The general principles of caring for babies remain the same as those described above.

Working as a nanny

A nanny provides child care in the child's own home, usually while the parents are at work. A nanny has sole charge of the children – so ideally will have a recognised childcare qualification. However, not all nannies are trained and there are no legal requirements for a person applying for a job as a nanny. There are various opportunities for working as a nanny:

- **Live-in nanny**: lives with the family they are working for, who provides them with food and a private bedroom in addition to their salary.
- **Daily nanny**: comes to the family home each day. Babysitting in the evenings might be arranged as part of the terms of employment, or in exchange for extra pay.
- **Nanny-share**: this is an arrangement whereby a nanny is shared by two families. If a nanny is shared by more than two families, he or she may be required to register as a childminder.

Childminders

Registered childminders are professional day carers who work in their own homes to provide care and learning opportunities for other people's children in a family setting.

By law, all childminders must:

- be registered with the appropriate regulator, according to the national law
- complete a basic registration course, including first aid training (England and Wales only): CACHE also has a course specifically for childminders – CACHE Level 3 Diploma in Home-based Childcare
- have their home inspected regularly, to make sure it is safe and suitable for young children
- be insured, in case a child they are looking after has an accident or damages someone else's property
- be checked by the Independent Safeguarding Authority (ISA), as must everyone else aged over 16 who lives or works in the childminder's home.

Childminders are usually registered to look after up to three children under five years and three children aged five to eight years, including their own children.

Mother's helps

These usually work alongside the parent(s), helping with child care and general household work. Mother's helps are unlikely to have formal childcare qualifications, but may be experienced.

Maternity nurses

These are specially trained to take care of new babies for up to three months after the birth. They generally live with the family.

Foster carers

Foster care is a way of providing a family life for children who cannot live with their own parents. It is often used to provide temporary care while parents get help sorting out problems, take a break, or to help children or young people through a difficult period in their lives. Often children will return home once the problems that caused them to come into foster care have been resolved and that it is clear that their parents are able to look after them safely. Others may stay in long-term foster care, some may be adopted, and others will move on to live independently.

How to work with other professionals in a multi-agency team

See Chapters 5, pages 213–17, for detailed information on working with other professionals in a multi-agency team.

Safeguarding and protecting children from harm

The principles of safeguarding and protecting children from harm are discussed in Chapter 3.

Look back at Unit 3 and remind yourself of the possible signs and symptoms of abuse in babies. As part of your role in safeguarding babies, you also need to be able to recognise signs when parents may need additional support. For example, although very few women with postnatal depression physically harm their babies, they may find it difficult to respond to all their babies' needs.

Postnatal depression

About half of new mothers will feel a bit weepy, flat and unsure of themselves on the third or fourth day after having a baby. This is a feeling of mild depression caused by hormonal changes, tiredness and reaction to the excitement of the birth. It is usually called the 'baby blues' and it passes after a few days. **Postnatal depression** is different from the 'baby blues' and usually develops within the first month following childbirth. Around one in ten mothers experience postnatal depression. It may or may not develop out of the 'baby blues', and the mother will show similar symptoms to those seen in 'ordinary' depression:

- **Feeling low, miserable and tearful** for no apparent reason: these feelings persist for most of the time, though they may be worse at certain times of day, particularly the morning.
- **Feeling resentful and angry**: this may be particularly noticeable in first-time mothers who feel that they are not enjoying having a new baby in the way they anticipated.
- **Feeling constantly tired**: disturbed sleep patterns are a natural part of looking after a new baby. However, mothers with postnatal depression find it hard to go to sleep even though they are tired, or they wake early in the morning.
- **Feeling tense and anxious**: the normal worries and anxieties that any mother feels for a new baby may become overwhelming. Also some mothers experience 'panic attacks': episodes lasting several minutes when they feel as if something disastrous is about to happen, such as collapsing or having a heart attack.
- **Feeling unable to cope**: when people are depressed, they sometimes feel that there is no way out of their problems and even the simplest of tasks seems too much.
- **Loss of appetite**: mothers may not feel hungry and forget to eat at a time when they need to have a good healthy diet.

Nobody knows why some mothers become depressed after childbirth, although it may occur partly because of the hormonal changes following childbirth.

Treatment for postnatal depression

It is treated in much the same way as ordinary depression. The following measures are helpful:

- Talking about the problem with somebody, such as the health visitor or GP.
- Getting extra support and help with looking after the baby from partner and close family members.
- Medication in the form of antidepressants may be necessary.

In severe cases of postnatal depression, the mother and her baby will be admitted to a psychiatric hospital for more intensive therapy.

Postnatal depression should not be confused with the much more serious condition **puerperal psychosis**: this is a very rare mental illness, affecting fewer than 1 in 500 women, which *always* requires treatment in a psychiatric unit.

Shaken baby syndrome

Some parents or carers may lose control and shake their baby in a moment of frustration or anger. This is particularly likely if the baby will not stop crying. Most people do not realise the damage that shaking can do; some may even think that it is preferable to smacking the baby.
Shaking can cause serious, permanent injuries or even death, because:

- A baby's head is big and heavy compared with the rest of the body.
- Unless supported, the head flops around because the neck muscles are not yet strong enough to hold it still.
- Shaking makes the head move back and forth very quickly and with great force.
- When this happens, tiny blood vessels can tear and bleed inside the baby's brain, causing one or more of the following: blindness, deafness, seizures, learning difficulties, brain damage or even death.

Signs that a baby has been shaken include floppiness, difficulty in breathing and drowsiness. CT scanners are used to determine the nature of the head injury.

Sources of support for families

Families under pressure

Families come under a lot of pressure from friends, from advertising companies and from television programmes to provide the very best clothing and equipment for their new baby. The idealised picture of happy, smiling parents cuddling their precious bundle of joy is hard to resist; advertisers use these images to bombard the new parents with a dazzling array of objects that are deemed 'essential' to happy parenthood. You are in an important position to advise on the basic principles when choosing equipment. Parents should prioritise their needs by considering all factors relevant to their circumstances:

- **Cost**: how much can the parents afford to spend? What may be available on loan from friends who have children past the baby stage? Can some equipment, such as the pram, be bought second-hand or hired cheaply?
- **Lifestyle**: is the family living in a flat where the lifts are often out of action, in bed and breakfast accommodation, or in a house with a large garden? These factors will affect such decisions as pram or buggy, and where the baby will sleep.
- **Single or multiple use**: will the equipment be used for a subsequent baby – in which case the priority may be to buy a large pram on which a toddler can also be seated? It may be worth buying new, high-quality products if they are to be used again.
- **Safety and maintenance**: does the item of equipment chosen meet all the British Safety Standards? What if it has been bought second-hand? How easy is it to replace worn-out parts?

Factors that can cause stress to parents

- **Financial**: if both parents have to go out to work, this can be stressful. One or both parents may need to reduce the hours of work or they may need to pay for child care.

- **Age of parents and support available**: very young parents or parents who are at the upper end of the child-bearing age range may have less support from their peers and find the adjustment to parenthood more stressful. Some parents lack support from the **extended family** who may live a long way away.
- **Tiredness**: having a young baby can disrupt parents' sleeping patterns; this is particularly stressful if both parents have to get up to go to work.
- **Responsibility**: some parents find the responsibility of looking after a young baby overwhelming; they may worry that they cannot cope or find that 'the baby' has completely taken over their life.
- **Conflict**: parents may have several other children to care for, all with their own needs. The needs of the new baby may conflict with the established routine within the family.

Access to health care and support

All parents can experience feelings of isolation and the need for support from time to time. Practitioners who work with babies and young children are in a responsible position. Staff members who are closely observant and who have a sound understanding of child development are often ideally placed to offer the support and information that parents need. There are many voluntary organisations that can offer help and support to parents of young children. The health visitor will be able to advise parents about local groups, such as parent and toddler groups and **Home-Start**, which is a voluntary organisation that provides trained volunteers to work with families under stress.

Potential problems

Occasionally you might come across parents who have difficult or challenging attitudes towards the staff and the setting generally. You should always be patient, even when *you* are exhausted at the end of a busy day! There could be any number of reasons for a sudden, angry outburst and you need to react

in a professional and caring manner. Several factors (including competition, guilt, and time constraints) may affect the relationship between a working parent and staff in an early years setting. For example:

- **Competition**: the parents may feel they are competing with you for the baby's affection, since both you and they have formed strong attachments to the baby.
- **Jealousy**: parents may feel jealousy if their baby takes his or her first steps in your presence – rather than at home.
- **Guilt**: parents often feel guilty; they may resent having to 'abandon' their children by leaving them while they work. This is even more difficult when separating from their baby causes *each* of them distress.
- **Time**: employed parents may feel that they have many roles and duties to perform but not enough time to perform them. Consequently, they often feel overwhelmed when they turn up to collect their children.

Outreach and family support

Considerable research shows that children's development and learning can be greatly enhanced with the support of parents and availability of play opportunities at home. This research can lead practitioners in two possible directions:

1 A social control model of teaching parents to bring up their children. This means the staff show parents examples of what to do, hoping the parents will copy 'good models'. The parents and the home environment they provide are considered to be deficient: there will often be a list of resources and activities which parents are told they should provide.

2 A developmental partnership in which professionals do not try to tell parents how to bring up their children. Instead, they seek to find out what the parents think and feel. They respect parents' views and help them to build on what they already know about and want for their children, offering knowledge, information and discussion.

Case Study — Parents involved in their children's learning (PICL): an example of a developmental partnership

Pen Green Centre for Children and their Families has led practice in involving parents in understanding and supporting their children's development. This programme includes:

- Action for the parent: helping parents to reclaim their own education and build up their self-esteem.
- Action for the child: encouraging parents to child-watch, to be involved in and respectful of their children's learning process and development.

In a system of parents involved in their children's learning, professionals and staff work closely together, sharing and shaping joint understandings. The parent's unique knowledge of the child is respected; and professional knowledge about child development is shared with the parent, including:

- understanding children's wellbeing and involvement as they play
- noticing and working with children's schemas.

Videos of the child, taken both in the family home by parents and by staff in the nursery, provide a way of observing and reflecting on children's play.

Find out more about PICL by going to www.pengreen.org or search online for 'Parents Involved in their Children's Learning (PICL)'.

Progress check

- Can you think of a difficulty which could come up in a key person's relationship with a parent? How could this be handled?
- What are some of the different ways of sharing information with parents about the educational programme and care routines?

Promoting a non-judgemental approach when working with babies and their families

All parents can experience feelings of isolation and the need for support from time to time. Practitioners who are closely observant and who have a sound understanding of child development are often ideally placed to offer the support and information that parents need. However, parents are usually quick to notice if you are critical of them – and they will be reluctant to share concerns with you if they feel you are likely to judge them.

Being non-judgemental means showing sensitivity to other people's needs and opinions, and trying to understand issues from a parent's perspective as well as from your own. You need to respect and value the knowledge, skills and experience that parents have, and be willing to try different approaches to fit individual circumstances.

It is also important not to make assumptions about any individual, as this can lead to stereotyping (see Chapter 1). It is very important that you get to know the children in your care – and their parents – and that you consider each child as an individual with his or her own unique needs.

Assessment practice

- List the factors that influence the health and development of babies in the first year of life.

- How can you ensure that both the indoor and the outdoor environment for babies are safe, reassuring and stimulating?

- Describe the holistic development of babies at *either* three months, at seven months or at ten months. How can you provide play activities that will promote the baby's development?

- How can the needs of babies be met in either group child care or in home-based child care?

- Describe the importance of well-planned care routines, the key worker system and an inclusive approach when working with babies and their families.

- How have the theoretical perspectives of development and attachment influenced current practice with babies under one year of age?

 Useful resources

Leach, P. (2003) *Your Baby and Child* (4th edn). London: Dorling Kindersley.
Meggitt, C. (2012) *An Illustrated Guide to Child Development* (3rd edn). Oxford: Heinemann.

Index